T0202483

Lecture Notes in Computer Science

Lecture Notes in Computer Science

Edited by G. Goos and J. Hartmanis

81

Data Base Techniques for Pictorial Applications

Florence, June 20–22, 1979

Edited by A. Blaser

Springer-Verlag
Berlin Heidelberg New York 1980

Sponsorship: IBM Europe
　　　　　　　IBM Italy
Local Organization: Scientific Centers of IBM Italy

Programme Committee:

　A. Blaser (Chairman), Heidelberg Scientific Center, IBM Germany
　M. Felix, Paris Scientific Center, IBM France
　F. Greco (Local Organizer), Pisa Scientific Center, IBM Italy
　R. Hartwig, Heidelberg Scientific Center, IBM Germany
　J. Jimenez, Madrid Scientific Center, IBM Spain
　M. E. Senko, Heidelberg Scientific Center, IBM Germany
　B. Smedley, Winchester Scientific Center, IBM United Kingdom

American Co-ordinator:
　P. E. Mantey, IBM Research San Jose, CA

Asian Co-ordinator:
　T. Takeda, Tokyo Scientific Center, IBM Japan

AMS Subject Classifications (1970): 68 A 45, 68 A 50
CR Subject Classifications (1974): 3.14, 3.63, 3.7

ISBN 3-540-09763-5 Springer-Verlag Berlin Heidelberg New York
ISBN 0-387-09763-5 Springer-Verlag New York Heidelberg Berlin

Library of Congress Cataloging in Publication Data. Main entry under title: Data base
techniques for pictorial applications, Florence, June 20–22, 1979. (Lecture notes in
computer science ; 81) Proceedings of a conference sponsored by IBM Europe and
IBM Italy. Includes bibliographies and index. 1. Image processing--Congresses. 2. Optical
data processing--Congresses. 3. Computer graphics--Congresses. 4. Cartography--Data
processing--Congresses. I. Blaser, Albrecht. II. IBM Europe. III. IBM Italia. IV. Series.
TA1632.D36 621.3815'48 80-11561

WELCOME

The theme to be explored during this conference is that of pictorial data, in itself a difficult matter to define. Very likely, there are many conflicting definitions. The conference memorandum says, that pictorial data is that which relates to the shape of an object or its location in physical space. In planning the conference, the organizing committee was only too aware of the multitude of applications which encompass data meeting such a definition. It is obvious that these applications are very important in many areas of today's world. It was suggested that this conference works towards a first understanding of the various pictorial application areas and their potential and then tries to identify the underlying commonalities, especially as far as data is concerned, its representation, structuring, and storage.

Why are the Scientific Centers of IBM Europe interested in that subject and why are they sponsoring a conference on pictorial data? An outline of their role might provide the basis of an answer to these questions.

As technology advances and as scientific achievements become greater and technical development more rapid, we feel that the establishment of Scientific Centers is increasingly important in order to conduct long and medium range research, and to develop applications which meet the needs of modern society. The projects undertaken by IBM's Scientific Centers represent a wide range of topics in computer applications research, in advanced studies in system/user interfaces as well as system design and programming, and in many problems of information science encountered by computer users. Among these topics there has been work in pictorial applications and data base issues for many years. Some of the relevant work of the Scientific Centers might be mentioned:

- The Scientific Center at Heidelberg has worked in the past on the processing of scintigraphic images and is now dealing with man-machine interaction and with related information management.

- The Italian Scientific Centers are engaged in a wide range of problems in areas such as natural sciences, econometrics, and computer networking.

- The Scientific Center in Haifa deals with the design of computer systems for agriculture, for medical research, and for aquifer management.

- The newly established Scientific Center in Winchester is initiating work on image processing in medicine and on social sciences.

- The Madrid Scientific Center works in image processing of remotely sensed data, e.g. for the identification and assessment of earth resources.

- The Scientific Center in Paris is also engaged in this field as well as in speech signal processing with the objective to teach deaf children through visual feedback how to speak.

The result of this work is published in the scientific community. Very often, research is done in collaboration with academic and scientific institutions. Examples are the studies with the University of Pisa, the Italian National Council of Research, the University of Vienna, the Institute of Molecular Biology in Madrid, and the Universities in Berlin and Heidelberg. We consider these joint studies an ideal vehicle for the exchange of expertise and for cross fertilization.

This conference, too, is directed towards an open exchange of knowledge and results of research. It is with such an open exchange of expertise that the growth of new ideas is encouraged and science thrives. And it is in this spirit, that I would like to express my welcome and my gratitude to the participants for coming and sharing with us today's knowledge about data base techniques for pictorial applications.

I want to thank IBM Italy for the offer to host this conference in wonderful Florence and for the organizational and administrative effort undertaken to make it a pleasant and beneficial experience for all the participants.

Paris, June 1979   R. Aguilar
                         IBM Europe
                         Director of Scientific Centers

INTRODUCTION

Over the years, technological trends in hardware and software have significantly improved the processing power of computers, their primary and secondary storage capacity and accessing speed, their telecommunications facilities, as well as their user interfaces via general and special purpose terminals. This has facilitated, among others, the advancements of integrated data bases and of their administration on the one hand, and of graphical and image processing (in brief: pictorial) applications on the other.

Developments in these two fields have traditionally been unrelated. Integrated data bases have been and are still being nearly exclusively used for commercial and administrative applications of batch or transactional type. Conversely, pictorial applications have been pursued mainly in technical, scientific, and planning disciplines as diversified as architectural and engineering design, biochemistry, air traffic control, robotics, utility and geographical mapping, urban and regional planning, meteorology, medicine, and in the analysis of remotely sensed data e.g. for earth resources and agricultural inventory development and environmental protection.

There are, however, several strong arguments for an integration of data base techniques with pictorial applications. To mention just a few of them:

(1) The processing of pictorial data poses quite severe computational problems and the volumes of data to be manipulated and analyzed grow larger and larger. Therefore, much attention must be given to choosing between the various methods known for structuring and retrieving this data.
(2) Pictorial (as conventional) information is an expensive resource which should profitably be used for as many applications at as many places as possible. As an example, the same remotely sensed data can and should be used e.g. for earth resources identification, environmental protection, agriculture, and meteorology. This calls for an organization of this data on which to build a variety of different applications.
(3) Graphical and image applications enter into commercial and administrative environments. Business (or data presentation) graphics and facsimile are just 2 subjects to be mentioned. This is to some extent due to the fact that advanced problems in business and administration call for similar modes of operation (e.g. interactive problem solving) as known in technical and scientific disciplines, where graphical presentation of information is an indispensable tool.
(4) Many applications require pictorial data in combination with conventional data (computer aided design can be

mentioned as an example). This calls for the management
of both types of information in the same system.

IBM Scientific Centers have traditionally been active in
pictorial applications research (e.g. in engineering,
medicine, remote sensing applications), as well as in data
base research (e.g. in relational data base management
systems and interactive enduser interfaces). Recognizing the
needs mentioned above, some projects began to investigate
scientific problem solving on the basis of prototyped data
base management systems accommodating pictorial information.

To assess the work which has been going on for several years
in application and data base fields and to discuss data base
features necessary or desirable for pictorial applications,
the Scientific Centers of IBM Europe organized this
international conference. More precisely, its objectives are
to seek an understanding of the various application areas
which involve the use of pictorial data, especially to
consider their requirements for the structuring, storage,
and analysis of such data, and to identify commonalities and
differences as well as to learn of relevant data base
research. The emphasis is placed on the interaction between
data base and application experts to exchange their views on
the data base needs of, or the facilities for, pictorial
applications.

To meet these objectives and to create a basis for mutually
beneficial discussion, application oriented contributions
were invited to particularly address the needs of their
respective application for data regarding its volume,
structure, storage, search (the algorithms used and the
types of searches), and the extent to which data access can
be pre-defined or needs to be dynamic and flexible. Data
base contributions were encouraged to emphasize those
features of their work which are relevant to pictorial data
and applications.

The agenda has been structured according to our assessment
of the conference subject and of the expected commonalities
and differences in data related aspects of the applications.
The first two sessions deal with geographic applications,
e.g. in geographic and utility mapping and in urban and
regional planning. The third session addresses the
administration and accessing of data representing two- or
three-dimensional geometric objects as they occur for
instance in architecture, engineering, and biochemistry. The
fourth session is devoted to remote sensing and image
processing applications, among others in water resources
management, agriculture, astronomy, meteorology, and
biomedicine. The fifth session, eventually, covers some
related data base research.

This is one of the first conferences totally devoted to the

subject. It is supposed to draw its success from pointing the applications oriented audience to the common problem of organizing and accessing pictorial information and to the solutions already visible, and in making the data base researchers aware of unresolved problems deserving their attention. There will be conferences on that subject in the years to come. We would be pleased if this one could play a kind of pioneering role for the others.

The conference was instigated by the Chief Scientist of the IBM Corporation. It was sponsored by IBM Europe and IBM Italy, and locally organized by the Scientific Centers of IBM Italy. Nevertheless, the contents of this introduction and of the conference contributions express the authors' own personal opinions and not IBM's.

I would like to express my gratitude and appreciation to all the lecturers and session chairmen, to the sponsors, to hosting IBM Italy, to the members of the programme committee, to the local organizers, and to the many contributors within and outside of IBM, who gave advice and assistance in preparing, organizing, and running this conference.

Heidelberg, June 1979   A. Blaser

TABLE OF CONTENTS:

DATA BASE REQUIREMENTS FOR GEOGRAPHICAL MAPPING

by

RICHARD L. VITEK

The rapid and significant improvements in computer technology have caused a
virtual explosion in the use of digital processing and digital products within
the mapping community. The availability of large volumes of mapping data in
digital form presents both an opportunity and a challenge. The opportunity to
provide more cost effective and responsive systems and the challenge to do it
well and as soon as possible. This paper defines a concept of operation which
uses digital source data bases to support the production of multiple products;
an approach and the status in establishing data base requirements in terms of
content, structure and format; and the data collection and software problems that
inhibit a simple solution. The use of this source data by other national as well
as international users is also addressed in terms of the need for flexible formats
and coding structures.

Defense Mapping Agency
Building 56, U.S. Naval Observatory
Washington, D.C. 20305

Introduction

The primary mission of the Defense Mapping Agency (DMA) is to provide map, chart and geodetic data to the U.S. Military Services. The primary purpose is to provide the user with geographic information on a global basis. This information has historically been presented in the form of a map or chart, that is, an abstraction of the real world in graphic form. The increasing use of the computer throughout the military is showing up as a demand for products in digital form. The content remains essentially the same as the graphic product but the form and format are changing. We now distribute digital maps and terrain elevation matrices in addition to the standard map and chart products. We are also turning more and more to the computer and automation to trim costs for our in-house production which is still very labor intensive. Digitizing is used in many cases as part of the production process even though the final product is a graphic. Over 50 percent of our manpower is devoted to digital products and digital processing.

We see the large volume of digital data as presenting both an opportunity and a challenge; an opportunity to be more cost effective and responsive, and a challenge to do the job well using data base techniques and state-of-the-art technology. Since the cost of collecting digital data is high, we must insure that the data which is collected is utilized to the maximum extent possible through efficient exchange procedures. The ideal situation is to collect data once and use it for as many products as possible. This idea leads one to consider the building of multiproduct data bases. By collecting and maintaining the data in digital form, we can, of course, provide quicker response. Besides the data that DMA collects there are also other sources of digital data. DMA is only one organization in a community of national and international producers of geographic data and products, all with very similar digital problems. Therefore we are working with the other producers and collectively developing exchange standards to take full advantage of all the digital data that will be collected.

A major consideration in the development of data base requirements is to provide a viable interface between the current and future data bases and files which will allow for phased, well-controlled change. Such an interface will provide for maximum use of new techniques and technology with minimum impact on current production. The data base requirements for DMA are not for a single data base but rather a set of management and production data bases, storage and exchange formats, data elements, and the associated environment which shapes their development and specifications. The exchange format plays a key role in providing the desired interface. This paper covers a concept of operation of that set of data bases to support multiproduct applications and an approach to establish the data base requirements in terms of the content, format and structure. There are collection and software problems which will be discussed later that inhibit a simple near-term solution; however, we feel a well-planned phased approach will allow us to meet the challenge of the future and take full advantage of the opportunities associated with the availability of digital data.

Concept and Model

The basic concept is to provide a unified set of management and production data bases which will comprise the DMA data bank. The unified set of data bases will consist of data in graphic, analog and digital form. A blend of the old and the new, existing simultaneously, which may be physically separated but will be centrally managed and logically integrated. The logical integration would insure minimum overlap or gaps in the total set of data bases by building

3

interfaces and/or physical integration. Physical integration will only be attempted where the integration can be shown to be cost effective and still meet or exceed all current user requirements.

In the idealized model of a data bank (see Figure 1) all data bases would contain evaluated and organized data. All data would be edited and evaluated on the way into the data bank and all products would be generated from data accessed from the data bank. The intent is to gradually, over time, develop such an idealized data bank which would consist of analog and digital production data and the required associated management indices and algorithms. New indices and algorithms would be developed as components of on-line management data base systems to allow a rapid determination of what source material is on hand, how good it is, where it is located, and the products that can be made from it. The data would then be retrieved and processed with automated equipment to furnish completed products to the user. The ideal model would contain standard procedures, data elements, data bases and data base systems. The standardization would evolve through development and procurement of new systems rather than retrofitting into existing systems. New systems would be developed and tested in parallel with the older systems to insure proper operation. After the new system is demonstrated, it would be placed in operation and the old system phased out with minimum disruption of the production process.

Standardization

Additional cost savings can be achieved by minimizing data and system redundancy and their associated high maintenance costs. This approach involves developing specifications to define existing data and procedures as well as developing standards where data and procedures are essentially the same or close enough to be made the same. Standardization then becomes a means to achieve cost reduction.

In the standardization process there are many elements to be considered from total systems to specific data elements. In analyzing systems, one may consider software, hardware, procedures and the individual data bases. In the storage and exchange of data one must consider the determination of specific media, forms, format or structure, and content of files. As the content of particular data bases is explored in detail, then one must also determine the data elements, data sets, area or cell sizes, resolution, feature types and reference systems. In any specific system or data base one must determine which of these many elements should be standardized and to what degree. The elements and the degree of standardization as they relate to specific management and production data bases will be discussed in the following paragraphs.

Types of Data Bases

It is helpful to define the various types of data bases to aid in a discussion of current and future operations. The two broad categories of data bases are management and production, these are shown schematically in Figure 2. The management data base contains facts about requirements, resources and production status. This type of data is frequently described as metadata or data about data. Typical management data bases in DMA are contained in the DMA Management Information System (DMIS). The DMIS includes a family of data bases such as, Production (DMIS/P), Equipment (DMIS/E), Area Requirements and Production Status (ARAPS), and Product Maintenance System (PMS) to name a few. Indexes, automated and manual, are also considered a type of management data base. There are many automated indices for maps, charts, photography, names, and other items used in the production process.

The production data bases contain the physical data which is used as input to (source) or results from (product) the production process. Source data bases are either as collected (raw) data or preprocessed to bring the data up to a specified level of readiness for further processing. The intent is that the processed digital source data should be stored as a single class, used for the detection and recording of new or changed data, and designed to service multiple products. The product data base is a synthesized set of data (features) from several classes of source data used to support the production of a specific product or family of products. DMA currently produces terrain elevation data in a standard format for multiple applications, this data is considered as a source data base. DMA also stores data such as reproduction material which is ready for production, as well as copies of digital products such as the Digital Land Mass Simulator (DLMS) data. The graphic reproduction material and the DLMS data are considered product data bases. The data has been collected into specific sets for a specific product. Hard copy graphics are also stored as an inventory of available products and listed in our military map catalog.

Data Base Systems and Functions

A brief description of a typical data base system is needed to aid in subsequent discussions. A data base system is defined as that total set of procedures, software and hardware for the utilization of a predefined set of data. The components may be manual or automated. A functional flow of a typical data base system is shown in Figure 3. The data bases are shown separated from the functions to be performed. It is important to look at this separation of functions and data to obtain a better perspective on standardization and integration of data bases and software. For example, each data base must be considered as part of a system to insure that all input and output requirements and functions of the system are defined. However the overall set of data bases must be reviewed as a group to determine redundancies and to plan for integration of similar sets of data.

The input functions of collection, editing, and validation generate a qualified transaction for entry into the data base. The storage and retrieval functions allow for update, query, and products. The production of products is through the output application programs. Products are predefined data sets for one or more users on a regular basis. The queries are for ad hoc or non-predefined data sets. The schema is the logical structure of the data which is different than the internal physical structure of the data base. The user view of the data base is through its products and schema.

The distinction between the logical and physical views of the data is important. It is this separation which allows the internal storage structure of the data to be independent of the applications using the data. Reorganization, consolidation or integration of the internal data is transparent to the user. The schema or logical view of the data can also be applied to magnetic tape systems and is discussed in more detail in the following sections.

Exchange Format Compared to Schema

Exchange formats for digital data on magnetic tape are very common. In fact, there are national standards for labels and codes to be used in exchange formats. Discussion of schemas to be used in data bases are also very common in the literature. However a comparison of the characteristics of schemas and exchange formats is not very common, but it does lead to some very interesting conclusions.

The schema, i.e., the logical structure of the data shows the data elements and their relation to one another. These relationships are generally classified as hierarchical, network and relational. The schema shows the data elements in sets, groups, or records; the different groups that exist; and whether or not they will occur more than once as repeating groups (see Figure 4). The schema itself does not contain any values, the data values are in the data base.

Magnetic tape exchange formats are very similar to the schema. The tape format is the order in which data is to be placed on the tape. The sequential nature is not important in this comparison. The format does not limit the quantity or values of the data but rather only the logical order in which the data is to be placed (see Figure 5). The tape format includes record, file and tape levels. These levels would show the order of data elements within the record, the order of records in a file, and the order of files within the tape. The exchange format can be thought of as the external users' view of the data set (see Figure 6) and satisfies the same query function for non-predefined data sets. The exchange format also provides the same isolation as the schema and allows the physical internal storage to be independent of and transparent to the users. When considered in this way the exchange format can then become the key link between departments within the same organization, between agencies, and between older files and new data base management systems.

Exchange Versus Storage Formats

A look at exchange formats and storage formats provides a different perspective but leads to a similar conclusion about the value of the exchange format. The following example also shows a case for the correct degree of standardization. Assume a group of six users whose primary concern is to be able to exchange data (see Figure 7). If there is no standard format and they each wish to exchange with all other producers, then each one of the six users will have to develop five conversion programs for a total of 30 programs. If any one user changes his internal format, five others are affected. If on the other hand they can agree on and develop a standard exchange format, then each user only has to develop two conversion programs: one to and one from the standard exchange format for a total of 12 programs. If any user changes his internal storage format, the change is transparent to other users and no one else has to change their conversion programs. One could go one step further and try to use the exchange format for internal storage. This would eliminate reformatting the data for exchange purposes but does not tell the whole story. Other internal operations for update and production may require reformatting because of the use of the exchange format. If this is the case then one must select the format which causes the least amount of reformatting. The conclusion to be drawn from the analysis is that if a group of users wishes to exchange data, they should develop a standard exchange format but leave its use as an internal standard a free choice of the individual users. The exchange standard should facilitate the maximum utilization of the total set of data without constraining the internal operations of any of the producers, and the storage standard should be oriented toward optimizing internal operations.

Exchange and Storage Specifications

Both the exchange and the storage specifications will contain a format, data elements, data items or values for the data elements and codes for the data items. A brief definition of these terms follows. An example of a data element is "month of the year." The data items are the values, that is, the

names of the months, January through December. The data items can also have
abbreviations or codes to minimize the number of characters needed for storage
of the data item. For example one could use the numbers 1 to 12 to represent
the months. For the more complex data elements such as geographic (map)
features there are a large number of data items, and the codes and coding
system for the codes then become very important. The coding system may be
used to define categories, types and so on. The storage specifications should
also define standard data sets to be stored.

The exchange format must be very flexible to accept a wide range of data
types and values because it must meet the needs of the whole community of users.
For geographic data the format should allow for variable area or cell size,
resolution, and reference systems. The data elements, data items and codes
must be a standard set published in a catalog or dictionary for access by all
users. The coding system used to establish the specific codes must be comprehensive, expandable, and the categories and types of data must be mutually
exclusive. The exchange specifications must be able to handle the data for
all current users and be expandable for additional data types from current and
new users.

The storage specifications should be oriented to internal needs. The format
should be designed to minimize the reformatting required for update, production
and exchange operations. The coding structure can be less complex than the one
for exchange codes because the internal set of features is only a subset of the
total exchange set. The only requirement on internal coding structure is that
it should allow for some expansion to collect additional data elements as
changes or needs arise. The internal codes must also have a one-to-one
unambiguous relation to the exchange set. This can normally be handled by
generating the proper code in the exchange set and is not a constraint on the
internal codes.

Standard Data Elements

The first step in developing an exchange specification is to develop a set
of standard data elements. Developing such a set of standard data elements
(DE) for geographic (feature) data is a formidable task. Each DE has its own
name, abbreviation, data items, data item codes, and most important a unique
and unambiguous definition. The definition is essential so that all users not
only know what data is available but also so they can identify synonyms. To
establish a standard set of data elements one must first define the set of DE
for each user (see Figure 8). The initial set of users would be internal to
the agency but would be expanded to include external users who wished to
participate. By using the definitions for each user's subset one must then
identify common elements. These are synonyms; that is, elements which are
meant to be the same but may have different names or formats. The next step
is to determine if a standard DE already exists in a Federal or National
Standard Set and if not, then one must be established. The task of identifying
synonyms and standards is aided greatly by using a DE Dictionary. Many DE
dictionaries, software packages, exist which provide for on-line storage and
query operations. These dictionaries facilitate analysis and selection of
synonyms and the subsequent printing of the synonyms and selected standard DE's.
The resources to identify the user's subset of data elements as well as the
final exchange set can be significant. However it should be recognized that
the cost of identifying the DE is small in comparison to the data collection
cost and the benefits of developing standard DE's will far outweigh the costs.

The above process is further complicated by the fact that many geographic
features have attributes that must also be identified. The attributes are also

data elements and as such have their own definitions and codes. For example, a road is a feature which has physical attributes, such as number of lanes, width, composition, and weight bearing capacity. Each user may have different attributes associated with their features. Therefore, after determining the common features one must then define the union of attributes for each set of common features.

A data element chain is used to define the feature and attribute list. A chain is a particular combination of data elements, such as the three data elements day, month and year to represent the data element chain for date. A typical geographic feature chain would include a DE for the specific feature and a repeating DE for attributes. This would necessitate a variable chain length to accommodate differing numbers of attributes.

Types of Exchange Formats

For geographic feature data DMA has established two standard formats: one for terrain elevation data and one for cartographic data. The terrain elevation data uses a format for a uniform matrix of points. The cartographic data format is for points, lines and areas and its format is suitable for sets of connected points, random multiple points, and text. These two formats when generalized can handle all of the types of geographic features. However some special high volume uses of data may dictate two more formats. As digital imagery and raster scanning and plotting are used more in production, it may be desirable to develop a standard format for raster data. It may also be desirable for large numbers of geodetic control and gravity points to develop a special random point format. The four formats would then be matrix, line, raster and random.

Exchange Format Enhances Transition to DBMS

Data bases and data base systems have many advantages but there are some associated disadvantages. The advantages include eliminating redundant data, reducing file updates, and providing quick and direct access to data. However the disadvantages are that one must give up some local control of data and in general change operations. If an existing system is not performing satisfactorily then a change may be welcomed as hopefully a change for the better. If on the other hand the present systems are performing satisfactorily then the big question is why change. The answer to that question is simply that while local systems may be optimized, there are further economies to be gained by looking to a global (agency or community) optimum. However, there are many cases in which data base systems were not as successful as originally anticipated. So before being committed to a completely new system, it would be highly desirable to be able to demonstrate some degree of success and proceed toward data base systems as benefits and priorities dictate. This can be done by <u>first</u> establishing an exchange standard and <u>then</u> proceeding to a data base environment.

Figure 9 shows the relationship among the internal storage files, the exchange standard and the external users. The external users would include both national and international agencies. After the exchange standard is established each internal user must develop the conversion programs to and from the standard. Each of the internal users can then exchange data through the standard format. For example, user A can convert to the standard and send the tape to user C, who then converts from the standard to his storage format. In addition any internal user can convert data to the exchange standard for an external user. The exchange then becomes the communication link between internal users as well as between internal and external users. Establishing an exchange standard and developing the conversion programs thus make all the data readily available to all other users. It should be mentioned that the conversion programs should be efficient in terms of CPU time and should not require any human interaction for decisions in the conversion process.

The exchange standard does not solve all the problems, however. Redundant data may still exist between internal files and updating some data elements may require multiple file updates. There are still economies to be gained by moving to a data base system. The exchange standard also provides the communication link in this transition. Figure 10 shows the transition from a file management system (FMS) to a data base management system (DBMS). The exchange standard is the link between the two. The schema for the DBMS must use the standard data elements and the DBMS must be capable of writing and reading a standard exchange format tape. If file A is converted to operate under the DBMS, data is still available to users B and C through the exchange format. All users do not have to transition to the DBMS simultaneously to maintain access to the total data set. As the FMS transition to the DBMS the systems become standardized in the sense that they now use standard data elements and the same DBMS. It is important to note that the files do not have to be integrated into a single file when transitioning to the DBMS. They may retain their separate identities and be updated and controlled by the same organizations as under the FMS. The main difference is that more people will have the ability to access the data; there will be no need to maintain the redundant DE's, and no conversion in DE's or formats will be necessary once under the DBMS. With this scheme, conversion from the FMS to the DBMS can be scheduled to fit the user's needs.

Macro View of Data Base and Files

Figure 11 shows an overview of data bases and files using an exchange standard and schema which allows the simultaneous existence of data bases and files with full exchange capability between internal and external users. The diagram is equally applicable to management and production data bases and files. Within DMA we have mostly file management systems which are single application oriented and use magnetic tape as the medium. Our first step in developing a capability as shown in Figure 11 is to establish an exchange standard and then develop conversion programs which will allow exchange of data between internal users as well as external users. Most of the producers of data would be expected to develop conversion routines although there might be some exceptions. The second step is to implement a DBMS with a selected set of files providing the greatest net benefit to the users. The DBMS must be able to read and write exchange formatted tapes. The transition to the DBMS can maintain the exchange link and also provide direct access to the data for on-line quick response. Additional files can be converted to the DBMS at any time without disrupting any exchange links. The decision to convert to a DBMS will be dictated by individual cost benefit analyses and production priorities. The exchange first and then DBMS approach is most applicable to our geographic feature files; however, it can also be used for the management files if desired. Some specific problems and characteristics of DMA management and production data bases are given in the following paragraphs.

Management Data Bases

The DMA management information systems such as finance, personnel and production planning and control are not directly related to the production data files and will not be discussed any further in this paper. The indexes are management data bases directly related to our source material and digital data bases and will be discussed. An index is a set of records which describes items of a collection and a pointer to where the items may be found. Current indexes both automated and manual are related to types of source material such as, maps and charts, documents, photography, geographic names, and digital data. As the transition is made from FMS to DBMS, indexes for the same type of source material will be consolidated into a single data base. For example, where our two Centers currently both maintain a FMS for maps and charts, these will be consolidated into a single data base to meet both Centers' requirements. However, further integration of indexes for different types of source material is not anticipated. In some cases security classification levels require a separation of the data. However, even where this is not the case the advantages of a single integrated index are outweighed by its disadvantages. After consolidation, each index will be for a different type of source material and data redundancy will be minimized. Where possible the indexes will be operated under a common DBMS and therefore data will be accessible through the same terminal and language. The individual organizational elements now responsible for update and operation of files for specific source material and their associated indexes can continue to be responsible for the indexes under a DBMS. Conversion from FMS to DBMS will then have minimal impact on the organization and its personnel. The major difference in operations under an on-line DBMS will be that other staff and department personnel will now have direct access to the index data and therefore can answer their own questions.

The data base management system eventually selected must be able to answer the following queries. A typical query would be to ask for all maps in a specific geographic area. The geographic area would be defined by latitude and longitude limits or geopolitical codes or names such as state, country, etc. A summary list of all maps in the area could be printed by producer, scale, quality or similar qualifiers selected by the user. If more detail is required a listing of the full record for selected maps could be requested. In some cases for maps and in most cases for photography, a simple listing however, is not adequate. The user normally wishes to know the coverage of a particular scale of map or photo. In this case a CRT terminal would be required to provide a graphic display of coverage for the maps or photos. A background outline of the geopolitical area would also be desired. It is anticipated that a separate data base of country outlines would be available for that purpose. A typical CRT query would: ask for a geographic area and be presented the country outline; call up maps or photos by scale and other qualifiers and see their outlines displayed with identifying codes; call up names or geodetic control and see the items as points with identifying codes or names. In this manner a user could browse through any or all the source material in a specific geographic area very quickly. A copying device should be available for making a take away hard copy if desired. The system must also be prepared to assist new users, by prompting, to select the correct data base and then the desired data from a specific data base.

Production Data Bases

The production data bases as shown in Figure 2 were the source (raw or processed) and product data bases. The intent is to develop digital source data bases which can be used for multiple product applications. A source data base for terrain elevation data has been developed. This data base conforms to the definition of source data base in that it is a single class of data and is used for multiple product applications. It is used as a product by itself and is also transformed and reformatted into other products. The development of an equivalent source data base for geographic feature data is much more complicated and is progressing much slower. Some details on each type are given in the following paragraphs.

The exchange of data is relatively straightforward. The data must be evaluated, organized and stored in a manner which allows ready access and efficient conversion for exchange. By developing an exchange specification and then conversion programs, any inherent problems will be surfaced and can be addressed and solved. The detailed descriptions of the data elements required for the exchange specification will also surface other problems. It may be that the data collected was so oriented to the specific product for which it was collected that it has no real value for other products.

For example, since the production lines are currently product oriented, the collection is tailored to be compatible with available software. In collecting road data on two parallel roads the operator may recognize that when symbolized the roads will overlap. Since the software and interactive systems to make post collection corrections are not yet available, the operator moves the road before digitizing. The data fits the product but it no longer represents the real world. One solution is to digitize the road twice; once for general use and a second time as offset for a specific product use. After software or systems are available to make the change automatically then the second digitization would not be required. A general rule is that the data as collected should represent the real world as accurately as possible. Distortions of the real world to fit a specific product or use of a product may make the data virtually valueless for other applications and may result in a complete recollection. Present production procedures for collection will have to be reviewed in detail to see what, if any, revisions are necessary.

A second problem also exists in the mapping area because of symbolization. Data is collected showing correct positions; however in later steps, in checking overlays of data, such as the symbolized roads and buildings, the building locations are moved because of symbol overlaps. The final product data base is valid for the product but not for general use. In this case the original data which shows the correct position must be saved for exchange purposes.

The preceding discussion was all related to exchange of correct data and only addressed the collection of data elements for a single product but in a way which would facilitate exchange. The next phase is the actual collection of multiple product data; that is, the collection of additional attributes and data elements for other products which are available from the same source material. This operation could save on preparation and set up time of the source material but has some inherent problems. First, it will take extra time since additional data is being collected, and priorities and completion schedules may not permit the extra time. Secondly, it means rewriting production procedures and retraining personnel, since current procedures are single product oriented. Production programs would have to be analyzed to determine the cost effectiveness on a case-by-case basis.

Even if the original collection could be made product independent and additional attributes and data elements could be collected in a cost effective manner, there is yet another problem. In the magnetic tape storage environment, data would still be collected and stored in product sets for convenience, even when this results in redundant data. The true source data base, which contains individual classes of data, for multiple product use, will happen almost automatically when the physical data moves to an on-line DBMS environment. This condition will have the same impact as the exchange format had for the terrain elevation data. If data from two products moves on-line under the same DBMS they represent an integrated set within the computer. It will no longer be necessary or justifiable to maintain duplicate data elements which

Terrain Elevation Data Base

The current DMA standard for terrain elevation data, product specification (1977), defines the format for a uniform matrix of elevation points and is used for both exchange and storage within DMA. As originally defined the standard called for one cell size, a one degree by one degree cell. However the header label has since been modified to allow for a variable cell size. Internal to DMA we will store the one degree by one degree cell as a standard data set. If users require other than the one degree cell size the data can be abstracted or merged to other cell sizes which can be accommodated by the exchange format.

Figure 12 shows how the exchange standard has been useful in introducing the source data base concept into the production process. The diagram shows the exchange and storage formats. It also shows that storage includes product and source formats. In this case the source storage format is equal to the exchange format; however, that could be changed in the future.

Some terrain elevation products P1 and P2 were being produced prior to the introduction of an exchange specification. To make existing data available the exchange specification was established and then conversion programs were developed to and from the exchange format from P1 and P2. In addition software was developed in-house to generate the standard storage cell size; to plot, smooth, perform accuracy tests and fully qualify the cells; and to merge and smooth borders to provide contiguous data. As pointed out before the standard cell size is also offered as a product.

Once the capability to produce standard storage cells exists, there are some interesting consequences. Any new product such as P3 must consider the generation of the standard first and then conversion to the product as a prime alternative. The production of P3 direct from raw source would require the development of special software (see dashed lines) to qualify the new cells. This development would be an additional cost and would be difficult to justify. In addition, P1 and P2 can also be produced from the exchange format because of the original conversion process. If requirements develop for different products in the same geographic area, the obvious way to produce them is to produce the standard first and then the final multiple products. Note that the standard has been introduced into the production process without interruption of any current production procedures. The addition of the exchange format and the conversion programs gives the producers for P1 and P2 an option to produce their products by two methods. After the standard to product procedures have been fully tested and qualified the old procedures can be discontinued. This is a virtually painless and certainly safe way to introduce standardization into the production process.

Geographic Feature Data Bases

To make production operations more cost effective, one approach is to minimize redundant data and eliminate duplicate activities. The collection, processing and storage of data all have an associated cost. The relative values (are collection) high, processing medium, and storage low. If we have a choice of storing finished data between requests or reprocessing the raw data each time, it would be cheaper to store rather than reprocess in most cases. Since collection costs are the highest we certainly do not want to be forced to collect the same data twice. Very briefly we would like to exchange all collected data and fully utilize collection resources by collecting multiple product data whenever it is cost effective.

require additional space and multiple updates. As additional attributes or data elements are collected, they can be added to the on-line set with ease. It may be necessary to add product codes to data elements and attributes to make storage and retrieval more efficient; however, that will be a small price to pay for an on-line unified multiproduct data base. If we can solve all the exchange problems the move to an on-line environment should be relatively easy.

Research and Development

DMA does not have an R&D facility directly within its organization but relies on facilities associated with the military services; such as the Engineering Topographic Laboratories (ETL) of the U.S. Army and the Rome Air Development Center of the U.S. Air Force. In addition we let contracts directly to commercial R&D organizations. In the data base area we are not attempting to develop any data base management systems (DBMS) specifically for our use, but rather are looking to test and apply available commercial systems.

ETL is testing several relational data base management systems such as Ingres and Oracle to determine their advantages and disadvantages relative to the hierarchical and network DBMS. In addition, ETL has also directed a study on topological data structures, Sharpley and Leiserson (1978) which is also a relational approach. This system uses modes, line segments and polygons to describe a given environment and relate the areas to lines and lines to points.

The Rome Air Development Center is directing a study on product independent data bases. The primary purpose of this study is to determine the feasibility of developing product independent data bases, what their characteristics should be, and an approach. Preliminary findings of this study have already shown product independent data bases to be feasible, the problem is to determine when they will become practical and cost effective.

Summary

The goal is to provide more cost effective and responsive operations. This can be accomplished through the application of data base techniques to both our management and production data files. The data base requirements must be developed for a large set of data bases and will take considerable time and resources. A concept of operations has been established which will guide the overall effort. Perhaps the single most important idea in the concept is the use of the exchange format as the link between old and new systems as well as between organizations. This exchange link provides maximum use of all collected data and allows a smooth, tested transition to new systems and technology. The major effort during the next year or two will be to develop exchange and storage specifications and the associated conversion programs. Future plans will include the gradual transition to an on-line, source, multiproduct data base as the long-range goal.

13

References

Sharpley, W.K. and Leiserson, J.F. (1978). A Unified Approach to Mapping, Charting, and Geodesy (MC&G) Data Base Structure Design. *U.S. Army Engineer Topographic Laboratories Report ETL-0144*.

Product Specification (1977). Defense Mapping Agency Product Specifications for DMA Standard for Digital Terrain Elevation Data.

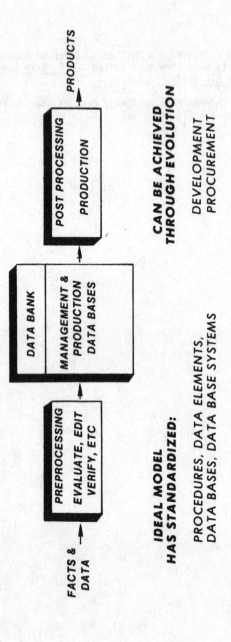

Figure 1 - Simplified Functional Model

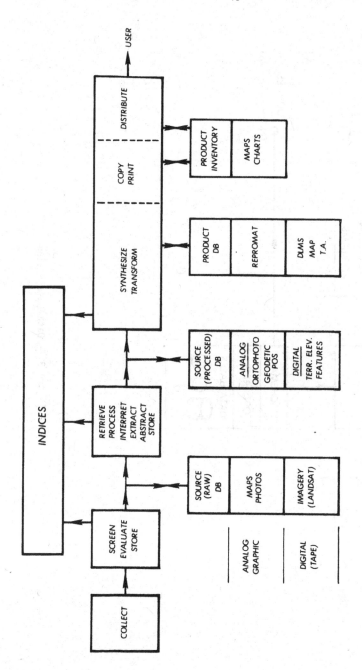

Figure 2 - Expanded Functional Production Flow

16

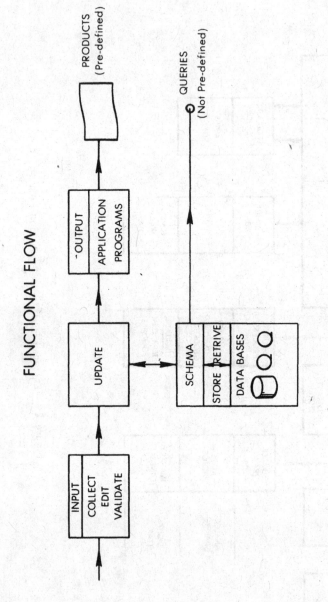

FUNCTIONAL FLOW

Figure 3 – Data Base System

17

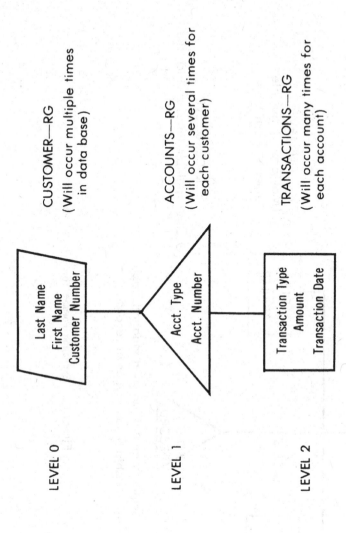

LEVEL 0 — CUSTOMER—RG
(Will occur multiple times in data base)

Last Name
First Name
Customer Number

LEVEL 1 — ACCOUNTS—RG
(Will occur several times for each customer)

Acct. Type
Acct. Number

LEVEL 2 — TRANSACTIONS—RG
(Will occur many times for each account)

Transaction Type
Amount
Transaction Date

Logical structure of data base showing relationship among data elements.

Figure 4 – Schema for Banking Data Base

18

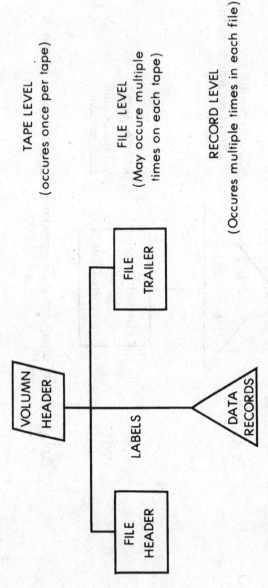

TAPE LEVEL
(occures once per tape)

FILE LEVEL
(May occure multiple times on each tape)

RECORD LEVEL
(Occures multiple times in each file)

VOLUMN HEADER

FILE TRAILER

FILE HEADER

LABELS

DATA RECORDS

Logical structure/format of data on magnetic tape showing relationship among types of records.

Figure 5 - Exchange Format for Typical Magnetic Tape

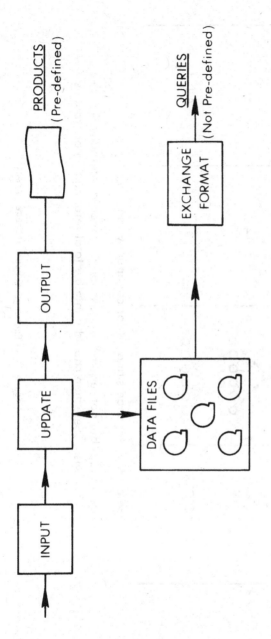

Figure 6 - Exchange Format - External View

EXCH vs STORAGE ALTERNATIVES	SET OF 6 USERS	CONVERSION PROGRAMS NEEDED TO EXCHANGE	USERS IMPACTED BY STORAGE FORMAT CHANGE
NO STANDARD	 ALL STORAGE ○○○○○○	30	5
EXCH ≠ STOR	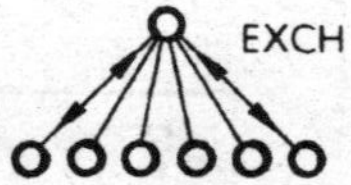 EXCH / STORAGE	12	0
EXCH = STOR	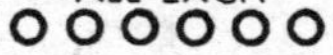 ALL EXCH ○○○○○○	0	All

Select an exchange standard for community use

User may (but not require) use exchange standard internally if they wish. Selection should minimize total reformatting operations.

Figure 7 - Exchange Versus Storage Format

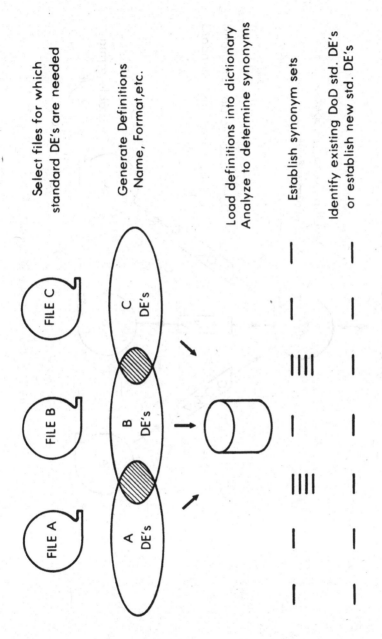

Select files for which standard DE's are needed

Generate Definitions Name, Format, etc.

Load definitions into dictionary Analyze to determine synonyms

Establish synonym sets

Identify existing DoD std. DE's or establish new std. DE's

Figure 8 - Developing Standard Data Elements

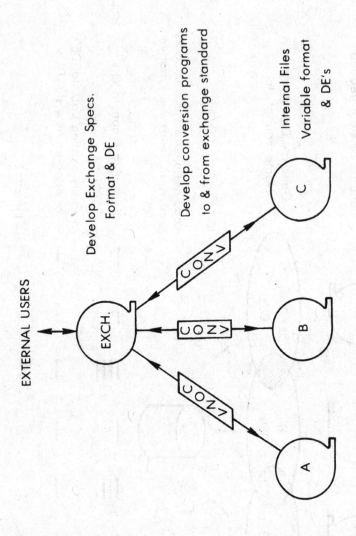

EXTERNAL USERS

Develop Exchange Specs.
Format & DE

Develop conversion programs
to & from exchange standard

Internal Files
Variable format
& DE's

Figure 9 - Develop Exchange Capability

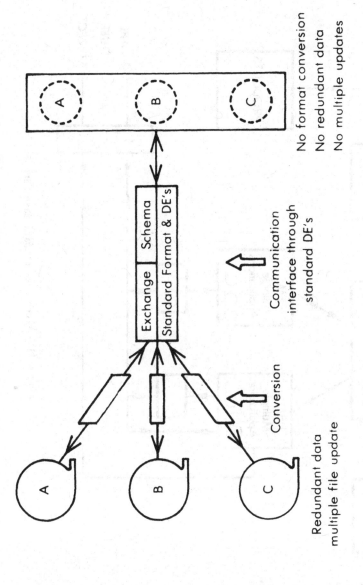

Figure 10 - Transition from FMS to DBMS

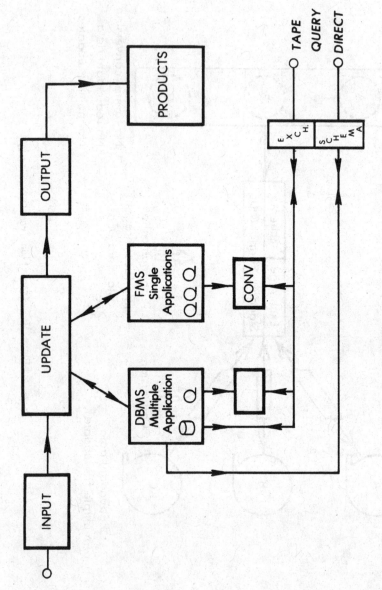

Figure 11 - Macro View of Data Bases and Files

25

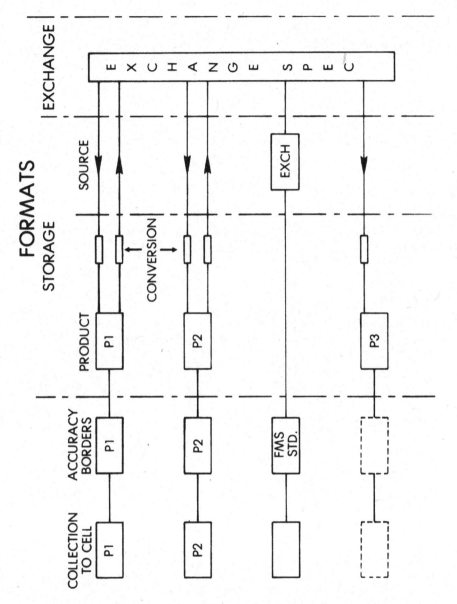

Figure 12 – Terrain Elevation Production Flow

DATA DEFINITION AND MANAGEMENT TECHNIQUES
FOR INTERACTIVE GEO-FACILITY APPLICATIONS

Carol J. Berry; Roger W. Holliday; William G. Tuel, Jr.

Abstract - All utility systems face the problem of producing and maintaining accurate records on their geographic facilities -- those facilities located throughout a geographic area for the purpose of providing service to the utility's customers. These records commonly include both alphanumeric and graphic information, such as distribution maps, circuit diagrams and design specifications. Some early attempts to apply computers to cope with this problem have attacked a single piece -- for example, map drafting systems have been designed to faithfully reproduce and edit the final graphic report (maps). However, in such systems, the alphanumeric data vital for engineering and design calculations are often lost.

This paper describes a comprehensive geo-facility system. In this system, data management techniques are used to preserve the relationships between a facility and other facilities, and between a facility and the various components of its description. The description of a facility is developed using data definition techniques for both facility attributes and graphic presentation.

The geo-facility workstation supports an x-y tablet input device. A variety of specialized operations can be invoked by pointing to menus located on the tablet. The design of these menus and the relationship of these menus to the facility definition requires additional data definition.

The interaction of the various definition and management functions described above is illustrated with a sample design session.

IBM Scientific Center, Palo Alto, California, USA

INTRODUCTION

All utility systems face the problem of producing and maintaining accurate records of their geographic facilities, i.e. those facilities located throughout an area for the purpose of providing service to the utility's customers. These records commonly include both alphanumeric and graphic information. Examples include distribution maps, circuit diagrams, and design specifications. The alphanumeric data include a facility's identification number, its engineering parameters, and accounting information. Graphic data show the location of the facility and its relationship to other facilities. It is often the case that several sets of records are kept, and often the alphanumeric data are maintained separately from the graphic data. For example, a transformer file containing ratings is kept separate from the distribution maps showing the location of transformers in the vicinity of an overloaded transformer. The necessity to cross-reference two (or more) files is a burdensome task for the electrical designer.

The problem of accurate record maintenance is compounded in high activity areas in which several projects may be active simultaneously. It is important for a designer to have up-to-date information on committed and scheduled projects. However, facilities records are usually updated only after all construction is complete and all facilities assigned to the proper accounting category. Thus the designer must frequently review a long list of open work orders to research whether a particular project affects his proposed design.

Early attempts to apply computers to cope with this problem have viewed the situation narrowly as a map maintenance problem. For example, map drafting systems have been designed to faithfully reproduce and edit the major graphic reports (maps). Such systems do not attempt to capture design information, and the alphanumeric data vital for engineering and design calculations are often lost. Data fields retained as textual annotation must be manually interpreted, and are not usable by analytic programs such as feeder loading. It is also difficult in most cases to express the required relationship information - how a transformer is connected, for example, or the proper relationships between a fuse and a disconnect on the same pole.

An effective solution must view the problem as it really is, viz., a facilities records maintenance problem (Tuel, 1978),reporting and data entry in which maps and design documents arereporting and data entry tools, not ends in themselves. Solutions to computerized records problems involve data management, data base, and data definition techniques. This paper describes a comprehensive geo-facility system and shows explicitly how data definition and management techniques are used to enter and maintain the relationships among facilities.

INTERACTIVE GEO-FACILITIES GRAPHIC SUPPORT SYSTEM

The Interactive Geo-Facilities Graphic Support (IGGS) System (IBM, 1979) is composed of graphic input/output devices connected to an interactive, time-sharing processor port. The graphic I/O device configuration is used as a design or drafting workstation. The workstations communicate with a host data base(s) for retrieval of primary data, storage of permanent facilities changes, and interchange of project data. The major hardware components are shown in Figure 1 and described below.

Components of IGGS

o   Processor/Storage - The processor executes the data control functions and calculations necessary to acquire and display records information. The particular software relationships required are described below. Facility data records are stored in high speed random workspace storage. Bulk storage for saved workspaces and program residence is provided.

o   Display Control - A single control unit which accepts alphanumeric, graphic, and control information from the processor, and returns input data from the alpha-numeric keyboard, the storage display cursor, or the digitizing tablet.

o   Digitizing Tablet - A large, flat electronic worksurface, equipped with a pen, mouse, or puck. When the pen is pressed against the surface, the x-y coordinates of the point touched are transmitted to the control unit.

o   Alphanumeric display and keyboard - A CRT alphanumeric display for tabular and formatted output; the keyboard permits alphanumeric data entry into the CRT display.

o   Storage display - A vector driven storage tube for presentation of graphic displays. It also has a cursor that may be positioned manually by the joy stick.

o   Joy Stick - A two-dimensional manual positioning mechanism for the storage display cursor.

With the exception of the dual displays, the configuration is not dramatically different from a map maintenance work station. What is significantly different is the organization of the components by the IGGS software. In particular, data definition techniques are used to define the facilities, their pictures and how tablet pointings are combined to create new entries in the work space.

DATA DEFINITION - THE KEY TO FACILITY RELATIONSHIPS

Although graphic documents contain large amounts of information, there are relatively few different types of objects represented. This is also the case in design. A designer works with a set of predefined objects, such as vaults, conduits, transformers, etc. His design consists of the selection and configuration of instances of these objects. In IGGS, the predefined objects are called entities.

Entity Definition

The entity is the basic unit of definition in IGGS. An entity is a generic definition for which data are acquired and/or displayed. Examples include: facilities, (e.g. primaries, fuses, single phase transformers); subfacilities, such as customer service drops; facility related data such as work order history and outage data; pictures (graphic diagrams) of facilities or subfacilities. Each entity may have fields containing definitions of relevant data. For non-picture entities, such fields usually contain engineering or accounting data. Picture entities contain general descriptions of the graphic presentation desired. Figure 2 shows the entity definition for a primary conductor and transformer in an electric distribution system.

Each entity definition specifies the name and numeric ID of that class of facility (e.g., PRIMARY 105), its attachment type (see below), layer (e.g., E for electric, G for gas), associated picture definition, default pointing rule (i.e. how tablet pointings are to be interpreted), and several fields which may be initialized to default values when an instance of that entity is created.

Each instance of an entity is associated with a geographic position and is related to other entities. The type of relationship is fixed by the entity

```
            NAME         ID      TYPE    LAYER    DEFPIC
            ------       -----   ----    -----    ------
FACDEF   :PRIMARY        105     2       E        5103
```

```
                                        Picture ID
                                   Entity layer
                              Attachment type(II)
                         Entity number
                   Entity name
            Definition type
```

```
            Name of pointing rule program
               Default pointing rule number

        DEFRUL   :ADD         9105

        FIELD NAME  TYPE REP     DEFAULT VALUE
        ----------  ---- ---     -------------
```

```
            Field name
                Type: 1 = character; 3 = integer;
                      4 = floating point;
                         Length of field
                                Default value
```

```
    FIELD  1:CIRCUIT    3    1      1234
    FIELD  2:MATERIAL   1    4      'ACSR'
    FIELD  3:SIZE       1    4      '4/0'
```

```
            NAME         ID      TYPE    LAYER    DEFPIC
            ------       -----   ----    -----    ------
FACDEF   :TRANSFRM      101     3       E        5101
DEFRUL   :ADD          9101

        FIELD NAME  TYPE REP     DEFAULT VALUE
        ----------  ---- ---     -------------
    FIELD  1:RATING     4    1      25.0
    FIELD  2:SERIAL     1    12     'AA-NNNNN-NNN'
    FIELD  3:NUMPHASE   1    1      '1'
    FIELD  4:PHASES     1    2      'AN'
```

Fig. 2. Entity Definition Examples

definition, and is diagrammed in Figure 3. Figure 3 is hierarchical. For example, each absolute point is uniquely connected to a layer. Each layer may have hundreds of points connected to it. Facility entities are assigned types (I, II, or III) depending on whether they connect to only one point (I), two points (II), or one point with two connector ends (III).

The entire body of data is structured in this way and stored in the workspace of IGGS. "Connections" are indicated by pointers which chain various entity instances together to explicitly indicate electrical connectivity and sub-facility association with a facility.

The entity definitions are predefined and stored separately in the workspace.

They are interpreted whenever a new facility is to be added to the workspace. The new facility's connections and position are established according to <u>pointing rule definitions</u>.

Pointing Rule Definitions

A pointing rule is a method for defining specific facility and picture locations in terms of the existing facilities and physical pointings to the tablet surface in the vicinity of a facility. Pointing rules are required for two reasons:

o   "exact" pointing to a facility is impossible by a human operator. Digitizing tablet resolutions extend to .02 mm (.001 inch), far finer than can be tracked by hand. Thus, a criterion for nearness or "correlation" must be invoked.

o   The desired location may be inaccessible due to drawing congestion or due to graphics deliberately offset from the facility's true position for clarity of presentation. Rules for determining true position of specified types of facilities are required. Positions generated by IGGS on the basis of pointing rules are called <u>logical points</u>.

Figures 4 and 5 illustrate a set of pointing rules for defining a primary conductor that must connect to the end of an existing primary. The graphic presentation is offset for clarity, but the two primary lines must graphically intersect. The rules, selected by rule codes specifying the logical points involved, allow the system designer to maintain precise geographic position for sets of facilities, as well as to produce uncongested graphic reports.

```
        DESC    :PRIMARY POINTING RULE
                 PTGDEF ID
                 ------
        PTGDEF  :9105    (Pointing rule number)

                 PHYSICAL/   ACTION    C O R R E L A T I O N
                 POINTING    RULE      ACTION         TARGETS
                 --------    ----      ------         -------
        LOG PT 1:1            0        2 (1)          3105
        LOG PT 2:2210 (2)     0        0
        LOG PT 3:2010         1 (3)    0
        LOG PT 4:2            0        0
        LOG PT 5:3            0        0
```

Notes:
(1) Correlation required on indicated target to validate pointing. ID 105 is the number of the PRIMARY entity.
(2) Derived points are specific combinations of previously defined logical points. General format is NABC, where N is a case, A and B are logical points, and C is a distance modifier. For the cases here, 22B0 means near end of facility picture for logical point B, 20B0 means point at near end of correlated facility associated with logical point B.
(3) Action mode defines the attachment assumptions. For the program ADD (add a facility), mode = 1 signifies attach facility to existing point connector at the point. Otherwise, signal an error. Mode = 0 signifies no action taken.

Fig. 4. Primary Extension Pointing Rule Example

One or more sets of pointing rules (for different attachment situations) are specified for each entity facility, and provide the link between a facility definition and its picture definition.

Picture Definitions

In addition to entity and pointing rule definitions, pictures of facilities must be defined. A facility picture is a workspace segment related to, but distinct from, the facility data segment. A facility may have multiple pictures. Thus different pictures may be drawn at different display scales. The defined picture is displayed in the appropriate location when a facility is added to the workspace. Its defining coordinates are the logical points generated by the pointing rule in use when the facility is created. Picture fields include: line segments of various types and weights, arcs, arrows, symbols, and justified text strings. Visibility at various scales can also be defined, so that detailed pictures can be suppressed on large area drawings.

Once created, a picture may be manipulated separately from the facility that it represents. Thus graphics can be offset or adjusted without losing the necessary facility connection relationships. It is also possible to provide text annotation derived from a facility data field. Thus, in Figures 6 and 7, the transformer represented by a triangular symbol at point 1, has its serial number, field #2, added to the drawing right justified on the line indicated by logical points 1 and 2. It would also be possible to orient the annotation independently of the transformer symbol by defining a picture using a third logical point.

The set of symbols used is specified independently and can be tailored to the usage of any IGGS workstation.

Several types of picture and pointing rules can be used with an entity definition. The selection of which set of entities and rules and which workspace function to use is made dynamically by the operator using function menus, separately defined by the user for the set of operations anticipated, and represented as a set of "paper function keys" located at an arbitrary position on the digitizing tablet.

Menu Definitions

The final definition element in IGGS is the set of menus. A menu array consists of a reserved area of the digitizing tablet, subdivided into a rectangular grid, with each element of the grid being definable as a key or a stack of keys and subkeys of varying sizes and extents. Generally speaking, each key defines a program name to perform some action. Subkeys provide selectable data for the program, including the possibility of alphanumeric keyboard input. Keys can be defined to make a particular entity definition active (current); set field values such as material or size; set the workspace function (for example, add, delete, edit, move); select specific pointing and picture rules; and invoke standard graphic display functions such as zoom, re-center, move in compass direction, etc. (Figures 8 and 9). Since keys can be stacked, a single menu pointing can accomplish several things, such as 1) adding a 2) 25 KVA 3) single phase 4) transformer between the 5) primary and the secondary at the point to be indicated by the sketch pointing location (see Figure 10).

```
DESC    :TRANSFORMER PICTURE

           Picture ID      Graphic Class      Visiblity flags

PICDEF  :5101            3                 1       1

            Logical point, local reference orientation (1)
               Offsets from logical point to base point
               Logical point defining local y-axis

BASE PT :100    0      0      200     0     0

            Line Type      Visible scale range (visible at all scales)
ATTRIB  :4              63

         Logical position and local reference
            Offsets
               Rotation angle from local x-axis (degrees)
                  Alignment (2)
                        Scale type (3)   Size   Symbol code

SYMB    :100  0    0    0   231   1         20      348

FTEXT   :100 -eps delta 270  344   1       15       2

                          Source data field
```

Notes:
(1) Code is three digits. First digit is logical point, second is orientation code, third is scale type (absolute inches or data units).
(2) Alignment refers to positioning of text characters with respect to reference point indicated by a three digit code. For the case here, 231 means centered, 344 means right justified below base line.
(3) Scale type defines measurement unit for scale size. Unit may be in absolute inches, or in geographical units.

Fig. 6. Picture Definition of Transformer Symbol

IGGS provides a set of "building block" programs for graphic manipulation, workspace management, and rule selection. By proper menu design each user can organize the IGGS components to support a wide variety of drawing and design styles. Specialized user functions can be added to those supplied by IGGS and invoked identically to IGGS functions.

ILLUSTRATIVE EXAMPLE

Figures 11 - 20 show a partial set of definitions for entities, rules, pictures, and menus which might be used in the design of primaries, laterals, secondaries, and service transformers for an overhead radial distribution system.

To illustrate the operation of IGGS, consider the operation of tapping a primary to create a lateral, setting pole locations on the lateral, locating a secondary tap, and indicating the service transformer size installed. The individual tablet pointings are numbered in Figure 21 and are explained in Table 1.

```
DOCUMENT    SHARE    20DX  15DY;
R;
R    AREA AND BLOCK DEFINITIONS;
R;
A    Q1(20,15)       0X    0Y    20DX      15DY;
B    Q2       =      Q1(6-18,2-13);
B    Q3(2,3)  =      Q1(9-16,4-12);
R;
R KEY/LOCATION/ FUNCTION ; SUBKEY/LOCATION/ID/DATA; NOTES;
R;
R    "ADD" KEY FOR ENTIRE MENU;
R;
K    Q1   1 SELECT;  S = 1 ADD;   N ;
R;
R    POINTING RULE 9101 FOR TRANSFORMER;
R;
K    Q2   2 RULE  ;  S = 1 9101;  N ;
R;
R    MAKE TRANSFORMER ENTITY CURRENT AND ENTER FIELDS;
R;
K    Q3   3 ENTITY; S = 1  101;  N ;
R;
R    SET NUMBER OF PHASES FIELD;
R;
K    Q3   4 FIELD ;  S  Q3(1,) 3  '1'; N ;
                     S  Q3(2,) 3  '3'; N ;
R;
R SET KVA RATING;
R;
K    Q3   5 FIELD ;  S  Q3(,1) 1  100.0; N 100.0    KVA;
                     S  Q3(,2) 1   50.0; N 50.0     KVA;
                     S  Q3(,3) 1   25.0; N 25.0     KVA;
```

Fig. 8. Menu Definition for Adding Transformer

SUMMARY

Proper maintenance of facilities records requires the use of data management and data definition techniques. In this paper, the data definition aspects of an Interactive Geo-Facilities Graphic Support System have been presented and illustrated. The definition of the facility relationships makes it possible to produce meaningful graphic documents and to maintain a structured facilities data base.

The authors would like to acknowledge the contributions of the many persons associated with the development of IGGS, particularly Mr. Don Skiba and Mr. Dick Martin of IBM.

BIBLIOGRAPHY

(1) William G. Tuel, Jr. and Carol J. Berry, "Data Bases for Geographic Facility Design and Analysis." ASCE Conference on Computing in Civil Engineering, Atlanta, Ga., June 1978.

(2) IBM Corp., Interactive Geo-Facilities Graphic Support (IGGS) General Information Manual GH20-2152, May, 1979.

```
LAYER    :ELECTRIC   E
*********************************************************

          NAME        ID     TYPE    LAYER    DEFPIC
          ------      -----   ----    -----    ------

*********************************************************
FACDEF   :POLE       102     1        E       5102
DEFRUL   :ADD        9102

          FIELD NAME  TYPE REP   DEFAULT VALUE
          ---------   ---- ---   -------------
FIELD   1:SERIAL      1    4     'NNNN'
******                                      *********
FACDEF   :LATERAL     103    2        E      5103
DEFRUL   :ADD         9103

          FIELD NAME  TYPE REP   DEFAULT VALUE
          ---------   ---- ---   -------------

FIELD   1:CIRCUIT     2    1     1234
FIELD   2:MATERIAL    1    4     'ACSR'
FIELD   3:SIZE        1    4     '4/0'
******                                      *********
FACDEF   :SECNDARY    104    2        E      5104
DEFRUL   :ADD         9104

          FIELD NAME  TYPE REP   DEFAULT VALUE
          ---------   ---- ---   -------------
FIELD   1:BLANK       1    4
FIELD   2:MATERIAL    1    4     'ALUM'
FIELD   3:SIZE        1    4     '10'
******                                      *********
FACDEF   :PRIMARY     105    2        E      5103
DEFRUL   :ADD         9105

          FIELD NAME  TYPE REP   DEFAULT VALUE
          ---------   ---- ---   -------------
FIELD   1:CIRCUIT     2    1     1234
FIELD   2:MATERIAL    1    4     'ACSR'
FIELD   3:SIZE        1    4     '450M'
******                                      *********
FACDEF   :TRANSFRM    101    3        E      5101
DEFRUL   :ADD         9101

          FIELD NAME  TYPE REP   DEFAULT VALUE
          ---------   ---- ---   -------------
FIELD   1:RATING      4    1     25.0
FIELD   2:SERIAL      1    12    'AA-NNNNN-NNN'
FIELD   3:NUMPHASE    1    1     '1'
FIELD   4:PHASES      1    2     'AN'
```

Fig. 11. Electric Distribution Entity Definition

```
DESC    :ADD POLES - MAY CORRELATE ON A LATERAL(103) OR BACKBONE (105)
PTGDEF  :9102
            PHYSICAL/DERIVED POINTING   ACTION   CORRELATION RULES

LOG PT 1:       1                  0       1 (1)     3103 3105
LOG PT 2:       1110 (2)           2 (3)   0
```

(1) Point may correlate on specified targets, but is not required to
(2) Derived point code (1AA0) means use logical point A
(3) Action rule 2 means "add facility to new point connector"


```
DESC    :ADD LATERAL - TWO POINTINGS - 1) POLE/PRIMARY, 2) POLE OK
DESC    :EXISTING PRIMARY IS SPLIT AND LATERAL ATTACHED
PTGDEF  :9103
            PHYSICAL/DERIVED POINTING   ACTION   CORRELATION RULES

LOG PT 1:       1                  0       2       3102
LOG PT 2:       2010               4 (1)   2 (2)   3103 3105
LOG PT 3:       2                  0       1       3102
LOG PT 4:       2030               2       0
```

(1) Action rule 4 for "ADD" means split correlated facility into two parts and
     connect current facility at the created node (point connector)
(2) Correlation required on either correlation target


```
DESC    :ADD SECONDARY - THREE POINTS: 1) POLE/PRIMARY, 2) OFFSET SIDE,
DESC    : 3) POLE AT END OF SECONDARY. PRIMARY SPLIT AND SECONDARY IS
DESC    : ATTACHED.  PICTURE OFFSET BY SPECIFIED AMOUNT TOWARDS 2)
PTGDEF  :9104
            PHYSICAL/DERIVED POINTING   ACTION   CORRELATION RULES

LOG PT 1:       1                  0       2       3102
LOG PT 2:       2010               4       2       3103 3105
LOG PT 3:       2                  0       0
LOG PT 4:       3                  2       2       3102
LOG PT 5:       2040 (1)           0       0
```

(1) Establishes base point for end of secondary


```
DESC    :ADD TRANSFORMER - ONE POINTING - 1) SECONDARY
DESC    : SECONDARY BROKEN AT PRIMARY, TRANSFORMER CONNECTED
DESC    :SYMBOL LOCATED AT POINTING POSITION
PTGDEF  :9101
            PHYSICAL/DERIVED POINTING   ACTION   CORRELATION RULES

LOG PT 1:       1                  3 (1)   2       3104
LOG PT 2:       4210 (2)           0       0
```

(1) Action rule 3 for "ADD" means break nearest connection of correlated facility
     and connect current entity between old and new connection points
(2) Derived pointing 42A0 means find the far end of the correlated facility. This
     point is used to establish the local y-axis for symbol orientation

Fig. 12. Electrical Design Pointing Rules

```
DESC      :POLE PICTURE WITH SERIAL NUMBER ANNOTATION
          ID        CLASS (1)   DISPLAY (2)   DETECT (3)
          ----      -----       -------       ------
PICDEF  :5102        1           1             1


          BASE PTN  OFFSET(X,Y)  Y-AXIS PTN  OFFSET(X,Y)
          --------  -----------  ----------  -----------
BASE PT :120        0    BETA    0           0    0


          LINE TYPE     VISIBILITY
          ---------     ----------
ATTRIB  :1             63


          PTN  DELX  DELY  ANGLE REFPOS SCTYPE SIZE  ID
          ---  ----  ----  ----- ------ ------ ----  --
SYMB    :000  0     0     0     231 (4) 1      10    214 (5)


          PTN  DELX  DELY  ANGLE REFPOS SCTYPE SIZE FLD.
          ---  ----  ----  ----- ------ ------ ---- ----
FTEXT   :000  000   GAMMA 90    132     1      10    1 (6)
```

Notes:
(1) Arbitrary picture class. May be used for display layer separation
(2) Normally visible. May also be specified as normally invisible.
(3) Normally detectable (correlatable). May be specified as not.
(4) Symbol/string adjustment digits -- 231 means centered on reference point calculated from PTN and DELX,DELY offset; 132 means left justified text vertically centered on reference point
(5) Symbol ID from symbol table in use (separately defined)
(6) Entity field number to be used for source of text

Fig. 14. Electrical Design Picture Definition (Pole)


```
DESC      :PRIMARY PICTURE (LATERAL OR BACKBONE)

          ID        CLASS      DISPLAY      DETECT
          ----      -----      -------      ------
PICDEF  :5103        2          1            1


          BASE PTN  OFFSET(X,Y) Y-AXIS PTN  OFFSET(X,Y)
          --------  ----------- ----------  -----------
BASE PT :200        0    0       0           0    0


          LINE TYPE VISIBILITY
          --------- ----------
ATTRIB  :1         63


          PTN1 DELX  DELY  PNT2  DELX  DELY
          ---- ----  ----  ----  ----  ----
LINE    :200  0     0     400    0     0
```

Fig. 16. Electrical Design Picture Definition (Primary)

```
DESC     :SECONDARY PICTURE

         ID           CLASS      DISPLAY  DETECT
         ----         -----      -------  ------
PICDEF   :5104        3          1        1

         BASE PTN   OFFSET(X,Y)  Y-AXIS PTN  OFFSET(X,Y)
         --------   -----------  ----------  -----------
BASE PT :200         0    0       300         0    0

         LINE TYPE  VISIBILITY
         ---------  ----------
ATTRIB   :4           63

         PTN1 DELX  DELY  PNT2  DELX    DELY
         ---- ----  ----  ----  ----    ----
LINE    :200  0     0     200   0       ALPHA
LINE    :200  0     ALPHA 500   0       ALPHA
```

Fig. 18. Electrical Design Picture Definition (Secondary)

```
D    SHARE           20DX        15DY;
R;
A    Q1(20,15)  OX    OY    20DX     15DY;
B    Q2              = Q1(6-18,2-13);        R  RULE 9109 KEY;
B    Q3(2,3)         = Q1(9-16,4-12);        R  TRANSFORMER ENTITY KEY;
B    FACILITY(1,4) = Q1(2-6,11-14);          R  FACILITY TYPES;
B    MATL(1,4)       = Q1(2-3,3-10);         R  MATERIALS;
B    SIZE(1,8)       = Q1(4-6,3-10);         R  WIRE GAUGES;
B    PHYSPARM        = Q1(2-6,3-10);         R  ALL WIRE PARAMETERS;
R;
K    Q1 1 SELECT;  S = 1  ADD; N ;           R  "ADD" KEY FOR ENTIRE MENU;
R;
K    Q2 2    RULE;  S = 1 9101; N ;          R  ESTABLISH RULE 9101;
R;
K    Q3 3 ENTITY;  S = 1  101; N ;           R  MAKE TRANSFORMER CURRENT;
R;
R    SET NUMBER OF PHASES FIELD;
R;
K    Q3 4  FIELD;  S  Q3(1,)  3 '1'; N ;
                   S  Q3(2,)  3 '3'; N ;
R;
R    SET KVA RATING;
R;
K    Q3 5  FIELD;  S  Q3(,1)  1  100.0;  N 100.0      KVA;
                   S  Q3(,2)  1   50.0;  N 50.0       KVA;
                   S  Q3(,3)  1   25.0;  N 25.0       KVA;
R;
R    SET ENTITY FOR FACILITIES;
R;
K    FACILITY  6  ENTITY;  S  FACILITY(,1)  1  104; N SECONDARY;
                           S  FACILITY(,2)  1  105; N PRIMARY;
                           S  FACILITY(,3)  1  103; N LATERAL;
                           S  FACILITY(,4)  1  102; N POLE;
R;
R    MATERIAL AND SIZE FIELDS;
R;
K    PHYSPARM  7    FIELD;  S  MATL(,1)  2  'ACSR'; N ACSR;
                           S  MATL(,2)  2  'CU  '; N CU;
                           S  MATL(,3)  2  'ALUM'; N ALUM;
                           S  MATL(,4)  2  'CWLD'; N CU WELD;
                           S  SIZE(,1)  3  '600M'; N 600 MCM;
                           S  SIZE(,2)  3  '450M'; N 450 ;
                           S  SIZE(,3)  3  '380M'; N 380 ;
                           S  SIZE(,4)  3  '211M'; N 211    4/0;
                           S  SIZE(,5)  3  '2/0A'; N 2/0 AWG;
                           S  SIZE(,6)  3  '1/0A'; N 1/0;
                           S  SIZE(,7)  3  '2A  '; N 2;
                           S  SIZE(,8)  3  '6A  '; N 6;
```

Fig. 20 Electrical Distribution Design Menu Definition

Table 1. Explanation of Sketch and Menu Pointings

Map of existing primary and poles is already registered on tablet and displayed on vector storage screen; menu is already registered on tablet (multiple menus may exist)

Pointing	Item Touched	Description
1	MENU ADD LATERAL	"Lateral" becomes the current entity and a temporary facility is created; the material and size keys are enabled for the lateral data fields; the lateral "add" pointing rule and picture definition are established.
2	MENU MATERIAL ASCR	The material code 'ACSR' is entered into the material field of the lateral entity.
3	MENU SIZE 380mcm	The size code '380M' is entered into the size field of the entity.
4	POLE PICTURE	The pole from which the lateral is to extend is indicated; a connection is made to the existing primary.
5	SKETCH LOCATION	The other end of the lateral is indicated; the new lateral is added to the workspace along with its picture; the picture is displayed on the vector storage screen.
6	MENU ADD POLE	"Pole" becomes the current entity, and a temporary facility is created; the material and size keys are disabled (in practice, the menu would normally include pole height definitions, serial number, etc.); pointing rule and picture definition for "POLE" replace those for the previous entity.
7,8,9	LATERAL PICTURE	For each point touched on the lateral picture, a pole facility is added to the workspace and its picture displayed offset from the lateral as defined.
10,11,12	MENU SECONDARY	"Secondary" becomes current; the size and material fields are set, in this case to #6 ALUM.
13	POLE PICTURE	The pole from which the secondary is to extend is indicated; the secondary is connected to the lateral at this point.
14	SKETCH LOCATION	A point indicating on which side of the lateral the secondary picture is to appear.
15	POLE PICTURE	The pole on which the secondary terminates is indicated; the secondary is added to the workspace and its picture displayed offset as shown.
16	MENU TRANSFORMER	The transformer entity becomes current, and the data fields are set to single phase, 25.0 KVA.
17	SECONDARY PICTURE	The secondary connection to the primary is broken; the transformer is inserted between the secondary and the primary; the transformer symbol is displayed.

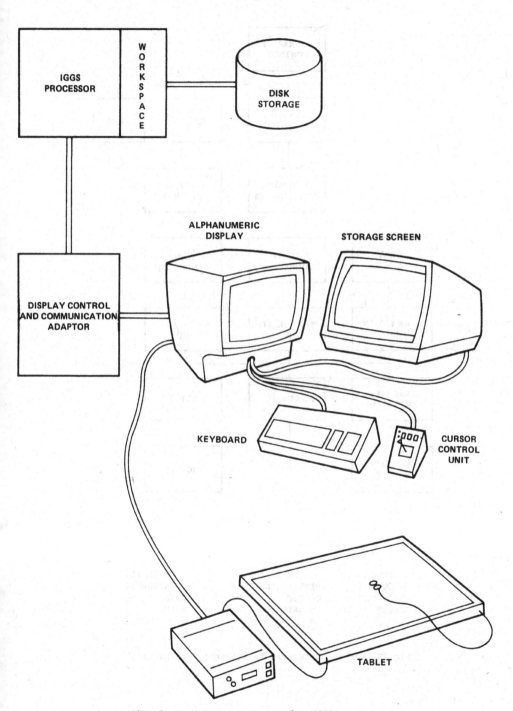

Fig. 1. Hardware components for IGGS

42

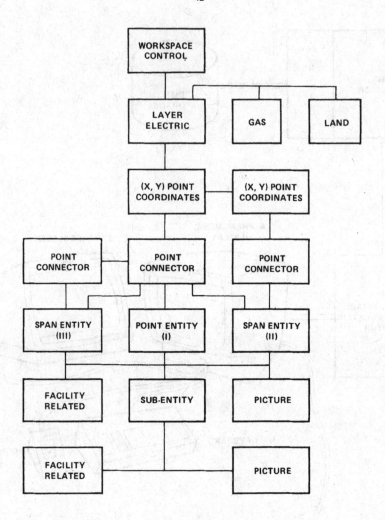

Examples:

```
    TYPE I           TYPE II              TYPE III
  POLE           PRIMARY CONDUCTOR     TRANSFORMER
  CAPACITOR      CONDUIT               FUSE
  VAULT          GAS MAIN              VALVE
```

Fig. 3. Workspace Segment Relationship Hierarchy

EXISTING PICTURE

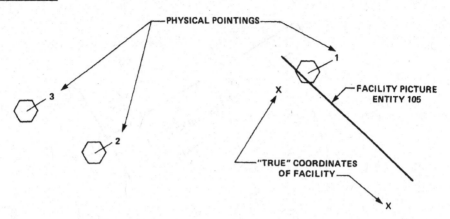

DESIRED PICTURE

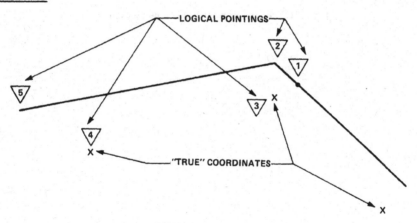

Fig. 5. Primary Extension Pointing Rule Illustration

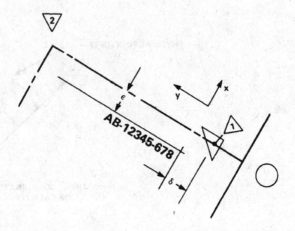

Fig. 7. Transformer Symbol Illustration

45

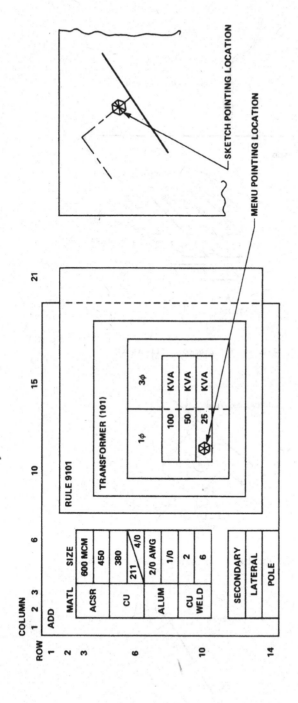

Fig. 9. Menu Document for Adding Transformer

46

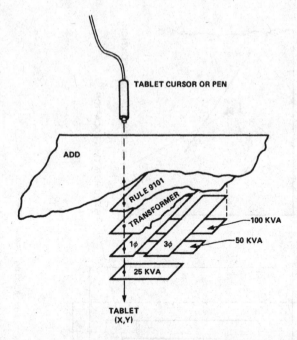

Fig. 10. Key Stacking Illustration

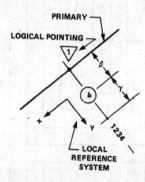

Fig. 13. Electrical Design Illustration (Pole)

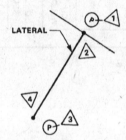

Fig. 15. Electrical Design Illustration (Primary)

47

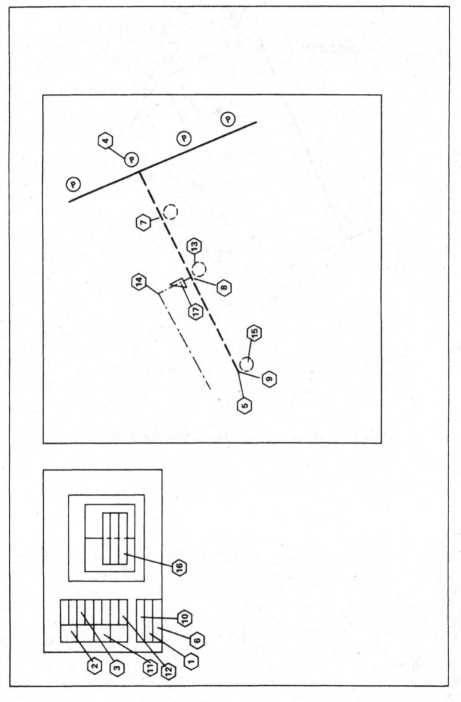

Fig. 21. Tablet Pointings to Add Distribution Facilities

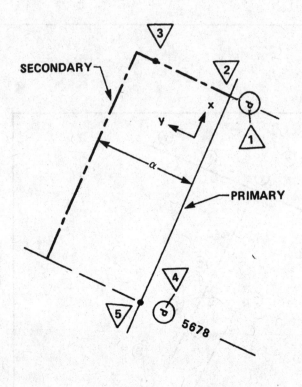

Fig. 17. Electrical Design Illustration (Secondary)

MAPPING WITH CENSUS DATA AND LANDSAT IMAGERY

Albert L. Zobrist

Computer analysis of Landsat data can provide several types of useful information in urban and near-urban areas. Thematic classification gives a map of land cover or land use and multi-pass registration can detect areas of change or urban growth. These derived products have roughly the same character as Landsat; they are computer compatible, are in image format, and have a peculiar map projection. Geographic operations on these data require integration with standard digitized (vector) representations of point, line, and area data. One example is generation of maps superimposing image and boundary data. Another example is tabulation of the image data by district polygons.

The approach described here uses image processing technology to perform spatial or geographic operations and concentrates upon the use of the image raster as a general representation for spatial data. Operations are provided for conversion of graphics (vector) data to image format, and for linking of image data to tabular files.

Jet Propulsion Laboratory
California Institute of Technology
4800 Oak Grove Drive
Mail Stop 168-527
Pasadena, California 91103

1. Preface

The particular problem of concern here is integration of Landsat data, which is in image raster format, with U.S. Bureau of the Census data, which is a combination of tabular and graphic (vector) data. However, Landsat is a prototype of the new and expanding class of remotely sensed data, and Census data are typical of the more traditional forms used by geographic information systems. The crucial challenge is to integrate these radically different data types for purposes of analysis.

2. Data Characteristics

The term Landsat refers to any of a series of three NASA earth orbiting satellites. The primary data collection instrument on each is a multispectral scanner which produces digital imagery in several visible and infrared frequencies. The familiar Landsat "pictures" of Earth can be made from these data but more important uses can be made of the digital version which can be ordered on computer tape. A single Landsat frame covers an area 185 kilometers on a side with a picture element resolution of less than 80 meters, thus, an order for one Landsat frame delivers from 20 t0 50 megabytes of data in four spectral bands. Aside from the great size of Landsat data sets, further problems are present. First, the area of interest to an application may straddle two or more Landsat frames requiring complex operations to rectify the analysis. Second, there is a problem with obtaining the true geolocation of Landsat data. It would be useful if the Landsat images were map projected, that is, if the image coordinates translated directly into some map coordinate system. As an alternative, Landsat data can be used as a geographic base and other types of data can be registered to it.

For reasons of economy and personal privacy, census data are available primarily as aggregations over various kinds of geographical units, for example, census tracts. Two files are needed for geographic information system use. One file is a table of statistics including the names of the aggregation units which serve as a key or geographic link. The second file is a graphics or vector file giving the name of an aggregation unit and a digitized boundary file which defines the true geographic location of the aggregation unit. In some cases, the boundary might be stored as directed segments with information on the right and left hand neighbors stored with each segment. An example is the DIME file as described in a publication by the U.S. Bureau of the Census (1970). The link between these two files is the name field. A name such as 'Manhattan' will have its statistics in one file and its boundary in the other. In terms of size, these files are much smaller than Landsat frames. Geolocation is not a problem since the boundaries are given in a geographic coordinate system. Geographic accuracy and file integrity are sometimes a problem.

These two data types, raster and vector, are natural ones for representing their information, and it is hard to imagine a common format that would be widely accepted. The two data types have not been used well together because raster format leads to image processing technology and vector format leads to graphics technology and it seems that a hybrid of these two technologies is needed.

3. The Image Datatype

Until recently, the image format has been used primarily as a computer process-able equivalent of a photo, with the value stored in each cell of the image representing a shade of grey or a color. But if the image is of a geographical area, then the value in the cell can be a datum for the area corresponding to that cell. A principle advantage of the image representation is that data for a geogrpahical point can be accessed immediately by position in the image matrix. Figure 1 illustrates the calculation of memory address of the data value from a latitude-longitude pair. This assumes that the image is map projected. If the image is not map projected, correlative data analysis is still possible if several data sets have been registered so that the same position in each image matrix corresponds to the same geographic point. It is a goal of image processing technology to make these operations efficient. The image datatype appears to be a powerful and general representation for spatially distributed data, and the range of uses can be divided into several broad categories.

Physical Analog. The pixel value represents a physical variable such as elevation, rainfall, smog density, etc.

District Identification. The pixel value is a numerical identifier for the district which includes that pixel area.

Class Identification. The pixel value is a numerical identifier for the land use or land cover, or for any other area classification scheme.

Tabular Pointer. The pixel value is a record pointer to a tabular record which applies to the pixel geographical area. This is similar to the key link mentioned in connection with Census files except that it would be inefficient to store long names in an image.

Point Identification. The pixel value identifies a point, or the nearest of a set of points, or the distance to the nearest of a set of points.

Line Identification. The pixel value identifies a line, or the nearest of a set of lines, or the distance to the nearest of a set of lines.

This range of uses requires that the system be able to handle images composed of words of varying length. For example, to identify census tracts in Los Angeles County requires 1500 different pixel values and elevation maps can require 15,000. This is more than the usual 256 grey levels handled by photographic image processing systems.

A negative aspect of image representation is the tremendous redundancy incurred in most cases. Most of the representations above have a more compact equivalent in graphics format. Several of our projects have involved over a billion bytes of data in image format.

A second concern is with accuracy of raster representation versus polygon representation of areas, lines, or points, or of physical variables. For example, to reduce the error of approximation to a curved border by half, a graphics data set needs twice as many vectors but a raster needs four times as many cells.

4. Data Analysis

The purpose here is to give a systematic arrangement of the basic capabilities needed for a hybrid raster-vector geographic information system. The particular system developed at JPL has been described in a previous report (Bryant and Zobrist, 1977). The basic capabilities are grouped under the subheadings that follow here.

4.1 Graphics to raster

The most important case here is the conversion of a region boundary file to a raster file containing a unique identifier for each region in the cells corresponding to each region. An associated tabular file is created to link image identifier with region names from the graphics file. In some cases it is desired to convert only lines or boundaries to raster form. A set of routines to accomplish these tasks consist of the following:

    A. vector linear transformation routine
    B. vector to raster scribe
    C. raster connectivity routine
    D. point overlay routine
    E. map color assignment routine

Routine A operates in vector mode only to transform a geographic coordinate in a linear fashion to agree with an image coordinate system. Routine B writes a raster file, setting raster cells to a selected value corresponding to the geographic locations of lines in a vector file. Routine C finds connected regions in the file produced by Routine B, marking each with a unique identifier. Since the border lines constitute a significant amount of area, they must be assigned in a systematic or random manner to neighboring regions. Routine D uses a tabular file containing centroids of regions and their corresponding names to perform lookup of raster identifiers to create a link between names and raster identifiers in the tabular file. Routine E is used to produce a visual product from the raster region file. It assigns four colors to a set of regions so that no adjacent regions have the same color. This routine operates with a heuristic instead of an algorithm, but is backed up by a guaranteed five color algorithm.

4.2 Surface approximation

Problems here can be categorized according to type and according to mathematical requirements that the surface must meet. The types of problems are handled by the following routines:

    F. point to raster surface
    G. vector contour to raster surface
    H. aggregated region tabular data to raster surface
    I. generation of raster surface by mathematical function

Here, the term raster surface refers to an image in which the cell value represents a geographic Z-value. Routine F is commonly used where point measurements of a physical variable are used to extend to a surface. A variety of techniques are known which can give a mathematical surface approximation to the points, and the raster is calculated from the mathematical surface. Routine G is a difficult and highly specialized routine. Its most likely use is to obtain raster elevation from elevation contour data because so much of these data exist.

However, the new generation of photogrammetry machines are producing raster elevation directly. Routine H might be used to create a population density surface from a map of regions and a table of population by regions. See Tabler and Lau (1978) for methods of obtaining a continuous surface while maintaining correct aggregates by region. Routine I is useful in a variety of modelling situations.

4.3 Raster processing

The system considered here will have to handle images of varying sizes and should handle up to 4000 x 4000. The most useful image processing routines are in the following categories

    J. file handling
    K. thematic classification
    L. mathematical function

Routines in J include image copying, cutting, and pasting. Routines in K convert raw Landsat into a raster representation of ground cover or land use. See Bauer, et. al. (1979), for a view of the status of these techniques. Routine L allows a user specified mathematical function to be applied to one or more images, resulting in an output image. An expression compiler is needed for the user specified function and a hash table is used for storage and lookup of computer results to save computation on large images.

4.4 Spatial registration

This is necessary when two maps or data planes are not in positional agreement when overlaid. In simple cases where the maps are accurate, agreement can be obtained by changing scale, aspect, or rotation (affine transformations). More commonly, the maps disagree by a complex distortion surface. The distortion is usually measured by obtaining the location in each data plane of a set of control points. The following routines can register data sets using control points

    M. random to grid control point transformation
    N. raster rubber sheet
    O. vector rubber sheet

Routine M is needed because randomly spaced control points do not allow efficient image processing in routine N. One of the surface fitting techniques used for routine F is used here to fit the random points and the fit is applied to a rectilinear grid of control points. Routine N distorts an input image according to a grid of control points to obtain an output image. The distortion is precisely followed at the control points and interpolated in between. An interpolation is also carried out to obtain the cell value in the output since it usually corresponds to a between-cell location in the input. Routine N is very complex because one line of the output is often calculated from more lines of the input than a computer can hold in main memory. Routine O applies the same operation to a vector data set but calculations are much simpler here.

4.5 Raster to tabular

Two operations are important here. Measurement of overlapping areas of two data planes and spatial integration of a surface data plane by regions in another data plane.

P. polygon overlay
Q. spatial integration

Routine P reads two inputs and creates three columns in a table. The cell values are placed in two columns and a cell count is placed in the third (a simple joint histogram). Hash table storage is usually useful for this routine. Routine Q is similar except that the cell values in one input are summed for the regions represented in the other input. A combined version of these routines that integrates a surface over the intersections of two region rasters is also useful. These routines can be used for point and line representations as well as areas.

4.6 Tabular to raster

Routine H falls in this category. A simpler version is:

R. chloropleth mapper

This routine reads a table which contains region identifiers and some derived statistic that is to be mapped into colors or textures in that region. The raster that contains the region identifiers is converted into a chloropleth map by table lookup.

4.7 Tabular processing

A basic set of tabular operations gives the system enough power to support a variety of applications.

S. sort
T. report
U. aggregate
V. delete on key
W. merge correlate
X. mathematical function
Y. concatenate

Routine S should operate on numeric or alphabetic keys occupying one or more columns. Routine T should allow column selection, specification of headings, column headings and numeric format, and subtotaling of selected columns using a control column. Routine U allows totalling or other operations for groups of records specified by a control column. Routine W merges columns from two files based on matching keys. Routine X allows a user specified function to be applied to values in the file placing the results in the file.

4.8 Interface

The essential interfaces are as follows:

Z. tabular input merge correlate
AA. tabular output copy
BB. graphics internal format conversion
CC. image internal format conversion
DD. remote sensed data cleanup

Routine Z is exactly like routine W except that one of the merge files can have external labels and format, such as a tape from the U.S. Bureau of the Census.

Routine AA outputs tabular files in arbitrary format. Routine(s) BB are needed because a number of different external formats for graphics data exist, but routines such as A, B, and O need a particular internal format. Since external formats may or may not be chained, the internal format should allow both so that chaining routines will not be necessary. Usually one new routine is needed for each new application. Routine(s) CC serve an analogous function for image data. An example of image format conversion is the disinterleaving of multispectral components of Landsat to produce a single spectral band image. Routines for DD fall into a highly complex area of removing sensor aberrations as necessary to perform an application. An example would be de-skewing a Landsat image to compensate for Earth rotation. There is a trend for the data providers (such as NASA) to provide ready to use products but it is likely that data customers will still find it necessary to perform these operations. Some customers prefer to begin with raw data while others find that the ready to use product has had an undesirable step performed.

5. Data Management Considerations

For each datatype, the overriding consideration is usually getting the data into the system, for it is in this area where greatest costs and difficulties are usually incurred. Figure 2 depicts data input as a three stage process. The first stage, called data capture, includes all operations up to the point where a data file is computer readable. Data capture costs are enormous for many basic kinds of data, for example, demographic and economic data gathered by the U.S. Bureau of Census. These data are then made available on computer tape at nominal cost to any user. Another common method of data capture is coordinate digitization of boundaries or linear features from a map. The map is not computer compatible but the digitizer output is. Manual photo-interpretation (for example, manual determination of land use boundaries) is a common step prior to coordination digitizing. Landsat imagery is a particularly attractive data source because it is already computer compatible and gives up-to-date coverage of large areas at nominal cost. Editing costs vary widely depending upon the nature of the data source. Reformatting can also be a major operation where large data files are involved. A good example is community analysis where data are gathered by various districtings (police, fire, sewer, census tract, etc.) but must be reformatted to a common districting so that analysis can be performed (for example, to obtain police calls per capita). The final stage of data input is to obtain a temporal baseline. For example, police calls in 1976 cannot be divided by 1970 population to obtain a per capita figure because of a temporal difference. Establishing a temporal baseline involves projection and modelling of the initial data to one or more common points of time.

Because data input costs dominate, the overall system design must give first priority to minimizing these costs. It is worth giving a bad example here. Suppose that for convenience of analysis, all data were recorded at an atomic level, for example, recording the nearest street address of each police call. Then police calls could be aggregated to arbitrary kinds of districts by totalling the calls within any district. Analysis is made simple and precise in this system, but gathering police calls by address results in enormous costs and difficulties, and gives a loss of privacy as well. Several principles can be stated here. First, data gathering agencies should prepare data bases that are computer compatible and are in a general form that is best suited for the range of applications that the data will be used for in a manner that makes economic and social sense, but should not be too concerned with formatting details of analysis systems. As an example, the U.S. Bureau of the Census DIME file, which is segment oriented, can easily be reformatted into a chain code format, but users of this latter format would be completely out of luck if the DIME file did not exist. There is one outstanding case today of a large data base which cannot easily be reformatted to meet a range of needs. This is the case of elevation or topographic data in contour graphic form. Computer methods of converting these data to an image raster format are not well developed yet. The second principle is that analysis systems should have good capabilities for reformatting from the various data bases. This allows data gathering agencies to get on with their data capture and editing tasks. In the case of remote sensing data, severe storage, archival, and retrieval problems are also present.

A system that deals with raster, vector, and tabular datatypes is technically rather complex but must be made handy for users such as geographers or planners. This requires some form of menu driven operation or macro sequence operation. The menus or macros are created by expert technicians or programmers for use by applications. Since the system will have hundreds of primitive functions that operate in user-specified sequences, the system datatypes should be as few and as general as possible.

Additional capabilities are necessary for a general geographic analysis facility, for example, statistical analysis and stochastic modelling and tabular data management. There would probably be some benefit from a direct integration of systems into a unified "super-system".

The raster-vector system described so far appears to be a user system as opposed to a data producer agency system. But in fact, it seems most appropriate for an intermediate role. It can perform basic types of processing on remote sensed data sets such as Landsat to produce simpler data sets that can be used more widely.

6. Application to Orlando, Florida

The Geography Division of the U.S. Bureau of the Census was interested in the urban growth of the Orlando region during the period 1970-1975. Typical remote sensing analysis could not be extended for this application since Landsat 1 was not placed into orbit until late 1972. Rather than integrating two Landsat data sources, the integration of two different types of data was required to produce the final product. A land cover map produced from analysis of a 1975 Landsat scene was utilized as the current date data source. Population statistics collected in the 1970 census were required for the construction of a map depicting urban land cover in 1970 and were the early date data source.

The application necessitated the use of IBIS software for the construction of a 1970 urbanized land cover map based on population density levels. The Census Bureau has loosely defined a census tract as being urbanized if the population density of the tract equaled or exceeded 1,000 people per square mile. Based on the criterion, a 1970 urbanized land cover map was derived (Figure 3). With the completion of the 1970 urbanized area map, the 1975 Land cover map was integrated to produce a new product emphasizing urban expansion (Figure 4). Additionally, tabular reports indicating the statistical importance of the transition of non-urban to urban land between 1970-1975 was derived (Figure 5).

7. Application to Portland, Oregon

Preliminary work in Portland was similar to that in other cities. Landsat data were thematically classified to obtain land use information over the metropolitan area. Three overlays of political districts were created using the rubber sheet reprojection and rasterization techniques. Figure 6 shows the classification map of Portland with an overlay of Census tracts.

Two crosstabulation applications were applied to the Portland data. In the first case, population statistics were allocated to traffic zones from census tracts in proportion to the distribution of residential land use. Normally such allocation tasks are performed by constructing area correspondence tables that assume an equal distribution of population over both kinds of districts. As the assumption of uniform population distribution is never valid, any distribution estimate based upon a residential land use map that is better than fifty percent accurate (i.e., equivalent to random) assures a better allocation of population. The proportionate allocation of population by traffic zone will permit planners to combine census and traffic data with residential and commercial land use acreages to predict automobile trip generation.

The second application was the assignment of population from the 1973 update of Census statistics to the 2 kilometer grid map of pollutants used by the Oregon Department of Environmental Quality. Again, the distribution of land use was used to more accurately allocate the population data. Multiplying population times pollutant level gives a measure of health impact by grid cell (Figure 7). Transferring these values back to a map of Portland would show areas of high impact in a graphic fashion (Figure 8). The grand total of health impact is important for modelling purposes. If the physical model from which pollutant levels are derived can be rerun for the hypothetical siting of a factory or freeway, for example, then the change in the grand total will measure its health impact. The ability of IBIS to handle population update and population projection will greatly aid modelling applications which involve population data.

8. Acknowledgements

The author is indebted to Steven Z. Friedman, Thomas L. Logan, and Nevin A. Bryant for their help and insightful discussions on the work reported here.

9. References

Bauer, M.E., Cipra, J.E., Anuta, P.E., and Etheridge, J.B. (1979). Identification and area estimation of agricultural crops by computer classification of Landsat MSS data. Remote Sensing of Environment 8, 77-92.

Bryant, N.A., and Zobrist, A.L. (1977). IBIS: a geographic information system based on digital image processing and image raster datatype. IEEE Transactions on Geoscience Electronics, GE-15, 13, 152-159.

Tobler, W., and Lau, J., (1978). Isopleth mapping using histosplines. Geographical analysis, 10, 3, 273-279.

U.S. Bureau of the Census, (1970). Census Use Study: The DIME Geocoding System, Report No. 4, Washington, D.C.

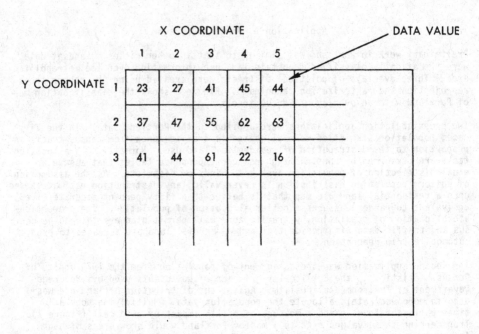

LOCATION FORMULAS:

$$X = \left[A \times LAT + B \times LONG + C \right] \text{ NEAREST INTEGER}$$

$$Y = \left[D \times LAT + E \times LONG + F \right] \text{ NEAREST INTEGER}$$

$$\text{MEMORY ADDRESS} = BASE + KX + Y$$

Figure 1. Image raster as a spatial data representation.

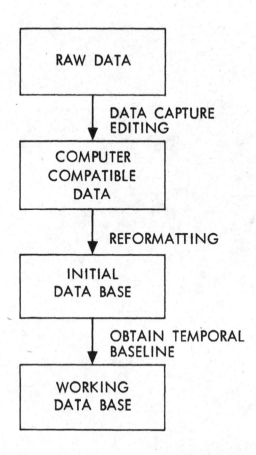

Figure 2. Data input stages.

60

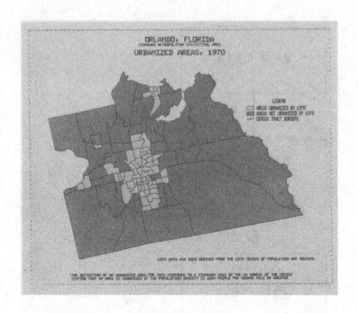

Figure 3. Chloropleth map of Orlando, Florida urbanized areas in 1970.

Figure 4. Orlando, Florida areas of change, 1970 to 1975.

URBANIZED LAND COVER STATISTICS FOR THE ORLANDO SMSA
ORLANDO, FLORIDA
1970 AND 1975

1970 STATISTICS BASED ON THE 1970 CENSUS OF POPULATION AND HOUSING
1975 STATISTICS BASED ON URBAN CHANGE DETECTION FROM LANDSAT IMAGERY

CENSUS TRACT NUMBER		TOTAL ACRES PER TRACT	1970 POPULATION STATISTICS		1970 URBANIZED LAND COVER STATISTICS		1975 URBANIZED LAND COVER STATISTICS		URBANIZED LAND COVER CHANGE BETWEEN 1970 AND 1975		
			NUMBERS OF PEOPLE	DENSITY PER MILE SQUARED	ACRES	PCT	ACRES	PCT	ACRES	PCT	MAJOR
102	NO TRACT	1161155	0	0.0	0	0.C	0	0.0	0	0.0	
66	166.00	88141	2224	16.1	0	0.C	6	0.0	6	100.0	
91	112.00	64934	2111	21.0	0	0.C	0	0.0	0	0.0	
67	167.00	157868	9379	29.9	0	0.C	1483	0.9	1483	100.0	
71	171.00	76679	3817	31.9	0	0.C	2406	3.1	2406	100.0	
86	207.00	21553	1637	48.6	0	0.C	671	3.1	671	100.0	
89	210.00	1803	943	74.4	0	0.C	684	5.7	684	100.0	
79	179.00	30379	3533	86.4	0	0.C	2036	6.7	2036	100.0	
70	170.00	24780	3345	87.8	0	0.C	1351	5.5	1351	100.0	
92	143.00	26394	3620	98.0	0	0.C	0	0.0	0	0.0	
75	178.00	30054	6600	99.1	0	0.C	1694	5.6	1694	100.0	
68	168.00	41116	6369	137.5	0	0.C	2864	7.0	2864	100.0	
48	148.00	15705	3371	177.0	0	0.C	1278	8.1	1278	100.0	
93	214.00	6035	1650	190.4	0	0.C	636	10.5	636	100.0	YES
95	216.00	11830	3919	199.2	0	0.C	1243	10.5	1243	100.0	YES
87	208.00	12496	9889	214.4	0	0.C	1383	11.1	1383	100.0	YES
35	135.00	5125	1717	215.0	0	0.C	442	8.6	442	100.0	
75	206.00	4949	1461	253.1	0	0.C	294	6.8	294	100.0	
65	175.00	14725	5823	279.3	0	0.C	1327	9.0	1327	100.0	
64	165.00	9319	4067	364.9	0	0.C	0	0.0	0	0.0	
49	164.00	7620	3959	368.5	0	0.C	687	9.3	687	100.0	YES
72	149.00	5100	3908	467.3	0	0.C	739	14.5	739	100.0	
60	172.00	1749	1007	513.6	0	0.C	0	0.0	0	0.0	YES
31	211.00	3579	2610	535.9	0	0.C	1260	35.3	1260	100.0	YES
100	131.00	3565	2945	546.5	0	0.C	0	0.0	0	0.0	
47	221.00	1503	1259	564.1	0	0.C	1048	69.7	1048	100.0	YES
50	150.00	4526	3865	581.8	0	0.C	726	16.0	726	100.0	YES
94	215.00	4014	4556	604.9	0	0.C	662	19.2	662	100.0	YES
101	177.00	5227	4962	662.4	0	0.C	285	5.4	285	100.0	
17	217.00	2705	5693	664.4	0	0.C	480	8.7	480	100.0	
96	217.00	1167	5120	764.5	0	0.C	72	2.6	72	100.0	
51	141.00	4705	5620	798.4	0	0.C	489	10.4	489	100.0	YES
69	169.00	5075	6331	890.0	0	0.C	130	2.6	130	100.0	
36	136.00	1702	5391	871.9	0	0.C	403	23.7	403	100.0	YES
43	141.00	3943	5801	874.1	0	0.C	1376	34.9	1376	100.0	YES
23	123.00	4247	4045	1043.2	2484	100.C	301	7.1	301	100.0	
		2484	6448	1140.5	3629	100.C	2484	100.0	0	0.0	
		3629					3629	100.0	0	0.0	

Figure 5. Tabulation of change statistics for Orlando, Florida.

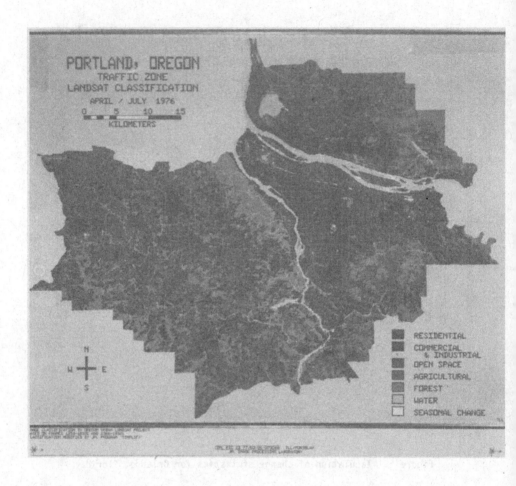

Figure 6. Land use from Landsat classification with political boundary overlay in Portland, Oregon.

PORTLAND, OREGON
POLLUTION BY GRID CELL

GRID CELL	POPULATION	POLL VALUE	POLL INDEX	COVERAGE
2,10	116	28	3236	92
3,10	147	29	4266	100
3,11	112	30	3363	100
3,13	1140	28	31911	91
4, 9	100	29	2912	100
4,10	135	29	3929	100
4,11	152	29	4397	100
4,12	294	29	8513	100
4,13	1155	29	33490	100
4,14	1279	29	37098	96
4,17	79	28	2203	100
5, 9	132	29	3832	100
5,10	199	28	5559	100
5,11	163	28	4554	100
5,12	118	28	3311	100
5,13	766	29	22207	100
5,14	827	30	24820	100
5,15	479	30	14368	100
5,16	96	28	2697	100
5,17	71	28	1990	100
6, 9	146	29	4220	100
6,10	145	29	4192	100
6,11	160	28	4476	100
6,12	102	28	2855	100
6,13	470	29	13620	100
6,14	538	29	15599	
6,15	774	30	???	
6,16	127			
6,17				100
				100
				100
			28228	98
	1028	30	54844	100
35,12	2606	31	80775	100
35,13	1120	31	34708	100
35,14	974	30	29227	93
36,11	825	30	24751	100
36,12	599	30	17982	100
	915092		36101440	

Figure 7. Tabulation of health impact by grid cell in Portland, Oregon.

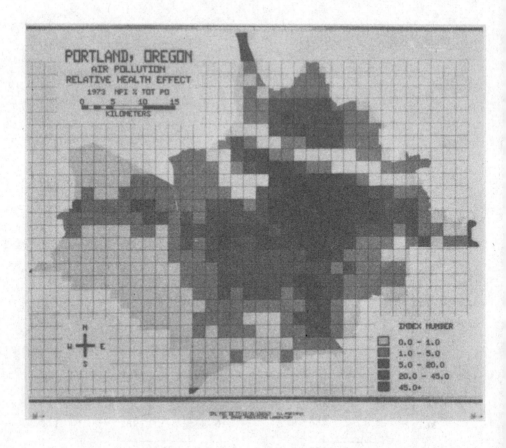

Figure 8. Chloropleth map of health impact by grid cell in Portland, Oregon.

THE DEVELOPMENT AND USE OF DIGITAL CARTOGRAPHIC DATA BASES

Stephen C. Guptill

The increasing demand of the Nation's natural resources developers for
storage, retrieval, manipulation, analysis, and display of large quantities
of earth science data have necessitated the use of computers and the building
of sophisticated computer information systems. As the needs of resource
managers and analysts were identified, it becomes obvious that cartographic
data in digital form were required. The Geological Survey is gathering
digital cartographic data in several forms including base category data (such
as boundaries, hydrography, transportation, etc.), elevation data, and land use
and land cover data to meet these and other needs. As we gather data, we are
beginning to identify some of the problems unique to organizing cartographic
data in form suitable for storage, retrieval, and analysis.

The ability of software to direct the storage, retrieval, and analysis tasks
is dependent not only on the efficiency of the software, but also on the
structure of the spatial data. The key elements and formats required by
spatial data handling systems must be identified and incorporated into spatial
data structures. The requirements of and approaches being taken by the
Geological Survey in performinng these tasks reflect our need to manage and
use large quantities of complex digital cartographic data.

U..S. Geological Survey
Geography Program, Mail Stop 710
12201 Sunrise Valley Drive
Reston, Virginia 22092
U.S.A.

Introduction

The Nation's natural resources developers face increasing complexities in their decisionmaking. The planner and manager must consider earth science, natural resource, biological, and socioeconomic information in order to identify alternatives for development, devise systematic procedures for evaluating alternatives, and reach   sound conclusions.

For example, the National Environmental Policy Act (1969) and the Coastal Zone Managment Act (1972) have significantly affected national resource development and have forced managers and planners at all levels to consider large amounts of environmental, economic, and resource data in reaching their decisions. On the other hand, growing resource shortages put pressure on these same people to increase the development of known resources to meet the needs of the Nation. Because decisions must be made within a relatively short time, management has less time to analyze the data and more pressure to make the decisions that have significant long-term implications. These complex deliberations require rapid manipulation and flexible use of data from a variety of sources.

Traditional Data Forms

While decisionmakers have many graphic and tabular sources of basic earth science information available to them, incompatibility of data from different sources make the information difficult to use in solving a given problem. The increasing demands for storage, manipulation, and graphic display of large quantities of earth science data have necessitated the use of computers and the building of sophisticated computer information systems.

Traditional data formats and manipulation techniques are inadequate to meet the demands of today's resource managers. In the past, most data were presented as maps, tables, and textual reports. Each organization collected data in a different way and produced their output in various formats. The scales of graphics, such as maps, are different; the data codes used to identify certain elements vary from agency to agency, and it is difficult to correlate with data in another format; for example, geologic data in map form are difficult to correlate with census tabulations in computer-readable form. Such data formats are difficult to change, thus slowing the evaluation process. Often data prepared and presented in a form to address specific problems do not lend themselves to the consideration of alternatives, and it is time consuming to incorporate new data into out-of-date graphic materials. To help overcome these problems, computers can provide a common language.

Computer-Based Geo-Information Systems

In the early development of digital computers, researchers recognized the potential for storing cartographic and earth science information in digital form. However, the development of this potential is just starting to be realized. The delay has been due in part to the high cost of specialized systems to convert graphic map data to an error-free digital form, the cost of devices to produce high-quality output from the digital data, the expense of computer resources to process the data, and the lack of computer software to manipulate the data. Only recently has the reduction in hardware costs and the increasing sophistication of computer hardware and software made it feasible to assemble and use data bases containing large amounts of digital spatial data.

The ability of modern computers to store, manipulate, and retrieve massive amounts of data gives management the ability to answer complex questions quickly. For example, a county planner interested in possible future sites for commercial development could ask for a map and acreage tabulation for underdeveloped sites on slopes of less than 10 percent and within 5 miles of a four-lane highway. If sufficient data are contained in the data base and the computer software and hardware exists to perform the operation, the planner could obtain the tabulations and graphic within minutes. Based on the results obtained, the planner might decide to rephrase the question and delete from consideration any land within a flood plain or a wetland. Further iterations might include consideration of current zoning regulations and the proximity of other commercial and industrial facilities and rail and air transport. A number of systems with some of these capabilities have been developed.

Geological Survey Activities

As the needs of resource managers were identified, it became obvious that cartographic data in digital form were required. The Geological Survey began production of digitized land use and land cover maps in 1973 and started the Digital Cartographic Applications Program in 1978 to provide digital cartographic data equivalent to the 1:24,000-scale topographic maps.

Land Use Data

Land use and land cover maps and associated overlays for the entire United States at 1:250,000-scale are currently being produced. These maps are compiled, digitized, edited, and incorporated into a digital data base that will be available in both graphic and digital form.

The maps satisfy a longstanding need for a consistent level of detail, standardization of categories, and uniform scale for data used by government land use planners. This benchmark series is scheduled for completion about 1984; updating of the maps, starting in 1979, will provide a much-needed tool for analyzing local and regional problems, trends, and changes in land use patterns.

The set of maps includes: (1) Land use and land cover map, (2) Political unit map, (3) Hydrologic unit map, (4) Census county subdivision map, and (5) Federal land ownership map. Selected areas also include a State land ownership map.

The land use and land cover maps are compiled to portray categories such as
residential, commercial, cropland and pasture, and deciduous forestland.
This classification system provides the user with a basic framework to which
subdivisions of the categories may be added if required.
described by Anderson and others (1976),
Maps portraying either natural or administrative information provide the
user with the opportunity to use the land use and land cover maps and data
either individually or collectively to produce graphic or statistical data.
This system is constructed in such a way that the graphical and statistical
land use and land cover data fits the basic topographic information and can
be related to other resource fields such as soils, geology, hydrology, and
demography.

Digital Cartographic Base Data

With experience in providing land use data in digital form, it became apparent
that additional data were required to support resource managers. The fundamental data needed to tie resource information systems together are found on
Geological Survey topographic maps. These data provide the common reference
and foundation upon which all systems must be built to adequately serve
today's resource managers. As a result the Geological Survey began the
Digital Cartograhic Applications Program (DCAP) in 1978 as part of the
National Mapping Program.

The objective of DCAP is to provide the following basic categories of data
in digital form:

Reference systems--Geographic and other coordinate systems not including
the public land survey network.

Hypsography--Countours, slopes, and elevations.

Hydrography--Streams and rivers, lakes and ponds, wetlands, reservoirs,
and shorelines.

Surface cover--Woodland, orchards, vineyards (general categories only).

Non-vegetative features--Lava rock, playas, sand dunes, slide rock,
barren waste areas.

Boundaries--Political jurisdictions, national parks and forests, military reservations. This category does not fully set forth land ownership or land use.

Transportation systems--Roads, railroads, trails, canals, pipelines,
transmission lines, bridges, tunnels.

Significant manmade structures--buildings, airports, dams.

Geodetic control, survey monuments, other survey marks, and landmark
structures and objects.

Geographic names.

Orthophotographic imagery.

Other data categories of high volumes, such as the United States Public Land Survey System, will be selectively included. Standard formats and codes, required to enable other agencies to incorporate their data into the National Mapping Program, must be developed, and the system must be structured to meet the requirements of a broad spectrum of users.

The files for the base categories are grouped into two basic forms. The first of these, called a digital line graph (DLG), is linear map information, such as transportation, hydrography, and boundaries, in digital form. The second, called a digital elevation model (DEM), consists of a sampled array of elevations for a number of ground positions that are usually, but not always, at regularly spaced intervals.

The land use and land cover and associated overlay map files, DLG files, and DEM files may be created from a number of data sources such as map plates or profiles or terrain models scanned in stereoscopic photogrammetric equipment or digitizing orthophoto equipment. The files will be managed by an automated data base management system and will be distributed through the National Cartographic Information Center at USGS in Reston, Virginia.

Spatial Data Handling

As we gather digital cartographic data, we are beginning to identify some of the problems unique to organizing it in a form suitable for various spatial data handling functions. These functions include data capture and storage, data management and retrieval, and data manipulation and analysis. Data capture processes concern the collection of data, their digitizing, and the creation and storage of error free files of digital data. Data base management systems place individual files into a standardized structure and manage access to the data base. Data manipulation and analysis techniques include such processes as the generation of graphics and other products which aid the user in forming mental models, formal models, and the printing of final products.

The ability of computer systems to perform these tasks is dependent not only on the efficiency of the system but also on the structure of the spatial data. The key elements and formats required by spatial data handling systems must be identified and incorporated into spatial data structures. In addition to creating a spatial data structure amenable to a broad range of tasks, consideration must be given to the size of the data base in the system. The management of spatial data, particularly large quantities of spatial data, is an area which has not been explored very thoroughly. Researchers have typically dealt with either small quantities of complex data or large quantities of simple data. Under these circumstances, questions of data organization have not been critical. As large sets of spatial data are compiled, the necessity of having an efficient, comprehensive data structure becomes apparent. A well thought-out and optimized logical and physical structuring of the data may mean the difference between the success and failure of a large project.

In the 1960's researchers began investigating various ways of
encoding and structuring spatial data. The problem of taking an n-dimensional data set and placing it in a linear (sequential) format for processing
by a sequential computer has not yet been completely solved. The works of
Palmer (1975) and Puecker and Chrisman (1975) provide an overview of the
common encoding and structuring schemes. The newly emerging computer archi-
tectures such as array processors, pipeline processors, and independent processors connected by a common communication path may require totally different types of encoding schemes and data structures than are presently being
used.   Sutherland and Mead (1977) discuss the implications of computer design
on algorithms in further detail. Further complications arise since a data
structure or encoding scheme which may be efficient for any one task may be
less than adequate for other aspects of spatial data handling. The problem
becomes one of whether to design task specific structures, which need to be
changed when the task changes, or to design compromise structures which can
handle a number of tasks in an adequate fashion.

Mitchell and others (1977) describe the
system developed for land use and associate
polygon maps.

Basic Spatial Elements

In any discussion of spatial data it is essential that the fundamental terms
being used be described. In this paper we will refer to the term "basic
spatial element." This serves as a comprehensive term covering any number
of ways to partition space and thus describe spatial data. Some common
"basic spatial elements" such as nodes (points), arcs (lines), and areas
are shown in figure 1. Other often used "basic spatial elements" include
grid cells, a lattice of points, or tesselation of triangles. The use of
the "basic spatial element" phrase is necessary to the concept of divorcing
the way in which space is partitioned (i.e., which of many basic spatial
elements will be used) from the characterizations and classification of the
information contained in a spatial data structure. The classification scheme
for data structures presented in the next section is independent of the
"basic spatial element" chosen to partition the space.

Classification of Data Structures

In order to simplify the discussion of spatial data structures, a classification scheme has been devised using three parameters. The parameters are
illustrated as the x, y, and z axies in figure 2.

The evaluation of a spatial data structuring scheme by these parameters
provides a qualitative measure of its complexity and provides a single means
to compare the characteristics of various spatial data structures.

The first parameter "amount of explicit spatial information" refers to the
number of explicit spatial relationships contained for each basic spatial
element in the data structure. Spatial relationships such as adjacency, contiguity, connectedness, and nearest neighborhoods can be determined and
stored with each basic spatial element in the data base.

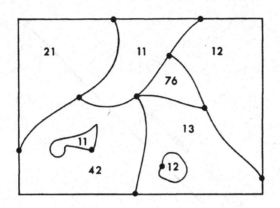

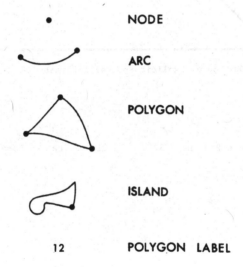

NODE

ARC

POLYGON

ISLAND

12   POLYGON LABEL

Figure 1 -- Sample Basic Spatial Elements

72

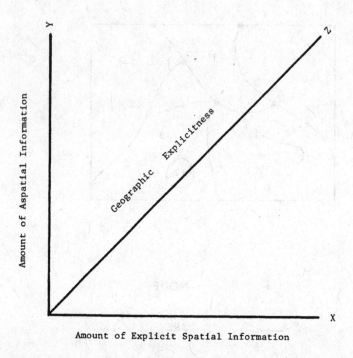

Amount of Explicit Spatial Information

Figure 2 -- Data Structure Classification Parameters

The second parameter "amount of aspatial information" measures the information content or the values associated with each basic spatial element. For example, a spatial data base representing a census tract map could contain for each tract the hundreds of socio-economic values collected for it. This "aspatial information" parameter may also contain spatially-related information such as area or length.

The final parameter "geographic explicitness" refers to the way in which the basic spatial element is located on the surface of the earth. A non-explicit structure would require a large amount of computation in order to locate the basic spatial element on the earth. An explicit structure would provide an unambiguious location for each basic spatial element. A data base containing information about earthquake epicenters, located by latitude and longitude, would be highly geographically explicit. An array of Landsat pixels, with only a nominal center of scene location would not be very geographically explicit.

Task Optimization of Data Structures

Using the classification parameters discussed in the previous section, it is possible to simply describe a single structure (data base) that is optimized for the individual 'tasks of: data capture and storage; data management and retrieval; and data manipulation and analysis. This will note the conflicts between these various tasks, and serve as the basis for establishing compromise structures. Table 1 summarizes the parameter values assigned for each of the task structures.

In a data base designed for data capture and storage tasks, the amount of explicit spatial information is low. Typically it is the minimum amount of information required to topologically define the basic spatial element (e.g., the left and right side attributes of a bounding arc). This amount of data is minimal because it is expensive to capture and/or compute as well as requiring a relatively large number of bytes for storage. Similarly, the amount of aspatial information is low, again because of the data capture costs as well as the burdensom storage requirements. The aspatial information may consist of only a unique identifying code plus a non-unique value or attribute. The geographical explicitness is low, usually consisting of "control point" records which can be used for calculating the true location of the spatial data. The bulk of the locational data is often left in whatever locating scheme that is produced by the data capture device (e.g. the machine coordinates as generated by a manual x, y digitizing table).

Optimization of a data base structure for management and retrieval tasks adds some new requirements. The amount of explicit spatial information desired increases to meet the demands of spatial retrievals (e.g. find all the residential land next to water bodies). The amount of aspatial information would probably increase only slightly with the addition of some spatially-related information such as area or length, and perhaps references or pointers to the appropriate locations in related non-spatial data bases. The geographical explicitness of the locational data also increases, again to facilitate spatial retrievals (find all data within 10 miles of 77°W long, 40°N lat).

Table 1.--Classification parameters for task optimization of data structures

Classification Parameters	Tasks:		
	Data Capture and Storage	Data Management and Retrieval	Data Manipulation and Analysis
Amount of Explicit Spatial Information	Low	Medium	High
Amount of Aspatial Information	Low	Low	High
Geographical Explicitness	Low	Medium	High

Table 2.--Classification parameters for a cartographic data base

Classification Parameters	Level
Explicit Spatial Information	Low
Aspatial Information	Low
Geographical Explicitness	Medium

The data manipulation and analysis tasks require the most information from
the data base. A great deal of spatial information and geographic explict-
ness may be necessary to answer complex questions. For example, to locate
a possible wildlife nesting area, an analyst may require a display of all
coniferous forest stands larger than ten acres, above 3000 feet in elevation, and further than 5 miles from any road, and located on public land.
Similarly, the analyst may require a great deal of associated aspatial
information. To answer a question such as display all the residential
land areas within each census tract of an SMSA where the industrial land
occupies 20 percent or more of the area and the tract residents have an
income less than $10,000 and have gone to an average of 10 years of school
or less, would require a large number of aspatial, socio-economic data elements.

A Data Base Structure for Cartographic Data

As illustrated in the previous section, various tasks can place quite different demands upon a data base and data structure. One of the missions of
the Geological Survey is to collect and distribute various earth science
information including cartographic data. In this environment, a Geological
Survey cartographic data base will have structure parameters that optimize
data capture, storage, and retrieval tasks. The parameters of such a data
base are shown in table 2.

The amount of explicit spatial information is limited to the amount of information necessary to topologically structure the information and to check
its attributes for consistency. The amount of aspatial information is sparse,
typically only a unique identifying code as well as a value or attribute code.
These attribute codes may serve as links to related aspatial data bases.
A moderate amount of geographical explicitness is required to make the data
more useable by the general public. For example, all positional data could
be transformed into map projection or geographic coordinates.

These general characteristics are incorporated into three of the spatial
data bases in existence at the Geological Survey. These data bases are
the digitial elevation models (DEM), the base category digital line graphs
(DLG), and the land use and land cover and associated map data. Explicit
details are available for the DEM's (Digital Applications Team, 1979a), DLG's
(Digital Applications Team, (1979b) and land use data (Guptill, 1978). When
complete, these data bases may contain as much as 10^{11} bytes of data.

Using Digital Cartographic Data

In previous sections we have given several examples of the types of uses of
digital cartographic data. It is important to recognize that analysis of
environmental and resource problems requires the input of spatial data to
incorporate distance, direction, and locational information into the analysis. Thus, linkages must be established not only between spatial entities,
but also with aspatial entities to permit comprehensive analysis. Rather than
provide further examples, it may be useful to categorize the types of tasks
that are necessary to perform various analytical operations as follows:

(1) Extract a selected study area from the data base. This may involve merging map sheets together and subsequent extractions from the data sets.

(2) Overlay or logically interest spatial data sets having the same geographic coverage, creating one data set with complex attributes.

(3) Calculate various spatial relationships (adjacency, contiguity, linkages) not stored in the data base as needed for the analysis.

(4) Merge aspatial data bases with appropriate spatial entities.

(5) Using the results of steps 1-4, query the resulting study area data base with spatial and non-spatial questions. Use the data or question results in product generation and model formulation.

What combinations of data structure, data base management, and analytical software will allow the widest user community to use digital cartographic data in an efficient, operational mode?

Operational Scenario

The number of possible uses of digital cartographic data are quite large. For a data gathering agency such as the Geological Survey to bias its data structure towards any given task while at the same time perhaps compromising other aspects of the data base system would be presumptive at best and irresponsible at worst. Thus the cartographic data bases will probably not be biased towards any one applications area.

This strategy creates two levels of data base management systems. The level I system, used ,to accomplish data collection and dissemination tasks, is concerned with task 1 in the above list, the spatial retrieval of information about a given area. The level II system is oriented towards analysis and applications users, and would perform tasks 2 to 5. Second level systems would be able to assimilate the appropriate subsets of spatial and aspatial data bases and place that data in a structure suitable for the users specific application and type of analysis. Since a subset of data is involved, the management and computation burden may be reduced to a reasonable size.

The Geological Survey is developing several level I type systems to manage the various spatial data bases. Other Federal agencies, such as the Fish and Wildlife Service, who have resource management responsibilities, are developing level II type systems. It is vital that the data gatherers and the data users communicate to insure the synergistic development of level I and level II systems.

Conclusions

The potential applications of cartographic earth science data in computer readable form are enormous and have just begun to be seriously developed. The Geological Survey is aggressively moving to provide these data in a comprehensive structure so the full potential of computer-based resource information systems can be realized. The problems faced by resource planners and managers are real and complex but the development of digital cartographic information systems can greatly aid their solution.

References

Anderson, J.R., Hardy, E.E., Roach, J.T., and Witmer, R.E., 1976, A land use
    and land cover classification system for use with remote sensor
    data: U.S. Geological Survey Professional Paper 964, 28 p.

Digital Applications Team, 1979a, Computer files and attribute codes for
    digital line graphs: U.S. Geological Survey, Topographic Division,
    520 National Center, Reston, Virginia 22092.

Digital Applications Team, 1979b, Computer files and attribute codes for
    digital line graphs: U.S. Geological Survey, Topographic Division,
    520 National Center, Reston, Virginia 22092.

Guptill, Stephen, C., 1978, A digital cartographic data base for land use and
    land cover and associated maps in Proceedings, International User's
    Conference on Computer Mapping Software and Data Bases: Cambridge,
    Massachusetts, Harvard University, 33 p.

Mitchell, W.B., Guptill, S.C., Anderson, K.E., Fegeas, R.G., and Hallam, C.A.,
    1977, GIRAS: a geographic information retrieval and analysis system
    for handling land use and land cover data: U.S. Geological Survey
    Professional Paper 1059, 16 p.

Palmer, J.A.B., 1975, Computer science aspects of the mapping problem in Davis,
    J.A., and McCullagh, M., 1975, Display and Analysis of Spatial Data:
    New York, New York, John Wiley and Sons, p. 155-172.

Peucker, T.K., and Chrisman, Nicholas, 1975, Cartographic data structures in
    The American Cartographer, v. 2, no. 1, p. 55-69.

Sutherland, I.E., and Mead, C.A., 1977, Microelectronics and computer science
    in Scientific American, v. 237, no. 3, p. 210-228.

GEOLOG PROJECT

DELARCY DA SILVA VICENTE MATTA

The Geolog Project was developed for the city of São Paulo, wich is the largest industrial, cultural and most populous center in Brazil.

This is the first Geoprocessing project undertaken in Brazil and its objectives is to provide the city's administration with improved means for allocating public resources more efficiently.

Conceptually, the project consists of compiling physical data (by geographical coordinates) and relating this with informations already existing in the city's files.

This report basically describes the process followed in defining the data required and structuring the respective files.

PRODAM - Cia. de Processamento de Dados do Município de São Paulo
Parque Ibirapuera, Pavilhão Ciccillo Matarazzo
São Paulo (SP) Brasil

1. INTRODUCTION

1.1 Review

The GEOLOG Project - Public Site Geocodification is actually the most important measure of a sequence of steps which have been taken by the Municipal Government of São Paulo and by PRODAM - Companhia de Processamento de Dados do Município de São Paulo (Data Processing Company of the City of São Paulo), towards developing a Geocodified Data System.

Although it was the objective since the beginning of our studies (1972), such a System implementation lacked until recently, in Brazil, the technical conditions, which were non-existent or of difficult access, as, e.g., digitizing and plotting equipment, etc. On the other hand, there is no doubt that both the technical personnel and the user himself underwent during this time a maturing process, rendering now favorable a receptive atmosphere for such ideas. It should also be noted that even the data files already existing at that time also developed towards better quality and reliability of the data they contained.

The entire evolution process directed itself from the start in a sequence of "objectives/feasibility", which we can describe as a "Search for the Existing Reality". Therefore, e.g., instead of associating the information to its geographical location by means of coordinates (x, y), we started to use the address concept (street, number); instead of associating an information to the public site segment, we did it using the public site level as a whole, and so forth.

In this way, the path we actually followed was inverse to the one desired, that is, in the involution sense, until feasible objectives were reached; after that, we started again the evolution process: each stage, when accomplished, allowed us to aim at more advanced objectives, temporarily disregarded in the past.

As a consequence, the puzzle's pieces started fitting together, so that by mid-1977 we already had a sound foundation, which allowed us to design a first Geocodified Data System.

1.2 CADLOG System

The entire development process which resulted in GEOLOG can be seen in Figure 1, and it should be mentioned that the work start was based on the file called TPCL - Real Estate Municipal Registry, and the set of Fiscal Maps (containing the city division into sectors for real estate tax assessment purposes).

These two sources were processed by specially developed programms (Address Standardization System-PADEND), which made possible the identification and standardization of all existing public sites in São Paulo, constituting a "Public Site Master Index - IML" file.

The next step was to associate data at the public site leve, and thus the CADLOG System - Public Site Registry was developed, containing among other, the following main information:

- Public Site code

- Complete denomination

- Associated blocks

- Block Face (Public Site/Block)

- Real estate at Block Face level

- ZIP Code at Block Face level

- Square meter value at Block Face level

- etc.

Thereafter, the CADLOG System was related to other operational systems, thus constituting a set of integrated files, making available information at the Public Site and/or Block Face levels, such as:

- Pavement

- Use of ground

- Physical change forecast in Blocks and Public Sites

- Building regulations

- etc.

There was an idea to develop, in a subsequent stage, a   System with data at the Public Site Segment level (SEGLOG);   however, since the Block Face concept was already operative, this proved not to be necessary, as the public site division in   segments corresponding to the Block Faces was already meeting the users' needs.

2. GEOLOG SYSTEM - PROJECT

2.1 Scope

The GEOLOG System, even though still closely related with the "Public Site" aspect, arose almost as a natural consequence to the entire former development, but now already using digitizing techniques, geographical data-bases and plotting.

As a concept, the GEOLOG System can be regarded as composed of two Sub-systems:

- GEOLOG Sub-system - Public Site Geocodification
- HVS Sub-system - Traffic Signalling

Their objectives, although modest, bear, due to their pionner nature, a complexity level which justifies them completely:

GEOLOG SUB-SYSTEM - PUBLIC SITE GEOCODIFICATION

OBJECTVE

- Establishment and upkeep of a geographical data ground work.

INPUTS

- Digitized data from the Metropolitan Cartographic System Maps (1:5000)
- Physical changes in the city, pointed out by new aerophotogrammetric surveys and by data existing in already operative Administrative Systems.

AVAILABLE INFORMATION

- Maps showing:
  . Sectors and Blocks
  . Public Sites (Code/denomination)
  . ZIP Code

HVS SUB-SYSTEM - TRAFFIC SIGNALLING

OBJECTIVE

- Establishment and upkeep of a System to process traffic signalling information.

INPUTS

- Data on traffic signalling associated to the geographical base

AVAILABLE INFORMATION

- Maps showing:

. Traffic signalling

. The entire geographical base

2.2 Procedure

The Project was developed by work teams, with totally integraded groups, even though with well defined tasks (Figure 2).

The first team, called "Software" deals with the System's structure from the computer viewpoint, either in the file definition (Geo-data-bases), or in the digitizing/plotting/application programs.

The second team, "Geocodification", was entrusted with the selection, preparation and analysis of maps, as well as, and very important, the definition of a digitazing procedure.

As to the last team, the main approach is given to the users, viewing the definition and qualification of data to be processed by the System; this team is particularly in charge of identifying the relationship type among the data, as well as its access form (questions).

The procedure used to define the sub-systems was based on a preliminary survey of the users' information needs (Finance and

Transportation Departments).

These needs were documented in a "Users Needs Matrix" where the combinations Input (Geographical Element) x Outputs (Type of Information) required by each user were recorded (Figures 3 and 4).

Based on the Finance Department and the Transportation Department matrixes, the sub-systems were designed as a DATA BASE STRUCTURE, that is, information to be held in the files and its interconnections.

Thereafter, each user's needs implantation priorities were defined, also taking into consideration the implantation feasibility and mainly the data updating.

Finally, according to those priorities, the Inputs and Outputs group was identified, as well as the corresponding part of the Data Bank, which is to be implanted in a first phase, to comply with the most pressing needs.

This procedure led to a general view of the system including the elements with priority in terms of implantatiom, and those which will possibly be implemented in future stages, which allowed an expansion of the systems to be developed and implanted during 1978, to meet future needs.

2.3 Data Structure

2.3.1 Data File: GEOLOG

The GEOLOG Data File is composed of the information set needed to represent in a digital form areas of the city of São Paulo, in terms of Blocks and Traffic Network.

The GEOLOG Data Bank was designed to bear the growth and development of new applications which use the same geographical reference data, minimizing the impact on already developed applications.

The structure and specifications of the Data Bank are the results of a careful analysis of various options, taking into consideration the application needs and the system's development facilities.

Its objectives are:

- To provide the system with various logical data structures, enabling the resolution of various problems.

- To provide for various and efficient mechanisms for storing, updating and retrieving information.

- To provide for control mechanisms, viewing the data integrity and an optimizad performance.

The GEOLOG Data Bank is composed of three physical Data Bases, logically listed:

- "Cell" Data Base

- "Block" Data Base

- "Public Site" Data Base

2.3.2   Cell Data Base

This Data Base contains all necessary cells to reference the city blocks and nodes already implanted in the system. The cell represents the division of the geographical reference system into abstract squares of 100 x 100 meters. The cells are the common base necessary for the geoprocessing of information referring to positions given by coordinates.

This Data Base is related with the following DB's:

- Block Data Base, by means of virtual pairing.

- Public Site Data Base, by means of unidirectional pointers, from the cell nodes to the links or the minimum public site stretches.

The Data Base is composed of 4 segment types, arranged in three levels.

The updating is a consequence of the digitizing and geocodification of the city maps.

2.3.3 Block Data Base

This DB contains all city blocks, including those not subject to taxes, such as: traffic islands, public squares, parks, etc., with the following information:

- Block's fiscal code

- Coordinates of the block defining points

- Cells and faces associated to the block

- ZIP code and public site stretches, associated to each block face

- Points of the block face with information to write symbols associated to the face

This Data Base is related with the following DB's:

- Cell Data Base, through the virtual pairing

- Public Site Data Base, through the virtual pairing

The DB is composed of 5 types of segments, arranged in three levels.

The updating will be performed by the Finance Department, in the manner foreseen in the GEOLOG and projects.

2.3.4 Public Site Data Base

It contains the following data:

- Codes and names of all city's public sites (streets, avenues, squares, etc.)

- Block faces and nodes associated to each public site stretch

- Reference to write symbols associated to the traffic network (i.e., codes and name of the public site).

This Data Base is related to the following DB's:

- Block Data Base, through virtual pairing with direct pointers

- Cell Data Base, through unidirectional pointer of that DB

The Data Base is composed of 4 types of segments, arranged in three levels.

The updating will be performed by the Finance Department, in the manner foreseen in the GEOLOG and CADLOG projects.

3. GEOLOG SYSTEM - IMPLEMENTATION

The implementation of the GEOLOG System was divided into two major stages: we initially concentrated our efforts in the implantation of the GEOLOG Sub-system, that is, the sub-system devised to render available the geographical base data, while the HVS - Traffic Signalling Sub-system had its development delayed in the project phase.

In this way, viewing to meet the objectives proposed in this sub-system, the data was structured in two basic modules:

- Geographical Base

  It represents in a digital form the Map of the City of São Paulo in terms of:

  . Block boundary
  . Traffic network - Node
                   - Link

- Fiscal Base (Real Estate Taxes)

  Data from the Finance Department added to the base:

  . Fiscal Sectors represented by Fiscal Blocks
  . ZIP Code (CEP)
  . Square meter value

The Geographical Base was associated to cells of equal size common origin, providing the system with flexibility to meet requests not previously geocoded, although transformable in a region represented by the coordinates (x,y).

The adopted data structure renders possible the production of maps of any region with the information of interest, in accordance with application.

- Public Site or Public Site Segment

- Public Site Intersection

- Area defined by coordinates

- Fiscal Sector

Maps characteristics:

- Geographical Base Elements reoresenting the chosen region (Blocks, Traffic Islands, Viaducts, etc.)
- Public Sites represented by Code and Name
- Other associated information:

  . Fiscal Block Code
  . Fiscal Sector Code
  . ZIP Code (CEP)
  . Square meter value

- Scale defined in the request

3.1 Data sources

The data source alternatives for the establishment of a Geographical Base which would meet the objectives were:

- Aerial photos in 1:40,000 and 1:8,000 scales
- Maps of the Metropolitan Cartographic System (SCM) in 1:10,000 and 1:2,000 scales
- Fiscal Maps (Official City Map - MOC) in a 1:5,000 scale

The fact that aerial photographs need more advanced technology for the information retrieval than the maps, allied to the lack of Brazilian know-how in geoprocessing, caused us to abandon its use during that stage.

The SCM 1:10,000 maps did not show advantages over the others, neither regarding accuracy; nor updating, besides being very poor in details.

Therefore, a decision had to be taken between SCM 1:2,000 and MOC 1:5,000 maps.

Even though the Fiscal Maps (MOC 1:5,000) offered less details and a lower accuracy tha the SCM 1:2,000, we decided to use

them, taking into consideration that they presented the
following advantages:

- They are "worked on" containing fiscal information: sector,
  block and code of the public site; expediting therefore the
  geocodification work.

- They are more updated (produced by enlarging and reambulation
  of the SCM 1:10,000 maps).

- They are compatible with the CADLOG - Public Site Registry
  implanted by the PMSP (São Paulo Municipal Government) in form
  of maps.

From the non-geographical viewpoint, the main source of already
structured data and which was used in preparing the GEOLOG Data
Bank was, as already foreseen, the CADLOG -Public Site Registry
file itself, which is at the present time being converted into
a Data Bank.

3.2 The Complete Process

The GEOLOG System operational philosophy consists basically in,
starting from a set of prepared Maps, to effect the digitizing
of the points of interest, generating, in this way, the Data
Base corresponding to the geographical referentials. To this
geographical base, the non-geographical data originated from
already operating Systems (in our case, from CADLOG   - Public
Site Registry) will be associated. Starting from this Data Base,
now complete, the maps would be extracted, containing associated
information, meeting the user's specifications (Figure 9).

3.3 Next Stage

Even though the establishment and implementation of GEOLOG
brings all advantages of geocodification to the data treatment,
the System is not being designed to substitute the now existing
maps, either for the information poverty, or for the same's
accuracy. It is not intended to obtain through   the   System
(plotted), maps with an accuracy at engineering project levels,

nor in the other extreme, which only attend to the planning
needs. The results accuracy will be compatible with the one
found in the data, that is, maps in a 1:5,000 scale.

We can foresse in the future, in a short term, activities
viewing the enrichment of the data base now created, either by
means of information addition, or increasing its use by the
development of programs which allow for the application of
algorithms and other techniques specifically viewing the user.

In a second phase, the next step could be, by means of adding
data collected in the field or by aerial photographs, the
evolution of the present System to such a level that will allow
for, if not totally,at least in specific cases, the preparation
of maps starting from magnetic files which will effectively
replace the present ones.

In that phase, we will be able to say that we are doing
Numerical Cartography.

FIGURE 1

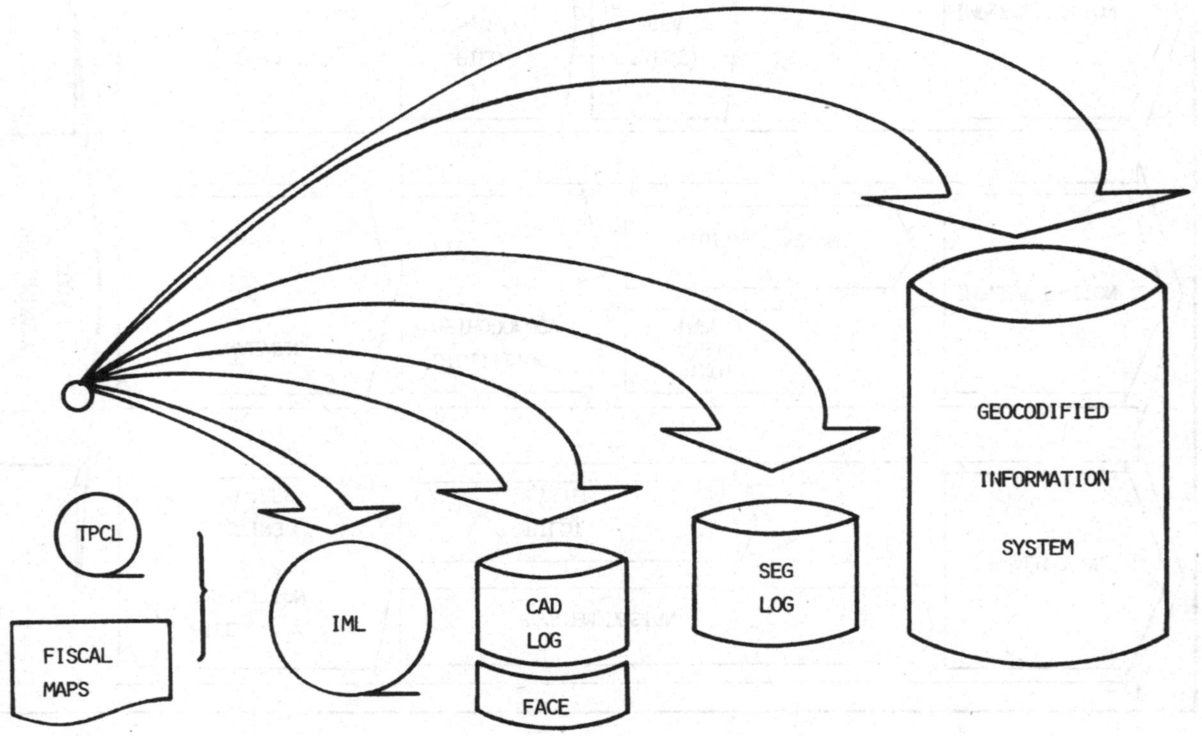

GEOCODIFIED INFORMATION SYSTEM

SEG LOG

CAD LOG

FACE

IML

TPCL

FISCAL MAPS

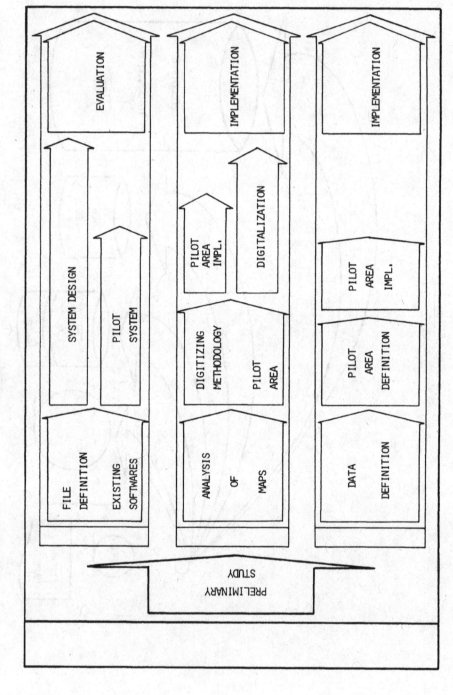

FIGURE 2

FIGURE 3

GEOGRAPHICAL REFERENCE	X,Y		BLOCK FACE
INFORMATION PACKAGE	SECTOR BLOCK	PUBLIC SITE CODE	
GEOGRAPHICAL INPUT	BASIC MAP		ZIP CODE
BLOCK FACE	✕		✕
BLOCK	✕		✕
PUBLIC SITE	✕		✕
SECTOR	✕		✕

96

FIGURE 4

GEOGRAPHICAL REFERENCE	X,Y	LINK	X,Y	X,Y	X,Y	X,Y	X,Y	X,Y LINK
INFORMATION PACKAGE / GEOGRAPHICAL INPUT	BASIC MAP	TRAFFIC DIRECTION	ADVERTIZING SIGNALLING	ORIENTATION SIGNALLING	HORIZONTAL SIGNALLING	SEMAPHORIC DATAS { POSITION PHISICAL DATAS, OPERATIONAL DATAS, SIGN }	GEOMETRICAL DATAS	
SEGMENT	X	X	X	X	X	X	X	X
NODES	X	X	X	X	X	X	X	X
AREA DIFINED BY STREETS	X	X	X	X	X	X	X	X
STUDY AREAS	X	X	X	X	X	X	X	X

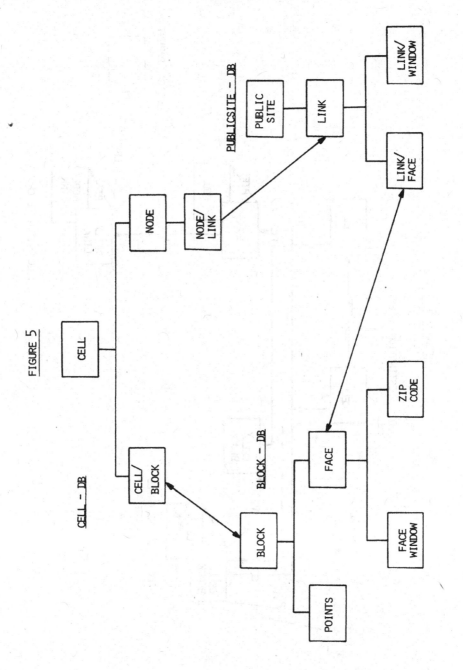

97

FIGURE 5

98

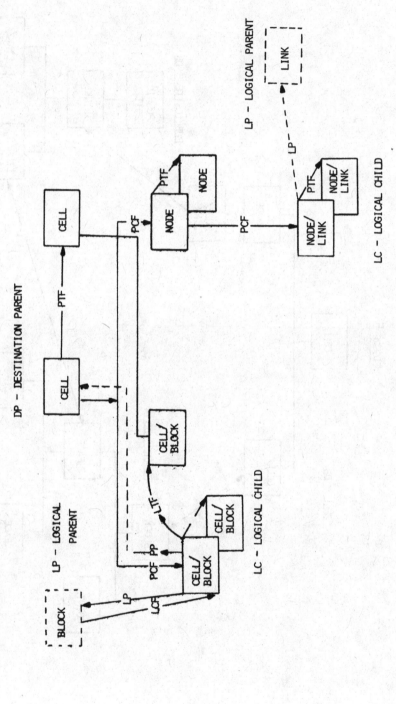

FIGURE 6

FIGURE 7

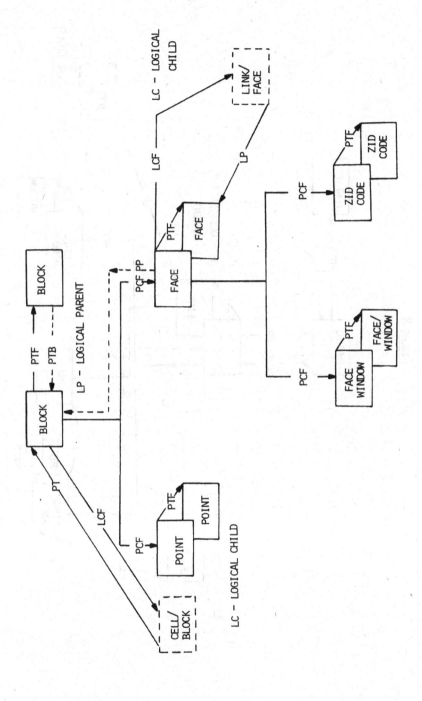

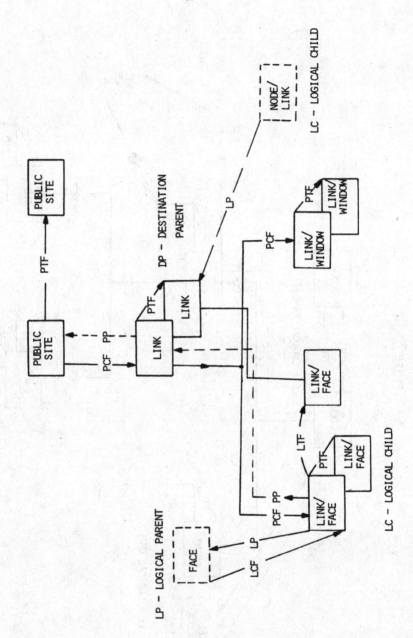

FIGURE 8

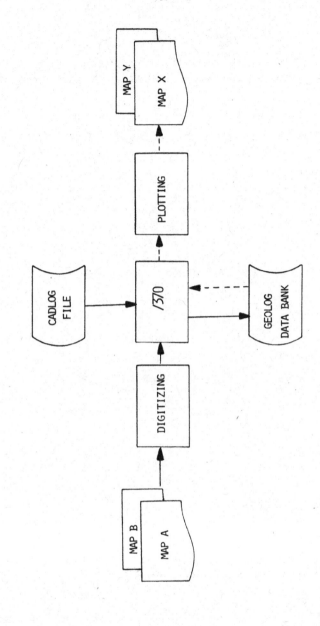

FIGURE 9

"Application Survey - Planning".

Bevan Smedley

This paper will survey the application of geographic-based systems in Urban and Regional planning. A discussion on the nature and requirements of the planning process will be followed by a review of significant implementations and research.

The growth of applications in this area has not been as marked as elsewhere. Reasons for this are proposed, and the implications for system design are considered. Emphasis throughout will be upon the vast data requirements of planning, coupled with the need to consider their distribution both over time and space.

The feelings of users with regard to the significance of geo-processing to planning, vary from those of complete disinterest, through scepticism, to outright support. This is reflected in the design of existing implementations, and until these views are fully understood and, in some cases, countered, the future potential for geo-systems in planning will not be as great as it should be.

IBM UK Scientific Centre,
Athelstan House, St Clement Street, WINCHESTER, Hampshire SO23 8UT,
England.

Definition of Planning.

Planning has been defined as "the art and science of ordering the use of land and the character and siting of buildings and communication routes, so as to secure the maximum degree of economy, convenience and beauty" (Keble).

At first glance, this old definition makes planning seem a straightforward simple profession. However, a second look at the definition soon reveals the process to be complex. Firstly, it is both an art and a science (critics of planning would say that they cannot make up their minds which it is) so that this implies that quantitative methods cannot, by themselves, provide the complete solution to any planning problem. Secondly, note the conflict between the demands of economy, beauty and convenience. It is impossible for any solution to be optimal as far as all three are concerned, at the same time. Thirdly, the planning process involves all levels of government, each with varying degrees of power (albeit very limitied) to implement plans - depending upon the country involved. Fourthly, the nature of planning is such that significant issues are involved and, once made, it is difficult to change plans in mid-stream.

As the years have progressed, planning has widened its horizons, and moved away from a concentration upon land use as the sole means of regulating development. Certainly in the U.K. planning now encompasses the social and economic, as well as the physical, systems of an area. As such, the variables to be studied cover a wide range of activities, as shown below :-

Population	Employment	Income	Resources
Housing	Industry	Commerce	Transport
Shopping	Education	Community	Recreation
Conservation	Utilities	services	Minerals

The Situation.

The ecological, social and economic environments are placing new and unprecedented demands on the planning and administrative abilities of today's local government officials. A constantly shifting population and economic structure, resulting from constantly increasing personal mobility, are straining local government administration. The rural population is moving into urban areas, while the inner city population is moving into suburban areas. Some results of this phenomenon are "urban sprawl" and the demise of many inner cities as viable socio-economic areas.

The brunt of these problams fall on local government administrators. They are faced by the dual problems of deteriorating productivity and increasing demands for new services - all this in the face of shrinking budgets. Faced with these problems, local government officials are beginning to ask complex policy questions. Many of these questions require data from multiple functional and geographic areas. For example :

"What impact will a proposed development have on schools, transportation, conservation, drainage, water and sewer facilities?".

"How should current police patrol resources be redeployed to cover changing crime and social patterns without sacrificing public safety?".

Tackling problems like these requires a multi-disciplinary approach, involving professionals from the many operating departments of local government, and co-operation with regional and central government. The problem situations are typically those which cannot be solved by direct action. The degree of government control over social, economic and physical systems varies widely. In most cases only negative control can be achieved (viz. "thou shalt not ...").

Furthermore, decisions once made have far-reaching and long-lasting significance and cannot be easily undone.

These complex policy-level problems cannot be addressed with information systems that support only a functional orientation. Data must be gathered across functional and geographic boundaries. Without adequate answers, effective administration and planning are impossible in today's complex ecological, social and economic environment. An integrated approach is required.

The Solution : Geo-processing.

Geo-processing is a recent data processing technique developed to meet the information requirements of state and local government agencies. Basically, it can relate geographic location to existing data bases (for example : geographic location can be related to police incident files, school population files etc.); geography is the common denominator that can link virtually all data.

Geo-processing can best be thought of as a three-step process :

1. Analyze the physical or geographic relationships between the various relatively stable features of the environment.

2. Using spatial and statistical data from the various departmental data bases, determine the activity patterns generated by the various land uses.

3. Analyze the proposed changes to land use, facilities or services that will affect these activity patterns.

All three of these steps could consume countless man-hours if done manually. Files from many different departments would have to be researched. With geo-processing however, a computer could do all the searching and correlating of data.

A geo-processing system can be thought of as a tool whose value is entirely dependent upon the skill and experience of the user. The system enables the user to aggregate and display geographic data, quickly. It provides information to help managers and administrators make effective decisions — it does not actually make the decisions.

Applications of Geo-processing.

The true value of a geo-processing system should be measured in terms of increased productivity for all its applications. These applications exist in every municipal department. Some (e.g. fire and police emergency) are done continuously. Others (e.g. re-zoning) are done only occasionally, as a planning function. Still others (e.g. building permits and inspections) are done routinely. Examples are :

Base map (engineering) - maintaining accurate engineering maps to eliminate the need for preliminary surveys.

Police dispatch - dispatching of police resources based upon geographic assignment and local event history.

School districting - planning optimal use of educational facilities based on geography of school population.

Transportation planning - planning of most efficient mass transit based on the location of riders and destinations.

Environment impact - analyzing impact of proposed developments on the ecology and municipal agencies.

Urban planning - analyzing impact of urban decisions on all local government agencies.

Note the apparent contradiction between the degree of complexity of geo-processing and the quality of graphical output in the above. This list is in increasing order of complexity of geo-processing, but decreasing in required (carto)graphic output.

The Nature of Planning.

Planning is a discipline which has a comparative lack of computing experience. The typical planner is professionally-qualified, usually in a non-numerate discipline, and relies upon other resources for any computing.

His data requirements are most diverse. Some data, usually surveys, censuses and maps, he maintains himself. For other, local, data he relies upon the operational departments of the local government, but has little say as to its content or format, but at least has reasonable access. The rest of his data comes from external sources, usually central government, over which he has no control at all.

Planning cannot be structured and therefore there is little scope for pre-programmed routines. Neither can planners wait for the conventional systems analysis approach. Solutions have to be devised in 'real-time'.

The planning process comprises :

DEFINING the problem and the data describing it.

DESCRIBING the relationships between variables, by means of

statistical analysis and modelling.

PREDICITING possible future consequences of alternative courses
of action.

PRESCRIBING that which is most suitable.

IMPLEMENTING the chosen plan.

MONITORING actual development against expectation, and
determining if another problem has to be defined, or the
original one re-examined.

Note the range and volume of data which can be involved. Data must
be analysed over time and space, as well as by topic. One estimate is
200 million bytes per annum, involving 8 separate years - 2 historical
(for past trends), the current year, and 5 points in the future -
typically spread over a 25 to 35 year period.
Above all, the process must be performed consistently and in an
integrated environment which enables each step to be linked with the
others in a coherent manner.

Current Approaches and Problems.
Although there have been some significant developments, notably in
the areas of information and related systems and in the production of
symbolic and plotted maps, the overall impact has been rather
disappointing, when compared to other local authority applications.
This is especially so in the case of modelling where experience both
in the UK and the USA has shown a movement away from the construction
and use of large-scale, technique-oriented models (which were popular
in the 1960's). What progress that has been made has tended to be
piecemeal, so that instead of a comprehensive system being
established, there exists instead a disjointed collection of packages,
models and techniques which it is almost impossible to merge into a
coherent amalgam with which to create a planning system.
Notable exceptions exist, especially in the management information
system area e.g. LAMIS in the establishment of property and other
urban data bases. Another significant development is the NIMS system
which couples an urban data base to an allocation model to investigate
accessibility problems in planning for municipalities in Scandinavia.
In considering why progress in computing has been slow, a variety
of factors can be submitted for consideration. Firstly, planning is a
dynamic discipline and techniques are changing. This is especially so
of quantitative techniques which only relatively recently have been
widely accepted. Consequently practising planners, whose experience is
backed by academic training gained several years ago, lack the
necessary numerate background in order to utilize such disciplines.
This is also true of training in computer science and appreciation,
which has only recently been introduced into the appropriate courses.
Secondly, the installation of computer hardware in local
authorities has been such that it has concentrated, at least
initially, upon batch financial applications. As hardware became more

powerful and relatively cheaper, on-line applications could be developed, but the necessary resources for developing them still tended to be managed by the financial department. Alternatively, application packages could be purchased to overcome this, but still the data processing department would be responsible for their evaluation, installation and operation.

Another factor is the lack of data in suitable format and in the right media for data processing. Most planning information is created from surveys, reports, and maps all of which have to be transposed by manual or semi-manual means into punched cards or tape, or directly to magnetic tape or disk. Automatic scanning of maps or photographs - or even the ground itself (i.e. by satellite) is possible, but the generated image still has to be interpreted. The sum total of such data is so large that unless the cost of collection can be partially or wholly justified by other means (e.g. shared with other applications, with other public bodies or must be collected because of statutory requirements) then it may be felt to be too expensive and outweigh any possible benefit which might accrue. Again, even if the data is collected, the cost of storage in computer media may prove to be too expensive, because of the volume involved, certainly if it is to be held on-line rather than in backing store (i.e. tape). The data problem is compounded because data which is available is collected by different organizations, and held in different formats and therefore must be held in some compatible format in order to be used and compared in physical planning.

Finally there has been dissatisfaction expressed with some of the techniques mentioned above. Models are a typical example. These tend to be developed as research, by academics and other interested parties, possibly in collaboration with practising planners. Consequently once the collaboration (i.e. research) is over, the planners are left with a 'black box' which, it is claimed, will solve all their problems. Putting this black box (the model) inside a bigger one (the computer itself) is sufficient to create a great deal of mistrust among the users and, to a certain extent, experience has proved them right.

Models are expensive to construct, both in terms of manpower and time, and then have to be calibrated against a known situation. One county in the UK has estimated that it took 10 man-years to construct and calibrate an allocation-type model which explored the relationship between employment and population over the county. Admittedly nearly 50% of this effort was spent in collecting the necessary data, which was an extremely useful exercise in its own right, but especially in this time of no growth and restraint upon public expenditure, such efforts are not seen to be paying their way.

Two other drawbacks in the use of models are that they seem to be insensitive to changes in input, and impossible to transfer and/or apply to different localities and situations. These criticisms really follow on from the 'black box' approach, where users do not understand the logic nor the data requirements of a model, hence any attempt to use it for a different state of affairs is quite likely to give rise to erroneous results and hence disbelief in this model in particular and all models in general.

A more general complaint, but one which is highlighted by the above discussion, is that models and data do not mix. Models are not written to utilize available data, but rather data has to be collected and formatted to suit the model. This problem is compounded by the various levels of aggregation of planning data and the spatial units in which it is gathered. Thus population data is available by enumeration district, whereas employment data is by employment area - two totally different zoning systems created by separate organizations.

In addition, some models expect data which it may not be posssible to collect at all - the most notable example being income data. Hence the would-be user must resort to various techniques (some scientific, others intuitive) in order to obtain the necessary data to satisfy the model's input requirements. This problem - the lack of suitable data - is illustrative of a process which is common in planning, and probably elsewhere too. It is best described as 'fudging', and defined as the process whereby an experienced professional uses his unique knowledge of a situation based upon training, intuition and local knowledge, to manipulate, modify or even create information. Such a process will be an implicit part of the physical planning process, certainly for some time to come. The drawback is that it is not systematic, is difficult to describe and justify, highly individualistic, and almost impossible to repeat consistently.

Another aspect of data in relation to models is the inadequate treatment of spatial information. Currently models treat this numerically (i.e using zone numbers); distances etc. are input not calculated. True handling of spatial information, by the recognition of a spatial data type, would improve any model's capabilities.

A final criticism of models lies in their individuality. They are always developed in isolation and never as a package with which to explore a total situation. Little or no consideration is given to using the output from one model as input to another. Consequently, in the real world, problems with single models become compounded when, as in the case of physical planning, a suite of models is required to explore and explain fully the intricate series of inter-relationships which are involved in a large-scale planning problem.

System Implications.

The nature of the planning process has many implications for the design of a geo-processing system.

Data base techniques are required to handle the vast amount of data coherently, and these must be backed up by further functions which analyse and manipulate the data.

Geo-systems require a new data type - locational (geo) data. Existing systems have not recognized that geo-data must be handled by the system in the same way as other data i.e. allowing analysis, conversion, calculation and other operations to be performed on it, rather than treat it as something special.

Means must be provided to enable relationships to be modelled within the information system, and allow access to statistical and graphical packages in order to understand and present the nature of the relationship to the user. Ideally, the system should be a framework which enables user-chosen routines to be added, interfacing with the information base through common paths - again a reason for a common approach to geo-data. (The concept of a 'framework' will be developed later).

Above all, the user must interact with the system. Only then can the 'distributed data base' (which is the experience, professionalism and intuition of the planner) be connected to the information base, and so enable complex problems to be tackled.

Overview of Systems.

Development has proceded upon functional lines. Some systems have concentrated upon specific requirements e.g. mapping – either to produce output of as high a quality as possible to match existing cartographic methods, or to use the speed of computer output devices to display complex planning information more readily, and in a succinct manner.

Other systems have tackled the time-consuming task of spatial data input, conventionally done by manual digitizing and subsequent verification by plotting.

Some development has been concerned with establishing data bases for specific functions e.g utilities mapping or property administration. Others have approached the problem-solving nature of planning by providing a visual graphics capability enabling the user to interract with the data and the display, or alternatively, attempted to interface models with a data base to give a different problem-solving capability. Examples of some of these are :

a) IBM Japan Scientific Centre : 'CARPS – Computer Assisted Regional Planning System', which aims for the integrated operation of data, models and applications in the context of regional planning.

b) IBM Federal Systems Division : 'GGIS – Generalized Geographic Information System', whose objectives are compatibility with existing geographic base (e.g. DIME) files, applicability to demographic and resource data, application independence, and geographic data structure compatibility.

c) IBM Research Division : 'GADS – Geo-data Analysis and Display System', whose emphasis is on the solution by non-programmers of problems involving data which can be related to a geographic location. GADS provides a data extraction technique for accessing data in a variety of files, and a set of conversational data analysis and display functions.

d) IBM UK Scientific Centre : 'SIMPLE – Statistics, Information and Modelling for Planning the Local Environment', a framework for a planning system which enables the whole gamut of planning processes i.e data analysis, modelling, statistics and forecasting to be performed within one integrated system by an end-user, interactively.

It is instructive to note that CARPS, GADS and SIMPLE all adopt the relational, or tabular, approach to data management, whereas GGIS is based upon the hierarchical approach, using DL/1. Thus it would seem that both approaches are feasible, although the interactive systems favour the relational one.

The performance problems associated with large amounts of data was tackled in GADS by using data extraction and aggregation techniques prior to the analysis session, whereas the experience with SIMPLE is that this problem is a necessary overhead in order to give the end-user complete freedom to access the data and to aggregate it in whatever way he so chooses.

Any real attempt to compare the differing approaches of the above systems could only be based upon a subjective consideration of the various documentation. The physical distances between the 'competence centres' would make any objective exercise extremely expensive. Besides, the diversity of approach is most probably a reflection of the differences in the application areas as they exist in the various parts of the world, and the level at which they were approached. Hence any comparison would not be on a like-for-like basis.

The Framework Approach.

After due consideration of the analysis of the physical planning process and the current problems relating to the use of computers, it was decided that a new approach was needed in order to make progress in the application of computers to physical planning.

A system design is too restrictive because it imposes specific techniques upon the user and is inflexible. The claim that a system can be extended is often made but is very hard to justify in practice. It usually requires an in-depth knowledge of the components of the system before any extra facilities can be added.

Consequently, a framework rather than a system is proposed. The difference is that the framework provides a basic set of tools which the user can use to perform certain limited functions, whilst the real function is provided by the user himself, selecting the techniques which he understands and has faith in and proved in the past, and adding such routines to the framework to create his own unique system. Thus a framework is an extensible system (by definition) which must be extended by the user before it can perform any useful work. Such extensions must be capable of being made with little effort on the part of the user, and not require any knowledge of the inner workings.

As has already been stated, the framework itself provides a basic set of components which experience has shown will be universally required. These are :

        Data management
        Data analysis
        Data manipulation
        Spatial data support
        Interactive terminal support
        Library interface
        Data interface.

Because of the large amount of data required for physical planning, it is vital that such data can be maintained in a consistent manner. Hence the requirement for a data management sub-system to store all the data in a structured yet flexible way, so that the user can retrieve easily, whatever information he requires. Coupled with this is the need to analyse (count,select, calculate means, totals etc) and manipulate the basic information according to the particular requirements of the problem in hand. Thus certain data may need to be selected and aggregated to a particular level (e.g. zone or district) for one problem, while a completely different set aggregated to another level for the next.

It has been argued that a data base system is not required for physical planning, since only aggregated data is involved. However, the conclusions of this research are that the ability to manipulate the basic data gives a much increased flexibility, and a greater power, and allows many alternative strategies to be explored. It also enables the interplay between structure (strategic) and local (detailed) planning to be easily achieved, since the same data base is involved in both operations.

In the past, a conflict has arisen between the flexibility required to allow the exploration of data, and the performance aspects necessary to enable efficient and speedy access to individual items or records. Previously, limitations of both hardware and software have meant that this conflict could not be resolved, and so different systems evolved separating the two basic requirements. The ever-increasing power of computers relative to their cost, both in speed and storage capacity, plus improved software technology, now means that this conflict can be resolved, and both approaches combined, with advantages to all.

Physical planning imposes an additional requirement upon any data sub-system, namely the ability to handle spatial data. This is inherent in the nature of the task. Analysis of the distribution of variables over physical space must be considered as a basic part of the planning process. Some approaches treat spatial data as variations of character or numeric values (e.g. addresses, postcodes, separate X- and Y- co-ordinates, grid squares, segments). However, there are many advantages to be gained by treating it as a new data type, and recognising it as such in the basic data sub-system by providing suitable functions which can operate on it in as similar way as possible to other functions which operate on character or numeric data. This is impossible or, at best, inflexible and coarse, with other forms of representation. The subject will be re-addressed later, after other aspects of the framework have been considered.

A vital component of the framework is that which provides interactive terminal support for the user. The drawback of batch systems is that they separate the thinking process of the user from the information process of the system. If turnaround is more than one or two hours, then the separation becomes so great that the power of the computer is lost and it is effectively reduced to a mere filing system. Only by providing interactive support can any system couple the two vital pre-requisites of any problem-solving process : the experience and professionalism of the problem-solver, and the information and processing with which the problem can be solved.

The last two components of the framework are those which distinguish it from any other systems approach. Firstly there is the underlying assumption that the user will wish to bring to the framework certain functions by which he can create his own system, and that these fuctions will exist as a library of routines. Hence one component must enable the automatic selection of the appropriate routine from the library and its inclusion in the framework, resolving any linkages which may exist between the two, or for that matter with any other sub-routines. The second component provides the missing link – namely the transference of data, under user- or routine- request, from the data sub-system to the model or whatever routine is selected, as input and vice-versa. In this way, output from a model can be fed back into the data sub-system and then treated exactly as any other set of information (and therefore used as the basis for input to another model).

This approach re-inforces the need to treat spatial information as a data type, rather than to hold it as special indices or representations. Only in this way can the framework approach be utilized in physical planning, to enable the automatic linkage of data, spatial functions and graphical routines, and so provide spatial processing and output. Additionally, allocation-type models rely upon spatially aggregated data for input, and provide similar output. Within the framework, the user can take his basic data, aggregate it by some spatial operation, and then interface it to his selected graphical or model routine.

Conclusions.

Most importantly, the role of geo-data in planning must be recognized. It plays a varied role, combining three functions :

a) assisting in the presentation of output – spatial distribution of topic variables (i.e. maps).

b) as values in their own right, enabling additional processing e.g. calculation of surface areas, densities, distances and distribution coefficients. Also, and very importantly, enabling allocation models to spatially distribute variables more meaningfully, being aware of distance, location, neighbourhood etc.

c) as the sole means of linking multi-disciplinary variables and understanding complex relationships e.g population-transport-employment.

Consequent to the above, it must be recognized that geo-data is another data type and that systems which process this information should do so in a manner consistent with the other data types – as far as this is logically possible.

Finally, geo-data is important as one of the vital ingredients of both of the two large data bases required for planning :

1). the information base (200m bytes per annum).

2) the distributed or 'experience' base of the user himself.

These two data bases must be linked by a system which is both flexible enough to handle a variety of data formats, and versatile enough to handle unstructured operations by varied users.

DEFINITION AND MANIPULATION OF

GRAPHICAL ENTITIES IN

GEOGRAPHIC INFORMATION SYSTEMS

Richard L. Phillips

Geographic information systems have much in common with generalized data base management systems. Both types of systems require the definition of items, attributes, and higher level constructs involving them, e.g. records. Geographic information systems deal in addition with graphical entities, a concept unknown in data base management systems. Not surprisingly, geographic systems have little in common; each one is a new "invention." This paper explores the graphic requirements of two typical geographic information systems with the aim of identifying how such entities are defined, used, and stored in a data base. Examples are drawn from a cartographic system where only graphic display is important, and a query system where graphical entities play an important role in both extraction and display of data. Conclusions are drawn in terms of the shortcomings of generalized data base management systems with regard to data definition, data storage, and data manipulation. The interdependence of these operations is discussed, illustrating that the way in which a graphical entity is manipulated by the user impacts on its definition and storage.

Professor Richard L. Phillips
Computer, Information, and Control Engineering
The University of Michigan
Ann Arbor, Michigan, 48109
U.S.A

Definition and Manipulation of Graphical Entities In
Geographic Information Systems

1. Introduction

Geographic information systems typically deal with two distinct kinds
of data--spatial data and aspatial data. Spatial data defines the location
of some object in geodetic coordinates while aspatial data is all other
information associated with that object. Aspatial data can be described in
terms of entities and the relationships among the entities. The entities
in turn are described by their attributes. Relationships have no attributes
and no values associated with them.

Manipulations of aspatial data consist of retrieving values of attributes
of the entities or values of attributes based on the relationships between
the entities. Commercially available generalized database management systems,
whether hierarchical or network, can adequately handle aspatial data. They
provide facilities for defining attributes, entities, and relations, and
for querying the database according to specified criteria.

Spatial data, on the other hand, poses problems in definition and
manipulation that no current database management system addresses. These
problems are generally due to the fact that manipulations of spatial data
result in values for relationships rather than values for attributes of
entities. This situation can best be exemplified by the following list of
tasks that users might require of geographic information systems:

1. Find nearest point to a member of a set.

2. Find the nearest point to a non-member.

3. How many points lie within x units.

4. Select all points within a user polygon.

5. Find the elevation of point A.

6. Find the area of land between two elevations.

7. Find the slope at point A.

8. Find the volume of material to be removed for a highway.

9. Find the highest place.

10. Find the average elevation within a user-defined polygon.

11. Find the total area leased to Company A within 10 miles of the
    coast from Houston to Galveston.

12. Find the total length of common boundary between areas leased to
    Company A and Company B.

13. Find the largest area of contiguous leases held by one company.

14. Given independent maps showing a) leases and b) some other spatial partitioning which does not respect lease boundaries, e.g., sea floor geology, find the total area of leases to Company A on geology type X.

15. If the value of a lease is a function of geology, find the value of leases held by Company A.

16. Find the shortest distance between A and B.

17. Find the nearest ride to point X on the graph.

18. Find the mean shortest distance from A or X to all nodes.

19. Find all nodes downstream of A.

20. Given estimate of input at all nodes, find the flow in all edges.

Fortunately, not all of these operations are required of a single geographic information system; they are usually specialized to a class of data and applications. In what follows, we shall consider in detail the data definition and manipulation requirements of two such specialized systems; one dealing with water quality data and the other with production information for off-shore oil leases.

2. A Water Quality Data Base

2.1 Overview

During the last 15 years, various U. S. Government Agencies (currently
the Environmental Protection Agency) have been monitoring the chemical
composition of the Nation's streams and rivers by samples taken at some
500,000 stations situated throughout the country. These data, mostly values
of chemical parameters such as zinc concentration, fecal coliform count,
percentage of dissolved oxygen, etc., have been placed in a large database
called STORET (Green, 1966). Various agencies, both state and federal, have
long had the ability to interrogate this database and retrieve information
that is useful for long term water quality monitoring, the assessment of
hydrological trends, the design of expanded monitoring networks, and perhaps
to aid in enforcement actions against major polluters.

The sheer bulk of STORET (currently about 1200×10^6 bytes) coupled
with a relatively inefficient mode of retrieval very nearly prohibits an
interested agency from making timely and meaningful use of the available
data. Moreover, even given the availability of a fast, efficient retrieval
program, a printed output is certainly not the best way to present the information. Strong and significant geographical relationships exist among
the data which cannot easily be detected from a tabular output. This suggests
the applicability of graphically aided retrieval and display techniques.

A system has been developed that makes it possible for a user to display
on a cartographic background the locations of selected water quality monitoring stations. The stations are shown not only in relation to each other
but also in relation to the surrounding hydrological features, state/county
boundaries, and municipal outlines. Parameter data which have been acquired
at the stations shown can be displayed graphically or in tabular form. A
time history of measurements for a particular parameter can be graphed or a
perspective display of a selected reach of a river can be requested, with
parameter values super-imposed as a bar graph at station locations. Being
interactive, the system allows a user to investigate hundreds of water
quality situations in the space of an hour or two. Then, guided by what
he sees, he can pursue interesting patterns of water quality degradation,
rejecting all those cases that seem to be of little value. The user thus
quickly gains an insight which might otherwise be masked by the volume of the
data and the labor involved in interrogation by nongraphic means.

2.2 Map Manipulations - Fixed Maps

2.2.1 Since the system is geographically oriented, the first step a
user must take is to select a reference map. That is, he specifies the
geographic region in which he wants to study water quality data. This can
be as vast as the continental United States or as small as a single county.
In selecting his map the user is in effect asking for one or more state
outlines, the state being the basic cartographic unit in the system. Later,
the user can embellish his map with other features, to the extent that the
available data allows. A reference map can be specified by explicitly
naming one or more states, or by defining a longitude/latitude window. If
these description formats do not provide the user with enough flexibility,
he can modify the map by shrinking or expanding the display scale, by a
zoom or a pan with respect to the original data, or by designating a polygonal portion (a county, for example) of the display as the reference map.
Additional geographic features such as county boundaries, river traces,
lake outlines, and municipal boundaries can be selectively added at this
point by requesting that they be overlaid on the state outlines. A user

can redefine a reference map at any time and as often as he wishes.
Figures 1, 2, 3, and 4 represent a sequence of reference map selection
operations, starting with a map of the continental United States. In
Fig. 1, the user has "pointed" to a portion of the U.S. that he wishes to
examine in more detail. For the zooming operation the user points to the
lower left and upper right corners of a rectangle that contains a portion
of the current map which is to be expanded to fill the display screen.
Fig. 2 shows the result of a zoom based upon the rectangle in Fig. 1.
Fig. 3 shows the addition of county lines to the basic outline map.
Hydrological features can also be overlaid as will be seen in Fig. 4.

2.2.2 Map Modification

At many points in a typical program session the user will want to
effect various types of map modification. For this the user can effect
arbitrary scale change and map translation, he can measure distance and
area, overlay the map with a local geographic grid, control map generalization by setting plotting detail, determine the longitude/latitude of a
specified point, and if identifying features have been shifted off screen
he can determine in which state a point lies. In addition, the user can
control switches that determine whether or not county lines or rivers or
city boundaries will be plotted. The original reference map can always
be regained no matter how extensively it has been manipulated.

Examples of several of the map manipulation capabilities are shown in
Figs. 4 and 5. In Fig. 4 the zoom and grid overlay features are demonstrated.
The user has outlined the southern tip of Florida on a larger map and asked
to have that area enlarged to fill the screen. He can, of course, request
successive zooms in order to examine smaller and smaller portions of the
reference map, but eventually he will reach the resolution limit of the
original digitized data. Shown in Fig. 4 as well is a geographic grid
overlay feature, which provides the user with a quick longitude/latitude
reference for locating points on the map. Fig. 5 is a composite display of
the state of Connecticut showing the features of state name retrieval, area
calculation, distance calculation, and longitude/latitude determination.
For the latter, the user moves the cross-hair cursor to a desired point and
presses "?". The point is marked and the geodetic coordinates are printed
beneath it. For area and distance calculations the user moves the cross-
hair cursor along an arbitrary path and, depending upon the original request,
either the distance or area is printed close to the path. The name of the
state in which a specified point is located can also be retrieved, as can
the county name if so specified.

Another type of map manipulation is used in conjunction with a qualitative display of water quality data. The user can ask to see a three
dimensional perspective display of selected stations, the country surrounding
them, and the specified parameter measurement shown as a vertical bar graph.
An example of such a display is shown in Fig. 6.

2.3 Map Manipulation - Variable Maps

For the most part cartographic data plays a passive, overlay role in
the system. Except for determining which water quality stations will be
visible on the display screen, the map database does not participate in
the water quality data selection and manipulation process. There is one
aspect of the system, however, that involves the definition and manipulation
of variable maps. These are actually user-defined polygons in geodetic
space. These are called water quality standards zones and are used for
specialized retrieval of stations that have reported standards violations.

Standards zones can be created either interactively or from a predefined file. The current version of the reference map is displayed and the user is asked to outline a zone. Once the zone is described, the user is asked to attach one or more attributes (standards) to the zone. Each attribute is specified by a STORET parameter number, a standard value or limit for that parameter, and a short name (up to 8 characters) for the parameter. The zone is stored in a specially structured file and the user is asked if he wishes to annotate the zone. If the response is positive the user can position the cursor in or near the zone and enter a notation or comment which will be useful or informative when the zone description is subsequently recalled.

The zones currently in existence for the present reference map can be displayed at any time. All zones or parts of zones that will be visible will be drawn and the attached comments, if any will be displayed at the location where the original annotation was placed. Also, a tabular listing of all zone attributes will be displayed.

If one wishes to change one or more aspects of a zone he can edit the zone and its description. There are five edit commands which allow the user to change, insert, and delete an attribute, insert a comment, and delete a zone. An example of standards zones display and editing is shown in Fig. 7. There, the user asked to have an attribute deleted, #300 in zone number 4 (the zones and attributes are fictional). The deletion of the attribute is signalled by crossing out the row. It will not appear the next time the zone is displayed. Finally, a zone and all attached attributes can be deleted; the zone is shaded to indicate deletion.

In order for a zone to be used as a standards comparison in retrieving water quality data the user must declare it to be active. Once this is done the user can ask the system to find all stations that are in violation with respect to a selected parameter. From a retrieval standpoint the system must do the following:

.perform point in polygon comparisons to find stations that are visible and fall within active zones.

.determine a subset of those stations for which the selected parameter has been measured.

.further restrict the subset to those stations that have ever reported a measured value in excess of the standard attribute assigned to the zone.

2.4 Cartographic Data Manipulation Requirements

As stated earlier, the major function of the map database is for base map overlay. Thus, structuring the database for update transactions was not a consideration. Rapid retrieval was, however, of great importance so considerable pains were taken to facilitate searching a large data base. There are actually three databases, one for state and county data, one for hydrological data and one for city outlines. The common key for all of them is latitude/longitude.

Each database has a directory portion which contains latitude/longitude extrema for every feature contained therein. Thus, anytime a feature from any of the databases is needed, the extremes of latitude/longitude currently displayed on the screen are used as a search window to isolate the features needed for superposition. A binary search of the appropriate database directory results in response times of less than two seconds. The static map database comprises a few million bytes.

121

The database used for water quality zone definition must be rapidly updated as well as searched. Not only can the spatial characteristics of a zone be modified but its spatial attributes, such as parameter type and parameter value are subject to variation as well. A direct access data structure was used for the zone database, with a retrieval key defined as a hierarchical combination of state identifier. The zone database is seldom larger than a megabyte, for a single user. There can be many such files in existence, however.

3. An Integrated Database Management System
for Offshore Oil Lease Information

3.1 Overview.

Since 1954 the federal government has leased over 2800 tracts off the
Gulf, Atlantic, and Pacific coasts to approximately 200 firms for gas and oil
development. The Conservation Division of the U.S.G.S. has been keeping data
on sales, production, and royalties for these leases for some time. Recently,
these data have been brought together in a single Lease Production and Revenue
database (LPR), along with geographic information necessary to map various
subsets of the data. Typical items in the LPR database are annual oil
production, annual rent and royalty, lease identifiers and attributes, company
names and bidding activity, and detailed cartographic information.

The database is used for such activities as prediction of discovery of
hydrocarbons from sale data, identification and display of similarities
among companies, and study of the distribution of bids for an individual
lease. To facilitate studies of this sort, the database system had to be
designed to provide convenient access for

> .statistical analyses

> .graphical products summarizing both the data and the
> analyses.

> .maps illustrating various characteristics of the data.

3.2 LPR Geographic Data

3.2.1   Map Production

Two different types of data are needed to produce maps: thematic and
geographic. Thematic data are associated with the individual leases and
provide information (for example, gas production, annual royalty, etc.) we
wish to portray. Geographic data provide the physical and legal description
of lease boundaries necessary to produce the map. These two types of data
are compiled in somewhat different ways.

From time to time offshore tracts are offered for lease through local
offices of the Bureau of Land Management. Data from each sale are put into
machine-readable form and gathered into a centralized data base. The Bureau
of Land Management gives these data to the Conservation Division of the
United States Geological Survey, and the Division adds identification codes
for each tract. As leases come into production, data on the volume of
production and the royalties paid are added to the data base.

Geographic data are necessary to describe the physical location of
each tract involved in the map. Since tracts are offered for lease using a
legal description based on the public land survey, the first step in compiling
the geographic data is to obtain geographic coordinates (latitude and
longitude) for the Outer Continental Shelf survey. These coordinates are
obtained in machine-readable form from the National Oceanographic and
Atmospheric Administration. The survey is organized in a hierarchical
manner with each state subdivided into areas that are further subdivided
into blocks. The coordinates locate the ends of all survey lines for a
given area.

The coordinate description of the survey data is necessary but not sufficient to produce maps. The thematic information must be linked to the block descriptions. The block identification number, which is specified in the legal description of the lease, is often all that is necessary to make this link since the lease is defined as occupying the entire block. However, in many cases, the lease occupies only part of a block, several parts of a block, or parts of several blocks. In such cases the legal description is phrased in familiar terms such as "the north-west quarter of the south-west quarter of block 117 and the north half of the south-east quarter of block 116." Such phrases are converted to a numeric code when they are added to the data base. During the mapping procedure, the code enables the system to subdivide the block appropriately so that only the correct portion is included in the lease.

Figure 8 is typical of the types of maps produced by the LPR system.

3.3 Querying

Aside from being used for automated map production, the LPR cartographic data plays a role in querying the database. Neighborhood queries are common and can be exemplified by the following:

    i) Find all leases within five miles of Galveston, Texas.

    ii) Find all leases inside a three mile limit from Houston to Galveston.

    iii) Find all leases belonging to Company A that are within twenty miles of lease B.

For queries of this type, place directories have to be part of the data base, that is, coordinates must be provided for Galveston, the mouth of the Rio Grande, etc. In addition, coast line and political boundary data must be an integral part of the database.

Another requirement is to answer queries regarding adjacent leases. These might be of the form

    i) Find all leases adjoining lease A.

    ii) Find all leases adjoining the coast line of Louisiana from City A to City B.

    iii) Find all leases belonging to Company A that are not surrounded by those belonging to Company B.

These queries imply that information regarding the identity of leases on either side of a boundary line segment must be stored in the data base.

In order to facilitate graphical queries, two relational operators have been defined. They are denoted as .ADJ. which is used to indicate adjacency and .NGH. which is used to indicate neighborhood attributes. Thus, one can form a query which has an element of the form entity.ADJ.entity, which indicates that an adjacency condition must exist for the entities on either side of the operator in order to satisfy the query.

Finally, the user can query by pointing at locations or areas on a map which show some or all of the entities of the data base. The user can outline a collection of leases and ask for production information or company ownership. This operation permits processes such as spatial aggregation prior to applying statistical procedures. Pointing can be used in conjunction with traditional alphanumeric querying in order to allow a user to satisfy his requests as efficiently and quickly as possible.

Clearly, the data structure required to permit the cartographic data to be used in the above manner must be quite flexible. The cartographic data is considered to consist of nodes, chains, lines, polygons, and points. A point is an ordered pair (x,y), representing longitude and latitude. A node is a point, together with an attribute value table, e.g. a road junction would be a node. A chain is an ordered set of points where the first and last points are nodes. A line is an ordered set of chains such that the last point of each chain is the first point of the next chain. Finally, a polygon is a line where the start node of the first chain coincides with the end node of the last chain. Each polygon is named so with every chain there is associated a left polygon and a right polygon as one travels along the chain from its start node to its end node.

3.4   Implementing a Database Management System.

In general, geographic information database systems require raw data storage structures which are heavily linked to one another and retrieval operations which may give rise to computation-bound tasks. These two facts imply that general database management systems will not be able to manage geographic data since they do not allow either the richness of the data structure linking required and they do not have the special algorithms to do the computations required by most spatial operations.

A general geographic database system must allow data structures which are convenient for simple retrieval, input, update, and mapping or displaying coordinates for point objects, curve or line objects, and region or polygon objects. Because the number of coordinates can be quite high, the data structures must be economic in terms of pointers. Otherwise, there could easily be more pointers than data and the cost of the overhead becomes a dominating factor.

Besides the data structure required for simple retrieval operations and/or manipulation operations (union, intersection, convex hull, etc.), the general data structure must allow the data to be structured as the computation-bound algorithms require. In other words, the algorithmic operations will, by their very nature, dictate or strongly suggest that certain types of information be readily available. Since it is the data structure which makes information readily available, the data structure must be, in fact, algorithmic-dependent.

In Section 1 we discussed the nature of aspatial and of spatial data. Often in geographic data aspatial data is only related via spatial relationships among them or is of interest only via the spatial relationships. For example, in a query such as "Find all leases within 5 miles of each other and 2 miles of a harbor," only the spatial relationships are of interest in retrieving the data. The data retrieved, however, is aspatial data. Other queries such as "Find all leases within 2 miles of a given pipeline which have produced more than 10,000 barrels of oil in a given time interval," require manipulation of both spatial and aspatial data. It appears that the structuring and manipulation of the two kinds of data require quite different facilities.

They must, however, be related in some way; current database management systems do not seem to provide the facilities necessary to make the connection.

The concept of managing graphical attributes in a database system is relatively new. Williams (Williams, 1976) and Go (Go, 1975) have implemented graphics-oriented systems which are based on a relational data model, but the basic software is experimental and not widely available. The network DBTG (CODASYL, 1971) data model, however, appears to offer as much flexibility as does the relational model, while the hierarchical model does not easily lend itself to describing topological relations among graphical entities.

For the LPR system a host language network-type database management system was selected. The database is implemented in ADBMS (Hershey, 1975), a system developed by the ISDOS project at The University of Michigan. ADBMS implements a subset of the CODASYL-DBTG specifications and, being a host language system, it provides low level subroutine calls for its data manipulation language. This means that to implement a high level query language, one must develop strategies for traversing the network schema and accessing specified data items. It is of interest to briefly discuss the organization of the LPR database. In accordance with DBTG terminology a database is organized as a collection of <u>records</u> of different types. A <u>record</u> is a grouping of <u>items</u> that have some relationship to one another. The overall structure of the database is determined by the linkages that exist between <u>records</u>, a property established by the data definition. Figure 9 is a diagrammatic representation of what is essentially the data definition for the oil lease database. The rectangles represent <u>records</u> with the labels being arbitrarily assigned mnemonic names. The arrows joining the <u>records</u> are called <u>sets</u> and represent allowable relationships among <u>records</u>. The <u>sets</u> that begin and end on the same <u>record</u> are related to a master <u>record</u> called SYSTEM, or CALC records.

Because the network data model permits the definition of such general relationships among entities, it is difficult to develop a high level query language that permits a casual user to pose unambiguous yet powerful queries. Languages for traversing network data bases have been developed by Bandurski (Bandurski, 1975), Bonczek (Bonczek, 1975) and Deheneffe (Deheneffe, 1976), but their systems all require that the user be familiar with the underlying schema to make effective use of the system. Moreover, none of the systems treat the manipulation of graphical entities.

A detailed discussion of the query language is inappropriate for this paper. The interested reader is directed to (Phillips, 1977).

4. Future Work

Future plans for both the water quality information system (STORET) and the LPR database management system call for more complicated tasks involving cartographic data. The analysis capabilities of STORET will be enhanced by the addition of a stream reach database. A reach is that portion of a river which extends downstream from the confluence of two rivers (or from the uppermost end of a river) to the next encountered confluence

The database comprises 22,000 reaches totaling 350,000 miles of U.S. streams. Among the data available for each reach are a unique identifier, reach length, path value (river mileage from head of reach through all downstream reaches to terminal point of the waterway), arbolate length (the summed lengths of all reaches upstream from the head of a reach), reach identifiers of connecting reaches, latitude/longitude extrema, and of course the geodetic coordinates for plotting the reach. Since the topology of the entire U.S. stream network is available it will be possible to perform flood forecasting, downstream transport modeling for hazardous substance spills to estimate concentrations and times of arrival at critical points, and to improve water resource statistics organization.

The stream reach database will be static so there will be no need for update and integrity considerations. Because of the flexibility of its intended use, however, efficient retrieval poses some problems. They are, as yet, unsolved.

The LPR system will be significantly expanded by the addition of several new types of cartographic data. This will include

1) Geophysical data (seismic)

> geodetic coordinates of shothole
> line number
> shothole number
> contractor name

2) Well element data

> geodetic coordinates of well
> well status
> identification number
> operator
> associated lease
> directional survey information

3) Other data

> platforms
> pipelines
> fairways (ship lanes)

These data will be used largely in automated production of the following map types:

1. Strip maps - Seismic - Sometimes referred to as prospect maps, etc. showing geophysical seismic data in an area.

2. Strip map - non-seismic - These maps depict fairways, coastlines, lease data information, surface and bottom hole well locations.

3. Pipeline map - These depict platform locations, straight holes, lease data, pipeline locations and sizes.

4. Field study and field plat maps - These are utilized in the field evaluation work and contain all lease information, production levels, directional surveys, fairways and coastlines.

All of these data are subject to error, modification, and updating so they will not comprise a totally static database. The frequency of change will, however, be small so a heavy transaction load is not expected. What will prove challenging is the fact that the three new databases will continue to exist as separate entities, probably at three separate locations. Thus, the current LPR database system will have to link to them. In principle this should be straightforward because latitude/longitude is a key common to all databases. Administrative problems may, however, prove more challenging.

References

Bandurski, A. E. and Jefferson, D. K. (1975), "Enhancements to the DBTG Model for Computer-Aided Ship Design," Proc. Workshop on Data Bases for Interactive Design, Waterloo, Canada, ACM, Inc.

Bonczek, W. D., Haseman, W. D., and Whinston, A. B. (1975), "Structure of a Query Language for a Network Data Base," Tech. Rept., Krannert School, Purdue Univ., West Lafayette, Ind.

CODASYL Data Base Task Group, (1971), April 1971 Report, ACM, New York.

Deheneffe, C. and Hennebert, H. (1976), "NUL: A Navigational User's Language for a Network Structured Data Base," Proc. Int'l Conf. on Management of Data, Washington, D.C., ACM, Inc.

Go, A., Stonebraker, M., and Williams, G. (1975), "An Approach to Implementing a Geo-Data System," Proc. Workshop on Data Bases for Interactive Design, Waterloo, Canada, ACM, Inc.

Green, R. S. (1966), "The Storage and Retrieval of Data for Water Quality Control," U. S. Government Printing Office, Washington, D.C.

Hershey, E. A. and Messink, P.W. (1975), "A Data Base Management System for PSA Based on DBTG 71," ISDOS Working Paper No. 88, The University of Michigan.

Phillips, R.L. (1976), "The Oil Lease Database Query System," ISDOS Newsletter, Vol. 8, No. 3, App. III, ISDOS Project, University of Michigan, Ann Arbor, Mich.

Williams, R. and Giddings, G.M. (1976), "A Picture Building System," IEEE Transactions of Software Engineering, Vol. SE-2, No. 1, pp. 62-66.

RFMP

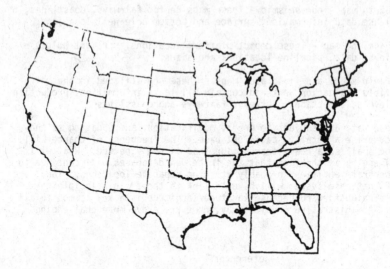

Figure 1

Reference Map of Continental United States.

MAPM

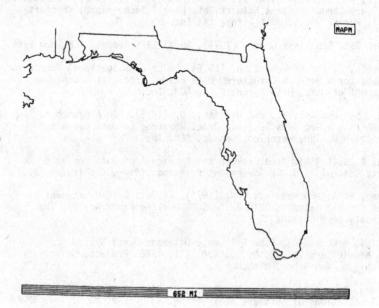

652 MI

Figure 2

Zoom-Derived Outline Map of Florida

129

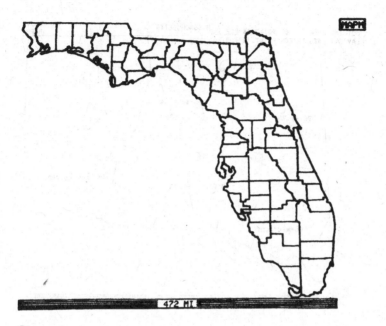

Figure 3

County Overlay Map of Florida

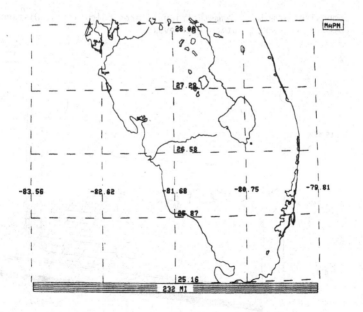

Figure 4

Zoom-Derived Map of Southern Florida with City Boundaries, Lakes and Rivers, and Geographic Grid Overlay.

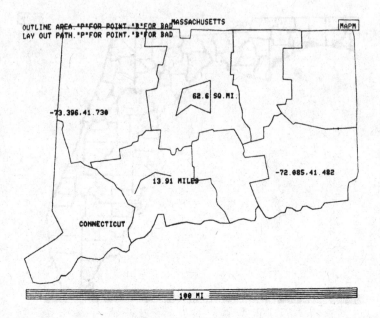

Figure 5

Composite Example of Name Retrieval, Area Calculation, Distance
Calculation, and Location Retrieval.

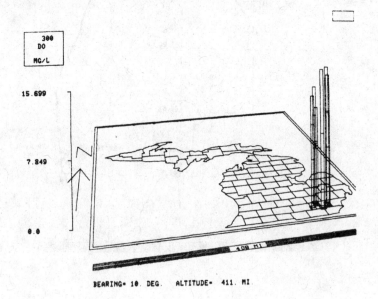

Figure 6

Perspective Data Display.

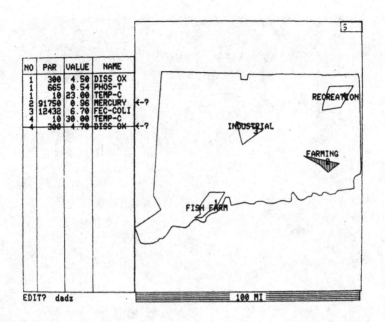

Figure 7

Example of Water Quality Standards Zones Display and Editing.

Offshore Gas Producers
Texas and Louisiana

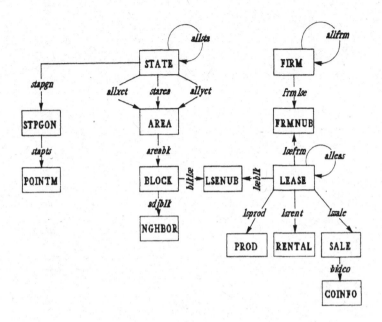

Figure 9

Schema Diagram for LPR Database.

LAND USE: PROBLEMS AND EXPERIENCES

I. Casazza - IBM Pisa SC, Italy

C. Galli - IBM Genoa Italy

G. Mazzarol- IBM Venice SC, Italy

Abstract

Starting from the observation of the current lack of knowledge of the external land use structure, a simple model
is proposed as a tool for an ordered collection of applica
tions and relevant data in "application layers", such that,
in a further step, such layers could be implemented as
views on a shared data base.
The characteristics of the data and of the user interfaces
relevant to an information system for land use, are discus
sed, with the aim of finding out whether there is any pecu
liarity which make them different from those commonly used
in other information systems.
The Land administrative structure, spans over many sites
which are logically and physically separated (region, district, province, etc.).
This observation together with that relevant the huge num
ber of data, suggests that on information system for land
use should be conceived as potentially dinstributable.
Some experiences which have been got by the application of
the currently available software tools to the land use pro
blems, are briefly described in the appendix.

INTRODUCTION

A first look at the Land use topic enhances some aspects of
the relevant problems which are briefly discussed in the pa
per.

- Lack of reference structure. The data structure of the
information systems are a mapping of the external organizations of the "worlds" which are to be managed, into the avai
lable software and hardware technology.
In the case of Land use, such an external organization (or
reference structure) doesn't exist.
Therefore a first rough model is proposed, which is to be
conceived as a framework, for assembling the various aspects
of the Land use problem.

- Peculiarity of data for Land use. Some aspects of data e.g.:
a) heterogeneity of data sources
b) the presence of a large number of relationships among data
c) the need to represent data both graphically and in a more
   traditional way
d) the need to keep historical series, helpful in planning
   activity

are discussed.

Moreover the data are tentatively classified as external data
(i.e. as they appear before the entry into an information system for landuse) and as internal data.
External data are related with the relevant information sources
while internal data are related to the supplied model.

- Characteristics of the user interfaces. The main tools which
must be given to the user, are discussed with the aim of finding
out those tools, if any, which are particular for accessing an
information system for Land use.

- Distribution. The large amount of data, the different views
from which different sites (region, province, district, ...)
use to look at the same problem, the low level of updating
suggest that an information system for Land use should be con
ceived as potentially distributable.

1) LACK OF A REFERENCE STRUCTURE

The design process of an information system, starts from the
observation of the organization of the world (e.g. a factory),
which is to be managed, and ends with the mapping of that organization into the available Software and Hardware technology. Unfortunately, as far as land use is concerned, such an
organization is not fully clear, at the moment.
As a matter of fact, many applications exist (manual or compu
terized) each covering a single aspect of the land use, but
each of them is conceived as isolated and not as a part of a
unique information system for land use. In other words the
current sight to the land use problem is application oriented.
In some way, the situation is comparable with the first approach
in the process of the computerization of manual procedures within
a factory (see for instance salary procedure, order entry procedu
re and so on) in which each procedure was looked at as a world
physically and logically separated from the other. In the recent past, the data base phylosophy has replaced this approach,
but this substitution has been helped by the existing organization which suggested the way to establish relationships among
the worlds that was first conceived as isolated.
Now, in the case of the land use, the approach should be rever-
sed, in the sense that the current data base philosophy should
help the land administrators in the construction of a "Conceptual Land Structure".
Bearing in mind that this paper does not intend to give defini
te solutions to the land use problem, the construction of a
Conceptual Land Structure means:

- to find out the universe of the land aspects (agriculture,
  geology, energy distribution system, communication system,
  etc.) which are to be managed;

- for each land aspect, establish the detail levels at which
  it is to be managed. As a matter of fact the current land's
  administrative structure (region, district, province, ...)
  can be helpful in establishing those detail levels;

- for each land's aspect and detail level within it, define
  an "application layer", i.e. the most meaningful applications
  for that land's aspect, and data needed by those applications.

The problem of defining the "Conceptual Land Structure" has not
only technicals aspects but also political and human ones that
should be properly evaluated before making any attempt to build
an information system for the land use.

Technical aspects (i.e. data base philosophy) involve an
uniform view of the conceptual data structure through the
different sites which will use that structure, and moreover
imply the concept of data sharing and data consistency main
tenance through different layers and through different detail
levels of the same layer. Political aspects could also affect
this process.
Human factors must be taken in considerations in establishing
the land resources which are to be managed, and the maximum
detail level at which any resource can be managed.

2) A PROPOSAL FOR THE CONCEPTUAL LAND STRUCTURE

The previous discussion leads us to conceive the conceptual
land structure as a pile of disks, each one corresponding
to an application layer (i.e. to a set of applications for
land use and relevant data).

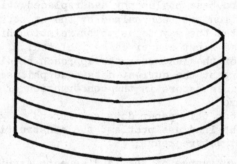

Fig. 1 - A framework for the conceptual land structure

Disks superimposition displays the concept that each layer is
not isolated from the other ones, meaning that they will likely
share some   data. This fact, in a following step, will suggest the implementation of those layers as views on a common
data base for land use once the proper programming tool for
the views creation is provided.
Moreover each disk or layer is composed of many tracks each
corresponding to a certain detail level within the layer (fig.
2).

Fig. 2 - Detail levels within an application layer

The detail level grows from the cylinder axis to the peri-
phery. Starting from the outermost track which corresponds
to the maximum detail level, the other tracks should be ma-
terializes through a synthesis process. Even in this case
the views mechanism can be used to implement the synthesis
process which gives rise to the various levels.
An obvious observation is that, to allow the consistency
maintenance, the data base should be built at the maximum
detail level. Unfortunately such an hypotesis seems to be
unfeasible as outlined later in this paper.
Within each layer the main activity seems to be that of
planning which can be roughly described in this terms.
Given a certain aspect of the land use, land administrators,
once observed the present and the past situations relevant
to that aspect, design a future situation for it.
From this moment on, the land administrators will check the
time progress of the plan, performing updates which essentially will result in moving the future in the present and
the present in the past (if needed for future plans, other
wise it will be cancelled).
This implies that each layer as far as relevant data are
concerned, should be conceived as   divided in three sectors
(fig. 3), the bigger one relevant to the past, since it will
contain the history of that side of the land, and the other
two ones relevant to the present and the future.
Once again a views like mechanism can be conceived as a tool
for implementing the time dependencies of data for land use.
The disk-track-sector model must be conceived as an empty
framework for the land administrators, which is to be filled
with meaninful applications and data.
It represents only a suggestion about the technique is to
be used for collecting applications and relevant data.

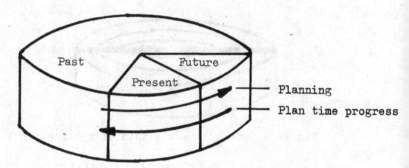

Fig. 3 - Time dependency of land use data

The current (manual or computerized) activities within the
land use environment should be mapped into proper application layers, while the current region-district-province
structure should be properly mapped into the track, or detail level structure.
In this model there is moreover, an implicit advice about
the need of cutting down the number of input data sources
hopefully of having a unique input data source at the maxi
mum detail level (i.e. at the outermost track of each disk)
since data relevant to the innermost levels, can be obtained
by a synthesis process, which allows the consistency maintan
ce through the levels.
Once filled that framework, and upon the observation of the
data shared among layers and detail levels, should the system designers be able to build the data base structure for
land use, and once provided the proper user interfaces, con
ceive the implementation of the application layers, detail
levels, and time dependencies in terms of views on a shared
data base.
So far, only a suggestion has been given to set up our mind
for land use problem's analysis.
Nothing has been told about data and relevant structure.
This topic will be briefly discussed in the following chap-
ters.

3) PECULIARITY OF DATA FOR LAND USE

Some aspects of data for land use are discussed, to find out
whether there exist any peculiarity which make them "different" from those commonly used in traditional information
system, or not.

3.1) HETEROGENEITY OF DATA SOURCES

At the moment, each land use application, uses data gathered
from the input source which is more suitable for its purposes. To mention some them, there are data obtained by satellites sensors, aerophotogrammetry, maps, census and sam
ples. To simplify the problem, we put our attention only on
two data sources: maps and census. As a matter of fact, da
ta coming from satellites sensors or aerophotogrammetry, on
ce processed (see ERMAN II), results in the creations of
maps. One can distinguish between two classes of maps. In
the first class there are those maps where, once established
a certain geographical reference system and a certain land
particle size and position (pixel) the land is described in
terms of attributes (or themes) relevant to each particle.
To give an examples of the "list of attributes" we mention
types of cultivation, slope, geological status and so on.
From now on, maps belonging to this class will be mentioned
as T-maps (where T stays for thematic).
In the second class, there are those maps which describes
in terms of shape and of geographic relationships, objects
and characteristics of the lands. Such maps describes
roads, railroads, rivers, contour levels, houses, etc.
From now on, map belonging to this class will be mentioned
as P-maps (where P stays for punctual).
It is important to stress that this classification (T-maps
and P-maps) is relevant to the data as they appear out of
system, and not as they will be internally stored.
As a matter of fact, while it is conceivable a mapping
between an external T-map and an internally stored table
(TMAP (particle, "list of attributes")), an external P-map
cannot be directly mapped in one corresponding internal
object.
What that can be done for storing an external P-map is:

- or derive from it T-maps (which can be stored as tables),
  therefore loosing information about the shapes of the
  objects represented in the P-map,

- or derive from it the descriptions of the shape, geographical position of the objects (description which can be
  internally represented in terms of tables), therefore loo
  sing information about the geographical relationship among
  the objects.

However a P-map can be conceived;

- as an input tool from which the proper internal represen
  tation is built (T-maps or a set of table for each category of objects), or

- as a working tool, built by a proper algorithm, to put
  together in an unique geographical reference system, dif
  ferent categories of objects, with the aim, for instance,
  to find out some geographical relationships among them.

In most cases, the shape or position of an object, as obtai
ned from an external P-map are not sufficient to fully describe the object itself.
Therefore, shape and position are only attributes among the
others which can be obtained by census.
In some cases (e.g. user interaction with displayed maps 4.5)
they can become the key for accessing the occurrencies of
that object in the underlying tables.
Fig. 4 is a tentative to find out a relationship between the
previous classification of the input data sources and detail
levels within an application layer. This figure enhances
the following things:

i) it is possible to establish an ordering among the classes
   of data (tables, P-maps, T-maps) in terms of detail levels

ii) as told before, an external P-map can be internally sto
    red as a T-map or as tables describing the shape and
    position, within a certain geographic reference system,
    of each object of the map

iii) each application on a class of internally stored data
     give rise to an object of the same class or to an ob-
     ject of a lower class

iiii) since it has been supposed that data of lower classes
      can be obtained by applications on data of higher
      classes, to allow consistency maintenance, all data
      should be entered at the maximum detail level (i.e.
      at the tables level)

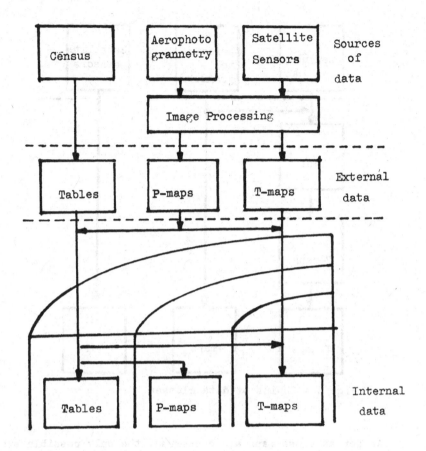

Fig. 4 - Relationships between land use data and
detail levels within a layer.

Unfortunately the last suggestion (iiii) is unfeasible, due
to the large amount of work (and of time) needed for gathering all data at the census level.
Therefore there will always be the chains of data classes
depicted in fig. 5.
Consistency can always be assured along vertical lines. The
figure shows that within a certain data class there will be
maps originated from different input data sources.

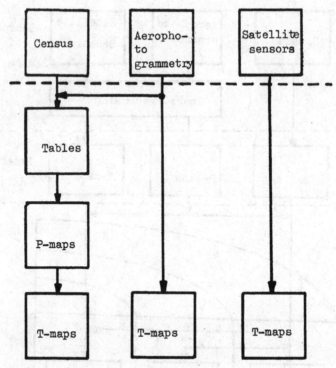

Fig. 5 - Chains of data classes

As far as those maps are concerned, the only possible state_
ment, at the moment, is the following one:

- Either they are relevant to different land characteristics
  (i.e. T-maps coming from census describe the density of
  population which is an item never detectable by the other
  data sources), and in this case there will not be any need
  of consistency maintenance among them.

- Or they are relevant to the same land characteristic, and
  in this case it is possible to establish an ordering based
  on the precision or reliability, for example, among T-maps
  of the different origin. So a T-map originated from census should be more reliable than a T-map originated from
  aerophotogrammetry, and this, in turn, more reliable than
  a T-map originated from satellite sensors. This ordering
  can suggest the usage of more realible data as "testers"

of less reliable one, in order to reduce their inaccuracy factors.

3.2) HETEROGENEITY OF THE GEOGRAPHICAL REFERENCE SYSTEM AND SCALE (GRS)

At the present time, each land use application uses the GRS for data which is more appropriate for its purpose and the situation will hardly change in the future.
This fact is probably due not only to the current lack of "Data Base mentality" but also to the intrinsic nature of some geographical entities, which can be described only within a certain GRS.
In 4.3 the maps definition facility is mentioned as a an user tool, which will result in an assembly of objects likely referred to different GRS.
Therefore the GRS relevant to each object must be maintened in the data structure, and moreover an automatic mapping fa cility among different GRS(s) must be provided.

3.3) TIME DEPENDENCY OF DATA

This point has already been discussed in paragraph 2. Even in this case, a time reference system must be established for the data, and fixed in the relevant data structure.

3.4) A TENTATIVE MODEL FOR LAND USE DATA DIRECTORY

So far, in land use environment, it has been found out that land use data can be internally represented in two ways:

i) The land particles (pixel) which can be looked at as the elementary objects of a T-map table. In this context each particle (or pixel) is described in terms or values assumed within that particle by a certain set of attribu tes. An internal T-map table can be looked at as internal representation of a corresponding external T-map as obtained by aerophotogrammetry or satellite pictures, on ce the relevant image processing work has been done, moreover,as hinted later in this paper, a T-map table can be conceived as the result an user application on other T-maps or on tables for objects description.

ii) Tables for objects description. An external P-map can
be conceived as the graphic representation of:

- the shapes of some categories of objects (roads, rivers, houses, ...),
- their position within a geographic reference system,
- the geographic relationships among them.

In most cases, those data do not complete the description
of the object itself.

As a matter of fact, the shape or position of a house can
be looked at as a part of the other description relevant
to it (floors within the house, apartments within floor,
etc.), generally not included in the P-map, but detectable
by census. Therefore P-maps and census data can be internal
ly represented as categories of homogenous objects where ho
mogeneity means that objects belonging to a category can be
described by the same set of tables.
Of course, the geographic relationships among the objects,
as they appear in an external P-map, are not explicitly represented in this model. Nevertheless, as hinted later in
this paper, those relationships can be restored,issuing,once the
proper programming tools will be supplied, the construction
of a P-map, which essentially will result in the selection
of the shapes of objects belonging to different categories
and their mapping in an unique geographic reference system.
The previous discussion, allow us to try a first rough
structure for land use data directory.
3.4.1) T-maps

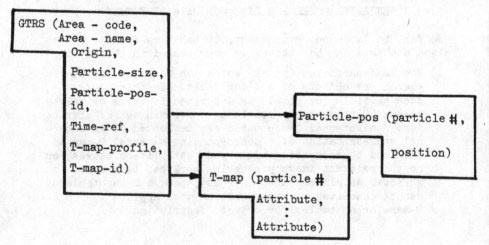

Fig. 6 - A tentative model for T-maps

A first table (GTRS: Geographic and time reference system) gives some information relevant to each T-map as a whole like:

- The area code and name of the area which the T-map is re levant to,

- The origin of the geographical reference system

- The land particle size

- The PARTICLE-POS-ID is the identifier of a table (PARTI-CLE-POS) which describes the relative position of each land particle.

- The time reference of the T-map table

- The T-map table profile. This is an entry which mainly describes for each attributes, the conventions about the values assumed by that attribute within the land par ticle (i.e., presence/absence, percentage of the particle area occupied by that attribute, average value of that attribute within the particle, and so on)

- Finally the T-map-ID is the identifier of the T-map table (T-MAP) defined as a collection of land particles, descri bed by a certain set of attributes

        T-MAP (particle , ATTRIBUTE, ... ATTRIBUTE)

3.4.2) Objects description

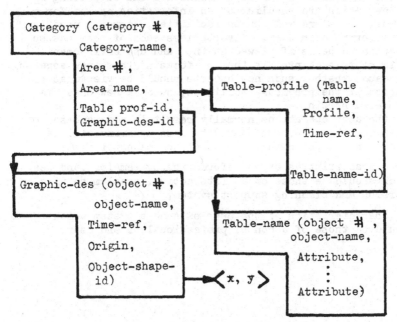

Fig. 7 - A tentative model for land's objects

Fig. 7 represents a tentative for the internal representation
of objects belonging to the land.
Categories are defined whenever it is possible to find an
homogenous group of objects which can be described by the
same set of tables. Once defined, the categories are referred to the land area in which the relevant objects lie.
The profile of the tables relevant to each category of
objects is described in the TABLE-PROFILE table, which in
turns give the entries to actual tables (TABLE-NAME).
As far as the graphic description is concerned, the CATEGORY
table gives the entry to GRAPHIC-DESCRIPTION table, which in
turn for each object identify the set of points describing
the shape and/or the position.

4) CHARACTERISTICS OF THE USER INTERFACES

The main interfaces which must be given the user to properly
access an information system for land use are the following:

- Query facility
- Computation facility
- Maps definition facility
- Maps outputting facility
- Interaction facility
- Views definition and maintenance facility.

With the exception of the maps definition and outputting fa
cilities, which are peculiar of an information system for
land use, those are well known facilities, commonly used in
other information system. Nevertheless each of them has so
me peculiar aspects if viewed in the land use environment.
The aim of this chapter is that of focusing those new aspects.
The question whether such new aspects should be viewed as an
extension of the previous facilities, or as a new ones, is
not covered herein.
Since the user operations normally result in a data base mo
dification, the problem of the data base updating will be
hinted. In the following discussion one cannot forget;

- the characteristics of an information system for land use
  which should be those of an interactive, problem solving,
  decision and planning support system,

- the characteristics of the user of such a system which
  should be those of a non DP professional or end user.

4. 1) QUERY FACILITY

The query facility, as implemented so far, is such that,
once provided a certain parameter list,the user can select
from the data base those data which satisfy it.   In the
land   use environment, the query facility will probably
cover some new aspects like:

- Questions about geographical relationships among the o-
  bjects.
- Classifications of objects and use of the inference.

4.1.1) Geographical relationship among the objects

Questions regarding the geographical relationships among
the objects are very likely in the land use environment.In
a previous chapter, has been supposed that such geografical
relationships as represented in an external P-map will not
be stored in the data base, due to their complexity and
number.
This decision implies two needs, at the system level and
at the user level. At the system level, some generalized
algebraic routines must be provided, such that, given the
shapes and positions of two objects within the relevant ge
ographical reference system,can map them in an unique GRS
and compute the requested geographical relationship.
At the user level, tools must be provided to define the re
quested relationship and to call the proper routine.
Those tools can be conceived as an extension of the query
language, or as an user interaction with displayed maps.
This second aspect, which seems the most feasible one at
the moment, will give rise to a "device dependent" language, and it will be partially covered in the paragraphs 4.3,
4.4, 4.5.

4.1.2) Classification of objects and use of the inference

An important use of the data base by the planner's point
of view concerns the objects classification according to
some "intuitive" variables, meaning that they represent on
ly the way of thinking of the planners, and therefore they
must be heuristicly mapped into the real variables (i.e.
the variable by which the objects are described), to perform the classification.
Due to this fact, the power of the classification process
becomes poor, frequent checks are needed to adjust the map
ping between intuitive and real variables, giving rise to
a very cumbersome work if carried on by hand.

Another important use of the data base is that of finding
out the possible correlations among facts relevant to the land
stored in data base. Both these activities could be sped-
up if some operators, derived from the clustering techniques of the statistics, will be available at the language
level. This topic will be better discussed in the appendix
concerning the experience of the Cittadella town.

4. 2) COMPUTATION FACILITY

Two techniques are used, at the moment, to make computations on retrieved data

- Embedding the query language in a host programming language
- Switching the retrieved data to application programs.

The first technique has the advantage of leaving the user
within the application environment in which he is working.
The second technique forces the user to a continuous switch from the application environment to the query one and
viceversa.
Nevertheless the second technique seems to be more suitable in the land use environment, since the characteristics
of the relevant information system, which should be an interactive problem solving, decision and planning support
system, and those of the user which should be a non DP pro
fessional.
As a matter of fact, the first technique is normally used
in the commercial environment in which applications are
preplanned, recursive, and directly coded by the programmer.
Conversely in the land use environment, where the applications are mainly unpredicatable (by the points of view of da
ta which are to be selected, and of computations which are
to be done on the selected data) and not-recursive, the
first techniques will give rise to the construction of a
program library unuseful in the future. Moreover the user
of a land use system could hardly afford the work of coding complex mathematical and statistical routines.
To speed up the switching between the query and application environments, an effort should be done in the direction of managing an application program library with the
data base philosophy.

4. 3) MAPS DEFINITION FACILITY

In a previous chapter the possibility of creating P-maps
and T-maps from the data base has been outlined (fig. 4).
The importance of this facility lies in the fact that it
can be used as a tool for defining views on the data base
(e.i. for implementing the disk-track-sector model) and/or
for creating an adequate support for further user interaction once the map is displayed on a graphic terminal.
User's and system's tools must be provided for implementing
this facility.
User's tools will mainly concern the choice of a land area,
of the objects and relevant attributes within that area
that will compose the map. System tools will mainly concern
the mapping of the shape and position of different objects in
an unique geographical reference system, and the supply of
the mechanisms for the maintenance of the collection of o-
bjects composing the map as an user view.

4. 4) MAPS OUTPUTTING FACILITY

User interfaces must be provided to output T-maps and P-
maps. Outputs can be addressed to hard-copy devices (printer, plotter) or to display devices (interactive graphic
dispaly).
The interfaces needed for the actual outputting will not
be mentioned herein since they are normally strictly device dependent.
Conversely, some hints will be given, as far as "output
dressing" operations are concerned, with the aim of think
ing about the tools that must be given the user to perform
such operations.

4.4. 1) Dressing operations for T-maps

As told before, a T-map is internally represented by a table, whose elementary objects are the land particles (pixel) described by a certain set of attributes. The easiest
way to output a T-map is that of choosing one attribute (or
theme) and graphically describe the land in terms of that
attribute.
The main operations which must be performed for dressing a
T-map are the following:

For each attribute which is to be outputted:

- Establish the range of values assumed by that attribute
  within the T-map table.

- Establish some values classes for that attribute

- Rewrite the T-map table in terms of those classes of values.

- Establish graphic conventions (colours, graphic symbols) for each class of values.

- Establish rules for the legend's display.

4.4. 2) Dressing operations for P-maps

A P-map is internally represented as a collection of objec
t's composing an user view which has been defined through
the facility mentioned in the paragraph 4.3.
To actually display such a map one must establish graphic
conventions;
- to distinguish categories of objects
- to distinguish objects within a category
- in some cases, to distinguish different values of the sa
me attribute within an object (the attribute "number of
lanes" can assume different values within a road)
Moreover rules must be defined to display the names of the
objects, and for legend's display.

4.5) INTERACTION FACILITY

The user operations on a map (both T-map or P-map) displayed on an interactive graphic device are briefly discussed.
Such operations span   the query and the data base updating environments.

4.5.1) Interactions for query

This section can be viewed as a subset of the query facility mentioned in 4.1.
Some examples will be given with the aim of giving the feeling of the relevant operations.

- Queries about the geographic relationships among objects.
This question can be roughly answered superimposing to
the displayed P-map a certain grid system. More precisely, this query can be asked detecting the objects, entering the relationship name (i.e. distance, lenght; etc.)
and therefore linking the relevant algebraic routine which evaluate the relationship.

- Queries about geographical relationship among objects

identified through a contour line and a keyword (WITHIN, ALONG, OUTSIDE, etc.) entered by the user.

- Queries about non geographical properties of objects identified through a detection or a contour line and the relevant keyword.

In the last case the identification process is only a key for accessing the underlying tables and for flagging the occurrencies of those objects which the user is interested in. From this moment on,a standard query (4.1) can be entered.

The result of a query can be also saved as an user view.

4.5.2) Interactions for updating

One can interact with a displayed P-map identifying some objects, and updating the relevant occurendes in the underlying tables. However the possibility of updating the graphic content of the screen is doubtful. The question is whether such changes can be reflected in the underlying tables.
One can enter a new road simply tracing a line on the screen, but probably, due to the resolution power of the screen,the question is whether this is the best way to do this job.
In the case of a displayed T-map, the attribute's value relevant to each land particle, has been supposed to be graphically represented in terms of classes of values (i.e., at a synthesis level which is higher than that of the underlying table).
Therefore any graphic change entered through the screen can not be reflected back to the relevant table.
One can suppose that such changes, if any, can be saved as user copies of the screen, or stand alone user views, where "stand-alone" means that such views are out of the updating procedures for the data base consistency maintenance.

4.6) VIEWS DEFINITION FACILITY

So far, many user's tools for view definition have been mentioned.
In the land use environment, since the relevant management system should be conceived as distributable (Chapter 5) the concept of view should be enlarged.
As a matter of fact, a view definition can result:

- or in the storing of the relevant statements which, running on the user request, will materialize the view,
- or in the creation of the proper set of indices which allow the user the navigation through the view,
- or in the physical data migration through the disk-track-sector model.

The relevant choice must be taken upon the evaluation of some parameters like:

- concentration versus distribution
- amount of updates
- need to speed up local processes
- degree of local autonomies.

4.4) DATA BASE UPDATING

A data base for land use is, of course, a time varying entity. Nevertheless the land is a "world" which changes very slowly if compared with other ones (a firm for instance). One can make a rough distinction between two kinds of updates:

- Periodic updates
- Applications driven updates.

Periodic updates are caused by the input data sources, which periodically refresh the internal data (tables, T-maps). Those updates must be reflected on the user views whenever they result in data migration through the model. Of course one must keep track of the updates "topology" and establish triggers which allow the data base consistency maintenance. The applications driven updates are those caused by the users through their interfaces.

Fig. 8 indicates the main channels through which the data base updates are performed. The two arrows labelled (P), in the top of the figure indicate the channels relevant to the periodic updates, and the other ones relevant to the application driven updates.

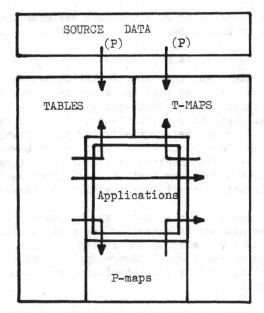

Fig. 8 - Main channels through wich updates are
         performed

5) DISTRIBUTION

Land administration is a function which spans many sites,
i.e. region, districts, provinces municipalities, physical_
ly and logically separated by the other ones.

Each site is inserted in a hierarchy which coordinates the
activities.
Nevertheless, a large amount of autonomy exists within each
site.
The conceptual structure composed of layers and detail levels within a layer, has been conceived taking care of this
situation, and once implemented, it can, in turn, be helpful,
in the assignment of the activities to each site.
Another observation is relevant to the amount of data needed
for a land use information system, which is extremely large,
expecially if one take in consideration the needs of managing
a certain aspect of the land at different detail levels, and
that of a systematic maintenance of future, present and past
data.
To summarize:

- The large amount of data,
- the low rate of updates due to the nature of the land and
  to the autonomies of local processes,

- the conceptual possibility of a definite assignment of
  the activities to each site, in terms of layers and detail levels,
- the need to speed-up local processes,

give rise to the statement that an information system for
land use should be conceived (and therefore designed and
implemented) as potentially distributable.
Against this statement there is the fact that very likely
there will exist a strong heterogeneity of the software
and hardware among the various sites, in terms of power and
types. In fact the implementation of a land use information
system is a multistep job, the last and major step being that
one which is relevant to the interconnections of heterogenous
worlds.
Therefore, heterogeneity in software and hardware power
gives rise to the problem of extending the distribution needs
not only to the data but also to the system functions, while
heterogeneity in software and hardware types gives rise to
the need of suppling generalized interfaces for connecting
hetereogenous worlds.

C O N C L U S I O N

At the present time the land use problem appear to be like
a wool skein, whose end must still be found to be properly
unwounded.
Therefore this paper must be looked at as an unstructured
overview about some major problems relevant to the land use,
with the aim of hopefully finding out some starting points
which allow us to access the problem.
The layered conceptual structure suggested at the beginning
of the paper,despite its roughness, is only an empty frame
work which, once accepted, must be filled by land administrators with meaningfull applications and relevant data.
The various layers and detail levels have been conceived as
communicating worlds, meaning that they can be implemented
as different views on a shared data base. Traditional
query language facility and logic for automatic maps creation facility have been mentioned, as tools for implementing
such views.
Data have been tentatively classified as tables, P-maps,
T-maps, and their relationships with the detail levels has
been discussed.

The importance of a geographical and time reference system
for each data relevant to the land use,such that it
must be fixed in the data structure, as been stressed.

Lastly, the assertion that an information system for land
use must be conceived as potentially dinstributable, will
constitute a kind of brake for those, if any, thinking that
implementation time is in the air.

APPENDIX A
TITLE: The experience of Cittadella

Introduction

Cittadella is a small town placed in the venetion area,
which was built in the 13th century as a fortress.
Today, within the original walls, the urban aspect of the
town is still intact.
However, in the last 20 years, the growing of the industrial
activity in the region, deeply altered the role and the
function of the city in relation to the territory in which
it lies.
Many undesirable phenomena related to this situation led
the Local Administration to set up the preliminary studies
of a detailed plan for the urban center.
Planning is the main intervention tool according to the
italian laws, since it can establish the future development
of the city, in term of objectives and relevant tools.
A joint project between the IBM Italy Scientific Centers
and Local Government started, with the following tasks:

- to build an information system for urban planning, merging
  different experiences and skills

- to deduce hints for the development of software tools
  tailered for this kind of applications.

1) Tha data

According to the most recent planning methodologies, developed in Italy (e.g. Piano Regolatore Generale di Bergamo
1969) several social-economic-architectural variables have
been chosen (about 300), which could reasonably describe
most of the phenomena involved.
These variable, can be classified as attributes of the fol
lowing entities

- buildings (e.g. geographical coordinates, status properties, usage etc.).

- place of abode (e.g. n° of rooms, rooms status, surfaces,
  inhabitants, ages, etc.)

- individual characteristics (qualifications, jobs, social
  needs)

- business activity (kind of activity, dimensions, relation
  ship, future developments)

- social status (a number of social informations for every family).

A big effort has been done both for choosing the appropria te set of variables and for collecting the relevant informa tion. The sources were mainly State Archives, maps, census and inquiries in the whole city (fig. 9).

2) The data base

As a worting tool, the MIDA system (Casazza, 1977),which is a prototype of a relational DBMS developed in the IBM Italy Scientific Centers has been chosen.
In a first stage of the data base design process the collec ted information has been mapped in to five flat tables (one for each entity previously outlined).
          The Entity - relationship model for the data (Chen, 1977) and Entity - relationships diagram (Chen, 1977 b)have been extensively used both to detect the complex re lationships among the variables, and to generate the appro- priate data model.
Thereafter about forty 3 NF relations, were obtained which have been represented in the Entity - relationships diagram as a connected graph, which ensured that the relations are all joinable on request.
So, for example, objects selected from the data base can al ways be referred to their geographical position, simply joi ning them with the relation where the coordinates were stored.
To exploit this facility, a one way bridge has been establi shed between the MIDA DBMS and an APL written package for the management of the TEKTRONIK 4015 graphic device.
Of course, for sake of semplicity, the APL capabilities were hidden and only some built-in functions for graphic outputs, imbedded in the language for the MIDA DBMS manage ment, were accessed by the end user.
In this way the system achieved the ability to produce cur ves, histograms, and maps.
Examples of those maps are supplied in fig. 9 and 10.

3) Problems encountered during the work

Let's start with the following observations:

i) the need of not loosing information forced us to gather data at the maximum detail level (remember the 300 varia bles previously mentioned)

ii) an important part of the work, done by the planners, was
that   concerning the classifications of objects according to the law's requirements and the verification of
some work hypothesis.

iii) The variables used for that work (ii) were such that
they can hardly be one to one mapped in to the variables used for describing the Cittadella town.

Let's give an example. If one wants to classify the buildings
on the basis of their status, this variable doesn't exist in
the data base. This was due to the intention of the planner
of trying to rationalize some intuitive concepts, like "valuable building", "building to be restored", etc., mapping
these concepts in terms of data base variables. This difficult task has been done in an heuristic way, and is briefly
described later.
From now on, the "STATUS" - like variables will be mentioned
as u -variables where u stays for user , while the set of variables in which it can be mapped will be mentioned as r-va-
riables(where r stays for real) since they belong to the set
of variables by which the town has been described.
Our feeling is that such a situation will be very common in
this environment.
Now it is possible to distinguish between two types of usage
of the data base:

- the straighforward use, which implies selections on the
basis the r-variables. This point will not been discussed
hercin   since it is supposed that any data base user is
familiar with it;

- the statistical use, which implies selections on the basis
of the U-variables. Two examples will be given, the first
one relevant to a classification work, and the second one
relevant to an inferential use starting from a work hypothesis.

3.1) Classification

To establish the future of each building (e.g. total preser-
vation, or changes in the structure and in the usage), according to the italian law, all the building must be classified
in terms of appropriate u-variables.
A Tree-like set of queries has been established (fig. 11).
At each level of that tree the following difficulties have
been encountered.
- To find the r-variables (e.g.domains and relevant relations)
in which to map the u-variable.

- To find the most appropriate logical operators (AND, OR,
  ...) by which to link the r-variables relevant to that
  u-variable.
- After the run of each level of queries it has been obser -
  ved that,
  - or some tuples were missed (e.g. the number of building
    in the leaves was less than the number of building of
    the root (too strong query),
  - or the number of buildings in the leaves was higher than
    that of the root, which implies a certain overlap among
    the leaves showing that the separation power of the que̱
    ry was poor (too soft query).

This situation inplied a continuous rearrangement of each le̱
vel of queries in terms of r-variables and/or relevant logic
operators.
After such an heavy and cumbersome work, has been possible
to properly classify about 4/5 of the buildings of Cittadella.

3.2) Inferential use

To give an example, the hypothesis "old people live in old
houses in apartments whose area is bigger than the average",
can be verified through the following steps:
- compute the average of the areas and of the ages of the
  apartments.
- select from the data base a relation (say R1) with the
  clause that the people age is over 70.
  R1 (HOUSE #, FLAT #, PEOPLE #, HOUSE-AGE, FLAT-AREA)
- select from R1 those occurrencies having the HOUSE-AGE
  and FLAT-AREA values bigger than the relevant average,
  and store them in R2.
An inspection of the cardinality of R1 and R2, will show,
for instance, that in R2 there are 80% of the tuples of
R1. In this case the hypothesis is verified and properly
quantified (80%).
But, there could be a lot of other facts, related to the
initial assumption which even an expert can not suspect.
To exploit all theese possible correlactions among facts
which can exist, stored in the data base, the previous steps
can be repeated performing equijoins of R2 with other domains
(of other relations) which result in the adding of new domains to R2 whenever the correlation is verified.

Of course this procedure in unpractical by the user point
view.

Conclusion

The statistical use of the data base, seems to be very fre_
quent in land use and urban planning environments.
The examples given herein show that the manual procedures
for objects classification and use of the inference are ve_
ry cumbersome and unpractical by the user's point of view.
Therefore it would be appealing the disposal, at the language level, of the clustering techniques (DURHAM 1974,
ANDERBERG 1973).

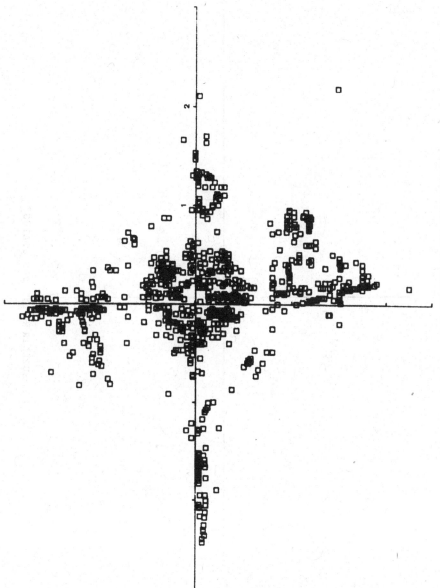

FIG.9 - THE BUILDINGS INCLUDED IN THE CENSUS

164

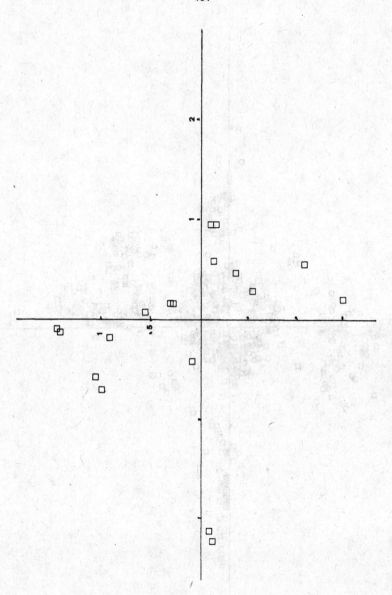

FIG. 10 - BUILDINGS IN "BAD STATUS"

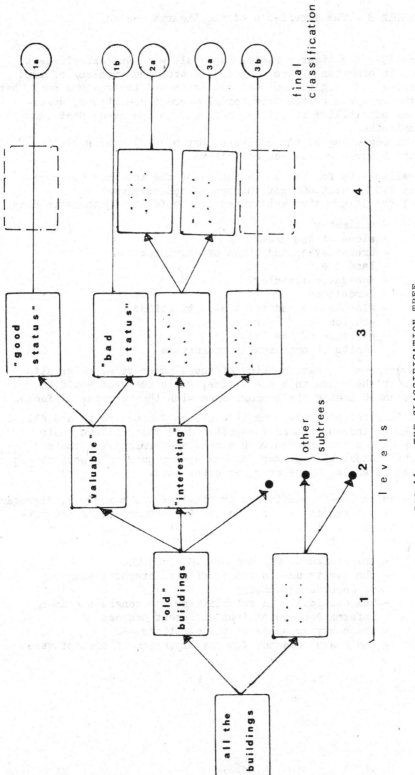

FIG 11 – THE CLASSIFICATION TREE

APPENDIX B - The experience of the Liguria region

Since 1977 the Liguria region has dealt with the extablisment
of an information system directed towards the problems of land
planning and singling out methodologies and instruments such that,
by the analysis of the territorial present conditions, specify the possibility for other uses, and so the needs that can
be satisfied.
At the beginning of the analysis (March 1977), the situation
of the Liguria region was as follows:

- availability for the whole region of the thematic cartography I.G.M. 1:25.000 got through aerophotogrammetry
- All the information subdivided in the following thematic clas
  ses:
  - altimetry
  - slope of the ground
  - urbanization and lines of communication
  - land use
  - schematic lithology
  - landslides
  - glasshouses and terrace-cultivations
  - erosion
  - exposure of the lands
  - limits of municipal corporations

- Awareness   that the size of these paper-files makes difficult their use in a short time, while the maps would be
  out-dated losing their congruence with the territorial facts.

As a first step of the work,it has been decided to record all
the known information on a magnetic disk which allows their
revision and examination with a display-terminal and their
graphic output by a plotter,for the uses requiring a perfect pre
cision of scale, by printer,for other uses.

The maps have been subdivided in pixel of 100 m x 100 m, disregar
ding the alternative way of storing the natural lines determining homogenous fields which of course is superior in term of
precision, but became unprofitable for other reasons like:

  - the limits of the maps I.G.M. 1:25.000
  - the limits due to the difficult interpretation
    of aerophotogrammetry
  - the difficulty in establishing the congruence among
    information coming from different sources
  - the heavy expenses of the digitizer
  - the heavy expenses for the expansion of the software

The size of the pixel (100m x 100 m) implies an error due to the choice, within that pixel, of the theme which assumes the prevalent value, but it has been considered that such an error is comparable with that of the input map.

The choice of a that pixel size is convenient according to the morphologic characteristic and the prevalent typology of the installations in the Liguria region, but expecially because this choice makes possible to obtain a large quantity of information without losing too many details and because a smaller size makes the input procedure difficult and increases the size of the file.

On the other hand, in order to reduce the limits due to the size of the pixel, whenever significant details smaller than 100 m x 100 m were found, the relevant pixels have been flagged.
The data entry has been made, transcribing the interpreted values on optical forms.

A single disk-file of the land has been obtained processing the tapes obtained by the optical reader. This file includes 588. 500 records, one for each pixel of the Liguria region and the Key is formed by:

- **north U.T.M.** coordinate of the low left corner of the kilometre including the pixel

- east U.T.M. coordinate of the low left corner of the kilometre including the pixel

- progressive number (1 to 100) of the pixel within the kilometre

(U.T.M. means universal translation of Mercatore)

The data-area of the record is planned for 33 fields of which, up till now, the first 19 are filled:

```
1 - altimetry
2 - slope of the ground
3 - urbanization
4 - railways
5 - motor-ways
6 - roads
7 - coastal - works
8 - re-ascending equipements
9 - hydrology
```

```
10 - quarries and dumps
11 - land use
12 - schematic lithology
13 - landslides
14 - terraces and glasshouses
15 - erosion
16 - exposure of the lands
17 - limits of municipal corporation
18 - urban development plans
19 - historic centres
```

while studying the constitution of new social economic thematic classes:

```
20 - population density
21 - population characteristics
22 - contamination
23 - sanitary instruments
24 - epidemic distribution
```

Some procedures have been implemented to follow the evolution of the land conditions through the display terminal 3270 at the pixel level.

The content of the file may be returned in form of maps in two versions, by batch procedures:

- by the production of an interface tape and the use of an off-line plotter. The return scale is 1:25.000.
  It is possible to make a choice of the graphic characters for display. This procedure is used to supply the cartography to the local governments.

- by a direct print on computer. The return scale, not integer, is different on the two axes.
  This procedure is mainly used to control the records correctness.

The realization, if it were limited to the study described up till now, it would have resolved, however, only the problem of the fast obsolence of the cartography while the results would not substantialy help the urban planner who is always forced by his job to heavy investigations of the whole region.

In a second and more important stage of the project, some T.P. procedures have been realized, such that it is possible to select from the data base, in an interactive way, those

pixels which satisfy a boolean expression defined on the pos
sible values of the recorded thematic classes.

Here is an example of a logic equation:

(altimetry = from 0 to 100 m.) AND (landslide = from 0 to 6%)
AND (urbanization = a lonely house)
BUT NOT (landuse = olive grove OR vineyard).

The selected pixels and their coordinates are automatically
transferred by the system in a work space for statistical or
mapping purposes.
This facility is mainly used to find the portions of the regional land where it is possible a different use from the pre
sent one.
Through the display-terminal it's also possible to extract
the pixels described in an equation like:

Origin = x, y AND n. times - thematic class = value

Where the pixels are accessed by a spiral which starts from
the given origin.
This facility is addressed to define the land area closest
to given origin which is under the influence of the phenomenon.

The difficulties encountered

Realizing the just described system, at least two kinds of
difficulties have been encountered:

- those due to the management of a large quantity of data
  (for the Liguria region about 11 million of fields,
  requiring about 140 millions of bytes).

- those due to the pictorial characteristics of the
  data.

Both these difficulties come out from the absence of software tools
expecially prepared for the pictorial data base management.
This has involved the creation and the maintenance of a series
of index-files by user-written programs, lengthening enough
the realization's time.

The Benefits Obtained

The transposition on a direct access magnetic support, the
inquiries and updating possibilities by display terminal, have
improved the validity of a land planning instrument such as
the thematic maps.

The interactive facilities, due to the implementation of a logic
search by display-terminal, allow a complete utilization and
an easy   retrieval of data, which is unthinkable in a manual
environment. This system permits the realization of a real sup_
port for the well known territorial planning needs of the local
government.
At the end, the obtained experiences will very likely permit
the extension of this software to other land-planning instruments too, such as the technical maps 1:5000, that, if compared
with the thematic maps (1:25000), will imply a greater difficul_
ty in their management.

REFERENCES

Aldred B.K. and Smedley B.S. (1974). UMS Technical Overview. IBM U.K. Technical Report UKSC0050.

Aldred B.K. and Smedley B.S. (1974). UML User's Guide. IBM U.K. Technical Report, UK0052.

Anderberg M.R. (1973). Cluster Analysis for Applications. Acad. Press, New York.

Bennett J.L. (1977). User-oriented Graphic Systems for Decision Support in Unstructured Tasks. IBM Research Report, RJ 1940.

Bergamaschi S., Bonfatti F., Camporesi R., and Olivelli S. (1978). Il linguaggio di qualificazione del Sistema Informativo OSIRIS, C.N.R. Centro di Studio per l'Interazione Operatore-Calcolatore, rapporto 39.

Bergamaschi S., Bonfatti F., Camporesi R. and Olivelli S. (1978). Considerazioni sul Progetto di Sistemi Informativi Relazionali di Grandi Dimensioni. C.N.R. Centro di studio per l'interazione operatore-calcolatore, Rapporto 38.

Berman R.R. and Stonebraker M. (1977). GEO QUEL A System for the Manipulation and Display of Geographic data. ACM Computer Graphics 11,2,186-190.

Bonfatti F. and Tiberio R. (1976). A Data Structure for Land Description and Investigation, Proc. of the Fifth Biennial International Codata Conf., Pergamon Press, 263-257

Bonfatti F. and Tiberio P. (1977). A Computer-Assisted Procedure for Analysis and Forecast of Human Resources: Application to Agricolture District Planning. Proc. International Conf. on Cybernetics and Society 33-37.

Casazza I. and Marini G. (1977). MIDA. A Relational System for Data Management, IBM Italy Technical Report, G513-3565.

Chamberlin D.D., Astrahan M.M., Eswaren K.P., Griffiths P.P., Lorie R.A., Mehl J.W., Reisner P., and Wade B.W. (1976). SEQUEL 2: A Unified Approach to Data Definition, Manipulation and Control. IBM Research Report, RJ1798.

Chen P.P. (1977). The Entity Relationship Model - Toward a Unified View of Data. ACM Trans. on Database Systems, 1, 1, 9-36.

CHEN P.P. (1977). The Entity Relationship Model - A Basis for Enterprise View of Data. N.C.C. '77 AFIPS PRESS, 77-84.

Durham B. and Odell P. (1974). Cluster Analysis: A Survey Springer Verlag Press, Berlin.

Kriger M.P. (1976). SUGAR: A High-Level Programming Language for Geographical Analysis and Mapping. ACM Sigplan Not. 11, 6, 40-48.

Mantey P.E., Bennett J.L. and Carlson E.D. (1973). Information for Problem Solving: The Development of an Interactive Geographic Information System, IEEE International Conference on Communications, ii, 44-47.

Mantey P.E. and Carlson E.D. (1975). Integrated Data Bases for municipal decision-making. N.C.C. '75 AFIPS PRESS 487-493.

Phillips R.L. (1977). A Query Language for a Network Data Base with Graphical Entities. ACM Computer Graphics 11, 2 179-185.

Williams R. and Giddings G.M. (1976). A Picture Building System. IEEE Trans. on Soft. Engineering, SE-2, 1,62-66.

Weller D.L.and Williams R. (1976). Graphic and Data Base support for Programming, IBM Research Report, RJ1744.

INTEGRATED GEOGRAPHIC DATA BASES: The GADS Experience

P. E. Mantey and E. D. Carlson

A large class of problems faced by decision makers requires access to information with geographical attributes. Examples of such problems include facility siting, resource allocation, assignment of sales or service territories, development of advertising strategies, urban planning, etc. In problem solving utilizing data with geographical attributes, the data can often be best understood when it can be displayed and interpreted in the form of a map. An interactive decision support system called GADS (Geo-data Analysis and Display System) has been developed to provide decision makers with interactive access to geographic data and to provide them with functions supporting both "problem finding" and "problem solving". This system has been successfully utilized by a variety of decision makers solving real problems in both government and private industry.

The GADS system supports interactive use of an extracted data base which contains a set of attributes for each of the polygons composing a map of the relevant geographical area. This extracted data base can be imagined as a three-dimensional array or cube with the dimensions being polygon, attribute, and time period. The map related to this cube of extracted data is defined by a set of nodes and (labeled) boundary lines. In addition to these two data bases, GADS supports user access to large source or "event" files. With interactive access to these event files, the user is able to create an extracted data base suitable for the specific set of problems being addressed by that decision maker.

This paper provides a brief description of the GADS system and the applications in which it has been utilized by non-programmer decision-makers. The data base requirements for the extracted data base, its corresponding polygon map, and for the (set of) event files being used, are examined in terms of their type, volume, structure, retrieval and search characteristics, and frequency of use. Also, the large geographic reference file (e.g. the DIME file of the U.S. Census Bureau), which is used in developing the polygon map and in determining geographic location of events in those source files (by programs external to GADS) is examined. Finally, some ideas on data base support for functions not in the GADS implementation (i.e. image) are considered.

IBM
5600 Cottle Rd.
San Jose, California 95193

INTRODUCTION

The GADS system (Cristiani,et.al., 1973), (Carlson, et. al., 1974) makes an integrated geographic data base accessible for supporting interactive problem solving by non-programmers. Geographic data is made available to the decision maker in the form of an "event" data base and an "extracted" data base. Geographical interpretation of the event data is accomplished by reference to a corresponding polygon map file. This polygon map file provides a framework or index for relating data from the event data base, in terms of their spatial relationship, and thereby enabling the development of the extracted data base. The polygon map file plays a role in development of the extracted data base that is analagous to that played by a "chart of accounts" in developing aggregate or summary files from the financial transaction records of a business. GADS offers the user an interactive system supporting retrieval and display of data from the event file, development of an extracted database from the event file, retrieval and display of data extracted from the event file, as tables, or maps, and aggregation operations on the polygon map which correspond to further aggregations of data in the extracted data base. Data base support for these functions is not directly provided by any known data management system, even though most of the needed data base functions are not unique to geographic data, but rather are required for any decision support system which builds an extracted data base from an "event" or transaction file. In this paper, the implementation of these functions as offered in GADS is described, and the desired extensions and generalization are discussed.

SYSTEM DESCRIPTION

GADS ARCHITECTURE

The Geodata Analysis and Display Sytem (GADS) is a system to support non-programmer decision makers in problem finding and problem solving: a Decision Support Sytem (DSS). GADS provides support for decision making where the data of interest are related geographically. The GADS architecture (Figure 1) contains two major components:

1. Extraction functions for subsetting, displaying, and aggregating data from event files and for constructing an extracted data base for a given polygon map.

2. A set of analysis and display functions that are used with this extracted data base.

EXTRACTION

The extracted data base is an aggregated and integrated geographical database. It corresponds to a particular polygon database map as a reference, and contains data extracted from multiple event files. The reduction of data from a variety of event files, via reference to an index or reference (e.g. polygon map, address-zone index or chart of accounts) is called extraction. In GADS, for extraction based on spatial relationships, these event files are geocoded (either as part of the transaction or by a separate process, described later). These geocodes in GADS are generally "x,y" coordinates. Other geocodes used on event files are zone or polygon

identifiers (e.g. Census tracts, zip codes, etc.) The source files are
usually the operational transaction or "event" files of the organization,
such as police or fire calls, building permits, business licenses, etc.
They may also be "external" files, such as Census data or market survey
data. The geocodes are the fields of the record which are used to support
subsetting or grouping of data based on geographical relationship. For
example, in developing an extracted data base for a given polygon map, the
event data may first be searched for a type of event (e.g. residential
permits), then those corresponding to each polygon in the zone map are
determined by a routine (point-in-polygon) which finds which (unique)
polygon contains the "x,y" coordinates of that event. Further aggregation,
via extraction, would produce entries in the extracted data base such as
the number of residential permits issued for each polygon, the dollar value
of such permits by polygon, or the number of bedrooms being built by
polygon and house price.

The process called "geo-coding" is that which produces an appropriate
geocode for each event; e.g. an "x" and a "y" coordinate. Generally these
are not part of the original transaction record in the event file. In GADS,
geocodes are appended to the event files as a step prior to extraction.
Geocoding utilizes a "geographic base" file. This file has been of two
forms in GADS. One is a table giving "x" and "y" coordinates for each of a
list of place names or street intersections. In some cities, such a file
is maintained for all valid addresses in the city. Thus, via table look
up, the address or place name in the original event record is used to link
to the specific "x" and "y" coordinates to be appended. The other geofile
used in GADS is a computerized map called the 'DIME' file. Using this file,
"x" and "y" coordinates for any address can be developed. Details of this
geocoding process will be deferred until the structure of the DIME file is
given.

GADS data extraction is configured essentially as shown in Figure 2
(Carlson, 1975). The data base structure and management can be described
using Codd's relational model (Codd, 1970). Each logical file in the large
data base is a relation (set of N-tuples). The subsetting operations
correspond to projection and join operators defined by Codd, and
aggregation is an addition of several N-tuples to form a single M-tuple
(this operation is beyond the scope of Codd's relational operators). The
extracted data base, therefore, is another relation (or set of relations).
Figure 3 gives an illustration. The extracted data base, needed for
solving a police manpower allocation problem, is formed from a large data
base containing data on crimes, population, land use, and geographic codes.
The resulting extracted data base is a relation containing the crimes by
type, residential acreage, total acreage, and population for each block.
Using the interactive data extraction of GADS, adding another crime type,
acres of commercial land use, or re-aggregating by block groups takes only
a few minutes.

Figure 4 gives examples of the data description and subsetting
capabilities. The data description implementation allows different formats
to be used for the same file or the same formats to be used for different
files (Figure 4a). Using one line per field (data element), the user gives
field name, data type, length, and starting position (if not consecutive),
and can use any remaining space for comments. The subsetting language

includes constructs for: subsetting based on any arithmetic or logical combination of the items in a file, creating of new items, conditional subsetting or creation (IF, THEN, ELSE), and function calls (Figure 4b). Results from subsetting can be displayed as lists (Figure 4c) or as locations on a map (Figure 4d). Using the display capabilities, two dimensional subsetting is possible. That is, the user can draw a polygon on the screen, and select only those elements of a file whose location is within the polygon. This facility is much more user oriented than algebraic specifications for subsetting, and other graphic subsetting operators would be useful (e.g., display all the crimes of the same type as the one being pointed at). The aggregation operations in the implementation are restricted to forming the extracted data base for the GADS problem solving functions. This data base is aggregated by polygons of a map (blocks in the example of Figure 3). In GADS, data extraction might be used to analyze crimes by location, or to aggregate crimes by type and by police beat. It could be used to display residential locations of workers, or to aggregate the number of workers living within transportation zones. Except for the geocoding, the extraction functions are not uniquely "geographical". Once the corresponding polygon has been determined for each event (or the subset selected) from the event file, the subsequent aggregation has no special geographical flavor.

EXTENSION AND GENERALIZATION: Extraction

Extraction in GADS assumes explicit geocodes, either x,y coordinates or polygon (zone) number, are appended to each event record in the source files that are input to extraction. However, it appears attractive to specify more general extraction functions so that geocoding becomes only a special case.

The general form suggested for extraction is

EXTRACT (Name) = (query) WITH RESPECT TO (reference) USING (function)

where;

"Name" is the name to be given the extracted variable;

"query" is the selection rule--an arithmetic or boolean combination of data elements of the event file--used to develop the extracted variable of the given "name";

"reference" is the index giving membership classes for the extracted database (e.g. polygon map, chart of accounts, or organizational directory);

"function" is a predefined and stored function which specifies an aggregation, grouping, or matching to be used in forming the extracted variable. Examples of functions include geocoding, which determines the zone or polygon containing the site of this event; or via chart of accounts "reference", determination of which expense category this expenditure belongs.

An example is:

EXTRACT(BURGLARIES)=(SELECT FROM CRIME FILE WHERE CRIMECODE=459)
WITH RESPECT TO (SAN JOSE MAP1) USING (COUNT-IN-POLYGON)

Thus "name" is the name of the column of the extracted data base which this
EXTRACT operation is to build, "reference" is the description of the set of
columns of the extracted data base, and "query" and "function" are used to
describe and determine how the variable of the given "name" is to be
developed from the data elements of the event file, with respect to the
given reference.

The set of functions is, of course, application dependent. With geographic
data, however, two that would find broad use are:

COUNT: Counts the number of occurrences of the selected event within
categories or classes specified by the "reference".

SUM: Sums the values of each of the event records selected for each of
the categories or classes specified by "reference". For example, sum
the dollar value of building permits issued by polygon, or the total
of expenditures by each department in each of the polygons of a map or
in each account of a chart-of-accounts.

COUNT-WITHIN-DISTANCE( ) or SUM-WITHIN-DISTANCE( ): These are
variations of the above which use as "reference" a table of points
("x" and "y" coordinates) for each class. The argument supplied by
the user defines the boundary for inclusion in that class (and
corresponding row of the extracted file). For example, if the
interest is in customers within a specified distance of a set of
proposed facility locations, and the event file contains customers
with addresses, then this function will use the addresses, the
geographic base file to convert these to "x,y" coordinates, use the
table referenced to determine the facility locations and aggregate
those meeting the distance criteria. Thus, for this example:

EXTRACT(CUSTOMERS)=(SELECT FROM CUSTOMER FILE)
WITH RESPECT (LOCATIONS MAP)
USING (COUNT-WITHIN-DISTANCE(1 MILE))

ANALYSIS AND DISPLAY FUNCTIONS

To support multiple users and applications, the analysis and display
functions must be applicable to different extracted data bases. A data
access program provides a direct-access interface between any extracted
data base and the analysis and display functions. Using an index and
parametric read-and-write subroutines, variables are accessed by name.

There were three important design goals for the analysis and display
functions. First, the functions were to support a set of applications
using geographic data. Second, the functions were to be powerful enough to
meet the data manipulation requirements of users who are application
specialists, but simple enough so that each function could be learned in a
few minutes. Third, the functions should support, not impose, the users'
problem solving processes. To achieve these three goals, the following
strategies are used. The analysis and display functions, chosen on the

basis of our study of potential applications, are presented as a set of
major functional groupings which the user can learn and invoke depending on
his appraisal of the problem requirements and his solution approach.
Within each grouping, functions are divided into levels. A user can
progress from the basic levels to the more complex during problem solution.
Finally, data storage and display in terms of maps serves as a natural
framework for unifying the functions.

Although it is not possible to give a complete description of the analysis
and display functions in this paper, the following paragraphs briefly
describe the functions. Table 1 summarizes the functions and Figure 5
gives illustrations.

(i) Statement Language (Figure 5a)

The statement language enables the user to formulate questions about the
extracted data base and to manipulate data in that data base. In a
statement the user refers to data items by name and table number. Each
reference is to an n-tuple in a table (one variable for all n-zones of a
map).

A display statement creates a map display of symbols, a symbol per zone
based on arithmetic and logical expressions given in the statement. The
display statement syntax is:

Table 1. Analysis and Display Function

1. Statement language (Figure 5a)

In a statement, data is referred to by name and table number. Each
reference is to an n-tuple in a table (one variable for all n-zones of a
map). A display statement creates a set of symbols for display on a map,
one symbol per zone. The display statement syntax is:

symbol: expression;

An assignment statement is used to compute values for existing or temporary
variables. The syntax is:

: expression @ name;

Expressions in statements can specify any logical or arithmetic
combinations of n-tuples. Sets of statements can be combined to form a
page. Other features of the statement language permit the user to:

a. invoke dynamic aggregation using an overlay map (see 3.);
b. save sets of display symbols;
c. use built-in functions (e.g., sum);
d. generate reports (print statement);
e. provide comments;
f. save pages of statements in a statement library;
g. edit statements (e.g., copy, delete).

2. Map display (Figure 5b)

These functions support the display of statement-created symbols on a map.
The user may:

    a. display one or more maps and one or more sets of display symbols
        simultaneously or consecutively;

    b. expand maps around any symbol;

  . .c. eliminate lines between zones containing the same symbol;

    d. display the zone number and data values for any symbol.

3. Overlay construction (Figure 5c)

These functions provide the ability to:

    a. create overlay maps which are combinations of the basic zones of the
        special purose map;

    b. save overlay maps in a map library.

4. Graphs (Figure 5d)

Graphs are a second method of data display. With these functions the user
may:

    a. create one, two, or three dimensional graphs having one point (or
        line in 3-D) for each zone;

    b. identify points by zone number;
    c. automatically or manually scale axes;
    d. cumulatively sum the y-axis variable.

5. Table display and correction

The third data display mode is tables. The table-based functions can be
used to:

    a. view an index to tables and a dictionary of variable names;

    b. display any table;

    c. alter values in a table and log the changes;

    d. print hard-copies of tables

                        Symbol: expression

               e.g., *: TOT_POP(44)/TOT_HH(44) > 3.5

Execution of the sample statement would create a set of symbols for a map
display, with an "*" in each zone where the average population per

household given in Table 44 (a specific year) in the extracted data base was greater than 3.5. Several statements can be combined to form a set of symbols for a map display and the symbols can be saved.

An assignment statement computes values for existing or temporary variables. The assignment statement syntax is:

: expression @ name;

e.g., :TOT_POP(44) + TOT_POP(45) @ TEMP(1);

Execution of this assignment statement would add (zone by zone) the values of TOT_POP in Table 44 and those in Table 45 and store the results in a temporary table (with one column).

Statement execution is done by an interpreter. Expressions in statements can specify any logical or arithmetic combinations of n-tuples. Sets of arithmetic and display statements can be combined to form a page. Other features of the statement language permit the user to:

a. invoke dynamic aggregation using an overlaymap (see iii);
b. save sets of display symbols;
c. use built-in functions (e.g., sum);
d. generate hard-copy reports;
e. insert comments;
f. save pages of statements in a statement library;
g. edit statements (e.g., copy, delete);
h. chain pages of statements together.

(ii) Map Display (Figure 5b)

These functions support the display of the symbols created with statements. The user can display one or more maps, with one or more sets of symbols, either simultaneously or consecutively. Maps may be expanded around any zone, and lines between zones containing the same symbol may be eliminated to form a sub-map of areas with similar data values. The user may select a symbol in a zone to get a display of data values for that zone. A typical display would contain 1000 lines and over 250 symbols. During use of these functions, several displays might be requested (e.g., change scale, change symbols, change map).

(iii) Overlay Construction (Figure 5c)

The overlay construction functions are used to create, alter, retrieve, and save maps. These overlay maps must be formed from combinations of the basic zones in the special purpose map supplied from the Geographic Base File. To identify zones one can display statement-created symbols, dots, or numbers in each zone. By selecting the identifiers, existing zones can be extended or new zones created from combinations of existing zones. All maps can be enlarged to facilitate overlay construction. Because overlay maps can be saved in a map library, they can be referred to in the statement language to form map displays or new variables based on data values aggregated according to an overlay map.

Use of the overlay construction functions usually requires frequent map redrawing to reflect changes.

(iv) Graph Display (Figure 5d)

Scatter diagrams are a familiar mode of data presentation and are the second data display mode in GADS. With these functions the user may create one, two, or three dimensional scatter diagrams. Each point (or line in 3-D) on the scatter represents one zone. The zone number for any point is displayed if the point is light-penned, and any zone number can be entered and the appropriate point on the graph will be flagged. The scatter diagrams are automatically scaled, unless the user enters specific scales on each axis. The user may request a cummulative summation of the y-axis variable.

(v) Table Display and Manipulation

The third data display mode in GADS is tables. The table-based functions can be used to: Display any table in the extracted data base (either any n-tuple in a table or the values of all variables for any basic zone), alter values in a table and log the changes, and print hard copies of the tables. These are also functions which permit the user to display an index of table names and numbers and a dictionary of names of the variables in the tables. This dictionary can be used as a reference in constructing statements. As a simple data protection mechanism, the user may create one or two working tables in the extracted data base and move data between these tables and other tables in the extracted data base. Only the working tables may be edited. The urban planners who helped develop GADS provided an urban-growth model which can be used to construct (forecast) new tables based on specific, existing tables (Cristiani, 1973), (Crable, 1974).

IMPLEMENTATION

The prototype GADS implementation is in FORTRAN and PL/1. The system has been run on a variety of IBM 360 and 370 systems under OS, MVS (with and without TSO), and VM; systems in size ranging from a 370/145 on up. The graphics routines built for GADS support use of direct-view storage display taerminals, raster refreshed terminals, or vector refreshed displays (with minor changes to the translate tables of the telecommunications support used by the operating system; e.g. TCAM with TSO on MVS). Without utilizing virtual memory, the full GADS system requires 250k bytes of main storage (using overlays). The user interacts with the display via light pen or joystick-driven cross-hair, and an alphanumeric keyboard.

APPLICATION EXPERIENCE

Over a period of several years, via joint study agreements, GADS was employed in seventeen case studies involving over 100 users. Table 2 breaks the applications into seven groups, gives the number of types of applications and references (where available) to details of these studies.

Table 2. GADS Applications

1. Police (Carlson, et.al., 1974)

   a. manpower allocation   (1 application)

   b. burglary analysis   (1)

   c. calls for service analysis   (2)

2. School (Holloway and Mantey, 1976), (Grace, 1975)

   a. attendance boundary formation   (4)

   b. school closing   (1)

3. Urban planning (Cristiani, et. al., 1973) (Crable, 1974)

   a. urban growth policy evaluation   (1)

   b. urban growth modeling   (1)

4. Fire

   a. inspection planning   (1)

   b. fire equipment planning   (1)

5. Human service delivery evaluation   (1)

6. Commuter bus route planning   (1)

7. Shopping Center location   (1)

8. Territory assignment of equipment   (1)
    repair personnel
    (Sutton, 1978)

DATA BASE ORGANIZATION

The data used in GADS applications can be categorized, as suggested in Figure 1, into four parts. Of these, the extracted data base, the polygon boundary set, (special purpose maps in Figure 1) and the source or "event" data are accessible via GADS. The geographic base file is a supporting file, used for the development of the polygon boundary set, and for geocoding (appending explicit geographic coordinates) to the event file.

EXTRACTED DATA BASE

The extracted data base of GADS is a three dimensional array or cube with dimensions being polygon, attribute and time period.   An example of the extracted data base is shown in Figure 6. Use of this extracted data in GADS applications takes three forms. These are discussed below in the order of frequency of occurrence.

<u>Attribute(s) For All Polygons</u>. This is the most frequently requested data
by GADS users: the values of an attribute or set of attributes for all the
polygons in a map. Corresponding to Figure 6, this represents selection of
a column or columns of the extracted data base. Any map display of
information from the extracted data base requires columns of data from the
extacted data base for a particular time or, if time comparisons are being
made, from the same column of different tables. The GADS statement
language is written to handle only the columns of the extracted data base.
If the map of interest is a subset of the polygon map corresponding to the
extracted data base, the entire column is still processed by the statement
language subroutines as specified, and the results selected to correspond
to the subset of polygons of interest (usually the field of view of the
display). Also, the histogram and scatter plots of GADS operate on columns
of the extracted data base.

One Attribute, One Polygon vs. Time. This data access is required for
time-series analysis. Functions to support development of time series
plots were included in one early version of GADS, but were not found to be
required by GADS users in the applications investigated, and are not
included in the current version of the system. (However, users of GADS do
make time comparisons of data, but do it for all polygons at once, for a
variable or a function of variables, and access the data by columns from
the extracted data base).

Because access by column is the more frequent requirement to support GADS
applications, the data base is organized so that a record is a column of
the extracted data base of Figure 3; i.e. values of an attribute at a
specific time for all zones. The data base is organized accordingly; the
polygons or zones are numbered and the value of an attribute for a
particular zone numbered 'n' is always the same element of each attribute
record. When data for a single zone is required (one or more attributes),
the corresponding attribute records are read and the elements of the
record(s) for that zone are used.

The portion of GADS that accesses the extracted data base is written in
FORTRAN. Data base calls are via subroutines: GETREC reads data records by
attribute name and time period name. PUTREC writes out data records to the
data base DBAS by attribute name and time period name. The DIRECTORY is
used by GETREC and PUTREC to translate attribute name and time period name
into record number.

During the design of GADS data base, an objective was to provide equal
support to access either the rows or columns of the extracted data base.
If the entire DBAS could have been contained (economically or practically)
in main memory, then access to rows or columns could have been supported by
treating DBAS as a two (or three) dimensional FORTRAN array. However, in
view of the size of DBAS and the system environment at that time (1971) in
our laboratory and especially in the computer facilities of our joint study
partner, the County of Santa Clara, this was not practical. Instead, the
records corresponding to columns of the extracted data base were stored on
disk, and DBAS via the DIRECTORY was accessed by GETREC and PUTREC using
the direct access support of FORTRAN.

184

POLYGON MAP

The polygon map can be considered as a file with three different lists of data. First, there are the nodes. These are the x,y coordinates of the ends of the line segments composing the polygon map, along with an assigned number, as shown in Table 3 for the simple map shown in Figure 6 (Evey and Mantey, 1974).

Table 3. Node List

Node Number	x	y
1	0	6
2	3	6
3	5	6
4	0	4
5	3	4
6	2	4
7	5	3
8	0	2
9	3	2
10	0	0
11	3	0
12	5	0
13	2	3
14	2	2

If x and y are in state-plane coordinates (as has been true in most maps used with GADS) then x and y represent the distance north and east respectively of some (arbitrarily chosen) reference point, and will be always positive values.

The segment list has, for each segment in the polygon map, the "beginning" and "ending" node for the segment, and number of the polygon on the left (when traversing the segment from beginning node to ending node) and the polygon on the right. The structure of the segment list is illustrated in Table 4, for the simple map of Figure 7.

Table 4. Segment List

Beginning Node	Ending Node	Left Polygon	Right Polygon
1	2	0	1
2	5	4	1
5	6	4	1
6	4	1	2
4	1	0	1
2	3	0	4
3	7	0	4
7	13	5	4
13	6	2	4
13	14	5	2

14	8	3	2
8	4	0	2
7	12	0	5
12	11	5	0
11	9	3	5
9	14	3	5
11	10	0	3
10	8	0	3

A third list contains the x,y coordinates of the "centroid" of each polygon. This list is identical in structure to the node list. The "centroid" is a point chosen for each zone where data or symbols associated with that zone are to be displayed.

OVERLAY MAP

Overlay Maps or Superzones are aggregations of the basic zones. Each basic zone is assigned--via the "create" or "aggregate" functions--to one (and only one) superzone. Thus the storage of overlay maps of superzones requires only the maintenance of list of length equal to the number of basic zones, and with each entry mapping that basic zone to the superzone of which it is a constituent.

EVENT FILES

The support for access to event files in GADS is limited to fixed format files with no hierarchies or repeating groups. Simultaneous access to multiple files is not supported, but shared access to single or multiple files is possible. Extractions from multiple files are handled by consecutive extractions from the individual files. Sequential and direct access I/O are provided. Character, fixed binary, packed decimal, and floating point (binary) data representations can be used. The entire large data base is stored on disk, and there is a utility for loading files from tapes or private disk packs.

GEOGRAPHIC BASE FILE

A Geographic Base File (GBF) (Mantey and Carlson, 1975) contains data to support the relating of data from other files to geographical location and also to display this data on a map. Several different approaches to the structure and contents of this file have been taken to development of a GBF.

The simplest GBF is a file sometimes called a Property Location Index (PLI) which contains a list of the valid addresses in the muncipality and an x,y coordinate for each. This approach is the one used in Lane County, Oregon, (Stichrod, 1973) and by the Assessor in Santa Clara County, California. To make this Lane file more useful, a list of public place and street intersections and their x,y coordinates is appended. With such a GBF it is then possible to automatically convert addresses (in the police call file for example) to x,y coordinates. If the GBF also contains the police beat, census tract, and municipality for each address, then it is very simple to count the number of calls in each beat. Evaluation of calls by census tract would also permit consideration of socio-economic data with the crime data (of course, police officers could also encode calls by beat and census tract, but this approach is liable to significant errors and seems to be a poor use of manpower).

The most detailed GBF's contain digitized land parcel boundaries, easement locations, building outlines, utility placements, and even topographic information, along with street address information on all parcels and names of all public lands and buildings. This GBF is at the level of detail of surveyor's data, and is suitable for engineering applications and detailed map building. Ottawa, Canada's National Capital Commission (Symons, 1970) has pioneered in the development of this kind of GBF.

The most common GBF in the United States at the present time is the result of work by the U.S. Census Bureau in conjunction with the 1970 Census. Using the Metropolitan Map Series, a massive feature labeling and digitization was performed for 200 major metropolitan areas in the United States. The resulting computerized maps were called the DIME (Dual Independent Map Encoding) files (US Bureau of Census, 1970). Each entry (record) in the DIME file represents a line segment (a portion of a street segment, railroad, creek, city limit, etc.). Figure 7 shows a sample record and the map data from which the record is derived. The segment has a "From" node and a "To" node, as well as a Left and Right side. Thus, each entry describes its two ends and its two sides. The description of the nodes includes x,y coordinates, produced by the Census Bureau's map digitization. The nodes are labelled as falling on a particular map of the series, and given a sequential number within map and census tract. The other data on each entry is feature identification for the segment and its sides. Each feature is identified by a prefix, name, suffix, type (e.g., North Army Southwest Street); only name and type are required (e.g., Coyote Creek). The description of a side actually describes the adjacent land. The census tract number, the block number, and the place (city) code are included for each side. High and low address ranges for the street segment sides are also given. The records are ordered by feature name and low address (features without addresses have no secondary ordering). Administrative overlays (e.g. beats, census tracts) can be readily defined in terms of segments of this file. Used in combination with "point-in polygon" routines, these computerized overlays facilitate development of counts of events in areas of any specified polygon map.

The structure of the DIME GBF is conceptually the same as the polygon map and contains more data. However the DIME GBF file merges the segment and node file into one, as is illustrated by the sample record of Figure 8. Each record contains substantial detail, in particular the address ranges on each side of the segment. (In the latest GADS implementation, the polygon files are also stored in DIME file format).

DATA BASE PARAMETERS

SIZE

The sizes of the data bases used in GADS applciations have covered a rather wide range, depending on the data available and the complexity of the issue being addressed by the decision makers. Table 5 shows the sizes of the event and extracted databases. The sizes do not include system variables, header, records or wasted space.

Table 5. Data Base Sizes

	Minimum (bytes)	Typical (bytes)	Maximum (bytes)
Event Files	200K	1M - 2M	8M
Extracted Data Base	64K	0.5M-1M	2.5M

The extracted data is kept on disk, and the event files either on disk or tape. The actual space required, because of headers, waste, etc. is found to be 1.5 to 3 times the amount indicated in Table 4. Our joint study partner, the Center for Urban Analysis in Santa Clara County, uses, as an estimate, 300 tracks on a IBM 3330-1 disk drive (4M bytes) per application.

The DIME GBF for a metropolitan area such as Santa Clara County, contains 80,000 segments, with 200 bytes per segment, or about 16M bytes.

USAGE

Extracted data base usage was observed for the police application (Carlson et. al, 1977). In that study, it was found that police officers could apparently assimilate only a small amount of data at any given time. Of 700 variables contained in the extracted data base for this application (25 variables for each of 30 sample days) the users worked with only two or three at a time. The users initially envisioned need for a very large amount of data, especially socio-economic data. The entire data requested was not included in the extracted data base because for some of it, the event data required was not available, while for other analysis indicated that the costs of geocoding would not be justified. Of the data provided in the extracted data base, only two variables (total calls and total consumed time) were heavily used.

Data use differed among users and for a given user over time. The number of data items requested and used usually started out at a high level, but rapidly decreased to those required for the solution approach being developed by the problem solver. Data use then increased in the evaluation part of the problem solving process.

The group of problem solvers working on the same problem used data from what may be considered as a "working set" of data. This working set was characterized by a small set of relatively constant data (with some overlap among problem solvers) and a large transient set of infrequently used data which varied among users and over time for a specific user. Some data was not used by some (and other data by more) of the users.

Figure 8 illustrates the relationship of total data available (A), the average amount of data used in a given session (B), and the average amount of data consistently used during a session (C), in the police case study

(Carlson, et. al., 1977). The relationship held for individuals as well as for the group to of problem solvers. The data items represent by the curve (C) were stationary, or changed very slowly with time for a given user. The data selected from the available set, and represented by the area between curves (B) and (C) were much more transient.

IMAGE DATA

Using a color raster refresh (TV based) display (Carlson et.al., 1977), the mixing on the display screen of TV-scanned images with GADS output has been found to be very helpful to users. The user sees a map on the screen as an electronic overlay, and (after reference points are identified to the system by the user), sees GADS data--particularly event data--displayed "on top of" this familar frame of reference. The current implementation uses a paper map, source (and storage) scanned in via a monochromatic television camera. LANDSAT images have also been used in this fashion. The electronic storage, scaling and manipulation of (color) images for this purpose would be very attractive, but was not considered affordable in the current GADS application.

SUMMARY AND CONCLUSIONS

In this paper we have described the data bases used in GADS and the functions applied to develop and use these data bases. Extraction is a powerful tool for supporting decision making from large source files, and is not limited to geographic data. The support required by the extraction function is not included in any existing data base system. The extracted data base is a table that is accessed by users as columns and as rows. The "pictorial" data in GADS--the map files--are tabular data with graphical and non-graphical attributes. Image data support would be very useful in the geographic data applications that have used GADS, particularly for creating overlays for output. The system support for these images has yet to be designed.

REFERENCES

Carlson, E.D., Bennett, J.L., Giddings, G.M., and Mantey, P.E. (1974). The Design and Evaluation of an Interactive Geo-data Analysis and Display System. Proceedings of the IFIP Congress 74, North Holland Publishing Company, Amsterdam

Carlson, E.D. (1975). Using Large Data Bases for Interactive Problem Solving. IBM Research Report RJ1585, IBM Research Division, San Jose, California

Carlson, E.D., Giddings, G.M., and Williams, R. (1977) Multiple Colors and Image Mixing in Graphics Terminals, Proceedings of the IFIP Congress 77 North Holland Publishing Company, Amsterdam, pp.179-182.

Carlson, E.D., Grace, B.F., and Sutton, J.A. (1977) Case Studies of End-User Requirements for Interactive Problem-Solving Systems. Management Information Systems Quarterly, Vol. 1, No. 1, March 1977, pp.51-63

Codd, E.F. (1970). A Relational Model of Data for Large Shared Data Banks, Communications of the ACM 13, pp.377-387

Cristiani, E.J., Evey, R. J., Goldman, R. E., and Mantey, P.E. (1973). An Interactive System for Aiding Evaluation of Local Government Policies. IEEE Transactions on Systems, Man and Cybernetics, Vol. SMC.3, No.2 pp.141-146

Crable, P.A. (1974) Analyzing an Urban Growth Policy Using an Interactive Computing System, National Confeence, American Institute of Planners, Denver, Colorado, October 1974.

Evey, R.J. and Mantey, P.E. (1974) An Algorithm for Simplifying Map Displays by Elimination of Superfluous Boundaries. IBM Research Report RJ 1350, IBM Research Division, San Jose, Californi

Grace, B.F. (1975) A Case Study of Man/Computer Problem Solving-Observations on Interactive Formulation of School Attendance Boundaries. IBM Research Report RJ 1483, IBM Research Division, San Jose, California.

Holloway, C.A. and Mantey, P.E. (1976) Implementation of an Interactive Graphics Model for Design of School Boundaries, Graduate School of Business, Stanford University, Research Paper No. 229, Stanford, California.

Mantey, P.E. and Carlson, E.D. (1975) Integrated Databases for Municipal Decision-Making AFIPS-Conference Proceedings Vol. 44, AFIPS Press, Montval N.J., pp.487-493.

Stichrod, R. L. and Martin, L. C. (1973) Data Processing: Analysis of Costs, Benefits, and Resource Allocation. Lane County Management Report, Lane County, Oregon.

Symons, D. C. (1970) A Parcel Geocoding System for Urban and Rural Information. National Capital Commission, Ontario, Canada.

U.S. Bureau of Census (1970). The DIME GEOCODING SYSTEM. Report No. 4, Washington, D.C.

Sutton, J. A. (1978) Evaluation of Decision Support System: A Case Study With the Office Products Division of IBM. IBM Research Report RJ2214, IBM Research Division, San Jose, California

Williams, R and Giddings, G.M. (1976) A Picture Building System. IEEE Transactions on Software Engineering, Vol. SE-2, No. 1, pp.62-66.

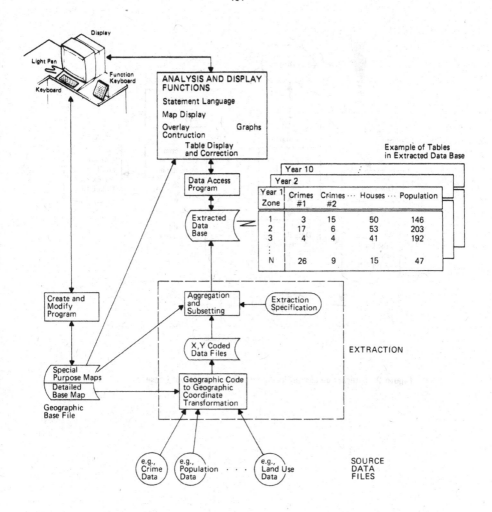

Figure 1. GADS architecture

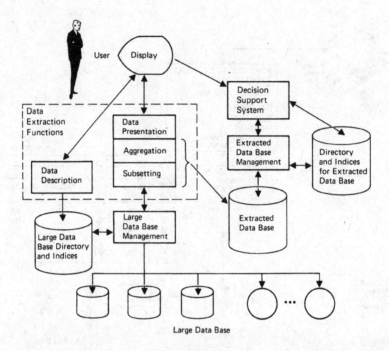

Figure 2. Interactive extraction interface to a large data base

193

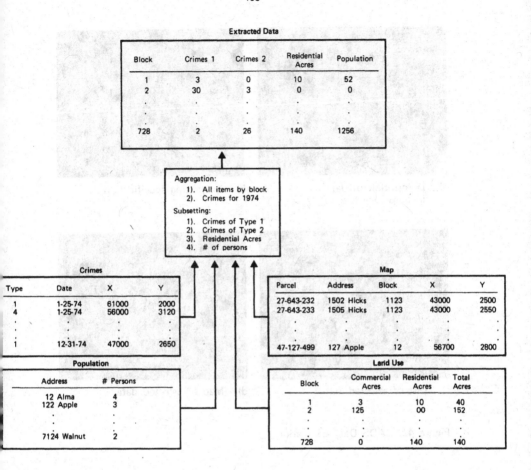

Figure 3. Extraction example

194

a). Description of data
in employee file

b). Subsetting specification

c). List of selected data

d). Map of selected data

Figure 4. GADS Data Extraction.

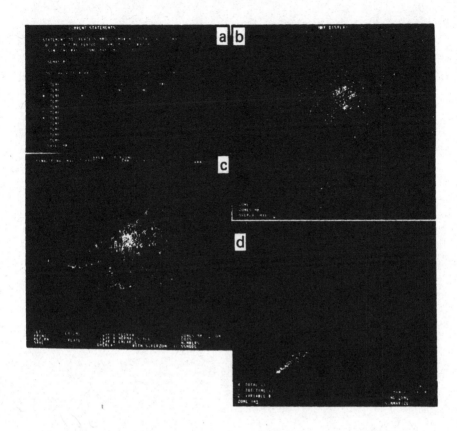

Figure 5. Example of GADS functions

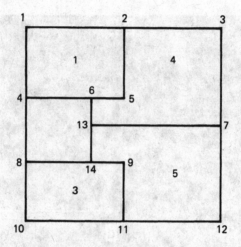

Figure 6 Example Map

197

Source Map

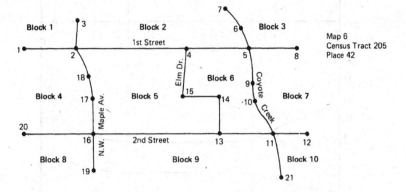

Map 6
Census Tract 205
Place 42

Number of Segments

Maple Av.	5
Elm Dr.	3
Coyote Cr.	6
1st St.	4
2nd St.	4

= 22 segments (records)

Contents of a Sample Record

Contents

Maple Av. N.W.

2	1530000	31000	6
18	1530100	30100	6
205	205 42 42	5	4
100	198		
101	199		

Legend

Name Type Suffix

From node number, x, y, map number
To node number, x, y, map number
Left tract, right tract, left place,
    right place, left block, right block
Left low address, high address
Right low address, high address

Figure 7. 'DIME' geographic base file structure

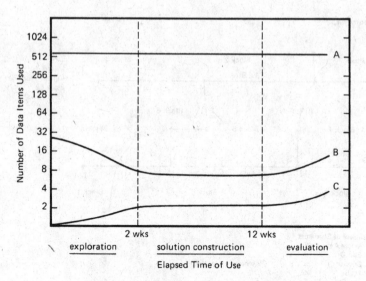

Curve A : Total data available
Curve B : Average amount of data used per session
Curve C : Average amount of data used consistantly
in consecutive sessions

Figure 8. Data usage

Interactive Cartography Using APL-Graphics

Yehonathan Hazony

The integration of efficient graphical processors into the standard
VSAPL system results in APL-Graphics as a powerful tool in the
management decision-making process. The system provides a high degree
of flexibility in the interactive analysis of large data bases. Fast
cartographical summaries allow the decision-maker to incorporate his
intuition into the iterative process of problem-solving. The present
report addresses the flexibility and improvisation power provided by
APL-Graphics in a dynamic problem-solving environment where problem
definition evolves together with the solution but under firmly imposed
deadlines. Illustrations of "instant-coding" will be given for
situations requiring instant but one-shot solutions.

Interactive Computer Graphics Laboratory, Princeton University
Princeton, New Jersey 08544

Introduction

The Interactive Computer Graphics Laboratory has been involved in several projects based on extensive use of interactive cartography. The major effort is an ongoing one, undertaken jointly with Princeton University's Transportation Program, and deals with analysis and planning for the Federal railroad system in the U.S. This project is based on the use of a variety of thematic maps as fast intermediate as well as final output of interactive analytic sessions, in which the "what-if" games of management are played (Hazony, 1979; Lutin et al. 1979a,b).

The main characteristics of this mode of analysis are that problem definition evolves together with solution, and that the size and contents of the basic data base are in a permanent state of flux. The only firm components in the process are deadlines, which are typically imposed by legislative acts. The basic graphical network model consists of about 20,000 links and a similar number of nodes accompanied by a digital representation of a variety of link and node attributes. An important "background" data base contains the geopolitical boundaries of the U.S. derived at the necessary level of detail from the U.S. Census data base. The most voluminous data base is the one containing the 1% Waybill data, which is a seasonal data base and is of the order of 10^8 bytes per season. In a typical analytical process, the 1% Waybill data base (or an arbitrary subset of it) is flowed through the network model (or subset, or a modified version of it). The output of the network-flow process provides statistical summaries which are presented as cartographical displays, overlaid on a graphical representation of the network under consideration. The supporting interactive graphics system must provide fast access to multiple sets of 10^8 bytes of data in conjunction with flexible analytical tools for subsetting, arithmetic and Boolean manipulations, as well as statistical summaries.

The Support System

Because of the permanent state of flux in the data structure and content, our "management information system" is in fact the VM370 operating system and the variety of software tools available under it. The main application tool is VSAPL which is augmented by the user controlled variable workspace size available under the VM370 operating system. VSAPL has been enhanced by a local implementation of an efficient graphical auxiliary processor driving Tektronix 4013/15 storage tube terminals. Additional data management utilities and all the conventional programming languages are provided through CMS. The system also supports on-line digitizers and plotters. This interactive environment is supported by an IBM 370/158 computer, with a 2 M-bytes core storage and a variety of disk and tape storage devices. Our experience has been shaped to a large extent by the use of a 2 M-bytes IBM 360/91 batch computer, communicating to the interactive 370 system through a VMRSCS linkage. The entire system is being replaced this summer by an 8 M-bytes IBM 3033 computer.

Some Overall System Considerations

In the current 360-370 configuration, the IBM 360 machine is used in batch mode for some data preprocessing required to reduce the 100 M-bytes chunks of data to subsets more manageable by the VM370 system. This particular mode of computer utilization is painful but is dictated by the availability of the underutilized and fully amortized IBM 360/91. The replacement of the entire system by a single 3033 will encourage a much more rational resource utilization through a unified pricing policy which will eliminate the financial incentive for sacrifice of flexibility and human effort in return for "cheaper cycles." Although these considerations are seemingly beyond the scope of this paper, they are mentioned because they have represented a substantial hindrance to the full development of the application and the methodology. Although this particular computer configuration represents a unique situation, other installations face different unique circumstances where past investments haunt future applications.

The experience obtained in our environment indicates that a 2 M-bytes IBM 370/158 computer operating under the VM370/CMS/VSAPL environment is just about powerful enough for the development and application of interactive cartography for large scale management information systems. The nature of the particular problems at hand indicated that in order to be able to manipulate a meaningful subset of the 100 M-byte data base, we had to use a typical workspace size of 4-6 megabytes and sometimes 16 megabytes. These are practical figures derived from experience with our particular computational environment, in which the interactive system supports comfortably about 40 time-sharing users. The typical user is provided access to a 512K-bytes virtual machine; many users have access to 1.5 M-bytes machines; some users are authorized to increase the size of their virtual machines up to 5 M-bytes; and a 16 M-bytes machine may be used only under special circumstances.

It is important to note that with 2 M-bytes of real core, the VM370 system in the above environment comfortably supports several 4 M-bytes concurrent virtual machines. More importantly, the interactive user can carry out a useful session with his 4 M-bytes virtual machine contending for and obtaining sufficient resources of the real machine.

The internal workings of VM370 are too complex for the above outline to provide a complete characterization, but the above summary does provide the end-user who is not a (computer) systems analyst an indication of the system's capabilities.

In moving to the environment of an 8 M-bytes 3033, one can make the following extrapolations:

1. with everything else being equal, it is reasonable to expect that a user will be able to comfortably utilize a virtual machine twice the size of the real core, namely 16 M-bytes, and

2. with the raw speed of the 3033 being about 5 times that of the
    158, the new computer configuration will certainly be able to
    back up the increased availability of 16 M-byte virtual
    machines as well as provide significant performance
    improvements.

Some Future Requirements

The readily available 16 M-byte virtual machines will substantially
alleviate the annoyance of repeated batch preprocessing of data down
from the initial volume of 10^8 bytes. Furthermore, the waybill data
base used represents only 1% of the full volume of data which may be
made available for some applications. In addition, some aspects of
railroad management may require a much more detailed geographical model
of the network to effectively address such issues as maintenance of way,
for example. This problem may easily require a data base of the order
of 10^8 bytes and up.

Other important contemporary issues which would require this kind of
management information system are, to name a few, energy resources on
the global as well as industry level, environmental resources on the
Federal as well as the state level, etc. Trying to deduce from our past
experience the nature of necessary future developments in the area of
management information systems, one can point out two major areas:

1. _Address Space_. In moving to the environment of the IBM 3033, we
are in fact reaching the limit of 16 M-byte address space available
under current architecture of 24-bits addressability. Notice, however,
that in our environment this limit forces us to switch back and forth
between the agonizing process of batch subsetting and interactive
analysis. This is definitely a handicap, which will be entirely
alleviated by moving to a 32-bits addressability, which will not require
a major deviation in hardware architecture. Such an address space will
integrate the entire data analysis process under a VM-type environment
and will represent a major step toward an entirely user-driven or
application-driven system.

2. _Data Flow_. The typical analysis of such a large data base
entails very large array manipulations. However, the present
hardware-software architecture of the 3033, as announced, will not
permit utilization of the full speed of the machine for array operations
because of the lack of "pipeline" facilities. In other words, it is
very difficult to deliver the data to the CPU fast enough to take
advantage of its full speed. This issue is extremely important in the
interactive environment, where the tremendous advantage which can be
realized with an order of magnitude speed-up is obvious.

The Interactive Problem-solving Environment

As pointed out above, in a typical application the problem is defined initially quite vaguely, though it is clear that a problem exists. The nature of the problem may become clearer following exploratory data analysis. However, further clarification may be obtained as a result of the failure of the designed solutions to accomplish the set objectives. The interactive process calls at this stage for the next iteration of problem redefinition. The objective of interactive cartography is to offer the problem-solver and policy-maker the opportunity to go through more than one iteration in the process of "what-if" analysis.

Since ambiguity and uncertainty are inherent to the process, the tools of interactive cartography should be flexible enough to permit improvisation as a way of life. The major advantage of the VM370/CMS/VSAPL (Graphics) system is that it permits the analyst to grow with the application. In other words, in the initial approach to the problem where the data is scant and the methodology not yet proven, the analyst may use a rather crude approach which may not require the full power of the system. In particular, the exploratory data base is small and may be handled in a small virtual machine, thus not taxing the resources of the machine overwhelmingly. The fact that the user has the incentive to and can dynamically adjust the size of the virtual machine is key to the efficiency of VM as a time-sharing environment. In a multi-user environment an equilibrium is reached when different users are at different stages of their problem-solving process resulting in an efficient temporal resource sharing of the system.

The flexibility provided by VM is complemented by the analytical flexibility offered by APL and its graphical extension. The significance of the above statement is clear to the reader who is already familiar with the APL environment, while for other readers the following illustrations may serve to make the point without an actual introduction to the system, which is certainly beyond the scope of the present paper.

The following examples illustrate some of the early improvised solutions which are simple enough to illustrate the flexibility of the system. Consider a data base consisting of an $\ell \times m$ node table having in the first column a node identification code, in the second and third columns XY coordinates data, and in the rest of the columns, node attribute data. It is useful to be able to visualize the geographical distribution of a certain attribute in relation to its magnitude. A common way of providing such a graphic representation would be placing a square (or any other polygon) centered at each node with its size proportional to the magnitude of the specific attribute. Choosing for the display the attribute described in column 4 of the data set DATA, the executable instruction reads

$DATA[;4] \ SQUARE \ DATA[;2 \ 3]$

where the dyadic program SQUARE accepts the ℓ-elements attribute vector as a left side argument and the $\ell \times 2$ coordinates matrix as a right side

204

argument. Note that the respective data arrays are extracted out of the data table using simple APL indexing with DATA[;4] producing the attribute vector while DATA[;2 3] produces the respective coordinate matrix.

The SQUARE program may be simply written as follows:

```
        ∇ A SQUARE B
[1]     DRAW 4,B,12,A,0,13,(-A),A,13,(-A),(-A),13,A,(-A),13,(ρ
        B)ρA,[1.5],A
        ∇
```

This one-line program will draw any number of squares, provided the number of elements in A is consistent with the number of rows in B. If A contains a single number, all the squares will come out equal. Figure 1 demonstrates the responsiveness of the present system to such a request. Suppose that the nodes represent rural communities, and the attribute in column 4 of the data base represents average income in the communities. Furthermore, let us assume that the present stage of an ongoing analysis deals with middle income communities and calls for the geographical distribution of such communities. Figure 1 includes 100 communities and is cluttered by the representation of communities which do not belong to this category. What is required is a windowing capability which subsets the data by attribute rather than geography. The following command will do that

```
        4 10 25 SUBSET DATA
```

and results in the partial display shown in Figure 2. The dyadic program SUBSET calls for the data as a right argument and a 3-elements vector as a left argument. The first element of the vector specifies which attribute column is to be considered and the other two numbers, 10 and 25 in the example, represent an arbitrary set of window boundaries. The reader familiar with APL vocabulary and syntax will recognize the simplicity of the solution

```
        ∇ A SUBSET B
[1]     IND←(1=+/B[;A[1]]∘.>A[2 3])/ι1↑ρB
[2]     B[IND;A[1]] SQUARE B[IND; 2 3]
        ∇
```

The unfamiliar reader will recognize the insignificance of the effort required for writing a 2-line program once the problem at hand is understood. The first line of SUBSET identifies the subset of data and the second line applies the previously discussed SQUARE program to the data subset. Inspection of Figures 1 and 2 may suggest that both displays are unsatisfactory. While the first is too cluttered, the second lacks some measure of relationship to the missing subset of data. Another representation may subset the data to several groups where each group is represented by a different size square, the smaller, medium, and larger sizes representing the lower, middle, and upper income groups respectively. This display mode may be generated by the following program

```
     ∇  A SUB B
[1]    (2×2*+/B[;A[1]]∘.>0,1↓A) SQUARE B[; 2 3]
     ∇
```

which is invoked by the statement
      4 10 35 *SUB DATA*
as shown in Figure 3. The number of elements in the left-hand side
argument vector determines the number of distinct subsets to be
displayed; the first element indicates the attribute column; the rest of
the elements include the subset boundaries. The above instruction
called for three subsets with the values of 10 and 35 as partition
values. Using the vector 4 10 25 40 as left hand side argument
      4 10 25 40 *SUB DATA*
would have resulted in four subsets with the values of 10 25 and 40 as
subset boundaries. The sizes of the squares would have been 4, 8, 16,
and 32 respectively. The progression of a factor of two has been chosen
for clarity of display. It would limit, however, the number of subsets
to be displayed without resorting to overly large squares for the higher
categories.

The above three examples demonstrate the ease of programming in the
context of the application. This power of improvisation is even more
useful in more complex situations. Everyone involved even once in the
process of generating a digitized cartographic data base is familiar
with the problem of weather- and time-related distortions of paper base
maps. Matching information available on different copies of the same
base map is difficult and often impossible. The program given in
Appendix I has been developed under deadline pressure to match any
tetragonal geographic window to any other tetragonal window. Assuming
that it is possible to identify corresponding sets of reference points
on two maps, the program transforms one of the maps (or a section of it)
in such a way that a set of four reference points matches exactly with
the corresponding points on the second map.

No attempt will be made to call upon the familiarity of the reader
with APL to understand this program. It is the mathematical idea which
requires the effort on the part of the problem-solver, and once the
appropriate idea is arrived at, the rest of it is coding, which is
trivial. The mathematical transformation employed is based on the
homogeneous coordinates representation of perspective drawing and is
embedded in lines 16-19 of the code (Appendix I). The rest of the
program includes service routines designed for the demonstration shown
in Figure 4. This tool was originally improvised and put to use in one
day with an hour of programming effort. Figure 4 demonstrates the
mapping of an image from a distorted to a rectangular frame.

A more powerful cartographic subsetting is shown in Figure 5
(Kornhauser et al., 1979), where a three-dimensional projection is used
to illustrate the interrelationships between two subsets of the Federal
railroad system. The power of this illustration is constrained by the
single color of the display. In the actual applications the results are
produced as multicolor high resolution maps.

Effectiveness and Efficiency

The following comments are made for the benefit of the reader who is used to the traditional batch mode of operation and is not familiar with the interactive environment. The five displays shown above appear on the screen instantly following the entry of the instructions. CMS time stamps are shown in Figure 3 indicating the timing information before typing the instruction (top) and after completion of the resulting display (bottom). The full session lasts less than one minute of connect time and less than one second of total CPU time (including overhead of the time-sharing operating system). This responsiveness, which is expected to improve on the IBM 3033, is key to the effectiveness of the system in the problem solving environment, and is due partly to the power of the VM370 operating system and partly to APL being an interpreted rather than compiled language.

It is a common but erroneous belief that the interpretive nature of APL results in high computational inefficiencies. This is not true, particularly in cartographic and large data base applications, where most required computations may be accomplished through large array manipulations. The actual mapping transformation illustrated in Figure 4 is performed in line 27 of the MATCH progam shown in Appendix I. This is accomplished through an inner product between the data matrix D and the transformation matrix T. Figure 6 displays the CPU time required for an APL inner product operation between two vectors, as a function of the length of the vector. Extrapolating to zero computations, one sees that the overhead due to the pass through the interpreter is about 4 millesecond CPU time (on the IBM 370/158) which represents 50% overhead for 500 computations and an entirely insignificant overhead for arrays requiring several thousand operations. Cartographic and large data base applications lend themselves ideally to large array manipulations, where the overhead due to the interpreter is insignificant.

Figure 6 serves also to illustrate another analytical aspect of APL-Graphics, providing instant displays of statistical summaries in a rich variety of formats.

Pictorial Data Processing

The expression pictorial data processing may be read in two distinctly different ways:

1. pictorial processing of data, or

2. processing of pictorial data.

From the point of view of the end-user, the digital methodology for processing of pictorial data, which is the way the underlying system processes pictorial data, should remain as transparent as possible. One does not have to acquire profound knowledge of computer graphics in considerations. For a discussion and demonstration of the power of multicolor displays the reader is referred elsewhere (Hazony, 1979). Our graphical facilities permit the user to design the multicolor display on the regular graphic screen and route the final output to an on-line multicolor plotter.

Concluding Remarks

With the appropriate graphical terminal, the methodology of pictorial processing of large scale data bases could become the obvious natural way of computer applications not only in cartographically related data bases but in engineering and scientific applications in general. The illustrations given above demonstrate that this approach has certainly come of age in terms of currently available hardware and software technology. The effectiveness of this approach will be substantially increased if future developments in hardware and systems can be more explicitly geared toward pictorial data analysis.

order to use pictures of the kind shown above. One cannot, of course,
analyze data subsets without knowledge of the data analyzed as well as
the purpose of the subsetting and extraction processes. However, the
application specialist who knows what data base and what attribute are
under study and how many subsets he is interested in, as well as the
subsetting boundaries, will find no difficulty in invoking the
instruction
        4 15 35 *SUB DATA*
which produced Figure 3, or, in the way of exploration,
        4 10 17 35 *SUB DATA*

    The exercise in topological mapping shown in Figure 4 is also handled
in a manner which does not require understanding beyond the application
subject matter, having to do with the inherent distortions of paper base
maps. A detailed matchup between two extensive cartographic data bases
could be accomplished entirely pictorially without requiring the analyst
to consider or manipulate a single number. The reader familiar with APL
may note that the programs given in Appendices I and II are relatively
long by APL programming standards. This is so because the actual
transformation algorithm is imbedded in service routines designed to
permit the user to stay completely away from programming and numerical
manipulations and still accurately accomplish his data processing goals.
The program COMBINE (Appendix II) is a dyadic function expecting the
name of the reference data base as a left argument and the name of the
edited data base as a right argument. If the respective names are NYA
and NYB, the process is invoked through the command
        NYA COMBINE NYB
The service routines display the two maps side by side on the screen in
a compressed scale; the crosshair cursor then appears, permitting the
analyst to identify four windows in each map. Next the two set of four
windows are presented sequentially in an expanded scale permitting
accurate graphical designations of the respective reference points
through the use of the cross-hair cursor. The expansion scale is under
user control when the respective windows are being set up. The final
result is a new coordinates dataset with a name derived automatically
from the original name affixed with the characters 'XY'. Thus in the
above example the name of the new dataset will be NYBXY. Assigning a
different name to the edited version of the map gives the analyst the
option to review, accept, or reject the new version, and also to retain
the two versions pending later decision on which, if any, copy is to be
deleted. In a real application case this procedure invokes extensive
numerical manipulations, yet the analyst is free to choose to entirely
ignore the numerical aspects of the process, since his involvement is
purely graphical.

    Figures 1-3 illustrate one of many ways of producing graphical
representations of nongraphical data and consequently extend the
applicability of the methodology of pictorial analysis to many if not
most other aspects of management information systems. An extremely
important dimension of pictorial analysis is multicolor display, which
cannot be reproduced in these Proceedings because of cost and time

References

(1) Hazony, Y. (1979), Interactive Cartography An Analytical Tool for Management Information Systems, Computers & Graphics (in press).

(2) Lutin, J., Alexander, K. and Hazony, Y. (1979a), Application of Management Information Systems to Environmental Planning: Coastal Zone Management, Coastal Zone Management Journal, Vol. 5 (in press).

(3) Lutin, J., Hazony, Y. and Kornhauser, A.L. (1979b), An Interactive Network Model for Railroad Traffic Flow Analysis and Cartographic Display, Transportation Research Records (in press).

(4) Kornhauser, A.L., Hornung, M., Hazony, Y., and Lutin, J. (1979), The Princeton Railroad Network Model: Application of Computer Graphics in the Analysis of a Restructured Railroad Industry, to be presented at the Harvard Graphics Conference, July 1979.

Appendix I

Typing the instruction
        MATCH
the following program will clear the screen and prompt the user to
graphically enter four corners of the first window, followed by the four
reference points for the second window. Once the two windows are
delineated, the user is prompted to enter control points for an image in
the second window. A SPLINE routine generates an image out of the
defined control points. The control points are transformed to conform
with the first window by a transformation which matches the corners of
the second window with those of the first one. The SPLINE routine
creates the left image out of the transformed control points. The
transformation matrix T is computed by lines 16-19 while the rest of the
code is service routines.

```
        ∇ MATCH;X;X1;XA;Y;YA;T;D;DA;OM;XP
[1]     ERASE
[2]     'ENTER FOUR GRID POINTS'
[3]     D←X←Y← 0 2 ρ0
[4]     LY:Y←Y,[1] YA←1↓VCURSOR
[5]     2 SQUARE YA
[6]     →LY×ι4>1↑ρY
[7]     DRAW 4 5 5 5 5 ,Y[4,ι4;]
[8]     HOME
[9]     ''
[10]    'ENTER NEXT SET OF FOUR GRID POINTS'
[11]    L:X←X,[1] XA←1↓VCURSOR
[12]    2 SQUARE XA
[13]    →L×ι4>1↑ρX
[14]    DRAW 4 5 5 5 5 ,X[4,ι4;]
[15]    ⍝FOLLOWING 4 LINES DERIVE TRANSFORMATION MATRIX T
[16]    XP←⊟X[1 2 4 ;],1
[17]    X1←Y[1 2 4 ;],1
[18]    OM←((Y[3;],1)+.×⊟X1)÷(X[3;],1)+.×XP
[19]    T←XP+.×(3 3 ρOM, 3 3 ρ0)+.×X1
[20]    HOME
[21]    2 1 ρ' '
[22]    'ENTER DRAWING IN SECOND WINDOW, TYPE S TO STOP'
[23]    L1:D←D,[1] 1↓DA←VCURSOR
[24]    2 SQUARE 1↓DA
[25]    →L1×ιDA[1]≠115
[26]    SPLINE D
[27]    D←(D,1)+.×T
[28]    SPLINE 0 ¯1 ↓D÷D[; 3 3 3]
        ∇
```

Appendix II

The following COMBINE program imbeds the same transformation but applies to real cartographical data. The more extensive service routines are invoked here by name rather than by explicit code. This reference mode invokes external programs to provide the needed services.

```
        ∇ LEFT COMBINE RIGHT;PL;PR;X1;XP;OM;T;WINL;WINR
[1]     WINL←WINR← 0 4 ρ0
[2]     PL←PR← 0 2 ρ0
[3]     'L' SETWIN LEFT
[4]     'R' SETWIN RIGHT
[5]     'L' GETP LEFT
[6]     'R' GETP RIGHT
[7]     XP←⊞PR[1 2 4 ;],1
[8]     X1←PL[1 2 4 ;],1
[9]     OM←((PL[3;],1)+.×⊞X1)÷(PR[3;],1)+.×XP
[10]    T←XP+.×(3 3 ρOM, 3 3 ρ0)+.×X1
[11]    ⍎RIGHT,'XY←(',RIGHT,'XY,1)+.×T'
[12]    ⍎RIGHT,'XY←',RIGHT,'XY[;1 2]÷',RIGHT,'XY[;3 3]'
        ∇
```

212

FIGURE 1

Graphical display of attribute data. The size of the square
corresponds to the magnitude of the attribute.

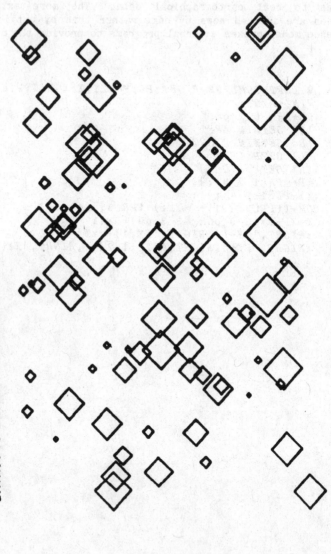

213

FIGURE 2

Windowing in attribute space: selective display nodes with
attribute value between two given limits.

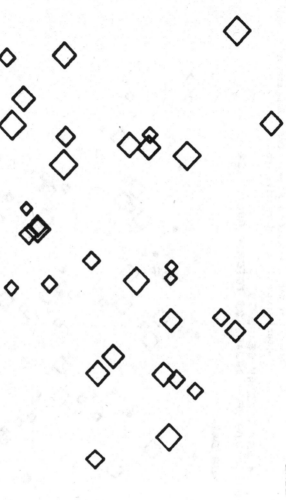

FIGURE 3

Subsetting in attribute space: attributes classified in three categories defined by two subsetting boundaries and represented by three distinct sizes of squares. CMS time stamps illustrate responsiveness of the interactive system.

```
CMS·G T'
TIME IS 13:41:14 EST TUESDAY 05/08/79
CONNECT= 00:04:00 VIRTCPU= 000:01.29 TOTCPU= 000:04.02

4 10 25 SUB DATA
```

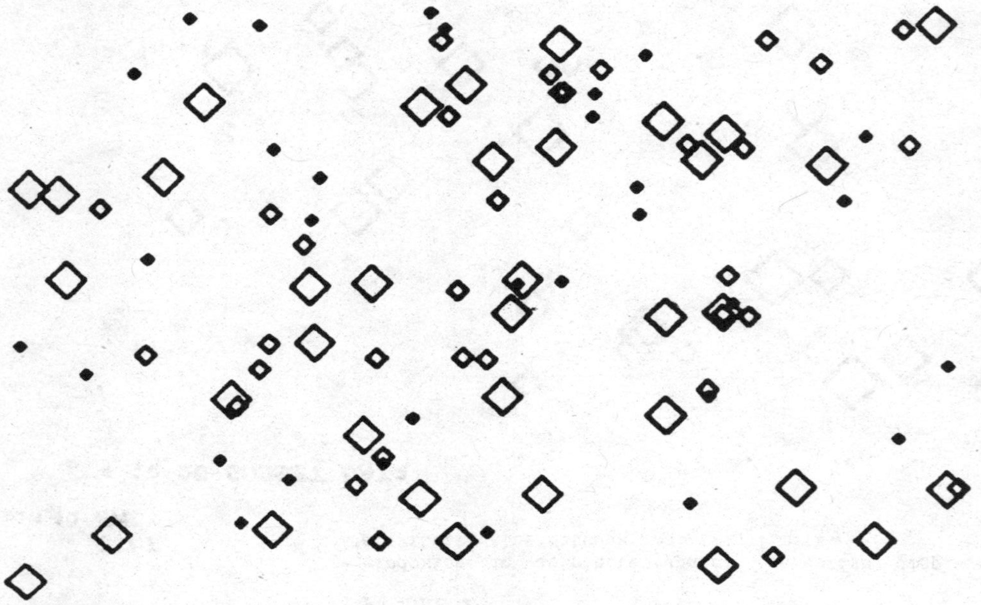

```
CMS'Q T'
TIME IS 13:41:53 EST TUESDAY 05/08/79
CONNECT= 00:04:38 VIRTCPU= 000:01.68 TOTCPU= 000:04.90
```

215

FIGURE 4

Topological matching of distorted windows: The image shown in the distorted window (right) is transformed to conform with the regular window (left).

ENTER FOUR GRID POINTS
ENTER NEXT SET OF FOUR GRID POINTS
ENTER DRAWING IN SECOND WINDOW. TYPE S TO STOP

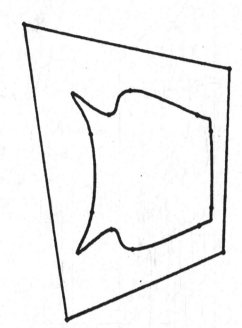

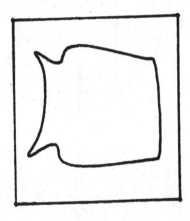

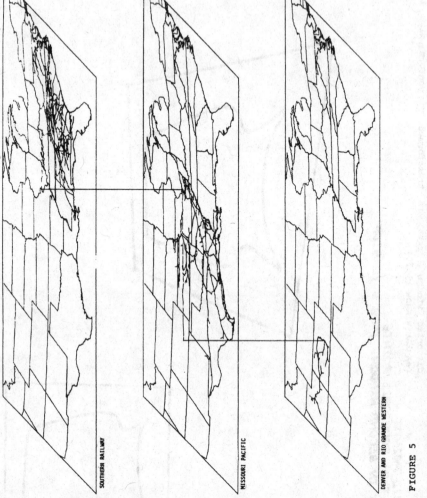

SOUTHERN RAILWAY

MISSOURI PACIFIC

DENVER AND RIO GRANDE WESTERN

FIGURE 5

3-D display of network subsetting: heavy line delineates a minimum path for train route moving on three subnetworks of different ownership. The final output of the analysis is reproduced on a multicolor plotter.

217

FIGURE 6

APL overhead for large array manipulations. The overhead due to the interpreter is obtained by linear extrapolation to zero array size. This test is performed on the inner product operator which is commonly used in graphical applications. Overhead becomes insignificant for 1000 operations and up.

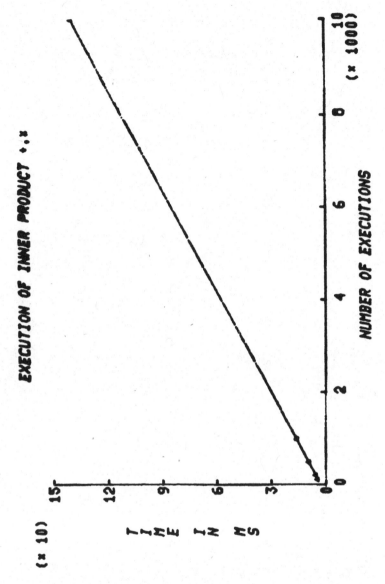

EXECUTION OF INNER PRODUCT +.×

THE STRUCTURE OF QUERIES ON GEOMETRIC DATA

J. Jimenez

J.L. Navalón

A geometric object is an abstraction of reality and many of its properties can be studied without direct reference to the absolute coordinates of its elements. We have developed a coding method that uses this fact to simplify the manipulation of vectorized n-dimensional geometric schemes and used it to reduce those manipulations to a small set of basic operations. We have built a subroutine package implementing these operations that works on a workspace extracted from a very simple data base. A pilot project is described in which this package is used in the management of map information for a geometrical data base.

IBM Scientific Center, Castellana, 4.
Madrid, SPAIN.

INTRODUCTION

This paper is written in two levels. At one level it deals with maps and geography.
We have established a small geographical data base and developed a coding and manipulation method for maps. The results of this experiment are presented.

At a second level it deals with geometry. The maps are coded into an algebraic structure that is a generalization of a graph and the basic operations among map elements
are reduced to algebraic operations. The process is generalizable to higher dimensions and is described in some detail. The result is a system in which geometric
objects are treated as variables of a new type with atributes (rank, dimensions, etc.)
which are purely geometric. Operations have been defined among these variables and
the whole system has been put together into a PL/I subroutine package which is described briefly.

In addition the range of applicability of these ideas to geographical data bases is
discussed, specially as it relates to the two possible ways to code a two dimensional (or higher dimensional) object: as a raster coded image or as a vectorized skel-
eton. We argue that both methods should coexist in general and we try to identify
the specific fields on which each one should be preferred.

MAPS AND IMAGES

There is a story (Borges, 1972) about a king who ordered his cartographers to produce
a map of his kingdom. When he was presented with the map, a magnificent parchment
document, he was pained to find that there were features in the kingdom that were
not reflected on the map, and so ordered that a new map, on a larger scale, be constructed. The process went on for years always producing maps of increasing accuracy,
and size, until eventually the cartographers compiled a map that coincided in size
with the kingdom, reproduced it exactly, and of course precisely overlaid it. The
story ends by telling us how travellers in the western desserts can still find in
places the ruins of the map, stuck in the deeper ravines and inhabited by nomad
tribes and wild animals.

We cite this story here because it points to the superficial similarity but the
profound difference between a territory, or a satellite mosaic covering it, and a
map. Consider a river; in the mosaic there will be a collection of pixels that can
be classified as water, and a good clustering algorithm will presumably be able to
isolate a contiguous subset of them and label it as a particular hydrographical
network. The concept of "river" however will be difficult to isolate by any present
day computer, and it is not even clear whether such entity exists at all outside the
perception of cartographers that draw maps of the region. The "river" concept, on
the other hand, has an important clarifying influence in the world model of people
living near rivers and is everywhere deeply ingrained in the legal and administrative
structure of life.

In a much simplified way it can be said that a satellite image contains "reality"
or a part of it, while a map contains the human interpretation of this reality
(Robinson and Petchenik, 1976). The same difference exists between a digitized hologram of a mechanical part and an engineering blueprint. Both representations serve
different purposes and should not be considered as mutually exclusive alternatives
for the codification of geometrical objects in general. It is however a valid question whether data bases should contain maps or images.

Many reasons have been given in favour of each approach. Images, grids, have the
advantage of fairly easy capture, storage and display of data and they have been
used very often in the past. The tendency has been increased lately because satellites provide large amounts of data already coded in the form of digital images and

because techniques are becoming generally available to treat those images in a practical way. Vectorized maps, polygons, have been defended in terms of storage. The
idea is that the number of elements needed to code a given feature in terms of a
grid increases quadratically with accuracy while it increases only linearly when the
same feature is coded as a polygon. This is unfortunately not true in general.

When a line is approximated by a polygon with an accuracy δ, the number of sides
needed changes like δ^{-D} where D has been defined by Mandelbrot (Mandelbrot, 1977) as
the "fractal dimension" of the line. Regular lines have a fractal dimension of 1,in
which case the statement above is justified; in fact this case is singular because
the coeficient of δ vanishes and the number of sides increases only as $\delta^{-1/2}$. Natural lines tend to have larger fractal dimensions. Borders, coasts and rivers have
been measured to have $D \sim 1.25$ (Richardson, 1961; Hack, 1957) and in this case polygons still have an advantage over images. Man made features and administrative divisions, such as census tracts, catastral plots or engineering drawings tend to be
smoother, closer to $D = 1$, and in many cases, even consist of straight segments in
which case polygons are obviously the natural representation. On the other hand
there are natural features whose fractal dimension approaches 2 and, for them, there
is no a priori difference between the two storage methods. Hydrographical networks
are one such example (Mandelbrot, 1977), and probably land use and land cover maps,
in which there is no lower limit to the scale of natural partitions, also belong to
this class.

Our own experience with a data base containing mainly administrative borders and
roads, digitized manually from a printed map, is that the number of sides goes as
$\delta^{-.8}$. This is intermediate between the exponent 1/2 characteristic of regular lines
and the higher exponents of natural fractals, and probably reflects as much the properties of the lines themselves as those of the digitization process.

The form of future data bases is however unlikely to be decided only in terms of
storage. The land surface of Spain covers approximately half a million square kilometers which, if digitized in a 10 x 10m grid, will produce an image with 5 x 10^9
pixels. While this number is large, it is not unreasonably outside the capacity of
modern storage methods. It is our believe on the other hand that, independently of
the way information is actually stored, maps will always be needed in the use of
this information by man. First, as noted above, the human world model and the cultural structure of the land are expressed in the form of maps, not images. Second
the storage saving can be spectacular in those cases in which only specific types
of information are required. A map of all national roads in Spain expressed as an
image will contain the same number of pixels as the whole data base, while a polygon
representation will have enough with a few thousand vertices.

In the next section we present a summary of our work in the manipulation of maps.
Deep in the coding philosophy is the idea that a map, in particular, and a geometrical figure in general, are only references to an underlying reality. In the particular model used in our implementation this reality is represented by a table of
points, the "universe", which contains the coordinates of all the points used in
the map, while the map itself is expressed in terms of indexes over this table. This
is not strictly necessary for our argument. There is no reason why the universe
could not be substituted by an algorithm that would assign to each index a particular pixel in a reference image. The general structure of the geometric manipulation
will not be affected.

CODING THE GEOMETRY

Consider the scheme given in figure 1, and let it represent a polygonalization for
the map of a city near the ocean. A road, a river and part of a lagoon are also
shown. The map contains a number of significant points such as vertices and inter-

sections and these points can be labelled in some arbitrary way such as the one
given in the figure. Let the list of these coordinates form a matrix U which we will
refer from now on as the "universe" of the scheme. It is clear that this matrix has
to be included in one form or another into any description of the scheme, and that
a point can be identified by its row index in U.

Polygons could now be written as vectors of the indices of their vertices. Thus the
road would be given by the vector

$$ROAD \leftarrow 10\ 4\ 6\ 8\ 9,$$

the city outline by

$$CITY \leftarrow 3\ 4\ 5\ 6\ 7,$$

and single points like the bridge of the road over the river by a scalar such as

$$BRDG \leftarrow 6.$$

This representation has several drawbacks from the point of view of data management.
In the first place it is ambiguous. Thus, the city is the region inside a polygon,
while the road is the polygon itself. Also, if no constraints are imposed to it, a
polygonal line is a complicated structure with a lot of possible subcases and exceptions in its treatment. For example, the operation of finding the area inside a
given border is in no way trivial and is full of pitfalls and special cases that
must be treated separately.

The common problem to all these difficulties is that in our simple minded representation the position of the points was given but their topological properties were
not specified. Going back to our concept of map, we have given a picture of the
territory, but we have not drawn the conceptual map. What we would like to make explicit is not only that the city has something to do with the lines on its perimeter,
but that it is the region inside them. Also it would be nice if we could reduce all
our lines to simple ones, our areas to simply connected and convex components, etc.
This can be achieved if we break our polygons into elements that are labelled specifically as line elements, our regions into area elements, etc. We can use these
simple building blocks for all our geometric manipulations and, later, reconstruct
the complete geometric objects as "vectors" built from elements which are no longer
points but those basic topological entities.

With points this is easy to do. A point is a point. Lines, as represented by polygons, can readily be broken into segments. A segment is the simple figure defined
by its two end points. Its properties are readily computed and the geometrical relationship between two segments, or a segment and a point are also trivial to investigate. Areas are not so obvious. We would like a surface element that can be used
to represent the interior of any line, that can do this without introducing any
superfluous point, and that is itself easy to describe. Moreover, we would want something that is in line with our previous definition of point and segments. The simplest answer is the triangle. It is given univocally by its three vertices, its
properties are simple, any surface can be divided into them, and this partition can
always be done using the existing vertices without introducing new ones.

Points, segments and triangles can be considered as building blocks for point sets,
lines and surfaces, and, it is clear that this procedure can be extended to any
number of dimensions, with volumes being decomposed into tetrahedrons, and higher
dimensional objects into generalized n-hedrons defined by sets of n-points. In this
way general lines become vectors of segments, areas, vectors of triangles, etc.

This representation is easily translated into algebraic notation. A segment is described by the two-dimensional algebraic vector of the indices of its end points, and
a triangle by a similar three-dimensional vector. These are the basic scalar elements. General objects can be broken into geometric "vectors" of these scalars and
represented by algebraic matrices. The column dimension of these matrices gives im-

mediately the category of the objects they represent. Thus, the river in figure 1 is given by the 5 x 2 matrix

$$RIVER \leftarrow \begin{matrix} 1 & 2 \\ 2 & 3 \\ 6 & 3 \\ 6 & 5 \\ 5 & 11. \end{matrix}$$

Each row represents a graphic scalar which contains two points and, therefore, corresponds to a segment. Thus, the object referenced is a line.

Note that now it is easy to distinguish between the coast line

$$COAST \leftarrow \begin{matrix} 11 & 12 \\ 11 & 19 \\ 19 & 14 \\ 14 & 13 \end{matrix}$$

and the ocean, which is given by (see figure 2)

$$SEA \leftarrow \begin{matrix} 11 & 12 & 19 \\ 19 & 14 & 13 \\ 19 & 12 & 13 \end{matrix}$$

It is seen now that an object needs for its definition two sets of data. First the universe, the list of points and its coordinates, has to be specified. This is the table given in figure 1, and may be common to several objects. In this particular example the same universe is used to describe the whole map which is, in general, an advantageous procedure since it avoids duplication of information, and by making explicit that two figures share a point in common, simplifies many of the operations between them. Second, for each object we need the matrix describing the components themselves, such as in the examples given above. This we will call the associated vector.

These two elements contain different kinds of information. The universe consists of coordinates and therefore relates mostly to the positional or metric aspects of the data. The associated vector contains the connections among the points and so describes the topological aspects of the map; it shows whether we are dealing with a line or a region, whether the object is connected or not, etc. In fact many geometrical questions can be answered without any reference to the metric information in the universe.

Consider now a map containing only lines. Using the code developed above, it can be represented by the set of points in its universe U, and the segments in its associated vector. A segment is just a pair of points in U x U and, therefore, our representation satisfies the algebraic definition of a graph. In fact we have set a correspondance between geometric segments and lines in the map, and edges and paths in an algebraic graph.

A hypergraph (Berge, 1973) is defined as a simple extension of a graph. We still keep the universe U, but the edges are taken not from the pairs in U^2 but from the n-tuples in U^n. Its properties are akin to those of classical graphs and they can be shown to form a boolean algebra when suitable operations are introduced. It should be clear at this point that our representation for areas and volumes was just a reduction of the topology of the set of significant points to a hypergraph. Thus, segments are edges of rank 2, triangles of rank 3, and so on.

We now introduce operations between our graphic scalar segments. Since they are just point sets, the meaning of union and intersection are obvious. Their implications are, however, of some interest.

Union, or cartesian product, is the tool we use to build higher rank objects from simple ones. Thus, a segment can be constructed as the union of two points, and a triangle as that of a point and a segment. A tretrahedron is formed either from a point and a triangle, or from two segments (figure 3).

Define rank, ρ, as the number of points in a scalar. This operator is most useful when used together with the intersection. Consider two scalars A and B, and define the dyadic rank as

$$A \rho B = \rho(A \cap B).$$

The two scalars would share a point, a segment, or nothing depending on whether $A \rho B$ is 1, 2 or 0 (see figure 4).

In fact this operation contains several of the questions normally asked about sets. Thus it is easy to see that two objects are connected iff

$$A \rho B \neq 0,$$

and that one is contained in the other,

$$A \subset B \quad \text{iff} \quad A \rho B = \rho A.$$

Actually all the operations on maps that do not depend on the coordinate of the points can be reduced to set operations on the associated vectors. We will refer to these manipulations that do not use the information in the map universe as topological. They act on the point set originally defined on the scheme, and map it into itself.

It is clear, however, that there exist geometrical manipulations that create new significant points and an obvious example is the intersection of two lines. The point of intersection of the segments is not needed to define any of the original lines but becomes significant after the intersection is carried out, and should be added to the universe. Thus we find the first example of a new kind of operations that we will call metric. The defining characteristic of this class is that it uses the positional information in the map universe. Although the operations in it are not as easily formalized as the topological ones they can be broadly divided into two types.

First we have the "Rubber-sheet" operations which are those modifying only the positions of the points without changing their topological structure. This class includes all the deformations allowed in classical topology, such as rotations, scale changes, point translations and stretchings. They form a closed group of operations that is both very simple and important. They do not use the information in the associated vector, and create no new points.

Second are operations which need both the universe and the associated vector. The most important one of this kind is the metric intersection or "cut". To understand it properly we need to look at our scalar elements in a new way. Take the triangle in figure 4. Up to now we have considered it as little more than a set of three points, but the space bounded by them is empty. The segments 1-4 and 2-3 do not intersect at 5, since this point is not included in the definition of any of them. When using metric operations, however, the space bounded by the points in the n-hedron is considered filled, and the figure becomes an "n-solid". Thus the "cut" of the "2-solids" 1-4 and 2-3 is the point 5, and the cut of the solid 1-4 with the "3-solid" 2-3-1 is the solid segment 1-5.

It is easy to see that the solid derived from a general n-hedron is always convex, and that all the possible (n-1)-faces and (n-2)-edges that can be defined among its points are indeed part of it. Thus the task of cutting two scalar n-solids or two general figures is reduced to a few simple operations.

A related question which is also considerably simplified by the convexity of the
scalar objects is whether a point is inside a figure or not. It is clear that in
general any operation on general objects can be reduced to manipulations on scalars
and simplified accordingly.

Some other basic operations have not been mentioned up to now but play an important
part in any practical system. Examples are those which compute properties of solids
such as lengths, areas and diameters. Another broad class is formed by the input-
output package needed to interact with some kind of graphic terminal. It is to be
noted that only the basic output operations have to be defined and that the facilities of the language can be used for most of the display activities.

THE GEL PACKAGE

All these ideas have been incorporated in an experimental subroutine package that
we call GEL (for GEometric Language). The package was first implemented as a set of
APL functions, and APL syntax was used as much as possible in the design of the
operations; this syntax has been used implicitly in the examples given in the previous section and has been conserved in later implementations of the package.

A unique universe, with an standard reserved name, was assumed to exist for all objects in the workspace and a new type of variable was introduced to accommodate the
associated vectors of individual objects. While APL was found to provide an ideal
environment for interactive work, a series of performance considerations, concerning so much the efficient utilization of CPU as the easy interaction with the files
needed in a data base, made us abandon this approach and recode the package as a
set of PL/I routines, an outline of whose structure, together with a list of the
most important functions, is given in table I. Most of this table is self-explana-
tory, except for the names of individual functions, but parts of it require some
comment.

It is very seldom that a map consists of just one geometric object. A typical
example might be a map of lakes in Finland, where each lake is an individual object,
an area, and the collection of all of them is the map. Since it is often useful to
operate with maps as single entities we have defined a new type of variable, the
collection of objects, which is essentially a list containing under a single name
a set of geometric objects, together with their attributes, possibly their names,
and auxilliary data which may be found useful in later processing. All functions
in the table have entries to operate on collections as well as on individual objects
and, when applicable, on geometric scalars, and a separate group, listed as "object management", has been provided to create, break up and combine the collections.
This group is not strictly geometric but is important in dealing with a data base.

The workspace functions assume that both the universe and the associated vectors
are in main memory, and thay can be used either to introduce (cvect) or extract
(vect) an object from a collection. Since elements in collections contain information regarding name and nongeometric properties and since geometric properties can
be computed using the GEL functions, this is enough to build all queries on objects
residing in the workspace. An special case has been found to be particularly useful
and a function (xtract) is provided for it; given a collection and a rectangular
window, it produces a new collection with those objects, or parts of objects, contained in the window.

Even if most of the GEL package assumes that the information resides in memory there
exist a small subset of disk functions whose purpose is to interact with a small
data base contained in disk, extract it and update it. These functions assume the
existance of three files, one containing the universe, another the objects and a
third one that contains data allowing us to stablish the correspondance between the

list of points in the universe in the data base and the extracted list in the workspace. When a collection of objects is extracted from disk in response to a query,
a function (xtrdsk) collects all the points contained in those objects and copies
them from the universe disk, adding them to the universe table in the workspace,
and, since in doing so the row indices of the points are changed, it also relabels
the objects copied from disk before adding them to the workspace. The correspondance
used in this relabelling is stored in a special file to be used in updating back
the data base (regen). Only two disk queries are supported at the moment, and they
are used to extract a workspace either by numerical key and name (look) or by key
and geometric window (vendsk).

The geometric functions were presented briefly in the last section but a couple of
high level functions can be cited here; the routine "fill" is used to produce an
area variable from the line variable difining its border (or a volume from its surface, etc), while the "border" function does the opposite operation. The function
"dist" computes non only the distance between points but the closest distance between two general objects and is used often in deciding whether two objects are in
a given neighbourhood of each other.

Finally the coding-decoding group provides an interface with the classical polygon
representation in which lines are given as lists of points. The "code" function
takes a polygon and produces a GEL line using as few points as possible while approximating the polygon to a given accuracy. The "decode" routine inverts the process
producing as many ordered polygons as disjoint parts there are in a GEL linear object.

An example of the use of this package in a pilot geographical project is given in
the next section.

AN EXPERIMENTAL APPLICATION

To provide a practical test for these ideas we have initiated a pilot project in
cooperation with the Spanish Geographical Institute, relating to the exploitation of
a small geographical data base for one province in Spain (Malaga). The original data
base contained roads, county lines, cities, canals, railroads, some land use and
geological information and statistical data relating to these features. The geometric data was given in the form of polygons and we have recoded it into GEL notation.
Since our interest was mainly in the geometric and map manipulation modules the data
base itself was simulated by two indexed files, one containing the geographical coordinates of the points in the "universe" and another containing the GEL objects, together with their names, statistical information, etc. As the user comes into the system his first task is to set a workspace containing an extract of the data base.
These extracted data are kept in main memory and constitute the material available
to the geometric module at any moment. More data can be added to the workspace along
the session, either as the result of a geometric operation or directly from the data
base, and there are options to delete selected data at some moments.

An object in the data base can be addressed either by name, by code (road, city, etc)
or by geographical location selecting an area on an interactive graphic terminal. An
object already in the workspace and displayed on the terminal can be identified in
addition by just pointing to it on the screen. A display module is available that is
used to display any object or collection. Different colours can be used for different
codes and the display zoomed on any selected part of the map. At present the system
supports two different terminals, a RAMTEK raster interactive color monitor and a
4015 TEKTRONIX black and white screen. Since all the geometric manipulations needed
for the display and the interactivity are done at the level of GEL objects, the
change of terminals implies only the substitution of a few basic gaphic access method
subroutines. Interaction with the system is achieved either through the terminal

keyboard or by pointing on the screen with a cursor. No effort has been done to optimize the data base access method and most of the classical questions (such as "all cities whose population is bigger than 100,000") are either not supported or answered in a relatively inefficient way. Considerable thought has been given, on the other hand, to the geometrical part of query computation ("All objects within a given neighbourhood of other object") and this part has been designed to be as independent as possible of the access method used. The whole system could thus be translated to serve a fairly generalized data base with relatively little effort, provided only that objects are coded in GEL notation.

Since one of our interests was to explore the interface between remote sensing and geometrical data bases, the display module includes an image manipulation option that displays parts of one or several raster coded images on the colour screen, together with objects from the workspace. The scale and orientation of the objects are then automatically adjusted to that of the image.

To this basic vehicle we have added two application programs. These programs were written using GEL notation and functions, and interact with the data base through the workspace. These applications were developed in answer to needs detected through the use of the original system and it is significant thay they were developed in a relatively short time (3 months). We believe this to be due in part to the fact that most geometrical questions were already solved by the subroutines in GEL. These applications are described below.

The graphic editor

A problem that appears very often in data base management is the correction of data errors, and, when these data are geometric, especial tools are needed for the correction. Geometric errors are introduced at many stages in data capture and manipulation and are very difficult to avoid. Typical examples are digitization inaccuracies resulting in secondary roads which do not intersect the main highway, coastal cities that lie on the ocean, etc. The correction of these problems can be attempted either automatically or interactively.

Our experience is that it is practically impossible to devise an automatic editor able to predict all, or even most of the possible inconsistencies that may appear on a map. Even when such a map is displayed several times, using different scales and color codes, it is often hard for a human observer to decide what is wrong and how it can be fixed. Our approach has been to use automatic checks to point to problem areas in the map, usually inconsistencies in the connectivity of a given element, and then use an interactive graphic editor to further isolate and correct the problem.

To use the editor an object is chosen and displayed on the screen together with neighbouring objects that might be useful to aid the correction. This display can be changed as many times as required to isolate details or to get a different vision of the map. The editor functions can then be used on the chosen object and finally the result can be replaced on the data base if the modification is felt to be successfull. A list of the editor functions might be of some interest and is given here:

- Change the geographical coordinate of a point in the "universe".

- Change all the pointers referring to a given point to a different, existing point. All segments containing the old point are changed to contain the new one.

- Include a new point in a segment, thus breaking it into two segments.

- Erase a point from an object, together with all segments containing it.

- Add a new point, and possibly a new segment.

- Delete a segment.
- Enlarge an object by the addition of other objects.
- Erase an object.
- Rename an object.

These functions can all be used interactively, normally using inputs given through the cursor. We have used the editor to correct the geographical inconsistencies in our data base and some of the functions mentioned above are the result of that experience. Naturally, although our data are now consistent there is no guaranty that their geographical accuracy is better than it was. This is probably a limitation common to all editors.

Image vectorization

The graphic editor was developed in view of the large amount of errors present in the data originally provided to us by the Geographical Institute. These data were digitized from a printed (1:200,000) map by an skilled operator using a good quality digitizing table, and they probably represent the best possible accuracy attainable from the original material. The average positional error of the points was estimated from such things as the mismatch of common borders in adjacent counties and found to be of the order of 200 m, corresponding to .8 mm in the original lines. To avoid these errors as far as possible we have started an experiment directed towards extracting digitized lines directly from thematic LANDSAT images or from digitized photographs of printed maps. The idea is to extract contours from specific classes in the image, segment these contours into disjoint closed curves and reduce the areas within them to GEL-coded objects.

The process begins by selecting a subset and a class on the thematic image and producing a binary subimage of the chosen class against all other. Next an edge detection and line following algorithm (Montoto, 1977) are applied to this image to extract the borders of the class in the form of a set of arcs of consecutive points. These arcs do not form continuous closed curves because the line following algorithm is sensitive to noise and is unable to follow the borders without occasional errors. The arcs are approximated by polygons and coded as GEL lines, and a syntactic module then tries to join them into longer lines according to the proximity of their endpoints and to their connectivity.

All this process is automatic except for the initial choices of subset and class and for an interactive adjustement of the polygonalization threshold. As a result the contours are generally reduced to two or three long arcs per area. The final adjustement is done using the graphic editor.

As noted before land use maps, which are the main results of LANDSAT data are complicated and have a high fractal dimension. Because of this the coding of an image produces a large number of individual small areas. We routinely smooth the classification images to clean them from small "islands" and "lakes" and the syntactic module erases isolated arcs that cannot be joined to neighbouring ones and are shorter than a given length. This is consistent with the approximation of lines by polygons. With these precautions it is possible to get reasonable vectorizations of thematic images coded as geometric objects, with errors that usually do not exceed 2 pixels; on a LANDSAT image this is equivalent to about 100 m.

CONCLUSIONS

Our experimental data base covers an area of about 8000 Km^2, approximately 100 x 160 Km in outline, and containing some 650 geographic objects of 20 different classes. These objects were originally given by the Geographic Institute in some 35000 points with a precision that was estimated in 200 m, and, using the "code" facility with an approximation threshold of 100 m, we recoded them into 5500 points. This information is enough to contain all major physical and political features in the area and can be stored in two files occupying less than 80 Kbytes. This size is small enough that it can be managed into a memory workspace and that the response time of the system is reasonably short. Even in cases in which the data base contains many more objects it is unlikely that a single map may need a much larger workspace. If this proves to be true, the only mission of the data base access method will be the extraction of the workspace plus all the classical, non-geometric query processing.

This is probably also true in spaces with higher dimensionality in which geometric processing is likely to take a larger part of the query computation, but where the volume of information should not be expected to be much larger than in two dimensions.

A major unsolved problem that is not treated in this paper is the management of image data were geometric processing is easy, but the volume of data is huge. We have shown, on the other hand, that properly coded vectorized data can be treated easily and economically.

REFERENCES

Berge, C. (1973), "Graphs and Hypergraphs". North Holland, Amsterdam.

Borges, J.L. (1972), "Historia Universal de la infamia". Alianza Editorial, Madrid.

Hack, J.T. (1957), "Studies of longitudinal stream in Virginia and Maryland". US Geolog. Surv. Prof. Paper 294-B.

Mandelbrot, B.B. (1977), "Fractals, form, chance and dimensions". Freeman and Co., San Francisco.

Montoto, L. (1977), "Digital Detections of linear Features in satellite imagery". Proc. Int. Symp. on Image Processing, Graz, pp. 149-153.

Richardson, L.F. (1961), "The problem of contiguity", General System Year-book 6, pp. 139-187.

Robinson, A.H., Petchenick, B.B. (1976), "The Nature of Maps". The University of Chicago Press, Chicago.

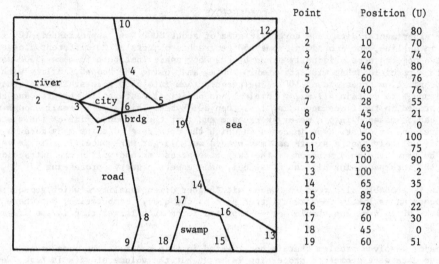

Point	Position (U)	
1	0	80
2	10	70
3	20	74
4	46	80
5	60	76
6	40	76
7	28	55
8	45	21
9	40	0
10	50	100
11	63	75
12	100	90
13	100	2
14	65	35
15	85	0
16	78	22
17	60	30
18	45	0
19	60	51

Figure 1. The Scheme of a map and its universe

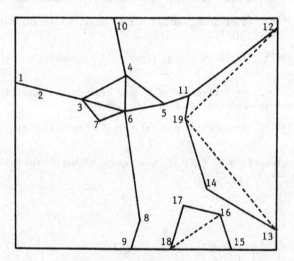

Figure 2. The objects broken into their basic
scalar components.

231

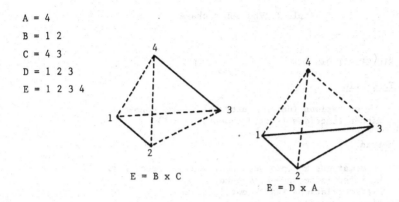

A = 4
B = 1 2
C = 4 3
D = 1 2 3
E = 1 2 3 4

E = B x C

E = D x A

Figure 3. The product of low rank objects can be used to
create more complicated ones.

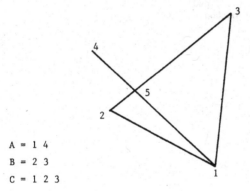

A = 1 4
B = 2 3
C = 1 2 3

Figure 4. The topological scalars A & C have only the point 1 in common.
The corresponding metrical objects cut at the segment 1-5.

Table I: The GEL package

GEOMETRIC OPERATIONS

   a) <u>Topologic</u>

       Set operations (union, intersect, rank, connect)
       Higher functions (sect, segment, border)

   b) <u>Metric</u>

       Deformations and projections (escala, presc, desc)
       Measures (size, grank, wbound)
       Dyadic relations (dist, cut, inside)
       Higher functions (fill)

OBJECT MANAGEMENT

       Workspace functions (vect, cvect, xtract)
       Disk functions (regen, xtrdsk, look, vendsk)

DISPLAY

       Object display (phd, psd)
       Terminal access method.

CODING/DECODING

       Code
       Decode.

CANONICAL GEOMETRIC MODELING
FOR
COMPUTER AIDED DESIGN

Hideo Matsuka
Sakae Uno

Abstract

The objective of this paper is to describe a unified and flexible geometric model which is called a canonical geometric model.

The canonical geometric model is composed of three models:

(1) wire-frame model
(2) area model
(3) volume model

These models are canonically represented in the form of a directed graph using a relational model and are accessed through a geometric model handler. They are applicable to various computer aided design systems and manipulated by an application program and by a designer at a graphic device.

This canonical geometric model has been utilized in many application areas; topography, landscaping, and office building design.

Tokyo Scientific Center
IBM Japan, Ltd.
1-4-34 Roppongi, Minatoku
Tokyo 106, Japan

1. INTRODUCTION

The design of large modern structures is a top-down process from conception to detail specification, involving many engineers. To design an object throughout its development phases, or to transmit information of the design object to many designers, systematic and flexible geometric modeling of the structures become extremely important. The term, ''geometric modeling'', was first used in 1976 by the CAM-I project in the U.S.A. The objective of this modeling technique was to specify the description and manipulation of the shape of machine parts. We define 'geometric modeling' as the description, representation and manipulation of the shapes, not only of machine parts, but of many kinds of objects.

1.1 CLASSIFICATION OF OBJECTS TO BE DESIGNED

All objects to be designed are viewed from two spaces: 'existence space' and 'material space'. 'Existence space' is the Euclidean space in which the objects exist and it is either 2 dimensional (2-D) space or 3 dimensional (3-D) space. 'Material space' is the space that represents the structure of the objects. It has wire-frame, area (region, surface) and volume (solid, compartment) structures. Table 1 shows how the objects are viewed from these two spaces.

Table 1.   CLASSICATION OF OBJECTS

Material Space Existence Space	wire frame	area	volume
2-dimensional	W2	A2	--
3-dimensional	W3	A3	V3

Examples
W2: wire printing, plate or sheet shape, engineering drawing
A2: house layout, plant layout, building floor plan, land use/district
W3: piping, frame structure (tower, building, etc.)
A3: land form, hull or shell structure (vehicle body, etc.)
V3: machine parts (solid), building room, ship compartment (compartment)

For example, engineering drawings belong to the category of 2-D wire-frame structures, shapes of automobile bodies to 3-D area structures, frames of steel structures to 3-D wire-frame structures. Once a structure is represented in a computer, it is called a 'model'.

235

1.2 DEMANDS FOR GEOMETRIC MODELING

As an example, consider a design object, a beam, which is primarily a volume structure. It could be a wire-frame or area structure, depending on the designer's intention. The beam's cross section shape is the polygon shown in Fig. 1.

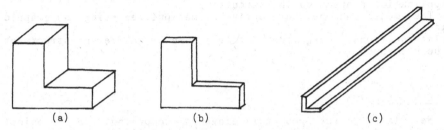

(a)   (b)   (c)

Fig. 1 CHANGE OF OBJECT BY ASPECT RATIO

When its width, length and height are approximately equal as in 1(a), it is abstracted to a volume model. When the width of the beam is smaller as in 1(b), it is abstracted to a 2-D area model. However, when the width is relatively bigger as in 1(c), it is abstracted to a 3-D wire-frame model.

Thus, the design objectives should be considered together with the shape when an object is abstracted. The usual modeling techniques which were developed in the past (CRAFT(Armour,1963), DIME(IBM,1973), TIPS-1(Okino,1973), PADL(Voelcker,1977), BUILD(Braid,1973), GEOMAP(Hosaka,1977), GBUILD(Reinschmidt,1970), CASGAP(Carlson,1974)), were sufficient if an object were represented with one concept of abstraction throughout whole design process.

However, the structure of an object changes through its design phases. In addition, a realistic object has a complex structure compounded of three structures. Under the usual modeling techniques, it could be difficult to map one model into another model, or to calculate an intersection between different type structures. These problems arise because these geometric modeling techniques have their own different representations and algorithms which depend on on the processing method. For these reasons, the usual geometric modeling techniques should be reconsidered.

2. CANONICAL GEOMETRIC MODELING

We do not build an individual geometric model which depends on any particular application. Instead, we propose a canonical geometric model, under which design objects with different characteristics can be processed in a common way. This canonical geometric model can uniformly represent each of the three types of structures: wire-frame, area andvolume structures shown in Table 1. We use a relational data model as the basis for this geometric model since this is simpler and more powerful than others.

The canonical geometric model has the following characteristics:

(1) Shapes of objects of wire-frame, area and volume structures can be canonically modeled in the form of a directed graph.
(2) The model is adaptable to fit individual applications.
(3) The model can be easily accessed from an application program through a geometric model handler.
(4) The model can be dynamically defined, deleted and modified from an application program during execution.
(5) The model can be interactively manipulated using a graphic device.
(6) Intersections among models of the same or different structures can be processed.

2.1 REPRESENTATION

We classify the geometric elements composing the canonical geometric model into four classes: 'vertex', 'edge', 'face' and 'body'. Within these classes, there are many legions. For example, edge has legions as follows:

```
(class)edge : (legion) line (infinite straight line)
                     offset (sequence of line segments)
                     circle (arc)
                     etc.
```

The wire-frame model is composed of geometric elements in vertex and edge classes, and the area model is expressed by those in the vertex, edge and face classes. The volume model needs the elements in the body class in addition to the elements representing the area model.

Now, to build the canonical model, we need four kinds of relations: attribute, link, set and group relations.

(A) Attribute Relation

This relation is a set containing only geometric elements of the same legion. For each legion of geometric element, one relation is defined, as shown in Table 2. Its columns contain geometric properties of an element. These properties are expressed in (x,y) space when it is in 2-D space, and (x,y,z) space when in 3-D space. This relation can have attribute columns other than geometric property ones. For example, a column of edge style can be added to the attribute relation to indicate output style (dashed line, dotted line and so on) to graphic devices. Geometric elements needed for a class are application dependent and not defined a priori. Although the system does not limit the number of geometric elements, the representation of a newly defined legion should be compatible with a convention of the structure proposed here.

Table 2 GEOMETRIC ELEMENTS

	Geometric Element	Example
	PONT (Point) Column: x,y,z Coord.	• (x,y,z)

Vertex	GRID (Grid Point)
	  Column: Grid Base Key
	       i,j,k No.
	- - - - - - - - - - - - - - - - - -
	GRBS (Grid Base)
	  Column: dx, dy, dz Span
	       x,y,z Origin
	       θ,φ,ψ Rotation
		(i,j,k)

Edge	LINE (Straight Line)
	  Column: l,m,n Direction Cosine
	       x,y,z Pass Point
		n m l (x,y,z)

	CRCL (Circle)
	  Column: Radius
	       x,y,z Center Coord.
	       l,m,n Normal Vector
		(l,m,n) r (x,y,z)

	OFST (Offset)
	  Column: Points No.
	       LKOF Start, End Key
	       Xmin,Xmax,Ymin,Ymax,Zmin,Zmax
	- - - - - - - - - - - - - - - - - -
	LKOF (Auxiliary OFST)
	  Column: Forward, Backward Key
	       x,y,z Coord	

	:	:

Face	PLNE (Plane)
	  Column: l,m,n Normal Vector
	       x,y,z Pass Point
		(l,m,n) (x,y,z)

	FCYL (Cylinder Surface)
	  Column: Radius
	       l,m,n Normal Vector
	       x,y,z Center Coord.
		t s r (x,y,z)

	COON (Coons Surface)
	  Column: x,y Grid No.
	       LKCN Start Key
	       Grid Base Key
	       Zmin, Zmax
	- - - - - - - - - - - - - - - - - -
	LKCN (Auxiliary COON)
	  Column: COON Key
	       i,j Array
	       Coons Equations Coef.	

(B) Link Relation

This relation expresses topological relationship between different classes of geometric elements. There are three possible link relations.

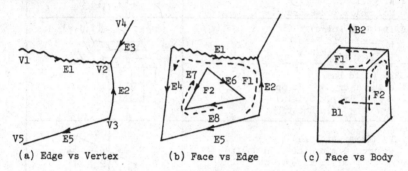

(a) Edge vs Vertex   (b) Face vs Edge   (c) Face vs Body

Fig. 2 RELATIONSHIP AMONG GEOMETRIC ELEMENTS

E-VV relation, which shows relationship between edge and vertex, has 6-degree columns composed of edge-legion, edge-key, start vertex-legion, start vertex-key, end vertex-legion and end vertex-key. An example of the relation is shown in the Table 3(a) which corresponds to Fig. 2(a).

F-EE relation expresses connection of a face and its surrounding edges and has six columns: face-legion, face-key, edge-legion, edge-key, next adjacent-key and back adjacent-key. Since the number of surrounding edges is not fixed, it is difficult for boundary information of the face to be expressed within a tuple. Therfore, a tuple of the F-EE relation expresses one of surrounding edges of the face and the whole information of surrounding edges is expressed by the same number of tuples as edges. Edge order information is expressed by 'next adjacent-key' column. A value in its column is a pointer to another edge which is counterclockwise adjacent to it, if these edges are the outer boundary of the face in the 'face-key' column. As for the inner boundary of the face, the next adjacent-key means a clockwise one. The adjacent information of an edge (next/back adjacent-key) may seem useless, but it provides an efficient way to search for the boundary edges. If a direction of an edge is not same as the loop direction of a face, the edge key is described with minus sign. In order to represent a face composing a 'lake' or an 'island', an auxilary LKFC relation is added to this relation. Table 3(b) shows an example of relations corresponding to Fig. 2(b).

F-BB relation expresses the relationship between face and body. This relation has six columns: face-legion, face-key, outer body-legion (space in direction of face-vector), outer body-key, inner body-legion and inner body-key. An example is shown in Table 3(c) and Fig. 2(c).

Table 3 LINK RELATION

```
+----+
!E-VV!     (a) Relationship between Edge and Vertex
+----+------------+------------+-----------+
     !    Edge    !Start Vertex!End Vertex !
     +------+----+------+----+------+----+
     !Legion! Key! Legion! Key!Legion! Key!
     +------+----+------+----+------+----+
     !  OFST!  1!  PONT!   1! PONT !  1 !
     !  CRCL!  2!  PONT!   3! PONT !  2 !
     !  LINE!  3!  PONT!   4! PONT !  2 !
     !  LINE!  5!  PONT!   3! PONT !  5 !
     +------+----+------+----+------+----+
```

```
+----+
!F-EE!     (b) Relationship between Face and Edge
+----+------------+------------------+---------+
     !          !          !Next     !Back     !
     !  Face    !  Edge    !Adjacent !Adjacent !
     +------+----+------+----+---------+---------+
     !Legion! Key!Legion! Key!   Key   !   Key   !
     +------+----+------+----+---------+---------+
     ! PLNE !  1 !OFST ! -1 !    2    !    4    !
     ! PLNE !  1 !LINE !  4 !    3    !    1    !
     ! PLNE !  1 !LINE ! -5 !    4    !    2    !
     ! PLNE !  1 !CRCL !  2 !    1    !    3    !
     !  ..  ! .. ! ..  ! .. !   ..    !   ..    !
     ! PLNE !  1 !LINE !  6 !   10    !   11    !
     ! PLNE !  1 !LINE !  8 !   11    !    9    !
     ! PLNE !  1 !LINE ! -7 !    9    !   10    !
     ! PLNE !  2 !LINE ! -6 !   13    !   14    !
     ! PLNE !  2 !LINE !  7 !   14    !   12    !
     ! PLNE !  2 !LINE ! -8 !   12    !   13    !
     +------+----+------+----+---------+---------+
```

```
+----+
!LKFC!
+----+------------+-----------+
     !   Face     !F-EE Start !
     +------+----+-----------+
     !Legion! Key!    Key    !
     +------+----+-----------+
     ! PLNE !  1 !      1    !
     ! PLNE !  1 !      9    !
     ! PLNE !  2 !     12    !
     +------+----+-----------+
```

```
+----+
!F-BB!     (c) Relationship between Face and Body
+----+------------+------------+-----------+
     !   Face     !Outer Body !Inner BODY !
     +------+----+------+----+------+----+
     !Legion! key!Legion! key!Legion! key!
     +------+----+------+----+------+----+
     ! PLNE !  1 ! OBJC !  2 ! OBJC !  1 !
     ! PLNE !  2 ! OBJC !  1 ! OBJC !  2 !
     +------+----+------+----+------+----+
```

(C) Set Relation

There are four pairs of set relations corresponding to four classes: vertex, edge, face and body. Each pair is in the form of (a, b), where a= a relation of set names, and b= a relation of all members in these sets. An example of the set relations is shown in Table 4 and Fig. 3.

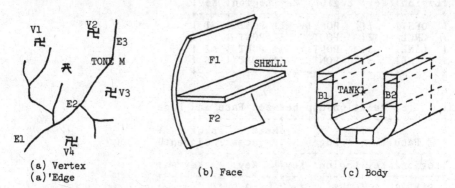

(a) Vertex
(a)'Edge

(b) Face

(c) Body

Fig. 3 EXAMPLE OF GEOMETRIC ELEMENTS SET

(D) Group Relation

This relation is a catalog of relation names representing wire-frame, area or volume model. For example, as shown in Table 5, a wire-frame structure is expressed by vertex relations, edge relations, E-VV link relation, vertex set and edge set relations. The names of these relations are stored in a group relation. In the area structure, attribute relations for face, F-EE link relation and face set relations are necessary in addtion to what needed in the wire-frame structure. In the volume structure, attribute for body, F-BB and body set relations additionally. It has some columns expressing user's name, transformation matrix, unit and so on, in addition to relation names. This is a sort of user's directory of the whole relations composing geometric model and is used to activate or deactivate the whole relations in one tuple identified by user's name.

Table 4   SET RELATIONS

(a)   Vertex   Set

!VSET!

Vertex Name	Usage
SYMBOL1	TEMPLE
SYMBOL2	TEMPLE

!LKVS!

Vertex Set		Sub Vertex	
Key		Legion	Key
1		PONT	1
1		PONT	3
1		PONT	2
1		PONT	4

(a)'   Edge   Set

!ESET!

Edge Name	Usage
TONE.M	RIVER

!LKES!

Edge Set		Sub Edge	
Key		Legion	Key
1		OFST	1
1		OFST	2
1		OFST	3

(b)   Face   Set

!FSET!

Face Name	Usage
SHELL1	SHELL

!LKFS!

Face Set		Sub face	
Key		Legion	Key
1		FCYL	1
1		FCYL	2

(c)   Body   Set

!BSET!

Body Name	Usage
TANK1	OIL

!LKBS!

Body Set		Sub Body	
Key		Legion	Key
1		OBJC	1
2		OBJC	2

Table 5 A GROUP RELATION

(a) Wire-frame Model

```
+----+
!WIR3!
+----+----+----+----+----+----+----+----+----+----+----+----+
     !NAME!VRTX!VSET!LKVS!PONT!GRID!GRBS!EDGE!ESET!LKES! .. !
     +----+----+----+----+----+----+----+----+----+----+----+
+----+
!WIR2!
+----+----+----+----+----+----+----+----+----+----+----+----+----+
    !NAME!VRTX!VSET!LKVS!PNT2!GRD2! .. !*XCO!*YCO!*THT!*SCL! .. !
    +----+----+----+----+----+----+----+----+----+----+----+----+
```

(b) Face Model

```
+----+
!FAC3!
+----+----+----+----+----+----+----+----+----+----+----+
     !NAME! .. !FACE!FSET!LKFS!F-EE!LKFC!OBJC!PLNE!FCYL! .. !
     +----+----+----+----+----+----+----+----+----+----+----+
+----+
!FAC2!
+----+----+----+----+----+----+----+----+----+----+----+----+
    !NAME! .. !GRB2!EDGE!ESET!LKES!E-VV!LIN2!CRC2!OFS2!LKO2! .. !
    +----+----+----+----+----+----+----+----+----+----+----+----+
```

(c) Body Model

```
+----+
!BODY!
+----+----+----+----+----+----+----+----+----+----+----+----+
    !NAME! .. !BODY!BSET!LKBS!F-BB!*XCO!*YCO!*ZCO!*THT!*PHI! .. !
    +----+----+----+----+----+----+----+----+----+----+----+----+
```

2.2 MANIPULATION

The canonical geometric model can be accessed through CALL statements by a geometric model handler. Functions of the geometric model handler are as follows:

(1) Define/delete geometric element
   -to define/delete some tuples of attribute, link and set relations related to one geometric element.

(2) Read/write attribute data in a relation.

(3) Find explicit relationships among geometric elements.
   -to find geometric elements, such as both-ends of an edge, all edges sorrounding a face or bodies separated by a face directly from link relation.
   -to search and find geometric elements such as all edges crossing at a vertex, faces separated by an edge and all faces enclosing a body indirectly from link relation.

(4) Find implicit relationship among geometric elements
   -to get relationship of vertex vs vertex, vertex vs edge, vertex

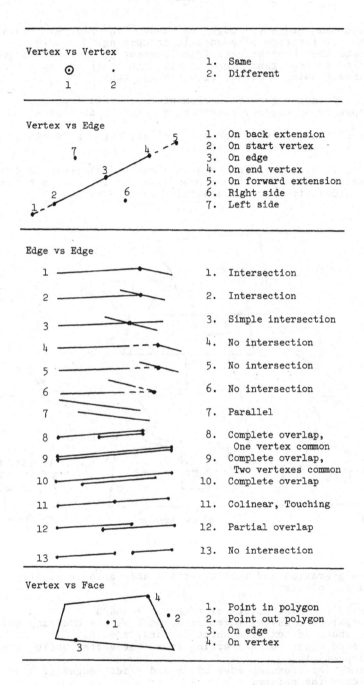

Fig. 4 IMPLICIT RELATIONSHIP BETWEEN GEOMETRIC ELEMENTS
(TWO DIMENSIONAL SPACE)

vs face and edge vs edge as shown in Fig. 4. This is a
fundamental function of geometric processing.
-to find the closest geometric element to a given coordinate.
This is an important funcion in the case of an interactive
environment using a direct view storage tube.

(5) Separate/combine geometric elements with same legion
  -to sepatate an edge by a vertex, a face by an edge and a body by
  a face.
  -to combine edges connected by a vertex, faces adjacent by an edge
  and bodies connected by a face.

(6) Execute a set operation between geometric elements in 2-D space
   Geometric elements can be processed by logical set operation,
that is, union/difference/intersection as in Fig. 5.

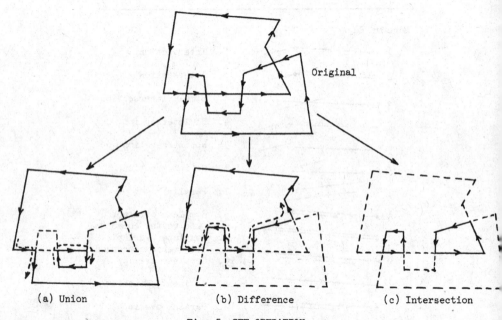

(a) Union   (b) Difference   (c) Intersection

Fig. 5 SET OPERATION

   Union operation of the objects A and B in Fig. 5(a) will be
processed as follows:

  (i) Find crossing points of edges of A and B.
  (ii) Separate crossing edges of A and B at the crossing points.
  (iii) Find a vertex of A which is outside of B.
  (iv) Trace edges of A starting from the vertex up to one of the
  crossing points.
  (v) Find the crossing edge of B and trace edges of B up to the
  other crossing points.
  (vi) Find the crossing edge of A and trace edge of A up to start
  point.

(vii) Erase name A and B and give a new name C.

The operation of difference is the same process as union, except that the edges of B are traced clockwise. In case of intersection, it is similar to union, except that tracing starts from a vertex of A which is inside of B.

(7) Calculate characteristics of geometric element
   -to calculate length, area, volume, center of gravity and so on.
   -to calculate extremes, inflexions, cols and so on.
   -to interpolate and fair edges and areas (surface).

(8) Process group relation
   -to activate or deactivate a group relation.
   -to include/exclude another group relation in/from the activated group relation.
   -to copy all relations in one group relation to another group relation.
   -to extract a wire-frame or area model from a volume model, and a wire-frame model from an area model.
   -to generate an area model from a wire-frame model, and a volume model from an area model.
      Automatic generation from a wire-frame model to a volume model is impossible in general. However, if a surface is reprsented by wire-frame on each cross section, this wire-frame model could be converted into a 3-D area model. If an object is specified uniquely by plan, elevation and side views (2-D area models), a volume model could be generated from these 2-D area models.
   -to transform a volume model into a 2-D area or a 2-D wire-frame model, a 3-D area model into a 2-D area or a 2-D wire-frame model and a 3-D wire-frame model into a 2-D wire-frame by projection (orthographic, oblique, or perspective projections).

3. ACCESS METHOD USED FOR CANONICAL GEOMETRIC MODEL

For DB handling of the geometric model mentioned in the preceeding sections, an access method named BAsic Relational Table Handler(BARTH) has been used. BARTH is application independent and self-consistent. It is a rapid access method suitable for use in a conversational application. It provides tuple-wise operations and runs under VM/CMS and TSO (Uno,1975).

A relation is named by a Relation IDentifier(RID) and a tuple by a Tuple IDentifier(TID). The RID and the TID are assigned by BARTH when the relation is created and the tuple is inserted, respectively. A control relation named the Master Relation(MR) is introduced to manage relations. A tuple in the MR contains infomation about a relation. A RID of a relation is a pointer to such a tuple in the MR, which describes the relation. This mechanism is shown in Fig. 6. On the other hand, a TID of a tuple in a relation is a serial tuple number within the relation. Thus, the identifiers allow direct access to the relation or the tuple.

Since the cardinality of a relation is unfixed, a paging technique is employed. If tuples are inserted beyond the page capacity, a new page is allocated to the relation. Tuples are consecutively stored within a page according to the order of the TID's. It is noted that any page can contain only a single relation to assure the consecutiveness of tuples. This mechanism provides rapid retrieval of a tuple through scanning a relation. The size of a page is installation dependent. All the accessible relations are brought into main storage. This has a problem when a relation is extremely large, or when too many relations are accessible.

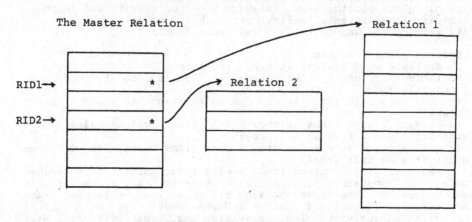

Fig. 6 RELATION CONTROL MECHANISM

Recently RIX (IMS/VS Relational Interface Extension) was developed by IBM Japan as a Country Implemented Program. This is a sub-system of IMS/VS and complements its functions. It enables both the hierarchical and the extended relational models to co-exist. All operations, including definition, deletion of a relation and retrieval, are executed by CALL statements from a user's PL/I or FORTRAN program (IBM Japan,1978). RIX is one of the most suitable data bases to build the canonical geometric model.

4. APPLICATION

The canonical geometric model is applicable to various kinds of CAD application areas. The following are some examples employing the canonical geometric model.

(A) Map/ Topography

Here we show overlayed pictures produced by processing simultaneously many kinds of models. For example, topographical information expresses terrain, land-use, administrative boundaries, public service utility network and so on. Terrain information can be represented in a 3-D area model, land-use in a 2-D area model, public utility network in a 3-D wire-frame model. When one model is activated, intersection between the model and another model can be processed by using the inclusion function in the geometric model handler

References

/1/ Armour, C., and Buff, B. (1963). A Heuristic Algorithm and Simulation Approach to Relative Location of Facilities, Management Science, Vol. 9, No.2.

/2/ Braid, I.C., and Lang, C.A. (1973). Computer-Aided Design of Mechanical Components with Volume Building Bricks, Proc. of 2nd PROLAMAT 73.

/3/ Carlson, C.M. and Cebulski, D.R. (Oct. 1974). Computer Aided Ship Arrangement Design, Naval Engineers Journal.

/4/ Feder, A. (Aug. 1975). Test Results on Computer Graphics Productivity for Aircraft Design and Fabrication, AIAA 1975 Aircraft Systems and Technology Meeting.

/5/ Hattori, S. (1971). Graphic Processing for Ship Lofting, NKK Report, No.54. (in Japanese).

/6/ Hosaka, M., and Kimura, F. (1977). Geometrical Processing with Interactive Graphics, Proc. of 3rd European Electro-Optics Conference, SPIE.

/7/ Hosaka, M., and Kimura, F. (Aug. 1977). An Interactive Geometrical Design Systems and Technology Meeting.

/8/ IBM Federal System Division (Nov.,1973), Impact Zoning Requirement Analysis, Vol.2.

/9/ IBM Japan (July, 1978). IMS/VS Relational Interface Extension: User's guide, N:SB10-6969(in Japanese).

/10/ Matsuka, H., Kawai, T. and Uno, S. (June, 1975). Integrated Designer's Activity Support System for Architecture, Proc. of the 12th DA Conference, SIGDA.

/11/ Okino, n. and Kubo, H. (1973). Technical Information System for Computer-Aided Design, Drawing and Manufacturing, Proc. of 2nd PROLAMAT 73.

/12/ Reinschmidt, K.F. (1970). Building Data Management, R70-55, Civil Engineering System Lab. MIT.

/13/ Sutherland, W.R. (1966). On Line Graphical Specification of Computer Procedures, Tech. Rep. 405, Lincoln Lab. MIT.

/14/ Uno, S., and Matsuka, H. (Aug. 1979). A General Purpose Graphic System for Computer Aided Design, 6th Annual Conference on Computer Graphics and Interactive Techiques, SIGGRAPH.

/15/ Uno, S. (1975). Basic Relational Table Handler, TSC Report, GE18-1816, IBM Japan.

/16/ Voelcker, H.B., and Reguicha, A.G. (Dec. 1977). Gemetric Modelling of Mechanical Parts and Processes, Computer, Vol. 10, No. 12.

Fig. 7 shows an isometric picture produced from both terrain and land-use information. Fig. 8 shows a thematic map retrieved from the topographic information.

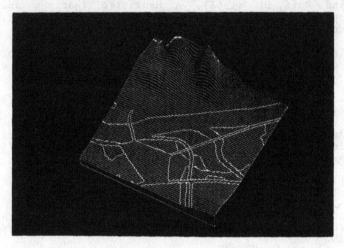

Fig.7 TOPOGRAPHY

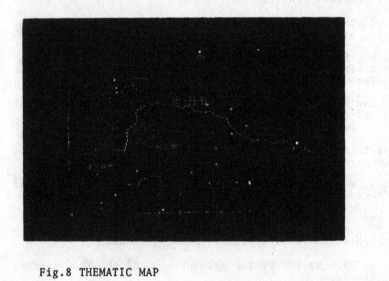

Fig.8 THEMATIC MAP

(B) Landscape

This example introduces an advanced technique of external representation of the model. A volume model representing designed objects can be projected into a 2-D area model. When the face relation has attribute data expressing color or texture, a user can hatch or color each face in a simple manipulation. In a more complex manipulation, he can put an extracted texture pattern on each face. In Figs. 9 and 10, objects which are generated from a volume model, are laid over a scenery photograph.

Fig.9 URBAN LANDSCAPE

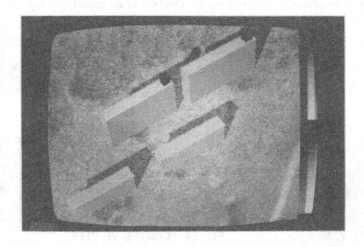

Fig.10 RESIDENTIAL LANDSCAPE

(C) Office Building

Here, we show some trials to extend the canonical geometric model. One is to admit parametric representation in the model and another is to introduce a bill of material (BM).

A standardized office building or a prefabricated house is constructed by standard parts. There are many parts whose topological structures are same but whose dimensions are different. Therfore, the cannonical geometric model is extended to permit parametric representation of dimensions. When a designer selects a part with parametric representation, it is converted into normal reprsentation. Now, he can manipulate the part with dimensions on a schematic floor plan, checking the tolerance among parts. As a result, information on part name and its location is stored into the BM.

Figs. 11 and 12 show shapes of standard parts generated from parametric representation. Figs. 13,14,15 and 16 show a configuration of a building designed by these parts.

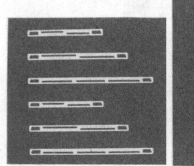 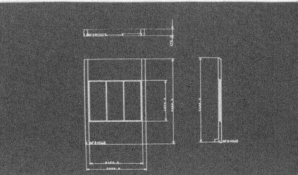

Fig.11 STANDARD PARTS   Fig.12 ENGINEERING DRAWING

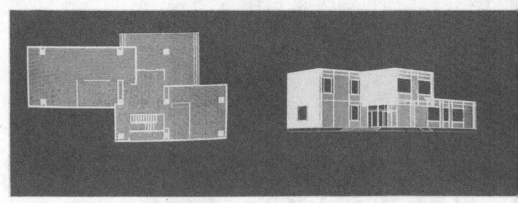

Fig.13 FLOOR PLAN   Fig.14 PERSPECTIVE VIEW

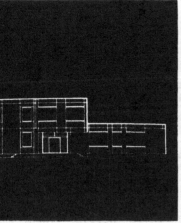
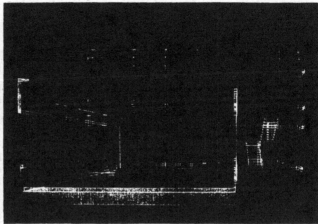

Fig.15 FRONT VIEW   Fig.16 CROSS SECTION VIEW

5. CONCLUDING REMARKS

Although many CAD systems have been implemented in the world, the majority of the systems are designed to solve specific problems and are not equipped with flexible and expandable functions. Therefore, the specific sysetm prevents itself from growing and establishing a total engineering system.

The canonical geometric model proposes a remarkable notion on design of an engineering application system. To establish an application system, a most suitable model structure can be selected. According to the structure, relations to be used and their columns are determined. This model is manipulated uniformly, and is displayed as a wire-frame picture or a full color image onto many kinds of graphic devices.

Today, we have been developing a CAD system named Advanced-IDAS for topography, road, building and so on using the canonical geometric model (Matsuka,1975), (Uno,1979). The model will be evaluated and enhanced through various kinds of CAD applications.

We hope that the notion of the canonical geometric model will be widely adopted in a variety of CAD systems.

Appendix

STATUS OF THE GEOMETRIC MODELING TECHNIQUES

We classified objects to be designed into two spaces as Table 1. Along this classification, we review usual geometric modeling techniques which have been developed.

(1) Wire-frame model

A wire-frame model is represented by infromation of edge segments and their topological relationships. This model has been widely used in computer graphics after SKECHPAD (Sutherland, 1963) was developed.

A typical example of a 2-D wire-frame model is GLOFT, that deals with the shapes of steal plates composing ship-hulls (Hattori, 1969). And a 3-D wire-frame model is used in CADAM for general engineering drawings (Lockheed, 1967).

(2) Area model

A area model represents the shape of faces encompassed by boundary edge segments. There are two possible area models: a 2-D area model (regional model) dealing with area structure in 2-D space and a 3-D area model (surface model) dealing with area structure in 3-D space.

The regional model has two representational methods. One method is to represent the shapes of the face in the form of grids. The other is to represent them in terms of boundary edge segments in the form of directed graph. The former was used in CRAFT (Armour, Buff, 1963) for room arrangements, SYSMAP (Harvard Labo, 1968) for districts and regional maps. The latter method was implemented in IDAS-A (Matsuka, 1975) and DIME (IBM, 1973).

The surface model mathematically represents the surface form of such objects as ship-hulls, automobile and aircrafts bodies. This method generates a smooth and fair surface under condition that parametric derivatives are continuous at the boundaries of each of the small patched faces. As mathematical representations, Coons, Hosaka and Bezier's equations are famous.

(3) Volume model

A volume structure has two sorts of objects. One is a 3-D solid such as machine parts and the other is a 3-D compartment such as enclosed space.

The solid modeling has two approaches. One is boolean method that deals with fundamental shapes (cubic, sphere,...) by mathematical set operation (TIPS-1 (Okino, 1973), PADL (Voelcker, 1977)). The other is graphic method that is represented in terms of faces of fundamental shapes and topological relationships among these faces (BUILD (Braid, 1973), GEOMAP (Hosaka, 1977)).

The compartment modeling is usually represented by graphical method (GBULLD (Reinschmidt, 1970), CASGAP (Carlson, 1974)).

3D GEOMETRIC DATABASES FOR MECHANICAL ENGINEERING

Robert N. Wolfe

Abstract

3D geometric data bases for mechanical parts and assemblies are a new and promising development in mechanical engineering. 3D data bases for sculptured surfaces of airplanes and automobiles have been used for many years, but the possibility of a data base containing the complete 3D description of all the parts of an airplane, car, printer or typewriter, and the impact it could have on the entire design / develop / manufacture / maintain product cycle is motivation for an increasing amount of work in 3D geometric data base applications, both inside and outside IBM. This paper examines 1) uses of these data bases in the 4 above mentioned product cycle areas and the benefits (reduction of duplication of effort, shorter lead times, better communication and understanding, etc.) resulting from the data base, 2) information content, file structure, file size and the integration of geometric and non-geometric data and 3) ways people want to access the data.

IBM Corporation
Thomas J. Watson Research Center
P. O. Box 218
Yorktown Heights, N. Y. 10598

INTRODUCTION

This paper discusses the uses, benefits and requirements of 3D data bases in mechanical engineering and manufacturing. It does not deal with the design or development of a database management system to satisfy these requirments. The first half of the paper attempts to show the need for 3D databases in mechanical engineering. The remainder of the paper deals with requirments.

It would be helpful to first look at the system function that could be built around a 3D geometric data base. The graphic system would probably have all the 2D geometric construction, design and drafting function embodied in existing 2D CAD systems such as Lockheed's CADAM® (IBM,1977) and many other existing 2D systems. In addition, it would have the following function:

1.Direct input and modification of 3 dimensional geometry, using an isometric or other axonometric projection on the graphic display, with the ability to tilt, pan and zoom to look at and interact with the physical object from any angle

2.Automatic production of views from the 3D model (Voelker, Requicha, 1977).

    a)orthographic views, including principle views and auxiliary views at any angle
    b)section views and cut-away views
    c)isometric views with hidden lines removed, including cut-away views and exploded parts views
    d)fully shaded and colored pictures of any isometric view, produced on a display screen for softcopy distribution or on a raster plotter or photocomposer for hardcopy distribution

3.Automatic tolerance analysis and dimension checking (Fitzgerald, Shelton, Wolfe, 1977) (Hilliard, Braid, 1978) based on information stored with the 3D model

4.3D interference analysis for mechanisms and assemblies, and graphic simulation of motion.

To achieve the function described above, the 3D data base would contain:

    a)Complete vertex, edge, surface and volume information for each part
    b)Dimension and tolerance information, properly related to the geometry of parts and assemblies
    c)All attachment relationships for parts, sub-assemblies and assemblies, for both rigid and non-rigid attachment
    d)Material type and density data
    e)Surface fabrication and finish information

A good review of 3D CAD and graphics in mechanical engineering was done recently by Elliot (Elliot, 1978).

USES AND ADVANTAGES OF A 3D DATA BASE

Engineering- Conceptual Design and Layout

From the very early conceptual design phases (including design of external shape and aesthetics of a machine), data would be captured in the 3D model. Fully colored and shaded pictures, with cut-outs and sections, would assist in communicating conceptual physical design information from engineer to engineer and from engineer to management. Through better documentation, communication and understanding, conceptual designs and their approvals would be done in a shorter time with fewer errors. Since all the conceptual design would be captured in the 3D data base, conceptual design and design layout could be more of a continuous operation with easier and faster iterations.

In the layout phase (and the detail design phase described below), analysis programs operating on the 3D data would provide the engineer with tolerance, interference analysis, stability, graphic simulation, NASTRAN and other design aid computations to refine and verify designs before detailing is done and prototype hardware is built. However, there are still many logical and computational problems to be addressed in this area.

Engineering- Detail Design

Detailed design would be aided by availability of the layout design in the 3D data base and by the 3D geometric construction facilities. The designer would be able to extract 3D objects or pieces of objects from the data base, add to them in a combination of both 2D and 3D geometric construction, producing a 3D model of each part. From the models, the system would automatically draw the principle orthographic views, all auxilliary views at any angle, sections, cut-outs and isometrics. At the U. of Rochester, attempts are being made at automatic dimensioning of orthographic views from the 3D model (Voelker, Requicha, 1977).

All prototype hardware would be built from the design data base so that accurate, current and easily understood information would be provided to model builders. They would have access to the 3D data base via graphic displays to examine isometric as well as orthographic drawings. The number of errors, iterations and time spent in model building and testing would be reduced. Graphic simulation of mechanisms and other 3D analysis computations would reduce the amount of model building and reduce the scrap and rework costs resulting from design errors.

The 3D parts file has significant potential for savings. At the Boing Commercial Airplane Company, an effective technique for improving productivity and cutting costs in the design and fabrication of piece parts has been reported (Thompson, 1976). At present it is a manual system, but in its final form, it would make use of a 3D data base of all Boeing parts. Called Boeing Universal Classification and Coding System (BUCCS), it provides for designing and classification of parts from standard functional shapes and veriations thereof. Each functional shape is represented by a parameterized 3 dimensional generic part or subpart. Any given detail part is built up from the standard parameterized shapes. Each part is given a hierarchical code derived from the codes of the generic shapes comprising it. Advantages are significant. Designs are more standard and design avoidance is made possible by a search for "equivalent" or "similar" parts, based on the BUCCS part code. The part codes are based on families of shapes producible by given manufacturing machines, therefore, manufacturability is assured or improved. In an automated system, time could be further reduced because the parameterized shapes would be stored as 3D geometric models and could be quickly combined at a graphic display, resulting in a 3D model of a new part.

Manufacturing- Communication of Information

When a 2 dimensional computer aided mechanical design system and a 2D data base are used by engineering, manufacturing benefits by receiving more accurate information and receiving it sooner. Engineering change information is more current and a tighter coupling between engineering and manufacturing is achieved.

A 3 dimensional design system and its 3D data base provide more information to manufacturing in a more easily understood form. Isometric drawings and 3D shaded pictorials make understanding easier and faster. This is particularly advantageous where a large percentage of manufactured parts and assemblies are subcontracted. Vendors will be able to respond more quickly with more accurate estimates and, most probably, lower price quotations because contingencies for unforseen problems will be reduced.

Manufacturing- Process Planning

Computer Aided Manufacturing- International, Inc. (CAM-I), is a not-for-profit R and D corporation whose international members act together to improve manufacturing productivity through the application of computers. CAM-I has a tremendous interest in pursuing the development of an advanced generative manufacturing process planning system. They believe two very important items must come into existence before such a system can be created. These are 1) a 3D CAD part modeling system and 2) a comprehensive manufacturing technology database. "CAM-I considers 3D CAD part modeling as essential for the total control of information to the factory. Without it, the system cannot be complete nor can automation occur totally within the factory" (Claytor, 1976).

Manufacturing- Numerical Control

For many years the APT language has been the primary vehicle for programming numerically controlled tools. There is no concept of a volume model in APT, only tool movement commands which result in a physical part. Although illusive, the idea of automatically generating a tool path program from a computer model of a part becomes more realistic as geometric modeling techniques evolve (Downey, 1977). The next new standard NC language should be based on a complete geometric volume description of the part (Elliot, 1978).

Manufacturing- Automated Assembly

Automated assembly using computer controlled industrial robots is a recent entry in the manufacturing arena, with the potential for increased productivity, lower cost and increased flexibility in the assembly process. Although no production oriented system with a 3D database is yet in operation, automated assembly is being seriously pursued in universities, research institutes and industry (Nevins, Whitney, 1977) (Lieberman, Wesley, Lavin, 1978). These systems will become viable for the routine assembly of piece parts only with the development of 3D geometric modeling and the associated 3D databases. The database aspects of automated assembly are discussed in more detail below.

Product Documentation

One of the last tasks to be performed in the product development cycle is the generation of documentation for those who use, install and maintain the product. Because it is at the end of the product cycle, it is always time critical and vulnerable to last minute engineering changes which must be reflected throughout large numbers of manuals. A major advantage of the 3D database produced by engineering and manufacturing, is the automatic or semi-automatic production of isometric and perspective drawings for operation, installation and maintenance manuals. Done by hand, these 3D pictorials are costly, time consuming and require an artists skills. With the 3D database they come almost for free, encouraging more extensive use of them and therefore more easily understood manuals.

A new and increasingly important reason for having these 3D pictorials generated from a database is the trend toward electronic distribution of documentation via communication lines, and the output of this documentation on display screens or high speed raster printers. The objective is to provide current, accurate information that can be easily and flexibly packaged. But if a manual step (an artist drawing the 3D pictorials) is needed in the process, the accuracy and currency of the information is lost or diminished. Therefore, the 3D database becomes more important.

DATABASE INFORMATION CONTENT

A Complete Volumetric Description

One of the essential characteristics of a 3D geometric database for mechanical engineering is that it completely describes the volumetric aspects of each object it represents. It cannot use only wire frame representations (a set of 3 dimensional coordinate vertices connected by vectors). It must define each volume by its surrounding faces (surfaces) and each face definition must indicate where the material is (on which side of the surface the material of the object is located). The simplest and most widely used approach to this total volumetric description is a hierarchical arrangement of coordinates, vertices, edges and planar faces. At the lowest level in the hierarchy are x, y and z coordinates. Vertices (points) contain 3 coordinates, edges contain 2 vertices and faces contain 3 or more edges linked together, head to tail, to form a closed loop. A face with holes and protrusions is composed of an outside loop, with one or more loops representing the boundary of any hole(s) in or protrusion(s) from the surface. In addition, each face is described by 1) a unit vector in a direction perpendicular to the surface and out of the material of the object, and 2) the distance from the origin of the coordinate system to the plane in which the face lies. Such an arrangement of planar faces is called a polyhedral representation.

Modeling the Part or Assembly

Having defined a method of describing objects volumetrically as a series of planar faces, part and assembly descriptions must be defined by users and stored in a computer database. The most widely reported approach is to provide the user with a set of primitive volumes such as cuboid, cylinder, wedge, prism, sphere, etc. and the ability to combine them via the operations of union, intersection and difference to form the desired composite volume. The resulting model is a hierarchy of primitives and subparts.

At IBM (Lieberman, Wesley, Lavin, 1978) (Lieberman, 1978), some preliminary work has been done on the definition of a data structure to be used in applications of industrial robots. The representation chosen is a graph where each node represents a volumetric entity which is either an object component, an object or an assembly. Nodes are connected by directed edges indicating one of the 4 relations; part-of, attachment, constraint or assembly-component. Associated with each node are attributes such as:

Name- the name of the object or subobject represented by this node and all nodes below it

Polyhedron- a pointer to the polyhedron defining the geometry of the object at this node

Coordinate Transform- a 4x4 matrix to transform the points of a primitive or subobject into the world coordinate reference frame

Physical Properties- type of material, etc.

Primitive Parameters- e.g., the length, width and height of a cuboid

3D modeling applications consume large amounts of computer time and storage. One of the biggest consumers of storage are the polyhedra. To reduce storage requirements it is possible to store only the primitive parameters and not the polyhedra. This could also be done with parameterized generic parts (e.g., screws, bolts, fasteners,etc.). On the other hand, the program run time to compute the polyhedral representation from the parameterized primitives and subobjects is substantial. The PL/1 language data structure for the part shown in Figure 1 requires 24,992 bytes of storage with the polyhedra stored at all nodes. Without the polyhedra, 16,296 bytes of storage are required. The time to compute all the polyhedra is about 53 seconds on the IBM 370 model 168. The part is composed of 20 primitive cuboids and cylinders.

Braid (Braid, 1974) goes beyond the use of only planar faces and, with restrictions, includes cylindrical surfaces in the definition of volumes. Building on the work done at the U. of Rochester (Voelker, Requicha, 1977), Boyse (Boyse, 1978) has done the preliminary design of a very advanced geometric modeller which handles both planar and cylindrical surface representations in any orientation without restrictions. The design includes the numerical geometry mathematics, algorithms and data structure. The data structure is dynamic, with both the structure and data changing rapidly in an interactive graphic terminal environment.

System developers should be aware that the size and arrangement of data in cpu memory, optimized for fast execution of geometric algorithms, may be different from the most efficient size and arrangement of data on disk storage. Production graphics systems have usually sacrificed ease of accessing data for geometric algorithm processing speed.

A good review of geometric modeling was recently done by Woo (Woo, 1977).

Integration af Graphic and Alphanumeric Data

One of the important aspects of a database system which handles 3D geometric information is the integration of this information with non-geometric information and the ability to output a combination of both. The availability of the Graphic Attachment Feature of the IBM 3270 alphanumeric display now allows any 3270 user to output graphic information for a very small delta cost over the cost of the 3270. This should help to motivate the development of combined graphic and alphanumeric databases. The Boeing BUCCS file is an example of a large application of this mixed data. Another is the engineering records file where both the physical representation of parts and assemblies (now engineering drawings) and the alphanumeric records data, need to be integrated into a common database.

WAYS OF ACCESSING THE DATA

The standard ways of accessing parts and assemblies by part number and engineering change level or development level will still apply for 3D geometric data. The "where used" file will still exist as it does today to find all places a given part is used in a machine or a product line. The bill of material will still be used to find all parts and sub-assemblies belonging to a machine or assembly.

However, with a complete 3D volumetric description in the database, an engineer will be able to determine automatically, and with 100 percent confidence, all the parts and assemblies affected by changing the position, size or shape of a given part or assembly. This can be done by computing the intersection of the part in question with all other parts in the machine. Since the computation can be lengthy when done with preciseness on large complex objects, it will probably be done with a staged screening process where the first step is to retrieve all those items from the database which intersect with a cuboid volume circumscribing the desired 3 dimensional object. For this step the polyhedra would not be searched, but only the x, y and z extremes of the parts in the file would be compared. Or perhaps it would be useful to accept all the parts retrieved by a set of search cuboids oriented orthogonal to the axes of the database coordinate system. These checks would be fast and simple.

If the objective is to search for "similar" or "equivalent" parts based on shape or functional characteristics like those used in BUCCS, then a complex hierarchical indexing scheme would be required. It would be too time consuming to search serially through the polyhedral representations of the entire database. The BUCCS code of Boeing is divided into a 5 character shape/function code plus a 7 character material/finish code. There would be at least 4 levels of hierarchy in the database to support this particular application. The system now contains 130,000 parts classified into 9 categories at the first level in the hierarchy, 84 categories in the second and 4800 categories total in the first three levels.

More progress in 3D modeling and database systems has been made in architectural engineering areas than in mechanical engineering, and perhaps this progress will benefit mechanical engineering developments. One of the most widely reported systems in architecture is GLIDE (Henrion, 1977). It is 1) a 3D graphics system for displaying 3-dimensional objects, 2) a database management system, 3) a high level interactive language with Algol-like syntax and 4)a system for computer-aided architectural design. Its 3D geometric database uses a polyhedral representation of objects.

A system to handle the extremely large 3D databases required in the construction of nuclear power plants is being developed at the University of Michigan (Borkin, McIntosh, Turner, 1978). It uses a polyhedral representation of physical objects. It manages both alphanumeric and graphical data, and uses a relational database approach to make operations on both types of data appear uniform to the user. The user may for example, ask for the intersection of the sets "4 INCH CARBON PIPE" and "TURBINE ROOM NO. 2".

SUMMARY

3D geometric modeling and associated databases will be responsible in the next 3 to 5 years for a new generation of mechanical CAD systems which will significantly enhance the 2D design systems in use over the past 10 years. However, little work has been done on the requirements of a 3D database system for mechanical engineering. In order for the 3D systems to have the most impact and produce the greatest benefits, the database must accomodate a complete 3D volumetric description of objects and support applications spanning the entire product cycle from conceptual design through product installation and maintenance. Geometric data must be integrated (at least logically) with alphanumeric data. Many new applications will be possible, requiring large amounts of computing time and storage. Cooperation between application developers and database system developers will be needed to optimize the storage, access time and compute time trade-offs which will be necessary to make these systems viable in a production environment.

For those interested in the development of 3D databases, a survey of databases for physical system design was done by Eastman (Eastman, 1976). For mechanical engineering databases, I would recommend reading Boyse (Boyse, 1978). In addition, a tentative standard for the digital representation of physical object shapes (ASME, 1978) has been prepared by Subcommittee 26 of the American National Standards Institute, and is being distributed for review at this time.

ACKNOWLEDGMENTS

I wish to thank William Fitzgerald and Franklin Gracer for the use of computer graphics programs to input the 3D model of the part shown in Figure 1, and Michael Wesley for the Geometric Design Processor program used to process the model.

REFERENCES

ASME (1978). *Digital Representation of Physical Object Shapes,* American Society of Mechanical Engineers(ASME), United Engineering Center, N.Y., N.Y.

Borkin, H. J., McIntosh, J. F. and Turner, J. A. (1978). The Development of Three-dimensional Spatial Modeling Techniques for the Construction Planning of Nuclear Power Plants. *Computer Graphics*, ACM, N. Y.

Boyse, J. W. (1978). *Preliminary Design for a Geometric Modeller*, General Motors Research Publication GMR-2768, General Motors Research Laboratories, Warren, Michigan.

Braid, I. C. (1974). *Designing With Volumes*, Centab Press, Cambridge, England

Claytor, R. N. (1976). *CAMI's Computer Aided Process Planning System (CAPP)*, Society of Mechanical Engineers, Technical Paper MS76-341, Dearborn, Michigan

Downey, P. J. (1977). Geometric Modeling-"Solids" for NC Programming. *Proceedings of CAM-I 6th Annual Meeting of Members*, Nov 15-17, 1977, CAM-I publication P-77-MM-03, Arlington, Texas.

Eastman, C. (1976). Databases for Physical System Design: A Survey of U.S. Efforts. *Proceedings of CAD76*, ICL Press, London

Elliot, W. S. (1978). Interactive CAD in Mechanical Engineering Design. *Computer Aided Design*, March

Fitzgerald, W. J., Shelton, G. L., and Wolfe, R. N. (1977). *A System for Converting a Rough Sketch to a Finished Drawing*, U. S. patent 4,058,849

Henrion, M. (1977). *Glide Reference Manual*, Institute of Physical Planning, Carnegie-Mellon University Dept. of Architecture, Pittsburg, Pa.

Hilliard, R. C. and Braid, I. C. (1978). Analysis of Dimensions and Tolerances in Computer Aided Mechanical Design. *Computer Aided Design*, May

IBM (1977). *CADAM® User Training Manual*, IBM Publication No. SH20-2035, IBM Corp., Mechanicsburg, Pa.

Lieberman, L. (1978). *Model Driven Vision for Industrial Automation*, IBM Watson Research Center Report RC7314, Yorktown Heights, N. Y.

Lieberman, L. I., Wesley, M. A. and Lavin, M. A. (1978). *A Geometric Modeling System for Automated Mechanical Assembly*, IBM Watson Research Center Report RC7089, Yorktown Heights, N. Y.

Nevins, J. L. and Whitney, D.E.(1977). Research on Advanced Assembly Automation. *Computer*, December

Thompson, A. R. (1976). *Improving Productivity Through Classification and Coding*, Society of Manufacturing Engineers, Technical Paper MS76-727, Dearborn, Michigan

Voelker, H. B. and Requicha, A. A. G. (1977). Geometric Modeling of Parts and Processes. *Computer*, December

Woo, T. C. (1977). Progress in Shape Modeling. *Computer*, December

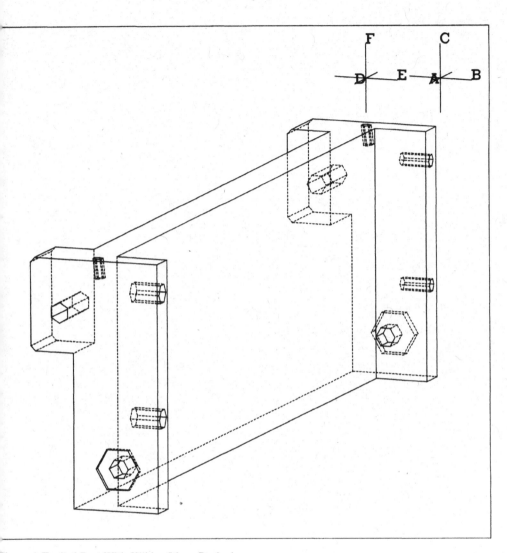

Figure 1 Typical Part With Hidden Lines Dashed

DATA BASE REQUIREMENTS FOR GRAPHICAL APPLICATIONS IN BIOCHEMISTRY

Karl D. Hardman*

SUMMARY

Although there are numerous areas of the life sciences that could benefit from having a general and universal data base for three-dimensional computer display systems, perhaps the most apparent is for structural studies of biological macromolecules (molecular graphics). Since the structure of the first protein (myoglobin, which contains 1400 non-hydrogen atoms) was solved by Sir John Kendrew and coworkers in 1962 by x-ray diffraction methods, no fewer than 80 different molecules of that size or larger have been solved. Probably in the next 5 years another 200 to 400 additional structures will be solved. These will include not only proteins, nucleic acids and polysaccharides, but complexes of these as well, where the total molecular weight may reach 10 to 50 times that of myoglobin (e.g. complete virus particles). The ultimate goals of the investigators are to discover the mechanism of action of these molecules and complexes, to predict three-dimensional structure and function of hypothetical molecules, and finally to be able to synthesize new macromolecules of new and predictable functions. In the past several years methods for solving large structures and refinement of models to observed crystallographic data have improved dramatically and will notably improve the accuracy of such models. It is quite clear that this improved accuracy will greatly aid reaching these objectives. Furthermore, these goals will only be possible if the present and future structural information can be thoroughly studied and assimilated. Computer graphics provides a reasonable hope and a sophisticated data base is an obvious necessity. Data base requirements for molecular graphics, not only those for display, manipulation and solving complex structures for they have been well demonstrated, but also those performing research studies on the accumulated results, are certainly within the grasp of current methods.

* IBM Thomas J. Watson Research Center, P. O. Box 218, Yorktown Heights, New York 10598

I. BIOCHEMICAL INTRODUCTION

A. General

This introduction to protein biochemistry is to present a glimpse of some complex structures and research goals to serve as a starting point for considering future needs to be accommodated in a data base for computer graphics. For general reading or additional references, see Metzler (1978) and Stryer (1976).

A "typical" living cell contains perhaps several dozen types of subcellular particles or organelles. Common examples of these organelles are ribosomes, mitochondria, lysosomes, chloroplasts, nuclei, plasmids, starch granules, microtubules, and even viruses, all with specific functions. Some of these particles are suspended in the liquid portion, the cytosol, which also contains a soup of many smaller molecular complexes or simple molecules while others are bound to membranes. Within these organelles, there is another level of organization and on expanding the scale, it can be seen that they are subdivided into smaller building blocks, packages or clusters of a few specific macromolecules. Currently to examine the functions of cells in practical terms we must study the physics and chemistry of these individual particles and, furthermore, we must divide these particles into their lowest common denominators, the individual macromolecules. Then the reconstruction begins.

There are, of course, different classes of macromolecules. Polysaccharides, for example, in starch and glycogen granules, are large molecular weight branched chains of glucose units used for storage. Lipids and lipo-polysaccharides in membranes form semisolid matrices for organization. Mitochondrial membranes contain packets of enzymes which are carefully organized to catalyze an orderly series of chemical reactions. Other enzymes are free in solution as single polypeptide chains while still others are aggregates of the same identical chains. The nucleus contains the chromosomes, which contain the genes, which contain the genetic code in double strands of DNA. Chromosomes contain DNA, RNA and proteins of various types, all of which are organized and held together in a very complicated geometry (Fig. 1). The underlying principle of complementarity and exact duplication, however, is quite simply understood in terms of the pairing of the base groups in the two strands of the DNA, which are held together by hydrogen bonds (weak dipolar interactions between NH groups and oxygen atoms from the different chains).

With respect to 3-dimensional structure, proteins have been by far the most extensively studied of all classes of macromolecules. They are chains of polymerized α-amino acids. Commonly, 20 different amino acids are condensed by enzymes which split out a hydroxyl from the carboxyl group (COOH) and hydrogen from the amino group (NH_2), forming H_2O and the peptide bond (Fig. 2). The amino acid side chains include chemical groups which are acetic, basic, neutrally charged but dipolar, and non-polar. Single polypeptide chains range in lengths of about 30 amino acids for the smallest proteins to over 400 for some of the largest.

Several examples of classical proteins follow. Myoglobin and hemoglobin are related proteins which are oxygen carriers. Both bind iron-filled porphyrin groups which in turn bind the oxygen. Myoglobin contains a single polypeptide chain of 153 amino acids which is coiled into 8 segments of α-helix and surrounds the iron porphyrin (Fig. 3). This was the first protein whose complete 3-dimensional structure was determined, which utilized X-ray crystallographic methods, Kendrew (1963). Hemoglobin contains four chains, each very similar in amino-acid sequence and coiled into distinct subunits similar to the 3-dimensional structure of myoglobin and contains 4 iron porphyrins and binds 4 oxygen molecules. Concanavalin A (Fig. 4) is of the class of proteins primarily from plants, known as lectins, which bind to the surfaces of certain types of cells and cause notable changes in the growth characteristics of the cells and are, therefore, of interest in various areas of cancer research. This protein contains another common structural feature known as the pleated sheet, or β-sheet. There are two basic types, parallel and antiparallel, where the directions of the chains are the same or opposite. These chains are also held together by a continuous lattice of hydrogen bonds between the amide hydrogen and carboxyl oxygens. Additionally, concanavalin A is a metalloprotein, containing Mn^{2+} and Ca^{2+} which serve to hold the polypeptide chain in that region of the subunit in a given 3-dimensional structure (conformation). This conformation, then, is capable of binding specific carbohydrates, which is its mode of attachment to the surfaces of cell membranes. At physiological pH values, a molecule of this protein is a tetramer of 4 identical subunits, each containing 1 polypeptide chain of 237 amino acids, 1 Mn^{++}, 1 Ca^{++} and 1 carbohydrate binding site. Carbonic anhydrase is an example of enzyme with a number of structural features mentioned. This enzyme catalyzes the conversion of CO_2 and H_2O to bicarbonate and

H^+. It contains 260 amino acids, more than 2000 nonhydrogens atoms several α helices, a β-sheet through the middle and a Zn^{++} ion in the catalytic site. The Zn is bound by 3 imidazale groups and binds a H_2O molecule, presumably the one which is combined with CO_2 to form bicarbonate. One of the smaller proteins, the hormone insulin, contains two different polypeptide chains, of 21 and 30 amino acids respectively, which are covalently linked together by disulfide bridges, forming one subunit. Under certain conditions, these subunits aggregate further to form larger molecules, e.g. dimers and hexamers. Numerous other proteins aggregate, such as hemoglobin (4 subunits, total number of atoms over 5000) and virus particles, such as tomato bushy stunt virus with 180 polypeptide chains per particle (40000 molecular weight each). Despite its huge size, its structure has been solved by X-ray crystallographic methods (Fig. 5).

A very important geometric property of some proteins is that they display what are called "allosteric effects". These are changes in shape in one portion of a molecule which produce concomitant changes at a quite different site, quite often more than 30 or 40 Å away. An example of an allosteric protein is hemoglobin. The binding of the first O_2 molecule produces 3-dimensional changes not only in the region of the molecule binding O_2 but in distant regions as well which increase the affinity of the other iron porphyrin groups for binding oxygen.

If we are going to piece together some of the puzzles of any of these examples of complex organization, then we must continually increase the sophistication of our methods. Since these are problems basically of 3-dimensional organization, then viewing and manipulating 3-dimensional images are the tools we will depend upon. The use of computer graphics for studies of large molecules is certainly not new (Levinthal, 1966); however, advancements in both the fields of biochemistry and computer technology (at all levels) has shifted this usage from a luxury to a necessity. An appropriate data base for biochemical macromolecules is a part of this necessity. Such a data base must be set up to accommodate nucleic acids, polysaccharides, proteins, lipids and complexes of more than one of the above types, such as glycoprotein (proteins containing covalently linked polysaccharides, e.g., the immunoglobulins) or gylcoplipids. Furthermore, the data base containing this structural information for different types molecules must be constructed so that it may be easily cross sectioned to extract common structural and functional properties, both those which are anticipated and those that are not.

B. Current Uses of Graphics

The 3-dimensional atomic coordinates have been determined for several proteins in different laboratories by building a molecular model into an electron density map, determined crystallographically, for example, Tsernoglou et al. (1977). Here, a portion of an electron density map is displayed on the screen (Fig. 6) which represents several amino acid groups. Atomic positions for the polypeptide backbone and side chains are fit into these densities by rotation, in real time, around the necessary bonds, until a best fit by eye and by some computed statistics is obtained. After completing one portion, the electron densities for the next several amino acid groups are brought onto the screen and the model fitting is repeated. Since the molecules are long chains which fold back on themselves many times and only several groups may be fit at one time, the fitting process stepping forward and backward along the amino acid sequence for satisfactory results. In some of these cases, difference electron density maps have been displayed, i.e., the difference between the observed and calculated crystallographic structure factors (magnitudes) are used to calculate both positive and negative contours (3-dimensional cages). These represent gradients which indicate where atoms or groups have been misplaced and the directions they should shift. After "refinement" of the entire molecule improved electron density maps, (or difference maps) are calculated and a new iteration of the refinement begins. Linked to this process have been programs which "idealize" standard geometric bond lengths and angles found in proteins so that the researchers may then correct any notable violations they may have produced before going much further. Similarly, energy minimization programs, e.g. Hermans and McQueen (1974), have been used to check the fit of the model by calculating and minimizing bond energies from standard chemical potentials, coulombic terms, and hydrogen bonds.

Two examples of more imaginative uses of computer graphics in biochemistry follow in this paragraph. 1) Model building of hemoglobin has been used in attempts to deduce the packing of sickle-cell hemoglobin in the fibers which are found in sickle cells, Levinthal et al. (1975). An optimum solution was found which satisfied the properties of the hemoglobin fibers. First some dimensions and properties of the fibers were assumed from prior crystallographic analysis of normal and sickle cells hemoglobin, electron microscopic and chemical information. Then sets of interactions between pairs of molecules tested by searching 6 degrees of freedom (3 rotation angles and 3 translations) to see if fibers found by these interactions would possess the prescribed properties. A "best" fit to the model was satisfied by only one set of contacts. Furthermore, the solution provides plausible explanations for several other properties of sickle cell hemoglobin which were not used in this test system. 2) Molecular graphics has been used to compare the crystallographic structures of a class of enzymes known as serine proteases, Kraut (1977). The positions of the chemical groups and the interatomic distances and angles in the active sites were compared in search of unusual chemical bands involving a proton donor group responsible for the catalytic activity.

C. Future Research Areas for Molecular Graphics

In order to establish requirements for any proposed data bases, we first need to briefly examine future research areas in molecular biology, particularly those whose attempts or success depend entirely on the existence of high performance data retrieval. Already mentioned were the areas associated with the display functions such as model fitting. As molecules and "particles" studied become larger, future research will include new methodology using on-line graphics for structure solving. With faster methods of data collection, such as area detectors, being developed, the rate-limiting steps of structure solving will be phase analysis. Rotation functions have been used to identify previously solved structures (or parts) in solved crystal data sets. This involved researching the new data (equivalent to a 3-dimensional frequency domain dataset) with a transform of test model. Methods using smaller and more general test models might be developed if decisions could be made interacting by the investigator as the search progressed. This would involve calculating dozens or more discrete Fourier transforms of perhaps thousands of points, comparing and displaying the statistics of the comparisons to the user, so that appropriate restarts or branches could be made. Automatic chain tracing algorithms (fitting of the polypeptide backbone to low or medium resolution electron density maps) will be incorporated into interactive model fitting procedures to take advantage of the computer power of the host to accompany the human decision making process. (For example, to possibly provide statistical guidelines as saddle points are reached. Incorporation of crystallographic least-squares and difference Fourier refinement procedures into interactive model fitting procedures also will need the uses of large Fourier transforms density maps and crystallographic data (calculation, storage and selective retrieval.)

For interactively comparing large numbers of structures or searching all molecules in the data base for proposed substructures, tightly branched data bases and appropriate algorithms will be necessary. Additionally, such studies will probably require temporary storage of intermediate results also with highly branched files. Substructural elements currently searched for in new structures are mostly limited to α-helix, β-structure, several types of bends in the backbone, and a limited combination of these three. The numbers and complexities of these elements will increase as interactive graphics improve techniques. Results will have to be statistically analyzed and stored. Some of the search procedures may possess similarities with pattern recognition methods. An example of this is some recent work by Liebman (unpublished results). A scalar quantity for "closeness" (inverse of the distance in 3-dimensional space) between each amino acid and every other amino acid is plotted versus the two sequence numbers, see Fig. 7, A and B. In these plots, the "closeness" along the diagonal is infinite ($1/0$), and immediately off the diagonal distinct patterns appear. These plots were computed by "batch" mode but indicate what could be done with interactive graphics.

Surfaces and complements of surfaces will need to be calculated, displayed, and manipulated (changing perhaps both geometry and chemical groups) to study molecules which would be expected to bind together. Searches for these complements will be necessary, for example, to identify recognition sites for enzyme substrates or inhibitors, for self assembly of fibers, multi-subunit proteins, and enzyme clusters. Calculation and fit of complementary surfaces could be used to predict, for example, antigen specificity for new antibody molecules, as they are discovered.

Search procedures will be needed for analysis and display of chemical features of molecular surfaces (Fig. 8), including distribution of charges, polar and non-polar groups, and attempts made to identify similarities among many molecules (as well as other surfaces on the same molecule). Such similarities will be correlated with parameters of biological activity, e.g., enzyme catalysis, or with binding specific chemical groups, molecules or classes of molecules.

An active area of future graphics research will unquestionably be the chemical mechanisms of enzymes (Figs. 9 and 10). Displays will be used to show the 3-dimensional structures of the enzyme activity site and substrate molecules, before, during and after the reaction and calculate how the energies of reactions are altered by changes in geometry of the atoms involved, including neighboring water and ions. Likewise such studies may be used to predict activities of unknown catalytic sites and eventually lead to the modification of known enzymes or the synthesis of new ones. The function of macromolecules in biological systems is obviously very dependent on their interactions with water. Interactive graphics will be used again here to display molecular surfaces (chosen selectively) and calculate positions and perhaps motions of surrounding water molecules. Similar work could be done then with ions found in solution also. This work is of vital importance, in fact, it will be used to redefine the concepts of "surfaces" of these molecules.

Perhaps a more difficult question than predicting the structure of a given active site may be the prediction of the 3-dimensional structure of the entire protein from its amino acid sequence alone. Proteins are syntheses from individual amino acids stepwise one amino acid at a time, into a long, flexible polypeptide chain, and fold spontaneously without any information other than the chemical information contained in the amino acid sequence and the solution around. Folding here refers to the conversion of the newly synthesized polypeptide chain, which is presumably random (or nearly random), to a unique 3-dimensional conformation. It is understood, however, that this unique structure has certain flexibilities and therefore motions in real time. It is currently accepted that the 3-dimensional structure of the native protein and the surrounding solution is one where the total free energy of the system is a minimum. Predicting complete structure from sequence is currently an active area, Levitt (1978), and will become more so with better computational and graphical tools. Much of past attention has been collecting statistics for interactions of neighboring amino acids of different sequences, for example, the frequency of occurrence and structural features of specific tripeptide sequences (20^3 possibilities) in known proteins. Statistics on many other parameters including longer range interactions, will have to be obtained and analyzed before principles of folding can be properly studied. This, however, is only the beginning once the capability to predict structure is possible, the normal progression will be prediction of function from amino acid sequences. Furthermore, the DNA code translates directly into amino acid sequence so that upon sequencing fragments of DNA, predictions of proteins of specific structures and functions would follow. (Biochemical methods for sequencing DNA have recently advanced very rapidly, in fact it is now possible to sequence an entire virus.)

Computer graphics have already attracted interest for the design of drug molecules with specific biological activities. During the recent meeting of the American Chemical Society (Honolulu, April, 1979) no fewer than 12 such papers were presented. With the advance of structural-functional areas in macromolecules, similar design experiments may be possible for protein hormones, hormone receptors, enzymes, enzyme modifiers and inhibitors, and DNA fragments which code for specific proteins. Production of insulin in bacteria, for example, has already been accomplished by incorporation of DNA fragments coding specifically for insulin into the cell.

II. USES OF DATABASES FOR BIOLOGICAL MOLECULES

There have been several large scale data bases formulated in the past for the retrieval of chemical information, and in some cases to be used with display devices. One of these has been set up specifically for protein 3-dimensional files. The data contained and the purposes of these files are different from any future data base envisioned for biochemical structural display and research. Furthermore, every installation to date using graphic displays for biochemical structures has, for the most part, created its own data base system. These have for the most part been primarily for the purposes of display and perhaps manipulation of molecular structure and not to handle queries of specific research questions. That is, the data bases have been set up to display one molecule (or portions), manipulate, and perhaps then ask further questions, but for the same molecule. In contrast, future data bases must emphasize the ability to ask global questions of all molecules in the file. Moreover, there has also been no attempt to design and create newer data bases at different locations which would have different ranges of uses and have them complementary, i.e., dovetail and share functions among various installations, as in "distributed" data bases.

A. Data Bases

There are currently 7 large data bases which are available to the public and cover the various disciplines of chemistry, Templeton and Johnson (1978). These only partially cover the areas ideally included in a biochemical structure data base. Their functions are obviously quite different than we wish to address but much should be learned from the utilization of these bases. Only one, the Brookhaven

Protein databank, is specifically biochemical in nature but is inadequate for future research needs and will be discussed later. Information in some but not all of these data bases fall into the categories of bibliographic citations, chemical information (compound names, molecular compositions and formulae, atomic connectivity, i.e. atom sets forming bonds, 3-dimensional atomic positions resulting from single crystal analysis, results from powder diffraction methods, and descriptions and comments). The ones mentioned below are the major ones of biochemical interest.

i. Cambridge Crystallographic Data File. This is the largest and most complete file with both structural (3-dimensional atomic coordinates) and biographical data, Allen *et al.* (1973). This data file contains entries of well over 10,000 compounds which are organic in nature (contain carbon) and whose 3-dimensional structures have been solved by x-ray or neutron diffraction. The purposes of the data base is to provide storage retrieval, and evaluation of these structures necessary for further work in areas such as theoretical chemistry, crystallography and molecular biology; however, it specifically excludes entries of polymers and proteins. The data base is divided into two separate files: (I) bibliographic and (II) structural and does not use particularly sophisticated techniques or numerous branches or nodes. Each entry is filed in one of 86 chemical classes and in card image format where the entry identifier occupies the last 8 characters. This reference code links the structural and bibliographic file entries. In the structural file, for example, all entries are ordered alphabetically by reference code within each class. The first 6 characters of each record identifies record type which includes those for information flags, crystallographic parameters, atomic coordinates, bond lengths, and connectively atom labels, and text. Preliminary checks for self consistency and completeness on new entries are performed by software, for example, symmetries of specific chemical bonds (bond lengths, angles, and valency are compared with previous data and various conditions such as gross or suspected errors are flagged and checked, if necessary by the original investigators. Acquisition of data for individual molecules may be made off-line through request directly to the Cambridge Center or several affiliated data centers throughout the world, or by on-line requests through various time-share networks. Accredited data centers have been established by lease of the data base (whole or in part) and serve either a large research institution or the scientific community of a given geographic region.

ii. Chemical Information System. Researchers from NIH and EPA have incorporated the Cambridge Crystallographic Data File into a much larger data base called the NIH-EPA Chemical Information System (CIS), Heller *et al.* (1977). In addition this contains files for mass spectra, nuclear magnetic resonance and x-ray powder diffraction data. These files can be searched interactive by chemical structure, i.e., queries can be formulated to locate all entries with one or more chemical structure or group, as well as other qualifications. For this, entries from the Cambridge Data File were assigned registry numbers used by the Chemical Abstracting Service as unique chemical identifiers. Also available are programs for analysis of complex NMR spectra, including ones for general curve-fitting and linear regression analysis, for calculating isotope enrichment from mass spectral data, and for calculating 3-dimensional conformations of small molecules in solution which are in the lowest energy states. This data base is located at the NIH computer center with its own communications system which permits worldwide, 24-hour access by qualified users via commercial telephone. For utilization of the crystal structure file, programs which are device independent and are available to all users on the network have been added to CIS to search, display and manipulate the structural data. The file may be searched by criteria such as molecular formula, molecular weight, coordinate data authors, and as in the other CIS files, by specific chemical groups or substructures. Upon identifying an entry, the molecule may be displayed in total or in part, inspected, edited, rotated, or displayed as a stereo pair for static 3-dimensional viewing. Interatomic distances torsion angles and dihedral angles can be calculated. This system can be accessed by a vector display or simple a low speed printer terminal, if that is all that is available to the user, however, the later obviously cannot utilize the graphical manipulations. Two-dimensional representations of chemical groups, etc., however, can be "drawn" in the printer terminals.

iii. Brookhaven National Laboratory Protein Data Bank. The bank is an archival file for structures of biological macromolecules, Bernstein *et al.* (1977), currently all but a few entries are proteins. The format and features are similar to the Cambridge Files but have not been upgraded with coding necessary for interactive use (as in CIS). The bank was started in 1971 to collect, standardize and distribute (to anyone, no restrictions) atomic coordinate from crystallographic studies. Currently the file contains about 100 entries with more than 20 megabytes of data and is distributed on mag tape, with the file names coded from the name of the molecule. Included are atomic coordinates, structure factors and phases and since most of the information is not generally published in primary literature, the comprehensiveness of the data is totally at the discretion of the original investigators. The text portion gives some basic biological information bibliography (which is currently being reorganized for interactive queries) authors, methodology used in the study. Problems, such as local disorder is regions of the molecule and refinement procedures, if any, are also stated. The amino acid sequence, sections of helix and β-structure are given in a portion of the file separate from the atomic coordinates. Separate records are included: (a) for atomic coordinates and connectivity nonstandard groups which are part of the protein, such as enzyme cofactors, substrates and metal ions; (b) amino acids involved in active sites; (c) disulfide bridges; and (d) operators for crystallographic and "local" symmetry elements.

Revisions and updates of such a file are extremely difficult. Minor changes are available to users on microfiche upon request, whereas major corrections are announced in newsletters. Future additions are to include "ideal" atomic coordinates for standard sub-structural elements, such as α-helix, β-structure DNA double helix. Programs supplied by Bank personnel are to be included which calculate various parameters for comparison, e.g., torsion and dihedral band angles. The Bank also will distribute and are currently soliciting programs supplied by any investigator which are applicable to any area of protein crystallography or research programs which use crystallographic data, such as coordinate refinement or calculations of total energy of the molecule.

iv. Macromolecular Structure on Microfiche. In order to put protein structural data (in graphics form) within each reach of the biochemist who does not have access to the necessary facilities, NIH has sponsored a microfiche atlas, compiled by Richard Feldman and commercially available (from Tracor Jitco Inc., Rockville, MD) under the name AMSOM (Atlas of Macromolecular Structure on Microfiche). The graphics sections presents standard view of each entry in stereo on 42x microfiche frames. The stereo is produced for the viewer by a small mirror device which mounts directly onto an inexpensive microfiche viewer. The standard views, perhaps 1000 per entry, show different orientations of the skeletal polypeptide chain, clipped views around each amino acid and designated regions of interest. A system of programs and files have been produced at NIH to automatically generate the microfiche masters and future supplements in a global manner. (After the standard views, etc., are selected and programmed, each molecule in the data base is processed in batch mode without special set up or intervention. Textual material (also on microfiche) contains a large variety of information including bibliography cross reference, biochemical information and a large section of all interatomic distances. Thus for less than $250.00 US, a library or biochemist may obtain complete microfiche files on about 100 proteins and nucleic acids and a stereo viewer to use with any microfiche viewer. Future supplements are to include features of each entry which are prescribed specifically by original investigators to exhibit the unique features of that particular molecule.

B. The National Resource for Computation in Chemistry (NRCC)

The NRCC is well described by its title. It was established in October 1977 by the National Science Foundation and Department of Energy located at Lawrence Berkeley Laboratory, supported as a national, common computer facility to supply the development and operating needs that cannot be met adequately by individual academic institutions. One of the areas of concentration is crystallography. Furthermore, an advisory committee workshop recommended a high level of support for development and use of molecular graphics, including hardware, software and information retrieval, Templeton and Johnson (1978). Specific recommendations for graphics were:
1. The development of a family of compatible graphics systems covering a spectrum of configurations of cost and performance; for use at the NRCC and at remote, time-share locations with intelligent terminals.
2. The dissemination of medium performance graphics systems,
3. The development and dissemination of device independent, general purpose graphics software for the NRCC community,
4. Establishing access to high-quality, color, computer generated (film?) and microfilm facility.
Recommendations for data base activities were for:
1. Data collection (acquisition), evaluation and data base construction (presumably updating also),
2. Data dissemination through data base accessibility,

3.   Education of the scientific community as to the contents, accessibility and potentials of the data base,

4.   Research on the data within the data bases and on the data bases themselves.

(Although stated as recommendations in their report, the committee apparently felt that items 1 and 2 do not require additional support from NRCC.)

III. REQUIREMENTS

While a future data base for structural applications in biochemistry is being formulated, a number of philosophical questions will have to be addressed and compromised. Who would the users be and how many? Would the data base be formulated for the relatively few crystallographers investigators who have a prior knowledge of structural research and computer science which is fairly sophisticated or would it serve a much larger group of life scientists, relying mostly on developing skills while using the system? The latter approach would not expect many investigators to contribute extensively to the improvement of the system. Users would primarily be from academic institutions, government and private research labs and medical foundations. How much usage and/or support could be expected from corporations, particularly at first? How would development and maintenance be supported, government contracts or grants, R & D?

Would it be designed for usage on large networks, worldwide with present or future communication facilities, or only for interactive usage very locally? If utilized by large networks, how would it be administrated? What types of hardware for graphics, hosts and interfaces or would it be fairly device independent? If designed for network usage, what would the minimum hardware be and cost, current and future? What network charges could be expected for the host, computing, shortage and software maintenance? Would it be language independent or perhaps would be the data base itself contain functions analogous to APL? Or even higher level languages? How accessible or protected would the results of each investigator be?

Possible requirements, without much speculation into future data processing capabilities and without unexpected quantum jumps in production of structural information, might look as follows: Accommodation of 500 entries for macromolecules with complete 3-dimensional structural information, and easily expandable in size and scope (the molecules would range in size from somewhat less than 1000 to perhaps 10000 atoms). Labels for atoms, amino acids (in sequence), substructure elements, classes of chemical groups, chemical functions. Multiple sets of three dimensional coordinates, error estimates and parameters of motion and disorder for all atoms. Lists of all atoms in all substructures (or beginning and end points). Elements of symmetry, crystallographic and noncrystallographic, with perhaps parameters indicating "exactness" of the latter type. Inclusion of alternate amino acids and all associated parameters, if structures are sufficiently isomorphous. File structure to accommodate and crossreference proteins, polysaccharides, nucleic acids (both RNA and DNA), lipids, covalent and noncovalently bound complexes of combinations of all these classes. Tables including standard bonding patterns for all standard groups, such as all amino acid side chains, common cofactors such as iron-porphyrin groups. Files of standard or typical 3-dimensional conformations and minimum energy information for the groups just mentioned, plus substructures such as β-sheets and helices (this is an example of the type of file which would be constantly expanding as the data base is used). Files of sequences of proteins and nucleic acids etc. where 3-dimensional structures are not known. Lists of parameters (classes) of biological functions for entire molecules or substructures. Labels or identifiers and structural parameters for all nonstandard atoms, groups or molecules bound, and all surrounding solvent molecules and ions. Proper data base structure for rapid cross sectioning and display by labels or keywords through all entries. Selected bibliographies and author indexes. Cross references to molecules of related functions. Sections within entries for a variety of physical information, including, for example, optical spectral data, nuclear magnetic resonance data, created with original entry or updated later. Ability to add software functions directly to data base. Convenient updating data and software functions.

Other requirements perhaps more related to usage of the data base and storage of intermediate results of the research on the primary data would include the following: Creation of temporary storage, working storage and archival files from the primary data base and update as needed, not only for the resulting graphical scenarios but for searches, sorts and merges and subsequent statistical analyses of the primary data. (How much should be stored as opposed to recalculated?) Easy editing of temporary files prior to film or video tape production (black and white and color). Assimilation of data files from other experiments. Automatic generation of cross-referencing and compressed files as updates occur.

A data base which would serve very well could certainly be constructed without many of the features mentioned here and total size would obviously depend on where the line was drawn. The Brookhaven Data Bank contains about 25 megabytes, as mentioned, accommodating nearly 100 entries which average about 3000 atoms each, with 80 bytes per atom. On reorganization, packing and adding most of the desired features, these same entries could easily be stored in much less than half this space. Therefore, in anticipation of growth to perhaps 500 entries, the expansion from 10 to 50 megabytes for the primary data base itself would be expected. However, it would be difficult to estimate secondary storage requirements for research performed on this data base and incorporation of auxiliary data bases, for example,the crystallographic structure factors for all entries (this could almost double the size) or the amino acid sequences of all proteins whose 3-dimensional structure have not been determined. It is apparent that even with generous allowances for these different expansion factors, the total data base size is not formidable.

If the longer range goals to determine the underlying chemical and physical principles by which these molecules function are to be achieved, then current and future structural data must be thoroughly analyzed. The dependence of such analyzes upon an appropriate data base must be properly understood and plans made accordingly.

ACKNOWLEDGEMENTS

I would like to thank S. Harrison (Harvard University), W. Wright (IBM SCD, Triangle Research Park, NC), M. Liebman (Institute for Cancer Research, Philadelphia), M. Rossmann (Purdue University), R. Feldmann (NIH, Bethesda, MD), H. Sobell (University of Rochester), Dr. Tsernoglou (Wayne State University), F. Richards (Yale University), and D. Metzler (Iowa State University) for kindly providing figures for this article. Those figures previously published have been reproduced here with the permission of the publishers.

BIBLIOGRAPHY

Allen F.H., Kennard O., Motherwell W.D.S., Town W.G., and Watson D.G.   (1973). Cambridge Crystallography data Centre, Part II, Structural Data File. Journal of Chemical Documents, 13,119-123

Bernstein F.C., Koetzle T.F., Williams G.J.B., Meyer E.F., Brice M.D., Rodgers J.R., Kennard O., Shimanacuchi T., Tasumi M. (1977). The protein data bank: A computer based archival file for macromolecular structures. Journal of Molecular Biology, 112,535-542

Feldman R.J., Bing D.H., Furie B.C., and Furie B. (1978). Interactive computer surface graphics approach to study of the active site of bovine trypsin. Proceedings of the National Academy of Sciences, USA, 75,5409-5412

Harrison S.C., Olson A.J., Schutt C.E., Winkler F.K., and Bricogne G. (1978). The tomato bushy stunt virus at 2.9 Å resolution. Nature, 276,368-373

Heller S.R., Milne G.W.A., and Feldman R.J. (1977). A computer based chemical information system. Science, 195,253-259

Hermans J., and McQueen J.E. (1974). Computer manipulation of macromolecules with the method of local change. Acta Cyrstallographica, A30,730-739

Kendrew J. (1963). The crystallographic structure of myoglobin. Science, 139,1259

Kraut J. (1977). Serine proteases: Structure and mechanism of catalysis. Annual Review of Biochemistry, 46,331-358

Levinthal C. (1966). Molecular model-building by computer. Scientific American, Vol. 214,6,42-52

Levinthal C., Wodak S.J., Kahn P., and Dadivanian A.K. (1975). Hemoglobin interaction in sickle cell fibers. I: Theoretical approaches to the molecular contacts. Proceedings of the National Academy of Sciences, USA, 72,1330-1334

Levitt M. (1978).   Conformational preferences of amino acids in globular proteins. Biochemistry, 17,4277-4284

Metzler D.G. (1977).   Biochemistry - The Chemical Reactions of Living Cells, Academic Press, New York

Rossmann M.G., and Argos P. (1978). The taxonomy of binding sites in proteins. Molecular and Cellular Biochemistry, 21,161-182

Sobell H.M., Tsai C.C., Jain S.C., and Gilbert S.G. (1977). Visuallization of drug-nucleic acid interactions at atomic resolution. Journal of Molecular Biology, 114,333-365

Stryer L. (1975). Biochemistry, W. H. Freeman, San Francisco

Templeton D., Johnson C., editors (1978). Computational methodology in crystallography: evaluation and extension. Report of the National Resource for Computation in Chemistry, Lawrence Berkeley Laboratory, University of California, Berkeley

Tsernoglou D., Petsko G.A., McQueen J.E., and Hermans J. (1977). Molecular Graphics: Application to the structure determination of snake venom neurotoxin. Science, 197,1378-1381

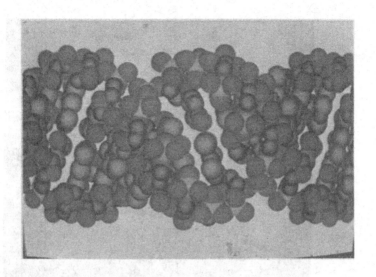

Figure 1 (A)

Models of double stranded DNA

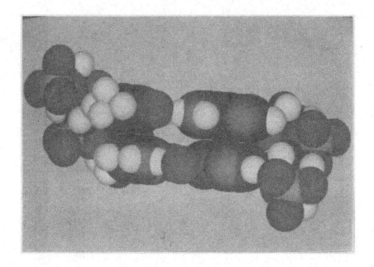

Figure 1 (B)

Two base pairs hydrogen bonded together as found in the double helix.

274

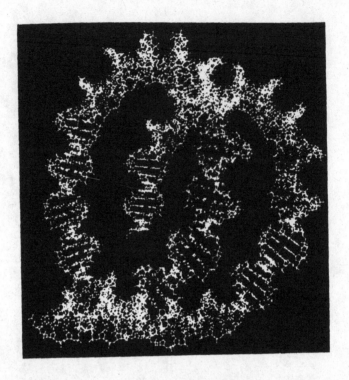

Figure 1 (C)

Super helix of DNA caused kinks at regular intervals

(A and B from R. Feldmann, C from Sobell, 1975).

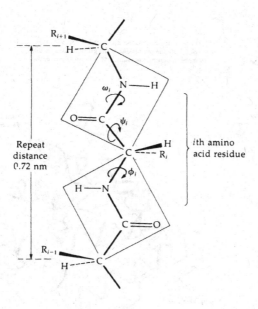

Figure 2

The peptide repeat unit of a polypeptide chain. This figure,
Figs. 3A, 3B, and 4C are from Metzler (1977).

Figure 3 (A)

Model of an ∝-helix, typical of those found in myoglobin.

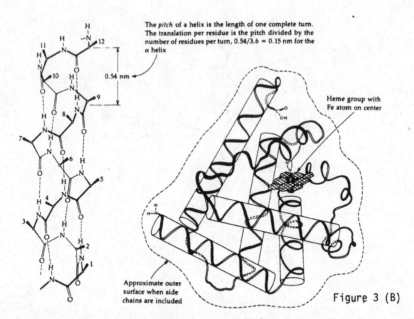

The *pitch* of a helix is the length of one complete turn. The translation per residue is the pitch divided by the number of residues per turn, 0.54/3.6 = 0.15 nm for the α helix

0.54 nm

Heme group with Fe atom on center

Approximate outer surface when side chains are included

Figure 3 (B)

An outline of the 3-dimensional conforma of the entire myoglobin molecule.

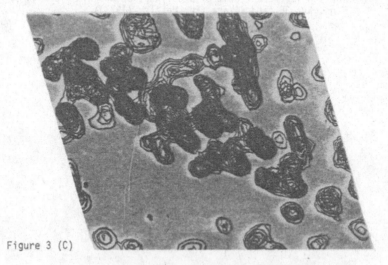

Figure 3 (C)

A portion of the electron density map of myoglobin from X-ray crystallographic data showing one section of an ∝-helix and the porphyrin group, with iron in the center.

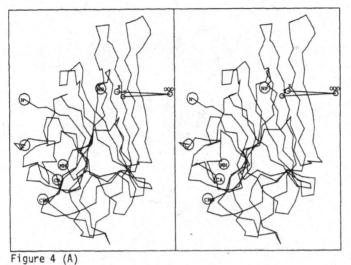

Figure 4 (A)
Computer graphics stereogram of the polypeptide chain of concanavalin A.
Every -cabon atom of each amino acid is connected with a vector.
Four identical chains make one molecule.

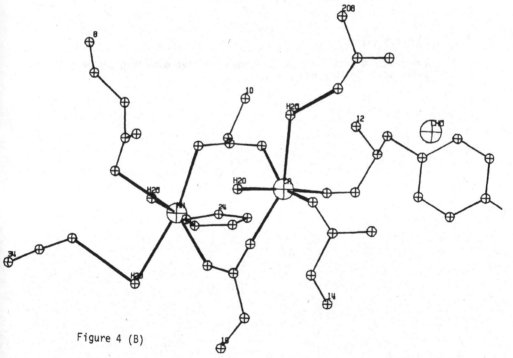

Figure 4 (B)

Graphics image of the atoms in the region of the Mn and Ca ions and
carbohydrate binding region.

278

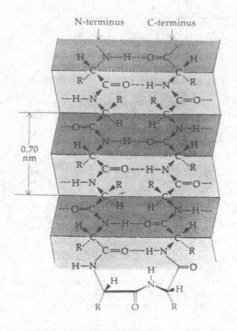

Figure 4 (C)

Two chains of anti-parallel -sheets involve more than 50% of all amino acids in Concanavalin A.

279

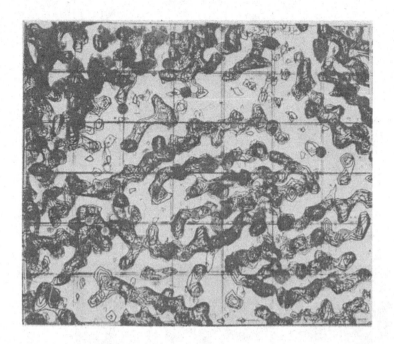

Figure 5

Portions of the electron density map of tomato bushy shunt virus, from Harrison et al. (1978). Multiple chains of -structure appear in the center and lower right.

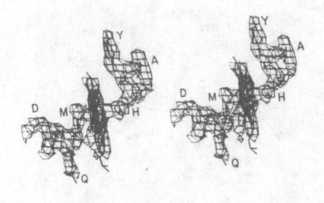

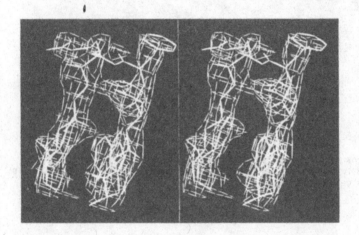

Figure 6

A photograph directly from the graphics screen of snake venom neurotoxin, Tsernoglou et al. (1977). Shown is a portion of the electron density map with the corresponding stick model of the atomic positions inside. In this work the complete atomic model was determined by fitting the atoms of the polypeptide chain into the 3-dimensional electron density map entirely on the graphics device, the GRIP molecular graphics systems at the Univ. of North Carolina facility (which is supported in part by IBM SCD, Research Triangle Park, NC).

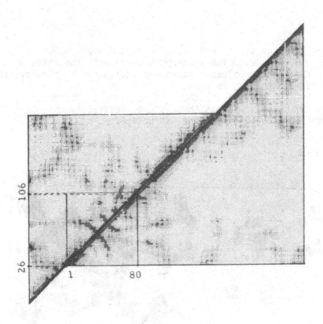

Figure 7 (B)

Two nearly identical regions in two different molecules are found by
"sliding" the two plots together along the diagonal. This can be done
by computer with a fraction of the time compared to 3-dimensional rotational
and translational searches on the two sets of atomic coordinates (from
M. Liebman, unpublished results).

Figure 7 (A)

Diagonal plots of "closeness" of each amino acid with every other amino
acid for the protein rhodanese. The x and y axes are both the amino acid
sequence number. The density values plotted are equivalent to the inverse
of the distance between the two amino acids.
Here, it is clearly seen at a glance that the molecule is divided into
two nearly identical halves, whereas this is not immediately obvious
from examining the complete 3-dimensional structure.

RHODANESE

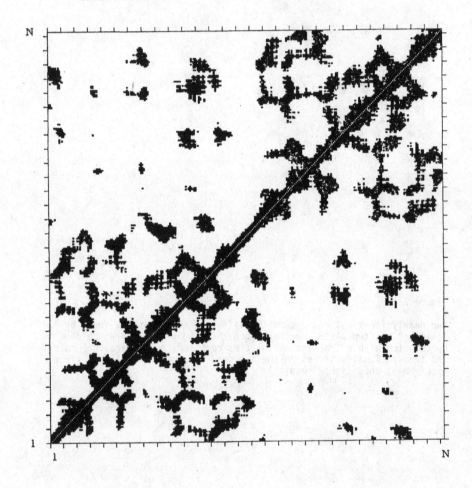

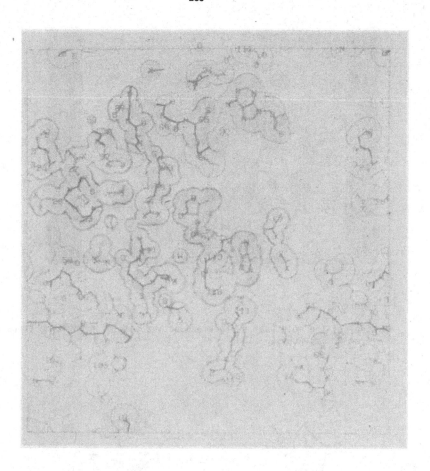

Figure 8

Van der waals packing diagram of a section through the ribonuclease S
molecule. The atomic model and the outlines of the packing volumes are
superimposed on the electron density map.

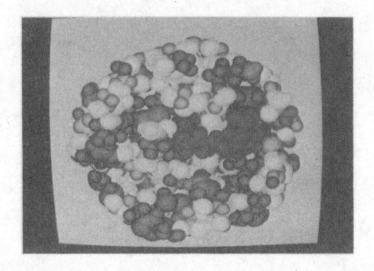

Figure 9

Model of the molecular surface and active site of the enzyme trypsin
(from R. Feldmann).

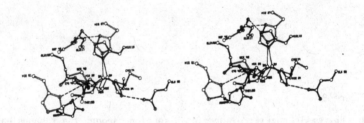

Figure 10

Stereo diagram of superimposed zinc binding regions of two different
enzymes, carbonic anhydrase and liver alcohol dehydrogenase, from
Rossmann and Argos (1978). In these enzymes, as well as others,
the Zn ions are an integral part of the active site.

A Survey of DB Requirements for
Graphical Applications in Engineering

J.Encarnacao and T.Neumann

Abstract

The problem of integrating the graphical and non-graphical information in one data base has not yet been adequately solved. The feasibility of solution has been shown in the literature (Williams, Giddings 76). This paper attempts to identify the specific features exhibited by graphical information structures as used in engineering application. It further focuses on the ways the users interact with the stored information. Bearing these features in mind, some requirements on data base management systems will be inferred.

Institut für Informationsverarbeitung und Interaktive Systeme
Fachbereich Informatik
Technische Hochschule Darmstadt

1. Introduction

The use of large integrated data bases in the commercial world has been by now fully established. Recently the need for similar data integration in engineering applications such as CAD, CAM systems has been recognized (Lillehagen, Oian 77). The question arises whether data base management systems designed for commercial users can be incorporated in industrial systems or if some modifications are necessary. This problem has been given some attention in the past. Williams (Williams, Giddings 76) has shown how design data (of graphical and non-graphical nature) can be stored using relational data description. Our contention is that to answer the above question three factors must be closely looked at: the structure and type of the information to be stored, the manipulation to be performed with this structure (usage) and users. In the following we shall analyse these three factors and try to infer some requirements on data management systems.

2. Why integrated data base

In this section we shall briefly recapitulate the basic thoughts in introducing the data base concept.
The data base technology can be viewed as a further step towards lessening the responsibility of application programmers to maintain their data. A programmer should see only the data and the relationships existing among them and disregard any detail of actual representation of his data in computer. Graphic systems are only seldom used as standalone facilities. More often they are incorporated in larger systems such as CAD/CAM facilities, cartographic systems, flight simulators and others.

Usually the data produced by graphic systems is used by the simulation or analysis programs and vice versa. Thus a common data base serves as a communication area between programs.

Systems like CAD facilities are used by a diverse community of users who also must communicate with each other (process the same data).

If application programs are to be of general validity they must be isolated from the specific representations of data they process. The transparency of detail of the data structure allows the programmer to concentrate on his primary problem. The separation of programs and data allows for definition of a standard interface. This, however, poses new problems: any information whether geometric, topologic, mathematical etc. must be modelled in terms of this standard interface. Moreover we require that the resulting structure can be manipulated in a straightforward way, that is by means of simple algorithms. In the next section we shall observe some features exhibited by geometric and structural information and infer some requirements on the data management system.

287

In summary the advantages of having centralized control over data are
(Date 76):

- Application programmers can be relieved of the task to
  maintain their data.

- Standards can be enforced

- Performance aspects can be shifted away from the application
  programmer.

- The amount of redundancy can be reduced.

- Problems of inconsistency can be reduced.

- Stored data can be shared.

- Data integrity can be maintained.

- Security restriction can be enforced.

3. Some observations on graphical information

3.1 Information modelling

If we are to state requirements on data base management systems, we have
to look closer at the information to be stored. In our case it is information
about graphical objects, or objects that can be presented graphically, (geometric description), the relationships between graphical objects (Topology),
as well as information of non graphical nature (electrical properties of
circuit components etc.). It often happens that non graphical and graphical
data are closely related (topology says something about how the circuit is
connected and how to draw a symbolic diagram).

Intuitively real world (graphical included) can be modelled in terms of facts
about things and in terms of relationships between ghings (Senko 73). For more
formal representation following concepts can be introduced (Blaser, Schauer 78):

- Entity represents anything that can be described by properties, some
  of which are uniquely identifying it.

- Property is an association of an attribute with an attribute value.

- An attribute value is a state of an attribute.

- An attribute is any characteristic to which a value can be.

- An attribute is any characteristic to which a value can be assigned.

Information may be represented in terms of entities and relationships among
them.
Diagrammatically the entities can be represented by entity types. Entity type
is a set of entities having common attributes. The relationships are then of
type 1:1, 1:many, many:1, of many:many (Fig. 1).

This information structure must in some way be modelled in the computer. Three
fundamental models have been developed for commercial information modelling:
hierarchical (IMS), network (Codasyl 71) and relational (Codd 70). Now the
question is can one model the objects of engineering world in terms of these
models? If so can one manipulate the resulting data structure in a simple way?

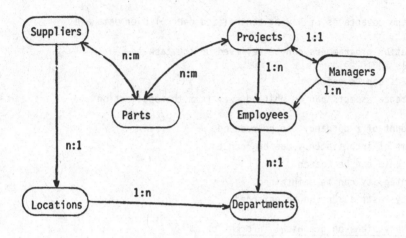

Fig. 1: Representation of facts and relationships of the real world

3.2 Relationships among graphic entities

We shall define a graphic entity as being one which has at least one
graphical attribute. Informally a graphical attribute is one which when given
a value can be perceived visually.

Conceptually representation of a picture can be visualized as an information
hierarchy. A picture is composed of faces, faces consist of edges and edges
consist of points.

The relationships between graphical entities are usually many to many (Fig. 3).
A simple example is an edge that belongs to several faces. Or the same type
of furniture can be situated in several rooms. An equivalent in modelling of
electrical circuits is one component type (subcircuit) belonging to more than
one subcircuit.

Fixed hierarchical structure such as outlined above is usually inadequate in
design databases. Imagine a description of a ship where compartments are devided
into smaller compartments (Bandurski, Jefferson 75). Similar situation may be
found in modelling an electrical circuit as mentioned above or in building
design where rooms are devided by walls into smaller rooms. An example of pure
topology would be a curve made up of several curve segments (Fig. 4). Thus the
possibility of defining homogeneous structures should be supported by the data
model.

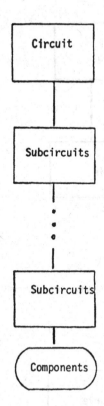

Fig. 2: Representation of a circuit

A complex design data usually cannot be represented by a simple tree structure. Rather the information can be better modelled in form of a network
structure. This is because entities can have more than one functional properties. For example compartments can be associated with the surfaces bounding
them but equally well with the compartments which comprise them (Fig. 5)
(Bandurski, Jefferson 75).

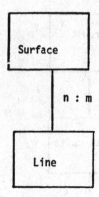

Fig. 3: One line belongs to more than one surface and one surface has more than one line.

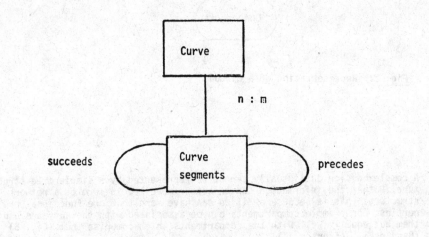

Fig. 4: Example of a homogeneous structure

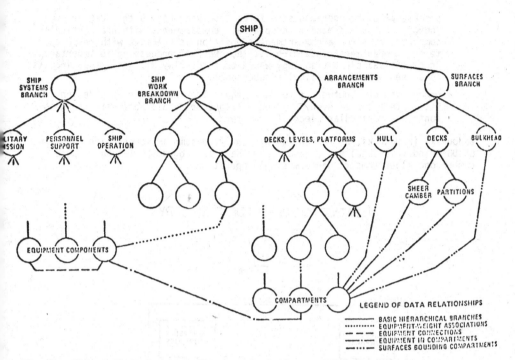

Fig. 5: Ship design structure (Bandurski, Jefferson 75)

Another example is the data structure for geometric modelling as given by
Lillehagen (Lillehagen 78) Fig. 6. Networklike and homogeneous structure
can be seen in this proposal.

3.3 Processing of an information structure

The primary purpose of structuring the information is to enable simple processing. As we have to model our information structure in terms of some
underlying data model a natural thing to ask is, the model to be such, as
to support simple programming of algorithms. Some of the representative
operations in applications with graphics are:

- traversing of hierarchical structures of arbitrary number of levels;
  this can be interpreted as displaying of pictures with increasing
  level of detail, such as the request to display internal structure
  of a gate.

- traversing hierarchical structures from bottom to top;
  e.g. find lines, planes, objects which have a common set of points.

- traversing through arbitrary number of intermediate levels to hide
  unnecessary detail of structure from the user.
  This can be interpreted as the user's request to display the furniture
  situated in each room. The intermediate building structure is immaterial
  to him.

processing of homogeneous structure; Observing Fig. 5 this can be looked upon as a demand to display all compartments within a particular compartment. Since a compartment's position is relative with respect to the compartment containing it, the order of processing is important. An electrical circuit analogy would be to display all gates (subcircuits) contained within a particular subcircuit.

- processing of a network structure. Again looking at the ship design Fig. 5 this can be seen as a request to display all compartments which contain a particular piece of equipment.

Bandurski (Bandurski, Jefferson 75) has analyzed some implementations in terms of DBTG and relational models and found that the programmer hat to compose cumbersome algorithms to perform simple operations.

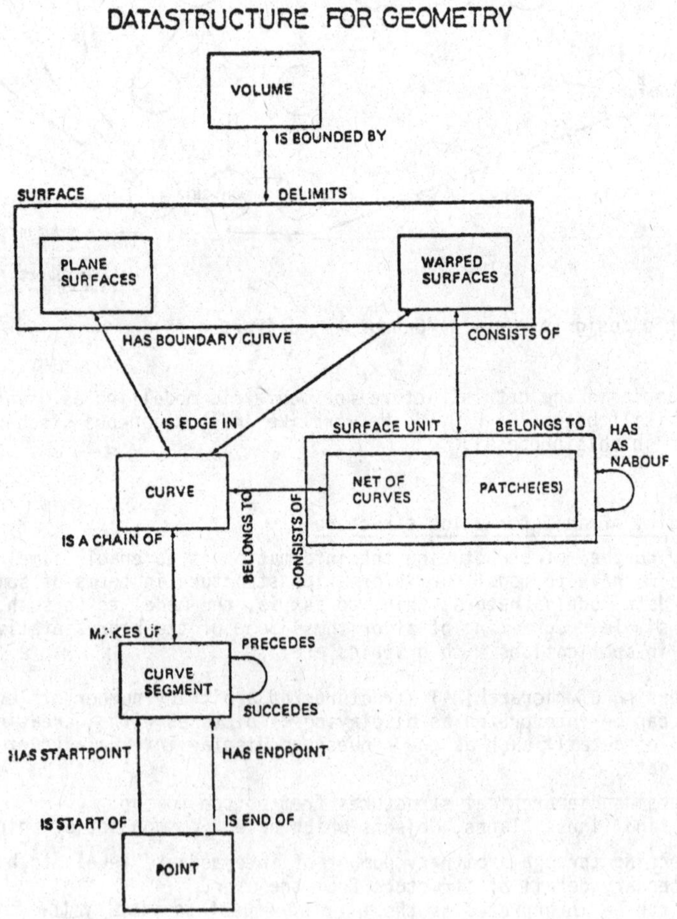

DATASTRUCTURE FOR GEOMETRY

Fig. 6: Data structure for geometry (Lillehagen 78)

4. The user

Let us now look at the potential user of our system.
The application programmer differs from a user of a commercial system in
terms of mathematical sophistication and familiarity with algorithms. He
is probably capable of learning to navigate through the data structure, though
he should avoid this activity as secondary to his task as oposed to commercial
dale processing where only relatively simple processing of data takes place,
once the data have been located.

An engineer (designer) is involved in a creative process and tends to pose a
large number of queries on the DBMS, each of them rather infrequently. The
user of a graphics system often invokes various complex functions (hidden
lines elimination) which demand a fast access to a large number of interrelated
data items.

People of various skill are often involved in a design process. Take for instance a building construction, architects, draftsmen, mechanical engineers,
electrical engineers, accountants etc., are involved. Each group is interested
only in information relevant to their work. Thus the DBMS must allow each
user to define his personal view of data and hide all unnecessary detail from
him.

5. The environment

Graphics systems are used within a number of applications. In this paper we
shall focus on computer assisted interactive design environment.

Design is a creative process. It differs from a process which merely extracts
information in types of queries. The number of queries tend to be large, the
number of repetitive queries small in contrast to a commercial application.
The designer wants to construct a large database representing his design, interactively as the design proceeds (Eastman, Lividini, Stoker 75).
He will want to make use of standard components or components designed previously.
The programs processing retreived data are usually complex.
The designer works interactively at a terminal and expects results to appear
'instantaneously'.

In view of this environment several requirements on the external view of information emerge.

- as types of queries are more difficult to predict, the navigational
  view of data does not seem ideal, as here formulation of 'expected'
  queries result in simpler algorithms, than those for 'unexpected'
  queries. Relational approach seems to be more adequate from this point
  of view. The problem is, how to assure adequate performance for unexpected access paths.

- a design process is an iterative procedure; it often happens, that data
  base must be reorganized as a result of newly found dependences between
  entities and attributes. In order to preserve existing analysis programs
  the data base management system (DBMS) must cater for queries referencing
  information structure which does exist but can be derived from existing
  information structure. This isolation of programs from conceptual view
  of data is usually termed as logical data independence. Again relational
  view of data seems to be more advantageous than navigational view, as
  it is relatively simple to define non-existent relations in user's view.
  The queries referencing fictitious relations are then translated to
  reference a set of relations (Held, Stonebraker, Wong 75).

- we can hardly expect a designer to be innovative if he is forced to think in only one mental model. Therefore the DBMS should support diverse user's views (Nijssen 77).

- the project database should be backed by library of often occuring components. The designer will compose more complex components using the standard ones (previously defined). After he has been satisfied with his creation, he may want to transfer it to the library for later use. This seems to be a major difference between a commercial and an engineering system.

- performance aspects - this is rather a difficult problem - though extremely important in the interactive graphics (design) environment. The generality discussed above is in contradiction with the performance requirements.

We feel that the performance aspects should not be brought to the user's view of information, but rather it should be delt with at a lower level (conceptual level).
Performance adjustments should not have any side effects on the user interface and it should be adaptable to the changing needs of the users. Implicit links are satisfactory to meet infrequent queries and explicit ones to satisfy the needs of application programs requiring fast access to data.
The performance might be enhanced by devitting the database into library and project files. The accesses to the library are relatively infrequent, which allows simple access structure.

- high versus low level query language.
Once the performance aspects have been delegated to a lower level, the purpose for a procedural (navigational) language seems to be lost. From the user point of view a set oriented language of type Sequel (Chamberlin, Boyce 74) should be sufficient.

6. Data type in CAD data bases

Ciampi and Nash (Ciampi, Nash 76) have pointed out that 4 types of data exist in a CAD data base. In terms of circuit development these can be explained as follows.

Type 1 data is the primary circuit description as entered say at an interactive terminal by means of a light pen.

Type 2 data is derived data such as printed circuit board diagram - secondary circuit description.

Type 3 data is data which is not a circuit description.

Type 4 data is pure descriptive data such as manufacturing data.

They also pointed out that type 2 is absent in commercial data bases.
There is not another input data description but the primary. This creates update consistency problems. If the primary circuit description is changed, the secondary description must be invalidated. Programs that generate it must be re-run.
Updates of secondary description should not be allowed. So it should be possible to prevent update selectively and to define consistency rules - such as invalidate type 2 structure if type 1 structure has been changed.

7. Conclusions

The problem of specifying requirements on DB can be reduced to the following problems:

- what information should be stored?
- what are the relationships between entities?
- how can this information structure be modelled in terms of some data model?
- what are the operations to be performed on the data structure?
- are the resulting algorithms simple enough?
- who are the potential users?
- in what environment should the DBMS be embedded?

We have looked at each of these items from the point of view of interactive computer graphics as used in engineering applications and identified some requirements on DBMS such as:

DBMS should support relationships of type many to many

- fixed hierarchical structures seems to be inadequate
- processing should be able to start at any node not necessarily at the root node.
- processing of the hierarchy from leaves to root should be supported.
- DBMS should allow for modelling and processing of homogeneous structures
- it should allow traversing from one level to another through an arbitrary number of intermediate levels
- access paths should be hidden from the user
- logical data independence is important
- diverse user's views of data should be supported
- performance aspect should not appear in the external view of data
- update consistency is more complex than in commercial systems due to existence of secondary (derived) input data; it should be possible to identify data which should be invalidated, should the primary data description change.

References

Bandurski A.C. and Jefferson D.K. (1975)
Data description for Computer Aided Design
Proceedings of the ACM Sigmod International Conference on Management
of Data. San Jose, California; pp. 193 - 202

Blaser A., Schauer U. (1977)
Aspects of Data Base Systems for Computer Aided Design (1977)
Informatik-Fachberichte, Band 11; pp. 78 - 119

Chamberlin D.D., Boyce R.F. (1974)
Sequel: A structured English query Language. Proceedings of 1974
ACM SIGFIDET Workshop. Ann Arbor, Michigan, April 1974; pp. 249 - 264

Ciampi P.L., Nash J.D. (1976)
Concepts in CAD Data Base Structures. Proceedings of 13th Design Automation
Conference. June 28-30, 76 San Francisco, Calif.; pp. 290-294

Codasyl Data Base Task Group (1971
April 1971 Report; New York

Codd E.F. (June 1970)
A Relational Model of Data for Large Shared Data Banks
Communications of ACM Vol. 13, No. 6 pp. 377-387

Date C.J. (1976)
An Introduction to Database Systems
Addisson - Wesley Publishing Company.

Eastman C., Lividini J., Stoker D. (1975)
A database for designing large physical systems
Proceedings of National Computer Conference 75; pp. 603-611

Held G.D., Stonebraker M.R., Wong E. (1975)
Ingres - A relational data base system
Proceedings of National Computer Conference 75; pp. 409-416

IBM, Information Management System, Virtual Storage Publications (1975)

Lillehagen F.M., Oian J. (1977)
Focusing on the internal Model in CAD and CAM Systems
Gilchrist (ed.): Information Processing 77, Proceedings if IFIP Congress 77
pp. 273-278; North Holland Publ. Company

Lillehagen F.M. (1978)
Modelling in CAD Systems.
CAD Tutorial, SIGGRAPH Conference Atlanta, Georgia, 1978

Nijssen G.M. (1977)
On the gross architecture for the next generation database management systems.
Information Processing 77, Proceedings of IFIP Congress 71; pp. 327-335

Senko M.E., Altman E.B., Astrahan M.M., and Fehder P.L. (1973)
Data Structures and Accessing in Data Base Systems.
ii Information Organization.
IBM System Journal Vol. 12, No. 1, pp. 45.- 63

Williams R., and Giddings G.M. (1976)
A Picture-Building System
IEEE Transactions on Software Engineering, Vol. SE-2, No.1, March 76
pp. 62-66

DATA BASE SYSTEMS FOR REMOTE SENSING

Fred C. Billingsley

Jet Propulsion Laboratory
California Institute of Technology
Pasadena, California, 91103

SUMMARY

Landsat and other satellites are returning ever-increasing amounts of data, with the eventual possibility of building a total data base of the order of 10^{18} bits. The data, from a multiplicity of sources, must be validated, calibrated, and accurately geographically located to be of highest value. Because increasing amounts of data are digital, the correlation of digital to non-digital data is required. Formats and cataloguing philosophy must be formulated soon to maximize compatibility of the data archives. The data are being used operationally, requiring of the system timely data delivery (both upon initial acquisition and upon retrieval from an archive), data in formats which are easy to use, and at reasonable cost. The various sources are essentially uncoordinated and diverse, resulting in archives which will require additional operations to accomplish the required formatting. Decisions on a number of issues must be made, some of them quickly; what type(s) of data are to be handled, expected customer base and data traffic (quantity and timeliness), geographic referencing schemes, formats, archive locations, pre-processing and data services to be provided, validation philosophy, cataloguing techniques, storage media, pricing policy, policy on conversion of existing data, technique of system build-up. Propositions for some of these are advanced.

1. THE DATA QUANTITY PROBLEM

Since the launching of the first Landsat in 1972, the satellite Earth Observations Program has attracted worldwide interest. It also generates extreme amounts of data -- for example, each Landsat satellite returns about 10^{11} bits per day to the United States archives. A ten-year program for one satellite thus results in about 3.5×10^{14} bits in storage. With the growing acceptance of satellite data, it is not unreasonable to consider that five satellites of similar -- or more -- capacity could be operational at one time: 2 Landsats in interleaved orbits, 1 or 2 satellites equipped with synthetic aperture radar, and 1 or more geosynchronous satellites for rapid monitoring of episodal events. Table 1 gives estimated data rates for some existing and planned future missions. Such a satellite group could return 10^{14} - 10^{15} bits per year. At the same time that this data bank is accumulating, we are swinging toward digital analysis, requiring that whatever other related data is used (for example, the census Dime File, surface elevation data, soil or land use maps or aerial photographs) be also converted to digital form. It is therefore not unreasonable to believe that we will be faced with a digital archive or perhaps 10^{17} - 10^{18} bits from which we must expeditiously retrieve the set of bits required to solve a particular problem.

Data produced in the Earth observing program may be divided into two general types: 1) that data collected to meet a specific need of a specific primary user. This is characteristic of data to be used in scientific investiga- tions, and no generally available archive is normally provided. 2) that data collected in a general survey mode with no specific end user in mind. Landsat data and general purpose maps are in this category. With the grow- ing sophistication of the analysts, more and more data are being called for by secondary users, so that the distinctions between these two types of data and the differences in the archiving and treatment of the data are beginning to disappear. We are coming to realize that data collected by or for a single investigator must be considered to be available to subsequent inves- tigators, and that for the solution of complex problems no one data source, data archive nor one data station will suffice. Accordingly, the NASA Office of Space and Terrestrial Applications is considering the possibility of a unified data system embracing the data concepts as sketeched in Figure 1 (GSFC, private communication). In this concept, data from various sources, in various possible states of preparation, and from various archives, may be retrieved by a given investigator to perform an analysis or solve a problem not necessarily planned as part of an initial flight mis- sion. This concept forms a major basis for the considerations discussed in the remainder of this paper.

A total information system may be considered to have a structure much as sketched in Figure 2. Considering that by the time a given bit is placed into an archive, it may have been part of some 50 computer operations, and that by the time it becomes part of a user decision it may have been part of another 50 operations, the need for an efficient system is evident. A major part of the system design is the partitioning of the total data processing load between the various parts of the system, including the analysts. In Figure 2 are listed a number of points to be considered in this partitioning of the system and the assignment of the functions.

2. DESIRED DATA ATTRIBUTES

The total system including the sensor, data processing and archiving, retrieval and data analysis requires data with a number of attributes, if the data are to be used. Some of these attributes which affect the design of a system are as follows:

- In these days of increasing analysis complexity even experimental use of the data requires sufficient analysis investment that guarantee of data availability is necessary. "Operational use" generally implies a commitment on the part of the user for repetitive receipt and processing. Dedication of facilities to satisfy both types of uses requires the entire system to be planned to avoid data gaps. Experimental use generally implies a short term program, giving some assurance of data availability. However, operational use is a long term situation requiring a commitment on the part of the data suppliers and archivers to program continuity.

- For many problems the timeliness of data delivery is critical either because the data must be acted on immediately or because the analysis must be complete before the next set of data is received to avoid a data pile-up. In addition, even for the "spur-of-the-moment" data user, rapid response from the archive is required to deliver data while a given problem is still being addressed.

- The data are of no use until analyzed and reduced to some decision. Thus in addition to being delivered to the analyst on time, the data must be in a form suitable for rapid and cost effective analysis. This may require that all calibrations have been applied or that the data be accurately registered to a known map projection before delivery to the analyst.

- The data must be available to the analyst at what appears to him to be an equitable cost. If it is not, one consequence may be that if the task cannot be accomplished in any other way, the task will not be accomplished at all. It must be recognized by the data suppliers that relatively few tasks will be dependent upon a particular source of data, and that if they wish their data to be used, pricing policy must appear to be reasonaable.

- There is a growing diversity of users, each with his own processing needs and techniques. Any given set of data may be manipulated and preprocessed in various ways for each of these users. This suggests that the data system should do a minimum of preprocessing before archiving, and provide specialized processing upon extraction, thus providing each user with the earliest possible generation data.

- Since users will obtain data from a number of sources, the design of archival and retrieval systems must allow the assembly of complete multi-mission data sets which will provide data to a given user from a variety of missions, all interrelated and formatted to allow their combined use.

- For the many studies which call for historical data, the data must be retained in its raw form for extended periods, along with the related cataloguing. As this may result in extremely large archives eventually, some criteria and procedures must be developed to allow screening of old data for disposal.

3. CURRENT PRACTICES

The ever increasing amounts of data being produced have some unfortunate characteristics:

- Various data are produced in unique formats. It has typically been true that each user in assembling data sets for his own problem has assembled and formatted these with little if any consideration towards standardizing formats and protocols with anyone else. Thus for him to use new types of data or for others to use his data, reformatting (at least) is required.

- Data are geographically distributed. While this should not cause a problem, the absence of cross-catalogues ensures that data will be difficult to locate and be effectively hidden from any but the original user. This is true for the Coastal Zone Color Scanner (CZCS) and the Heat Capacity Mapping Mission (HCMM) data, to given two examples.

- The data are stored in archives incompatible in formats and cataloguing. There is no correlation between the various methods by which data are geographically referenced.

- The data are accessed in ad hoc ways. There is no standard way of obtaining data from archives, no way other than mail for transmitting data to users, and the procedure for every archive is different.

It is therefore clumsy, intractable, and inefficient for multiple users to use a given set of data or for a given user to assemble a data set from a variety of sources. It begins to place on the distribution system a load which has not previously been experienced. It is now time to consider coordinated data systems which retrieve data from the various project archives and combine and deliver the data packets to users. A common approach will eventually propagate into the data system, and affect the archiving, formatting and retrieval from the various project sources. The first step in this coordination is data formatting.

4. NATURE OF THE DATA - THE FORMAT QUESTION

There are two levels of formats for space-acquired image data and related ground data: the "production/archive" tape used as a digital archive, and the "user CCT", whose data are extracted and reformatted from the production/archive tape to provide a product more suitable for the user. The production/archive tape is designed for optimum production efficiency, but this tends to limit the flexibility in meeting the diverse needs of the user community. It is not appropriate to try to define a world standard at the production level since individual archive formats differ depending on the hardware and software design preferences, contractor algorithms, equipment used, processing techniques and throughput requirement. The user format can be much more flexible and amenable to adoption as a worldwide format. Since the user CCTs can have a wide distribution, this is the area where most of the benefits are expected from standardization.

There are a few overriding general "requirements" which present conflicts in philosophy. For example, the format should be compact, precise and simple so that non-computer experts can understand it relatively easily. However, it must also be flexible, convenient, and suitable for a wide variety of data types from many sources. In addition, it should be possible to read the basic data without prior knowledge of its source. Flexibility and ability to read the data automatically tend to suggest a certain degree of complexity in the format, whereas simplicity is also desired.

4.1 Cellular or Image Data

The most important data type which must be accommodated in the CCT family structure is that of cellular or image data. This, of course, is the type of data available from the Landsat missions, and is the highest priority type of data. This most important data type might be obtained from multi-channel imaging sensors, be stereo imagery, or might be obtained from synthetic aperture radar or a scanning radiometer. Some of the requirements for such data include the need to handle compressed data which might mean variable pixel word lengths, forward and reverse scan, merging scan lines with different sensors which might not be synchronized. It should be possible to compute from platform parameters and other information provided with the data the exact ground location of each pixel to within some tolerance, which is a function of the product.

4.2 Polygon Data

This data type describes homographic areas by indicating the location of the boundaries, and is commonly used in geodata base systems. In this encoding, spatial features are defined using nodes and connecting line segments. Point form data are described using only nodes; linear form data consist of nodes and connecting line segments; and areal data consist of nodes and line segments forming closed regions, i.e., polygons. Polygons need not be contiguous nor completely cover the scene of interest. The organization of the encoded nodes and line segments is generally handled through lists. Linear encoding techniques include: (1) location lists, (2) point-dictionaries, (3) DIME files, and (4) chain/node encoding. Line encoding offers the most general type of geographic data representation and is particularly advantageous in terms of computer storage requirements in describing: (1) large uniform regions of data such as state or county boundaries, i.e., regions that are large in area in comparison with the basic data cell size, (2) regions of irregular shape, and (3) features that are characteristically linear.

4.3 Profile (Transect) and Point Data

An advantage of this linear form storage concept is the ability to describe not only data that are polygonal in nature, but also linear and point source data in the same logical structure. Linear data, e.g., river networks, are simply unclosed polygons. Point source data, e.g., water quality samples, are nodes. Hence, utilizing the same structure one can describe a watershed through a description of the polygonal soil patterns, linear drainage patterns, and point-source spring locations.

4.4 Alphanumeric and Numerical

The alphanumeric, numerical and logical linear lists include such information as the ancillary information, anotation information, cloud coverage, quality control factors, product descriptions, format definitions, possibly software, radiometric and geometric correction models, processing history, site locations, ground control points, in some cases test patterns, printing information, tick mark locations, etc. An expandable field should be available for providing text information to describe in plain language the processing history, etc., of the data. Of course, this field would not necessarily have to be present on the CCT when it is not used. A subset of this data type is the nominal list, in which the geographical location of the data is implicit by reference to another list (or to ancillary data fields within the list data set). These data may typically include statistical characterizations of a particular layer of geographical data or tables of aggregated information that correspond to features of interest which are delineated in another part of the data base.

4.5 Data Representation

The data types which should be allowed in all areas of the data fields should include at least logical, integer, fraction, real, complex, alphanumeric, and binary coded decimal. It is assumed that, except for the latter two, all numbers would be binary. Logical data are used to define map contours of thematic regions. The real and complex data types should be independent from scientific computer data representation.

It must be possible to record raw data with little or no ancillary information. Partially processed data or fully processed data with or without annotation must be supported. Specialized products may be accommodated in the format such as multi-temporal, pseudo-imagery, mixed data imagery, mosaic data, subscene data, thematic map data, various projections and various data ordering schemes such as band interleaved by line (BIL), band interleaved by pixel (BIP), band interleaved by pixel pairs (BIP2) and band sequential (BSQ). Multiple scenes from different sources must be accommodated as well as cross-references between data bases and scenes. It is important that there be no restriction on information quantity.

The often-discussed differentiation between "data" and "information" is irrelevant to the system design, as both will be represented by the same set of data types. However, it is more important that for "information", quality flags, derivation algorithms, and other data allowing information verification be included in the ancillary record.

305

5. SYSTEM ELEMENTS DEFINITION AND FUNCTIONS

● Source: Provides all data collection and processing functions up to the defined preprocessing point. Suggested preprocessing is reformatting, determination of radiometric corrections, location of geographical control points, determination of geometric warping function, annotation with all radiometric and geometric calibration data.

● Archive: Receives the data from the sources and maintains a catalogue of data available. On receipt of orders, duplicates and transmits data, either wholesale (i.e., bulk, non-selected) or retail (e.g., selected frame sets). Does no data modification, but may deliver segments of data to geographical coordinates.

● Outlet: Orders data from the archive and maintains a working store. On receipt of customer order, may provide value-added services by performing digital processing as necessary (e.g., geometric projection, radiometric correction), and produces the requested customer product. If a prime outlet is established, it may be the location of a central cataloguing facility to coordinate all sources. It may also be the location of non-space data which has been determined to be of widespread use.

6. SYSTEM DESIGN FEATURES

Some features and considerations in the design of a coordinated system to satisfy the data attributes are:

6.1 Data Handling Principles

● Data available in digital form should be stored and disseminated in digital form. In a large measure, the increased utility of the data has been allowed by the digital analysis and the use of the data in geographically addressable form.

● Data from various sensors and from non-space sources will be used together, and therefore must be annotated and formatted for easy geographical registration and segment extraction.

● Because of the bulk of data received and to allow delivery of earliest generation data, processing prior to archiving should be minimized. Suitable annotations must be made for ancillary data during initial handling to facilitate subsequent processing.

● To avoid the need for many users to have to scale or register the various data, and to allow the users to order only the quantity of data required, segment extraction, scaling and registration should be provided by the system upon user request.

6.2 Data Access

- Good browsing and cataloguing are required.

- Wholesale, bulk data at commensurate prices should be available, as well as the normally-expected retail orders.

- System design to meet user timeliness requirements may eventually require direct user reception of the data. This in turn may require the development of some on-board processing. The system must be designed to allow this evolution.

- Timeliness requirements may also require dissemination of the data from the archive by domestic satellite.

- Many problems such as those involved in watching changes will require repetitive data. Thus the system must be able to respond to standing orders to routinely deliver selected data.

6.3 Archiving

- The data recording medium used in the archives must be adequate to allow extended storage without repeated attention and at the same time provide random access to the data.

- For Landsat, all data should probably be considered "in the public domain" and should be archived. However, data utility undoubtedly decreases with time, so that it may be desirable to delete old data after some defined retention time. Also, data compression may be desirable in lieu of deletion.

- There is no archival need for the archive to be at the source. However, source people like to keep a copy of everything. This is useful for a short period, to assess the data quality and until it is assured that the data are received at the archive.

- It is not necessary that all archives the consolidated. If various data are archived at various locations, these should be complementary and not duplicate.

- If an outlet is established at a location having an archive, the two functions must be kept separate. If common equipment is used, an equitable cost sharing plan is necessary so that neither function subsidizes the other.

7. THE USER VIEW

The discussion so far has carried us to the point of delivering usable data to the analyst for his processing. Let us now consider some of the factors involved in a system which must use image type data and polygon and grid cell data from other sources (Billingsley and Bryant, 1975).

Polygon overlay and grid cell information systems access data for selected areas, but in general their data files are time consuming to generate and frequently costly to process. Updating of land use changes for such systems may become prohibitively expensive. A recent development has been to process Landsat and other digital imagery with classification algorithms to derive land cover maps. Such maps, however, cannot interface directly with existing geocoded information storage and retrieval systems. What is needed is the conjunction of existing geocoded data sets and information management systems with thematic maps and remotely sensed imagery. An approach to this is to use the capabilities of digital image processing systems to process raster scans made from maps and polygon data.

The basic premise in designing such a system is that a digital image processing language and its associated algorithms can efficiently execute file manipulation of spatially referenced data. The geocoded data set in the tabular data base can be referenced to a raster scan in which each pixel is equivalent to a grid cell or a polygon node. Current information on land use can be derived from Landsat imagery. Additional data sets will be generated through scanning photographs of thematic maps or converting digitized information to raster format. It should be noted that the raster scan data base is not designed to replace existing tabular data files and information and storage retrieval systems, but rather makes available additional data not originally included, and permits the entry of updated information by simply replacing the data plane. The referenced paper makes the arguments for the image mode processing; the question here is one of philosophy as to where in the total system which processes should be performed, and what ancillary data such as geographical coding is required in machine readable form to do the required processing. Figure 3 illustrates the user's view of such a system. It can be seen that this system follows the philosophy previously outlined under data handling principles: Minimize processing of raw data but append required ancillary data while the raw data is in hand and apply corrections only on retrieved data.

8. LOCAL DATA SYSTEM CONSIDERATIONS

Assuming that all has gone well in the world and that a suitable central system is in place, the local user still has the decision to make as to whether to use it. This decision will normally revolve around two factors: money (front end and/or operations) and data delays (which may be converted to money equivalent). The system design job has been to aggregate a very large number of potential users, to estimate their needs in terms of data traffic (quantity, allowable delays, and geographic distribution), and to provide a large system with low cost, minimum potential for failure, suitable cataloguing, browse, and query capability, and reasonable queueing performance. The local user, on the other hand, is concerned with these factors to a lesser extent (a local user, by definition, is one with a small number of analysts, within a relatively small geographical area), and has much less flexibility in invoking the law of large numbers. His driving forces include:

- Data must be accumulated from various sources at various distances; some from established archives, some via direct spacecraft transmissions, some by coordinated data packets through the central system, some generated and/or stored locally, etc. (Figure 4)

- He will have available a number of possible input data paths: e.g., satellite, landline, courier, and mail. Each of these will have a characteristic delay function (Figure 5), and costs depending on bandwidth, total traffic, and distance.

- He must understand the sensitivity of his analysts to data delays or to missing data, and plan backup data paths for critical data.

- He will be very concerned with costs: data charges, data transportation costs, and the costs in idle time or other hangups caused by transit delays, possible delays at his own location required for data preprocessing, makeup of data deficiencies, or for analysis.

- He must determine how much to rely on the central system and how much locally stored (on line and off line) data to provide.

8.1 System Tuning

The central system and the local system will each be trying to optimize the total performance by adjusting parameters under their control. However, the goals may - probably will - be quite different: the central system must identify the operations scenarios of all potential local users and design a cost-effective system satisfying all of the potential drivers, but (probably) not provide many specialized services; the local user, with many fewer analysts, has the choice of using the central system facilities (cataloguing, registration, etc) or not, and may provide both generic and specialized services to the analyst. Thus the "tuning" of the two systems may be quite different (Figure 6). The central system must be stable against failures, perhaps implying lesser services provided, whereas the local system, with its wider variety of services, may be more critically designed. Also, interactive activity on the central system will likely be mostly catalog query and data ordering, with the interactive analysis being done using the capabilities of the local system. (This prediction is based on the assumption that as computing costs continue to come down more computing may be afforded locally, and that remote processing as with the LARSYS terminals will decrease. It also assumes that much generic processing such as instrument rectification, data set geographical registration, and common formatting will be done by the central system.) Thirdly, the central system optimization can take only minimum cognizance of the delays and frustrations of the local analysts caused by singular lacunae in data delivery, whereas the local system must optimize operations including the analysts time, and instances of idle time caused by data delays are very visible. Table 2 lists some possible pitfalls in system acceptance of either level system.

9. ISSUES FOR DECISIONS

It can be seen that the question of designing national-class data bases for geographically coded data cannot be done without consideration of the multiplicity of sources, diversity of users, and data distributing requirements. Suggestions for some of the outstanding issues for which decisions must be made are outlined below:

- Data Types - This should probably be limited to that set of data required to solve geographically-related problems. In particular, it would include two-dimensional image data (in digital form, with a possible prior film version), map data (digitally coded via polygons or the like, with possible references to hard copy maps), two-dimensional data in image format but representing other variables such as surface elevation, geographically located point data such as individual temperature measurements at airports, geographically located demarcation data such as the census DIME File.

- Customer Base - If suitable formats can be derived for data as described above, there will be a very large defacto distributed data base available and along with it a large diverse group of possible users including various Federal agencies, various regional, state or local public

agencies, private industries such as geophysical or petroleum exploration companies, universities, and others. As the diversity of data
which is properly formatted grows, the diversity of users will also grow.

- Data Traffic and Timeliness - This requirement will evolve as the study
of data types and customer base proceeds. It is already evident that
some uses of the data require as little as two days throughput delay
after data acquisition and that most requirements are satisfied with a
seven day throughput. However, studies are needed to estimate the
distribution of allowable delays and the associated requested data set
sizes.

- Geographic Referencing Schemes - With the increasing fineness of
resolution of the data, data quantities are increasing. It is becoming
more important that the distributing centers be able to deliver data
blocks to customers only surrounding the desired area, rather than
complete (e.g., Landsat) frames. In order to be able to extract these
segments, precise geographical location parameters must be appended to
the archival frames. At this time it appears that most users would be
pleased with rectangular segments, bounded by latitude-longitude or
northing-easting, and desire pixel lines along these coordinates.

- Formats - The format philosophy outlined in the body of the paper when
fully developed should satisfy the users' needs for both data interchange and for use within geographically coded data processing systems.
The format design is intended to be recursive in the sense that a segment processed by a system would have appended the modified annotation
data to allow the processed image to be reentered.

- Archive Locations - Archives which presently receive two-dimensional
remote sensing data include EROS Data Center (Landsat and aerial
photos), National Space Science Data Center (NSSDC) (Heat Capacity
Mapping Mission, Coastal Zone Color Scanner and other "science" data),
NOAA Archives (weather satellite data), and others. In addition, various locations are generating other types of data such as the USGS (topographic map and land-use polygon data, and the surface to elevation
images), Census Bureau (DIME File). Further, it is anticipated that
many users will generate data which would be of use to others and which
could profitably be considered available.

- Data Services - In the case of Landsat, it has been found that a small
fraction, perhaps 5 percent of the data, have been requested in digital
form. It therefore seems inappropriate to completely process all of the
raw data before entering into the archive. It is therefore suggested
that the pre-archive processing be limited to the determination of
calibration parameters. An appropriate system service would be to
assemble data packets with data extracted from various archives,
registered and scaled according to customer requirements. It is probably not appropriate to do any actual processing on the data, although
this is an open question.

- Validation - Data in the various archives will be in various degrees of
correctness. As a minimum, the condition of the data should be indicated in the annotation; responsibility for this should be agreed to

between the data source and the archive. It probably should not be a data distribution system function, nor should the system assume responsibility for acquiring uncatalogued data on special order.

- Cataloguing Techniques - Given the limitations suggested above, the prime catalog reference is expected to be geographical with secondary references to cloud cover, time of year, time of day, data source, and perhaps data validity.

- Storage Media - Because of the requirement for extracting segments at the archive, data storage must not only be archivally permanent but randomly accessible. Traffic studies will determine how much data should be electronically on line. The most likely storage candidate at this point seems to be digital video disks manually mounted, with the possibility of "juke box" retrieval when traffic flow warrants.

- Pricing Policy - If the data base is assembled by Federal agencies, there is a requirement to have all data in the public domain. This implies some level of data services which would not be required of secondary sources. These services could well be subsidized, as would be the initial acquiring of the data. Only reproduction cost would be borne by the product price.

- Conversion of Existing Data to Standardized Formats - As there is beginning to be a large amount of data in the archives, a relatively small part of which will probably be digitally accessed, the conversion of this data does not seem warranted until ordered from the archive. However, cataloguing of the old data should be brought completely up-to-date so that it can be found.

- System Build-up - Since the set of data sources, set of customers, and traffic flow requirements will not be known initially and since in any event it is probably not desirable to incur a large front-end cost, the system should be built modularly with the ability to add sources, data links, and customers as demand grows. However, the formatting schemes and the cataloguing technique must be well thought through ahead of time, as both of these should remain relatively constant, independent of the size of the system.

10. CONCLUSIONS

The utility of Landsat or other satellite sensors and the general ability of analysts throughout the country to accomplish their tasks using remote sensing can be greatly helped or greatly hindered by decisions such as outlined above, the most critical being that of data formats and cataloguing. Data are already being used operationally and the archives are growing. Immediate attention is needed to the above topics to assure that the growth is orderly and that the data generated from various sources can be interrelated and used by a wide variety of analysts.

BIBLIOGRAPHY

1. Aepli, T., Brooks, J., Carafides, A., Dallam, W., Park, A., Smith, D. Landsat D: Corps of Engineers Interface with Advanced NASA Ground Systems Study, Report No. ETL-0151, General Electric Company for USACOE Engineer Topographic Laboratories, Ft. Belvoir, Va. 22060. (1978)

2. Anderson, J.R., Hardy, E. E., Roach, J. T. (1972), A Land Use Classification System for Use with Remote Sensor Data, USGS Circular 671, Washington, D.C. Revised as USGS Professional Paper 964, 1976.

3. Billingsley, F.C., Bryant, N.A. (1975), Design Criteria for a Multiple Input Land Use System, NASA Earth Resources Symposium, NASA TM X-58168, Vol. I-B, p 1389-1396.

4. Bryant, N. A. Zobrist, A.L. (1976), IBIS: A Geographic Information System Based on Digital Image Processing and Image Raster Datatype, Proc Symposium on Machine Processing of Remotely Sensed Data, Purdue University, W. Lafayette, Ind.

5. Chrisman, N. R. (1975), Topological Information Systems for Geographical Representation, 2nd International Symposium on Computer Assisted Cartography, Reston, Va.

6. Cicone, R.C., Malila, W.A., Crist, E.P., Investigations of Techniques for Inventorying Forested Regions, Vol. II, Forestry Information System Requirements and Joint Use of Remotely Sensed and Ancillary Data, Report No. NASA CR-ERIM 122700-35-F_2, Environmental Research Institute of Michigan for NASA Johnson Space Center, Houston, Texas 77058. (1977)

7. Davies, R., Scott, M., Mitchell, C., Torbett, A., User Data Dissemination Concepts for Earth Resources, Report No. NASA CR-137905, Aeroneutronic-Ford Corporation for NASA Ames Research Center, Moffett Field, Cal., 94035 (1976)

8. Deuker, K. J. (1972), A Framework for Encoding Spatial Data, Geographical Analysis, 4, p 98-105.

9. Deuker, K. J. (1974), Urban Geocoding, Annals of Assoc. of American Geographers, 64, p 318-325.

10. Dyer, H. L., et al (1975), Information System for Resource Management and Related Applications, Argonne National Laboratory, for the office of Land Use and Water Planning, 2 Vols.

11. Ellefson, R., Swain, P. H., Wray, J. R. (1973), Urban Land-Use Mapping by Machine Processing of ERTS-1 Multispectral Data: A San Francisco Bay Area Example, LARS Information Note 101573, Purdue University, W. Lafayette, Ind.

12. Faust, N.L., Furman, M.D., Spann, G.W., Design of a Low Cost Earth Resources System, Georgia Institute of Technology Engineering Experiment Station for NASA Marshall Space Flight Center, Huntsville, Ala. 35812, under contract No. NAS8-32397. (1978)

313

13. Holmes, R.A. (1971), Data Requirements and Data Processing Earth Resources Surveys, S.P.I.E. Journal, Vol. 9, January, 1971, p 52-56.

14. Kohn, C.F. (1970), The 1960's; A Decade of Progress in Geographical Research and Instruction, Annals of Assoc. of American Geographers, 60, No. 2, June, 1970, p 215.

15. Miller, W.R. (1975), A survey of Geographical Based Information Systems in California, Intergovernmental Board on Electronic Data Processing, State of California, May, 1975.

16. Power, M. A. (1975), Computerized Geographic Information Systems: An Assessment of Important Factors in Their Design, Operation, and Success, Center for Development Technology, Washington University, St. Louis, Mo., Dec, 1975.

17. U.S. Bureau of the Census (1970), Census Use Study: The DIME Geocoding System, Report No. 4, Washington, D.C.

18. Warner, P.A. (1974), National Geocoding, Annals of Assoc. of American Geographers, 64, p 310-317.

TABLE 1.

ESTIMATED DATA RATES FOR EXISTING AND PLANNED MISSIONS

GOES	1.5×10^{13}	bits per year
HCMM	1.2×10^{12}	bits per year
LANDSAT-3	2.6×10^{13}	bits per year
MAGSAT	6.0×10^{10}	bits per year
NIMBUS-7	2.9×10^{12}	bits per year
SAGE	1.6×10^{10}	bits per year
TIROS-N	2.0×10^{13}	bits per year
ERBE	2.5×10^{11}	bits per year
ICEX	3.7×10^{14}	bits per year
LANDSAT-D	9.5×10^{13}	bits per year
NOSS	1.6×10^{13}	bits per year
OERS	2.0×10^{14}	bits per year
STEREOSAT	1.5×10^{14}	bits per year
UARS	2.0×10^{12}	bits per year

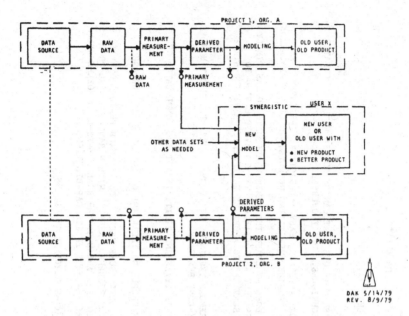

DAK 5/14/79
REV. 8/9/79

Figure 1. DATA ACCESS CONCEPT FOR A MULTI-SOURCE DATA SYSTEM SERVING
MULTIPLE USERS

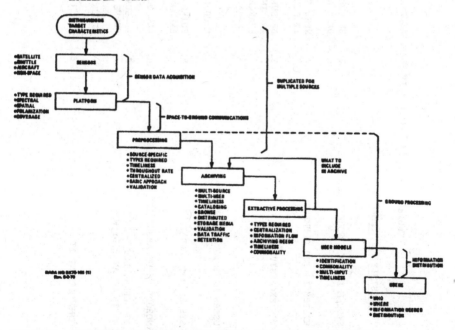

Figure 2. TECHNICAL COMPONENTS AND ISSUES OF TOTAL INFORMATION
SYSTEM STRUCTURE

Table 2 - SOME PITFALLS IN THE DESIGN AND USE OF A DATA SYSTEM

	POSSIBLE PROBLEMS		SOLUTIONS
1.	SYSTEM DOESN'T WORK TECHNICALLY	1.	BE SURE PROBLEM IS ONE THAT CAN BE SOLVED WITH ANTICIPATED DATA AND TECHNIQUES. DON'T OVERSELL.
2.	SYSTEM IS TOO CLUMSY TO USE	2.	NEED GOOD CAI APPROACH, EASY INTERACTION. FRIENDLY. KEEP IT SIMPLE. PROVIDE ONE-SITTING RESULTS. GOOD DOCUMENTATION.
3.	TOO EXPENSIVE	3.	BE SURE IT DOES AT LEAST THE MINIMUM ADEQUATE JOB AS SIMPLY AND INEXPENSIVELY AS POSSIBLE. TRY TO AVOID HAVING TO CHARGE FOR SERVICES TO AMORTIZE EQUIPMENT. MINIMIZE STAFF OPERATORS.
4.	USERS HAVE TO COME TOO FAR	4.	HOW ABOUT REMOTE TERMINALS VIA PHONE LINE? PSYCH OUT HOW MUCH CAN BE DONE REMOTELY.
5.	SYSTEM NOT VERSATILE	5.	BUILD FLEXIBILITY/EXPANDABILITY IF NOT TOO COMPLICATED OR EXPENSIVE.
6.	NOBODY KNOWS ABOUT IT	6.	LET OUTSIDE PEOPLE DO THEIR JOB ON THE SYSTEM. PUBLISH.
7.	IT WORKS, BUT DOESN'T DO ANYTHING ANYBODY WANTS	7.	BE SURE IT SOLVES SOME NEEDS. PUT IN EACH FEATURE ONLY TO SOLVE A KNOWN PROBLEM. KEEP IT WITHIN RANGE OF REAL PROBLEMS. IT MAY BE TOO FAR AHEAD OF THE REAL DAY-TO-DAY PROBLEM NEEDS. EDUCATE REAL ANALYSTS IN ITS CAPABILITIES.
8.	THEY RESENT IT	8.	DON'T BE A COMPETITOR TO THE USERS.

Figure 3. FEATURES OF AN IMAGE BASED INFORMATION SYSTEM FOR GEOGRAPHICALLY LOCATED DATA

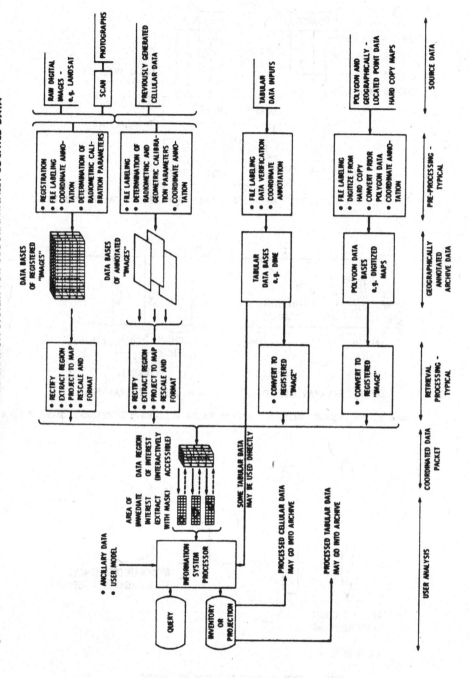

318

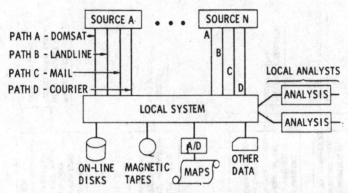

Figure 4.   THE LOCAL USER MAY OBTAIN DATA THROUGH SEVERAL ACCESS PATHS

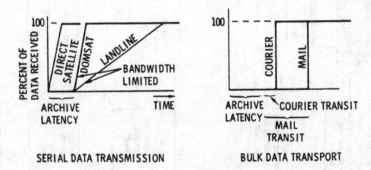

Figure 5.   DIFFERENT TYPES OF ACCESS PATHS WILL HAVE DIFFERENT TRANSIT DELAYS

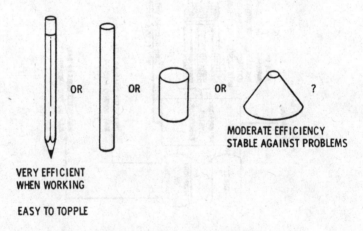

Figure 6.   A FINELY TUNED SYSTEM MAY NOT BE ROBUST

Data Base Requirements for Remote Sensing and Image Processing Applications

Ralph Bernstein

Summary

Remote sensing of the earth has evolved from a film based, manual interpretation technology to a digital multispectral and multisensor technology with significant machine processing for correction, information extraction, data management, and modelling. This transition is not without growing pains. Of the 10^{15} bits of data that are currently acquired per year in the NASA program, only about 10^{13} bits are utilized. Future programs involving higher resolution and wider spectral range sensors will increase the data acquisition rates by an order of magnitude. Technological problems exist today in data correction, information extraction, processing, storage, retrieval and dissemination. This paper will identify some of the data base requirements for future programs, and discuss technological approaches for improving the handling and processing of remotely sensed data. Fundamental to this approach is the concept of a global data and information base that is geographically accessible, contains data from all earth observation programs, and is easily and economically disseminated. This capability is needed, and the technology is available for its implementation.

IBM Corporation, Federal Systems Division, 18100 Frederick Pike, Gaithersburg, Maryland, USA 20760

INTRODUCTION

Earth observation programs for resource and environmental measurements are
currently in the exploratory phase and are rapidly entering an operational
phase involving routine use. Advanced technologies for sensing, communications, processing, and storing data have been developed and are beginning
to be utilized to support space science and applications activities.
Although advanced technologies exist today for supporting earth resource
and environmental measurements, systems and procedures for an integrated
and coordinated global data base have not yet fully developed. It is
essential that this be done soon, in that in excess of 10^{15} bits of data
are currently acquired by NASA per year, and it has been estimated that
only one-hundredth of the data acquired is currently being utilized.
Further, extensive time is being used to locate available data, and in
many cases needed data are not used because of lack of knowledge of the
existence of the data or inability of the user to process the data.
There is a need for the development of an integrated data base that is
cross-disciplinary, contains both data and derived information, and has
easy and broad accessibility. It is essential that this capability be
provided at a low cost in a computer compatible format, and the data
be available in a timely manner.

The interrelationship of data to support multidisciplinary programs is
becoming more important. For example, it has been established that for
accurate agricultural crop yield prediction not only is it necessary to know
what was planted where, but to also know, rather specifically, soil moisture
and other meteorological conditions. In the category of environment,
biological, chemical, and thermal processes all influence our weather and
climate. Data relating to these processes are needed in order to gain an
understanding of and to produce environmental models.

The earth resources program is a scientifically active program that has
been tremendously accelerated by recent satellite programs such as Skylab,
Landsat, Heat Capacity Mapper Mission, Seasat, and the supporting aircraft
programs. Future missions, such as the Naval Oceanic Satellite System,
Space Shuttle, Spacelab and future Landsats will provide more data and
support scientific investigations and operational program development.
Table 1 provides a listing of resource management activities that have
developed and are being supported as a result of these programs (Catoe, 1978).

The environmental program is equally active, having been based upon the
Tiros and Nimbus programs, and in the future being supported by the Tiros-N,
NOAA A-G, Nimbus-G, Sage, Earth Radiation Budget Satellite, NOSS, GOES, and
the Ocean Atmosphere Observation System. Table 2 provides a summary of
atmosphere and oceans programs that are developing as a result of these
programs (Nagler, 1978).

Table 1. Resource Management Programs (Catoe, 1978)

AGRICULTURE

o Survey U. S. Cropland to Prepare Statistical Summaries and Production Forecasts for Major Crops.

o Monitor U.S. Pasture and Cropland to Detect and Assess Insect, Disease, and Stress Damage.

o Survey U.S. Cropland to Evaluate Current Farming Practices and Classify Areas on the Basis of Productivity.

o Survey and Monitor U.S. Cropland to Calculate Short- and Long-Run Demand for Irrigation Water.

o Survey Major Crops on a Global Basis to Inventory Acreage and Forecast World Production.

o Survey Pasture and Range Areas to Prepare Statistical Summaries of Forage Acreage, Calculate Supportive Capacity for Livestock, and Assess Current Grazing Practices.

ENERGY/MINERALS

o Survey Geological Features to Detect Sites Indicative of the Location of Mineral Deposits.

o Survey Surficial Thermal Patterns to Detect Potential Geothermal Sources.

o Survey Waters of Outer Continental Shelf Areas to Detect Oil Film Possibly Indicative of Submarine Oil Deposits.

o Monitor Surface Mining and Oil Drilling Operations to Detect Resultant Environmental Pollution.

o Monitor Oil and Gas Pipelines to Detect Breaks or Other Environmental Dynamics.

o Monitor Deepwater Ports to Detect and Assess Oil Pollution.

o Monitor Powerplant Operations to Detect and Assess Thermal Pollution in Adjacent Waters.

FOREST

o Survey and Monitor Forestland to Prepare Forecasts of Timber Production, Classify Areas According to Productive Status, and Assess the Efficiency and Ecological Soundness of Timber Production and Harvesting Operations.

o Monitor Forests and Grassland/Brushland Areas to Detect and Assess Insect, Disease, and Stress Damage.

o Survey and Monitor Forests and Grassland/Brushland Areas to Assess Fire Potential, Detect the Outbreak of Fire, Assess the Dynamics of Fire, and Assess Damage.

LAND

o Survey and Map Current Land Use Patterns Within the U.S. in Support of State Land Use Planning and the Management of Federal Lands.

o Survey and Map the Vegetation, Landforms, Topography, Geology, and Soil of the U.S. Land Area.

o Continuously Survey Lake and Coastal Shoreline Morphology and the Navigational Channels Within the Coastal Zone in Support of Shipping and Recreation.

o Survey, Identify, and Map the Location of Geological Hazards Over the U.S. Land Area.

o Survey the U.S. Flood Plain Areas and Identify and Assess Potential Flood Hazard Areas.

MARINE

o Survey and Map the Physical and Chemical Properties of the Global Oceans for Optimum Ship Track Routing, Drilling Operations, and Other Open Ocean Operations.

o Monitor and Assess Those Dynamic Processes of the Ocean Potentially Harnessable as Sources of Energy.

o Survey and Map the Distribution and Quantity of Commercial and Sport Fish Species in U.S. Coastal and Off-Shore Waters, Their Food Supplies, and Other Environmental Factors Necessary to Predict Future Catches.

o Monitor the Health of the Global Oceans by Surveying the Source, Distribution and Movement of the Main Pollutants in the Marine Environment, and Marine Organisms.

o Survey and Monitor Hazards to Navigation on the High Seas, Such as Sea Ice, Icebergs, and Severe Wave Conditions.

WATER

o Survey and Inventory the Volume and Distribution of Surface and Ground Water to Assess Available Supplies for Urban, Agricultural, and Hydroelectric Consumption.

o Survey and Map Great Lakes Ice Cover and Type to Determine the Passibility of Navigational Channels, Optimum Routing of Lake Shipping, and Port Accessibility.

o Survey and Monitor Quality Surface Water Throughout the U.S. and Surrounding Coastal Zones with Particular Attention to Lake Eutrophication and Sources of Water Pollution.

o Survey and Monitor Surface Water, Snow Cover, Glaciers, and Ground Water Levels and Movement to Identify Potential Flood Conditions and to Trace the Movement of Floodwaters.

o Survey and Monitor the Surface Water Volume and Indicator Species of Vegetation in Wetlands and Estuaries to Evaluate the Ecological Productivity of Wetland Areas.

Table 2. Earth Applications Disciplines (Nagler, 1978)

ATMOSPHERE AND ICE

o Climate Research
o Upper Atmosphere Research
o Stratospheric Contamination
o Large Scale Weather Forecasts
o Small Scale Weather Forecast
o Weather Research
o Tropospheric Contamination
o Ice Forecasts
o Ice Research
o Glaceology

OCEAN

o Global Ocean Condition Forecasting
o Coastal Ocean Condition Forecasting
o Physical Ocean Research
o Ocean Engineering
o Marine Geology
o Ocean Geodesy and Bathymetry
o Living Marine Resources
o Biological Ocean Research
o Ocean Contamination
o Chemical Ocean Research

Scenarios for the years 1985-2000 suggest a number of imaginative and interacting programs for future earth observation. They range from high resolution sensors for localized disaster assessment to microwave sensors for measuring subsurface boundary layers. Table 3 summarizes these possible programs and their application characteristics.

DATA REQUIREMENTS FOR EARTH OBSERVATION MEASUREMENTS

Several studies have addressed the data requirements for earth observation program. Van Vleck, et al (1973) have summarized requirements by discipline, including resolution, area coverage and interval, and spectral bands. Rapid dissemination of earth observation data to the user community is needed. With reference to Table 4, the data coverage interval requirements for the conterminous U.S. range from weeks for agriculture, forestry, and hydrology to several years for cartography. As can be seen from Figure 1, similar data conditions exist in the environmental program where observation intervals range from hours for meteorological measurements to years for climate and glaciology measurements (Nagler, 1978). When all factors influencing data acquisition rates are considered, the resultant bit rate for all disciplines exceeds 10^{15} bits per year. Improved resolution sensors will likely increase these rates further.

FUTURE SENSOR DIRECTIONS

Sensor technology is a dominant influence in data processing and data management. With the advent of automated sensor systems on unmanned platforms using advanced detector technologies, a growth in data is inevitable. For example, in the Landsat program, the amount of sensor data that can be potentially acquired over the same area of earth will increase by a factor of 10, as noted in Table 5. Sensor technologies in the mid-1980's will improve sensors further, and also increase data rates and processing requirements.

A new technology that has great promise uses solid state linear arrays. An array of detectors perpendicular to the ground track scan the earth, are sampled, and the data are then stored or transmitted to ground. The advantage of this technology is that it replaces electro-mechanical devices with non-moving electronic components (such as oscillating mirrors), can provide 10 m resolution, will have improved signal-to-noise performance compared with conventional scanners, and will have excellent internal geometry characteristics (Thompson, 1979).

Table 3. Possible 1985-2000 Space System
Concepts (Aviation Week, 1979)

GEOSYNCHRONOUS EARTH OBSERVATION SYSTEM

Large telescope with 3m resolution for disaster assessment

GEOSYNCHRONOUS SYNTHETIC APERTURE RADAR

Radar coverage for disaster assessment, soil moisture monitoring
and resource observations

RADAR HOLOGRAPHER

Microwave measurement system with geosynchronous illuminator
and low-earth orbit collector to generate an earth hologram
for resource uses

LANDSAT-H

"Smart" multispectral linear array and synthetic aperture radar
for earth resources observations

THERMAL INERTIA MAPPER

Ground thermal emissivity measurements

SWEEP FREQUENCY RADAR

Microwave texture measuring system for identification and
classification of ground materials

MICROSAT

Passive radiometer for soil moisture measurements

TEXTUROMETER

Ground texture measuring system to classify ground materials

ELLIPSOMETER

Radar system for measuring soil moisture, vegetation moisture,
and vegetation height

PARASOL RADIOMETER

Phased array radiometer for measuring soil moisture

FERRIS WHEEL RADAR

Large radar for measuring subsurface boundary layers.

Table 4. Requirements for Earth Resources Disciplines
(Van Vleck, et al)

Discipline	Resolution (meters)		Coverage Interval (days)	Area Covered km³	Bands/ Sensors	Data Rate (bits/day)	
	Detailed Survey	Recon. Survey				Min.	Max.
Agriculture	10-30	30-100	7-21	3×10^6	12	2×10^{10}	5×10^{11}
Cartography	3-20	20-200	1825	9×10^6	3	3×10^8	2×10^{10}
Forestry/ Range Land	10-50	50-200	7-30	3×10^6	8	3×10^9	3×10^{11}
Geography	6-30	6-100	365	9×10^6	3	1×10^9	3×10^{10}
Geology	6-100	30-200	365	2×10^6	4	2×10^8	6×10^{10}
Hydrology	3-100	50-250	10-20	1×10^6	4	2×10^8	4×10^{11}
Meteorology	1000-2000	1000-4000	.25-1.0	30×10^6	2	1×10^8	2×10^9
Oceanography	20-300	200-1000	14-30	15×10^6	4	1×10^8	1×10^{11}

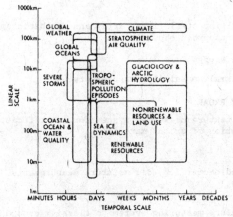

Figure 1. Requirements for Environmental Observations
(Nagler, 1978)

Table 5. Landsat Sensor Characteristics

Landsat	Sensor	Year	Resolution	Spectral Bands	Dynamic Range	Bits/ Scene
1	Multispectral Scanner	1972	79 m	4	6 bits	1.8×10^8
2	Multispectral Scanner	1975	79 m	4	6 bits	1.8×10^8
3	Multispectral Scanner	1978	79 m	5	6 bits	1.9×10^8
D	Thematic Mapper	1982	30 m	7	8 bits	18.4×10^8

A mid-1980 planned flight program after Landsat-D is the Operational Earth Resources Program. This program will have a new sensor called the Multispectral Resource Sampler (MRS). Table 6 compares the sensor characteristics of the MRS with the Landsat-D Thematic Mapper. It is noted that the MSR will have significantly narrower spectral bandwidth, improved spatial resolution, and the ability to point off-nadir. The planned technology will utilize multilinear arrays (2,000 detectors/band). The use of off-nadir can potentially contribute to some reduction in data processing and storage by limiting data acquisition to only those areas and spectral range for which data is required.

Table 7 provides the Thematic Mapper spectral bands that will be used, and the rationale for their selection. Although the dominant criteria has been to support the agricultural/forest/rangeland resources monitoring disciplines, it is apparent that the band selection has also been influenced by bathymetry, geological and land use disciplines and applications.

It is interesting to plot satellite sensor characteristics in the 1960-1985 time-frame to assess data and data rate increases. In Figure 2, it is noted that sensor resolution in the NASA and European programs will improve by two orders of magnitude reaching about 10 m by 1985, the number of spectral bands will increase from one to seven, and the detector dynamic range will significantly improve from about 32 to 256 levels. As a result, the number of bits in a typical scene (185 km x 185 km) will increase by over four orders of magnitude, and the data transmission rates by over five orders of magnitude.

DATA FLOW

The flow of sensor data from the spacecraft or aircraft to ground involves a conversion process and telecommunications. To date, tele-communications has not been a data flow problem.

Telecommunications

Telecommunications has progressed consistently since its inception. The increase in the capability to transmit data has increased by an average of a factor of ten every 17 years. Martin (1971) has plotted this growth in communications data rate, and is shown in Figure 3.

The Landsat-D satellite will have two earth observation sensors, a five-channel Multispectral Scanner similar to the Landsat 1, 2, and 3 sensor and a Thematic Mapper. The data rate of the Multispectral Scanner will generate data at a 15 Mbps rate and the Thematic Mapper

Table 6. Comparison of MRS and TM Characteristics (NASA)

	MULTISPECTRAL RESOURCE SAMPLER	THEMATIC MAPPER
Coverage	Sampling	Inventory
Temporal Coverage (One Spacecraft)	Every 2-3 Days	Every 16 Days
Spectral Range	0.36-0.95μ (20 Channels-Select Any 4) No IR	0.45-0.90 (4 Channels) 1.55-2.35 (2 Channels) 10.4-12.5 (1 Channel)
Spectral Bandwidth	≥ 20 nm	≥ 60 nm
IFOV	15/30 m	30 m
FOV (Swath Width)	15/30 Km	185 Km
Pointing	2 Axes: ±40° Across, ±55° Along	Fixed Nadir
Stereo Coverage	Sampling Basis	Sidelap Only
Technology	Multilinear Arrays (4 Bands) 2,000 Detectors/Band Pushbroom Scanning	Semiconductor 16 Detectors/Band Electromechanical Scanning

---

Table 7. Spectral Band Rationale (NASA)

0.45 - 0.52 μM

Bathymetry in Less Turbid Waters; Soil/Vegetation Differences; Deciduous/Coniferous Differentiation; Soil Type Discrimination

0.52 - 0.60 μM

Indicator of Growth Rate and Vegetation Vigor Because of Sensitivity to Green Reflectance Peak at 0.55 μM, Sediment Concentration Estimation; Bathymetry in Turbid Waters

0.63 - 0.69 μM

Chlorophyll Absorption/Species Differentiation; One of Best Bands for Crop Classification, Vegetation Cover and Density; With the 0.52 - 0.60 μM Band It Can be Used for Ferric Iron Detection; Ice and Snow Mapping

0.76 - 0.90 μM

Water Body Delineation; Sensitive to Biomass and Stress Variations

1.55 - 1.75 μM

Vegetation Moisture Conditions and Stress; Snow/Cloud Differentiation; May Aid in Defining Intrusive of Different Iron Mineral Content

2.08 - 2.35 μM

Distinguish Hydrothermally Altered Zones From Non-Altered Zones/Mineral Exploration; Soil Type Discrimination

10.4 - 12.5 μM

Surface Temperature Measurement; Urban Versus Non-Urban Land Use Separation; Burned Areas From Water Bodies

328

EVOLUTION OF NASA EARTH OBSERVATION SENSOR PERFORMANCE

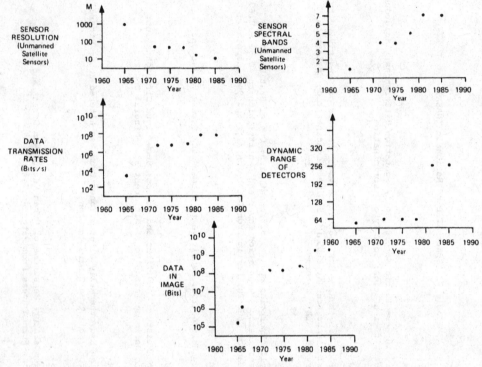

Figure 2.   Evolution of NASA Earth Observation Senses Performance

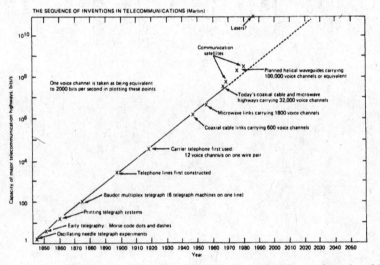

Figure 3.   The Sequence of Inventions in Telecommunications, (Martin, 1971)

at 84 Mbps. Thus, in 1982, the next generation earth resources satellite
will be sending data to the earth at a peak rate of about 100 Mbps.
This will be implemented with the aid of the Tracking and Data
Relay Satellite communications link, which allows for high data rate
relaying via the TDRS of satellite data to ground stations at 100 Mbps
using the S and Kv bands. It is anticipated that data rates as high
as 1-2 Gbps will be possible. This is accomplished by the use of higher
frequency and more efficient antennas, and improved modulation techniques.
Future plans also involve the geographical allocation of communication
linkages, as well as time and frequency allocations.

It appears that communications capabilities will not be the limiting
factor in earth observation data handling. The question is rather, the
rate which these data can be processed, converted into an information
product, stored, and used.

Data Processing

The flow of data from the sensor to the user involves a number of operations
involving both machines and man. A simplified processing flow is shown
in Figure 4. The sensor converts the energy that is emitted or reflected,
by the target or object into a voltage or digital value. Frequently,
restoration techniques are used for data compensation to reduce noise
and other degradation effects. The next step in the process is to
correct the data by the removal of radiometric (intensity) and geometric
errors caused by the sensor, platform or the scene (Bernstein, 1975).
Frequently, image to image registration is desirable in order to increase
scene information extraction potential (Anuta, 1970). Manual and machine
techniques are then used to convert the sensed data into information
products, compressed and compacted as needed, and then applied by the
user for his disciplinary objective (Bernstein, 1978).

Table 8 summarizes typical data processing operations commonly used by
investigators. The type of processing done is limited only by the
imagination of the investigator and his computational resources.

With the advent of advanced sensor technologies, a major problem has
been in processing the ever-increasing amount of sensor data. Under
contract to NASA Goddard Space Flight Center, IBM-Federal Systems
Division has developed a system for high-speed preprocessing and
registration of Landsat-3 and HCMM sensor data. This system, the
Master Data Processor, is an operational system capable of data input
rates of 4 Mbps and processing rates of 20 Mips (Schoene, 1977). The
MDP uses an Advanced Signal Processor developed by IBM for sonar signal
processing which contains both an arithmetic processor and a control
processor. The arithmetic processor contains two pipelined array
processors with a 16 x 16 bit array multiplier and a 32-bit 3-way adder.

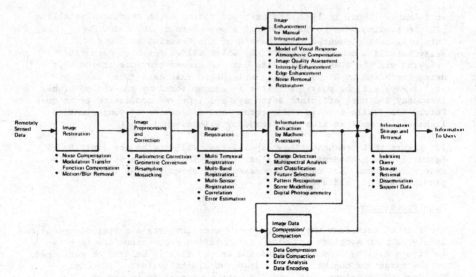

Figure 4. Simplified Earth Observation Data Flow

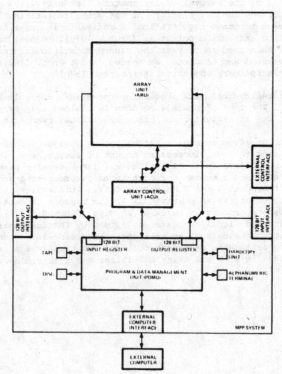

Figure 5. Massively Parallel Processor Architecture

Table 8. Common Image Processing Programs

SUPPORT PROGRAM

Histograms	Displays frequency of occurrence of each intensity
Grid	Superimposes graduated grid on image data
Grey Scale	Adds grey scale wedge to image
Annotate	Adds alphanumeric annotation to image
Statistic	Computes image data statistics
Report	Provides processing time and costs
Error Analysis	Computes accuracy of geometric and radiometric correction
Reformat	Changes image format from picture element interleaved to line or band separated format.

GEOMETRIC MODIFICATION

Magnify	Expands image size
Reduce	Reduces image size
Geometric	Implements two-dimensional image geometry correction
Rotate	Rotates image through specified angle
Mosaic	Geometrically combines two or more images and removes overlap
Resample	Implements selected intensity resampling algorithm.

RADIOMETRIC MODIFICATION

Intensity	Implements uniform intensity modification to image
Intensity (X,Y)	Implements spatially variable intensity modification to image
Normalize	Normalizes data so that average equals one

IMAGE MANIPULATION

Combine	Adds (or subtracts) two or more images
Output	Outputs image on tape, display, recorder, plotter or printer
Scroll	Advances displayed image at selected rate
Register	Translational adjustment to cause two images to be in registration

MEASUREMENT PROGRAMS

Area	Determines area (in appropriate units) of polygon defined by 3 or more points
Length	Computes length (in appropriate units) between two points
Contour	Generates isodensity contour line plots.

ENHANCEMENT PROGRAMS

Filter	Performs Fourier transformation and filtering of input image
Noise Removal	Eliminates noise from image data
Direct	Computes directional derivative of image
Ratio	Divides each element of one image by corresponding element of second registered image
Laplace	Computes Laplacian of an image
Adjust	Converts intensity values of an image using replacement table

INFORMATION EXTRACTION

Classify	Multispectral Classification/Feature Extraction
Rose	Generates a rose diagram useful for geological fault analysis

TEST IMAGE CREATION

Bar	Generates a test image of a resolution bar chart
Star	Generates a test image of a radial bar chart
LINWEDGE	Generates a linear gray-scale step wedge
SQ2WEDGE	Generates a non-linear gray-scale step wedge

UTILITY FUNCTIONS

Logon	Initiates a terminal session
Logout	Terminates a terminal session
Save	Permanently saves image under a user name
Table	Creates or updates a data table for input to the ADJUST, AREA, CLASSIFY, SHADE, or ROSE commands
Select	Selects an image area for further processing
Catalog	Lists images and tables saved by users
Whouser	Lists the IDs of the active users
Remove	Removes a specified dataset from the system
Change	Changes the name of an existing dataset
Reserve	Allocates and initializes disk space for an image
Size	Lists the size of an image (pixels and lines)
Clear	Frees all system files
Time	Displays CPU, execution, and session time used.

The processor can execute 20 million adds and multiplies per second, and implements image preprocessing and registration operations. The control processor is a general purpose processor and is used as a system supervisor, for general computation support, and manages the data. Sensor data is input and output via high-density tape (14-track, 20 Kbpi) at 4×10^6 bps.

For future programs, NASA has an R&D project to increase the computation speeds associated with information extraction by a factor of about 10^4 times compared with general purpose computers. This program is known as the Massively Parallel Processor program. The computer architecture for this program consists of an array of 128 x 128 processing elements that provide 16,384 parallel processors for image manipulation and information extraction (Computer Design, 1979). The MPP is designed to process images and two-dimensional data at six billion addition/subtractions per second or two billion multiplications per second. The MPP consists of an Array Unit, Array Control Unit, and Program and Data Management Unit (See Figure 5). The Array Unit functions as a single instruction multiple data stream computer and provides the computational power. The Control Unit supplies instructions to the Array Unit, and utilizes microprogramming and overlapped operations within an instruction cycle. The Program and Data Management Unit loads programs into the Array Control Unit, displays results and manages data flow. Data is transferred to I/O devices in 128-bit transfers every 10 nsec.

The MPP is being designed by Goodyear Aerospace Corporation for NASA/GSFC and will be built in a prototype form by 1982. It is anticipated that this processor will provide computational power for earth observation image processing applications, and the concept may eventually be implemented on-board satellites to provide real-time sensor data processing, so that information rather than data could be transmitted directly to ground for immediate use.

INFORMATION ORGANIZATION

Once data have been sensed, communicated to ground, and converted into information, it must be organized for use and application.

Information Understanding

Processors, such as general or special purpose computers, convert the data into an information product. This conversion involves a significant amount of man-machine interaction in that information categories must be defined and selected by man, and then detected and classified by machine. Many

different classes of materials exist on or near the earth's surface, and
may have many subtle intensity, spatial, and spectral variations. A
"knowledgeable orderliness" is required in order to understand and implement
the organizational process. Figure 6 shows an information tree in
which earth features have been categorized in a taxonomic manner (Landgrebe, 1976
and Wu, 1975). The tree shown displays the totality of classes that can exist.
At the top are the general classes of features, which are then divided and
subdivided into subfeatures which can then continue to the desired level of an
information product. Shown on this particular tree are only subclasses of natural
and cultural vegetation. The tree has many more categories than those
shown, and the more provided, the lower the probability of a multispectral
misclassification. Tree structures are commonly used in pattern recognition
where the number of classes is large and have a complex relationship.
Theoretical results and analyses have developed using this tool (Rosenfeld, 1969).

Given that this structure has been developed in a systematic and complete
fashion, a classification system can be established, standardized, and used
to define the region viewed. A standard land use and land cover classification
system has been developed by Anderson, 1976, et al. Shown in Table 9, are the
first and second levels of their system. It has three major attributes:
(1) it gives names to categories by using common and accepted terminology;
(2) it enables information to be digitally stored and transmitted; and
(3) it allows inductive generalizations to be made by man.

Once all data have been assembled, a geographically accessible multi-layer
information system can be structured, such as is shown in Figure 7 (Foster, 1977).
Thereafter, only changes to the data base need be entered. These data can
be digitally stored and retrieved.

Current Information Forms

Most information products are generated for local or regional areas,
and are in the form of a map or chart. They are easily interpreted,
inexpensive in quantity production, and can be readily transported. Their
disadvantages are: 3-5 years preparation and production time, significant
manual involvement in the preparation stage, and unsuitable form for computer
processing and rapid data dissemination. A listing of maps and charts
produced by the National Cartographic Information Center, along with
supporting data is shown in Table 10 (Wood, 1976).

Future Information Forms

With the advent high-speed computers, large mass memories, and interactive
displays, the possibility exists for a better approach to the storage,
retrieval, and display of earth observation information. It is entirely
practical in the near term for earth observation data to be acquired,
corrected, converted into information products, and stored in a large data
base, all in a digital form. The data base would be queried on the basis

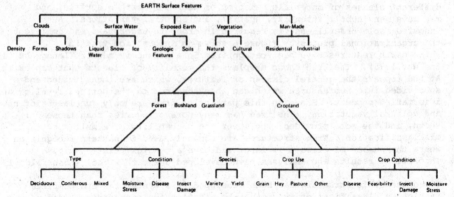

Figure 6. Earth Resources Information Tree (Landgrebe, 1976)

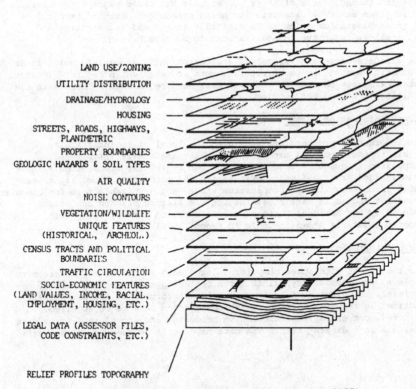

LAND USE/ZONING
UTILITY DISTRIBUTION
DRAINAGE/HYDROLOGY
HOUSING
STREETS, ROADS, HIGHWAYS, PLANIMETRIC
PROPERTY BOUNDARIES
GEOLOGIC HAZARDS & SOIL TYPES
AIR QUALITY
NOISE CONTOURS
VEGETATION/WILDLIFE
UNIQUE FEATURES (HISTORICAL, ARCHEOL.)
CENSUS TRACTS AND POLITICAL BOUNDARIES
TRAFFIC CIRCULATION
SOCIO-ECONOMIC FEATURES (LAND VALUES, INCOME, RACIAL, EMPLOYMENT, HOUSING, ETC.)
LEGAL DATA (ASSESSOR FILES, CODE CONSTRAINTS, ETC.)

RELIEF PROFILES TOPOGRAPHY

Figure 7. Multi-Layer Information System (Foster, 1977)

Table 9. Land Use and Land Cover Classification System for Use With Remote Sensor Data (Anderson, et al)

LEVEL I		LEVEL II
1 URBAN OR BUILT-UP LAND	11	Residential
	12	Commercial and Services
	13	Industrial
	14	Transportation, Communications, and Utilities
	15	Industrial and Commercial Complexes
	16	Mixed Urban or Built-Up Land
	17	Other Urban or Built-Up Land
2 AGRICULTURAL LAND	21	Cropland and Pasture
	22	Orchards, Groves, Vineyards, Nurseries, and Ornamental Horticultural Areas
	23	Confined Feeding Operations
	24	Other Agricultural Land
3 RANGELAND	31	Herbaceous Rangeland
	32	Shrub and Brush Rangeland
	33	Mixed Rangeland
4 FOREST LAND	41	Deciduous Forest Land
	42	Evergreen Forest Land
	43	Mixed Forest Land
5 WATER	51	Streams and Canals
	52	Lakes
	53	Reservoirs
	54	Bays and Estuaries
6 WETLAND	61	Forested Wetland
	62	Nonforested Wetland
7 BARREN LAND	71	Dry Salt Flats
	72	Beaches
	73	Sandy Areas other than Beaches
	74	Bare Exposed Rock
	75	Strip Mines, Quarries, and Gravel Pits
	76	Transitional Areas
	77	Mixed Barren Land
8 TUNDRA	81	Shrub and Brush Tundra
	82	Herbaceous Tundra
	83	Bare Ground Tundra
	84	Wet Tundra
	85	Mixed Tundra
9 PERENNIAL SNOW OR ICE	91	Perennial Snowfields
	92	Glaciers

Table 10. National Cartographic Information Center Products and Data (Wood, 1976)

MULTIPURPOSE MAPS AND CHARTS

Aeronautical Charts
Bathymetric Maps
City Maps
Extraterrestrial Maps
Flood-Plain Maps
Forest Maps
Geologic Maps
Land-Use Maps
Map and Chart Feature Separates
Nautical Charts
Orthophotomaps and Orthophotoquads
River Surveys and Damsite Maps
Slope Maps
Topographic Maps

GEODETIC SURVEY DATA

First- and Second-Order Control
Third-Order Control From Any Useful Source
Selected Fourth-Order Control
Photogrammetrically Established Control
Selected Private Survey Control
Land Plats
Census Subdivisions

AERIAL PHOTOGRAPHS AND SPACE IMAGERY

Photographs
Satellite Computer-Compatible Tapes
Photomosaics
Other Remote Sensor Data

CLOSELY RELATED DATA

Cartographic and Educational Materials Such as Atlases, Gazetteers, and Related Literature
Digital Data Representing Detail on Maps and Charts
Geographic Names

of key attributes, such as geographical position, and all data available for that area would be displayed in a suitable form (images, graphs, tables, maps, charts, etc.). One can visualize a particular region viewed at a small scale, and then queried using latitude and longitude or Northing and Easting as an address to search for and retrieve the data stored in that region (see Figure 8). All available data or information stored for that area can then be displayed in a selected form of presentation.

Size of Data Base

It is interesting to determine how much data would be collected if the entire earth were to be imaged at high resolution. The area of the earth is about 5.1×10^{14} m^2. If the earth were to be viewed with a multispectral sensor with 1 m resolutions, 10 spectral bands, and each sample were a 10-bit number, then the total number of bits that would be acquired would be

$$\text{global data bits} = 5.1 \times 10^{16} \text{ bits}$$

This is, of course, an unmanageable amount of data to store with current technologies, and only represents the raw data before any information extraction has been performed on the data. Consider, however, the global storage of information, as opposed to data.

Size of Information Base

For most applications, information areas larger than 1 square meter can be used. Further raw data can be converted into an information product (such as the type of crop in an information area, its ownership, etc.). Thus, a significant degree of data compression can be achieved, and useful and directly accessible information can be stored in a digital form. If we assume,

> 10 m x 10 m information areas over land,
> 32 bits of information per land and polar areas,
> 100 m x 100 m information areas over water,
> 16 bits of information per water area,
> 70% of globe area is water,

Then the total number of bits that would be stored for a global information system would be,

$$\text{global information bits} = 5.1 \times 10^{14} (0.3 \times 32 \times 10^{-2} + 0.7 \times 16 \times 10^{-4})$$

$$= 5.0 \times 10^{13} \text{ bits}$$

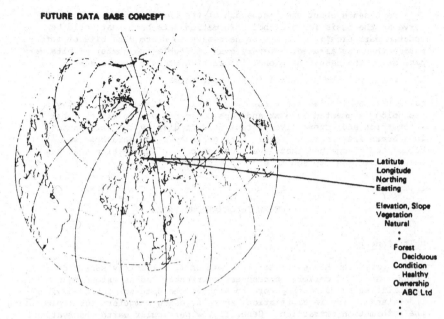

Figure 8. Future Data Base Concept

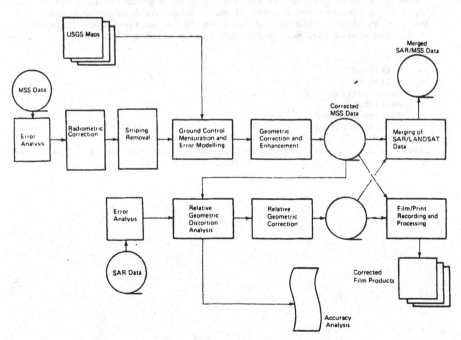

Figure 9.   Landsat and Synthetic Aperture Radar Data
Merging Processing Flow

This represents about one-thousandth of the original data, and could
serve as the basis for a global information data base that would be
updated periodically. It may be necessary to store more bits of information than was assumed; however, even if double the number of bits were
necessary, the resultant global information storage requirement,
10^{14} bits, will be practical in the near term.

Current mass memories store about 10^{12} - 10^{13} bits of data. Today's
technology augmented by disk and tape could be used to store global
information and interactive systems used to display the information
in a human interpretable form. Once generated, the data base would
be updated by changes that have occurred or new information that has
been derived, as opposed to storing all data.

FUTURE INFORMATION SPACES

Multi-Concept

In the past, man has extracted information from remotely sensed data
using visual and cerebral processes. Currently, he is extending his
capabilities by using computers to enhance the data for improved visual
understanding and interpretation, and also using computers for implementing
the information extraction. Generally, a particular earth observation
program and sensor are used to support an investigation. Recently,
however, investigations have begun using data from different programs,
sensors, temporal periods, elevations, etc. in combination in order to
improve the accuracy and process of converting data into information
and understanding. This concept is known as the multi-concept (Colwell,
1974), and states that more information is obtained by:

    Multistation
    Multiband
    Multidate
    Multipolarization
    Multistate
    Multienhancement
    Multidisciplinary

imaging and processing techniques. In essence, by the use of all available
data, the maximum amount of information can be extracted.

Example of Merged Sensor Data

An interesting experiment was conducted involving the merging of image and radar sensor data. Landsat data provides multispectral coverage of a region, while the radar data provides high resolution spatial data. The radar data were obtained from a synthetic aperture radar obtained from aircraft overflights. The experiment involved the merging of the radar data with the Landsat data, such that the merged data set would have both the spatial and spectral characteristics of the data sources.

Figure 9 identifies the processing flow in this experiment. The radar data had a resolution of 25 m, and the Landsat data 79 m. In order to maintain the resolution of the radar data, the geometrically corrected Landsat data were resampled to a 25 m picture element separation. The radar data were then geometrically corrected so that it had the same geometry as the Landsat data, and the two registered data sets were combined. Several methods of combination were used and are shown in Figure 10.

Clearly, more than two data sets can and should be used in order to support scientific and application experiments. The point, however, is that data with widely varying characteristics obtained from different programs, sensors, and platforms can be processed to have the same geometry, combined, and used in a synergistic fashion to improve our knowledge and understanding of the earth, and to better manage its resources and monitor its environment.

Phenomenon Modelling

A measure of understanding of a physical or biological process is how well we are able to mathematically characterize the process and predict future events. Examples of modelling processes abound in meteorology and biological growth. Earth orbiting satellites with repetitive coverage provide opportunities for obtaining sufficient information and understanding to allow the development of new models and to validate these models. Table 11 lists a number of model activities that have been and are expected to be developed.

The rapid acceptance of satellite data in meteorology accelerated the development of meteorological modelling and weather prediction in the 1960's. Currently, there is significant activity in developing local and national models in a number of disciplines. The U.S. Geological Survey and the Defense Mapping Agency have developed a national terrain (elevation and slope) data base and model for the United States. A number of regions are developing hydrological models useful for flood prediction and water management, and NASA and the Department of Agriculture have developed a wheat yield model and are extending it to other food crops. Air and water pollution models and even soil and geological models are being developed.

340

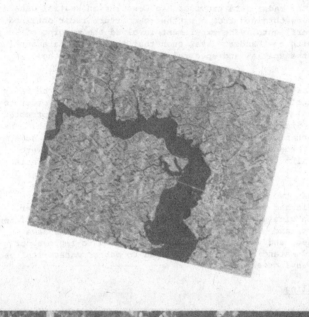

+ 25.4-METER PIXELS   PROCESSED BY IBM +

Figure 10b. Synthetic Aperture Radar Data Corrected
and Registered to Landsat Data

+ 25.4-METER PIXELS   PROCESSED BY IBM +

Figure 10a. Landsat Subimage Processed with
25 m Pixel Spacing

341

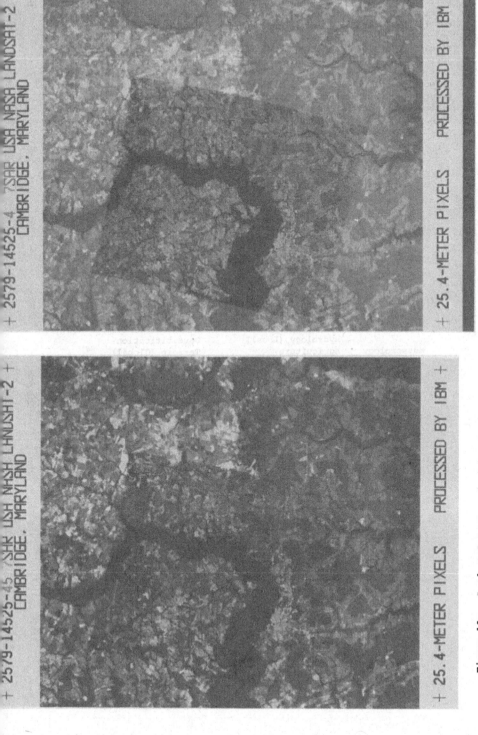

+ 2579-14525-4 7SAR USA NASA LANDSAT-2 +
CAMBRIDGE, MARYLAND

+ 25.4-METER PIXELS   PROCESSED BY IBM +

Figure 10d. Landsat Data Merged with SAR Data
(Bands 4, 7 + SAR)

+ 2579-14525-45 /SHR USA NASA LANDSAT-2 +
CAMBRIDGE, MARYLAND

+ 25.4-METER PIXELS   PROCESSED BY IBM +

Figure 10c. Landsat Data Merged with SAR Data
(Bands 4, 5, 7 + SAR)

It is anticipated that this effort will further expand in the future, both in terms of global coverage and new application areas. A global multidisciplinary information base is very important for this development, due to the interaction and interdependence of the disciplines.

Modelling involves significant multidisciplinary data. For example, agricultural production is heavily dependent upon soil moisture, thus crop yield is dependent upon knowledge of both what is growing and meteorological conditions. A data base containing information from many programs is thus needed to support scientific and application programs. Ultimately, even the models may be in the data base and interact with each other in order to gain a better understanding of global processes and to support environmental and earth resources applications.

Table 11. Physical Model Development

1960's	1970's	1980's
		Climate
		Agriculture (Global)
		Air Pollution (Global)
		Water Pollution (Global)
		Geology
	Soil (Local)	Hydrology (Global)
	Terrain (National)	Forest
	Water Pollution	Soil (Global)
	Air Pollution (Local)	Erosion
	Hydrology (Local)	Desertification
Meteorology	Agriculture	Terrain (Global)

CONCLUSIONS

Significant technological advances have occurred in the earth
observation program. Satellite sensors, systems for communicating
the data to ground, correcting the data, and extracting information
from the data have made impressive advances in recent years.
Technology is available to acquire high resolution multispectral

sensor data from satellites, transmit data to the ground at 10^8

bits per second and process the data at 10^{10} instructions per
second. Yet only a small portion of the data that has been acquired
has been effectively used. This is due in part to rapid advances
in sensor technologies and to the delay that has occurred in implementing advanced technology in earth observation data processing
and data management. Further, there is a lack of a multidisciplinary
data base that is easily, rapidly, and economically accessible.
What is needed is the rapid development of a data base and information
system, so that sensor data can be converted into information and
models that are readily available and accessible. The development

of a data base of about 10^{14} bits will be required in the near term
to support this need. It is anticipated that low cost, large scale
mass memories will allow internationally developed global data bases
to be shared that will significantly enhance the utility of remotely
sensed data and improve man's understanding of the earth, the utilization of its resources, and the protection of its environment.

REFERENCES

Anderson, J. R., Hardy, E. E., Roach, J. T., and Witmer, R. E.
(1976). A Land Use and Land Cover Classification System for Use
with Remote Sensor Data, U.S. Geological Survey Paper #964,
U.S. Government Printing Office, Washington, D.C.

Anuta, P. E. (1970). Spatial Registration of Multispectral and
Multitemporal Digital Imagery Using Fast Fourier Transform
Techniques. IEEE Transactions on Geoscience Electronics,
Vol. GE-8, pp. 353-368.

Aviation Week & Space Technology , (1979). Earth Resources
Concepts Proposed, March 26, 1979, pp. 46-53.

Bernstein, R. (1978). Digital Image Processing for Remote
Sensing. (Edited). IEEE Press & J. Wiley, pp. 121-174.

Bernstein, R. (1975). All-Digital Precision Processing of ERTS
Data. NASA Final Report, Contract No. NAS5-21716, FSD-75-0009.

Catoe, C. E. (1978). End-to-End Data/Information Systems Concept:
The Solution or the Problem? 8th Annual Remote Sensing Conference
Proceedings, Space Institute, University of Tennessee.

Colwell, R. N. (1974). Keynote Address, 1974 Annual Convention of
the American Congress of Surveying and Mapping, American Society
of Photogrammetry.

Computer Design, (1979). Parallel Processor Will Be Capable of
Performing 6 G Additions/S., pp. 55-56, March 1979.

Foster, H. D. (1977). A Remote Sensing System for a Nationwide
Data Bank, Proceedings, 1977 Machine Processing of Remotely Sensed
Data Symposium, Purdue University, Lafayette, Indiana.

Greenwood, L. R. (1978). Environmental Observations from Space;
Present and Future. EASCON 1978 Record, IEEE Publication 78CH
1354-4 AES, 1978.

Landgrebe, D. (1976). Computer-Based Remote Sensing Technology -
A Look to the Future. Remote Sensing of the Environment, Vol. 5,
No. 4.

Martin, J. (1971). Future Developments in Telecommunications,
Prentice-Hall.

Nagler, R. G. (1978). Satellite Measurement Capabilities for Environmental and Resource Observations. EASCON 1978 Record, IEEE Publication 78CH 1354-4 AES.

NASA 5-Year Planning, Fiscal Years 1979 through 1983. NASA Headquarters, Washington, D.C., March 1, 1978.

Rosenfeld, A. (1969). Picture Processing by Computers. Academic Press, New York.

Schoene, L. P. (1977). Master Data Processor, Technical Directions, FSD, Autumn 1977, Vol. 3, No. 2.

Thompson, L. L. (1979). Remote Sensing Using Solid-State Array Technology, Photogrammetric Engineering and Remote Sensing. Vol. 45, No. 1, pp. 47-55.

Van Vleck, E. M., Sinclair, K. F., Pitts, S. W., and Slye, R. E. (1973). Earth Resources Ground Data Handling Systems for the 1980's. NASA TMX-62, 240, p. 12.

Wu, C. (1975). The Decision Tree Approach to Classification. PhD Thesis, Purdue University.

Wood, J. T. (1976). Cartographic Data Available to Coastal Planners, 2nd Annual Pecora Symposium, ASP & USGS.

A GEOGRAPHICAL DATA BASE

Juan Fco. Corona Burgueño

Landsat images provide a great amount of valuable information that, when complemented with information from other sources, can be organized in a way that it is
useful for decision making in agricultural planning. This organization is formalized by means of a geographical data base whose components are described in this
paper. They include acquisition of information and its insertion into the data
base, the storage requirements, the logical structure which is basically relational,
geoprocessing and applications. Answers to queries can be graphics displayed
through the Ramtek system using two T.V. terminals or printed on an APL terminal
or a fast printer. This data base is currently being used in several projects
carried jointly with government institutions.

Mexico Scientific Center
IBM de México, S.A.
Cantil 150
Pedregal de San Angel
México 21, D.F., MEXICO

PRELIMINARIES

It is difficult to give an adequate definition of what a geographical data
base (GDB) is. We could say that a GDB is a collection of geographical data
arranged in such a way that, by processing it, we can obtain relevant information which is useful for planning and decision making. There are several drawbacks in this definition; first, what do we mean by geographical data?; second,
how do we arrange and process the data?; and third, planning and decision making
by whom and for what?.

We are not going to worry in giving a precise definition of a GDB and for the
purpose of this paper we will say, as does D. W. Rhind (1974), that geographical
data is that which requires at least two spatial dimensions to be referenced.
The arrangement, processing and use of the information depends very much on the
specific application.

In this paper, we will describe the components of a geographical data base developed at our center as is currently being used in several joint projects. The paper
is divided in seven sections, namely:
1.- System Overview
2.- Sources of Information
3.- Data Base Structure
4.- Geoprocessing Algorithms
5.- Query Language
6.- Applications
7.- Conclusions.

1.- SYSTEM OVERVIEW

The GDB is an interactive system which handles positional and non-positional
geographical information, v.gr., agricultural, hydrological, meteorological,
socio-economical and political boundaries. The logical structure of the data base
is relational and it will be described with more detail later.

In figure 1, we can see the relations between the different components of the
system. The data is collected and after several process which may consist in
registering, filtering or image classification, the information is stored into the
data base to be processed later.

In our system, we have different sources of information, being satellite images
only one of them and, in fact, most of the information comes from statistical
tables and standard cartographic maps.

There are also several processors for geographical information. One of them is
ERMAN-II, which is an image processing software package; other processors that we
have developed allow us contour and vertices extraction from classified Landsat
images processed by ERMAN, or geoprocessing of polygons which represent geographical regions.

In order to have graphic output through a CRT terminal, we also built an auxiliary processor written in Assembler. This processor enable us to communicate between
APL and a Ramtek system with two T.V. monitors attached to it. For efficiency purposes, we included some of the geoprocessing algorithms in this processor, obtaining so a fast response to queries formulated to the system.

2.- SOURCES OF INFORMATION

There are several sources of information for a GDB, among which we can mention
a) Landsat images, b) aircraft photographs, c) cartographic maps, and c) statistical tables. Any GDB should be able to combine and integrate in a single data
base these different types of data. One way of accomplishing this, is by using
the image-based approach which consists in representing the information by means
of matrices whose elements correspond both in position as in value to the different
zones of interest that appear in the area; figure 2, using an hypothetical example,
illustrates this concept. The disadvantage of this approach is that it requires
means for storing and processing large amounts of data when dealing with big zones
or when some accuracy is required. However, the geoprocessing algorithms are
very easily implemented besides of one being able to use existing packages for
image processing.

Another way of integrating information from different sources, is by using what
we called the contour-based approach, which consists in representing the data by
means of the coordinates of the vertices of polygonal lines approximating boundaries
or curves, in the case of zonal or linear information. In the case of punctual information, we store the coordinates of points of interest.

The approach we use is mainly the contour-based; one reazon being that most of the
information is obtained in this way; another reazon is to have the possibility of
adapting the GDB to small computers with small memories.

In the section on geoprocessing, we will describe some of the algorithms we have
developed to deal with the contour-based approach.

Next, we describe the digitization processes used in our system for each one of
the sources of information mentioned before, i.e., a) Landsat images, b) aircraft
photographs, c) maps, and d) statistical tables.

a) Landsat images.

These images undergo first a preprocessing for registering and filtering; then, with
ERMAN-II, they are processed until a good classification is obtained, next the
classified image is smoothed by a process that homogenizes the classes in the image
taking off the 'salt and pepper', that is, the isolated points that remain in the
different classes; once this process is completed, a class of interest is selected
and a binary matrix is built. This binary matrix has 1's in the elements corresponding to zones where the class is present, and 0's elsewhere. After this, the binary
matrix is processed by a series of APL programs which first extract the contour and
then the coordinates of the vertices of the contour, to finally store these coordinates in the data base. We repeat this process until all the classes of interest are
stored in the data base.

b) Aircraft photographs.

This type of data is digitized by using a microdensitometer, which scans the picture
giving to each pixel, a value representing its color or grey level intensity. This
is recorded on a tape which is then processed similarly as a Landsat image to finally
store the desired information in the data base.

c) Maps.

Map digitization is very difficult to perform it since there is not a completely
automatic way that does it. We have used several semiautomatic methods. One consists
in first taking a photograph of the map and then digitize it using the microdensitometer, next, the resulting image is displayed on the T.V. terminals to then
follow the contours of interest by using a trackball attached to the terminal. Only
the coordinates of the points indicated by the user are stored in the data base.
Both the display and coordinates obtention can be done by using the APL-RAMTEK
auxiliariy processor or the ERMAN-II system.

Another method we have used, consists in placing a ruled transparent paper over the
map and then read the coordinates of the vertices of the polygons which approximate
the contours, or just the coordinates of points of interest. Then, these coordinates
are stored in the data base directly using punched cards or with APL using the
auxiliary processor TSIO.

d) Statistical tables.

There is information like names of cities, number of inhabitants, average salary
in a given zone, and some other type of socio-economical information which can be
obtained from statistical tables and which any GDB should be able to integrate to
its data base and combine it with the other type of data. We have accomplished this

by associating to points or areas their corresponding socio- economical indexes or values.

3.- DATA BASE STRUCTURE

We classify the information in two types, namely, positional and non-positional. Positional information is just a set of coordinates representing points in a carte-sian plane; non-positional information is all other type of information which might be associated to a geographical position but itself does not have any positional meaning, for example, names of cities, population, and temperature. The non-positional information is stored as relations and the positional information by means of coordi-nates. The relational data base management system is written in APL and developed at our center. This system allows, through the auxiliary processor TSIO, the use of disks or tapes to read and store data; also with the APL-RAMTEK auxiliary proce-ssor, we can acces the Ramtek terminals from APL and thus have a graphic facility for our GDB.
Summarizing, we view our data base as a sequence of planes, figure 3, each one of them containing one type of information, for example, political boundaries. In this way, a geographical point, besides its positional coordinates, has a vector of attributes associated to it.
The structure we have for our data base enable us the use of views in our system. These view selections can be through an arbitrary shape geographical window and through any combination of attributes (planes), allowing the user to work, if he desires so, with a small subregion and few attributes, and in this way making possibly the adaptability of our system to small computers.

4.- GEOPROCESSING ALGORITHMS

The coding of data depends on its nature as well as its processing. We classify the data in three types: a) zonal, b) linear, and c) punctual. Examples of zonal data are the political boundaries (countries, states, municipalities) and land use maps; isolines, roads and rivers are examples of linear data; and positions of cities and data from meteorological stations are instances of punctual data. For geoprocessing, this classification is a little rough because, for example, when we process measurements of rain stations, for hydrological modeling, this data could be extrapolated to a complete river basin by means of Thiessen polygons, method which obviously cannot be used with data about cities.

Another important factor which has to be considered when coding the data, is the application. We have found in several projects that it is very important being able to obtain zones which satisfy certain conditions on different properties, v.g., the zone with height above sea level between 500 m. and 600 m., belonging to county 'A', and with average annual temperature between 25°C and 30°C.

Also it should be possible to measure areas, lengths and distances, as well as being able to find zones neighbors to a given one for, say, accesibility conditions or lengths of common boundaries. Concerning linear data, we should divide it in at least two types, one for isolines and the other for roads. The reazon for this, is that when processing isolines, one should be able to find the zone with parameter value (temperature, for example), between two given ones; therefore, unless the information is coded as zones bounded by isolines, besides the isoline itself, one should code the information specifying the side of the isoline in which the value of the parameter is larger.

Graphic output is very useful when dealing with geographical data therefore, we have to be able to print character maps or to colour polygons, for displaying them. Summarizing, we should code the information in a way which at least enables us to obtain:

a) Intersections and unions of zones,

b) Measurements of areas, lengths and distances,

c) Neighbouring zones,

d) Direction of increase of the terrain and meteorological parameters,

e) Graphic display and colouring of zones, and

f) Printing facilities.

We can use in our system the image-based and the contour-based approaches. When is possible to use the image-based approach, it results very convenient because it facilitates the implementation of the geoprocessing algorithms; also, it is very convenient when working with ERMAN, because we feed this system with the different matrices representing the attribute planes as if they were bands of the same image, which in some sense are, and take advantage of all ERMAN facilities for image processing and obtain valuable information to display it, store it, or print it.

In the case of the contour-based approach, we had to develop complex algorithms which perform the different processes mentioned before.

The algorithm which obtains the intersection of two polygons assumes that they
are coded in the positive orientation, in other words, if we walk on the boundary of the polygon following the order as the vertices were coded, then the region
of interest is to our left. This coding permits us to consider the complement of
a polygon just by ordering the vertices in the clockwise sense.

The algorithm for polygon intersection, figure 4, consists first in obtaining the
points of intersection between the edges of the two polygons; next, a point of one
the polygons that is inside the other, is chosen; starting with this point, we follow
the boundary of the corresponding polygon in the sense as it was coded until a
intersection is found, there we change to the other polygon and follow it until
the next intersection is reached to return to the original polygon. We continue in
this way, alternating polygons in the intersections, until we go back to the original
point completing one polygon. If there are edge intersections which have not been
considered, then we have to repeat the process with the remaining intersections in
order to obtain all parts of the intersection.

This algorithm, however, presents some difficulties when the two polygons have
edges or parts of these in common, or when a corner of one of the polygons is on
the boundary of the other. These cases are illustrated in figure 5, where it is
also illustrated the errors that might occur if these situations are not foreseen.
One method that avoids these problems is the following: instead of changing polygons
when an intersection is found, we consider the angles formed by the edge on which
we reach the intersection and the different edges which come out from this point;
we continue on the outcoming edge which makes this angle maximum. Figure 6 illustrates this idea.

In order to answer questions about neighbouring zones, we found very convenient to
code the zones as a sequence of boundaries which in turn are coded as a sequence of
vertices which are coded as a pair of coordinates; a boundary is defined as a sequence of vertices where the first and last vertices are shared by at least three
sides each, and no other vertix in the boundary satisfy this condition. This coding
is illustrated in figure 7. We adopted the convention that the vertices of a zone are
ordered in the sense that leaves the zone to our left when we walk on the boundary
folloing this order. If for a zone, one of its boundaries should be traced in the
sense opposite as it was coded, then, in the coding of the zone, a minus sign is
placed in front of it. An algorithm was designed and implemented which, by coding
each boundary only once with no attention to the order between them, forms the
different zones. This algorithm avoids inconsistencies in the coding and it is based
in the method of maximum angle mentioned before; first, we indicate which boundaries are shared by two zones and which are not, then we start with one of the
boundaries and go to its final vertix, there we analyze the angles in the counter-

clockwise direction formed by the last side of the boundary and each one of the
initial (last) sides of the boundaries that start (finish) at that vertix. Then,
we follow the boundary containing the side which makes this angle maximun; we
continue in this manner until we return to the original boundary, completing in
this way one zone; next, the remaining boundaries are used to form the other
zones; boundaries shared by two zones, are counted twice. This algorithm is illustrated in figure 8.
Other algorithms, like 'point in polygon' or 'polygon coloring' have been designed
and implemented. The algorithm to color polygons is useful both for graphic purposes and for the image-based approach to build the matrices representing areas.
Isolines are coded as a sequence of vertices ordered in a way that the parameter
value is larger to the left of the isoline.

5.- QUERY LANGUAGE

The language is based on APL and consists of a set of APL functions, some of
which are just connectors to give a more natural appearance to the queries.
These queries are sentences which look very much like Spanish phrases. The
connectors may be omitted without any problem if the user already has some
experience with the language. The language is described with more detail in
Aste (1979).
Answers to queries can be graphics displayed through the Ramtek system or
printed on an APL terminal or a fast printer.
Since the language is a collection of APL functions, an experienced user can
acces the data base directly from APL with or without the query language.

6.- APPLICATIONS

The GDB described in this paper is currently being used in several joint
projects , as a regional planning tool in hydrology, agriculture and forestry.
It is also being used in a project whose objective is soil classification
in order to have an efficient distribution of fertilizers. The GDB allows us
to obtain inventories, location of zones satisfying certain properties as
well as mesuration. Simulation is also possible, more specifically, it is possible to simulate the growing of a certain vegetables in zones with given
characteristics and analyze the possible production.
The implementation of mathematical models is also contemplated.

7.- CONCLUSIONS

The relational structure has been found very useful to handle geographical
information, therefore, this structure is recomended for a general GDB.
Another important characteristic that we believe is very useful in a GDB is
the property of handling information from different sources.
Batch capabilities, graphic output both through a color T.V. terminal and
a line printer are very desirable since these facilities give to the GDB
a great power for updating, model implementation, and visual interpretation
of the results.
Very often, the end user is a non-computer specialist, therefore, a natural and
simple query language is highly recomended.
We have found that the contour-based approach is very useful if we want to
have the possibility of adapting our system to small computers.

ACKNOWLEDGMENTS

I thank all members of the Mexico Scientific Center who directly or indirectly
have participated in the design and implementation of our GDB. Special thanks
go to our partners who are not only testing the applicability and usefulness
of our GDB, but also participate in the development and implementation of
algorithms useful to the projects.

BIBLIOGRAPHY

Aste, J. (1979) An APL relational data base. IBM Mexico Scientific Center,
Technical report CCAL-79.1

Flores, A., Silva, G. (1979) Logical approach algorithms for contour and
vertices extraction. IBM Mexico Scientific Center, Technical report CCAL-79.2

Rhind, D. W. (1974) The state of the art in geographic data processing - a UK view.
Seminar of geographic data processing. IBM UK Scientific Centre, Technical
report UKSC 0073

356

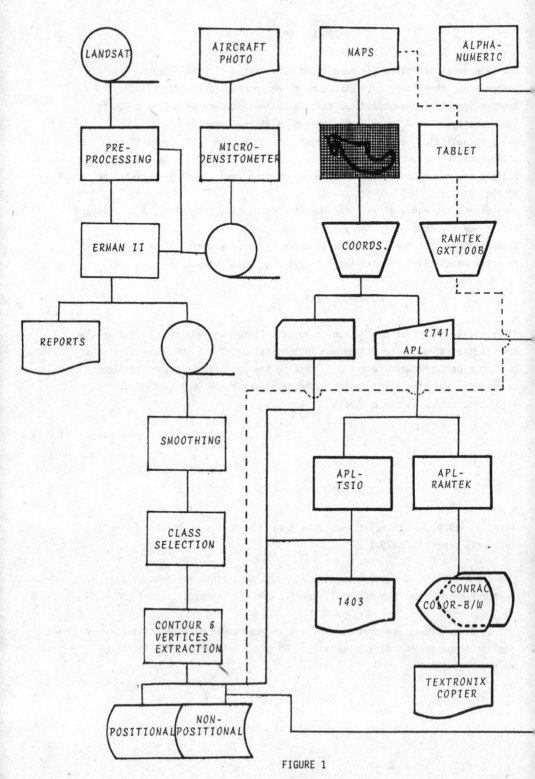

FIGURE 1

1	1	3	3	4
2	1	3	3	4
2	1	1	4	5
2	1	4	4	5
1	1	4	4	5

LAND USE

1: PASTURE
2: WATER
3: FOREST
4: AGRICULTURE
5: URBAN

2	2	2	3	5
1	2	3	4	4
1	2	3	4	2
1	2	2	3	3
2	2	2	3	3

HEIGHT ABOVE SEA LEVEL

1: BETWEEN 1980 AND 2000 M.
2: 2000 - 2020 M.
3: 2020 - 2040 M.
4: 2040 - 2060 M.
5: MORE THAN 2060 M.

1	1	1	2	2
1	1	1	2	2
1	1	1	2	2
1	1	2	2	2
1	1	2	2	2

POLITICAL DIVISIONS

1: COUNTY 'A'
2: COUNTY 'B'

FIGURE 2

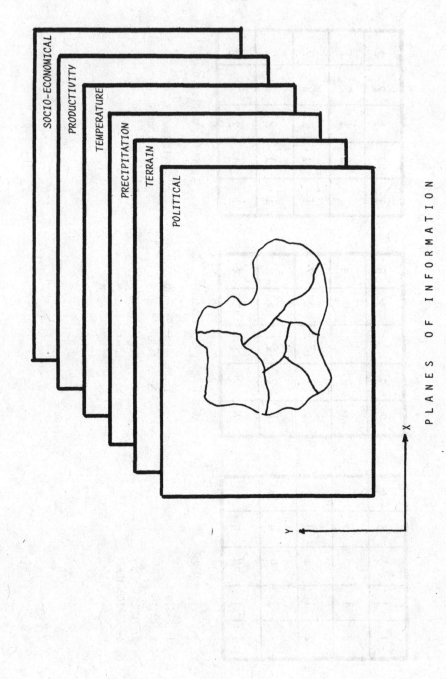

PLANES OF INFORMATION

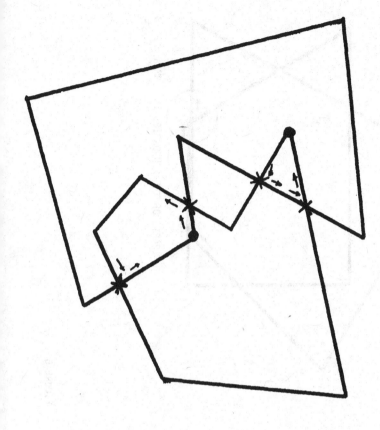

POLYGON INTERSECTION

FIGURE 4

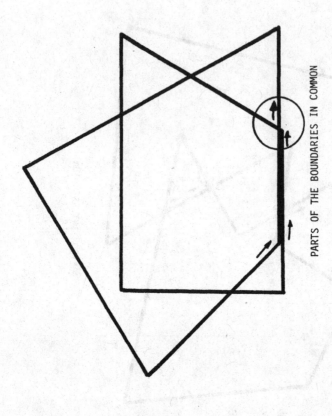

PARTS OF THE BOUNDARIES IN COMMON

CORNER OF ONE POLYGON ON THE BOUNDARY OF THE OTHER

FIGURE 5

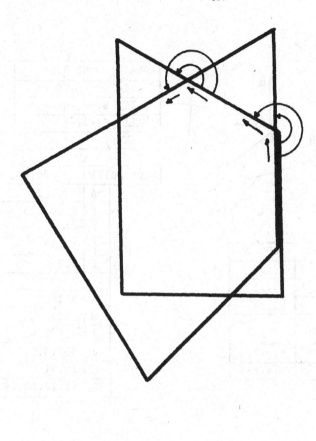

FOLLOWING 'MAXIMUM ANGLE'

FIGURE 6

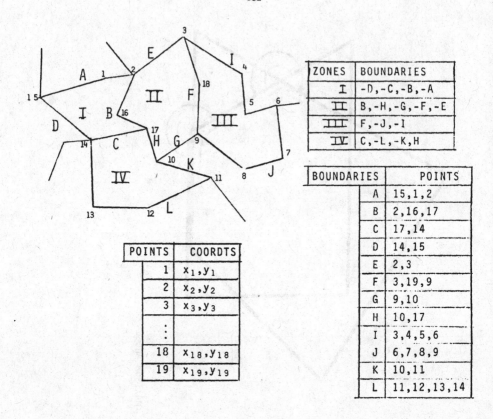

ZONES	BOUNDARIES
I	-D,-C,-B,-A
II	B,-H,-G,-F,-E
III	F,-J,-I
IV	C,-L,-K,H

BOUNDARIES	POINTS
A	15,1,2
B	2,16,17
C	17,14
D	14,15
E	2,3
F	3,19,9
G	9,10
H	10,17
I	3,4,5,6
J	6,7,8,9
K	10,11
L	11,12,13,14

POINTS	COORDTS
1	x_1,y_1
2	x_2,y_2
3	x_3,y_3
⋮	
18	x_{18},y_{18}
19	x_{19},y_{19}

FIGURE 7

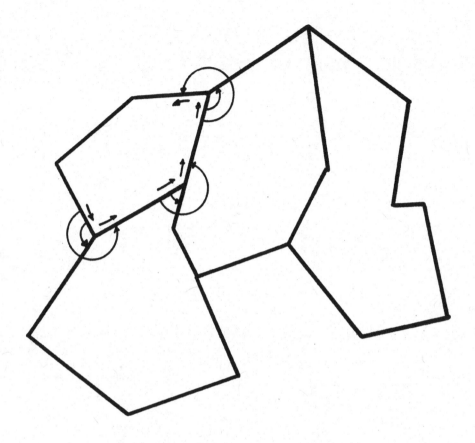

FORMING ZONES BY FOLLOWING 'MAXIMUM ANGLE'

FIGURE 8

COMPUTER - ASSISTED IMAGE ANALYSIS IN MEDICINE

BY

MAX ANLIKER

INSTITUTE FOR BIOMEDICAL ENGINEERING OF THE UNIVERSITY
OF ZURICH AND THE SWISS FEDERAL INSTITUTE OF TECHNOLOGY
IN ZURICH, SWITZERLAND,

The evaluation of images is a frequent task of doctors
particularly of radiologists. The visual evaluation process
is generally time-consuming and it often makes above-
average demands on the individual with respect to concentration and systematic procedure. This is particularly
true of light microscope studies and also of the analysis
of thermograms and computed tomograms. Moreover, in
many problems the observer is obliged by the criteria
employed to make subjective decisions which may compromise the reliability and comparability of the results.

For a long time, experiments with computer-aided analysis
of photographs and television pictures were unsuccessful
because either the time or the cost involved exceeded
reasonable limits. Today both costs and time have been
drastically reduced by use of   low-cost digital storage
units which permits on-line digitalization with an
image-element rate of 12 MHz and video image processing,
and by the introduction of modern microprocessors and
bit slicers.

Depending on the type and complexity of pattern recognition requirements and evaluation, image analysis with
the aid of the computer will afford many advantages in
medicine in the future. It also appears likely that
similar analysis facilities will be available for images
which are variable in time. However, the development of
the required computer hardware and programs is a difficult task, and it does represent a significant challenge
even to experienced specialists in the field of bio-
electronics.

In the following some aspects of medical image analysis
are described by way of examples chosen from on-going
research.

1. Breast Cancer Dedection by Computer Thermography

To establish a more objective method of idendifying
abnormal patterns of regional blood flow a new thermography system has been devised. It permits an on-line
digital mapping of thermograms and an immediate computer
analysis of the temperature distribution. For the purpose of breast cancer detection some of the conventional
visual evaluation criteria are replaced by empirically
determined thresholds of parameters which characterize
unusual features of the topographic temperature variation.
In a retrospective study of 120 cases with 16 breast
cancers and 41 benign tumors the results of biopsy,
mammography and computer thermography are compared.
A frontal, a half-right and a half-left thermogram were
recorded of each patient with the aid of a Spectrotherm
unit. Of particular significance proved a hot spot
index for the frontal thermogram and a parameter defining
the normalized difference between the mean temperatures
of the left and right mamma seen in corresponding side
exposures. With these quantities one can identify 14
of the 16 carcinomas whereby the false positive rate
is 16/104 or 15.4 %. Included in the false positive
rate are 10 of the 41 patients with various benign
tumors. One of the two false negative cases was also
interpreted as benign by mammography, the other can
thermographically be recognized when the hot spot index
is applied to the half-left and half-right exposures.

2. Computer-assisted Videomicroscopy - a Procedure for
Micropharmalogical Studies of the Microcirculation

It is difficult to obtain information on the life-
sustaining process taking place at the microscopic
level in tissues since they are, in most cases, not
accessible to direct observation. Videomicroscopy
and micro-engineering provide new possibilities of
investigating these processes under normal and patho-
logical conditions in human beings. For example, the
transport of molecules tagged with an fluorescent
agent can be followed in various regions of the body,
such as the conjuctiva or the nail fold, if the optical
magnification is high enough. Without computer-aided
analysis of the video image, quantification of the
transport and exchange phenomena mediated by the capillaries and other microvasculature would be a laborious
if not impossibly complex, process. Therefore an on-
line determination of the velocity of erythrocyte
movement in capillaries of the human nail fold, using

a microcomputer and image-storing unit has been
developed. This method can also be adapted for
studying the effects of pharmacological agents on
the transport of matter across the capillary walls.

3. Quantitative Computed Tomography

During the last 8 years, computer tomography has led
to a considerable widening in the scope of radiolo-
gical diagnosis. However, this new diagnostic concept
is very slow in producing an impact on medical research. This is partly due to the fact that commercial
equipment often fails to meet the specific requirements
of research projects, or that the equipment is reserved exclusively for clinical application. Moreover,
manufacturers of computer tomographs (CTs) tend to
regard know-how in this field as an industrial secret,
which makes it difficult for research groups at universities to construct their own equipment. However,
experience has shown that in spite of the major technical effort involved the construction of such an appara-
tus for research purposes can pay dividends.

Many groups working at universities are currently investigating, in theory and practice, the possibilities
and limitations of the diagnostic interpretability of
computer tomograms. The diagnostic limitations of the
reconstructed images are today often attributed to less-
than-adequate spatial resolution and the lack of sufficient differentiation of the densities in the structures
under study. These properties of resolution are in turn
determind by the scanner characteristics, particularly
the beam geometry, the radiation dose, and the reconstruction process. Computed tomography however not
only provides us with eye-catching pseudo images of
anatomical sections but also offers quantitative information on tissue distribution and tissue composition.
As such it adds a new dimension to diagnostic radiology
and may become an extremely valuable research tool. An
example ·indicating this is the quantitative low-dose
computed tomography developed for the purpose of
detecting gradual changes of bone mineralization,in
particular early signs of bone diseases and osteoporosis.

With the aid of a small computer tomograph utilizing
125_I as a radiation source and an analytical procedure
for calculating the density of the spongiosa in the
bones of the extremities, it is now possible in humans

to quantify changes in mineralization occuring over
a period of one or two weeks. The radiation exposure
needed for this measurement is only about 2 mrad and
it is therefore possible to apply the procedure to
healthy test subjects including children.

Measurements made on macerated femur with the aid of
this CT bone densitometer have shown that the sensitivity of the spongiosa density parameter with reference to osteoporosis is greater by a factor of 5 to
10 than that of the total mineral content of the related cross-section of bone. In vivo investigations
of mineralization at the distal end of the radius of
patients prompted the same conclusion. This finding
may also be regarded as confirming the hypothesis
that the breakdown and deposition of bone substance
takes place at a higher rate in spongy than in compact
bone, because the spongiosa has a richer blood supply
and the hormone-controlled cellular exchange of
calcium and phosphorus taking place there is more
intensive.

Computed tomography can also be used for longitudinal
studies in small animals. This was demonstrated in a
series of pilot investigations. At present, extensive
efforts are made to visualize anatomical structures
in three dimensions and to improve resolving power
in time to sufficient degree for a dynamic analysis
of the cardiac functions.

Concluding Remarks
—————————————

Medical image analysis with the aid of computers is
only in the beginning phase as far as clinical
applications are concerned. Its true success and
benefit to the patient will largely depend on cost
effectiveness and on a detailed scoutiny of all those
steps involved in the acquisition of the images
which can be modified in such a way that they
faciliate the deduction of the desired information.

ANALYSIS OF WATER REMOTE SENSED DATA: REQUIREMENTS FOR DATA BASES AND DATA BASES INTERACTIONS

P.Mussio (*)

R.Rabagliati (**)

SUMMARY

Requirements for data bases and data base interactions from users of surface and coastal water remote sensed data are presented.

The water surface system structure is presented, pointing out some of its multifaced interactions with the territory. The problem of surface water system observation, modelling and representation, which are carried out with different aims (description, design and management) is presented. The role, importance and the use of data base in reaching the different goals are shown.

Two main problems are pointed out: the construction of an interface between the users specialistics languages and the informatics tools and the problems of matching pictorial and traditional data.

Outlines of a user definable image description system and of a methodology for the construction of a user oriented query language are given. From these observations data bases requirements follows.

(*) LFCTR, National Research Council
(**) IBM Venice Scientific Center

CONTENT

1. Description and study of the surface water system.

1.1 Description of the surface water system in the territory.

The study of the surface water system is very important nowadays, because of the value that this resource has in several human activities (agriculture, industry)and urban needs. On the other hand, the many aspects (glacies, rivers, lagoons, etc.)in which this resource appear (all of them in active interaction with the surrounding environment) bring scientists involved in this discipline to consider the surface water system as an open system [1] , [2] .
We describe the surface water system with a series of parameters, with relations between the elements themselves and between the surface water system elements and the others subsystems elements of the territory (urban, agricultural, industrial settlements, echosystems, ecc.). Without giving a too detailed description we assume that the surface water system is distributed in the territory resources as glaciers and snow cover, rivers, lakes, lagoons and coastal waters.
Futhermore over the whole territory, the surface water system is distributed, with a different intensity, as humidity in the surface soils, and as water in ground aquifers.
As a subsystem of the territory the surface water system is related to the urban, agricultural and industrial settlements as they are the major water utilizers. Although this resource was quite available in North Italy, the water system is rather impoverished to-day and sometime even not available mainly because of a bad management and protection.
This means that the organization of territory data into a data base may help in management and protection problems solving, but the strong relations existing among the system elements of the territory, should be identified in advance and specified according to the different levels of the system knowledge we have.

In order to face these problems a certain availability of data is needed to start an explorative study and the construction of a model of the water system.

1.2   Study of the surface water system in the territory.

The study of water system is developed in this report
starting from traditional and pictorial data collected from
remote platforms to carry out system analysis and modelling.
We focus this description on glaciers and coastal waters
with some mention to lagoon waters [3,4,5] . This choice
has been done because of the tipical connection between
pictorial and traditional data existing in these two cases.
However it is necessary to underline that for other
elements of the water system, as lakes, rivers, and marshes,
the connection between traditional data and the information
from pictorial data (images) have been extensively
examined [6] , [8] .
As far as traditonal data are concerned, the Italian
Glaciers Register reports physical-geographical data that we
reproduce in tab. 1. The item number 25 in tab. 1 is the
result of the annual glaciological campaing (see fig. 1)
during which the distance (d_i) from the glacier front and
the observation angle (α_i) are measured for each signal
(S_i). From these data the annual movement of the front
glaciers is calculated.
An example of traditional data collected for the analysis
of coastal waters is reproduced in tab. 2. The measurement
of the water characteristics is related to the positition,
shown in fig. 3, of the Malamocco plume [5] .
The main characteristic of the traditional data is that of
being a measurement of one or more components of the state
variable in a particular space-time point (see fig. 3). In
particular the measurements of the different components of
the state variable are not simultaneous (at least not very
often).
As we have seen in tab. 1, scientists of differnt
disciplines have developed their own models and languages
starting from traditional data. We must underline that the
informatic instruments must match these scientific languages
keeping either the experience and the methodology and taking
into account that an informatic tool has always an
'influence, whether or little or not on user thinking
habits' [19] .

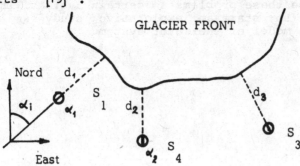

Fig. 1   Traditional measurements of the mouvements

of a front glacier.

Tab. 1 Glaciers data reported from the Italian Glaciers Register [7] .

1	Numero progressivo	1... 419..............800..
2	Nome del ghiacciaio	DISGRAZIA
3	Nome delle montagne	ALPI RETICHE
4	Nome del gruppo	BADILE DISGRZIA
5	Nome della valle	MALENCO
6	Latitudine	46° 16' 40"
7	Longitudine	2° 42' 30"
8	Bacino idrico 1	SISSONE
9	Bacino idrico 2	MALLERO
10	Bacino idrico 3	ADDA
11	Bacino idrico 4	PO
12	Bacino idrico 5	--
13	Bacino idrico 6	--
14	Nome del monte	DISGRAZIA
15	Quota del monte (m)	3678
16	Quota max. ghiacciaio (m)	3000
17	Quota del fronte	2600
18	Lunghezza massima (m)	1500
19	Larghezza massima (m)	2000
20	Superficie (ha)	210
21	Inclinazione	15
22	Esposizione	NORD
23	Tipo di ghiacciaio	PIRENAICO
24	Caratteri del ghiacciaio	PIANALTO-CIRCO DI VALLE
25	Variazione del fronte (m)	-900 (•)

(•) valore medio dal 1896 al 1957

Tab. 2 Chemical-phisical water characteristics in Malamocco inlet.

Vert. 1										

Vert. 2
....

Vert. 5		15-16 giugno 1977								
		PROFONDITA' [m]								
Tempo	Livello	0.50			5.50			11.50		
[hh.mm]	[cm]	vel [cm/sec]	sal [‰]	temp [°C]	vel [cm/sec]	sal [‰]	temp [°C]	vel [cm/sec]	sal [‰]	temp [°C]
20.40	68	78.	--	--	60.	--	--	32.	--	--
21.40	65	40.	34	22.1	30.	35	19.9	14.	35	19.1
22.40	57	0.8	33	24.	-24	34	22	-.8	35	20.2
23.40	35	-60.	33.5	22.	-44.	34	22	-30	34.7	21
.....	..	...	....	....	....	..	..	...	...	...
.....	..	...	....	....	....	..	..	...	...	...
12.15	20	26.8	31	25.5	8.	34	22	-1.7	35	20

As far as pictorial data are concerned we notice that they are a set of simultaneous measures of the electromagnetic characteristics of the earth surface [8] ; that is a variable depending on several components of the water system state variable. If we consider the components of the state variable $(s_1, s_2, s_3, \ldots s_n)$, not completely identified, we can say that the measure of the electromagnetic characteristics may be written as:

$$P(i,j) = \theta F * g(s_1, s_2, s_3, \ldots s_n) \qquad \text{(see fig. 3)}$$

This measure is associated to a specific area called pixel and referred to a set of coordinates.

The main characteristic of these pictorial data is the simultaneity, that is translated in the image processing phase with the grouping of the image points (as it can be obtained with a clustering tecnique).

An example of this characteristic is shown in fig. 3 where we have reproduced the results of an explorative image processing: (white class) represents the sea water, the 'black' categories represent the land structures and the other classes represent wetland areas and the plume of the Adige river [9] .

In the fig. 4 the land structure and wetland are put together in a single class. The same situation is shown in fig. 5 and fig. 6 for the plume and land structure of the Po river delta.

The experts of the different disciplines, used to tradictional data, are involved in the construction of their new scientific languages and models to take advantage of the new information contained in pictorial data.

As it is outlined in fig. 3,4,5,6 the statistic summary is not sufficient to synthetize these data, but is necesary to know how points are goruped in the image, to form real objects!

The meaning of the data doesn't depend only on the figures, they are or not in a class, but mainly on their belonging to some image structures. In our image processing these data structures are seen as a subsystem of the image, according to some previously defined rules.

1.3   Integration between pictorial and traditional data.

In order to describe the water system is necessary to integrate tradicional data and the information obtained form pictorial data taking into account the modifications introduced by these data in the system analysis method. Furthermore we have to notice that traditional and pictorial data are not coherent.

In fig. 7 the output of an image processing is shown together with traditional data in a comparison space. On the parallel planes /x,y/ the contourlines reproduce a grouping of $P(i,j)$ values considered 'similar' on the basis of a previously defined rule. The traditional data, as in fig. 7, $(t_1, t_2, t_3, \ldots t_n)$ are placed between the planes

/x,y/, or over them when the traditional measures are simultaneous to that of remote platforms.

Traditional measurements are the value of the water velocity at times t_i in the section S of Malamocco inlet (see fig. 7), and also the measure of the chemical-physical characteristics (salinity, temperature, organic composition, ph, etc.) collected in the points P_i at times τ_i .

The pictorial data on the planes /x,y/ are reproduced with grey tones (see fig. 3,4,5,6) and the corresponding figures are complex measures that take into account several varibels.

The integration among traditional and pictorial data (see fig. 7) is strictly related to the models set up for the space between the planes /x,y/. That is time evolution computation of the structures we have described on the /x,y/ planes, and the check of them at different times t , with non pictorial data [10] . So the image exploration is a preliminary analysis combined with a verification made with traditional data. Once the the image quality is verified, the explorative analysis is used to indicate the significant structures [11] .

1.4 The data base as an instrument for the study of surface water system.

In the study of the water surface system the data base is seen as one of the instruments that allows the data analysis and than the synthesis of models for the system simulation. The analysis is at the beginning for separate subsystems: data analysis of system elements as in tab. 1 and tab. 2. Than the analysis overcome the single subsystem analysis and the data of several elements are compared, associated and if possible correlated.

A possible result is a grouping of variables, that is the beginning of a formal model of the whole system.

The realization of a data base itself implies a choice of some data that are considered relevant for the system description. This choice correspond to explicit or implicit model formulation in which the relevant aspects of the system are establisched.

For the surface water system some elments as glaciers and rivers have been observed for hundred of years without taking into account the interactions with the other water system elements. Some subsystem models have been set up using experimental observations and analysis of the collected data.

Other subsystem of the surface water as coastal water structures are observed as a whole for the first time with the help of the images from remote platforms. For this reasons is not easy the model definition and the application of selective choices on the data. We have in this case the problem of what and how to store data in the data base.

The integration between traditional and pictorial data as

described in the previous paragraph identifie however the first requirements for data of different origin.

Further requirements of conformity come from the need of data analysis execution and relations identification with other territory subsystems.

The water system is connected with many human activity as agriculture, industry, ships traffic, etc. [12] . In tab. 3 we have reported the ships arrived at the port of Venice in 1974, classified according to the different class of maximum immersion. For the design of the entrance to the port of Venice (Malamocco inlet fig. 10) a choice of a plume with a staff rather long, which is useful in polluted water removal from the beaches, can be in opposition with the choice of inlet shape for ships traffic security and efficiecy.

As far as the utilization of the data is concerned to built models and to design system modifications, pictorial data are produced to modify or integrate the original one. The new pictorial data can be used for new system analysis and comparisons. Therefore we have to manage, to store and to use pictorial data on which the image processing schould operate; we have to identify objects, to insert or modify data within already defined structure.

2. Hypothesis on the use of data base according to the user requirements.

2.1 Specialized languages utilized by the user.

The data related with the surface water system are utilized by several users, according to the interdisciplinarity of the system analysis and system modifications design and system management.

As we have already pointed out(tab. 1 and tab. 2) specialists of different disciplines use their languages to describe phenomena and data.

As far as glaciers are concerned specialists speak of tongues, bodies, fronts, sun exposition, and of quantity and quality of snow and ice to obtain synthetic descriptions that give, together with traditional data (see tab. 1), enough information on the glaceiers state from which the front glaciers movements are computed.

In the same way specialists, involved in the study of coastal waters speak of staffs, bodyes, and contourlines of a plume to which they relate an amount of energy, a volume of water with different phisical-chemical characteristics to obtain a synthesis of the hydrodinamical circulation. The description of glaciers and coastal plumes, in the specialistic languages, are in certain cases not clear to everybody but sufficient to provide a correct transmission of the information. Infact the same elementary objects and names appear in both descriptions but with different meaning and associated computations; this situation becomes evident

with a simple comparison of fig. 16 and fig. 18.
The informatic processing of pictorial data can be the same
for the description of different objects, but the
comunication with the user must be different according to
the various disciplines and also to the following
computations.
What the 'information analist' is required to do is to
identify what can be coded in the user language; that is the
user is asked to design with the 'information analist' an
'intermediate language' which is the base of the query
language for the 'specialized data base'.
In such intermediate language are expressed the significant
data synthesis that must be stored in the specialized data
base. This methodology allows the user to query the data
base in a 'natural' way and to make decisions only about the
not yet coded words of his language.
However it is necessary to point out that there are several
phases in the system analysis and different users
behaviours; this mean different specilized languages not
even homogeneous in many cases.

2.2   Phases in system analysis.

In the first phase of the system analysis the specialist of
a discipline (data base user, from now on called user)
explores the collected data to find out preliminary
information on the data structures and significant
relations. For traditional data this exploration is of
statistical kind [13] , while for pictorial data is also
necessary to investigate the data structure [11] .
In the case of the Malamocco plume (see fig. 8) the
explorative statistical analysis, carried out observing
histograms of the whole image or of some windows, may
classify similar pixels potentially useful to identify the
coastal process [9] . The user can see the coastal
structures, like channel dams, and plumes but he has no
descriptions avilable for these objects studies.
The programs utilized in this research(*) allow a first
analysis of the identified structures, through a choice of a
pixel classes, using histograms, reflectance diagrams along
a previously determined path (see fig. 10 and fig. 11).
In this way the validity of the classes choice is tested:
in fig. 12 we have chosen the reflectance from 114 to 255,
which we presume is due to water with suspended materials.

(*) The programs have been set up at the LABORATORIO DI
FISICA COSMICA E TERRESTRE of the National Reseach Council
(Milan).

The user may now describe the structure that he can see in the image using interactive programs, that identify the vertices of the structure. From these vertices the expansion of many structures properties as the vertices description (see fig. 13) and an 'ITALIAN' description of the plume (see fig. 14).

We must underline that the meaning of image objects can be very different according to the users. For example the description of fig. 14 is made with sentences that are not significant to an hydrologist that prefer a synthetic description as in fig. 15. The user must therefore define the objects of his sythesis. These are the descriptions the user want to store in the data base, to compare them with the description of the same phenomenon in different periods as is shown in fig. 16 for the Malamocco plume.

The user must therefore define a language that allows himself to describe, store and analyze coastal structures in connection with land structures (see fig. 9 and fig. 3). We have to point out that land structures are very useful in the registration phase of the image processing [9] .

The definition of a 'user language' is not immediate because of the lack of experience in the use of these data. Only an accurate analysis of several examples, many trials and errors, with a suitable calibration can leed to the 'user intermediate language' definition. Such language is, in other words, a base for the definition of a model and of a formal representation.

If we come back to the problem of integration of pictorial and traditional data we can say now that the main problem is the use of the formal model for the identification of surface surrounding the data structures on the planes /x,y/ of fig. 7 and verified by traditional data t_i, τ_i .

So the program that realize the formal model must use both traditional and pictorial data (synthetic representations).

As the models are used as prediction instruments, they generate either images and synthetic structures. The images obtained from the models must be again analized with the image processing pakage to obtain suitables synthetic descriptions to be stored in the data base. The new image can be obtained with simple insertions or modifications of spatial data previously stored.

2.3   System design and management.

For the design of system modifications and for the system management are used programs that need synthetic descriptions chosen by the user and traditional data of the system elements and traditional data of other subsystem elements of the territory (tab. 3).

We notice the utility of the image generation from the computed data and from the results of the system simulations.

For the design of system modifications is very important

379

the modification of synthetic structures that is the description of the images.

3. Our experience in the image processing and relational description identification.

3.1 Outline of image processing for the image description using relations.

The image is a matrix of numbers. Using the TESI [14] , (Trattamento ESplorativo Immagini) the user find the minimum and maximum threshold of the pixel classes of interest (see fig. 17). In this way we have obtained an input for AIPL [14] an interacive program that runs under APL/VS directed by a series of tables defined by the user. AIPL is organized in four steps:

- selection in the image of the points belonging to the choosen pixels class (see fig. 18) and identification of the boundary points according to a relation with nearest points and described with a numeric code [18] .

- the boundary code allows the selction of boundary points with sorting procedures of each image objects. The fig. 19a reproduce a summary of 31 identified objects of fig. 18, which are 'blobs' or 'holes'. The described image is reproduced in fig. 19b where the necssary vertex for the description are indicated with their barycentres.

- the user can develop different relations choosing among a set of commands that give:the relations with other objects of the image, the characteristics parameters as area, perimeter, vertex number, their ratios, the barycenter, the axial ratio, x angle, and the 'inside outside' relations (see fig. 20 an fig. 21).

- the user define some elementary objects to be described with logical operators. The boundary of each image object is divided in syllables (vertex sequences), that belong to the same elementary object. The syllables are joined together to obtain sentences that represent the objects of user image (see fig. 22).

3.2 Methodology for the definition of a user intermediate language.

The analysis of the figures we have described, shows that they are associated to intemediate processing steps of experieces that are under way or accomplished by the staff of LFCTR of the National Research Council (Milan). Now we can made the following remarks:

a) the user seldom utilieze the whole image with a number of
pixels of the order 10exp6. If the user needs to have a
global information or he wants the interactions between
system elements, he use reduced or compressed images. For
fenomena well localized, as plumes, or glaciers, he will
locate 'windows' of the image around the particular he is
intreded in. In this case, according to our exeperiences
the order of magnitude of the pixels number is reduced to
the order of 10exp4.

b) Furthermore, on this window, the user can use the
synthetic descriptions, in which for instance the land
structures are summarized in a single line.
In this description we are only interested, with a maximum
of accuracy, to the ground control points (in fig. 4 the
Adige and Po rivers outlets) while the coast can be
identified and described in with less accuracy.

c) When the objects of an image are time dependent (fig. 9
and fig. 16) the comparison of the shapes can facilitate the
identification of significant variations.
On the other hand in the comparison of different images
(fig. 16 and fig. 17) we find objects with similar shapes
that are different for the users and that requires names,
meanings and processing completely different.
For the comma a) we require the definition of instruments
for the management of the whole image (non structured data
for which is not possible a query of this tipe: 'find the
images with more than five plumes').
These instruments must be able to reduce the image, to cut
windows and comunicate with successives programs.
The other remarks brought us to study the possibility of
storing descriptions in a way that has some meaning for the
user (he can ask for example: 'does it exist in this
position a plume?', where 'position' is a description). The
user can execute queries, comparisons in it own language: he
can define the elementary and complex objects and combine
the significant parameters.
These requirements are satisfied by means of some
interpreters (fig. 23) that allows the user to define: the
relations among neighbouring points, his own tokens
(elementary objects) and their names, his own operators for
the composition.
DEFN AIPL ask the user to obtain the set of boundary points
and it can solve some ambigous situations such as filiform
and crossed structures.
For example comparing fig. 18 and fig. 19 the elimination
process is evident for the filiform structures.
IU1 (user interpreter one) associate names to elmentary and
complex structure. For the examples we have seen the names
are connected to the coastal process (bight, gulf, bay).
IU2 (user interpreter two) allow the user to associate his
sentences to summaryes and relations developed form the
vertexes table (fig. 20). Using this interpreters and

geometrical figures the user define his objects and the object names.

He develops therefore a language that express his own 'tecnical dialect'. Such language (set of algorithms) doesn't satisfy all the user requirements, expecially as far as the decision process is concerned: for this reason such language is called an 'intermediate language'. There are three levels of such disciplinary language: for system analysis and synthesis, design and management.

On the other hand the relations establisched by the user with the interpreters and AIPL are translated in other relations as in fig. 24 where is exemplified the image of fig. 18.

4.   The requirements for the data base and its instruments.

The description we have made of data processing for the surface water system pointed out the most important requirements to store, and manage these data.

Our image processin for remote sensed data can reach the identification in the image of data structures. The experiments and tests we have done utilized traditional storing facilities with their problems. As we have shown the image processing usually start from window images (10exp4 pixels) that are processed several times for different descriptions. On these descriptions we apply than further statistics, descriptions, etc. All the images of this paper are expansions of an unique base structure (matrix vertexes) of the classified objects vertexes.

The interactive way of working lead to the following requirements:

a) Necessity of a good information search speed, new objects description, and deletion of useless objects facilities.

b) facility of partial correction of images descriptions.

c) data protection as several users can use them.

d) privacy check to allow the user not to perform prohibited operations. This means that not all the users are allowed to modify the definition of tokens sets and functions.

The data for this kind of analysis must be public. The data structures of the described image processing is uniform: each data structures we have examined are tables. The traditional data are already collected in this way. The pictorial data in this field are are always matrices numbers and after the first image processing step each object is associated to a set of matrices.

A row of the vertexes matrix contains the coordinates and the code. From this matrix vertexes all the descriptions we have seen are obtained. These descriptions are again matrices of characters and numbers in which every row has a significant item (fig. 24).

This tipe of structure is simmetric respect the image generation and recognition [17] . The goal of the recognition becomes the starting point of the generation, that is very important if we consider the predominant role of the data exploration.

The organization of the structures we have described requires a facility for the table updating: new quality in the objects descriptions, new tokens definitions,etc.

The instruments we have described are managed by means of a set of tables that are stored in the data base, which contains the data and the rules for their interpretations. This lead to a requirement that the data base should contain the interactive instruments to process these data.

For pictorial data simple interpreters are necessary and useful to allow the user his own tokens definition and his operators generation. This means that the user doesn't manage or define data strutures but the content of the structures for the data processing. For the tokens, graphically defined the user code them with a name, for the operators the user needs first an 'information analyst' and than he proceed as for the operators. We note that the kind of description allows the recognition of the same structures seen from different platforms.

BIBLIOGRAPHY

1 L.Van Bertalanffy, General System Theory Penguin Book, England, 1971.

2 S.Rinaldi, "Ingegneria Sistemistica Ambientale" Politecnico di Milano, 1974

3 R.Rabagliati, R.Serandrei Barbero, "Possibilita' di impiego del remote sensing da satellite per il controllo annuale dei ghiacciai" Rivista di Geografia Fisica e Dinamica Quaternaria, 1978

4 A.Annoni, A.Della Ventura, P.Mussio, Proposition d'analysis explorative des donnes d'un vol OCS au moyen d'instruments interatives" Proceedings Assemblee pleniere de la CIESM, Antalya, 1978

5 "Progetto scambi laguna mare: campagna di misure - 15/18 giugno 1978" LSDGM (Venezia) CNR, TR.91, 1978

6 P.Mussio et all., "Studio multispettrale da satellite sulle acque dei fiumi Po e Ticino alla loro confluenza", Atti 19 Congresso Nazionale per lo Spazio, Roma, 1978.

7 "Catasto dei Ghiacciai Italiani", Comitato Glaciologico Italiano, 1961.

8 "Manual of Remote Sensing" American Society of Photogrammetry, 1975

9 A.Annoni, "Analisi di parametri superficiali di sistemi marini mediante dati telerilevati da diverse piattaforme" Doctoral Thesis, University of Milan, 1979

10 C.Chignoli, R.Rabagliati, "A two-dimensional model of the Lagoon of Venice", IAHR, Baden Baden, 1977.

11 P.Brambilla, G.M.Lechi,P.Mussio, "What is a remotely sensed tree? A proposal for structural and pseudo spectral reconaissance", Proc.of Inter. Symp. on Remote Sensing for Observation and Inventory on Earth Resources and the Endarged Environment" Friburgo, 1978.

12 P.Rosa Salva, R.Rabagliati, "Indagine di fattibilita' di un modello per la pianificazione del territorio lagunare", Acqua e Aria, Novembre 1978.

13 J.Tukey, F.Mostella, "Data Analysis and Regression" Addison Wesley , N.Y., 1977.

14 P.Mussio et all., "Programmi per il trattamento di dati da telerilevamento" Atti Congresso Nazionale per lo Spazio, Roma, 1978.

15 R.Frassetto, "Ocean Colour Scanner over the Adriatic Sea" (in press)

16 P.Mussio et all., "Trattamento esplorativo di immagini da telerilevazioni" Atti 1 Congresso Telerilevamento, Gargnano, 1978.

17 U.Cugini, P.Mussio, C.Cavagna, "On an image generation and recognition system", Artificial intelligence and pattern recognition in C.A.D., J.Latomb Editor, p.p.429-480, North Holland, Amsterdam, 1978.

18 P.Mussio, G.Fresta, S.Zambon, "Un algoritmo per la codifica e la descrizione automatica dei contorni di immagini digitali" LFCTR, TR. 12, 1975

Tab. 3   Ships traffic in the port of Venice (1974).

Aziende	1/2	2/3	3/4	4/5	5/6	6/7	7/8	8/9	9/10	10/11	11/12	12/13	13/14	14/15	x/x	totali
Esso Standard	1 1	2 8	4 8	2 3	1 2	5 6	3 37	2 3	8 24						2 5	30 97
Ind. Italiana Petroli				2 2	2 3	3 10	3 10	5 24	2 5						3 3	21 57
Irom	1 1	2 7	8 97	2 5	7 8	1 3	4 7	2 2	11 42						5 29	43 201
Irom S. Leonardo										2 4	5 24	7 16	5 11	2 3	32 44	55 104
Costieri A. Adriatico		2 41	12 49	7 13	1 1	2 4	1 1								3 11	24 120
Api		1 3	5 46	3 74	2 28		1 1	1 1							3 4	20 157
Agip		2 8	5 9	4 5	4 5	1 2			1 1						1 50	18 80
Icip Total		1 5	1 1	3 6	4 7										1 13	7 25
San Marco Petroli		1 1			4 7	3 8	1 2	2 8	3 7						1 3	3 40
Sarom	1 4	3 18	13 69	8 13	9 14	4 14	3 8	2 8	3 7	2 2					6 28	65 186
M.E. Dep. Cost. Nord		3 5	1 1	4 7	1 6	4 41	2 21	2 6	7 10						2 2	22 88
M.E. Dipe 2 acc. 1	1 1		6 6	7 10	6 6	11 13	2 11	2 6	3 4	1 1					14 14	53 67
M.E. Dipe 2 acc. 2	1 1	3 8	13 32	6 19	10 17	8 42	1 10	4 4	3 3						3 7	46 137
M.E. Dipe 2 acc. 3		2 6	11 57	7 17	6 49	2 12	3 10								3 7	35 159
M.E. Dipe 2 acc. 4		3 27	15 56	7 22	12 13	2 11		1 1	1 1	1 1					5 31	46 162
M.E. Dipe 2 acc. 32-34		1 3	11 27	11 69	8 24	6 49		8 33	12 66	1 10					6 15	64 29
M.E. Dipe 1 acc. 5-10			6 17	3 3	11 16	9 34			2 2	1 1					7 8	42 94
Dipa N. Alumetal 1 Ammi			7 18	8 62	10 26	7 17	2 12	1 1	6 9	6 18	1 1				11 14	63 181
Dipa ovest			8 8	3 13	8 18	3 3	8 11	7 7	8 10						20 25	65 95
Enel I			1 3			1 1	1 1	1 1	1 1	1 1					4	4 6
Enel II		1 1	2 20	5 11	3 5	2 8	3	6 12	13 47	7 10	1 1				9 10	41 105
Vetrocoke			5 16			1 1		4 15	14 36	3 5					7 11	44 108
Dep. Generi Monopolio					1 35	1 1	1 1								3	3 37
Italsider			7 10	9 17	10 57	3 3	1 19	4 29							6 6	40 141
Petromar	5 7															5 7
Malteria Adriatica															5	5 5
Carbochimica			2 6	5 48	2 2	3 3									7	7 54
Eraclit Venier			4 5		1 1					1 1					3 5	8 11
Italiana Olii e Risi							2 2	1 2	1 1						4 13	13 19
Chiari e Forti II			1 2	4 7	1 1	3 3	2 2	1 1		1 1					4 4	13 13
Caffaro				2	1 2	2 2									2 2	9 14
Alucentro									3 7						5	5 9
Sava II			6 14	2 7	2 9	5 29									4 4	19 63
Sirma II			8 10	4 5	2 10	1 1	2 2	3 3							4 5	24 36
Cementir					2 23										2	2 23
Pagnan			1 1			1 1									2	2 2
Alumetal II				2 3	3 4	3 21									9	9 29
	10 15	27 141	163 588	120 443	131 389	100 339	51 187	63 164	103 280	25 53	7 26	7 16	5 11	2 3	171 373	985 3028

Class of 1/2 means ships with a maximum immersion from 1m to 2m.
For each class the number of ships and the number of arrivals are indicated.

386

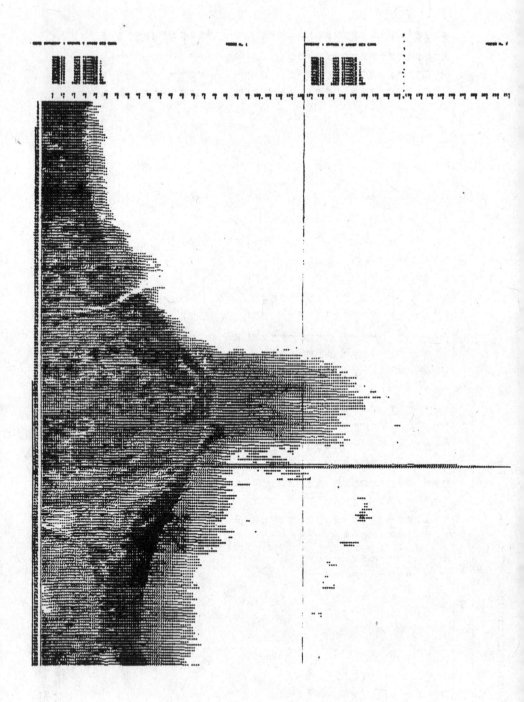

Fig. 3   Ocean Colour Scanner   Platform.   Brenta and Adige
rivers plumes.

Fig. 4   Ocean Colour Scanner platform. . Brenta and
          Adige coastal structures.

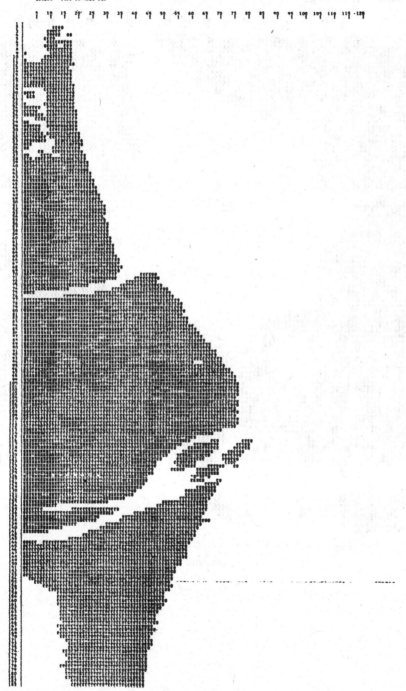

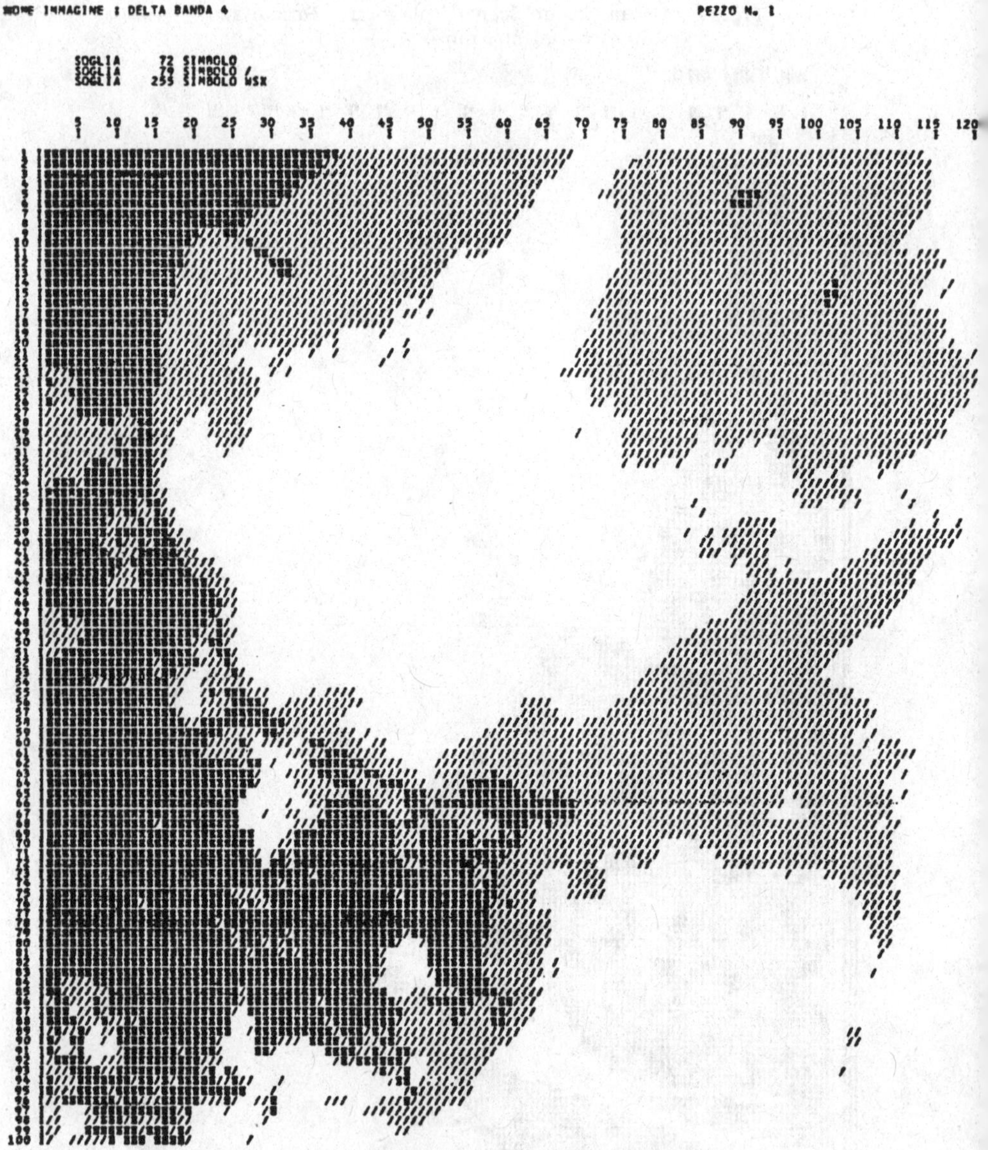

NOME IMMAGINE : DELTA BANDA 4   PEZZO N. 1

Fig. 5 LANDSAT platform (band 4). Compressed image (1:10)
of Po river plume and coastal structures.

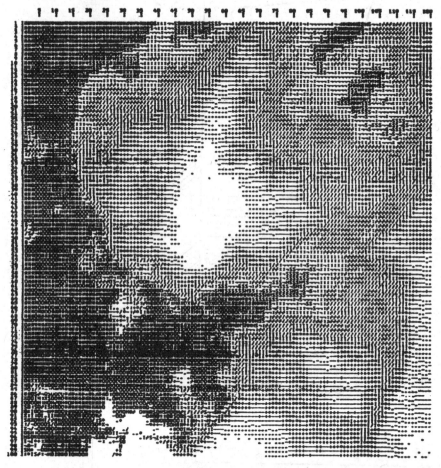

Fig 6 LANDSAT platform (band 4). Compressed image (1:10) of Po river delta with equidistribution.

390

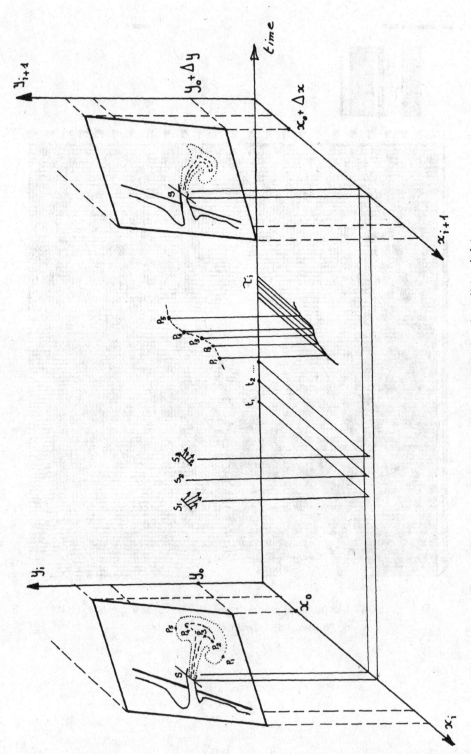

Fig. 7 Integration between pictorial and traditional data.

Fig. 8 O.C.S. channel 6. Malamocco plume identification with equidistribution representation of sea and coastal structures.

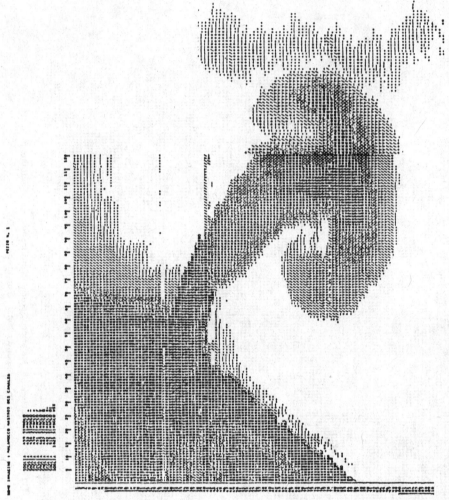

Fig. 9 O.C.S. channel 6 . Malamocco plume identification with the separation from coastal structures and sea waters.

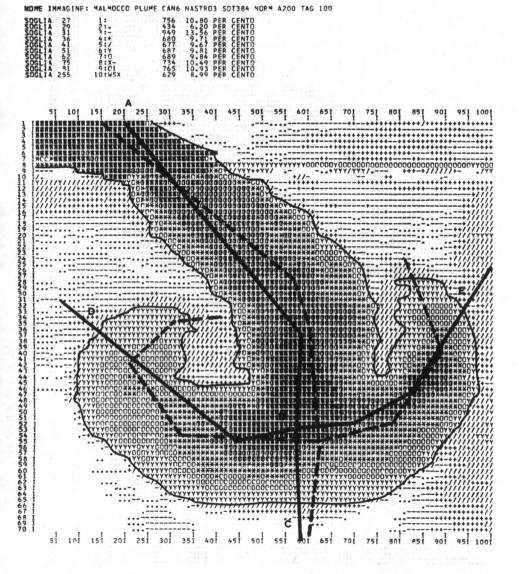

NOME IMMAGINE: MALMOCCO PLUME CAN6 NASTRO3 SOT384 NORM A200 TAG 100

```
SOGLIA  27     1:       756   10.80 PER CENTO
SOGLIA  29     2:       434    6.20 PER CENTO
SOGLIA  31     3:-      949   13.56 PER CENTO
SOGLIA  36     4:+      680    9.71 PER CENTO
SOGLIA  41     5:/      677    9.67 PER CENTO
SOGLIA  51     6:Y      687    9.81 PER CENTO
SOGLIA  62     7:0      689    9.84 PER CENTO
SOGLIA  75     8:X-     734   10.49 PER CENTO
SOGLIA  91     9:01     765   10.93 PER CENTO
SOGLIA 255    10:WSX    629    8.99 PER CENTO
```

Fig. 10 O.C.S. channel 6. Malamocco plume analysis with
radiance variations.

394

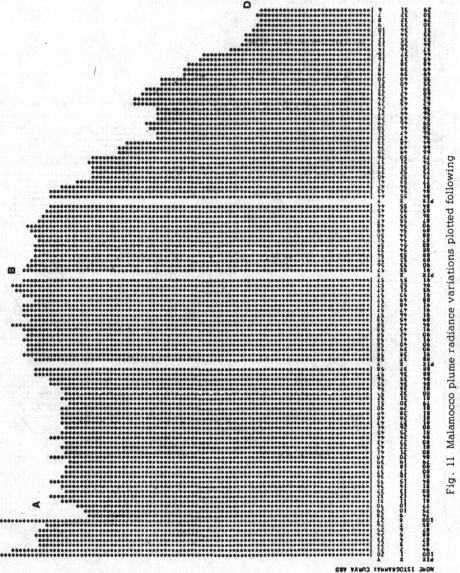

Fig. 11 Malamocco plume radiance variations plotted following the path A-B-D of fig. 10.

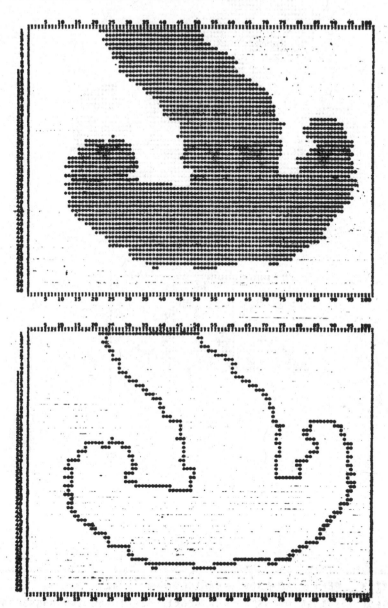

Fig. 12 Malamocco plume contours identification for the plume
structure description.

396

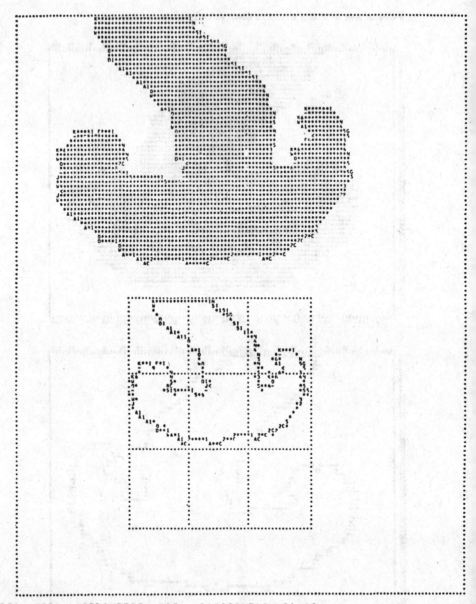

AREA= 2783   PERIMETRO= 305   BARICENTRO= 31 42
STRINGA VERTICI:
5151515G4515151N4N4NS8NS3456-OWK6F6<1AhK6-KIN45GS34NS85GS3E23SC2C2C2
C2CA12C2CA12CA1A1AhO1DO1A1A1AWJ<WJ-OWK6-KI9FIN4NSC28515156-J<1DOWO1AWO
1A1A1A1A1DOWKIN45

Fig. 13 Malamocco plume structure generated from the vertexes
         matrix. The area, the perimeter and the barycenter are
         shown.

Fig. 14 " ITALIAN " description of fig. 13 using " words " of geometrical applications.

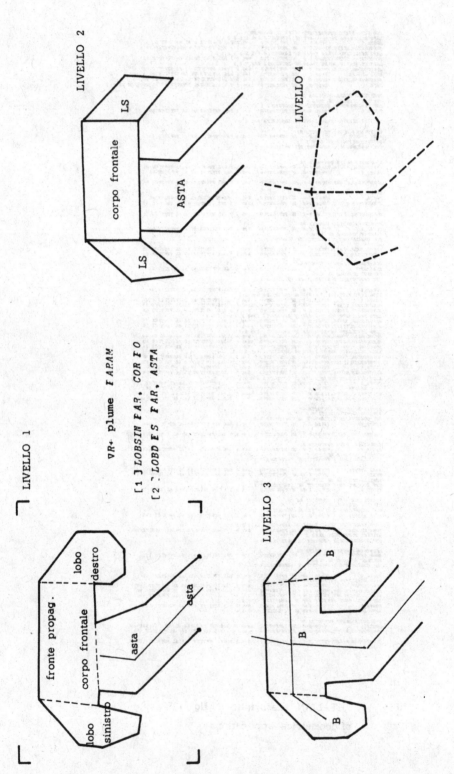

LIVELLO 1

LIVELLO 2

LIVELLO 3

LIVELLO 4

∇R- plume I A?A.M

[1] LOBSIN FA?, COR F O
[2 ? LOBD ES FAR, ASTA

corpo frontale

LS

LS

ASTA

lobo
destro

fronte propag.

corpo frontale

lobo
sinistro

asta

asta

B

B

B

Fig. 15 Synthetic description of Malamocco plume.

399

Fig. 16 O.C.S. channel 6. Malamocco plume evolution: 33minutes after the image of fig. 9.

400

Fig. 17a Preliminary identification of Badile-Disgrazia glaciers
and snow cover (white class).

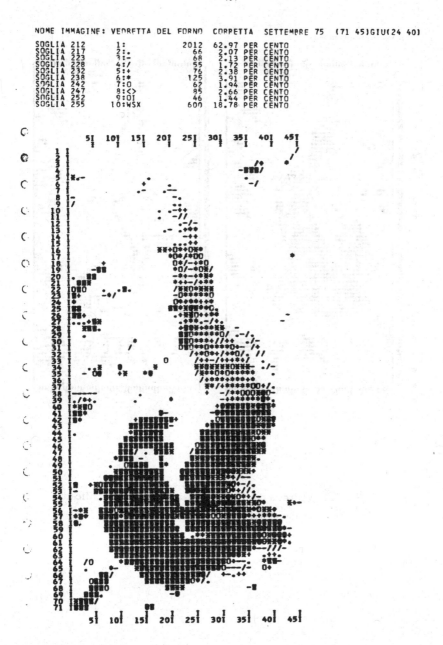

Fig. 17b Identification of the vedretta del Forno glacier.

402

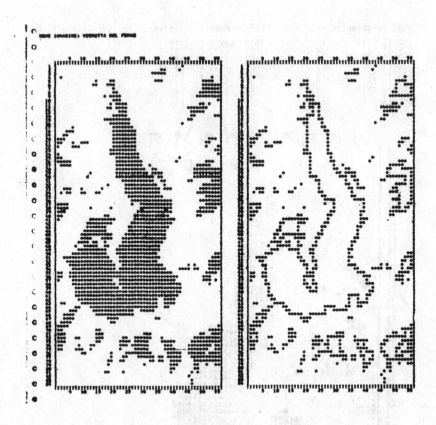

Fig. 18 Vedretta del Forno glacier: contours identification
for the glacier description.

403

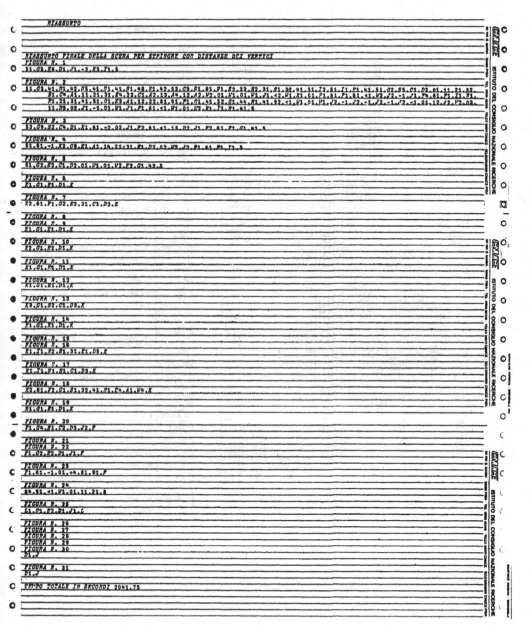

Fig. 19a   Summary of the objcts identified in the image of
the Vedretta del Forno (see fig. 18b).

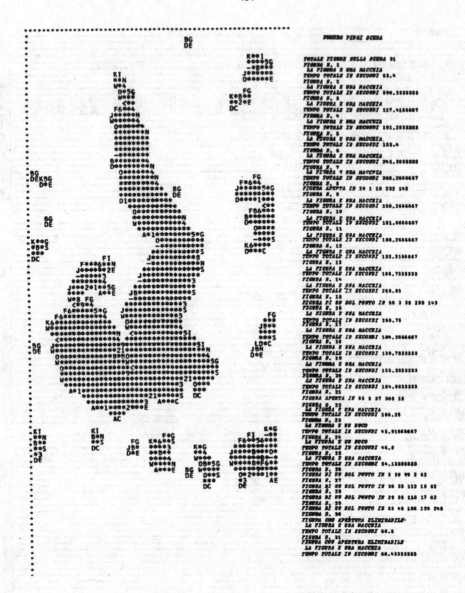

Fig. 19b Vedretta del Forno image generated
after the single object description.

Fig. 19c Summary of the objects
of fig. 19b.

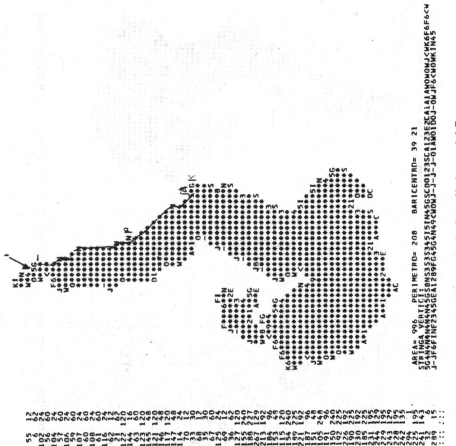

Fig. 20a   Description of the object N.2 of the Vedretta del Forno
image (see fig. 19b).

406

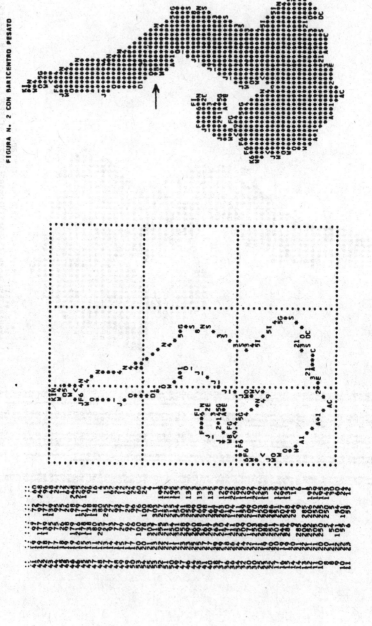

Fig. 20b Vedretta del Forno structure generated from th vertexes matrix.   Fig. 20c Object N. 2 with weighted barycenter.

```
(FIGURA 2) RELAZIONE CON TUTTI

    LA FIGURA 1 STA A NORD EST          RISPETTO ALLA FIGURA 2
    LA DISTANZA TRA I LORO BARICENTRI E 48.01041554
    LA FIGURA 3 STA A NORD EST EST      RISPETTO ALLA FIGURA 2
    LA DISTANZA TRA I LORO BARICENTRI E 30.41381265
    LA FIGURA 4 STA A SUD EST           RISPETTO ALLA FIGURA 2
    LA DISTANZA TRA I LORO BARICENTRI E 38.20994635
    LA FIGURA 5 STA A SUD SUD EST       RISPETTO ALLA FIGURA 2
    LA DISTANZA TRA I LORO BARICENTRI E 33.54101966
    LA FIGURA 6 STA A NORD NORD EST     RISPETTO ALLA FIGURA 2
    LA DISTANZA TRA I LORO BARICENTRI E 45.607017
    LA FIGURA 7 STA A NORD EST          RISPETTO ALLA FIGURA 2
    LA DISTANZA TRA I LORO BARICENTRI E 41.61730409
    LA FIGURA 9 STA A NORD OVEST        RISPETTO ALLA FIGURA 2
    LA DISTANZA TRA I LORO BARICENTRI E 31.144823
    LA FIGURA 10 STA A NORD OVEST        RISPETTO ALLA FIGURA 2
    LA DISTANZA TRA I LORO BARICENTRI E 28.28427125
    LA FIGURA 11 STA A NORD NORD EST    RISPETTO ALLA FIGURA 2
    LA DISTANZA TRA I LORO BARICENTRI E 20.1246118
    LA FIGURA 12 STA A NORD OVEST OVEST RISPETTO ALLA FIGURA 2
    LA DISTANZA TRA I LORO BARICENTRI E 23.85372088
    LA FIGURA 13 STA A NORD OVEST OVEST RISPETTO ALLA FIGURA 2
    LA DISTANZA TRA I LORO BARICENTRI E 23.40939982
    LA FIGURA 14 STA A SUD OVEST OVEST  RISPETTO ALLA FIGURA 2
    LA DISTANZA TRA I LORO BARICENTRI E 24.69817807
    LA FIGURA 16 STA A SUD OVEST        RISPETTO ALLA FIGURA 2
    LA DISTANZA TRA I LORO BARICENTRI E 34.71310992
    LA FIGURA 17 STA A SUD SUD OVEST    RISPETTO ALLA FIGURA 2
    LA DISTANZA TRA I LORO BARICENTRI E 26.92582404
    LA FIGURA 18 STA A SUD              RISPETTO ALLA FIGURA 2
    LA DISTANZA TRA I LORO BARICENTRI E 28.44292531
    LA FIGURA 19 STA A SUD SUD EST      RISPETTO ALLA FIGURA 2
    LA DISTANZA TRA I LORO BARICENTRI E 32.89376841
    LA FIGURA 20 STA A SUD EST EST      RISPETTO ALLA FIGURA 2
    LA DISTANZA TRA I LORO BARICENTRI E 29.61418579
    LA FIGURA 22 STA A SUD              RISPETTO ALLA FIGURA 2
    LA DISTANZA TRA I LORO BARICENTRI E 27.01851217
    LA FIGURA 23 STA A SUD EST          RISPETTO ALLA FIGURA 2
    LA DISTANZA TRA I LORO BARICENTRI E 40.31128874
    LA FIGURA 24 STA A SUD SUD OVEST    RISPETTO ALLA FIGURA 2
    LA DISTANZA TRA I LORO BARICENTRI E 11.40175425
    LA FIGURA 25 STA A SUD EST EST      RISPETTO ALLA FIGURA 2
    LA DISTANZA TRA I LORO BARICENTRI E 28.7923601
    LA FIGURA 30 STA A NORD NORD OVEST  RISPETTO ALLA FIGURA 2
    LA DISTANZA TRA I LORO BARICENTRI E 23.53720459
    LA FIGURA 31 STA A NORD EST EST     RISPETTO ALLA FIGURA 2
    LA DISTANZA TRA I LORO BARICENTRI E 28.17800561
TEMPO TOTALE IN SECONDI 3152.05
```

Fig. 20d   Summary of the relations between the object N.2 and the other objects.

```
      DESCRIVI FIGURA 2



DESCRIZIONE FIGURA N. 2
  AREA= 996   PERIMETRO= 208
  AREA/PERIMETRO = 4.7885
  NUMERO VERTICI/PERIMETRO = 0.64423
  TEMPO TOTALE IN SECONDI 139.3166667



      (IN 'DISGRAZI SET7 E') ELLITTICITA DI FIGURA 2


ANGOLAZIONE = 6.8027
RAPPORTO ASSIALE = 0.8243
TEMPO TOTALE IN SECONDI 292.0333333




      BUCHI INTERNO MACCHIE




  IL BUCO 23 E INTERNO ALLA FIGURA 4
  IL BUCO 24 E INTERNO ALLA FIGURA 2
  TEMPO TOTALE IN SECONDI 50.5
```

Fig. 21 Parameters and relations of the object N.2.

409

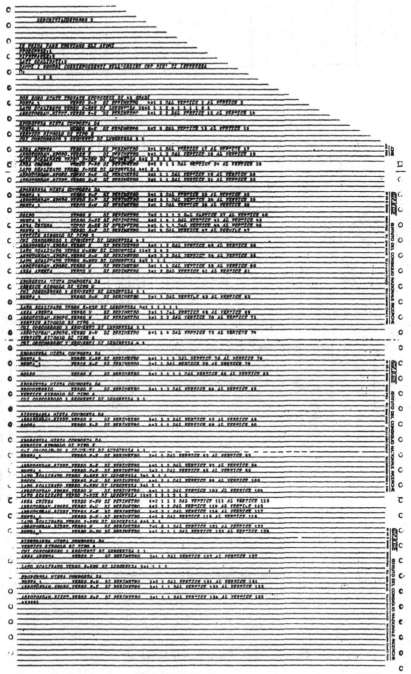

Fig. 22 " ITALIAN " description of contours of object N.2 in fig. 20.

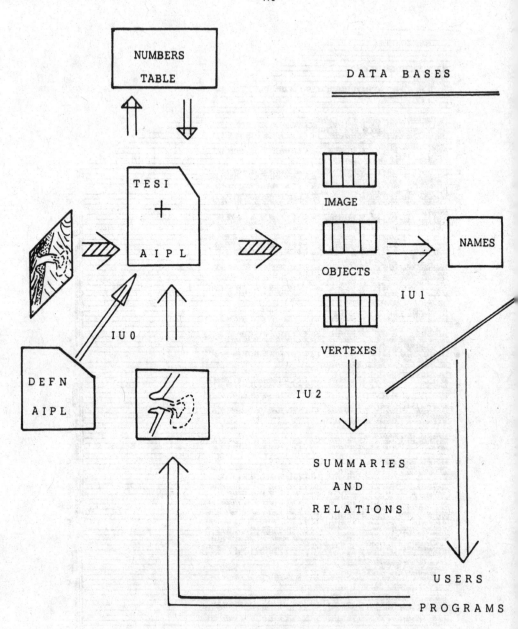

Fig. 23   Flow chart of the image processing pakage.

OBJ

OBJ1	NAME1
PART1	NAME1

IMAGE

obj1	nv/np	nv	a/p	Per. . . . .
. . . .				
. . . .				
obj31				

OBJECT n

Part 1	param	1	2	3	n

VERTEXES

name	x	v	type

Fig. 24 Relations at different synthesis levels.

Aspects of Handling Data from Astronomical Images

Dr A. Hooley, Dr E.J. Kibblewhite,

Dr M.T. Bridgeland and Dr D.A. Horne

Astronomical photographic data bases can have sizes ranging from a few thousand to many billions of bytes. Much of the data processing can be regarded as a filtering process which reduces these large input sets to very much smaller subsets. We give as an example the problem of detecting a complete set of astronomical objects of a specific type (QSOs), and describe in detail the algorithms, data structures and processing techniques used in the SRC Automatic Plate Measuring machine at Cambridge. This system completely analyses 4 billion bytes of data per day.

Institute of Astronomy, Madingley Road, Cambridge

1. Introduction

Astronomers have always been able to record information on photographic plates much faster than they could analyse it. A modern Schmidt telescope can record 10^6 astronomical images in an hour's exposure. About half the images are those of stars which are always point-like objects, and the rest are distant galaxies and other extragalactic objects (see Plate I). Each 14 inch square photograph contains 4 billion bytes of information so that in a single night, with one telescope, we may record 40 billion bytes of data.

These panoramic detectors are used either to search for specific types of objects for later study or for collecting statistical data on the Universe. At present, all plates are analysed visually by trained astronomers. Not only is this slow but serious bias can be introduced into the selection of objects since only objects strikingly different from their neighbours are usually detected by eye. Our perception of distant parts of the Universe can depend critically on what objects we choose to study and observational selection effects have plagued many areas of astronomy.

At Cambridge we have been developing an automated photographic measuring system (APM) for the U.K. Science Research Council. This system will be run as a national facility for U.K. astronomers and Guest investigators. It consists of a very accurate laser beam scanning microdensitometer to digitise the plate, and a series of on-line computers to analyse the data as it is being scanned. Although the system is designed for general purpose photographic analysis, it is uniquely suited for searching for specific types of objects. We will take as an example, the problem of detecting QSOs.

2. Detection of QSOs

Quasi-stellar objects (QSOs) are very active massive objects, possibly powered by a central black hole. They are as massive as entire galaxies and so bright they can be seen at distances such that their light takes billions of years to reach us. They are intrinsically interesting, and statistical studies of their properties may enable us to unravel the early history of the universe.

There are perhaps a hundred QSOs on an average Schmidt plate (35 square degrees of sky) and as photographic images they are virtually indistinguishable from stars in our own Galaxy. They can only be identified by comparison of a number of plates, each taken under different conditions, e.g. different wavelength bands, polarisation filters, or different times. It is apparent that there are at least two fundamental data bases in this problem; the original data on the plate, and the data on the QSOs. However, to generate the QSO data base we have to measure the properties of every image on the photographs and compare these properties between photographs. We therefore have to generate a third, inter-mediate data base of image parameters from all the plates and it is the generation of this data base that has proved the hardest technical problem. This is discussed in more detail below.

Fig. 1 shows the steps in the process of finding QSOs, and the amount of data generated at each stage. The plate is scanned point by point in a raster, and the samples are fed into a processor that detects all the images above the sky background, and determines their parameters. The parameters are then classified according to their shape using learning algorithms described in section 3. Usually this complete data base is stored on magnetic tape along with a classification of all images. We know QSOs are stellar in shape, so only point-like images are further processed. Thus all shape information may now be rejected and we are left with an 8-byte vector of position and intensity (2 x 24 bit words, 1 x 16 bit word) for each object. These data are stored on disc. We scan a number of plates of the same area of sky, taken in different colours, and the data for the same objects collated. The broad band spectra of the objects are then classified. Because we do not wish to throw away any candidate QSOs we use similar algorithms to those already mentioned for shape classification. These recognise 'common' types of spectra (due to stars) and once these are eliminated from the data base, we are left with a small sample of candidate objects all of which differ significantly from field objects. Nearly all of these objects are interesting even though a substantial fraction may be rare types of star, but we can only perform the final separation into stars and QSOs by further observation using big telescopes.

Thus the APM system has filtered out only a very small number of objects of specific type from the enormous amount of data available on the plate. Such on-line filtering allows us to optimise our search procedures for certain types of object in an essentially unbiased manner and at economic cost.

3. Image Processing Algorithms

3.1 Data Base Handling Problems.

For reasons of scanning speed and numerous engineering considerations, the plate is scanned continuously in a raster scan and looks to the computer like a 5 billion byte tape drive reading continuously at 300,000 bytes/sec for 5 hours. This is equivalent to 30 6250 b.p.i tapes read at 50 i.p.s. Apart from a short flyback time after every 256 samples, the data flow cannot be stopped, (if the mechanics of the scanner are to be efficiently utilised), and the physically dynamic nature of the data base restricts the choice of feasible processing techniques. The most important restriction is that the system can never go back through the data set to correct or modify previously processed data, in the light of information from the current scan line. Because of the raster scan process, each image is perceived as a series of slices from several or many scan lines. The data processing algorithms must therefore be structured to work on a line-by-line basis with sufficient details about image position, shape and connectivity being saved to allow complete image reconstruction. Because random access memory is relatively costly, this encoding must be performed efficiently. Once the algorithms had been developed and tested in software, they were implemented in a hardwired processor capable of processing the data as fast as we could scan it. The algorithms break down into three types:

1) Signal conditioning algorithms which reduce the amount of numerical processing the system carries out, without degrading the image data.

2) Connectivity algorithms that determine which data belongs to which images.

3) Image parameter algorithms that work out the centre of gravity, integrated intensity and shape of the images.

3.2 Signal Conditioning Algorithms

All astronomical images are recorded superimposed on a background (or more strictly, a foreground) caused by the night sky and photographic noise. This background must be subtracted from the data set produced by the scanner, and in general only intensities greater than a certain threshold level above the background are considered to belong to images. Even if no astronomical images were present, noise fluctuations appear above the threshold, and the nearer to the background the threshold is set, the more often the noise exceeds it. Unfortunately we can only distinguish faint stars from galaxies if the intensity profiles of these objects are measured to the faintest possible levels. Faint galaxies have a stellar (point-like) core with a faint diffuse halo. This requirement to measure image data as near to the background as possible means that we must not only measure the background extremely accurately, but also cope with the very large number of spurious 'noise images' which can be greater than 10^8/plate. In our system the background is measured using a special processor and noise images are removed by a non-linear shape filter.

Background Processor. There is no unique definition of background in the presence of images. We derive maximum likelihood estimators of the background by forming histograms of the number of times a given intensity occurs within areas of 64 x 64 pixels. These histograms are obtained by a pre-scan all over the plate. The maximum likelihood estimator gives the most likely value of the mode of the histogram. Special purpose hardware derives these modal values and two dimensional smoothing is applied to these data points (10^6 mode estimates all over the plate). We also determine the width of the histogram background bell and this gives us a measure of how good an estimate each histogram can provide; (see Fig. 2). We set a threshold at a fixed intensity above the local background, for every point scanned on the plate.

Noise Remover. Because atmospheric and telescopic distortions smear the images of point sources of light, all earth based astronomical images are at least 1 arcsec in diameter, or about 40 contiguous pixels in area on a Schmidt plate. We use a geometric window filter which rejects 'images' of less than n-points in maximum linear extent ($0 \le n \le 6$). Images smaller than this are removed from the thresh-olded data, while images larger than this are completely unaltered (Fig.3). This noise filter is highly non-linear and its parallel nature makes implementations on commercial computers very slow. In our system we store 8 sequential lines (256 pixels each) of data (the current and previous 7 scan lines), together with a 1 bit binary image of the threshold data (1 if a point is above threshold, 0 otherwise), in a set of serial shift registers(Fig.4). The final 8 locations of each of the 8 shift registers, are fed into logic which detects a contiguous set of zeroes around small images within this 8 x 8 window. By clocking the data sequentially through the chain of registers, the window effectively sweeps over successive sample points on the plate. The logic removes small images as they are detected so that the data stream out of the last register is considerably simpler than the input stream. Note that the logic is so programmed that portions of images greater than the maximum size to be removed, are left totally unchanged by the process. This filter is crucial to the operation of the system since it reduces the number of spurious images that have to be processed, by a factor of 10 to 100.

3.3 Image Reconstruction

To obtain adequate slope information, the spacing between raster scan lines is much smaller than the size of even the smallest astronomical images. Every image is therefore scanned in a number of 'slices', ordered in the data stream in a complex manner. (See Fig. 5). Images are assigned numbers (or 'names') in the order in which they are first scanned and in general this is different from the order of termination. Collation of all the slices of a given image is a non-trivial process since noise can (and does) produce complex connectivity relations between segments on different scan lines. The collation algorithm must recognise 5 basic connectivity patterns (and combinations of these - see Fig. 6). These are 1) Start of new image (or image segment); 2) Simple continuation of images; 3) Branching of image into 2 segments; 4) Merging of 2 image segments to form 1 image; 5) Termination of image segment. Some or all of these can conspire to form 'rings', 'halos', 'hairs', etc.

The processor which carries out this task works in parallel with a second
processor that determines the parameters (centre of gravity, moment of inertia, etc.)
of every image slice on the current raster scan line. These parameters are temporarily stored in a 16K x 24 bit word random access memory (RAM). This memory can hold
1024 blocks of parameters of data and serves to buffer the raster scan data (which
is continuous) from the asynchronous operation of the rest of the data processing
system. In fuction the memory acts as a whole set of First-In, First-Out (FIFO)
memories, one for each image in the scan area.

The function of the <u>Collation Processor</u> is to store these blocks of data in
the RAM and to keep track of the locations of all the blocks belonging to each
image. The RAM contents are thus a highly dynamic data base reflecting the recent
past history of the plate scan. We should note that after a merge has occurred,
the name of the merging image section is in general changed so that we must be able
to rapidly update its connectivity list. Early designs used associative processing
techniques to carry out this latter function. We now use a linked list structure
implemented in hardware.

The Collation Processor has three linked lists: 1) <u>The Block List</u>: This is
strictly a set of sublists, one for each separate image currently being scanned.
Each sublist points to the set of memory block addresses containing parameter
information from slices belonging to that image. The nodes of each sublist also
carry pointers back to the image name which owns the sublist. 2) <u>The Garbage List:</u>
A list of unused memory block addresses. 3) <u>The Parent List:</u> A list of unused
image names. At the start of the scan the first list is empty and the other two are
full. The Garbage and Parent lists each have a hardware register that stores the
head of each list.

When a new image is detected, it is assigned a block address from the Garbage
list and an image 'parent' name from the Parent list. Both lists are updated
by changing the head register contents to the pointer to the previous head's
successor. Every image has a number of blocks of data stored in the 16K memory,
and a name and a linked list of all the associated blocks stored in the Collation
Processor. Each parent (image) name has associated with it, two pointers; one
that points to the block list head (LH) and the other to the block list tail (LT).
All new images (condition 1 of Fig. 6) are given different parent names. If a
merge occurs, (condition 4, Fig. 6) the two parents must be combined. This is done
by joining the two linked lists (easy, because we know both the head and tail
pointers of each), and sequencing through the block list of the merging parent,
changing the parent name at each node. Special hardware is used to ensure this is
carried out efficiently. When a termination is detected (condition 5, Fig. 6),
the system checks to see if this is a final termination (it does this by keeeping
a count of the numbers of new segments, merges, branches and partial terminations
in a register associated with each image name). If so, all the block addresses
associated with that image are passed to the fourth and final processor called the
Arithmetic Unit (AU), (functionally equivalent to many of the commercially available
"Array Processors"). The AU, which is optimised for very fast bulk I/O overlapped
with simultaneous floating and fixed point computations, takes all the appropriate
data from the 16K RAM and combines it, to form for the one image; 1) Image centre
of gravity; 2) 2nd moments about C. of G.; 3) Integrated intensity; 4) Areal profile;
5) Number of pixels. As each block is removed from the RAM into the AU, its block
address is returned to the Collation Processor Garbage List for re-use. Finally,
the image name is returned to the Parent List.

The structural complexity of the hardware is needed to achieve the necessary
speed to handle the continuous stream of data fed from the scanner. Much of the
hardware memory is dedicated to storing data <u>about data</u>. This means that all part

processed image data is more or less directly addressable at all stages of the
process whenever needed, making potentially lengthy searches unnecessary. This
is a very efficient process and is applicable to a much wider class of operations
where more conventional methods characterised by the process loop; 1) Read in all
data; 2) Search for items to be processed; 3) Perform process and return items to
store or output; 4) Go back to 2); are slowed considerably by the search phase 2).
We have used hardware to gain speed but the approach is equally valid in software.
At a system level, the expense of extra memory for indexing the data base is often
less than the extra cost of a faster processor to implement the search algorithm.

4. Classification and Collation

4.1 Classification

One of the principal functions of the APM machine is to search for rare
objects. Also, most astronomical image classification to date has mainly a subjective basis, and it is likely that subtle undetected differences exist between
objects currently all assigned to the same particular type. With these considerations in mind, we have chosen to use a classification technique which presumes
very little about the results of the sorting process and instead, simply attempts
to divide an unknown distribution of objects into a number of maximally separated
bins. In this way we hope to derive an objective reclassification of the known types
of astronomical object, and also to discover rarer types of object that need large,
whole-plate searches for their elucidation.

Because these programs are still experimental in nature, I will give only brief
details about their organisation. Images of the same type of astronomical object at
the widely varying distances encountered in astronomy, can vary greatly due to resolution and spectral effects. This means that a template that well describes objects of
type A when they are close to the observer, may be a very poor match if the same objects
are viewed at high redshift. Thus a whole range of templates (or a single template and
a transformation function) must be available for each type of object to be classified.
The word template is here used very loosely, and might describe a geometrical profile,
a vector of parameters or a general region of search space.

Since we know that all objects look fainter as they are moved farther from
the observer, we have chosen to impose a 1-dimensional ordering on all images, as
a simple function of their observed integrated intensity. This reduces the region
of search space wherein a good match might be expected.

We proceed by loading as many image parameter sets into memory as possible,
ordering them by intensity. We define a metric on the n-space of image parameters
which can be used to compute an absolute difference between any 2 parameter sets.
Each successive image is entered as follows. We locate its approximate match area
by the intensity ordering, and perform a local search to find the nearest fit
already in memory. We have previously computed all the local relative fits of images
in store and in particular we know the best-fit pair. If the new image better
matches a neighbour than the members of the previous known best-fit pair match each
other, then it is combined with that neighbour, the template modified accordingly,
and the local fits recomputed. Otherwise, the 2 previously noted best-fits are
combined and modified similarly, and the new slot created in the memory space, filled
by the new input object. This process is continued until a large number of image
templates have been entered.

At this stage, common objects have combined to form well defined templates
spaced throughout the intensity range, with the rarer objects scattered in between.
We now have to relate different templates in different intensity ranges to the same
types of image. To do this we assume that a piecewise-linear function can reliably
transform a template of an object at one intensity to a nearby intensity range. We

do not yet know the form of this function, but this can be discovered by trial and error, each local search for a nearest neighbour in n-space yielding one section of the piecewise-linear function. Once the identity of each template is known, the updating of the templates may cease, and the set be used to classify more objects.

4.2 Collation of Images

Because, for example, the only reliable photographic method of separating QSOs from stellar images is by using a set of photographs taken in different wavebands, and comparing the intensities of every object in each waveband, we need a fast and reliable way of collating the results of image analysis from a whole set of plates. Since 1 plate may yield $10^6 \rightarrow 10^7$ images (roughly half of which will be star-like), a linear search technique would completely fail to keep up with the data rate if the image parameters from each plate appeared in arbitrary order.

We have again attempted to eliminate the need for a lengthy search by structuring the data before entry into the data base. Our rule for collation is simply that images detected at the same sky-coordinates on each plate are almost certainly due to the same object, and it is these that are to be collated. Now due to the various conditions of observation, telescope zenith angle, plate holder alignment, mean telescope temperature, photographic processing distortion of the gelatine, and because we cannot guarantee to load a set of plates into the scanner in an identical alignment, we would not expect scanned images to always appear in the same order from the raster scan stream.

To avoid such problems, we do a small pre-scan of a few objects well separated on the plates, and compute a set of curvilinear coordinates that relate physical x-y positions on each plate to the same sky-locations. These equations are fed into the scanning machine control circuitry so that during the main scan the laser spot is in fact deflected in the same sky-frame pattern on each plate (to within a few pixels). In this way, we guarantee that the vast majority of images are detected in exactly the same order on each plate, so that a simple serial comparison of the data output streams serves to accurately collate each set of data. Odd images not conforming are saved for a rapid second pass.

5. Concluding Remarks

In this paper we have provided an overview of our own work up to the present. This deals with the problem of handling massive numbers of images where the number of computations per pixel is relatively small. A major problem that we have not here referred to is the problem of overlapping images, where the light from two or more objects gets mixed up on the photographic plate. Techniques that can successfully separate the contributions from each object are as yet poorly understood. They are mainly akin to two dimensional iterative model fitting and involve a far greater number of computations per pixel than the methods we have discussed previously. However, in general one would only wish to apply such processing to relatively small numbers of images, as perhaps may be found in a television frame (512 x 512 pixels) and therefore we propose to tackle this problem using a general purpose computer of power equivalent to the IBM 4341 class. Similar techniques to those we have already implemented in hardware for organizing data may well be useful here, though we believe that these problems are essentially computer bound.

Plate 1.   Section of a Schmidt Telescope Plate, showing typical astronomical images.

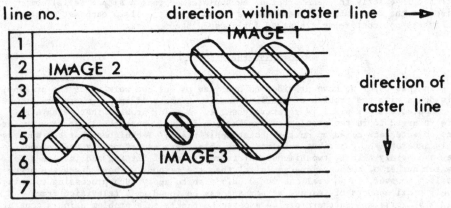

Fig. 5.   Illustrating how images are 'sliced' into sections by the raster scan process.

421

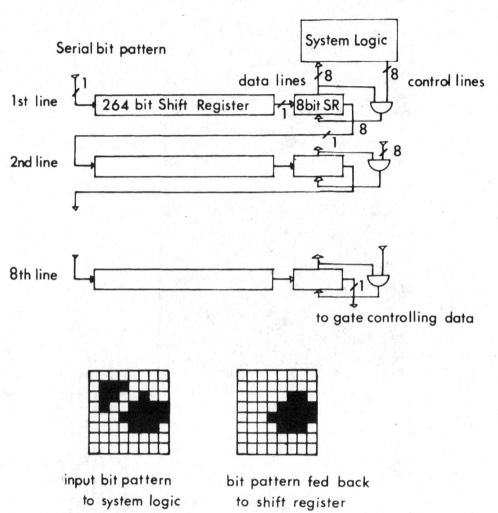

Fig. 4. Schematic layout of the non linear shape filter used for noise removal.

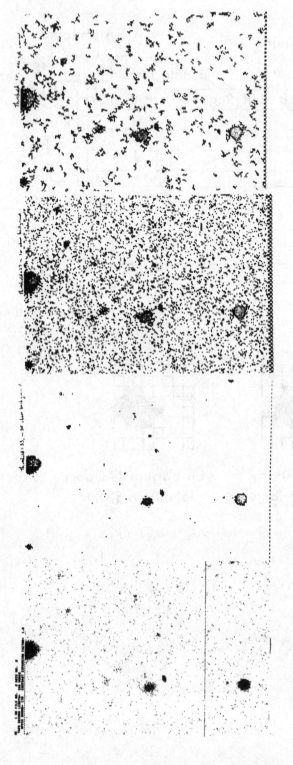

Fig. 3. Four views of the same area of scanned plate. The left hand view is a crude grey-scale representation of the samples. The second view is thresholded at 3 standard deviations (3σ) above background. Here we see little noise, but faint images are mostly lost. The third view is thresholded at 1σ and the faint images are now very apparent, but a lot of noise is also present, making processing very time consuming. The right hand view is also thresholded at 1σ but has been 'cleaned' by passing through our non-linear shape filter. Note that the outer structure of the faint images is unchanged.

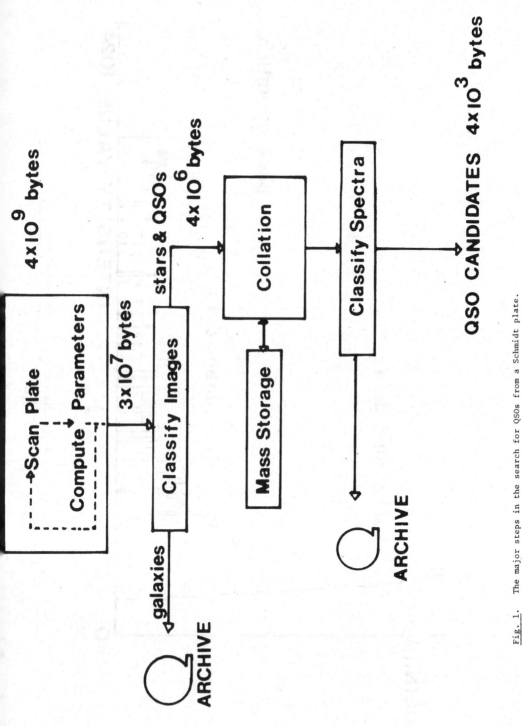

Fig. 1. The major steps in the search for QSOs from a Schmidt plate.

424

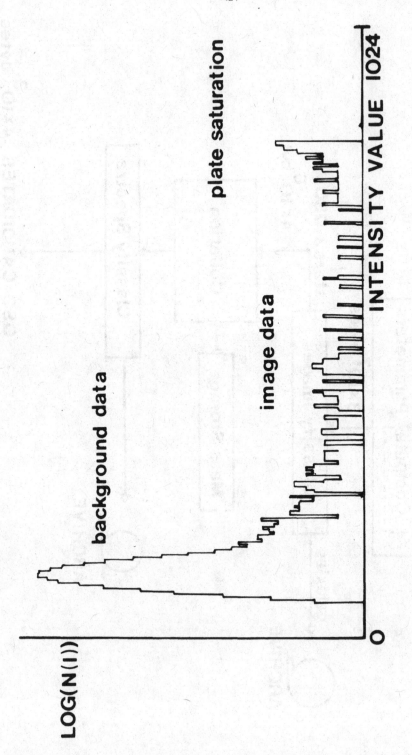

Fig. 2. A typical probability density distribution for the pixels on an astronomical plate. The major "gaussian" hump is due to sky background and
contains almost no information about images of interest.

425

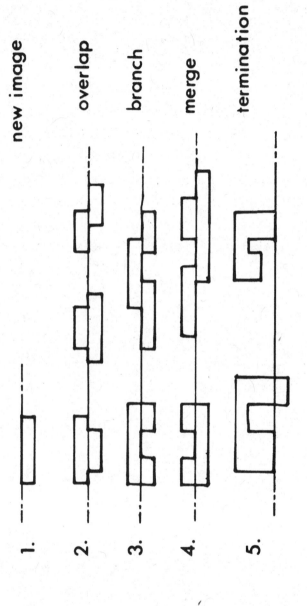

Fig. 6. The 5 basic types of image slice connectivity. 1) Start of image segment; 2) Simple continuation; 3) Branching into 2 segments; 4) Merging of 2 segments; 5) Termination of segments.

Title: Data Base Requirements in Meteorology

Session: Remote Sensing and Image Processing Applications

Author: J.P. Bourdette
         Manager of French Weather Service DP Center

Meteorological data can be defined as a combination of
weather parameters, time, place and data type. Usually,
these data are merged into sets on a geographical basis
rather than on a chronological basis. All observed data are
transformed into several types of processed data. To some
extent, as far as manual use is concerned, all final data
are to be produced in a graphical form. Observational data
are produced al over the world and processed data numerical
or graphical, are to be distributed worldwide. This leads
to the problem of meteorological data exchange. An
organization of meteorological data built on Data Base
principles could ensure an enhancement of the global system,
mainly by avoiding unnecessary redundancy of meteorological
data, facilitating the interfaces between users at all
levels of development, giving a more efficient access to
meteorological data in graphical form and improving global
performances of the system. Characteristics of such a Data
Base system are discussed as well as communication systems
needed to serve users and to feed data into the Data Base
system itself.

TITLE: DB REQUIREMENTS IN METEOROLOGY

All informations and opinions expressed in this
document are under the entire responsibility of
the author and do not involve organisms such as
WMO or national meteorological services.

1- METEOROLOGICAL DATA

1-1- Definition of meteorological data

Meteorological data are commonly understood as sets of
elementary meteorological data. Each element can be defined
as a combination of type of data, time, place, weather
parameters. Type can be measurement, forecasted value, or
interpolated value,... Time is time of measurement, time
range for an averaged value or time of predicted value.
Place is self evident and there is a wide set of weather
parameters such as pressure, temperature, wind and more
generally all physical parameters that can describe the
status or the evolution of the atmosphere.

These elementary data may be used for themselves particularly measured values, but usually users are interested in sets
of elementary data grouped on a chronological point of view
for a given place or on a geographical point of view for a
given time.

The chronological point of view is mainly retained in
climatology, and though it is an important aspect of meteorology, it will not be analysed further on in the limits of
this document. On the other hand the geographical approach
is the basic tool used for what we can call "synoptic"
meteorology.

1-2- Synoptic meteorology

Synoptic meteorology tries to answer two kinds of questions:

-    What is the weather now over some given area,

-    What will be the weather to-morrow or at the day J + N
     over a given area.

The second question is the usual short or medium range
weather forecasting based upon deterministic methods. The
answer to the first question is to some extent necessary to
the second one. Furthermore they both have the same characteristics as regard to data structure or graphical aspect,
so we will mainly analyse in the followings the meteorological problems linked to short-range weather forecasting.

429

1-3- The meteorological process

The techniques commonly used to produce weather forecasting
rely on a discrete representation of the atmosphere on a
regular grid. Starting of an initial status of the atmosphere, a discrete scheme of evolution derived from thermo-
dynamics laws is applied. This weather forecasting model is
at the end of what we call the meteorological process. This
process can be summarized as follows:

- Perform weather measurements at a given universal time
  wherever. a meteorological station is available.

- Collect all these observations.

- Make an interpolation of observations to have initial
  status of the atmosphere at the grid modes.

- Execute the numerical weather forecasting model.

The third step is necessary because the network of stations
of course does not coincide with the regular grid and a
regular grid is required for mathematical simplicity of the
model. This step, in fact answers the first question of
synoptic meteorology and is known as the meteorological
weather analysis. The complete process is performed twice a
day. The process described there is internally described and
its final output, a set of grid point values over a
geographical area is not generally in a suitable form for
external users of meteorology.

1-4- Users of meteorology

The main characteristic of the actual or potential users of
meteorology is their great diversity. Public organisms or
private societies are interested as well as individuals.
Some are concerned with temperature, other with snow, other
with wind, humidity, fog, ...

Though it seems to be difficult to draw a simple classification of requirements we can bring out two common remarks:

- It is quite impossible to communicate suitable meteorological information through words. This is mainly due to
  the diversity of users and the diversity of meteorological parameters involved.

-    As far as synoptic meteorology is concerned almost all
     users are interested in a geographical form of meteoro-
     logical data.

It appears clearly that a graphical presentation of meteorological information will be the most suitable form. However,
in some cases, meteorological information cannot be used in
a pictorial form, particularly if it has to be introduced in
another process, on a computer for instance. In such a case
a numerical presentation, such as grid point for instance is
more suitable.

   1-5- Graphical or numerical presentation

Mainly two kinds of meteorological images are produced by
meteorological services.

First (referred to as type A documents) are directly derived
from observational numerical data: around stations of
observation, meteorological parameters are plotted in a
numeric or symbolic form. That presentation is highly
suitable for all manual processing in centres that have no
automatic DP equipment to perform weather analysis and
weather forecastings. In such a case type A documents are
used as a basis for manual interpolation. In computerized
centres type A documents are also widely used because they
are the first synthetic information available before automatic analysis can begin.

The second ones (B documents) are derived from grid point
information and represent 2 dimensional fields of weather
parameters by iso-lines techniques: for instance one of the
most used is the height of a surface where the pressure is
constant ; temperatures at the same level of pressure can be
plotted on the same document.

One common objective of the two types is to present to
manual users meteorological informations under a form easier
to understand than its numerical equivalent. But it must be
noted that graphical and numerical form contain the same
amount of information, so that, generally speaking, synoptic
meteorological information can be considered as graphical
information. However these data are not processed in a
graphical way except for their final distribution.

   1-6- World wide aspects of meteorology

Obviously, meteorological phenomenas must be taken into
account on a world-wide basis and for instance a forecasting
model that would be restricted over a small area would fail
surely after a short range prediction because of the uncer-
tainties on the boundary conditions.

On another hand, though some users can be satisfied with local meteorological informations, many other such as sea or air transport need world wide informations.

The meteorological process described above requires that observational data be collected all over the world up to the processing place and that the output results be disseminated back also on a world wide basis. If we consider that usual weather forecastings do not excess a few days range (typically 2 to 4) ; the delays of transmission of data must be kept as short as possible. Of course that matter of delays is relevant of the telecommunication system used, but also of the organization of the data themselves.

2- THE WORLD WEATHER WATCH

In the first section we described the main features of meteorological data we will try to present a world wide organization of meteorological on data base principles. Such an approach is not implemented for the time being and it is useful for further discussion to give a short description of the present system.

The World Meteorological Organization (WMO) has settled up a system called World Weather Watch (WWW) in order to solve, among other problems, those raised in section 1. Three main sub' systems have been implemented

- The Global Observing System to coordinate observations as regards to time, parameters to be measured, network of observing systems,...

- The Global Telecommunication System, which is mainly a telecommunication network with specific procedures and an exchange program for all kind of meteorological informations (observational or processed data in numerical or graphical form).

- The Global Data Processing System, to coordinate processing of meteorological data.

This system has been running satisfactorily for several years and it is under permanent improvement, so that all the nations represented at the WMO can dispose of all the observational and processed data internationnally exchanged within reasonable delays. However some deficiencies remain:

- The telecommunication network is based on a ring structure and is very vulnerable to the outage of a mode or a
  link. Here and there some by-pass have been implemented
  but the procedures used cannot take then into account
  easily.

- A good global monitoring of the system in real time is
  very difficult to implement.

- The system is not flexible and is new techniques of
  transmission for instance are difficult to integrate.

- There is an important redundancy in handling the data.

Furthermore it does not seem possible to solve these problems by improving the existing system. One possible approach
is to think of the system in terms of data base.

3- INTERNATIONAL DATA-BASE FOR METEOROLOGY

3-1- Basic requirements

One of the major constraints to be considered is the fact
that all nations involved in WMO have not the same level of
equipments and that for a long time nations with important
computer system will coexist with nations with manual
procedures, so if we want to keep a good efficiency to the
system we must take into account a hierarchized structure.

We will try hereafter to give a list of basic requirements
of an international DB for meteorology.

In order to respect the basic WMO principles the "customers"
of such a DB will be the nations represented at WMO.

- Equality of access: each nation should have access to
  all the dates available in the DB on the same basis as
  each other.

- Nature of data: All the observational data should be
  available and also a predetermined set of processed
  data.

- Form of the data: the data should be accessed in numerical form and a graphical form. The former is the most
  adapted to further computer processing, the latter will
  be prefered wherever a manual use is expected.

- Avoid redundancy: in the present system there is no internationnally shared system to store and handle the data, so we come find as many points of storage as they are meteorological processing centres.

- Real-time performance: as far as only short range forecastings are available at the present time, it is essential not to loose a lot of time in waiting for the observational data before the beginning of forecasting model nor in distributing the processed data.

- Reliability: the DB system will be as most reliable as possible since in that concept an outage of that system will causes damage to the world community of meteorologists. Moreover the quality of the data, particularly the observational data, should be ensured at the level of the DB, to avoid duplication of efforts at national centres level, to check the data.

- Archiving of the data should be ensured at the level of the DB. It is essential that recent data (a few days namely) should be accessed in a real time mode by the national centres, especially for checkpoint facility in case of outage of a customer or of a link access to the DB. However archiving for long periods, it is useful for studies or special analysis, does not require real-time access.

- Diversity of formats: due to the diversity of national centres and potential users a great diversity of presentation of data, in a numerical as well as in a graphical mode, is required. This particular point will be developed hereafter.

As it is, such a DB system will present only weak requirements over some usual aspects of DB systems such as privacy, sophisticated language of interrogation.

The integration of meteorological data management into a DB system would improve its global efficiency reliability and flexibility. The implementation of processing programs would be made easier since they could access to data into a computer oriented format, rather than the manual oriented present format.

3-2- Implementation problems

Hereafter a non exhaustive review of expected implementation problems is reviewed.

3-2-1- Representation of graphical data

At the present time the meteorologists use graphical documents issued of a great variety of devices. A DB approach
must keep on the existing interfaces with the existing
devices in already equipped centres.

Two main kinds of formats are used:

- Vector mode format, particularly designed for incremen-
  tal plotters.

- Line mode format, designed for fac-simile transmission.
  The line mode can be in a plain fac-simile form or
  compacted because of the great amount of white areas on
  meteorological documents.

So graphical data can be internally represented under three
forms:

- numerical,

- vector-mode,

- line-mode.

For numerical representations a grid point format is suitable for B type documents and coded observational format for
A type document. Two approaches can be retained: either the
three modes are stored at the same time either one mode of
storage is selected and special transformation will be made
upon request for a particular device. First of all it must
be noted that only two transformations are possible:

    - numerical   vector-mode
    - vector-mode   line-mode

So at least the numerical mode is required. By all means it
was necessary since a lot of users are computerized. For
vector mode and line mode the solution to be retained is
probably an intermediate solution between the two extrems
because it results of a compromise between computation time
required for the transformation and space storage consumption. For informations that are likely to be distributed to
a wide lot of users, the best way is to store documents
under the three formats to avoid multiple transformations.
For informations asked occasionally and for a few users,
storage will be kept on a numerical mode. Line mode can be
made in a compacted way because the transformation involved
is easy to perform.

The average amount of storage needed for a typical document
is given below:

    - line mode (fac-simile)   1 to 4 millions bits

- line mode (compacted)   0.2 to 0.7 millions bits

- vector mode   60 000 bits

- numerical (grid point)   30 000 to 60 000 bits

3-2-2- Centralized or distributed DB

The DB system can be imagined as centralized in a selected
place with a star-shaped network. The main deficiency of
such a system is due to the high cost of the network
required to reach all the nations of the world. One can
reduce the cost of this network by implementing a
multi-point scheme but performances of the system will be
affected since all synoptic data are to be collected as soon
as possible after the synoptic hour, and on another hand
this will reduce the reliability of the network in case of
outage of a masterlink. It is probably more advisable to
design such a DB on a distributed basis. In such a case a
few centres would be implemented so as to minimize the
access network to the system. Local star-networks could be
used or public packet switching networks where they are
available. It is not necessary that all local DB store the
same data, because if some meteorological data are of a
world wide interest, many of them are only required on a
regional level. However it must be noted that, as a basic
principle, each user must have access to whatever informations exists in the DB.

The internal network of the DB must be implemented on high
rate telecommunications links to ensure low response time
between local DB and finally between the user and the DB.
Furthermore this network must be meshed enough to ensure a
good reliability on the global DB system.

This idea of a distributed DB will introduce more redundancy
in the storage of data since informations of world wide
interest will be stored in several local DB but this will
also add a supplementary level of reliability if some local
DB is not available or has lost its data. In such a case
only the regional set of data will be lost.

3-2-3- Amount of storage

It is difficult to imagine what changes in the meteorological practices will occur by implementing an integrated DB
system. In particular one can expect to have an increase in
the observational and processed data required by the users.
But that increase if it occurs will be limited by the
processing capability of the national centres and a pratical
approach taking into account the present amount of data is
likely to give a reasonable order of magnitude.

For each synoptic period a set of 200 documents can be retained that means 100 millions bits, according to figures of 3-2-1, for processed data. Observational data can be estimates at 50 millions bits.

Due to redundancy introduced by the idea of a distributed DB (a factor 2 can be estimated for 4 local DB for instance), 300 millions bits will be required for a synoptic period that is 1.8 billions bits for on line storage for 3 days for instance. Of course these figures do not take into account the overhead introduced by the DB system itself. If such figures are obviously too important for most of national centres, they show all the interest of an integrated DB shared on an international basis.

3-2-4- Integrated processing

Up to there we have only imagined an international DB system and all matters of processing were supposed to be under the responsibility of the national centres. As a matter of fact it seems to be reasonable to leave each country process their data as they are required to do by their own users. If we consider the particular problem of weather forecasting models, we can see the following situation:

- Some countries with big computer centres for meteorology perform daily a set of weather forecasting models. They perform first a world wide or at least an hemispherie model to have a general idea of the weather evolution but with poor details. Then a regional model with smaller grid mesh is performed using the results of the first as boundary conditions. In some cases a smaller model is used for fine detail.

- At the other end, some countries cannot support big computer centre and must use processed data of neighbour countries if available or try to make a manual analysis or forecast.

In the present WWW system some countries are committed to exchange interna. Finally their processed data, but due to deficiencies of the telecommunication system particularly in some regions of the world, these data cannot reach the countries where they are needed or at least arrive too late.

One could take full advantage of an integrated DB system by adding to its requirements for data processing.

Such an integrated system would be able to produce, with very good delay, weather analysis and weather forecasting on a world-wide basis and even on a regional basis in the case of a distributed data base. Each country could concentrate its efforts on producing very fine mash models for national utilization, or particular processing for their specific users.

437

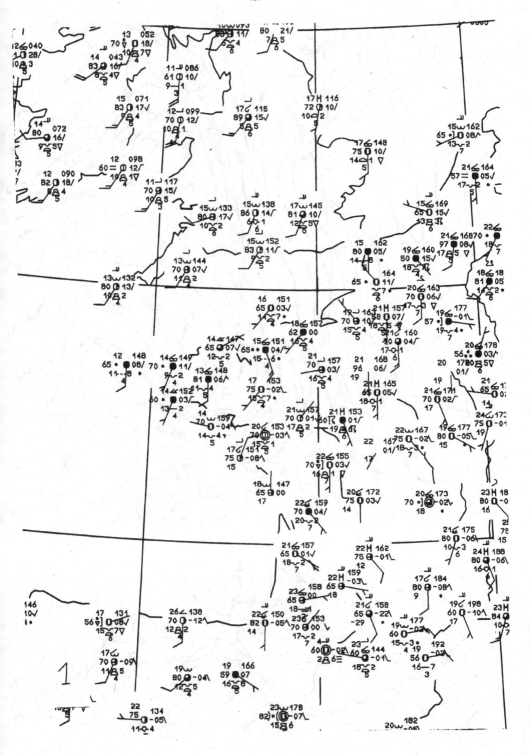

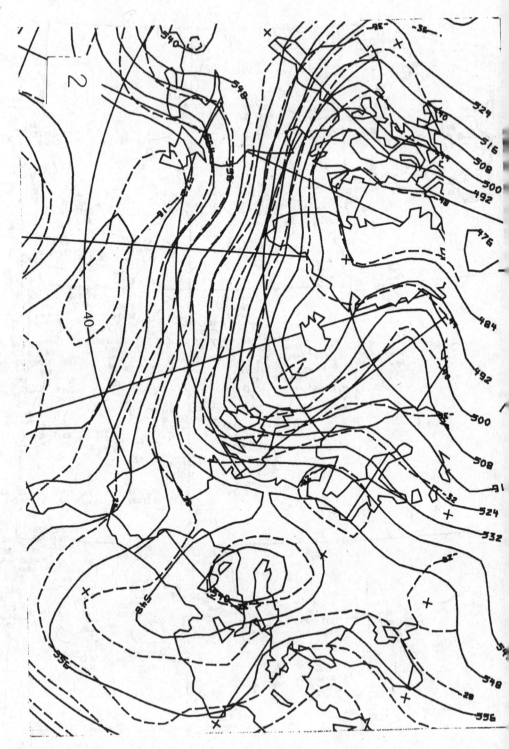

439

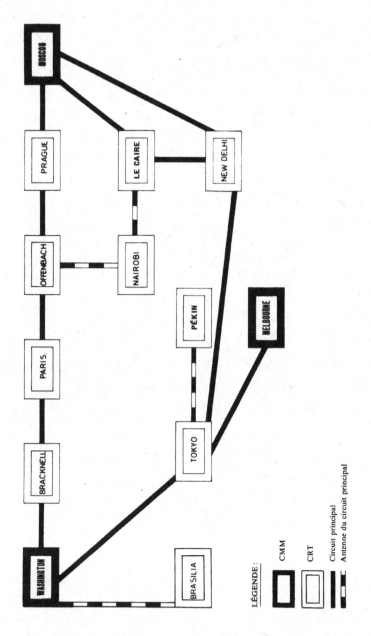

LÉGENDE :

CMM

CRT

Circuit principal

Antenne du circuit principal

3

DATA BASES AND STRUCTURES FOR A
GAMUT OF GRAPHIC APPLICATION
ABSTRACT

Dr. Irvin M. Miller

We will review a number of graphic applications that were developed
for the IBM 3277 Graphics Attachment Support to study the need and
structure of the data bases for these applications and the structure
of the data for creating the vector graphic displays. The first
will be in the area of Business Graphics, where we will show how
the nature of the application changes when we plot graphs from data
entered real time at the terminal to plotting it from a data base.
A few sample data base structures will be evaluated along with the
internal structure for the actual plotting of the graphs.

In the next application, we will look at the DIME files (mapping
data generated by the U.S. Census Bureau). We will discuss the
indices used during the interactive display of this metropolitan
street map file. Taking advantage of the interrelationship of the
data, we will generate various types of street maps.

Then we will discuss the data structure for the finite element methodology for plotting structural designs and the results of analysis.

Next we will consider the plotting of halftone images and the structures of these files so that we can electronically clip and manipulate
these images. The structures for these files can be very simple or
can be complex as the mapping files. We will also be discussing the
saving of the graphic orders and the data base operations required to
maintain the file.

Finally, we will discuss an application used for generating flow
charts, and pages of text that will allow us to merge the images
generated by the other applications allowing us to generate a composed
report. The data structure for this application has a generality
that allows us to integrate the results of the manipulations of the
previously described applications.

IBM Corporation
Dept. 83Y
1133 Westchester Avenue
White Plains, N. Y. 10604

Business Graphs

Before interactive graphics was readily available, graphs were often drawn by hand or at best, by low speed plotters. The speed in reviewing data was limited by how fast one could generate these graphs. Now with high speed, interactive, graphic display devices, one can generate graphs within seconds. This speed gives the user a healthy appetite for consuming the information on hundreds of graphs. To satisfy ones need for rapid access to data, it has become necessary to develop large data bases for graphical review.

The data for business graphics is often highly structured and usually temporally referenced. In Figure 1, we have used a stock market file as a sample generalized data file. The index file gives us a company identification, the beginning and ending year and month for the data, along with a pointer to the beginning of the data. This group of 28 bytes of index information allows us to select data for display or analysis purposes. The data itself is organized so that all data pertaining to a given year and month is stored in the same record. If we had many parameters defining the monthly operation of the data, we could extend the width of the data file. In files of this type, if data is not available for a given time period a special number such as .0001 could be used. For files with a large number of parameters, the names of the fields could be stored in a separate file.

For variable length data or for speed of retrieving individual data items, we could use an alternate approach for structuring the file (Figure 2). First we create an index defining categories of the data such as a company. This category contains a number of data items to which we have a pointer to the index for the first item. For the index, we have the data name, the data spacing (yearly, quarterly, etc.), the starting year, the starting time period and the number of data items, and a pointer to the data. We then enter the data in the data file. If the length of the data is greater than a single record, we may use several records to store the data. With an offset to the pointer, we could concatenate the data contiguously. This packing approach makes the deleting of data more cumbersome - if we want to delete data. In these files we have assumed the data to be numeric and of the same precision.

After the data has been retrieved from the disk we may wish to prepare it to be plotted. There are three files structures which are used (Figure 3). The first, the graph components, identifies the curve numbers for the various X-Y pairs of vectors. A curve can be plotted with one of the following types:

> Line
> Disconnected Line
> No Line
> Floating Box
> Shape

These types can be qualified by marketing and annotated values. These curves can then be qualified by shading, no shading, or stack bar linki parameters. This combination of types, qualifiers, and linking parameters can give us a rich combination of plotted curves.

Next we have a vector which gives us a curve number and the number of
points for that curve. The number of points summed is used as a pointer
into the third array - the data array.

Once we have created a graph (Figure 4) satisfactorily, we may want to
use this picture as part of a document. We would like to merge this
resulting graph with text and other pictorial data. In the merge
program we will discuss this concept.

Maps

As with data bases for business graphs, map data bases can also assume
different structures. For example, the U.S. Census Bureau has created
map data bases of various large cities in the U.S. These files consist
of a record for every street segment joining a pair of nodes. This
record is 300 bytes long and contains information such as:

> Street Name
> Left Zone
> Right Zone
> Low Left Street, Number
> High Left Street, Number
> Low Right Street, Number
> High Right Street, Number
> Longitude of First Point
> Latitude of First Point
> Longitude of Second Point
> Latitude of Second Point

In order to retrieve the data easily it is necessary to build indices
for this file (Figure 5). For example, we could create one for zones.
The first part of the index contains a zone number, number of records
that contain that zone and a pointer to the first set of record numbers
containing this zone. One then uses these record numbers to fetch the
data. Similarly, one can use street names instead of zone numbers.

Another way of storing data for boundary type maps is to have a dual
set of indices (Figure 6). The first set consists of areas and the
number of linked line sets that enclose this area. Fetching the link
numbers we then fetch the link indices. These indices point to node
numbers. We then look up the X-Y coordinates of the corresponding
node numbers. The storage of data in this form is primarily for maps
containing area related characteristics such as population, tax rates,
etc.

Whatever the form of the data, we eventually want to plot it as in
Figure 7. We can zoom in on areas, shade them, thicken the streets
or identify places of business or residence (Figure 8). The map data
can then be saved to be merged with other pictorial or textual information.

444

Finite Element Methodology

Finite element analysis is useful in stress-strain analysis, thermal
conductivity, and electrical conductivity of mechanical objects. The
method is basically a way of breaking an object into convenient and
meaningful areas so that one can solve the Poisson equation with a
numerical analysis approach. If we look closely at a finite element
grid we find that it looks like a map (Figure 9). Thus, the same
data structure used to define a map can be used in this area. We
can zoom in and out and identify areas in the same way that we could
with maps (Figure 10).

Images

A photograph is a three dimensional continuous domain of data. Besides
the two spatial dimensions, we have the third dimension of grey level.
If we define 0 as white and 255 as black, we have sufficient latitude
to define a high quality photograph, especially considering that a
newspaper has about eight gray levels. For existing display tubes 150
points per inch is sufficient to display a photograph, however for
zooming or printing purposes we might want better resolution. In our
work we have scanned photographs at 100 points per inch but stored
them at 50 points per inch discarding 75 percent of the data. Thus
an 10 x 8 inch photograph would be 500 by 400 points, giving a total
of 200,000 points. Since each point contains a grey level, we need
one byte to describe each data point.

A record length of 500 bytes is commensurate with the 10 x 8 photograph. Thus to store photographs we will use a data file whose record
length is 500 bytes. Since the records can be treated contiguously
a single scan could span several records or part of a record. All
stored photographs will start from the beginning of a record.

To find a record we have a separate index file in which each record
is 16 bytes long. The first 8 bytes is the name of the photograph,
the next set of two, is two bytes representing the width and length
of the photographs, and the last 4 bytes is the number of records
preceding the starting one for the given photograph. One could
concatenate the index records into longer records. See Figure 11 for
a pictorial description of the image files and Figure 12 for a picture.

Since we may wish to crop a picture, we can define the vertices of
the polygon enclosing that portion of the picture we want. We then
define the rectangle where we want to place the cropped picture. If
the aspect ratio is not conserved, the picture will be expanded to
fit the rectangle. If the new picture is smaller than the old, then
data is discarded. If it is larger, then we could interpolate or
duplicate adjacent areas. For simplicity, in this effort we will
duplicate adjacent areas for enlarged pictures. When we discuss
the merger of various data files, we will go into the details of the
data structure for cropping pictures.

Demo

To be able to display graphical orders quickly without having to
calculate the orders, it is convenient to store them on a file.
With certain lengthy calculations, it can take a lot of computer
power to generate the graphical orders. In order to show examples
of various applications, we took the generated orders and placed
them on a file. This file has a secondary application in that it
can be used for a checkpoint restart of a graphic application or it
can be used to store graphic patterns that one would like to retrieve
at a later time.

To achieve the filing of the data we made an entry in the device
write routine so that we could write the orders to a file as well
as the device. The device writes are concatenated as one record or
file. Each of the writes to the file has a begin graphic stream
(BGS) at the beginning and an end graphic stream (EGS) at the end.
Thus, when the file is retrieved, a routine searches for each of these
separators and writes them one at a time. All of the graphic data
order strings are concatenated in one large file.

In deleting a record, one moves the data following the record to be
deleted on top of the deleted file, and subtracts the length of that
file from all those following it.

The index record contains the name of each file, a pointer to the
beginning, and a length. The initial index record contains the number of files and the total length of all the files. If one adds files
or just deletes the last file, this scheme is very satisfactory. If
one did extensive deleting of files from other than the end, the
structure would be inefficient. See Figure 13 for an example.

Merge

One develops specialized applications to handle the human interface
and response in creating some picture such as a graph, map, halftone,
or drawing. Eventually this information must be brought together to
write a report or publication (Figure 14). In some cases a finite
element model may be used by a manufacturer for advertising purposes.
The program for merging this data will have a series of commands or
function keys which will allow one to retrieve and manipulate the
data. We could perform such operations as move, duplicate, scale,
and rotate. In Figure 15 we show the three arrays needed to describe
the graphical data. These arrays are concatenated on a file and
indexed by the structure shown below.

The type field in the descriptor can be defined as follows:

> 0 - Deleted Entity
> 1 - Point or Linked Lines
> 2 - Text
> 3 - Halftone
> 4 - Group
> 5 - Etc., special entities such as arcs
>   and arrows

The XY field gives the coordinates defining the object specified by
the type field. For example, an arc is defined by a center and the
end points of the arc, as opposed to a center, radius, beginning
and ending angles. This first definition allows a general transformation to be applied to scaling and moving. The number of X-Y pairs
for the line type tells us the node points for a linked line. In
the image definition it gives us the rectangle or polygon in which
the image is to be placed.

The qualifier field is used in three ways. First it gives us characteristics for lines such as type and thickness. For text it gives
us the size, font, and the text itself or a pointer to a text file.
For images it gives us a pointer to the picture file and the rectangle
defining the portion of the picture we wish to clip.

Summary

We thus have a total system consisting of the four data structures
described - Business Graphs, Maps, Images, and Merge and an undes-
cribed Text File. A pattern has begun to merge among these applications. The basic structure appears to consist of a data file, an
index into the file, and a qualifier or master index for the index
and data files. When we create several images this gives a fourth
structure which is the index to each image file. This structure implies
a generalized data base scheme. Since these schemes exist already,
we merely have to fit this structure into standard data base schemes
and have access to the data base operations which already exist.

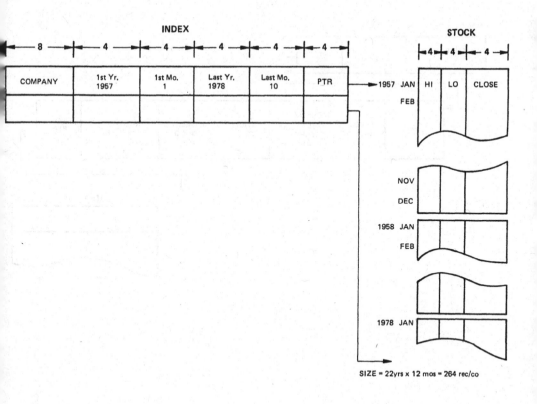

STOCK MARKET DATA STRUCTURE

FIGURE 1

448

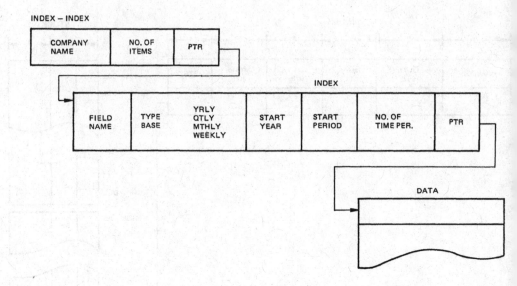

GENERAL BUSINESS DATA STRUCTURE

FIGURE 2

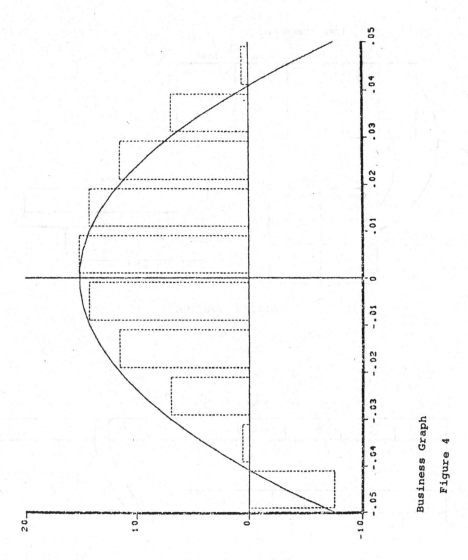

Business Graph

Figure 4

450

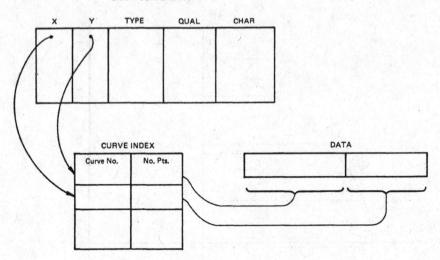

PLOTTING STRUCTURE

FIGURE 3

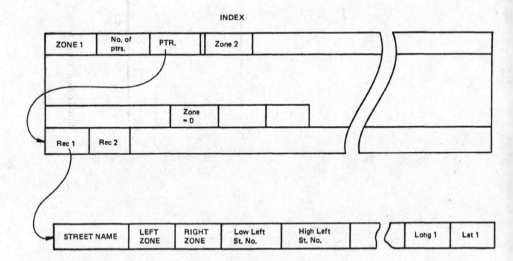

INDICES FOR DIME FILE

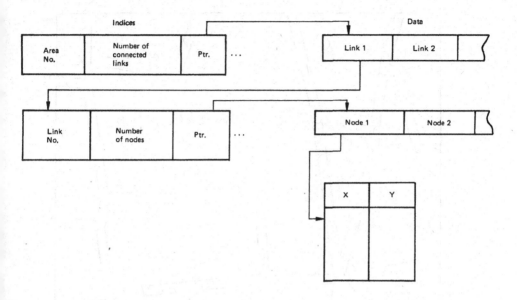

AREA MAPS

FIGURE 6

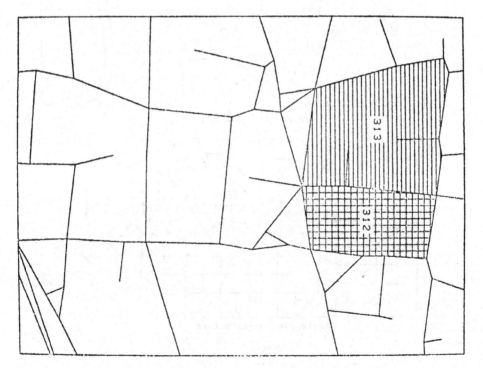

Map from Census Data

Figure 7

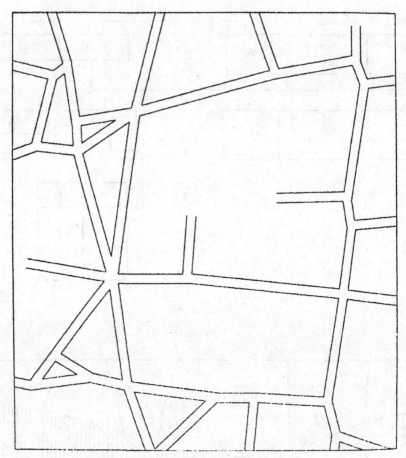

Zoom and Street Thickening

Figure 8

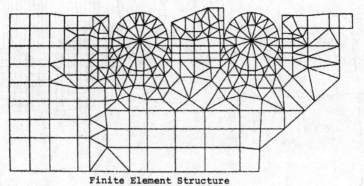

Finite Element Structure

Figure 9

453

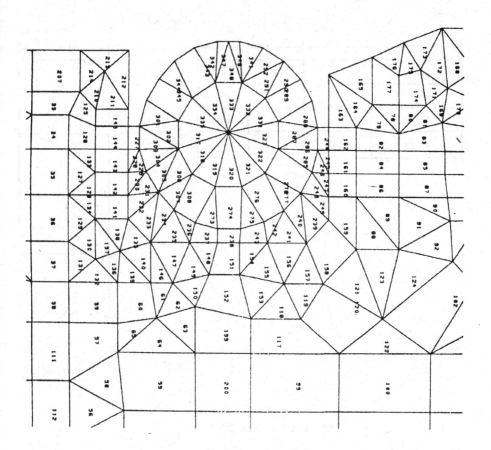

Magnification of Finite Element Structure

Figure 10

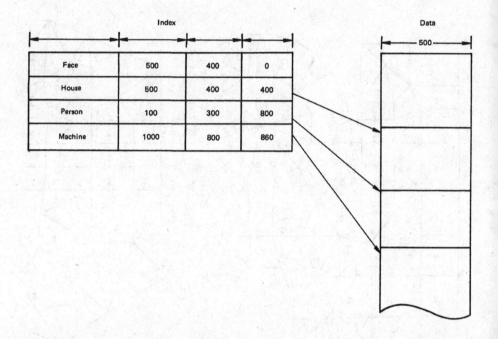

IMAGE DATA STRUCTURE

FIGURE 11

455

Halftone of a House

Figure 12

456

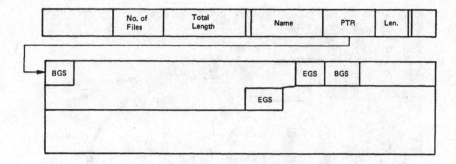

	No. of Files	Total Length		Name	PTR	Len.	

GRAPHICAL ORDER FILE

FIGURE 13

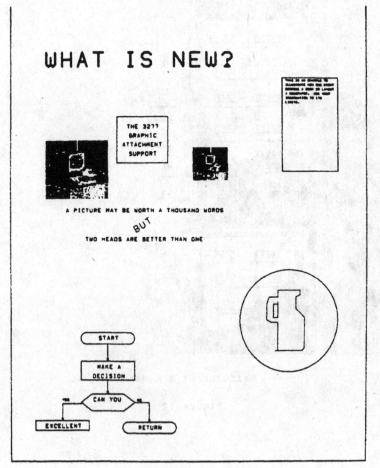

A Report

Figure 14

457

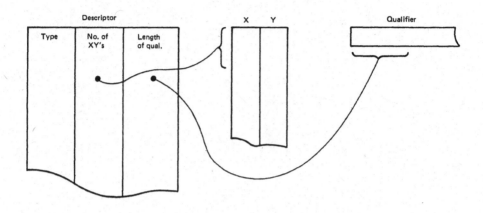

GENERALIZED MERGE

FIGURE 15

GSYSR : A RELATIONAL DATABASE INTERFACE FOR GRAPHICS

J.L. Becerril (*)
R. Casajuana (*)
R.A. Lorie (**)

ABSTRACT: PBS (a general purpose Picture Building System) is presently supported by a relational database (XRM), through an interface called GXRAM. A new interface (GSYSR) has been developed on top of System R, in order to allow PBS to use ordered relations, not directly supported by System R.

The GSYSR interface is used to create or delete ordered relations and to manipulate them when explicit reference to the ordering is made. Otherwise the usual data language interface of System R can be used on both ordered and unordered relations.

This paper describes the main features of the interface and discusses some essential features of a relational database system to be used for supporting a PBS-like system.

(*) IBM Scientific Center, Madrid, Spain.
(**) IBM Research Laboratory, San Jose, Ca, USA.

1. PREFACE

The GSYSR Relational Database Interface for Graphics is based on System R [Astrahan et al. (1976)]. It enables a PL/I programmer to define and manipulate ordered relations in System R. Although the main purpose of the project was to design an intermediate interface between the Picture Building System (PBS) [Weller and Williams (1976)] and System R, the design gives GSYSR as much independence as possible from the actual implementation of PBS, making it a valid interface for any other graphic system with a philosophy similar to PBS (From now on, in this paper "graphic system" will mean "PBS-like graphic system").

Sections 2 and 3 of this paper give a brief introduction to PBS together with some comments on a relational database previously used to support it. Section 4 describes the main features of System R.

The fifth and sixth sections describe the motivations, advantages and implementation of GSYSR, while the last section summarizes the requirements of any relational database system used to support a graphic system easily and efficiently. A list of the GSYSR routines is given in the appendix.

2. AN INTRODUCTION TO PBS

PBS was developped as an experimental general Picture Building System, consisting of the following major components:

- Relational Database System.
- Relational Editor (graphical editor and data structure editor).
- Display Handler.
- Graphical Interpreter.
- Correlation Handler.

In this paper we are interested only in the database component. A complete description of PBS can be found in [Weller and Williams (1976)].

A relational database system capable of supporting PBS consists of a set of relations, each of which must have the following features:

2.1. Graphical meaning.

With every domain is associated not only a data type (integer, character string,...) but also some semantic information called graphical meaning, which is specified by the user and chosen from a certain repertoire known to PBS. Some of the possible values and their corresponding semantic interpretations would be:

Value	Mnemonic	Meaning
4	SCALE	scale
12	COLOR	set color
14-16	X,Y,Z	position on corresponding axis
17	XYOPERATION	operation to be performed
22	DATA	nongraphical data

Thus graphical data is self-describing. It can be stored in the database with non-graphical data and still be identified and manipulated separately.

Let's consider the example in Fig. 1.

Catalog   ... Relation : TRIANGLES

Domain	Graphical meaning	Datatype
COL	12 = COLOR	50 = SMALL INTEGER
OP	17 = XYOPERATION	50 = SMALL INTEGER
X1	14 = X-COORDINATE	40 = FLOATING
Y1	15 = Y-COORDINATE	40 = FLOATING
X2	14 = X-COORDINATE	40 = FLOATING
Y2	15 = Y-COORDINATE	40 = FLOATING

Relation: TRIANGLES

COL	OP	X1	Y1	X2	Y2
3	10	0	1	1	-1
3	10	1	-1	-1	-1
3	11	-1	-1	0	1
4	10	0	1	1	-1
4	10	1	-1	1	1
4	11	1	1	0	1

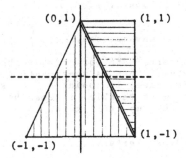

Fig.1. Example of picture and its relational representation.

The relation TRIANGLES contains six domains, whose names are COL, OP, X1, Y1, X2, Y2, and six tuples. The catalog of the database contains the graphical meaning of each domain in addition to the data types. The first domain, COL, has a graphical meaning of 12, which means COLOR, and the values in the tuples, 3 or 4, could be interpreted by PBS as "red" or "blue", for example. The second one, OP, is an XYOPERATION (graphical meaning = 17), which means that PBS will interpret the values as different actions to be performed, like: draw a line between two points (x1,y1) and (x2,y2), move the figure pointed to by the screen cursor to (x1,y1), draw a line from the point determined in the previous tuple to (x1,y1), etc. In the example, the value 10 is AREA, which means that the segment determined by the points (x1,y1), (x2,y2) is one of the boundaries of a solid figure. Succesive tuples with the value 10 in OP continue to define the rest of the sides, until a tuple is found with value 11 in OP, which is interpreted as CLOSEAREA. PBS would display the relation TRIANGLES as two solid triangles with a common side.

2.2. Ordered tuples.

An ordering must be supported on the tuples of the relations, since, as it is clear in the example, any change in the order of the tuples would produce a different figure.

2.3. Duplicate tuples.

Tuples in relations need not be unique, since there is an ordering to distinguish them. Points or lines can be common to several figures. In the example, if the colors of the two triangles were the same, the tuples corresponding to the common side would be the same; nevertheless, both would be necessary in order to have two triangles.

2.4. Tuple identifier.

A unique identifier must exist for every tuple in the database (TID). This is required by the correlation mechanism, that must identify every item on the screen with the tuple(s) representing it in the database.

2.5. Two way cursors.

Cursors, both forwards and backwards, must be supported along the ordering. When a user wants to delete a figure (a solid triangle, for instance) by pointing to, say, a point on the "last" side, the system must be able to scan backwards to identify the set of tuples which make up the figure.

2.6. Other features.

The database interface should allow the reference to relations and domains by mnemonic names, providing a comprehensive set of commands for all the usual database operations (insertion, updating, deletion, retrieval, ...).

3. OTHER DATABASE SUPPORTS FOR PBS

The first version of PBS was supported by a relational database called XRM [Lorie (1974)] through the GXRAM [Moorehead (1976)] interface. GXRAM supports named ordered relations, as well as a catalog including information about relations and their domains (data types, keys, graphical meaning, units, etc.). The commands can be classified in the following groups:

- Data control (open, close, save database, ...)
- Data definition (define relation, define domain, ...)

- Cursor management (open, position, move, ...)
- Binding and unbinding (variable, vector, structure)
- Data manipulation (update, retrieve, insert, delete)
- Catalog handling (attributes, names, ...)
- Auxiliary functions (type conversion, error message handling, ...)

This interface incorporates the concepts of _binding_ and _pointing_, making it possible to associate (bind) relation domains with program variables, and to point to one tuple using a cursor which can be moved along the relation. These steps are typically performed before reading, writing, updating or deleting tuples.

The experience gained by using PBS/GXRAM led to the specification of general requirements [Weller and Palermo (1979)] for a database system to support graphic systems such as PBS, independently of any particular data model (relational, hierarchical or network). It also became clear that one should try to integrate more closely the graphical and non graphical data. The ultimate goal should be to provide a comprehensive and coherent interface supporting the definition and manipulation of the same data from programs and from graphic and non graphic terminals.

As most of the functions expected from a general database system were supported by System R, it was decided to study the feasibility of using such a system to support PBS.

4. INTRODUCTION TO SYSTEM R

System R is an experimental relational database system developed at the IBM Research Lab. in San Jose, CA, in order to demonstrate that systems built around the relational model can be used in a real environment with performance at least comparable to today's existing systems.

As in any relational model, the user's view of the database is a set of relations, also called tables. There is no explicit structuring information between the tuples of the same relation or between tuples of different relations. Instead, the relationships between tuples are implicit in the values that the various fields take in the tables, and they can be exploited by the high-level relational data language called SQL. SQL can be used as a data language imbedded in a host language, such as PL/I, or as a stand alone interface for non-computer specialists.

The basic block of a query is the SELECT block. For example, referring to the relation TRIANGLES in Fig. 1, one can use in a program the following statement in order to retrieve the tuples that satisfy a given color condition (WHERE clause).

```
LET Cl BE SELECT OP,X1,Y1,X2,Y2
    INTO $VAR_OP, $VARX1, $VARY1, $VARX2, $VARY2
    FROM TRIANGLES
    WHERE COL = 4;
```

($ is used to distinguish host variables from SQL identifiers.)

The SELECT statement specifies globally a set (C1) of tuples and a classical OPEN, NEXT, CLOSE mechanism is used to retrieve one tuple at a time from the defined set. The INTO clause specifies a target list of host variables which will be used to store the returned tuple. The WHERE clause may also contain host variables instead of literal values, as in

WHERE COL = $VAR;

(If the language is used as a stand alone interface the INTO clause is omitted and program variables cannot be used).

At open time the value is taken from the host variable and the query is logically evaluated as if that value had appeared in the statement.

In such an example the statement is known at the time the program is written. This would not be true for ad-hoc queries, being constructed by program or entered from a user terminal. To support such ad-hoc queries an EXECUTE feature is provided in System R. For example, a program could contain the statement

PREPARE X AS S;

where X is a name and S is a character string variable which, at execution time, would contain an SQL statement. A following statement

EXECUTE X, p;

will automatically cause the execution of the statement with name X. (If S is a query then the OPEN statement also plays the role of EXECUTE.) The corresponding string S may contain one or several question marks denoting variables to be supplied at execution time. In such a case the pointer p is used to identify a structure containing the input parameters.

SELECT can also be used to retrieve set functions like SUM, AVG, MAX, etc. A WHERE clause can involve a set (for example in a test for membership) and such a set may be the result of another - imbedded - SELECT. The language also supports joins, groups, value ordering, and views. Single tuple and set updates, deletions and insertions are supported. For example, the color 4 can be changed into color 5 in a single statement:

UPDATE TRIANGLES
    SET COL = 5
    WHERE COL = 4;

In System R much emphasis is put on the dynamic environment. New tables can be created, old tables can be dropped, tables can be expanded by adding columns. Indexes that are used to speed up retrieval can also be defined dynamically. All these operations are part of normal processing and do not require offline utilities. These features are essential in an interactive graphics environment because the construction of a graphical picture requires the dynamic creation and editing of data structures as well as the input of data.

The architecture of the system exhibits two main components. The

lower-level component called RSS (Research Storage System), is
responsible for record management and for maintaining access paths to
the records. The most important access path is the index. It uses a
single tree structure to maintain a value ordering of the tuples in a
relation and to provide an associative entry given the key. RSS also
manages buffers and devices and is responsible for most of the
multi-user control features like locking and logging, and for
recovery. The higher-level component, called RDS (Relational Data
System), is responsible for mapping the SQL constructs onto the RSS
objects. When a data statement is submitted to the RDS, the statement
is parsed, names are resolved to RSS object identifiers, the best
access paths for accessing the requested data are determined by an
optimizer and a compact efficient machine language routine is
generated for executing such statement. Such an access routine is in
fact a series of calls to the RSS.

When data statements are part of a program the RDS process takes
place at compilation time. In the case of an ad-hoc, unanticipated
query the RDS process takes place at PREPARE time. Only input
parameters are bound at execution time. This approach is thus based
on the binding of the access mechanism to internal characteristics of
the data at the earliest possible stage. Such an early binding and
the generation of an actual access routine keep the overhead at
execution time to a minimum. Data independence is not sacrificed
because any change in the data representation or access paths
availability will force the automatic regeneration of the access
routine.

Among other functions supported by System R let us mention the
support of views, a complete authorization mechanism, the control of
concurrent access in write mode by several users and a recovery
mechanism for avoiding loss of data in case of machine malfunction.

5. INTERFACING PBS TO SYSTEM R

It is clear that System R presents, from the point of view of
supporting PBS, a series of advantages over XRM. Among them :

- Support of multiuser environment.
- Advanced authorization mechanism.
- Dynamic index definition.
- Relations can be expanded "horizontally" (Add domain).
- Symbolic reference to objects (Relations, domains, indexes,
  segments).
- Exhaustive set of catalogs.
- Variety of data types.

Also, System R is a complete database system while XRM is a lower
level access method.

But System R, like XRM, does not support directly the type of
functions available in GXRAM. Exactly as GXRAM was needed on top of
XRM, an interfacing package (GSYSR) is required between PBS and
System R. It is responsible for supporting ordered relations,
maintaining the PBS-related semantic information in the catalogs
(graphical meaning,...), and providing a set of commands similar to

GXRAM or the ones indicated in Weller and Palermo (1979) .

Furthermore, an important objective is that all relations be directly accessible via SQL sentences, although in the case of ordered relations it will be the user's decision to consider or to ignore the ordering.

In this way we can obtain an integrated database, where all relations will be accessible using the full power of SQL, and the ordered ones (which, in most cases, will contain data related to graphical applications), created through GSYSR, will be accessed by GSYSR and/or SQL from a user's program, and by PBS through GSYSR (See Fig. 2).

		PBS	USER'S PROGRAM
ORDERED RELATIONS	CREATION	GSYSR	GSYSR
	MANIPULATION	GSYSR	GSYSR/SOL
UNORDERED RELATIONS	CREATION	(*)	SQL
	MANIPULATION	(*)	SQL/(*)

(*) Expandible to GSYSR in a future release.

Fig. 2. Interface to relations.

6. GSYSR: DESIGN AND IMPLEMENTATION

In this section we show in some detail how the relational database requirements of PBS have been fulfilled in GSYSR. We follow the order used in section 2.

6.1. Graphical meaning.

System R maintains a catalog consisting of a set of relations containing exhaustive information about every item in the database (segments, relations, domains, users, ...). Two of them, SYSCATALOG and SYSCOLUMNS, are particularly suited to our purpose. SYSCATALOG has, among others, the following domains: TNAME (relation name), CREATOR (creator's ID), NCOLS (number of domains) and REMARKS, containing a tuple for every relation in the database. The interesting domains in SYSCOLUMNS are: CNAME (domain name), TNAME (relation name), CREATOR (creator's ID), COLNO (position of the domain in the relation) and REMARKS. The relation has a tuple for each domain in the database.

The contents of these relations can only be modified by the

system, except for the domain REMARKS, in which the user can store any information (up to 254 characters).

GSYSR uses REMARKS in SYSCATALOG to identify the relations created through the interface (the ordered ones). In SYSCOLUMNS, REMARKS is used by GSYSR to keep the graphical meaning, key, units, etc., that is, the complementary semantic data needed by PBS for every domain. In this way, all the related information is held in the same catalog, which, in turn, is efficiently handled by System R.

6.2. Ordered tuples.

System R does not support any ordering other than the one implied by the values of some columns in the tuples. Therefore, in order to keep track of the ordering needed to represent a picture, every relation has an extra domain (the first one), called LINE__ID, which contains a sequence identifier created by GSYSR for each tuple when it is inserted. This process is transparent to the user.

The problem of having to renumber the tuples periodically when insertions are performed is avoided by using a varying character string rather than a number to convey the sequencing, much like the Dewey classification scheme. Note however that byte strings rather than alphanumerics are used, providing a maximum of 255 bytes in the sequence field, where each byte can have 256 different values. This gives a practically infinite space.

6.3. Duplicate tuples.

Duplicate tuples are allowed in GSYSR, as they are in System R. However, since GSYSR introduces an extra domain (LINE__ID) with a different value in every tuple of a relation, duplicate GSYSR tuples are seen by System R as distinct ones.

A related question concerns the definition of keys (more properly called indexes) on one or more of the user defined domains, through GSYSR. GSYSR allows the following possibilities:

- No index.
- Non-unique index. Ascending or descending ordering based on the values of the affected domains. Duplicate values allowed.
- Unique index. Ascending or descending ordering based on the values of the affected domains. Duplicate values not allowed.

An index can be created or deleted at any time, the only restriction being that only one of them is permitted in each relation, when created through GSYSR. These indexes will only be used when the relation is accessed directly through SOL. Since the GSYSR scans always follow the order implied by LINE__ID, only the indexes automatically defined on LINE__ID will be used. (See 6.5. below).

6.4. Tuple identifier.

The graphic system makes heavy use of a unique tuple identifier. Although System R uses tuple identifiers internally, they are not accessible at the relational interface, and a special mechanism needs be implemented.

Whenever the graphic system asks for the identifier of a tuple (TID), the interface creates it, unless it already exists. To make the TID available, GSYSR maintains a relation with three domains, containing the relation name and the LINE__ID (this pair uniquely identifies the tuple in the database), and the TID generated by GSYSR.

6.5. Two way cursors.

Two SQL unique indexes, one ascending, the other descending, are automatically defined on the extra domain LINE__ID when GSYSR is used to create a relation of ordered tuples. This process, like all others related to LINE__ID, is transparent to the user.

These indexes permit two SQL cursors to be moved following the values of LINE__ID, one cursor following the ascending order, the other the descending one. Each pair of such SQL cursors supports a single GSYSR cursor, which can be moved forwards and backwards along the ordering.

6.6. Other GSYSR features.

The requirement of referencing objects (segments, relations, domains,...) by name through the interface is automatically fulfilled, since this is the way System R identifies them in SQL.

The interface provides a comprehensive set of commands (see Appendix). Since these commands will be used on ordered relations, the data manipulation operations are mainly cursor-position oriented, although very simple selections by value (queries) are also possible.

6.7. Some cursor implementation characteristics.

Let's consider in some detail the implementation of the cursor mechanism, describing the internal process which takes place when a cursor is opened, moved and closed.

As SQL cursors are defined in the application program, they cannot be dynamically created when required by GSYSR. However, a pool of cursors can be predefined in GSYSR and, when needed, GSYSR can locate a free cursor in the pool and allocate it to a specific relation scan.

What follows is a possible scenario of commands and the actions that would be taken internally in GSYSR.

a) Open a GSYSR scan cursor on a relation R1.

- Retrieve from the System R catalogs the information related to R1 (number of domains, domain names, types, graphical meanings,...).
- Store this information in a table called GRDES.
- Allocate and open an SQL cursor on R1, using the "ORDER BY" clause, so that it can be moved following the ascending values of

the domain LINE__ID.
- Insert a new line in a table called GSCANTB, storing information
  about the SQL cursor identification, direction of movement
  (up/down), the relation name, the LINE__ID of the tuple pointed to
  by the cursor at each moment, a pointer to the GRDES entry
  associated with R1, and a pointer to the area (in a table called
  GPVARS) reserved to store binding information for this cursor.
- Return to the user an identification of the GSYSR cursor.

b) Bind one or more domains to variables.

- GSYSR stores the addresses provided by the user in the GPVARS
  area.

c) Move the cursor forward.

- Move the SQL cursor (by issuing successive "fetch" calls).
- Update the LINE__ID entry in GSCANTB.

d) Move the cursor backward.

  Since the opened SQL cursor can only be moved along increasing
  values of LINE__ID, the following operations are required: (this
  function would be greatly assisted by a SQL cursor function for
  moving along decreasing values of LINE__ID; we shall return to
  this point in our conclusions)

- Close the existing SQL cursor.
- Allocate and open an SQL cursor, positioning it initially on the
  tuple identified by the corresponding entry in GSCANTB, and using
  the "ORDER BY" clause, so that it can be moved along descending
  values of LINE__ID.
- Update GSCANTB, reflecting the new direction of the GSYSR cursor.

e) Close the GSYSR cursor.

- Close the SQL cursor.
- Update GSCANTB, marking the cursor "closed".

  The pointers to GRDES and GPVARS are kept, and so is the
  information in GRDES.

f) Open a new GSYSR cursor on R1.

  The system is able to detect a "closed" entry in GSCANTB
  corresponding to R1, and only the following steps are necessary.

- Open the SQL cursor.
- Update GSCANTB (mark cursor "open").
- Return to the user the GSYSR cursor identification.

g) Open another cursor on R1.

  The steps will be the same as in a), except that it is not
  necessary to retrieve again the information from the catalogs, nor
  to duplicate the corresponding entry in GRDES.

  Whenever there is an entry in GSCANTB corresponding to a certain
relation, that relation is said to be "active". In general, this

situation implies a noticeable improvement in the efficiency of the "open-cursor" mechanism.

Both GRDES (domain information of active relations) and GPVARS (binding information) are stored in constant length tables, fixed at GSYSR generation time. Although unused space is freed up when a relation or a segment is deleted, these tables can become full. A garbage collection mechanism is activated when such a condition occurs.

7. CONCLUSIONS . REQUIREMENTS FOR A RELATIONAL DATABASE SYSTEM TO SUPPORT GRAPHIC SYSTEMS

One of the objectives of the project was to provide the implementers of PBS, and the end user, with a unified view of the data. On one hand System R offers a broad range of database management functions with a high level interface. On the other hand the development of a PBS like graphic system requires some specific features not directly supported by System R. An interfacing package (GSYSR) was therefore built to support these features on top of the System R interface.

The following comments and suggestions are based on our experience acquired during the development of GSYSR.

Firstly, as apparent already in GXRAM, the catalog plays an important role in providing an easy to use package. The System R catalog structures and functions revealed themselves to be complete, well organized and efficient. They provided the implementers with a straight forward means of implementing the symbolic interface and handling extra specific information (graphical meaning, units, etc.).

Secondly, the tuple ordering, so important for supporting graphics, was implemented without introducing any new concept alien to System R. The net result is that relations created by GSYSR can also be manipulated by the System R facilities, hence providing a highly integrated view of data. However, we would like to make some suggestions which would simplify our implementation of the ordering and certainly enhance the performance. In the current System R a cursor following, say, an index, cannot change direction nor can a tuple be fetched without moving the cursor, nor can a cursor be moved by more than one position at a time. All of these functions could be supported by a single index. In fact the lower level access method of System R (RSS) already supports the backward scan and RDS should be changed to make the feature available at the interface.

Another suggestion concerns the support of data partitioning. System R supports what is called segments, but at the RDS level all segments are shared and they are saved and restored together. In interactive sessions where a user can work for a long time on a clearly defined subset of the database it would be more efficient to be able to support private segments that could be saved and restored independently one from the others. Although such a feature was initially designed into RSS it is not supported at the RDS interface.

Finally we would like to consider two outstanding features of

System R and analyze how they affected the support of GSYSR. The first one is the high level of the data interface, the second the compilation approach used in System R. The high level data operations that can be specified in SQL (join, group, etc.) are not actually used in GSYSR. Up to this point experience has shown that only simple scans are needed for graphic support. However the availability of these functions does not penalize the simpler ones in any way and they are most useful for manipulating the data from SQL. The syntax is also high level, user friendly and english like. In a system like PBS in which commands are built by interaction with graphics, the string form of the command is generally not present. The GSYSR system therefore must build a string which will afterwards be parsed. This seems a waste of time but the alternative consists in using as an interface a structure which would contain all the parameters to be passed to the interface. For a simple scan the structure could be a linear sequence of parameters. But very quickly the structure would become more complicated: for example, a non trivial predicate on the scan calls for a tree structure (it could use a linear table only if restrictions are imposed, like requiring the predicate to be in a disjunctive or conjunctive normal form). To avoid future limitations or the progressive definition of a dual interface accepting the sometimes unnecessary parsing seemed to be the better strategy.

The compilation approach has been used in System R in order to enhance the performance of the system. If the data statement is known then the parsing, optimization and code generation can be done at compilation time and the performance at execution time is close to the performance of the access method. For ad-hoc statements the whole process takes place at execution time. However, the parsing and the optimization (trivial for simple statements) would be done anyway in an interpretive system and the overhead for code generation is in fact very small. As the retrieval of each tuple, for example, is done with better performance, the overhead for code generation is compensated by the gain in execution as soon as a few tuples are touched (which typically may be 10 or 20). Therefore, generally speaking, compilation is always advantageous. Of course, it is always interesting to decrease the number of compilations. This is why GSYSR keeps a table of cursors for which an access module already exists. In a sense this implements a buffer of access modules. It is hoped that there is a certain locality of reference which ensures that the same relation is accessed several times in a similar manner in a relatively short time so that recompilation can be avoided. A feature of System R which is very useful in this regard is the possible parametrization of data statements, even in a PREPARE/EXECUTE mode. Our project was instrumental in the decision to make such a feature available.

In conclusion, as can be expected in a project which maps specific requirements onto a general purpose system, some of the mapping techniques can be kept very simple, some may be less straightforward. The experience in developing GSYSR showed that no hard problem exists in using System R as database support for graphics. It is hoped that GSYSR may be used for several real graphics applications so that our design may be further evaluated.

472

ACKNOWLEDGEMENTS

The authors acknowledge the support of P. E. Mantey and R. Williams and the many fruitful discussions with D. L. Weller.

The work described in this paper has been done mostly during an assignment of J. L. Becerril and R. Casajuana to the San Jose Research Lab., and continued at the Madrid Scientific Center (Spain). Both wish to thank also W. F. King, D. D. Chamberlin, M. W. Blasgen and other members of the Database Systems department for their cooperation, as well as J. Rodriguez Rosell for many helpful conversations.

APPENDIX: GSYSR ROUTINES

A list of all the GSYSR routines follows, together with a brief mnemonic description.

- DATA CONTROL

GACQSGT   Acquire segment
GDELSGT   Delete segment
GRESTDB   Restore database
GSAVEDB   Save database

- DATA DEFINITION

GADDDOM   Add domain to an existing relation
GCORELD   Copy domains description
GDEFDOM   Define domains in a relation
GDEFKEY   Define index (key)
GDEFREL   Define relation (to be followed by several GDEFDOM)
GDELREL   Delete relation
GDOMKEY   Include domain in index definition
GDROKEY   Drop index

- CURSOR MANAGEMENT

GCLOALL   Close all scans in the database
GCLOREL   Close all scans in a relation
GCLOSCN   Close scan
GCOPSCN   Copy scan (open scan equal to an existing one)
GMOVCUR   Move cursor (up or down, n places)
GOPESCN   Open scan
GPOSCUR   Position cursor (at the Nth tuple)
GPOSKEY   Position cursor (by key)
GPOSTID   Position cursor (by tuple identifier)

- BINDING

GBNDNAM   Bind a variable to a domain identified by name
GBNDNUM   Bind a variable to a domain identified by number
GBNDSTR   Bind a structure to a relation
GBNDVEC   Bind a vector to a relation
GUNBNAM   Unbind a variable (by domain name)
GUNBNUM   Unbind a variable (by domain number)
GUNBREL   Unbind all domains of a relation

- DATA MANIPULATION

GCLOQRY   Close the current query
GDELCUR   Delete tuple pointed by a cursor
GGETCUR   Fetch tuple (by cursor position)
GGETNEX   Fetch next tuple
GINSCUR   Insert tuple (by cursor position)
GINSEND   Insert tuple (at the end of a relation)
GNEXQRY   Fetch the next tuple of the current query
GOPEQRY   Open a query on a relation
GUPDCUR   Update tuple (by cursor position)

- SYSTEM CATALOG INFORMATION

```
GCARDB    Find out the number of segments in the database
GCARREL   Find out the relation cardinality.(By name)
GCARSCN   Find out the relation cardinality.(By scan)
GCARSGT   Find out the number of relations in a segment
GCHKREL   Find out if a relation exists in the database
GDEGREL   Find out the relation degree
GDESDB    Find out the segment names in the database
GDESDOM   Find out the description of a domain
GDESREL   Find out the description of a relation
GDESSGT   Find out the relation names in a segment
```

- AUXILIARY COMMANDS

```
GCONGET   Convert internal PL/I type to text string
GCONINS   Convert text string to internal PL/I type
GCOPREL   Copy relation
GGENTID   Generate a tuple identifier
GNAMDOM   Return the domain name for a domain number
GNUMDOM   Return the domain number for a domain name
GRELTID   Convert tuple identifier into RELNAME
GSETED    Set or change the control of error messages
GSHOED    Display the message control variable
GSTART    Initialize the system
```

REFERENCES

Astrahan M.M., et al. (1976). System R. Relational Approach to Database Management. ACM Trans. on Database Systems, Vol 1, No 2. June 1976, pp 97-137.

Weller D.L., and Williams R. (1976). Graphic and Relational Database Support for Problem Solving, Proc. ACM SIGGRAPH Conference, Computer Graphics, Vol 10, No 2, July 1976, pp 183-189.

Lorie R.A. (1974). XRM-An extended (n-ary) relational memory. IBM Cambridge Scientific Center Report G320-2096. January 1974.

Moorehead W.G. (1976). GXRAM, Relational Database Interface for Graphics. IBM Research Report RJ1935. February 1976.

Weller D.W., and Palermo F.P. (1979). Database Requirements for Graphics. Proc. IEEE Compcon 79, San Francisco, February 1979, pp 231-234.

The Integrated Data Analysis and Management System for Pictorial Applications

H. Schmutz[x])

Abstract

IDAMS is a prototype of a general purpose system for interactive data manipulation. The paper analyzes the requirements for an interactive pictorial data base system and shows that the known requirements for pictorial application can best be met by a general purpose system such as IDAMS. Major features of IDAMS are:

o the powerful high level data manipulation language.

o the datatypes of APL plus extensions for interactive data analysis.

o the convenient extensibility of the system by functions written in FORTRAN, PL/I or ASSEMBLY language.

o the interactive extensibility via APL, both within and in addition to the data manipulation language.

o the convenient access to special purpose hardware including image processing devices.

The ease, with which the general purpose system can be adapted to a pictorial application, is contrasted with the problems and risks introduced by the development of a special purpose data base system for pictorial applications.

----

[x]) IBM Deutschland GmbH
     Heidelberg Scientific Center
     Tiergartenstrasse 15
     D - 6900 Heidelberg

1. Introduction

Our purpose is to analyze the usefulness of integrated data analysis and management for pictorial applications. The basic idea behind the Integrated Data Analysis and Management System (IDAMS) is the integration of tools which are needed by the interactive problem solver into one system with a consistent and userfriendly interface. IDAMS is "general purpose" in the sense that it was not designed with specific application areas in mind. A first prototype of IDAMS is operational and in use at several locations by partners who did not participate during the development and who are primarily interested in their application /13/.

The term "pictorial applications" is a generic term for all applications which use data connected to coordinates. Such data may be derived from geographic measurements like remote sensing or from computer aided design work. Several of these application areas have been addressed by preceding papers in this conference. We make the two following basic assumptions about the application areas:

1. The application requires problem solving , i.e. is based on creative interaction between human intelligence and the computer as a flexible tool with a priori unstructured use. Clearly, there are also well structured applications with, for example, geographically coordinated data such as the collection of climatological data into an archive. DB/DC systems like IMS /14/ are very likely the right tools for this kind of applications, if high volumes of data and high transaction rates have to be supported. Transaction oriented, parametric use of a pictorial data base is not subject of this paper. However, in general such data, if they exist, are of value to the researcher and should be accessible within the problem solving environment.

2. A number of tools have been specifically developed for pictorial applications such as (a) hardware like image display devices /4/ and special purpose computing equipment and (b) an open ended collection of algorithms /1-3/ like subroutines for finding an edge or for classifying patterns within an image. These hardware and software tools are considered pertinent to the application.

We are convinced that a special purpose data base system is not justified. No requirements for pictorial applications are known which are in conflict with the requirements for general purpose systems.

In order to show this we will first summarize the

requirements for an interactive data base system for pictorial applications. It will be interesting to classify the requirements as application independent or as specific for pictorial applications. Subsequently we will present a brief functional overwiew of IDAMS. In the conclusions we will come back to the requirements and discuss the use of IDAMS for the considered class of applications.

2. Requirements for an Interactive Pictorial Data Base System

In analysis of the needs for planning in the local or regional government, Smedley /15/ argues that any such system must include facilities for data storage, manipulation and analysis, for statistical analysis, for modelling and evaluation techniques to aid decision making and for graphics to present results. From experience, Smedley draws the conclusion that "a need for better descriptive facilities" exists. We can classify these requirements into the following categories:

- Data Storage
- Computational Facilities
- Special Hardware
- Interactive User Guidance.

We will discuss some of the important requirements for each category in more detail.

We expect the <u>data storage</u> requirements to be taken care of by the "data base system". The term "data base" is frequently used generically for different kinds of collections of data.

Firstly, there is the "operational data base" which is typically centrally controlled by a group of data-processing-experts. A careful design makes sure that the data remain consistent and that the data are only modified by authorized users via predefined and centrally developed application programs. As already mentioned, the operational database is typically supported by a DB/DC system, and does not, in general, satisfy the needs of the problem solver. However, as a large collection of data, the operational data base may be extremely valuable to the problem solver, which should at least have read access to a selected part of it.

Secondly, there is an archive as a collection of data on tape, in a mass storage system or in some other form. The archive itself should not be considered as part of the interactive data base. However, access to the archive is necessary for the problem solver for both, saving and restoring data collections.

Access to the operational data base or to the archive may remain simple in nature. It is sufficient if only predefined access paths are supported, i.e. selection according to predifined keys. The third data base needed by the problem solver is its own, personalized data base containing information under his own control. This data base, henceforth referred to as the Interactive Data Base (IDB), forms an integral part of the problem solving system and many of our data storage requirements relate to it.

A basic requirement for the IDB is a framework in which a user can describe and reference data. A data description facitlity enables the user to structure the data and to assign names and datatypes to the data items. A user references data by symbolic names and, where appropriate, by search values or search conditions on data items related to the information to be identified. For example, the IDAMS user views his IDB as a collection of named tables. Each table consists of a fixed set of named columns and a time-varying set of rows. Data attributes are tied to columns. The intersections of a row and a column is called a field. A field contains a data item of the type defined for the, columns.

The IDAMS framework for symbolic references to data should be considered as an example, although the tabular view of data has several advantages in itself. The requirement is the support of a tabular or some equivalent framework for referencing data.

A natural requirement for a pictorial data base system is the support of application oriented data types such as points, sets of points, lines, line sequences, and areas. Corresponding operators or built-in-functions should permit to specify search conditions such as "all towns (=points) located in the alps (=area)". Similarly, the data types necessary for statistical analysis should be supported.

It should also be possible to attach units of measurement to such quantities, so that a user may easily obtain, for example, the size of an area in square miles or square meters without having to bother about conversion factors.

A further important requirement is connected with the size of data. Datatypes like point sets, line sequences or areas are represented as aggregations of scalar values. Though it is unrealistic to keep large high resolution images defined by millions of scalar values as a single field value - as described earlier, such data should be stored in a kind of archive - the data resulting from image analysis may still be very voluminous. As an example, IDAMS supports aggregations with up to 32000 scalar values between 0 and 255 in one field, or up to 256000 bits.

The problem solving user of the IDB should feel free to modify in a trial and error mode the IDB without commitment to the modifications. After he has carefully verified the modifications, he should be able to make the modifications permanent. Otherwise, he should be able to recover to a previous state of the data base and retry. Conceptually, changes to the data should be made on a temporary copy and become permanent if the modified copy is saved. This is an extension of the active workspace concept with SAVE and LOAD commands as it is implemented in APL systems, now applied to large collections of data. The SAVE/LOAD mechanism should actually not involve copying of the data and duplication of the storage requirements. More efficient techniques are known and should be applied /8/.

The SAVE/LOAD facility together with a DUMP/RESTORE faciltiy form the basic set of integrity functions required for an interactive database serving problem solving users.

Performance plays a key role in the requirements for a pictorial data base system. The above described functions are only valuable if they can be performed within acceptable time. The basic functions of the IDB data management may be similar to those offered in a DB/DC system for operational data, however, complementary performance requirements apply. The operational data base is designed and tuned such that transactions require only a small number of accesses to secondary storage, frequently only between one and five. This is possible because access paths are known in advance. In contrast, for interactive data bases the access paths are unknown in advance. The system must build indices dynamically, sort extracted information and apply optimization techniques for fast answers to ad hoc queries. These techniques are of reduced importance in an operational data base system and therefore frequently inadequately supported in these systems.

The primary goal of <u>computational</u> facilities is the efficient combination of algorithms with the data. This is achieved via a Data Manipulation Language (DML). The DML should in level be higher than normal algorithmic programming languages and should be easy to use, expecially for the beginning computer user.

The DML must support the primitives for the expression of search conditions and data transformations. Examples are the usual set of arithmetic and string operators, the comparison operators and the boolean operators. Of course, the set of primitives must include those necessary to handle application specific data types and the data types necessary for analysis. As a more general requirement, the DML should use as much as possible the expression sublanguage of an existing programming language to avoid further proliferation of languages.

The expression sublanguage of the DML should be extendable. The user should be able to define interactively operators implemented as a function or procedure in a high level language. These operators should be employed within expressions the same way as the previously described primitives. It is important that the definition is possible in interactive mode and without termination of the DML session. This extensibility is crucial for the advanced user, because no set of primitives provided in a very high level language can be expected to cover all important situations.

Similarly, it must be possible to extend the DML interactively such that major existing application programs can be combined with the data. Such programs are typically, but not exclusively, available in FORTRAN or some other high level language and exist independent of a data base system. Examples are pattern recognition algorithms applied to images /1,2/ or models to predict the economical development in a geographical area /3/.

The same extension facility is necessary to incorporate algorithms for data analysis into the DML, e.g. a subroutine package for statistical analysis, or, software like the Graphic Analysis Package /16/ for making data visible.

The system must support these algorithms within the DML corresponding to their purpose: as regular, single-valued functions, as sources of data or as sinks for data. A typical source in an image processing application reads image after image from an archive. Each image is analyzed interactively with application specific algorithms. The result of image analysis are interrelated area, line, point and other data which may be further transformed and then stored in the interactive data base.

Any convenient, very high level DML will be limited in function. With other words: if an algorithm is complex, it is often easier expressed in a procedural language than in a non-procedural language. It is therefore desirable that the DML conveniently supports the extraction of data in a way that the data can be further processed in a general purpose, high level language such as APL.

The support of external devices such as image processing devices or device couplers is essential for pictorial applications. In addition a graphics device is necessary. The latter may be different or identical with an image display device /4/. New devices are likely to be in development in this area, and many varieties exist already. A data base system for the problem solver must offer the hooks which permit the integrated use of these devices in the DML for data entry, data editing and for making data visible.

The extendability of the DML described above for functions and operators provides exactly these hooks.

In summary we can say that the DML in a pictorial data base system is the focal point in which raw data, data from operational data bases, data from archives, data from external devices, data contained in variables, and, of course, data from the interactive data base can be processed by DML operators, user defined operators, FORTRAN subroutines, and results submitted to the archive, to external devices, to variables and, again, to the interactive data base.

A primary requirement for a pictorial data base system is the possiblity that an application specialist can start using the system without much preceding training. Though the above discussion was very general and restricted to the most important requirements, it is obvious that a useful system must offer a complex set of functions. User guidance must be provided via menus and "fill in the form" techniques such as Query By Example /5/ to guide the user through the system. This is almost self-evident, however, it is not sufficient. As discussed above, the pictorial DB system is during its use extended by data, functions or algorithms and devices. A user guidance facility is required, which permits the user, who extends the system, i.e. defines and adds a new data collection, a new algorithm or a new device, to extend the network of menus such that guidance to the newly introduced objects is subsequently possible. The user guidance subsystem must offer to associate explanatory text with user objects and to express relationships between objects, subjects areas and system functions in combination with information which helps to use the objects correctly within the system. Again it is self-evident that definition, extension, update and general maintenance of the guidance network is supported in an interactive, userfriendly way driven by menus and applying, where appropriate, "fill in the form" techniques to guarantee a consistent documentation and guidance within the application.

Table I summarizes the requirements discussed in this section. It was not our objective to present an exhaustive and detailed list. We have addressed only the major requirements, however, to an extent, which permits us to put the application specific aspects into perspective. After a brief discussion of IDAMS in the next section we will refer back to the summary to support our conclusion that a pictorial data base system is best based on a general purpose system such as IDAMS.

```
| Data Storage and Management                                      |
|       Self Describing Data                                       |
|       Data Reference by Name and Contents                        |
|       Geometric Datatypes                                        |
|       Datatypes for Analysis                                     |
|       Large Dataitems                                            |
|       Temporary Modification                                     |
|       Performance for Ad Hoc Query                               |
|                                                                  |
| Data Manipulation                                                |
|       Very High Level - Nonprocedural                            |
|       Access to Data Storage                                     |
|       Set of Basic Operators                                     |
|       Operators for Geometric Datatypes                          |
|       User-defined Operators                                     |
|       Open-ended for:                                            |
|             Picture Processing Algorithms                        |
|             Statistical Analysis Routines                        |
|             Graphic Display Functions                            |
|             Access to "Pictorial Hardware"                       |
|       Interactive High Level Language Environment (APL)          |
|                                                                  |
| Interactive User Guidance                                        |
|       System                                                     |
|       User-Objects                                               |
```

Table I Summary of Requirements for a Pictorial Data Base
Management System

3. The Integrated Data Analysis and Management System

IDAMS is described in /6,7/. The subsequent description is
essentially an extract of /6/.

Figure 1 shows IDAMS embedded into a system environment. The
upper part contains IDAMS with the interactive component and
a central interface permitting the convenient extension of
IDAMS to access program libraries, archives and the
operational data controlled by a DB/DC system.

The user interface offered by IDAMS consists conceptually of
five main components: the Interactive User Guidance
component (IUG), the closely related Data and Function
Definition component (DFD), the High Level Query Interface
(HLQ), the Graphical Display Formatting Component (GDF) and
the Function Execution component (FEX).

IDAMS is built around an extension of VSAPL under VM/CMS
which contains the convenient and efficient interface to the
environment. Figure 2 illustrates the implementation.
Except for the central interface, which is written in

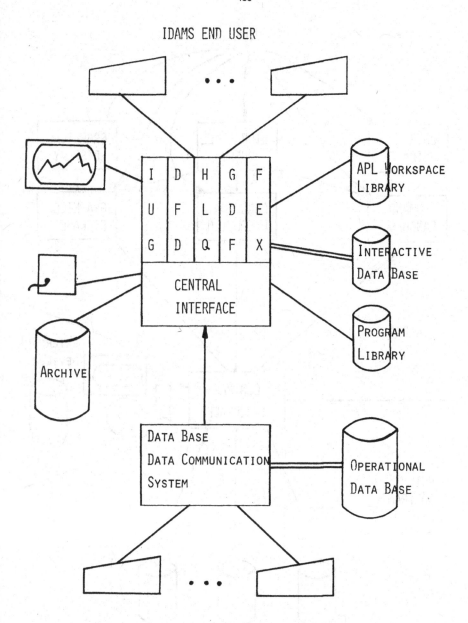

IDAMS END USER

PARAMETRIC END USER

FIGURE 1: IDAMS WITH ENVIRONMENT

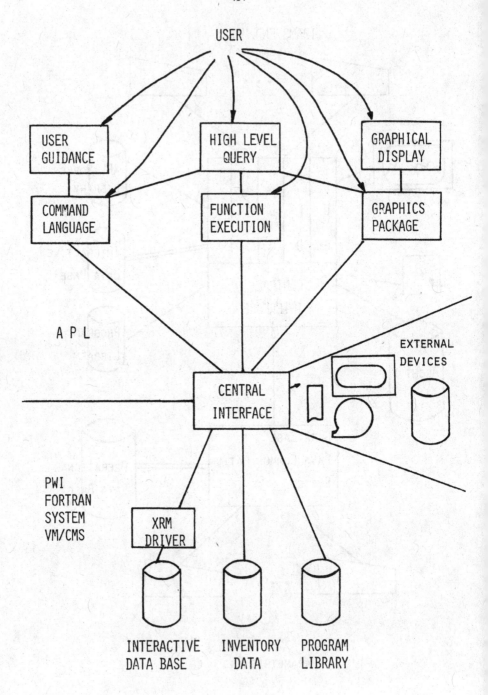

FIGURE 2: IDAMS SYSTEM ARCHITECTURE

Assembly language, and the Data Management drivers, which
are written in PL/I, all other components are programmed in
APL and therefore easy to maintain, test, and extend.

The interface to the data management drivers is based on a
"one record at a time" logic. It is straight forward to
connect IDAMS to a suitable data management system such as
XRM /8/, RSS /9/ or, VSAM /10/. XRM is currently supported
and RSS adaptation is in preparation.

The interface to drivers is such that the performance
options offered in these systems (inversions, sorting,
scans, etc.) can be utilized without putting the burden on
the IDAMS end-user.

In addition to the described type of data management IDAMS
offers the user an APL and CMS "internal" data management
based on keeping the accessed data in vectors within the APL
workspace. This is efficient for small collections of data.
The access to data in the Data Manipulation Language is
independent of where the data are stored, whether as
workspace tables, in XRM or in RSS.

The objects supported in IDAMS are TABLES for data
collections, FUNCTIONS for regular Single Valued functions,
or for SOURCES and SINKS, and UNITS of measure. Descriptions
of these objects and associated data are kept in Permanent
Dictionaries between sessions. Within an application several
of these dictionaries may exist. During an IDAMS session the
user copies the definition of a selection of objects into
the initially empty Active Dictionary. He may also add
temporary object definitions to the Active Dictionary. These
objects disappear at session end automatically together
with clearance of the Active Dictionary unless they have
been made permanent prior to session end. If a user makes
an object permanent, he is prompted for descriptive guidance
information to ensure consistency between existing objects
and the network of menus in the IUG component.

Independent of the notion of permanent and temporary
objects, IDAMS supports the SAVE/LOAD logic described in the
prededing section for tables.

The IUG component offers a guided tour to the pertinent
information based on successive selection from menus.
During search, the user controls the level of detail of
guidance information in terms of short and long form
explanations. A direct search facilily enables the user to
specify all he knows in one move, thus considerably speeding
up the information retrieval process.

As already mentioned IDAMS uses a tabular view of data for
Data Definition. Data attributes are tied to named table
columns. The following describes some of the data

attributes:

o IDAMS supports entries of arbitrary rank, e.g. scalars, vectors and matrices.

o· A datatype may be Character, Boolean, Integer, Real or Sampled Function: the special datatype "sampled function" consists of a sequence of real x and y values.

o Associated with real data is a unit of measure, e.g. kg, meter, inch-per-second, etc.

o Additional descriptive information relates to the method of storing (workspace, XRM, RSS) and to the representation of values. For example, it is possible to represent scalar values as one byte integers.

Function Definition involves for parameters the same datatypes as for table columns:

Further attributes are:

o the language , e.g. APL, FORTRAN, etc.

o the type , e.g. Single Valued, Source, Sink

o unit mapping, i.e. units of results expressed in terms of units of the input arguments.

A source is a function, which may be typically used to read data from an input file. It delivers data to the query in the format of a table, one row at each invocation. A sink is the reverse mechanism, at each invocation a row is passed to the associated function.

The High Level Query interface is intended for users with little APL-knowledge and virtually no data processing background. The language is table oriented and highly declarative. The user inserts "example elements", i.e. variables or literals into displayed skeletons which provide table/program names and column/parameter names. Further he specifies constraints, which must hold true for these example elements, in form of APL-expressions (predicates). The set of result values, satisfying the query may be

(1) inserted into a table (ready for further query processing),

(2) listed on his terminal (ready for further APL-processing),

(3) displayed graphically (ready for further display processing),

(4) put into APL variables without listing.

Using temporary tables allows to obtain the results of a
complex query by a sequence of simple queries (in principle
the approach of structured programming). Since each step is
performed by executing a compiled APL-function the whole
sequence can easily be put together into one APL-function.

A display on the terminal has the format of a table; the
contents of each column are assigned to APL variables, the
names of which are the particular column names. This allows
to further process displayed values by means of APL.

Displayed sampled functions get stored in a "pictorial data
base" from where they can be retrieved for further
processing by means of APL with a set of graphical
functions.

The results of a query are not limited to either one of
these possibilities; they may be used in combination.

The graphical display and formatting component is built upon
the Graphical Analysis Program /16/. In its current form
the main emphasis is on the display of sampled functions,
i.e., functions of one variable and on the display of
functions of two variables, using contour plots and cross
sections. During one session all displayed functions may be
kept in a "pictorial data base" for repeated usage, e.g.,
with changed scaling or for display in one ore several
frames together with others. The graphical display of the
results of a query is a valuable aid in data screening or in
exploring relationships between data.

The function execution interface allows to execute non
APL-programs within a query, and/or to provide a tabular
view for the usage of APL-functions. A tabular view helps in
case of APL-functions with more than two inputs and/or more
than one result (handled by means of global variables).

The IDAMS interface, which allows the switch of environments
within a VS APL machine has been built around a specially
developed auxiliary processor and is further described in
/11/.

It is one of the primary objectives of IDAMS to guide the
user through the system. It is therefore, despite the rich
offer of functions, expected to be easy to use. This is,
like with other interactive systems, best learned by using
it. Figure 3 shows a query to a data base containing
information on stock market data. The skeletons and headings
have been created by menu selection, the other information
has been "filled in" by the user. the APL symbol stands
for output. All other "fillins" relate the output "examples"
to information contained in tables. The Draw function

488

APL	EXPRESSION
□	ID, FULLNAME

DRAW	FORM	NAME	SF
	2 3	ID	TS

STOCK	ID	TITLE	VALUE
	ID	FULLNAME	TS

FIGURE 3: EXAMPLE OF AN IDAMS QUERY

displays the selected time series as shown in figure 4. The FORM parameter determines the partitioning of the display screen into 2 times 3 subscreens. The NAME parameter associates text to the graph and the SF parameter is the sampled function to be displayed.

4. Conclusions

If we go back to the points raised in section 2 and summarized in Table I, we identify at first IDAMS as a system which satisfies these requirements only in a general way. But, IDAMS offers a variety of hooks for extension and adaptation to an application area.

IDAMS does not offer the application oriented datatypes of points, lines and areas. Instead, IDAMS offers the more basic data structures of vectors and arrays. It is straight forward to map the application types in convenient way to the IDAMS structures. For example, we may represent a point in a two dimensional space as a vector with two elements. A line may be a vector of two points i.e. a vector with four elements.

In analogy, an area may be represented by the vector of points of a polygon. Once such a representation has been choosen, IDAMS may be extended by built-in functions like point in area, or the union and the intersection of areas. Examples for such routines are shown in figure 5. The development of such functions is not much more than an exercise in APL programming.

IDAMS per se does not offer application specific programs, such as edge detection in images, or conversational image analysis. Again, IDAMS is very flexible. Such algorithms may be defined as built in functions, or, as user functions with guidance information in the IUG component. These algorithms may be interactive and originally written in APL, PL/I or FORTRAN or in some other language but following the linkage conventions of either PL/I or FORTRAN.

Given that the major algorithms exist for a specific pictorial application area, the adaptation of IDAMS to this application area is a matter of a few person months. In contrast, the development of a system from scratch which matches the functions of IDAMS requires an effort which is in the order of a factor of one hundred greater.

Let us now look at the aspect of complexity. It may be argued that a special purpose pictorial data base system is less complex and better performing than a general purpose system like IDAMS. To this end it would have to be shown that some of the requirements can be dropped.

```
ID      FULLNAME

PCA     PACIFIC CANADIAN AIRLINES
AMC     AUSTRALIAN MINING CORPORATION
EIF     EUROEPEAN INVESTORS FUND
ODB     OVERSEAS DISTRIBUTION BANK
SDC     SCIENTIFIC DEVELOPMENT
MPS     MANPOWER SERVICES
```

(B) TERMINAL OUTPUT

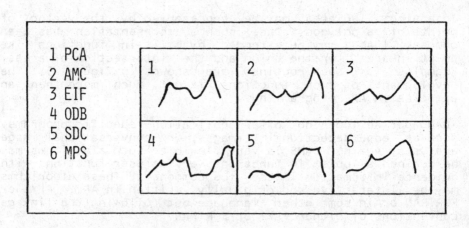

```
1 PCA
2 AMC
3 EIF
4 ODB
5 SDC
6 MPS
```

(A) GRAPHICAL DISPLAY

FIGURE 4: RESULT OF QUERY

```
      ∇PTINPOL[□]∇
    ∇ R←P PTINPOL X;I;J;K
[1]   ⍝ P=(X Y) IN POLYGON X=(X1 Y1 ..., XN YN)
[2]   J←P[1]≥I←((0.5×ρI),2)ρI←I,2↑I←,X
[3]   J[;2]←⁻1⌽J[;1]
[4]   J←(≠/J)/⍳1↑ρI
[5]   K←I[J-1;2]+(P[1]-I[J-1;1])×(I[J;2]-I[J-1;2])÷I[J;1]-I[J-1;1]
[6]   R←(~∨/K=P[2])×1=2|+/P[2] <K
    ∇

      ∇SHADE[□]∇
    ∇ R←SHADE B;C;D;E;F;R;□IO
[1]   ⍝ A SHADE POLYGON B WITH DIST A[1] AND DIRECTION A[2]
[2]   □IO←1
[3]   R← 0 2 ρ0
[4]   →(0≥1↑A←2↑,A)/0
[5]   L1:B←B+.×F←(1 ⁻1 ×ρF),[0.5] F←1 2 ○○(A[2]-90)÷180
[6]   C←⌊/B[;1]
[7]   D←⌈/B[;1]
[8]   L:→(D≤C←A[1]+C)/L0
[9]   →(2>ρE←(≠/E)/⍳1↑ρE←E,[1.5] ⁻1⌽E←C≥B[;1])/L
[10]  E←B[E-1;2]+(C-B[E-1;1])×(B[E;2]-B[E-1;2])÷B[E;1]-B[E-1;1]
[11]  R←R,[1]((ρE)ρC),[1.5] E[⍋E]
[12]  →L
[13]  L0:R←R+.×⌽F
[14]  HDRAW((1↑ρR)ρ 1 0),LR
    ∇
```

FIGURE 5: THE APL FUNCTIONS FOR PICTORIAL DATATYPES

As a tempting example, let us take the area of data types.
Could the special purpose system restrict itself to
pictorial data types (point, line, area, etc.) and scalars?
Unless the system is restricted to a very specific well
determined application the answer is clearly no! Questions
like the following are difficult to answer: is a point
determined by two, three or even four coordinates? Where two
coordinates are sufficient, four are an enormous waste of
storage. Offering three different point types makes the
system complex. The questions are even worse to answer for
lines, areas and other subspaces of higher dimensional
spaces. Lines may or may not need a weight, a thickness etc.
But even if all these types could be generally and
satisfactorily defined (which has not been achieved so
far!), would they be sufficient for the scientific problem
solver? Even in pictorial applications, data analysis is
not restricted to pictorial data types. Timeseries and
higher dimensional structures are appropriate for
statistical analysis. For example, in the analysis of
multivariate functions a point may have any number of
coordinates /12/.

IDAMS as a prototype is in investigation at several IBM
internal and external studies /13/. None of these
application oriented studies would have been or would be
feasible without the extendability of IDAMS. The fact that
IDAMS can easily be extended is also proven by the existence
of the Graphics Display and Formatting Component, which has
been added on top of IDAMS in a very similar way as IDAMS
has to be extended for a specific application area.

IDAMS is a prototype, which is certainly not in all areas
functionally complete. It is part of the objectives of the
above mentioned studies to determine deficiencies of IDAMS.
However, with the current experience we are convinced that
building and improving upon the general purpose solution is
the only way to succeed.

References

/1/ Sklansky, J. (Ed.): Pattern Recognition: Introduction
     and Foundation. Dowden, Hutchinson and Ross,
     Strondsburg, Pennsylvania, 1973.

/2/ Verhagen, C.J.D.M(Ed.): Proceedings of the Second
     International Joint Conference on Pattern Recognition,
     August 13-15, 1974, Copenhagen, Denmark. Available from
     ACM, IEEE catalogue number 74CH0885-4C.

/3/ Straszak, A. and Wagle, B.V. (Eds.): Models for
     Regional Planning and Policy-Making. Proceedings of the
     Joint IBM/IIASA Conference, Vienna, September 1977, IBM
     UK Scientific Center Winchester.

/4/ Williams, R.: Image Processing and Computer Graphics. IBM Research, San Jose, Techn. Rep. RJ 2336, September 1978.

/5/ Zloof, M.M.: "Query by Example", IBM Research Yorktown Heights, Techn. Rep. RC 4917, July 1974.

/6/ Schauer, U. et al: Integrated Data Analysis and Management in APL. IBM Scientific Center Heidelberg, 1978.

/7/ Erbe, R. et al: Integrated Data Analysis and Management System - Users Guide. IBM Scientific Center Heidelberg, 1978.

/8/ Lorie, R.A.: "XRM an Extended (n-ary) Relational Memory", IBM Cambridge Science Center, Techn. Rep. 320-2096, January 1974.

/9/ Astrahan, M.M. et al: System R: Relational Approach to Database Management. ACM TODS, Vol. 1, 97-137, 1976.

/10/ Virtual Storage Access Method (VSAM), Programmers Guide. Publ. GC26-3840, IBM Corporation, White Plains, N.Y.

/11/ Eberle, H. and Schmutz, H.: Calling PL/1 or FORTRAN subroutines dynamically from VS APL, IBM Scientific Center Heidelberg, Techn. Rep. TR 77.11.007, 1977.

/12/ Hoel, P.G.: Introduction to Mathematical Statistics. John Wiley and Sons, New York, 1971.

/13/ IBM Germany: Heidelberg Scientific Center Annual Report 1977. Techn. Rep. TR 78.04.003, April 1978.

/14/ Information Management System, General Information Manual. GH20-1260, IBM Corporation, White Plains, N.Y.

/15/ Smedley, B.S.: A Computer-Based Framework for Physical Planning. IBM UK Scientific Center, Techn. Rep. UK SC 0099, Winchester, July, 1978.

/16/ GAP - Installed User Program 5796-PFK, Program Description/ Operations Manual SH20-1752, IBM Corporation, White Plains, N.Y.

A Picture Drawing System
Using a Binary
Relational Database

G.C.H.Sharman

ABSTRACT

The Picture Drawing System is a prototype general purpose graphics system which uses the binary relational database system NDB. The prototype was developed to demonstrate that the full potential of graphics systems can only be realised with an effective database management subsystem, and that the binary relational database approach offers precisely the kind of support needed.

The required database structure is illustrated, and the basic picture interpreter and picture editor algorithms are described. The use of the binary relational database approach makes these algorithms essentially simple. As a result, the implementation of PDS, written in PL/I, occupies only 1000 lines of code.

IBM UK Laboratories Ltd
Hursley Park
Winchester
SO21 2JN
ENGLAND

496

Vector graphics systems, in which a writing mechanism - such as a CRT
beam or plotter pen - is programmed to literally draw a picture on a
viewable surface, have been well known for several years. These systems
have led to the development of graphics programming languages (more
properly, graphics extensions of other programming languages) with the
general characteristic of imperative commands such as:

        DRAW LINE   FROM(X_1,Y_1) TO(X_2,Y_2)
    or
        DRAW ARC   FROM(X_1,Y_1) TO(X_2,Y_2) CENTRE(X_3,Y_3)

These commands are interpreted with respect to a cartesian co-ordinate
system which is imposed on the entire picture. Several graphics programming languages already exist, and there has been a proposal to
define a standard for such languages [ACM].

During this period graphics systems have been expensive, and have been
employed only in specialised application areas such as vehicle design,
where the cost of programming graphics applications is a small component
of total costs. However, many people believe that graphics systems may
be much more widely applicable in, for example, the display of maps and
other conventional signs, the illustration of textual data, and the
presentation of business and technical information. For these purposes,
low cost graphics systems will be required, and these may not use the
original vector technology. Nevertheless, it is very likely that they
will continue to be programmed in the graphics programming languages
designed for the vector devices.

Programming in such graphics programming languages is not particularly
easy. A single picture may require a program of a few hundred lines,
which could involve conditional constructs and loops. Imagine a program
intended to generate a pie-chart of some business data. This will
involve drawing a circle, computing sector sizes and drawing radii to
delineate each sector, as well as superimposing textual data to describe
each part of the chart. Since the basic objective of all graphics systems is to speed up the rate of information exchange between man and
machine, many pictures will be required. It seems likely that the cost
of generating these pictures by programming will become significant in
relation to the cost of the hardware used.

Some pictures, such as the pie-chart, can no doubt be generated automatically from a set of input parameters by a standard program. Equally,
there will be many cases where this is not possible. For these cases,
some alternative method of picture generation is required.

The most general technique available seems to be the combination of a database management system with a picture interpreter which is capable of drawing any picture from definitions stored in the database. In this approach, the definitions are compactly stored and only one graphics application program ever has to be written - the picture interpreter. The data in the database defines each line, arc, point, or other picture element in the required picture as an individual entity. It is also possible to store a library of pictures by relating each of the picture elements to some identifier of the picture to which it belongs.

This approach has a further advantage in that the picture definition is now held as data, and not as a piece of program text. Should it be necessary to change the picture, we just update the database rather than editing and recompiling a graphics program. We may obtain even more flexibility by writing the picture interpreter in such a way that it can selectively display subsets of a picture, containing for example only the lines, or pictures can be nested within a picture. This would lead to a system which has the capability of rapidly building up pictures from standard 'picture parts' which are already stored in the database. The construction of flowcharts and circuit diagrams are obvious examples of this.

Where a picture contains some hundreds of picture elements, even updating a database will prove to be a tedious way of creating or maintaining the picture. In any case, it will be difficult for the database operator to visualise the effect of the changes which he is entering into the database. What we need is a way of specifying these changes in a direct graphical form using a picture editor. This is a program which accepts graphical input from a screen and converts it into data which is suitable for storing in the database. Using a picture editor, the task of creating a new picture is reduced to the simple human task of drawing it on a screen. After that, the picture may be retained and manipulated indefinitely. The picture editor may, of course, assist the initial drawing task by intelligently squaring up lines intended to be perpendicular, computing the best radius for an arc, and so on.

In a practical system, the picture editor and picture interpreter should work in close co-operation. It should be possible to display a partially completed picture whose definition is stored in the database and then add to it or change it and have the resulting changes stored in the database. In this mode, the combined database and graphics system becomes an extremely powerful tool for the graphics designer, which may be used in a manner resembling that of more traditional artistic media, but with much greater speed and flexibility.

IMPLEMENTATION WITH A BINARY RELATIONAL DATABASE

None of the features described above are unique or novel. In fact, they
have been incorporated into many of the specialised graphic applications
built over the last few years, and are also clearly visible in general
purpose graphics systems such as PBS [PALERMO].

Here we shall describe a prototype system of this type known as the Picture Drawing System. This was developed to exploit both the capabilities of character graphics terminals such as the IBM 3279, and of the
Binary Relational Database system known as NDB [WINTERBOTTOM & SHARMAN],
[SHARMAN & WINTERBOTTOM], [DMP]. The prototype does not claim to support a particularly sophisticated graphics facility. Its real interest
lies in the simplicity and directness of implementation which is made
possible by the binary relational database system.

A binary relational database [SENKO] uses only two basic concepts to
store any kind of data: the entity and the relationship. An entity is
simply an identifier for some "thing" in the outside world, and a
relationship is simply a representation of a link between two such
things. Entities are classified into sets of entities all of the same
type, while relationships are similarly classified into relationship
types. Relationship types are further characterised as many-to-many,
many-to-one, or one-to-one.

To illustrate the structure of a binary database, we draw a diagram
showing each entity type as a node and each relationship type as an arc
joining the nodes which it relates. These nodes and arcs bear the names
of the types which they represent. Arcs also carry an arrow indicating
the sense of the relationship represented: from one entity type to
another entity type. In this paper we shall assume that all relationships are many-to-one.

Figure 1 presents a simplified diagram of a database structure to store
a two dimensional picture consisting of any arbitrary combination of
points, lines, and arcs. This database would be capable of storing any
picture made up of such elements, and so it can be said to define a
class of possible pictures.

The diagram may be understood as follows:

• Each point in the desired picture is represented by an entity of
  entity type "point", which is a unique identifier. This is related
  via binary relationships to the X co-ordinate and Y co-ordinate at
  which the point is to be displayed.

• Each line is represented by an entity of entity type "line", which
  is a unique identifier. This is realted to "point" entities which
  define the start point and end point of the line. Many lines may
  share the same start point or end point.

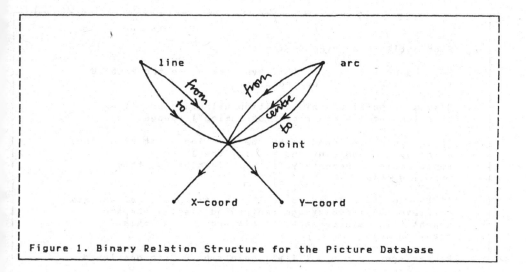

Figure 1. Binary Relation Structure for the Picture Database

- Each arc is represented by an entity of entity type "arc", which is
  a unique identifier. This is related to entities which define the
  start point, end point, and centre point of the arc (arcs are conventionally drawn in a clockwise direction). Many arcs may share
  the same start, end, or centre point.

With this database structure, a picture interpreter may be programmed
using the standard application programming interface of the binary relational database management system. The algorithm for drawing the picture would read as in Figure 2.

The essential advantage of the binary relational approach is that this
algorithm can be implemented very simply in the application programming
interface of the database management system, since the API allows direct
reference to entities and relationships. This makes it easy to implement a powerful and reliable graphics system.

```
1.   Find entities of type "point".

2.   For the next entity of this type, retrieve the related
     X co-ordinate and Y co-ordinate.

3.   Display a point at this position using the primitive
     functions of the graphics programming language.

4.   If the point is found to be the starting point of a line,
     retrieve its endpoint and display the line.
     Repeat this as necessary for all lines having this
     starting point.

5.   If the point is found to be the starting point of an arc,
     retrieve its endpoint and centre and display the arc.
     Repeat this as necessary for all arcs having this
     starting point.

6.   Repeat steps 2 - 5 until all points have been displayed.

Figure 2. Algorithm for Picture Interpreter
```

The database structure shown above is too simple for effective use. In practice, we need to store a library of pictures rather than a single picture, we need to be able to construct pictures from component pictures, and we also need more sophisticated graphics facilities. These might permit, for example, the use of colour, a variety of line types, the solid filling of closed figures, the inclusion of textual data, together with scaling, translation, rotation, reflection and windowing of the resultant picture.

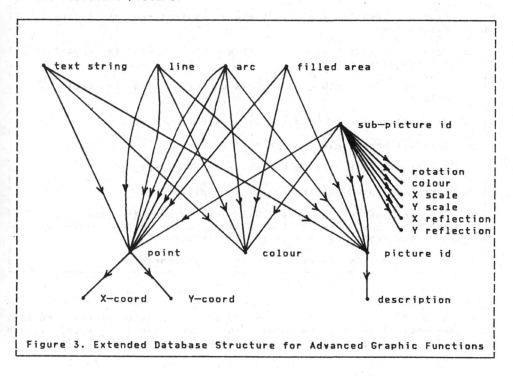

Figure 3. Extended Database Structure for Advanced Graphic Functions

A database structure to support most of these capabilities is illustrated in Figure 3.

This database is obviously more complex than that of Figure 1 on page 4. Nevertheless it is quickly recognisable as a development of the simple database, and can be understood in the same terms. Pictures are represented in terms of points, lines, and arcs as before, with the addition of text strings and filled areas as picture elements. Each picture element may have a colour attribute. The database can store an

502

arbitrary collection of pictures, since each picture element is related to a unique identifier of the picture to which it belongs. Pictures can be nested within pictures using the relationships between picture identifier and sub-picture identifiers. For example, these might be used to indicate that picture A should be included within picture B at a specified origin, and with specified changes of scale, rotation, reflection, and colour. This part of the database is analogous to the "bill of materials" structure widely used to specify the relationships between components and assemblies in a manufacturing environment.

---

1. Find the identifier of the picture required from the picture description.

2. Draw all points belonging to this picture, using the specified co-ordinates.

3. Draw all lines belonging to this picture, using the specified colour.

4. Draw all arcs belonging to this picture.

5. Fill all areas belonging to this picture.

6. Insert all text strings belonging to this picture.

7. Find all nested subpictures of this picture.

   For each subpicture, locate its picture identifier and perform steps 2 - 7 for that picture, applying the specified scaling, rotation, reflection, and colour.

Figure 4. Algorithm for Extended Picture Interpreter

The design of a picture interpreter for the database of Figure 3 on page 6 is somewhat different from that needed for Figure 1 on page 4 though not different in kind. The basic algorithm is described in Figure 4.

It should be obvious that step 7 involves a recursion to process nested pictures to an indefinite degree of nesting.

Even this algorithm is very over-simplified with respect to the facilities which the user might reasonably require. With the binary relational database support, it is straightforward to extend these capabilities in several different directions:

• To permit selective or step-by-step drawing of separate components of a picture, e.g. to display level by level, or colour by colour.

- To permit a search capability enabling the user to identify a picture, or group of pictures, by some of its characteristics, e.g. to
find all pictures containing a specified subpicture, or all pictures
containing arcs centred at a particular co-ordinate position, or all
pictures containing a certain arbitrary pattern.

- To incorporate the graphics information within a larger database
structure, so that the picture of an object, such as a manufactured
part, may be stored along with the other data specified about that
part.

These facilities would be regarded as very sophisticated in relation to
today's graphics systems. We shall not describe their implementation
here, but will emphasise that they are natural and reasonable extensions
of the picture interpreter described above, and would not involve vast
programming effort or vastly greater complexity than the basic interpreter described above.

Let us turn our attention now to the implementation of the picture editor. In order to achieve an acceptable user interface, we need a graphics input device with certain minimum characteristics:

*   The capability to specify a co-ordinate position visually (e.g. cur-
    sor, cross-hairs, light pen)

*   The capability to select from a set of available operations, picture
    element types, etc. (e.g. menu selection, program function keys).

*   The capability to enter textual or numeric data (e.g. keyboard).

```
|                                                                      |
|                                                                      |
| 1.   Identify a picture to be created, developed or edited.          |
|                                                                      |
| 2.   Prompt the user to specify an operation to be performed         |
|      (e.g. add, delete).                                             |
|                                                                      |
| 3.   Prompt the user to specify the type of picture element          |
|      (e.g. line, arc).                                               |
|                                                                      |
| 4.   Prompt the user to enter required co-ordinate positions         |
|      for the specified picture element (eg. start and end            |
|      points when adding a new line).                                 |
|                                                                      |
| 5.   Translate new screen positions into co-ordinates suitable       |
|      for storing in the database and store them; store or            |
|      delete a system generated identifier for the picture            |
|      element; and create the appropriate relationships               |
|      between them.                                                   |
|                                                                      |
| 6.   Call the picture interpreter to draw the newly specified        |
|      picture element, and repeat the process from step 2.            |
|                                                                      |
| Figure 5. Algorithm for Picture Editor                              |
```

With these facilities, the basic algorithm for a picture editor would be
as described in Figure 5.

There are clearly other facilities which such a picture editor ought to
support:

*   Validate the effect of a change against existing data before
    commiting it.

- Display the effect of a change before committing it. This would allow the user to erase and redraw a picture element which he does not like.

- Copy part or all of an existing picture.

- Select and view subpictures for inclusion in the picture being worked on.

- and so on.

Extensions to the basic algorithm are straightforward and will not be described here.

At the end of each transaction, such as adding a new line to the pic-ture, the database will correspond to the picture actually displayed. This means that the user always has immediate recovery in case of a sys-tem failure, and it also means that he can suspend his operations at any time and resume from where he left off. The integrity requirements in this area are similar to those for any other database application, and it should be possible to use existing database facilities.

Many graphics systems maintain elaborate main storage data structures to describe the picture which is being manipulated.   Such data structures may be dumped onto secondary storage at user specified checkpoints or when the user terminates his session. However, the user may be forced to back off to a checkpoint or suffer an integrity exposure in the event of system failure. The use of a database management offers clear advan-tages in this area.

The design of data structures is also an important factor in the per-formance and flexibility of a graphics system. In many cases, the design is application specific and therefore inflexible with respect to new application requirements. By using a database structure we have delegated these problems to the database management system, and ensured that the graphics system is fully general purpose.   Clearly, this does not mean that performance is no longer important, but it does mean that performance improvements should focus on the implementation of the data-base system and not on the graphics system per se.

A prototype of the system described was implemented in the summer of 1977. This consisted of a picture interpreter and a picture editor which supported a fairly large subset of the facilities described above. The implementation occupied about 3 person months, and ran to about 1000 lines of PL/I (including both graphics and database statements). At the time when this was completed, there was no graphics terminal available for testing and a 3270 simulation was therefore used. Clearly, this terminal has no graphic capability, but nevertheless it was possible to create a collection of around 20 pictures, and to edit and redisplay these in a degraded form.

The implementation was developed and run under VM/370. Picture editing could be performed at conversational speeds with medium load on the sys- tem. The time required to redisplay a picture containing 20 - 40 line segments was around 1 second, with no special attention being paid to performance tuning.

These figures seem to suggest that the implementation objectives were achieved, and that the database technology is feasible as a major way of using graphics. The speed with which it was possible to put together this graphics system is surely a tribute to the remarkable power of the binary relational approach.

APPENDIX A: REFERENCES

[ACM]   ACM, 'Status Report of the Graphics standards Committee of ACM/SIGGRAPH', SIGGRAPH Vol 11, no. 3 [1977]

[DMP]   IBM, 'Data Mapping Program: Program Description and Operations', IBM SRL SB11-5339, IBM Corp. [1979]

[PALERMO] Palermo, F. & Weller, D., 'Picture Building System', IBM Research Report RJ2436 [1979]

[SENKO]   Senko, M.E., 'DIAM as a Detailed Example of the ANSI/SPARC Architecture', Proc IFIP TC-2 Conference, Freudenstadt [1976]

[SHARMAN & WINTERBOTTOM] Sharman, G.C.H., & Winterbottom, N., 'The Data Dictionary Facilities of NDB', Proc VLDB4 Conference, Berlin [1978]

[WINTERBOTTOM & SHARMAN] Winterbottom, N., & Sharman, G.C.H., 'NDB: Non-programmer Data Base Facility', IBM Technical Report TR.12.179 [1979]

APPENDIX B: ACKNOWLEDGEMENT

My sincere thanks are due to Alison Long who was responsible for the implementation described, and contributed much to its design.   I would also like to express my thanks to Bryan Roberts for many valuable discussions, and for presenting this paper in Florence.

DATA ASPECTS OF GRAPHICAL APPLICATIONS

Experience from an Engineering Joint Study

Karl Soop[1]
1979-05-23

Summary

This paper reports on experience with an Application Support System, called SMART. The SMART prototype was developed to investigate DP techniques in the Engineering environment, including graphics. Several of these applications involve highly complex geometric and physical objects, which are manipulated on graphic screens. In many cases it is not possible beforehand to establish precisely which structures will best describe the application and help solve its problem. This observation holds not only for the application data themselves, but also for the picture and dialog structures that will eventually serve the user. Often modifications and additions are demanded many times during the life-time of an application.

SMART was proven to satisfy these needs for engineering applications. Moreover, the prototype was validated in a whole range of ancillary application types, some of which were in the administrative domain.

----

[1] IBM Nordic Laboratory
  Box 962, S-181 09 Lidingo, Sweden

1. The Joint Study

My talk centers around experience gained in a joint project
between Aerospatiale and IBM. The Aerospatiale plant in
Southern France manufactures helicopters, and our partner
group was the Engineering Department at the plant site. In
the project we studied the DP environment in this group, its
activities and its problems. The study led to a relational
data methodology and support system named SMART. SMART is
now used in production in a variety of applications; it is
currently in prototype status and runs under VM/CMS.

In this paper I will present both clear-cut results of the
joint study, and my own interpretation of some of the
results; their significance to data support in Engineering
and in general; their possible role in DB trends. The
results are highly pertinent to graphics; but, as will be
seen later, one conclusion was that it is generally not
possible to isolate one area of application support as
purely "graphic".

I will first present some of the characteristics of the
engineer's application environment, and in particular his
view of data. This leads to a number of general
data-support requirements, which have been validated by
extensive experience with live applications at the study
site. After this I go into a technical description which
includes a sophisticated graphic application as an example.
In the final section I try to extrapolate the significance
of our results in terms of possible forms for future
support.

2. The Engineer's Data View

Let me summarise some characteristics of the engineering DP
environment. The applications have all the familiar
properties that tend to justify relational support:
Unforeseeable, complex and changing data structures,
unplanned access paths, and unclear separation between
structure, function and the "data itself". The engineer
wants to enter these parts of an application quickly, try
them out, and be able to change and add as he pleases. He
will then rapidly arrive at a solution to his problem in a
stepwise, iterative manner. He wants to be able to connect
the new solution to other existing applications, without
having to convert data or develop costly interfaces.

In addition, the engineering community is notoriously
impatient with DP solutions that have to be expressed in
non-user terms and those that involve needless repetition of
detail. JCL cards, "file" and "record" are examples of

entities that have no meaning in an engineering problem. The fundamental requirement that the DP system remember the engineer's data (including structure) until he logs on to the next session, is so obvious that it should not even need a name. Therefore "data base" is a non-word in this context, and SMART provides relational support, not a "relational data base".

Our study took the engineer's own view of his data as the starting point for the design of SMART. Here "data" must be taken in a very broad sense, including not only the "problem" data of the application at hand, but also that part of the engineer's experience, know-how and even intuition, which is needed for solving the problem. It follows that the data embrace both factual and algorithmic knowledge. This is described in more detail later in the discussion of methodology.

In designing the support system we therefore departed from the usual bottom-up approach, where the user will ultimately have to depend on the capabilities and idiosyncrasies of the underlying low-level support, such as physical storage organisation, operating system, access method, etc (see left figure below).

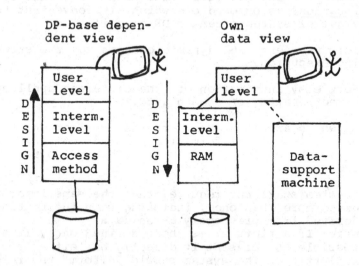

Bottom-up   Top-down alt.I   alt.II

Instead, we accepted the user's view of his data as the "correct" one in the sense that it best reflected the syntactic, and not least the semantic, requirements on the support system. Any low-level component which is capable of supporting this view (even though we may have to implement an intermediate layer) would suit us. In this case, we selected RAM [Lorie & Symonds, 1970], which at the lowest level reduces to a number of flat VM/CMS files (middle figure). But it would have been as useful, and vastly more advantageous to us, if we could have chosen a low-level support system that directly builds on the high-level data views, such as a relational machine (right-hand figure). In fact, our objective was to design SMART in such a way that it could be directly implemented in hardware; this facet of the study is reported in [Soop, 1979]. Indeed, when we speak about requirements on data structure, access and manipulation, we make no difference between the user's own view and the bottom-level support, since they should ideally be identical.

3. The Knowledge Bank

This section summarises some key properties of SMART, and can be regarded as a list of general requirements on the data-support system. I will elaborate on graphic-specific requirements in the later discussion of user interfaces.

- Accommodate any structure which is relevant to the application, as opposed one which is convenient to the physical or system-oriented DB organisation.

- Support frequent and dynamic changes to the structure during execution.

- Support easy integration of the different applications by direct sharing of common data.

- Data, which are irrelevant to the application, notably DP-base dependent information, should not have to be specified by he user. Examples: Physical screen size, record number.

- The system shall not require that the same information be given more than once, including when information can be derived from previously given data.
  Example: If a picture has been defined once, it should be possible to present it directly on either a screen or a plotter. The system should perform the relevant mapping.

- Describing the data to the system should be non-procedural as far as possible. In other words, unless procedurality is a genuine feature of the application, it should not be necessary to specify information in any particular order or with irrelevant dependency constraints. In particular, pictorial information can be specified with non-procedural means.

- Entry of data that cannot be captured by other means should be interactive. This includes application preparation (design, implementation, documentation...), and is required even if the application itself is passive.

- Application preparation can to a large part be carried out by the users themselves. The ability to participate in design, demo and test has proven of critical value to ensure that the user gets what he wants. Basic education in SMART takes only a couple of days.

- The user must be able to easily modify application data and function, including structure, as he gains experience and his requirements evolve, sometimes even during execution.

- There is no sharp limit between information that describes structure and data values ("problem data"). It is, e.g. not possible in a non-trivial dialog to separate part of a picture as being more static than others. A notion like a "map" which is "filled out" by "data" has little general use: What in one picture may be presented as the numeric character string '2.77' may another time be presented as a bar of length 2.77 in a histogram, or as the orientation angle of a shape component. Screen concepts like "fields" are relics from the time typewriters were the only interactive terminals.

- There is no sharp limit between information that describes structure and data types (or so-called "attributes"). For example, the condition that a value is numeric is a special case of a relation expressing domain membership. In engineering there are many other similar domains (e.g. complex numbers, standard part numbers, numbers between zero and one). It makes little sense to single out certain of those for special treatment, e.g. automatic checking.

- There is no sharp limit between "data" and "program" (or function) in actual usage. Functional relationships (e.g. algorithms) occur frequently in engineering (as in other) applications, and should be treated on the same footing as relationships between stored data. The only difference occurs in updates: It is not possible to modify a programmed relationship during execution, which is also in line with accepted implementation discipline.

The dilution of frontiers between information pertaining to structure, value, function and other data led us in the project to coin the expression <u>knowledge bank</u> (as opposed to "data base") for the joint repository of application information. One finds that by describing (or entering) the data to the support system, one actually describes part of the application. With SMART, we describe the <u>whole</u> application by relations in the knowledge bank. Since all this information is remembered in the knowledge bank, SMART can be regarded as both a support system and an application-development and maintenance tool. Furthermore, SMART satisfies the requirements on step-wise or ad-hoc implementation and testing, since the entered data can be queried at any time (the notion of "query" extends into general execution, along with the meaning of "data"). Further conclusions on the application aspect are summarised in the Appendix, since they are of less interest to graphics.

4. Validation

We have every reason to believe that the conclusions and requirements expressed in the previous sections are relevant to Engineering, as well as to many other application areas. This was clearly born out in a number of validation studies performed in the last phase of the project. Among the circa ten applications run were bill-of-material, administration of technical drawings and evaluation of a pilot survey.

The studies involved data collections representing up to 80'000 relation pairs per application. We found performance to be adequate in most cases: typically a simple query would take of the order of 3-10 seconds, but most of the delay seemed to depend on a rather overloaded central machine. In a few cases we made comparisons with an equivalent implementation on a hierarchical support system, and the result was astonishingly advantageous for SMART. In fact, only when queries were posed that directly exploited the pre-planned hierarchical structure did SMART perform less well than the compared system. The figures for application preparation were even more telling: Dependeing on the phase, it was from 8 to 16 times faster to develop with SMART.

The most challenging application validated on SMART was a graphics design package called Complex Shapes. Complex Shapes is one of the principal engineering applications in production at the study site. It contains elements of mathematics (tensorial definition of primitive shapes), topology (recursive definition of shapes), geometry and mechanics (properties of shapes and materials). Shapes are created, maintained and calculated upon, using the IBM 3250 graphic display. All elements, including graphic structuring (up to GSP level) are designed, modelled and executed in terms of binary relations. Complex Shapes was used as a highly successful benchmark application to validate many of the design decisions in SMART. I will return to the data properties of this important application below.

5. Relations in SMART

Two basic decisions in the design of SMART were to support only binary relations, and to support concrete and abstract relations alike. There were many reasons for these choices, one of which was simplicity of use.

5.1 The Binary Relation

It is often claimed that a relation in information processing is something like a table of values. This is supposedly a way to make newcomers feel more comfortable with relational methods, noting they are probably familiar with tabular presentation (in phone books, tax returns etc.). In connection with our work, this is a misleading and unfortunate trend for three reasons:

In the first place, the notion of a relation in SMART is strictly connected with the intuitive notion of a relationship between two objects and is further underscored by the presence of abstract relations (like LESS-THAN or SQRT-OF) [Abrial, 1973]. Secondly, tables are chiefly useful for non-volatile presentation, where one must display the information in its own context: lookup is manual. On a display screen the context is provided by the interactive session, and there is no reason why the query system cannot select for you the relevant information: lookup is automated. The fact that we had to live with hardcopy tables for a long time does not mean that this format is more "natural" than others (e.g. hierarchical) in any sense. Thirdly, one only has to note that proponents of the tabular (or n-ary) view invariably put column headings on the table, to see that what they really had in mind was a number of thus named binary relations.

5.2 The Relational Diagram

In summary, a SMART user is not forced to look at his application in tabular terms. On the other hand, he must describe his application as binary relationships. By this is meant that he must enter all information that appears to describe

      (a) his experience and know-how,
      (b) the problem.

Among (a) may be data, like the density of materials and
digitised drawings, that can be entered wholly or partly
through automated means. In fact, part of this
information is likely to exist already in the knowledge
bank from other application activities.

Now it turned out that the mere act of expressing the
problem in concise terms often leads directly to a
solution within the framework of the user's experience.
If it does not, the solution usually emerges after some
manipulation of the entered relations. We therefore have
the important result that once (a) and (b) have been
entered, a finished "application" is almost at hand.

The descriptions (a) and (b) are made in a <u>relational
diagram</u>, which forms the basis of the development
methodology. Relaticns are shown as arcs; for example,
the relation COLOR-OF is depicted

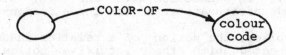

where the circles represent classes of <u>objects</u> that
exhibit the stated relationship. The classes are not
themselves represented in the knowledge bank, except as
the ad-hoc consequence of using objects in relations.
Their names are given by the designer only as an
aide-memoire; the left circle might here be named after
things that have a colour in this particular case, e.g.
"rotor-parts". Object classes are depicted as squares if
their contents are a priori known, which is the case e.g.
for real numbers and the days of the week.

The objects themselves, as well as relations must be
given names that are entered into and remembered by the
system. Relations may also be treated as objects if
relevant to the application. This further strengthens
the homogeneity of the knowledge bank: Classical "data",
such as personnel numbers or the length of a helicopter
blade are self-named objects like '271' (literals),
whereas a relation may be given a name like COMPONENT-OF.

5.3 Abstract Relations

A fully homogeneous knowledge bank comes from the
representation of function as abstract relations [Abrial,
1973]. Those must be specified by a DP programmer
(currently using a PL/I dialect). An abstract relation
is implemented as either a Generator, an Accessor or a
Tester program, depending on its properties (there are in
fact two kinds of Accessors). The abstract relation is
then used in relational expressions as any other
relation, and the system handles the invocation of the
correct program depending on the circumstances. For
example, an Accessor is invoked in single composition,
and a Tester in intersection. Refer to [Soop, 1979] for
a complete description of the relational algebra.

As mentioned earlier, all algorithmic information is
normally entered as abstract relations; ideally no
application code resides outside the knowledge bank. The
term "algorithmic" may, however, sometimes be misleading.
For the mechanism of, say, a Tester presents the relation
en bloc so that actual coding of the Tester program may
in practice be non-procedural. Only if demanded by the
application design itself, do procedures need to be
entered into the knowledge bank.

6. External Models

In the overview of the properties of SMART I have stressed
what is "relevant to the application". If you work in the
DP shop, your "application" may in fact be something quite
different from the normal user's. Here, you could still use
SMART to model your own universe; your relations would then
perhaps be named NEXT-RECORD, FIRST-ARGUMENT or the like.
They would form a platform for system-level applications,
which could then be included as system support in the
knowledge bank of the end users.

This is the manner SMART looks at graphic support. We can
regard the application proper as a description of the real
user problem and solution, thus excluding pictures, dialogs
etc. that are needed to actually run the application. The
latter components might then be implemented by specialists
in human factors, display terminals, data communication, and
so forth, SMART being perfectly capable of accommodating
also those corresponding structures.

This was the view we adopted in the project. For each
application model A, one or more external models are
developed to form access interfaces to A. With suitable
high-level tools, simple external models can be built by the
user; a few such tools were implemented in the project.

6.1 <u>Graphic Presentation</u>

As may be expected, the limit between what was perceived
as "graphic" data and what was "pure application" data
proved to be vague. For example, the application may
define a "point" as the intersection between two lines,
or as one of the end points of a line segment. It ·may
also be defined in a number of other ways, the most
obvious by giving its coordinate (in the user system):

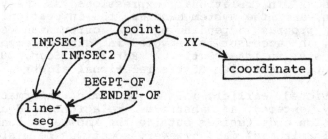

Graphic presentation, on the other hand, would probably
demand that the point be given in the latter way only
(but transformed into device units). Similarly, a line
segment would have to be given as a coordinate pair.
This can be expressed by abstract relations that check on
the actual definition and compute the coordinates (after
due transformation, clipping, etc.):

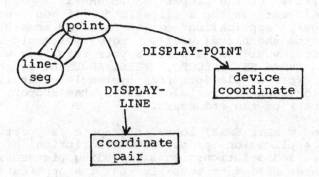

The result of a composition (join) with a DISPLAY
relation can then be directly shipped to the graphic
device. Characteristic of the approach is the mixing of
application and presentation information in the knowledge
bank (cf [Williams, 1974]).

It will be understood that the abstract display relations
depend on the device technology and available hardware

primitives; they therefore appear to violate the
requirements on DP-base independence. But those
relations belong to the external model, and hence to the
DP-professional's world. A display system using raster
technology with colour, might have the equivalent
interface:

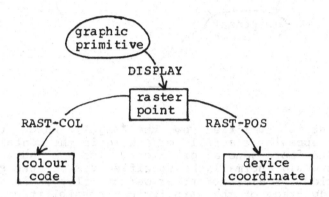

It is important to stress that the decision to select
this or that information for graphic presentation may be
taken ad hoc: The application deals with a problem
containing geometric, topologic, or purely numeric,
elements which may or may not benefit from interactive
display. The external model is applied simply by adding
the system relations (taken from a workspace of graphic
support) to the existing application structure.

6.2 The Complex Shape Application

In this application a geometric shape is structured into
a number of component shapes, unless it is a primitive.
This recursive definition is common to many graphic
applications, where one seeks to master pictorial
complexity by successive subdivision of the material to
be presented or handled.

The basic shape structure is depicted thus:

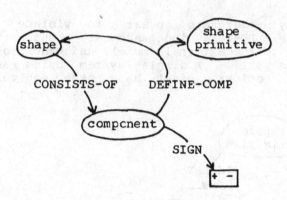

A component is qualified by the "sign", which tells
whether it appears as a fill or a hole in the containing
shape. With more general graphic support, a number of
parameters would normally be specified beside the sign,
e.g. position, scale, colour or detectability, in order
to take advantage of the structuring possibilities with
conformal shapes [Williams, 1974]. In a full dialog
structure, also the response on detection of the
component would be specified (e.g. a state transition).

In the engineering application one type of shape
primitive proved of almost ubiquitous value. It is a
planar or space curve, defined in polynomial form:

$$\vec{x}(u) = \sum_{i=0}^{n} \vec{T_i} u^i$$

where n is the degree and T a tensor of 2n or 3n
constants. The relationships are:

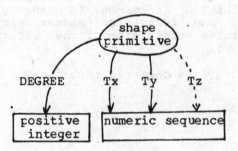

Once all above relationships have been entered, any shape
can be presented on the 3250 through the graphic access

method. We now add abstract relations to compute the
surface area of a shape, its center of gravity, and other
geometrical properties. These relations, like the
display relation, unravel the structure of the shape
under transitive closure:

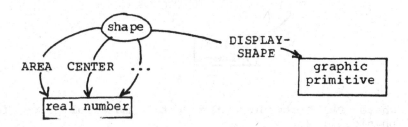

But this only forms the geometric part of Complex Shapes.
In order to introduce mechanical properties, materials
must be assigned to shape instances to form physical
parts:

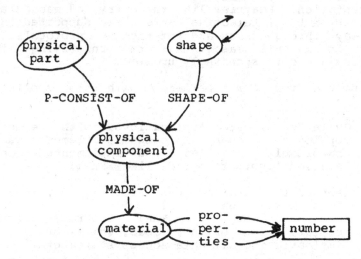

where "properties" refer to a number of relations like
DENSITY, ELASTICITY and the like. This makes it possible
to compute quantities such as the weight and inertia of a
physical part through new abstract relations (using
transitive closure). Similar relations would be defined
to produce bills of material.

Finally, one can add economic properties, and effectively
connect the application to cost sizing packages, e.g.
through:

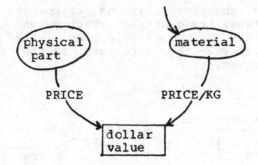

where PRICE computes the total material price for a physical part.

6.3 Summary

This brief overview of Complex Shapes merely hints at some of its capabilities in the area of data representation. Features like the entry and manipulation of shapes on the interactive screen are supported in the usual way through menus and interactive protocols. The effect is in all cases that the underlying binary relations are correspondingly updated.

We conclude from our experience with this application that:

(a) Quite complicated applications, with geometric, topologic, mechanical, economic elements can be comfortably modelled and implemented on a relational support system like SMART;

(b) Many of the key relations are <u>abstract</u>; they form what would be application programs with conventional support. SMART encourages a natural modularisation of this code, while at the same time obviating all data-access statements.

(c) There is a strong <u>coupling</u> between the information describing the application and its graphic presentation. Several relations play a role which may be said to be partly application-oriented, partly graphic.

7. Thoughts for the Future

In the previous sections I have conveyed some of the results of the Joint Project and discussed requirements on data support in general, and in graphics in particular. I will now try to extrapolate some of our conclusions in the light of current DP trends.

As earlier stated, the design of the relational support in SMART was strongly influenced by the possibility that it might ultimately be implemented as special machinery. Among key design decisions to favour this end were binary-only relations, equal role of abstract and concrete relations, economy of relational operators, equivalent use of relation names as objects, and attribute-free data objects. These aspects are covered in full in [Soop, 1979], and here I will only emphasise the significance for pictorial data.

One important conclusion from the study was the tight coupling between the application model and its external models, in which we include graphic dialogs. In advanced applications, this coupling is a necessity due to the unplanned nature of data presentation and interaction. On the other hand, performance may demand a functional separation between external and application models, since the former can be optimised in terms of the hardware it utilises.

In a traditional graphic system, like the IBM 3250, there is an attempt to separate a large portion of the picture-presentation function (notably character and line generation) and assign it to specialised hardware in the control unit. This yields a high performance for the static task (presentation) of the external model. On the other hand, it leaves it largely to the main processor to set up, maintain and control the dynamic task (event-response), which is an essential ingredient of the dialog. Today's graphic control units make no attempt to assist the dynamic task, beside some low-level identification of lightpen attentions and the like. In particular they do not provide picture updates based upon structured dialogs (such as state diagrams), which also belong in the external model.

I think dialog control is the major direction to expand graphic hardware. The Joint Study showed that the binary relational structure supports all structural information also in very advanced dialogs. Therefore the new-generation controllers should be based upon associative-memory techniques in the design of buffers and other control store [Symonds, 1968], and provide limited relational micro-coded support. Limited, because we are seeking to optimise only certain well-defined operations (namely picture presentation, event identification, update), and full relational support is not needed. My paper [Soop, 1977] discusses the theory behind this in detail, and shows that less than 30 relations are required to support the majority of dialogs. The control unit need then contain only a subset of the relational architecture proposed in [Soop, 1979].

8. Conclusion

The Engineering Joint Study has made a significant contribution to illuminate the properties and requirements of advanced data support for graphics. We believe the results and conclusions are valid not only in Engineering but in many other areas, including administrative data processing. The study has shown that it is possible to build a relational support system in software which meets the requirements of this environment as listed in Section 3. Furthermore, it has been argued that this support is especially suited for implementation in hardware if demanded by performance.

References

Abrial J.R. (1973)
Data semantics, University of Grenoble

Duwat G. (1979)
Development d'applications dans un bureau d'etude, Point de l'Informatique, IBM France (in preparation)

Lorie R. & Symonds A.J. (1970)
A schema for describing a relational data base, IBM G320-2059

Soop K. (1977)
A model for graphic structuring, IBM Nordic Lab

Soop K. (1979)
A data support system, IBM Nordic Lab (submitted for publication)

Symonds A.J. (1968)
Auxiliary-storage associative data structure for PL/I, IBM Sys J #3-4, p.224

Williams R. (1974)
On the application of relational data structures in computer graphics, IBM RJ1339, San Jose

Appendix

What is meant by an "application" in the knowledge bank?
Here follow some interesting conclusions from the study,
which can be used as hints for the design of future
application support:

* The support system does not provide a sharp limit
  between an application in preparation and in
  production. An application can be developed, tested,
  demoed, and run with SMART, and it is a purely
  administrative decision when and how (if ever) the
  cutover is made. This decision may involve activities
  outside SMART, such as compilation for another
  environment and shipping. The fuzziness occurs in the
  state of the application; obviously different tools are
  used in preparation and production.

* Likewise, an application has no clear-cut beginning and
  end date: it evolves. It often exists in embryonic
  state as outgrowths of other applications or as
  half-designed ideas, part of which may be stored in the
  knowledge bank. After a while in production, an
  application may turn into a new version or spawn off a
  new application -- again little but an administrative
  difference. This phenomenon was described (in another
  project) as the "evolving application organism".

* Consequently, there is no clear definition of what
  constitutes one application among the collection of
  information in the knowledge bank. This is, again, a
  decision which must be taken outside SMART, involving
  authorisation, versioning, etc. A large portion of the
  information in the knowledge bank is shared between
  users, versions, sessions, which may all be parametric:
  can we indeed talk about one or more applications in
  such a situation?

* Maintenance, in the traditional sense, disappears in
  the environment (except possibly when correcting bugs
  not caught in testing). Migration should present no
  problem since the knowledge bank has no DP-base
  dependent information. (This has actually not been
  validated -- the only DP base used was VM/CMS on the
  IBM S/370 series). Changing application requirements
  (such as new function, new business rules, new
  standards, improved human factors), are merely
  reflected as updates to the knowledge bank. They can
  be regarded as either application preparation or
  production running (the distinction is minimal, as seen
  before).

Activities tagged above as belonging outside SMART were not
explored in the study. Their nature indicate, however, that

they can favourably be expressed, in their turn, as
relationships within the knowledge bank, once the underlying
system provides basic control mechanisms (e.g. password
protection).

An Image-oriented Database System

Yoichi Takao, Shoji Itoh, Joji Iisaka

Tokyo Scientific Center, IBM Japan
Mori Building 21, 1-4-34 Roppongi
Minato-ku,   Tokyo   106   Japan

SUMMARY

This paper describes the concepts and facilities of
interactive database system named ADM (Aggregate Data
Manager), which facilitates the unified handling of image
data and conventional coded data.

The basic idea of this system is that, regarding 'image'
as one of the data-types, each image is treated as a data
element like a number or a character string within the
framework of a relational database. This approach enables
the usage of a simple but powerful relational data language
for storage and retrieval of both coded data and image data
in a unified way. Image data handled by this system are
categorized into two classes, i.e. binary images and
gray-tone images.

For the purpose of image data manipulation, Image Editor
is provided, which supports basic image editing functions
common to most image-oriented applications. On the other
hand, to meet diverse requirements of image processing, an
extension facility is provided, with which users can add
thier own commands and processing functions.

INTRODUCTION

Formatted database systems have contributed to the
information management in terms of conventional coded data,
i.e. numbers and character strings. Especially a
relational model of database (Codd 1970, Chamberlin 1976)
has made an epoch by opening the way for end-users to access
a database easily with the provision of simple but powerful
data model and data language.

On the other hand, there are pressing needs to broaden
the scope of database to other types of data e.g. texts,
graphics, images and so on, because they serve equally
important information as conventional coded data and they
must be also organized systematically to constitue an
effective information system.

As for image data, with the recent progress of hardware
and software technology, a wide variety of applications are
becoming practical, ranging from the business applications
like electronic document filing, electronic mailing, etc.
to the conventional research areas like remote sensing,
medical, etc. And most of these applications require the
database covering both image and coded data. To cover a
wide range of image-oriented applications, an essential
point seems to treat both of them equally at the level of
data model and to provide flexibility of data structuring
using both of them. However, this point is not generally
satisfied by the existing image processing system in which
coded data are treated only in a restricted way.

In order to facilitate unified handling of both image and
coded data, an interactive database system named ADM is now
under development at Tokyo Scientific Center. The database
of ADM is built within the framework of a relational model
mainly to utilize its simple but powerful data language.
ADM stands for Aggregate Data Manager and, here, the more
general term 'Aggregate' is used instead of 'Image' beacuse
it is possible to extend its scope to other types of
aggregate (non-coded or unformatted) data, e.g. texts,
graphics and so on.

SYSTEM OVERVIEW

ADM prototype system now under development functionally
consists of four subsystems, i.e. Interaction subsystem,
Edit/process subsystem, Workspace subsystem and Database
subsystem as shown in FIGURE 1.

Interaction subsystem controls man-machine interaction
through a workstation which consists of an IBM 3277
character display and a DVST (Direct View Storage Tube)
image display. The interface provided here is
command-oriented, and this subsystem analyzes the command

entered through keyboard and then dispatches an appropriate
other subsystem. The screen management of both character
and image display is done also by this subsystem, which
facilitates the scrolling of each screen. As an auxiliary
output device, a color display is also supported, which can
display color code images or natural color images consisting
of red, green and blue components.

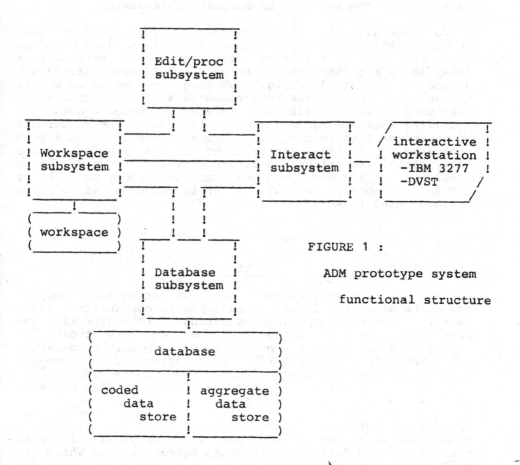

FIGURE 1 :

ADM prototype system

functional structure

Edit/process subsystem consists of Aggregate data editors
and User function manager. For each type of aggregate data,
an editor is provided to facilitate basic editing functions.
For example, image editor supports basic image editing
functions such as extraction, overlay, magnification and so
on, which are common to all image-oriented applications. On
the other hand, to meet diverse requirements of aggregate
data processing, User function manager is provided, through
which users can invoke their own processing functions.

Workspace is a collection of named temporary aggregate data which are kept only during a session. Aggregate data generated by editing/processing or data capturing are firstly stored into workspace and then, with related coded information, stored into database if necessary. Also the aggregate data to be edited/processed must be retrieved from database into workspace beforehand. This approach simplifies the user commands because database commands and edit/process commands can be completely separated.

Database subsystem controls database access and provides an easy but flexible interface to access both coded data and aggregate data in a unified way. From user's viewpoint, a database is a collection of tables (a relational database) and each aggregate data e.g. each image is treated as a data element like the conventional coded data i.e. a number and a character string, although internally coded data and aggregate data are managed separately due to the difference of their characteristics. The kernel component of database subsystem is SYSTEM-R (Astrahan et al. 1976) which is the experimental relational database management system being developed at IBM San Jose Research Laboratory and, hence SEQUEL (Chamberlin et al. 1976) is adopted as a data language also in ADM.

DATABASE

In ADM, a relational model has been extended to support aggregate data like images in addition to conventional coded data i.e. numbers and character strings. This extension has been done just by introducing the new data types for aggregate data and this approach makes it possible to retain the simplicity and flexibility of relational data language, i.e. SEQUEL in our case. Hence, from user's viewpoint, a database is a collection of tables and the data elements which appear in those tables can be not only numbers or character strings but also aggregate data, e.g. images. For clarity of further discussions, we call the conventional coded data which can be elements of the original relational model as atomic data in contrast to aggregate data which are newly introduced by ADM.

The data types of atomic data supported by ADM are integer, real and character string. These data types are just what SYSTEM-R supports and the data of these types are completely managed by SYSTEM-R itself.

Aggregate data are also categorized or characterized by the system-defined data types, but further classified into user-defined sets called domains. Domains of ADM are disjoint each other and comparison of two aggregate data is

valid only when they belong to the same domain. In other
words, domains can be regarded as subdivision of data types.
     Since aggregate data generally have completely different
characteristics, e.g. required storage space, from atomic
data, it is often inefficient or even impossible to manage
both of them equally at the physical storage level. And, in
ADM, aggregate data are generally stored into storage spaces
different from those for atomic data and internal
identifiers of aggregate data are stored into SYSTEM-R
relations along with atomic data to establish the
associations among them. Aggregate data are physically
clustered based on their belonging domains and their
internal identifiers are unique only within the cluster i.e.
the domain. This approach has been implemented as value
sets in PRTV (Todd 1975) or class relations in XRM (Lorie
1974) to manage character strings. Concerning this
approach, there are pros and cons in the case of character
string, but, in the case of aggregate data like images, it
seems to be the only plausible way because the access
efficiency will be heavily affected by physical clustering
and, in order to save storage spaces, it must be avoided to
keep aggregate data redundantly which could happen when the
same aggregate data appears in many places within a
database.

     The data types of aggregate data supported by the current
ADM prototype are as follows:

     - Binary image
     - Gray-tone image
     - Set

     Binary images are stored in compressed forms.
Compression is done through 1-dimensional run length coding
using 4, 8, 12 and 16 bit code words shown below.

(RUN LENGTH)		(CODE WORD)
0- 7	:	0XXX
8- 63	:	10XX XXXX
64- 511	:	110X XXXX XXXX
512-4095	:	1110 XXXX XXXX XXXX

Among various compression algorithms (Huang 1977) this
fairly simple one is adopted as a trade-off between
compression rate and process time because compression and
decompression are all done by System/370. That is; higher
compression rate can be attained if we use 1, 2 or 3 bit
code words for the run lengths of higher probability, but
then, bit by bit processing must be done, which is slow on
System/370. On the other hand, faster compression and
decompression can be achieved if we adopt byte-oriented code
words, but then, compression rate becomes very low. And,
hence, we use 4 bit (half byte) based code words as a
compromise. Another possibility of compression is to use

2-dimensional algorithm which generally achieves higher
compression rate than 1-dimensional one.   But we have not
selected 2-dimensional one because the DVST used as an image
display in ADM is essentially a vector graphic device and
1-dimensional algorithm matches vector graphics very well.
In compressed form of binary image, each line is represented
by a sequence of run length code words and, as a prefix of
each line, the line number and the number of bytes used for
the line are attached in order to make scrolling and editing
easier.

Gray-tone images are currently restricted to only 4
bits/pel (16 gray levels) format or 8 bits/pel (256 gray
levels) format and stored as they are, i.e. without any
compression.
Color images are not supported as a special aggregate
data type. However we can handle color images with the
current ADM, because we can regard a gray-tone image as a
color image by interpreting the pel intensities as color
codes, or we can combine 3 gray-tone images as red, green
and blue components to produce a natural color image.

Comparison operators for binary and gray-tone images,
which can be used in retrieval condition specifications, are
just equality and non-equality based on their internal
identifiers.

The final type of aggregate data is a set. A set is
literally an unordered set of atomic data i.e. numbers and
character strings. The purpose of providing set data type is
to facilitate easy and convenient description of aggregate
data, and, hence, the members of a set are restricted only
to atomic data in ADM. By analogy with the information or
document retrieval systems, it may be clear that sets (of
keywords) are the nice tool for characterization of
aggregate data like images and are also suited to the query
formulation with a high level language like SEQUEL.

Comparison operators for sets are defined based on set
theory as follows:

    a EQUAL TO b
    a NOT EQUAL TO b
    a COVERS ALL OF b
    a DOES NOT COVER ALL OF b
    a COVERS SOME OF b
    a DOES NOT COVER ANY OF b
    a IS COVERED BY b
    a IS NOT COVERED BY b

where, in the current ADM prototype, a is restricted to a
column name and b is restricted to a workspace object name
or an explicit list specification.

Sets are internally represented by binary relations of
SYSTEM-R. That is, for each domain of set data type, a
binary relation is set up, which consists of internal set
identifier column and member column. So, queries containing
set comparison operators can be processed just with query
modifications at the SEQUEL level and those modified queries
can be executed directly by SYSTEM-R.

USER INTERFACE

User interface of ADM is command-oriented, and its
commands can be roughly categorized into the following four
groups:

- Database commands
- Scroll commands
- Workspace commands
- Edit commands

Each group of commands is described in this section.
Commands are also categorized according to the modes in
which they can be used. The top-level mode is major command
mode and, in the followings, unless otherwise mentioned, the
commands are valid in the major command mode.

Database commands are completely SEQUEL statements e.g.
SELECT, INSERT, DELETE, UPDATE and so on. In these
statements, in order to handle aggregate data, the name of
aggregate data held in workspace can be specified in the
same manner as numbers or character strings are specified in
the original SEQUEL. And, as for the set data, it is also
allowed to specify explicitly using list notation, e.g. (
'ANIMAL', 'PLANT', 'MINERAL').
Database queries are done with SELECT statements and the
query results are presented as follows. The retrieved table
is displayed on the character display and, if image columns
exist in it, those columns are filled with identifiers,
while the image corresponding to the top of the leftmost
image column is displayed on the image display. Then ADM
enters table scrolling mode in which users can scroll table
and also choose the image to be displayed on the image
display using the following commands:

- TOP   - RIGHTEDGE
- BOTTOM   - LEFTEDGE
- UP   - RIGHT
- DOWN or NEXT   - LEFT

Users can also use workspace commands described below for
workspace object creation and so on in this mode.
From this table scrolling mode, ADM can further enter

image scrolling mode by ENTER command. In this mode, image scrolling can be done with the same commands as those for table scrolling and, in addition, with MAGNIFY and REDUCE commands.

Workspace commands are used to manage workspace objects i.e. aggregate data held in the workspace and includes the followings:

- CREATE
    Creates a new workspace object from the specified source which is the column name and the identifier when in table scrolling mode or the name of input device e.g. M/T or scanner when in major command mode.
- PURGE
    Purges a specified workspace object.
- REPLACE
    Equivalent to isuue PURGE and then CREATE with the same workspace object name.
- RENAME
    Changes the name of a workspace object.
- LIST
    Displays all the names of current workspace objects along with their attributes i.e. data types and domain names.
- DISPLAY
    Just displays the specified aggregate data with the defualt format and immediately returns to the major command mode. As for image data, display device must be specified.
- SCROLL
    This command is valid only for image data and the difference from DISPLAY command is that ADM enters the image scrolling mode in this case.

Edit commands are dependent upon the type of aggregate data and can be used only in appropriate edit mode. To enter edit mode, users issue the command EDIT along with the name of a workspace object, the type of which determines the appropriate editor to be invoked.

Set data editor is simple and just provides ADD, DELETE and REPLACE (member) as edit commands.

Image editor supports basic cut-and-paste type functions as follows:

- EXTRACT
    Extracts a subimage and discards other portion.
- OVERLAY
    Overlays two images of the same type i.e. binary on binary or gray-tone on gray-tone. As for gray-tone image, replaces the portion of overlaid

image by the overlaying one. As for binary image, two types of overlay is available, i.e. replace and merge (boolean OR).
- SUPPRESS
    Suppresses a subimage and sets this portion to uniform intensity of the specified value.
- REVERSE
    Reverses pel intensities of a subimage, i.e. converts positive image to negative one or vice versa.
- CONVERT
    Converts gray-tone to binary or vice versa. Gray-tone to binary conversion is done by fixed thresholding or by using threshold (dither) matrix (Jarvis et al. 1976). Binary to gray-tone conversion is done by mapping black and white respectively to the specified intensity.
- MAGNIFY
    Magnifies image by integral factor, say n, i.e. expands each pel to n*n pels which all have the same intensity as the original one.
- REDUCE
    Reduces image by integral factor, say n, just by taking every n-th line and every n-th pel in the line.

In these commands, a subimage is restricted only to a rectangle and the corner positions of a rectangle are specified with the cross-hair cursor of the DVST image display.

In addition to these system-supplied functions, user can add their own image processing functions like edge enhancement, smoothing and so on within the framework of the image editor to meet their application requirements.

FORMS-ORIENTED INTERFACE

Forms-oriented interface aims at providing end-users the means to access a database in a very simple manner. Through this interface, a database can be viewed as a collection of documents categorized by their forms and the only things users must know are the names of those forms. Although this interface is less flexible than SEQUEL interface, it seems more convenient for the document filing in office environment.

A form is defined in terms of the scanned image of a blank paper form and the position and type of each field within it. The types of fields are categorized as follows :

- Coded data field :

Numbers or Character strings
Single or Multiple occurrences
(This specifies whether, within the single data
field, only one data item can appear or multiple
data items can appear.)

- Check data field :
Single or Multiple check positions
Exclusive or Non-exclusive
(This specifies whether, among several check
positions within the check field, only one check
mark can appear or multiple check marks can
appear.)

- Image data field :
Binary, Gray-tone or Composite of them

Although we can think of any complex forms, only
single-level field structure is allowed here, i.e. nested
field structure is not allowed and the shape of each field
must be rectangular.

Queries through this interface are done as follows : A
user enters the name of the form i.e. the category of
documents that he needs, requesting the system to display
the corresponding blank form on the image display. Onto
this blank form, he enters the retrieval condition for each
field in a fill-in-blank fashion. After all the necesary
conditions are specified, the retrieval from database
occurrs with all the conditions ANDed. Then he can view the
retrieved documents one by one on the image display.

The documents to be stored into a database are scanned
and segmented into fields based upon the field position
specifications of the corresponding form definition. And
then the data in each field are processed separately
according to the field type. At present, the coded data
must be entered through keyboarding, although ideally they
should be encoded automatically from scanned images with
some recognition logic. As for the check fields, encoding
are automatically done using a data presence check algorithm
in the same manner as optical mark reading. The data within
binary or halftone image fields are simply stored into a
database in compressed or non-compressed forms depending
upon whether they are binary or gray-tone images. However,
as for the composite image fields, it is required to segment
or separate the image into binary and gray-tone portions.
To do this segmentation automatically, some algorithms are
now under development, which extract rectangular gray-tone
image portions embedded in a binary image, mainly based upon
the pel intensity statistics. This segmentation is very
useful from the data compression viewpoint, because
gray-tone images require far more storage than binary ones
and , without this segmentation, images even with small

gray-tone portions must be handled wholly as gray-tone images .

CONCLUDING REMARKS

ADM described in this paper are now partially operational under VM/370-CMS at Tokyo Scientific Center. It is coded mainly with PL/I, but the image handling portion is coded with ASSEMBLER because bit handling of PL/I is unacceptably slow. SYSTEM-R which is used as a basis of ADM is not modified at all and, hence, ADM runs as a usual PL/I application program on SYSTEM-R. At present, image data are stored in CMS files and ADM runs only in single-user mode due to the restrictions of CMS file sharing.

Although we cannot conclude definitely at this stage, from the viewpoint of required disk space and response time, binary images seem to be acceptable but gray-tone images are not. This is mainly because gray-tone images are stored without any compression. Although restricted, as one approach to solve this problem, some experiments are being done to compress gray-tone images using binary representation method such as an ordered dither and so on. However, since this compression is not exact i.e. degrades image quality, the critical point is how to measure image quality and how to determine the trade-off between compression rate and image quality, and this is still an open problem.

Finally, as mentioned in the first section, the scope of ADM is potentially extensible to other types of aggregate data e.g. texts, graphics, and so on. Generally, to add a new type of aggregate data, the following three constructs are required:

- Comparison operators for database retrieval
- Data presentation service
- Editor

And, with the current technology, it seems feasible to provide these facilities for texts, graphics and even for digital voice data (Zeheb et al. 1978).

ACKNOWLEDGEMENT

The authors are very grateful to Dr. M. M. Astrahan and other members of SYSTEM-R group of IBM San Jose Research Laboratory for helping them to install SYSTEM-R at Tokyo Scientific Center.

REFERENCES

Codd E.F. (1970). 'A Relational Model of Data for Large Shared Data Banks', Comm. ACM, Vol. 13, No. 6

Chamberlin D.D. (1976). 'Relational Database Management Systems', ACM Computing Survey, Vol. 8, No. 1

Astrahan M.M. et al. (1976). 'System R : A Relational Approach to Data Base Management', ACM Trans. on Database Systems, Vol. 1, No. 2

Chamberlin D.D. et al. (1976). 'SEQUEL2 : A Unified Approach to Data Definition, Manipulation and Control', IBM J. Res. Develop., Vol. 20, No. 6

Todd S.J.P. (1975). 'PRTV : Peterlee Relational Test Vehicle', Proc. Int. Conf. VLDB

Lorie R.A. (1974). 'XRM - an extended (n-ary) relational memory', IBM Cambridge Scientific Center Report G320-2096

Huang T.S. (1977). 'Coding of Two-Tone Images', IEEE Trans. Comm., Vol. COM-25, No. 11

Jarvis J.F. et al. (1976). 'A Survey of Techniques for the Display of Continuous Tone Pictures on Bilevel Displays', Comp. Graphics and Image Processing, Vol. 5

Zeheb D. et al. (1978). 'The Speech Filing Migration System', Proc. 4th ICCC

"Problems with geo-data"

Bevan Smedley, Barry Aldred

    This paper, which complements that given on "Data base research
and development at UKSC", will consider the implications of handling
geographic data in that context. It surveys the practical and
semantic problems of handling geographic data and summarises the
requirements that must be satisfied by a coherent support system. The
philosophy is presented of a geographic data type, taking an allowed
range of values, and associated with an appropriate set of primitive
operators. The implications of network geographic data are also
considered. The interface between the system and the problem
programmer is discussed, and implementation problems are explored with
reference to conventional geographic processing technology, noting the
inherent advantages and difficulties. An alternative strategy is
outlined which offers the possibility of overcoming some of the
present problems and acheiving significant advantages in terms of
simplicity and performance. The paper concludes with a discussion on
the potential for geo-data in processing as compared with that
required solely for graphic output, and hence considers the true role
of such data in pictorial applications.

IBM UK Scientific Centre,
Athelstan House, St Clement Street, WINCHESTER, Hampshire SO23 8UT,
England.

1. BACKGROUND TO THIS PAPER

This paper is a summary of seven years of research into geographic data processing, undertaken in both the Application Technology and the Advanced Application Departments of the IBM UK Scientific Centre. The research concentrated initially upon the requirements for a geographic information system for use by urban planners to assist them in the problem analysis stage of their work. Subsequently, effort was diverted into a development phase resulting in the production of three CIP's - the first incidently being a non-geographic version of the initial research. Further research was then undertaken into the application requirements of the complete planning process - from problem definition to implementation and monitoring of a chosen plan. (see paper in Geographic Applications - planning section).

Behind all this work is the reliance upon the 'relational' approach, as exemplified by the Relational Data Base Research, also undertaken at Peterlee, resulting in PRTV - the Peterlee Relational Test Vehicle. This paper must therefore be seen in the light of the paper by A.Sanders which describes the relational research and its position with regard to the hierarchical approach of IMS.

2. PROBLEMS OF SUPPORTING GEOGRAPHIC DATA
2.1 Introduction

Geographic data can be defined as information describing spatial location. This somewhat vague definition is in accordance with common usage and allows geography to manifest itself in a variety of forms. For example geographic data may reside on a map in pictorial form , or may be expressed numerically by Cartesian coordinates, or may be expressed indirectly by reference to another spatial description such as house addresses. Throughout this paper the emphasis will be on quantitative geographic data ie. that form of spatial description that can be numerically related to other such values. Qualitative geographic data, such as addresses, which are primarily processed as character strings and whose geographic significance is only secondary are already satisfactorily supported by existing systems and will not therefore be explicitly considered.

There has been a considerable growth of interest in geographic data processing over recent years (UNESCO,1972 NATO,1974) reflecting the current trend towards a quantitative approach not only in scientific disciplines such as geology, metereology, geography etc. (Rhind,1974a), but also in the more practically orientated activities such as public utilities management, highway design and urban planning. It is this latter area particularly that has provided much of the current stimulus for the development of techniques to assist in the handling of geographic information (URISA,1966 PTRC,1971). In this report examples, where given, will broadly relate to urban planning operations.

The rationale for geographic data processing techniques to the various application areas has been given elsewhere, eg. urban planning (DOE,1972 DOE 1973), and will not be duplicated here. However the problems of supporting geographic data have been much less clearly discussed and a proper understanding should form the essential background to any coherent attempt to develop a geographic data processing framework. Accordingly we shall first consider the implications associated with geographic storage and manipulation.

Difficulties in geographic data handling arise from:

- Practical problems concerned with the mechanics of data collection, data processing etc.

- Semantic problems concerned with understanding and interpreting the significance of the information.

Practical problems have received the most attention to date and, although by no means resolved, are at least well understood. Semantic problems are only now coming to the surface, in the wake of the early geographic data handling implementations, and are having a significant impact on subsequent systems designs.

2.2 Practical problems
The practical problems cab be subdivided to correspond to the four major components of the data processing operation:
- Data collection
- Data entry
- Data manipulation
- Data output

Data collection: Problems of data collection vary enormously according to the application area. In urban applications (Weald,1974 Tomlinson,1967) the principal data sources tend to be physical maps although other sources are achieving importance, for example aerial photographs. Difficulties include:

- Availability: getting hold of the basic geographic information at the correct level of detail for the information area of interest.

- Currency: keeping the geographic information up to date such that it reflects the existing situation

- Consistency: the problems of relating data from different sources eg. consistent data conventions, compatible data units etc.

- Completeness: the problems of ascertaining that all data items have been included without duplication or ommissions

- Representation: the difficulties in describing geographic values such that they are amenable to geographic data processing. In general this implies that a qualitative geographic data description be used such as cartesian coordinate referencing (DOE,1972), but other standards are in use, for example grid square encoding (SFIT), or network referencing techniques such as DIME (SCRIS,1970).

- Cost: geographic data collection can be very expensive, particularly when up-to-date maps are not available. Cost justification, of course, depends upon the application, for example in the urban planning field useful figures on collection cost versus subsequent benefits have been compiled in (DOE,1973).

Data entry: Much work has been done on data entry, eg (Trewman,1974 Gardiner-Hill,1971), and a great deal of progress has consequently been made in the translation from source form to internal machine representation. A particularly valuable compilation of data entry techniques is to be found in (UNESCO,1970). Data entry considerations include:

- Hardware devices: the most common instrument used for inputing data from maps is the manual digitiser, although some success has been achieved with line following instruments. Less common is the optical scanner approach. Numeric and character representations, if available, can of course, be input in the usual way.

- Errors: three kinds of errors can be distinguished ie. those present on the source document itself, those attributable to the hardware device and those attributable to operator error. Clearly random source errors cannot be removed automatically, but those due to quantifiable effects, such as distortion of the source document by stretching or shrinkage, can be handled algorithmically. Resolution of the hardware device can be a serious limitation and a cause of error in many applications, but in urban planning, for example, it can generally be neglected. Operator error is the most serious problem in manual digitising and it can become an expensive and time consuming process to correct all the errors introduced in this way. Certain errors can be detected by data processing, eg. range checks on the coordinate values, unclosed areas etc. but the most successful data checking and correction systems have involved interactive editing (Rhind,1974b).

- Cost: the cost of geographic data input is generally very high compared with its non-geographic equivalents. However, in most applications, the geographic data is only a small proportion of the total to be input.

Data manipulation: The problems of data manipulation include:

- Machine environment: conventional data processing equipment does not include support for geography at the machine instruction level; this, of course, contrasts with the more usual character and numeric data. Thus, for example, although there is generally a machine instruction available for multiplication of two numbers, there is not a similar one to perform the intersection of two areas. A suitable environment, provided by a compiler or operating system, may remedy this deficiency, but such provision is rare. Thus the programmer is faced with the difficulties of constructing the processing program from a set of tools not designed with geography in mind.

- Internal representation of geography: the internal representation chosen for the geographic information conditions the ease with which it may be later manipulated. Since there are not, as yet, any recognised standards for geographic encoding this representation is under user control. This can have unfortunate consequences in that a representation may be chosen for one application and not fully take into account future requirements. Moreover it leads to local installation standards, thus forbidding program interchange, and, much more serious, focuses the attention of the application programmer on implementation difficulties rather than user requirements.

- Geographic manipulations: geographic information can be considered in two different lights; as data in its own right, for example, to be manipulated in a manner analogous to numbers, or as index information and used as a retrieval key to other non-geographic data items. It is in this latter role that it has principally been used by urban planners (DOE,1972). In a general context there is no need to restrict geographic, or any other, information to only one of these two roles and indeed it will be shown later that tremendous power and flexibility comes from being able to switch freely between the two (Aldred,1974a). It is possible to specify an almost unlimited number of operations that involve geographic data items; quite clearly the only sensible way to implement these is to attempt to identify a set of primitives such, that when appropiately combined, they achieve the desired scope. Although this has not yet been done commercially for geography it is, of course, standard practice for arithmetic. Any loss of efficiency in implementing complex operations is vastly compensated by the supreme flexibilty offered by this approach (Aldred,1974b).

- Cost: it is invariably true that the data processing costs associated with geographic information exceed those normally associated with conventional data. This is a reflection of the considerable interfacing that has to be performed between the machine functions and their orientation towards numeric and character data and the geographic manipulations required.

Data output: Much effort has been devoted to geographic data output and the range of options open to the user is very wide. Output data formats available include maps to cartographic quality, vector displays of varying accuracies on display screens or hard copy, raster type output on line printers or television monitors through to alphanumeric representations. Output problems can be classified under:

- Hardware devices: the most common data output device is the graph plotter which is suitable for vector output of varying resolutions. Much lower quality output can be obtained by line printer mapping and many packages exist to assist with this process, perhaps the most widely used is SYMAP (Fisher,1968). Visual display units of both an interactive and non-interactive nature exist to produce transient forms of output. Just as for data input alphanumeric representations may be used to convey the geographic information.

- Output format: the output format is not only device dependent but also very user and application dependent. Many different visual representations are available to convey geographic information. Thus contour, conformal, proximal, vector etc. maps can be produced irrespective of the device used on output. The variety of output formats greatly exceeds those suitable for data input.

- Cost: data output costs are very considerably less than data input costs because of the absence of operator participation. Moreover the range of data output devices and formats allows considerable user choice in balancing cost against resolution and visual appeal. The attraction of line printer output is based almost entirely on its extreme low cost by comparison with vector based material.

2.3 Semantic problems

The main semantic problems are associated with:

- Spatial descriptions
- Spatial relationships

Spatial descriptions: Problems of data description arise from the necessary mapping that must occur between the physical reality of the information and its description to be supplied to the system. It frequently happens that the user description is constrained by the software support available, or by the practical problems of data collection etc. Thus it is invariably the case that only an approximate spatial representation is supplied to the computer system.
This mapping process can cause semantic confusion in the areas of:

- Dimensionality: All physical objects are, of course, three dimensional. However in many cases it is unrealistic to attempt to describe them as such, perhaps data to that level of detail is not available, or perhaps such a system complexity is inappropiate. In the urban planning application the third dimension (height) is not required to take part in spatial manipulations (although it may be required for other purposes). In this paper we shall only concern ourselves with a two dimensional representation of three dimensional objects. This is generally taken to be some projection of the 3-D shape on the horizontal (XY) plane. Such a process should result in all physical objects being represented by areas. However this can still bring with it certain difficulties, namely areas so produced are excessively detailed requiring too voluminious a description. It raises only problems of accuracy if the shapes are simplified. One common technique is to replace very small areas with single points, and very thin path shaped areas with lines. Such transformations create new problems, for the geometrical properties of these representations are not those of the original data. Thus it is no longer meaningful to ask for the site area of a property that has been represented by a point. The reverse situation applies to roads, thus the length of a line representation of a road is unambiguous but the length of an area representation of a road is not. More problems can easily be identified, for example if points are to be treated as infinitely small areas then no two can be known to be coincident, they can only be assumed to be coincident within the accuracy to which the system holds data; this is not the case for areas, since their expanse is known it can be stated that two areas overlap. If points are treated as areas of infinitely small dimensions then should it be valid to unite a point with an area to create a new value ? If roads are treated as lines then is the intersection of two roads a point or a line, or at what angle of intersection does a change in status occur ? This kind of exercise rapidly forces the conclusion that in our two dimensional representational world we must either:
1. Divide the representations of physical objects into three classes, viz. points, lines and areas, and not permit composite values. Very clear rules must then be constructed to control their interactions.
2. Treat the representations of physical objects as one class, namely areas and refine our definitions of properties such as length etc. to take this into account.

- Accuracy: Two kinds of accuracy can be distinguished: mapping accuracy that quantifies the discrepancy between physical reality and user representation, and operational accuracy, that controls the errors that may be introduced into spatial values by the geographic manipulations within the system.

A knowledge of the mapping accuracy associated with a data value is necessary if the system is to adequately reflect the behaviour of the real world entity. Thus, if an area of land has been correctly represented, say to within 10 metres, by a rectangle then the system can associate an area of uncertainty 10 metres either side of the supplied rectangular boundary. This subsequently allows the system to deduce that there is a possibility that a certain building lies within the area of land, because it falls within this area of uncertainty; it avoids a definitive result being given on data that was not sufficiently accurate. User point representations are transformed by this approach to circles of uncertainty, the system knowing that the correct spatial value lies within the circle but does not make assumptions as to exactly where.

Since the mapping accuracy is user defined a different mapping accuracy may be associated with each spatial value stored.

Operational accuracy is system dependent. In an ideal world the system should introduce no errors on its own account and hence the factor would be uneccessary. However, experience with numeric data illustrates that this is frequently an impossibility and allowance must be made for errors introduced in this way. In many cases there is a trade-off to be made between accuracy and performance and the ability to control the precision to which an operation is undertaken may often avoid unecessary computation.

- Distribution: It has been implicitly assumed so far that the spatial data has been discrete ie. that it is necessary to identify a particular spatial region, with the later intention of associating it with some other information, for example its name, or its value, or its owner etc. Problems arise when the data is not discrete but continuous, for example height above sea level or housing density. Two separate techniques may be applied if continuous data is to be mapped into a discrete data format suitable for information system processing. Firstly the contour line approach may be used, as on physical maps, although we now face special semantic difficulties ie. although we are using a line representation we are referring to area data. For example a contour line does not define the enclosed area but just the area actually under the line, all other areas to be deduced with reference to the whole set of contours. The second approach is the grid method, whereby the area of interest is divided up into discrete aerial units and a mean value is held for each unit.

Spatial relationships: The problems of spatial relationships are concerned with trying to understand what is implied by a spatial description over and above a purely physical identification of a region of space, that is concepts such as membership of a network, adjacency to other locations, or other spatial relationships between data items. It is important to distinguish between the data relationships that are a direct consequence of the physical data descriptions used, and the other data relationships that must also be maintained, but are a consequence of implicit user assumptions.

Clearly, in order for the system to cater for these assumptions, they must be made explicit. An example of the problem is provided by network data; if the road network is digitised then the intersections are truly common to the road sections meeting at that junction; the intersection spatial locations are not coincidentally the same but actually the same, and this is true irrespective of the accuracy of the representation. Thus, a car at the intersection of two roads is actually on both. A pedestrian subway may happen to have the same spatial description but this does not mean that it is to be considered a part of the road network.

The data relationships can be broken down as follows:

- Reference system relationships: An important spatial relationship to be considered is the one that exists between the descriptive spatial value and the quantitative referencing system in use. The difficulty of representing a three dimensional world in a two dimensional system is that for non-planar spatial regions distortions are inevitable. In most cases such distortions can be ignored but where accuracy is important over large areas then considerable sophistication is necessary to compensate for such effects. Many different referencing systems may be used as a quantitative base, for example planar ccordinates, polar coordinates, mercator projection etc. The choice of base system is, of course under the control of the user; it does not necessarily mean that the system itself must adopt a similar method internally, but that it must allow for the implications of the referencing base.

- Inter-dependent relationships: Many other referencing systems are in vogue besides those that are based on some absolute, or independent scale. The most common indirect referencing system is to specify geographic locations directly in terms of other spatial entities eg. address as a means of identifying property locations, eg. district name as a means of associating the spatial descriptions of enumeration districts. The DIME system of spatial referencing relates all properties to blocks, which are defined in terms of the street network. More subtle variations of indirect referencing exist. Thus, for example, the area of land required by a road may be defined as a strip of specified width along the centre line of the route. The advantage of this approach is that when the route of the road is changed the strip moves along with it, thus avoiding the necessity for the user to respecify or redetermine the parcel of land involved.

Network systems also involve an interdependency of data items. In a network of lines there is actual sharing of locations between the various components at junctions. Special recognition of this allows the system to distinguish the 'flyover situation' where sharing of location does not take place. It might be argued that the necessity for such a distinction is a consequence of the two dimensional representation of the three dimensional world but this is not the case; a network implies a connection between otherwise independent components. Three kinds of network may be distinguished; we shall refer to them as point, line and area networks. Point networks, not very common, can be illustrated by a group of mines that share some of the shafts; thus a spatial component of one spatial value belongs to another. Line networks are generally the best understood and are exemplified by road, rail and public utility links. They too have shared regions but introduce the new concept of flows. The emphasis in line networks is accessibility through the network and capacity. This brings about the need for direction along network links to be understood by the system. Area networks are illustrated by county boundaries or enumeration districts; a region of space is partitioned into spatial units which touch but do not overlap. The boundaries between such areas are shared and this knowledge allows adjacency to be understood and supported.

3. FUNCTIONAL REQUIREMENTS
3.1 Requirement overview

The previous section has presented an overview of the problems associated with geographic data handling. It is quite clear that only a subset of these problems are directly relevant to a computer system, although many of the practical non-DP issues need to be appreciated in order to understand the processing required (thus the problems of data collection influence the processing required on the kind of data that can be collected). From this point on we shall only consider the data processing component of the geographic data handling process.

The primary requirement to be appreciated is that geography is a new type of information that requires its own special computer provision. Although geographic information may be presented as character strings (eg. strings of Cartesian coordinates) it does not have the properties associated with character data. Thus one can, in principle, define a set of values that geographic data is allowed to take and a set of geographic properties that can be exploited by appropiate operators. All posible character string values are not meaningful geographic values, nor are operators such as concatenation or substring meaningful geographic operators (as opposed to union, intersection and difference for example). The situation is exactly parallel to that which exists for numeric data which again is expressed in appropiate character values for visual appreciation and is susceptible to appropiate numeric operators. Thus we propose that the requirement in geographic data processing is for a new data type - locational data - which existing software (compilers and application packages) does not recognize.

If we accept that geographic data is something new that existing interfaces were not designed to handle then we can see a need for the definition of two new interfaces:

1. The external system interface
   - a user orientated interface that maps between the computer user and the data processing system and presents a logical view of geographic objects
2. The internal system interface
   - an interface between the logical view of geographic objects and physical reality of computer objects (ie. a physical mapping of the logical geographic object)

3.2 External system interface

The external system interface should present to the user, in as simple a way as possible, a coherent and logical view of geography. The strategy that we propose is based upon the concept of the geographic data type and therefore includes four essential components:

1. A definition of acceptable geographic data values
2. A definition of the valid conversions between geographic data values and existing non-geographic data values (ie. character, numeric, logical etc.)
3. A definition of the system supported primitive operations on geographic data values
4. A definition of programmer access to internal components of a geographic data value to support functional extensibility

The advantage of this approach is that geographic support is restricted to the handling of geographic values of a pre-defined type with a limited and well known set of properties. Users have a simple interface to understand and are able to combine the basic primitives into complex geographical manipulations of their own choosing. The success of conventional high level programming languages illustrates the wisdom of this approach.

The difficulties lie in establishing the correct definitions such that the scope of the interface is broad enough to span the relevant application areas without being unduly difficult to learn or use, nor be too costly to implement. Although it is not the intention of this paper to provide a definitive description of an appropiate external geographic system interface it may be helpful to state some tentative ideas. It should be understood that these are based upon our previous work in the urban planning area and are subject to certain biases and preconceptions.

It would seem desirable that the interface should possess the following properties:

1. It should have the notion of closure.
There should be a limited number of object types supported (eg. geographic, character, logical etc.) and the various operators and functions should confine their input and output to these values. Thus the geographic output of one operator should be acceptable as the geographic input to another etc. This notion avoids the restrictions that arise when the result of certain operations is in a 'special form' and not generally acceptable for further manipulation.

2. It should be based upon the principle of minimality.
Thus the operations supported should be the minimum set that, when appropiately combined by the user, supply the required function. This avoidance of functional redundancy minimises implementation effort and reduces the quantity of information to be assimilated by the user. It may not contribute to the ease of use in all manipulations but this may well be compensated by the generality provided by a limited number of primitive operations.

3. The interface should support data objects whose values are:
a) Absolute
b) Defined

Absolute expression associates a data object with a value which is independent of all other data objects. Defined expression associates a data object with a particular relationship to other data objects. This relationship is independent of all future operations on those data objects although clearly the value at any point in time will vary to maintain the relationship.

4. The interface should be defined in such a way that allows it to be embedded in existing programming languages.
The value of this provision is that the development effort need only be concentrated upon what is actually new ie. the geographic data type provision. Since the interface includes conversion between geographic and conventional types maximum use can be made of existing support, besides the simple fact that even the most 'geographic application' is going to concern itself with a substantial amount of non-geographic data handling.

5. It should be implemented in such a way that an option remains open for the system to perform deferred operations.
Deferred operations allow the system the possiblity of reordering the operations specified by the user, such that it can achieve the desired result in a more optimal way. Such an approach removes, in part, efficiency considerations from the user and places them on the system. In the light of (2) and (3) above optimisation will probably be an important feature of a successful implementation.

6. It should be possible for the system to be stripped down and optimised for a particular application.
The price paid for generality is generally performance and complexity. In many applications it may be desired to use only a subset of the full interface provision but to do so efficiently. An obvious example is that, were a 3-D capability to be defined, it would be desirable that a 2-D subset could be used that did not excessively expose the suppressed third dimension to the user.

3.3 Internal system interface
There are two basic approaches to the internal representation of geographic values. The 'shape' of such a value may be described by a series of X,Y- co-ordinate values of points lying on the boundary line of the value, using as many points as necessary to describe the shape, and assuming either a straight line or a defined curve between each pair of points. Alternatively, the shape may be described by identifying those cells of a pre-defined grid which contain the shape in question.
In the absence of any hardware implementation of geographic data, the internal interface has the choice of many possible representations based upon those data types which are supported viz. string and numeric. This choice gives rise to problems of incompatibility between implementations, with consequent impact upon the transferability of systems, application packages and/or programmes. The lack of any standard for geographic data at this time does mean however, that the logical view of data can be shared, and even the same physical view can be sustained by varied implementations, only differing in the lower levels of code.
However, the representation of geographic data differs from that of string or numeric data in that it has requirements for secondary information to be recorded alongside the basic data. Some similarity exists with that for varying length strings — for which it is necessary to record both current and possibly, maximum length. A possible representation for geographic data is as varying length

strings - of co-ordinates, but even here there is a need for additional information, which can be considered to fall into four categories.

If a geographic object is to be regarded as a collection of point, line or area segments - or possibly a mixture of these - then there is a need to record the type and other characteristics (e.g. accuracy) for each segment.

The second category of additional information, can be classed as 'advisable' rather than 'essential' or, to apply existing terminology, 'virtual' rather than 'real'. This is information which exists implicitly in the string of co-ordinates, but which needs processing to extract it from the basic data, and which can simplify subsequent geo-processing because of its capacity to summarize the nature of the geographic data.

Examples of such 'virtual' data are the bounds of a geographic object i.e X- and Y- maxima and mimima; critical points on the object which define when the direction along the X- and/or Y- axis changes value; and a coded grid superimposed over the geographic object which extends the box-search capability beyond that of the overall bounds. All this data may be needed in order to be able to apply certain, improved, geographic algorithms e.g. point-in-polygon. The existence of such virtual data can greatly reduce the manipulation processing requirements, depending upon value, and the overhead of additional storage and initialisation processing can often be justified.

The third category of additional information which might be appropriate to accompany the basic data, differs from the second in that there is no additional data to be stored, but rather that additional information is implied. For example, the algorithms could assume that the co-ordinates defining the object are in sequence starting at the minimum X-, mimimum Y- value; that in the case of areas, the co-ordinates are ordered in a clockwise direction and close the area; and that a segment does not overlap itself, and only touches at an end. Such assumptions, if in-built to the algorithms will simplify an already complex piece of logic, and again, speed up processing.

A further assumption could be implicit, in that the accuracy value could be applied to reducing the number of co-ordinates defining the object. The simplest example is of an intermediate point near, but not on the line joining two points. If the distance from this line is less than that accuracy value, then the intermediate point can be ignored. This implicit processing should be applied whenever an object is registered to the system - either on input, or as the result of some geo-processing algorithm - e.g. the union of two area objects.

The fourth category depends upon the nature of objects supported by the system. If both absolute and defined geographic objects are to be implemented, then it may be advantageous to store procedural descriptions of geographic values, defering explication until realisation is necessary. This allows scope for optimisation, the re-ordering of sequences of operations or the substitution of special-purpose algoritms. If defined values are supported, then such a mechanism at the logical level at least is essential - to allow definition of shapes based upon named objects. It also offers much scope at the algorithmic level too - for defined shapes based upon absolute co-ordinates.

Three different approaches to an implementation of an internal system interface will now be described. Two of them have been coded and implemented as a geo-processing package (the first as a research prototype, the second as a CIP). The third approach has not been developed to a similar extent, but is proposed as an alternative method, probably complementary to the others but offering significant advantages in certain situations. None of the three methods to be described meet all of the conditions already prescribed, but each is an attempt to trade-off considerations in the light of practical situations.

The first method was used in the UMS prototype at UKSC between 1972 and 1974. It is based upon co-ordinate data, holding them in system-defined blocks not accessible by the user. Conceptually, the user can access a geographic object, by name or context, but in reality he accesses a pointer to one of three value tables according to the type of the object. The value table maps the object into segment values, recording for each segment the additional information described in categories 2 and 4 above, and a pointer to the segment table. This second table maps the segment into the points which define it, by storing pointers to the third table which records the absolute co-ordinates (as two separate integer values) for each point. This last table contains the known world - as far as the system is concerned - in that it holds the co-ordinates of every point described to the system. Such an approach provides for true network representation as well. Thus points or segments may be shared between values, if appropriate - but this knowledge is not explicit to the system.

Experience with this implementation revealed that the processing overheads associated with three levels of table search to obtain a list of co-ordinates, were too high to obtain satisfactory performance on large data bases. An interim solution was to combine some or all of these system tables at the start of an operation, in order to reduce the number of table searches. Even so, performance was not satisfactory.

Consequently, for the CIP, the decision was taken to remove these levels of indirection by recording the co-ordinates in place, thus removing the ability to share components of spatial descriptions between user-values. It should be noted here that the data management used in both implementations was PRTV - the relational data vehicle developed at Peterlee. This supports scalar objects only, with varying length character strings being handled through a value-set mechanism. Geographic objects were therefore treated as coded character strings, with header information in category 2 above, held as the first part of the string. This implementation did not support defined objects in user-tables, but did allow for variables (single-value items) with certain defined shapes.

Character strings of up to 4K bytes are required for this implementation. This is a theoretical rather than a physical limitation, based upon a restriction to 10 segments per object value, with up to 50 points per segment. This limitation has not been reached in practical use to-date in urban planning applications, except when uniting a series of areas or lines - a fairly rare occurrence.

The third method (Aldred,1974c) is intrinsically different and based upon a radical extension of the grid described in category 2 above. Each grid cell is coded either '0','1' or '2' according as to whether or not it fully or partially shares space with the object being coded. Subsequently, all '1' cells (partial sharing) are

expanded until sufficient accuracy is attained. The bit string which
defines the expanded grid can be compressed quite significantly. In
the limit the storage required being directly proportional to the
boundary length (or line path length) and the accuracy. Such a method
gains over the more conventional approach in the storage and
processing of complex shapes, and can handle mixed objects involving
combinations of points, lines and areas - since all are treated alike.
It loses on simple objects such as a straight line, of whatever
length, which can be defined by the other implementations already
described by just two co-ordinate pairs.

The 'grid' method also requires totally different algorithms for
geo-processing, and offers distinct advantages for the union,
intersection and difference operations on geo-objects, which are
extremely complex where co-ordinate data is concerned, but in this
method are simply bit-string operations. Perhaps the main
disadvantage of the 'grid' method is its inability to convert back to
an accurate set of co-ordinates, or to enable accurate calculations
such as length, or surface area, to be performed. Hence the conclusion
that the approach is complementary to the others, although such a dual
approach has not yet been attempted. One solution might be to maintain
data in the co-ordinate form, and then convert it to the grid
representation for complex operations (e.g. union) converting the
result back to co-ordinate form - with some loss of accuracy to offset
the additional capability.

4. IMPLICATIONS FOR NETWORK DATA

The implementaton of a geographic data type - as points, lines and
areas - has implications for certain applications, in particular those
which are concerned with geographic networks, notably of lines (e.g.
utility facilities) and areas (e.g. districts).

The treatment of lines and areas as described above has no
explicit concept of connectivity or adjacency. This can only be
realized by the use of geo-processing algorithms. Neither do line
values have any concept of direction. Obviously, such additional
information can be held as separate non-geographic attributes under
user-control, but in networking applications such data must frequently
be associated directly with the geographic value. Another issue is
whether to regard a network as a single value - in which case the
design limits will have to be increased greatly - or as a special case
collection of values. The single value approach does not seem
satisfactory in that the additional information (e.g direction, flow,
capacity) is segment not object dependent. One proposal, so far not
implemented, is to designate a block of entries as a network,
processing the entire block as a single value under certain
circumstances, but enabling the maintenance of the additional network
information at the entry, or segment, level. Either a network block
would have standard attributes for this additional information, or
else some form of internal descriptive material will need to be
developed to communicate with the networking algorithms.

Furthermore, the concept of a network block again implies the
necessity for some pre-processing to validate the network definition
for consistency, and closure.

Although networks do not, at first sight, seem to have relevance
to urban planning - the basis for all our work to date (whereas they
do for transportation planning, for example), there are still some
implications for the internal design of the system. There are

significant performance advantages to be gained when performing geoprocessing on networks. For example a point in polygon routine searching against a block of areas can cease once a 'hit' has been found – if that block is a network (since by definition the areas are non-overlapping). The search could also be reduced if the constituent areas are ordered in some pre-defined sequence e.g. in min-X, min-Y order. (A similar improvement could be made with any collection of geo-objects if an agreed form of ordering can be established, and the system left to either maintain this sequence directly, or by means of indices. Geo-data would then correspond even more closely with character and numeric data – which have an established collating sequence).

Intersection and difference operations on network elements are immediately reduced almost to the level of a no-operation, whilst unions will be made much simpler through the elimination of common segment boundaries.

Similarly, when plotting or displaying network data, any implementation which treats segments in isolation will incur unnecessary overheads of duplicate processing, and if the registration of the output device is not perfect, the resultant graphic could be marred by extraneous 'noise'.

5. CONCLUSIONS

The potential for geo-processing must not be minimised. There are advantages to be gained from the conception of a locational data type with the need to store and mainipulate it as such, rather than simply regarding it as a means to an end – graphic output. Because of this, consideration must be paid to the methods for the internal handling of this data. If input and output are the sole requirements then the storage considerations should be such as to relate directly the nature of the hardware involved – raster, vector or character. However, once the need to process locational data is recognized then the implications with regard to data formats must be taken into account in the manner described above.

The objective of this paper has been to widen the acceptance of the concept of the locational data type. The ultimate goal must be to standardize upon a representation format, initially in software, but finally in hardware. If this conference can make the first step along this road then it may turn out to be another giant leap for mankind.

REFERENCES
Aldred,1974a : The Case for a Locational Data Type. IBM UK Scientific Centre Report No. UK0054. Neville Road, Peterlee, Co. Durham, England. 1974.
Aldred,1974b and Smedley : The Urban Management System. IBM UK Scientific Centre Reports No. UK0050, UK0052, UK0053. Neville Road, Peterlee, Co. Durham, England. 1974.
Aldred,1974c : Locational Value Encoding Technique. IBM UK Patent Application No. 55910/74, December 1974.
DOE,1972 : UK DEPARTMENT OF THE ENVIRONMENT. GISP – General Information System for Planning. HMSO. 1972.
DOE,1973 : UK DEPARTMENT OF THE ENVIRONMENT. Manual on Point Referencing Properties and Parcels of Land. HMSO. 1973.
Fisher,1968 et al : Reference Manual for Synagraphic Computer Mapping (SYMAP), Version V. Laboratory for Computer Graphics and Spatial Analysis, Graduate School of Design, Harvard University,

Cambridge, Mass. USA. 1968.

Gardiner-Hill : Digitising and Editing Techniques. International Cartographic Association Commission. III Paris, France. 1971.

NATO,1974 : Proceedings of the Advanced Study Institute on Display and Analysis of Spatial Data. Nottingham, England. 1974.

PTRC,1971 : Urban Data Management Symposia sponsored by PTRC / DATUM / CIUT / CIDC / AFCET / NORDPLAN. Bonn 1971, London 1972, Paris 1973, Madrid 1974.

Rhind,1974a : State of the Art in Geographic Data Processing. IBM UK Scientific Centre seminar on Geographic Data Processing, Peterlee, Co. Durham, England. November 1974.

Rhind,1974b : An Introduction to the Digitising and Editing of Mapped Data. Automated Cartography edited by DALE P.F. British Cartographic Society. 1974.

SCRIS,1970 : US BUREAU OF CENSUS. The ACG/DIME Updating System and Interim Report. SCRIS report No. 4. 1970. Washington DC 20233.

SFIT : Swiss State Data Bank. Swiss Federal Institute of Technology. Zurich, Switzerland.

Tomlinson,1967 : An Introduction to the Geographic Information System of the Canadian Land Inventory. Canadian Department of Forestry and Rural Development, Ottawa. 1967.

Trewman,1974 : Automated Cartography and Urban Data Banks in the UK. 7th. International Conference on Cartography. ICA. Madrid. 1974.

UNESCO,1972 : Symposia on Geographical Information Systems sponsored by the UNESCO and IGU 1972, 1974.

URISA,1966 : Annual Conference Proceedings of the Urban and Regional Information Systems Association, Stockton State College, New Jersey, USA. 1966-1974.

Weald,1974 : The Price and Problems of Information Systems to support Urban and Transportation Planning - with special reference to Data Quality. CIDC / AFCET/ PTRC / NORDPLAN Symposium on Urban Data Management. Madrid 1974.

SOME DATABASE REQUIREMENTS
FOR PICTORIAL APPLICATIONS

Frank Palermo
and
Dan Weller

K52/282
IBM Research
San Jose, California

Abstract

In this paper we discuss some functional and
performance requirements on a database system to support
development of interactive applications dealing with
pictorial data. An effort has been made to specify
requirements that are independent of a specific
implementation philosophy.

Experience using a database system for interactive
applications has led us to determine some features that a
database system should have. The most important requirement
is that the user be able to access data by name, so that
programs are independent of the data that they access. This
implies that the data is self-describing. The database then
provides not only data values, but also a syntatic and
semantic description of the data.

An important use of the database is to interpret the
data in the file as a picture. This use of the database
requires support for ordered files, parameterized files, and
support of expressions as data values.

Some requirements for database support of interaction
in graphics applications are also discussed. The task of
managing tables for interaction is greatly simplified if the
database system provides support for self-describing data.
The response time constraint imposed on the database system
for supporting interactive applications is also discussed.
This includes response time considerations for drawing
complex pictures as well as the high-speed response for the
interaction with the user.

A sample database interface which meets the functional
requirements is included. Further research work is needed
to translate the performance requirements which are stated
in terms of response time for screen activity into database
performance requirements for the basic database functions.

Introduction

Applications which are interactive present a number of requirements on database management systems. These requirements can be divided into two categories: function and performance.

From an application programmers viewpoint, the database system should provide support for a simple tabular representation of data. Each table should be accessible by its name. The representation of a table should also include the syntax and semantics of the data. This is necessary to provide independence between the data and the application programs. Data independence makes it possible to write programs which can use different data tables. An example of this kind of general program is the interpreter which is used in the Picture Building System6.

The user should be able to specify the order of rows in a table. This is particularly important in graphical applications where a sequence of (x,y) coordinates represents a polygonal figure.

Many geometrical applications require that objects are related so that as one of the objects moves, the related objects also move. This can be accomplished by allowing the values in the table to be written as expressions involving a base value. There is also a need to have data items in a table maintain a common value. When this common value is changed all the data items dependent on it are also changed.

Parameterized tables allow an application to represent a class of similar objects with one table. Thus the number of different tables to describe a set of objects can be significantly reduced.

To support interaction the application programmer has to keep track of the images displayed on the screen. When the user selects an item on the screen, the application program must identify the selected item and perform the appropriate action to comply with the users request. These functions will be called the identication and linking functions. The identification function can be performed by using standard database retrieval functions tf the description of the items on the screen are stored in a table. This type of table has a high-speed response requirement. Because this requirement is not feasible for all tables, the database system should allow the application developer to specify the response requirement for each database table. The linking function can also use standard data base support if the information about the appropriate system responses to user actions are included in data base tables. When interactive application designers begin to use standard database support, the task of creating new interactive programs will be greatly simplified.

It is still an open question whether database systems can meet the response time requirements needed to support interactive applications. From our experience we have

identified some requirements and some features that we have
found useful in interactive applications. These
requirements include response time requirements that are
necessary to maintain smooth and meaningful interaction with
end users. When this is done the creation of interactive
applications will be greatly simplified.

In the following sections we discuss some requirements
of a database system to support a high-level application
development system such as the Picture Building
System126. Database interfaces have been designed for
the most part with little knowledge of the end application.
Here we discuss requirements from the application point of
view. Hopefully it will induce application developers to
present their database requirements, and that the resulting
dialog will be useful to database designers as well as
application programmers.

Data and Program Independence

A basic requirement of database systems is that the
application programmer should be able to write application
programs that are independent of the data stored in the
database.

Data used by an application program has four
components:
1. The data itself,
2. The syntax (format) of the data,
3. The semantics (meaning) of the data,
4. The access path to the data.
Usually the second, third, and fourth components are
implicitly incorporated into the program and the database
only keeps track of the data itself. The format of the
data, its meaning, and its access path must be known to the
application program.

If all these components of the data are stored in the
database, and the data can be retrieved by name (knowledge
of access path not needed), the data is said to be
self-describing. If the data is self-describing then the
application program need not keep track of the data's
syntax, semantics, or access paths. Self-describing data is
a necessary ingredient in achieving independence between
programs and data.

Database Organization

The database should consist of a set of named segments,
each of which is a collection of named tables. Each table
consists of an ordered set of uniform records. Each record
consists of a collection of named fields. Each record is a
row in the table and each field is a column in the table.
The reason for uniform records is that it allows a simple
tabular view of the data.

Information about each field is kept in the database along with the data. This field description information consists of at least the following:
1. The name of the field,
2. The data type,
3. The data length,
4. the semantic description.

At least the following data types should be supported: real numbers, integers, text strings, and bit strings. We have found that single precision (32 bit) floating point numbers and integers suffice for most applications. In addition character strings of up to 256 characters and bit strings of up to 2048(2K) bits seem to be sufficient. However; the system should allow the user to extend the types of data that are supported by the data base. Thus an application developer should be able to define extended precision floating point numbers and complex numbers as data types that are stored in the data base. In addition, data types which are vectors of (x,y) coordinates should be supported for geometrical applications involving polygonal figures. For adding data types to the system, the application developer should be able to define the data type, specify its set of valid operations, and add the appropriate support programs.

As an example consider the following triangle:

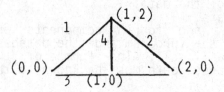

The triangle can be represented by the following table named 'TRIANGLE' with four rows and five columns:

	xstart	ystart	xend	yend	operation
1)	0	0	1	2	line
2)	1	2	2	0	line
3)	0	0	2	0	line
4)	1	2	1	0	line

The following table gives the attributes of the columns in the table 'TRIANGLE':

name	data type	data length	semantics
xstart	real	4 bytes	x-coordinate
ystart	real	4 bytes	y-coordinate
xend	real	4 bytes	x-coordinate
yend	real	4 bytes	y-coordinate
operation	integer	4 bytes	xy-operation

Since ordering is an important concept in interactive applications, the database must support ordered tables efficiently. Since ordering is used to distinguish records, a table may contain duplicate records. As an example of the need for ordering consider the following. A line figure can be described by giving a set of points describing the corners of the figure in the order in which they are to be connected. Even though there are other representations that would not require ordering, it would distort the application programmer's perspective to force this unordered point of view.

Data Definition and Manipulation

A user should be able to interactively define a table by specifying the name of the table, the number of fields, and the attributes of the fields. He should also be able to define a table by specifying that it have the same structure (fields and attributes) as another table.

Before data can be read from a database or written into a database, the source and target must be specified. The user specifies the source and target by binding fields of a table to program variables. The table is specified with an OPENSCAN command. The user may 'bind' each field of a table to a different program variable, or may 'bind' all the fields of a table to a vector. Selection of a record or set of records is either by record number (remember the records in a file are ordered), or by a match with some of the field values or ranges of field values. The scan points to the selected records.

After binding and selection have been done, a user may read, write, insert, update, or delete the selected records. When a user issues a 'GET' command, the bound program variables are filled in with the values from the corresponding fields in the selected records. When a user issues a 'PUT' command, the bound fields in the selected records are filled in with the values from the corresponding program variables. The data transmission is either direct or with conversion to the data type specified for the program variable. The user should also be able to read or write a record from a buffer or a structure with no conversion or binding. After the processing of a file is completed the user may issue a CLOSESCAN command, and possibly a SAVE command to save any database changes.

Consider the example of reading all the values of the fields 'xstart' and 'xend' in the file 'TRIANGLE' into the vectors VECTOR1 and VECTOR2. This can be done by using the following sequence of commands:

```
OPENSCAN('TRIANGLE',SCAN)
```

```
BIND(SCAN,'xstart',VECTOR1)
BIND(SCAN,'xend',VECTOR2)
SELSCANVAL(SCAN,'*')
GET(SCAN)
CLOSESCAN(SCAN)
```

The '*' in the 'SELSCANVAL' command means that all the records are to be selected. By changing the second argument of the 'SELSCANVAL' command one could read one record, a subset of records, or the whole file as shown here.

Interpretation of Data

In graphical applications, the data in the database can be used to describe a picture. In some sense a table in the database replaces a subroutine to draw a picture in a traditional graphics system. For each set of semantics (graphics is one set) an interpreter has to be written. PBS has an interpreter for the 50 graphical meanings (semantics) that have been defined. There are graphical meanings for rotation, scaling, shifting, X and Y position, etc.1. The graphical meaning of 'call' which names another table enables one to structure tables or pictures hierarchically.

Normally one only reads and writes data in a database, but now because the data in the database is interpreted to draw a picture, the need arises for data items to be expressions, for data items to take their value from parameters, or for two or more data items to have the same value. Some manipulations can be done by scaling, shifting and rotation of the file 'TRIANGLE', but allowing parameters with expressions allows the full power of analytic geometry for expressing manipulations.

For example, consider the following parameterized version of the triangle picture shown above:

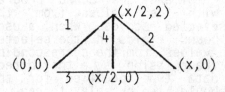

We could store it in a file 'PTRIANGLE(x)' as follows:

	xstart	ystart	xend	yend	operation
1)	0	0	x/2	2	line
2)	x/2	2	x	0	line
3)	0	0	x	0	line
4)	x/2	2	x/2	0	line

where 'x' is a parameter, and 'x/2' is an expression. Drawing 'PTRIANGLE(2)' gives the same picture as drawing 'TRIANGLE'.

The picture shows that line 1 is connected to line 2, but that information is not contained in the file. If we move the first line not realizing that the '2' in the second line should also change then the lines 1 and 2 will no longer meet in a point. We need to have the data value '2' of the second line reflect that it is the same as the data value '2' of the first line. The actual value could be stored in one data value and references made to it in other data values. One way to represent this is to introduce local names as follows:

	xstart	ystart	xend	yend	operation
1)	0	0	x/2	a=2	line
2)	x/2	a	x	0	line
3)	0	0	x	0	line
4)	x/2	a	x/2	0	line

Now if the first line is moved by changing the value of 'a', all lines connected to it are also moved.
When the data items to be identified are in different files then the "fully qualified" name of the data value should be used. The display of Bob's salary from a file with employee's salaries can be done in the following manner:

	xstart	ystart	operation	value
1)	10	20	output	EMPLOYEE.SALARY(Bob)

When this file is interpreted, the actual salary for Bob from the SALARY field of the EMPLOYEE file is displayed. Thus we can see the need for parameters, expressions, and two or more data items having the same value.

Correlation Data Management

Graphical data in a table can be represented as a picture on a display terminal by the interpreter. Correlation is the identification of a database item by pointing at its pictorial representation on a graphics terminal. Correlation is the basis for interactive graphics.
When a picture segment is presented to the user, information about the various items on the screen which are selectable is stored in a set of tables called the correlation tables. These tables contain information such as
1. The item name of the displayed item,
2. Its physical position on the screen,
3. The type of item(e.g. point,line,polygonal

line etc
4. Information about its relationship to other
   records in the data base
   (the access path to it or its display tree address)

For each pictorial segment in the display there is a
correlation table. In addition, there is a table to keep
track of the pictorial segments. This leads to a set of
interrelated tables which represents the picture and the
possible interactions available to the user.

A number of problems and requirements for supporting
interactive applications are discussed in reference 5. The
problems are stated from the point of view of the
application programmer. They include
   1. handling a large number of selectable items,
   2. identifying the structure of the selected item,
   3. maintaining meaningful tagsfor the selected item,
   4. resolving ambiguities among selected items,
   5. dynamic control of selection sensitivity,
   6. selecting an object by pointing inside of it.

If the management of the correlation tables is handled
by a database management system, the identification function
can be treated as a query on the correlation tables which
requests the data access path for each item that satisfies
the query. In case of multiple items meeting the query
specification the number of items which qualify is returned
and further qualifications can be appended to reduce the
qualifying list, or the list can be examined one item at a
time. The total set of access paths for qualified items can
also be obtained.

The problem created by a large number of selectable
items should be handled by a data management system. Such
systems typically manage large tables by getting storage
from the system when required and returning storage to the
system when no longer needed. This presents a requirement
on the data management system to manage the correlation
tables and provide efficient retrieval from them.

The table entry for each selectable item should be the
data access path, a vector of user understandable
identifiers , one for each leg of the structure tree for the
leaf item. In this case whenever an item is selected by the
user, the application program creates a query asking for the
access path vector for each item which satisfy the query.

For example, the query could be to return the access
path vector for all items which lie within .5 units of the
selected x and y coordinates of the selected position.

Ambiguities can be resolved by providing queries which
have fuller restrictions on the selected item. Thus for
example when the application program finds that more than
one item satisfies the original query, the distance
criterion could be made more restrictive or the query could

specify that some other attribute of the selected item have
a specific restriction for that item to qualify.   This
method thus allows for the dynamic control of selection
sensitivity.

The query which enables the application program to
determine when the user selected a point inside a fixed
object can also be formulated. For example in the case of a
rectangle the query would ask for all items which are
rectangles and whose lower coordinates are less than the
selected coordinate point and whose upper coordinates are
greater than the selected coordinate point. (note that the
rectangles are assumed to be parallel to the coordinate axis
in this case.

With database support for correlation the process of
correlation can be greatly simplified5. The ability of
the database to generate identifiers (GENID) for records and
to select a record based on such an identifier (SELID) is
sufficient to support the correlation process. When a file
is interpreted identifiers for the records can be generated
and stored. After the user interacts with the picture the
stored identifier can be used to manipulate the correlated
item.

Performance requirements

Interactive applications have certain response time
requirements which can be translated into response time
requirements for database functions. The user must be able
to use any of the functions in the listed interface
interactively.

In terms of what the end user sees in interactive
graphics applications, it has been observed that the display
of a picture on the screen should be done in less than one
second if the picture is a simple one (less than 100 lines.)
If the picture is more complex containing about 1000 lines
,for example, it should not take more than two seconds for
the entire picture to be completed. There should be at
least a part of the picture generated in less than one
second. The point is that there should be some activity on
the users screen throughout the process so that the user
does not lose interest. For raster data similar
requirements hold. Thus the screen should be filled in two
seconds with some screen activity taking place in less than
one second. The translation of this type of requirement
into database requirements is not simple. However a first
estimate is that the average time for retrieving the

response to a simple query should take less than 10 milliseconds.

The data stored in the data base that is used for interaction has a much more demanding requirement in terms of response time. When a user selects an item on the screen, the appropriate pick table must be searched and the selected item identified and its tag returned to the application program. Here the requirement is that this operation must take less than 100 milliseconds so that the redisplay of the screen for the new information can take place within the required two second response time.

Summary

Experience using a database system for graphic applications has led us to determine a number of features that a database system should have. The most important requirement is that the user be able to access data by name, so that programs are independent of the data that they access. This implies that the data is self-describing. The database then provides not only data values, but also a syntactic and semantic description of the data.

The database is organized as named ordered files. Data is manipulated by binding program variables to files by means of scans. Each scan is used to select a subset of the file. An important use of the database is to interpret the data in the file as a picture. This leads to the need for database support of parameterized files and expressions as data values.

For interactive applications, the drawing of a complex picture places response time requirements on the data base. For drawing a picture, the user should see a response within one second. For more complex pictures, there should be a smooth presentation with the initial part of the picture drawn within one second and additional parts being completed with no more than one second delays between activity on the screen.

For the tables that provide for user interaction, the retrieval time for performing the identification function should be very short. These tables should be given priority with respect to search algorithms so that the overall performance requirements can be met.

Reference

1 Weller, D. L., Williams R., 'Graphic and Relational Data Base Support for Problem Solving', Computer Graphics SIGGRAPH-ACM, Vol. 10 No. 2, 1976, pp. 183-189.

2 Meder, H. G., Palermo, F. P., 'Data Base Support and

Interactive Graphics', <u>Proc. Third Int. Conf. on Very Large Data Bases</u>, Oct. 1977, pp. 390-402.

3 Moorhead, W. G., 'GXRAM, Relational Data Base Interface for Graphics', IBM Research Report RJ 1735, 1976.

4 Williams, R., 'A Survey of Data Structures for Computer Graphics Systems', Computing Surveys, ACM, Vol. 3, No. 1, March 1971, pp. 1-21.

5 Weller, D. L., et. al., 'Software Support for Graphical Interaction', IBM Systems Journal, 1979.

6 Palermo,F.P.,Weller, Dan, 'Picture Building System', COMPCON Spring '79, Feb.,1979.

Appendix 1 - Database Interface

Definition
INVOKESEGMENT(segmentname) - invokes an old segment or
                                creates a new one
CLOSESEGMENT(segmentname) - closes the named segment
DELSEGMENT(segmentname) - delete the named segment
DEFFILE(filename,segmentname) - define a file in the named segment
DELFILE(filename) - delete a file in the current segment
ADDFIELD(filename,fieldname,datatype,length,semantics) - add a field
DELFIELD(filename,fieldname) - delete a field
SAVE - save the current segment

Binding
OPENSCAN(filename,scan) - returns a scan identifier and selects the
                                first record
CLOSESCAN(scan) - terminates the specified scan
BIND(scan,field,variable) - bind a field to a scalar or vector
BINDALL(scan,variable) - bind all the fields to a vector or matrix
UNBIND(scan) - unbinds all the fields of the file
UNBINDFIELD(scan,field) - unbinds a single field

Selection
SELNUM(scan,number) - selects the record specified by the
                            record number
SELVAL(scan,values) - selects the record or records whose
                            bound fields match the 'values'
SELNEXTINFILE(scan) - selects the next record in the file
SELID(scan,identifier) - selects the record associated with the
                            identifier generated by a GENID call

Input/Output
GET(scan) - gets the selected records from the database into the
                bound variables
PUT(scan) - creates a record or records from the bound variables
                after the last selected record
UPDATE(scan) - updates the selected records from the bound variables
DELETE(scan) - deletes the selected records
READINTO(scan,address) - reads a record into contiguous memory,
                            starting at 'address'
WRITEFROM(scan,address) - creates a record from contiguous memory
                            starting at 'address'
UPDATEFROM(scan,address) - updates a record from contiguous memory
                            starting at 'address'

Information
NAMECUR(scan,filename) - returns the name of the file the
                            scan points to
DEGREE(filename,degree) - returns the number of fields
SIZE(filename,size) - returns the number of records in a file
FIELDNAMES(filename,fieldnames) - returns a vector of the
                                field names of a file
FIELDDES(filename,fieldname,fielddes) - returns the data type,
                                length, and user value

for the specified field

Correlation Support
GENID(scan,identifier) - generate an identifier for the selected
                        records
NAMEFILE(identifier,filename) - returns the name of the file which
                                holds the identified records

Utility
LOAD(filename) - creates a database file from external source data
DUMP(filename) - creates external source data from a database file

AQL: a Relational Data Base Management System and its Geographical Applications

F. Antonacci, L. Bartolo, P.Dell' Orco, V. N. Spadavecchia

IBM Italia, Centro Scientifico - v. del Giorgione, 129 ROMA (Italy)

Abstract

AQL (acronym for: A Query Language) is a Data Base
management system based on n-ary relational model. It has
been designed to help the nonspecialist in data processing
in solving interactively unstructured problems, in building
applications, in running simulations. A rich pattern of
default options, synonyms, attribute definitions, inference
and a menu facility provide an easy-to-use interface which
combines data extraction facility and computational
capabilities of the host programming language (i.e. APL).
The extension of such a system to cover the geographic data
requires extensions in both the conceptual schema and the
language to represent and express concepts pertaining to the
geographic nature of data. Also, definition mechanism are
found to be extremely useful to represent aggregate concepts
in geographic data processing. The general characteristics
of AQL are widely discussed in (ANT78): here they will be
reviewed briefly, then the geographic extension will be
discussed.

1. INTRODUCTION

The relational model of data, first proposed by Codd in (COD70) has provided the non-computer professional user a powerful means to approach and solve unstructured problems, i.e. those which have imprecise solution criteria and multiple solutions, which have to be found heuristically, during the problem exploration phase. In fact, the simplicity, simmetry and semantic completness of the data model allows the user to think in terms of named tables, on which he can execute the familiar operations of table searching and extracting. A number of languages to support this process have been proposed, namely QBE (ZLO75), AQL (ANT78) and SEQUEL (CHA74). Among these, AQL has a number of features which provide a value added in terms of intelligence and flexibility avalaible to the user-regardless he is a computer specialist or not. These features are:
1. Descriptiveness, which allows the user to select data only by specifying the properties of the result data, leaving the system the task of how to get them;
2. Richness of default options, which allows the user not to specify large parts of the query, which is then completed by the system;
3. Interactive query completion facility, which complements default options in case of ambiguous queries;
4. Inference mechanism, which takes care of the navigation among relations;
5. Possibility of using synonyms and definitions for attribute names;
6. Open-endedness, which allows the user both to extend the language and to define synonyms for keywords, on the base of pre-existing functions, provided that the syntax is preserved.
An extensive description of AQL, which is based on APL (IBM1, IBM2, IBM3) and preserves its environment all along the query, is found in (ANT 78): here, a brief recap will be given, then the extensions proposed to cope with geographic data will be exposed. To help exposition, a set of examples will be used, referring to a data base (called: LANDUSE) containing the following relations:

POLZONE (ZID, NAME, POP, GPROD, AREA)
AGRIZONE (ZID, NAME, PRODUCE, PRODUCTIVITY, AREA)
GEOZONE (ZID, NAME, TERTYPE, AREA)
ADMIN (ENTITY, LEVEL, PARENT)
CULTIVATION (CROP, LEVEL, SPECIES)
INDUSTRIES (ZID, NAME, TYPE, LOCATION, PERSONNEL)

(Other relations will be introduced as soon we shall discuss the treatment of geographic data). The relation POLZONE represents the political zones (e.g. cities), of which ZID represents the zone identifier, NAME its name, POP the number of inhabitants, GPROD the gross product of that zone, AREA its area POLZONE is the least distinguishable political (or administrative) entity, which can be, for example, a city, a quarter, or a district: in our example, we choose it to be a city. The relation AGRIZONE is analogous: except that now we speak of PRODUCE (by which we intend the kind of crop produced) and PRODUCTIVITY (in terms of quantity of that crop per year). To study the soil nature, the relation GEOZONE is used, where TERTYPE is indicating the type of soil zone. The relation ADMIN represents the administrative hierarchy: ENTITY is the identifier of the administrative unit (e.g. city) PARENT is the identifier of the administrative unit at the immediately upper level (e.g. province), while LEVEL is the level of ENTITY in the hierarchy. Same considerations apply for the relation CULTIVATION, where CROP stands for the basic entities, and SPECIES stands for the upper level entities. The relation INDUSTRIES describes the industrial locations: ZID is the zone identifier, NAME is the industry name, TYPE is the type of processing performed in that industry, LOCATION is the ZID of the POLZONE where that industry is located, and PERSONNEL carries the number of people working for that industry. The phases of query, update and creation will be illustrated separately.

2. QUERY

The simplest query in AQL is the one requesting data from one attribute of a table, subject to a given condition on that attribute or another one. For example:

Q1. Zones where corn is grown

```
        AQL 'LANDUSE'
(NAME OF AGRIZONE)
WHEN
PRODUCE EQ CORN
```

The Data Base name (LANDUSE) is used as right argument of the function AQL, used to invoke the system, which unlocks keyboard and waits for input. The function WHEN has as its right member the condition list which, in our case, consists of the only condition: ''PRODUCE EQ CORN''. The system automatically refers PRODUCE to AGRIZONE, finds the occurrences in it of 'CORN' and then finds in the target list, left member of the function WHEN, the corresponding agricultural zone names. Referring attributes to the proper relation is only one of the possible default actions undertaken by the system; others can be seen by the following example:

Q2. Personnel working in industries

```
     AQL 'LANDUSE'
PERSONNEL
```

The system refers PERSONNEL univocally to INDUSTRIES, then, as no selection condition has been specified, all the values are taken. If we want to know the total number of employees in industries, we can sum up those numbers:

Q3. Total number of people working in industry

```
     AQL 'LANDUSE'
SUMUP PERSONNEL
```

Conditions may be linked one another by means of the logical connectors AND and OR; also NOT can be used. An example follows:

Q4. Name of zones where corn is grown which are larger than 1 million square meters

```
     AQL 'LANDUSE'
(NAME OF AGRIZONE)
WHEN
(PRODUCE EQ CORN) AND AREA GT 1000000
```

Queries may span more than one relation: this corresponds to a join operation, in terms of relational algebra (COD70). This can be seen in the following example:

Q5. Name of industries located in cities with more than 500000 inhabitants

```
     AQL 'LANDUSE'
(NAME OF INDUSTRY)
WHEN
LOCATION ISONEOF (ZID OF POLZONE)
               WHEN POP GT 500000
```

The inference process allows the user to express queries in more concise form, avoiding the navigation through relations: by use of inference,   the preceeding query may be expressed as follows:

        AQL 'LANDUSE'
(NAME OF INDUSTRY)
WHEN
POP GT 500000

and it will be restated by the system in the complete form. In this case, POP, although not belonging to INDUSTRY, may be univocally referred to POLZONE: the system does it, then the difference between the condition and target relations (POLZONE and INDUSTRY, respectively) triggers the inference mechanism. Whenever the attribute in the condition may be referred to more than one relation, and none of them is the target relation, the menu mechanism is triggered, like in the following example:

Q6. Total grown area

        AQL 'LANDUSE'
SUMUP AREA

In this case, no reference for AREA is possible, and the system prompts the user with a menu:

CHOOSE THE NUMBER CORRESPONDING TO THE PROPER RELATION
1. POLZONE
2. AGRIZONE
3. GEOZONE
▢:

The user states that the relevant relation is the second, types 2, and has the query completed and executed by the system.
The open-endedness characteristics of AQL - i.e. the possibility of expanding the language by adding new user-defined keywords - is particurarly useful whenever a query is frequently used and/or it is convenient to refer to it by a single word. This can be seen in the following example.

Q7: Define a function which gives   the upper - level administrative entity of a given one (for example: the province, region, etc... capital)

Supposing to call this function MAINCITY, the user will write

```
        'Z←MAINCITY CTY' AQLDEF 'LANDUSE'
(PARENT OF ADMIN)
WHEN
ENTITY EQ CTY
```

The functi̇ A AQLDEF builds and stores a function, named
MAINCITY, which executes the given query. In this way we
could ask, for example:

```
Q8.     MAINCITY 'PONTEDERA'
PISA
```

which is the capital of the province where Pontedera is
found; while, if we ask:

```
Q9.     MAINCITY 'PISA'
FIRENZE
```

which is the capital of the region where Pisa is found. We
can also build a function which gives the national capital
of any given city - i.e. the transitive closure of the
preceeding relationship - and call it CAPITAL:

```
Q10.    ∇Z←CAPITAL CTY; CAP
[1]Z←CTY                         SET UP THE RESULT
[2]→0 IF EMPTY CAP←MAINCITY CTY  IF CAP HAS NO CAPITAL THEN
                                 QUIT
                                 THAT'S THE CAPITAL
[3]Z←CAPITAL CAP                 ELSE, GO UP ANOTHER STEP
∇
```

We can now ask the capital city for Pontedera:

```
Q11.    CAPITAL 'PONTEDERA'
ROMA
```

through PISA and FIRENZE. Suppose now that we want to know
the total area grown with each crop: in this case, the
grouping facilities of AQL will be used, together with some
arithmetic function:

```
Q12.    AQL 'LANDUSE'
(DISTINCT CROP) CAT SUMUP (AREA OF AGRIZONE)
                        GROUPBY
```

CROP

The function DISTINCT takes each crop from the relation
AGRIZONE only once this list is catenated with the subtotals
of grown areas, grouped by CROP.

3. UPDATE

In AQL, the update operation is very simple, as it is
performed by two functions: namely, ADD (which will be seen
in the Data Definition section) for insertions, and REPLACE
for replacements and deletions, considered as a replacement
with the empty vector. The right argument of REPLACE
specifies, by means of a query, the places where the new
values will be written and its left argument carries the new
values. An example follows:

U1. Change, accordingly to a specified table, the locations
    of industries which are near to cities with more than
    1000000 inhabitants and which employ more than 500
    workers

        AQL 'LANDUSE'
NEWLOC REPLACE (LOCATION OF INDUSTRY)
                WHEN
                (PERSONNEL GT 500) AND
                POP GT 1000000

NEWLOC is the name of a table (APL variable) which contains
th e identifiers of the new locations for those industries.

4. DATA DEFINITION

Data definition in AQL is performed by a set of functions,
whose sintax is analogous to that of query. These functions
allow the user to create, modify and drop relation schemata,
add tuples to already defined relations, define, store,
modify and drop objects of the conceptual sub-schema (i.e.
views and copies). Let us see how a relation is defined:

D1. Define the relation INDUSTRIES (with the attributes
    already seen).

        AQL 'LANDUSE'

DEFINE (ZID WITH NAME WITH TYPE WITH LOCATION WITH
PERSONNEL)
OF INDUSTRIES

The system interacts with the user, asking him to specify
the features of each attribute (i.e. type, definition - if
it is a defined attribute...), then creates the schema for
the relation INDUSTRIES. The same function DEFINE may be
used to add a new attribute, while for dropping, we proceed
as follows:

D2. Drop the attribute PERSONNEL from INDUSTRIES

AQL 'LANDUSE'
DROP PERSONNEL OF INDUSTRIES

Note that this would drop also data possibly contained in
PERSONNEL Suppose now that we want to fill the relation,
i.e.:

D3. Add a number of tuples to the relation INDUSTRIES

AQL 'LANDUSE'
(ALLINFO OF INDUSTRIES) ADD VALUES

The function ALLINFO stands for all the attributes of the
relation INDUSTRIES, connected with the function WITH, while
the object values stands for one of the following:
1. Name of a given file ("bulk input" file)
2. List of names of APL variables, each ordinately
   corresponding to each attribute of the relation
3. An explicit result of a query
4. The empty vector, which means that data will be inputted
     from the terminal, in which case the system prompts the
     user with the attribute names and waits for data.
To experiment the effects of some changes in the system, it
is convenient to create a copy of the relation upon which
the changes have to be seen. For example:

D4. Make a copy of the zones grown with corn

AQL 'LANDUSE'
((ZID1 WITH NAME1 WITH PRODUCT1 WITH AREA1) OF CORNZONE)
ISCOPYOF
((ZID WITH NAME WITH PRODUCTIVITY WITH AREA) OF AGRIZONE)
WHEN
PRODUCE EQ CORN

The function ISCOPYOF builds and stores the relation
CORNZONE; changes on AGRIZONE will have no effect on
CORNZONE and vice versa. If we want this effect, we merely
make a view:

D5. Make a view of the zones where corn is grown

     AQL 'LANDUSE'
((ZID WITH NAME WITH PRODUCT WITH AREA) OF CORNVIEW)
ISVIEWOF
((ZID WITH NAME WITH PRODUCTIVITY WITH AREA) OF AGRIZONE)
WHEN
PRODUCE EQ CORN

In this case, only the selection condition(s) are stored,
and any query to CORNVIEW will be translated into a query to
AGRIZONE; in this way, updates on AGRIZONE will be reflected
on CORNVIEW. Next part will describe the impact of
geometric properties of data on the data base management.

5. INTRODUCING LOCATIONAL DATA- IMPACTS ON THE CONCEPTUAL SCHEMA AND THE LANGUAGE.

It happens, quite often, that the physical reality which is
modeled by the data base is, in a certain way, dependent
upon the location(s) where the phenomena described take
place. Examples of these facts range from the case of a
transportation network management to the problems related
with the land use and the urban plan management. In these
cases the very shape and conformation of objects is
relevant, concepts like "position" and "distance" are
central, and graphical output is the rule rather than the
exception. Storing these data in a relational data base
requires the conceptual schema be prepared to accept such
concepts as "point", "line", "surface", etc...., beside the
usual concepts, referred to the specific location.
Conceptual schemata, similar to this one and involving the
"point", "line" and "surface" data types may be found, for
example, in (ALD74). This, in turn, involves the problem of
finding a suitable representa tion of these concepts, in
order to extract the relevant information from them and
exploit the information which can be implicit. Also, this
means that a suitable reference system has been chosen (with
the possibility of dynamically change it), a scaling and a
projecting facility are supported by the system, and that a
general space description facility is provided that can
describe both space in itself and relationships of entities
in this space. To manage these concepts, express
relationships and operations on them, the language which

supports the system has to have both "computational" and "geographical" capabilities. These last involve operations on drawings (e.g. maps) which can be of the set-type like union, intersection and complement or belong to a graphic - editing class, like scale, rotate, overlay. The next section will describe some proposals for dealing with the representation problem, in the AQL environment, while the following will describe the language exten sions needed to accomodate these new concepts.

6. THE REPRESENTATION PROBLEM IN AQL

In attempting to represent a map in a form suitable to a computer system, one is essentially faced with the problem of capturing the semantics of the map. Various types of maps are known, each one concentrating on a particular "theme"- so, for example, political, geophysical, agricultural, etc.... maps are in use. The information they carry is often expressed by means of a "colour" given to the zone. The problem is then how to represent those zones (and the map in general). One method, proposed, for example, in (CAS75) and in (OHK77), consists in a previous subdivision of the map in a certain number of zones, each associated with a given code. Attribute values in each zone are given that area code. This method, although simple to implement, has as its major drawback the little precision in the facts localization, as the subdivision has been made independently on the phenomena to be described. Another method subdivides territory in square-shaped cells, each identified by a coordinates couple (see, for example (BON76)). For each cell, the values of the properties to be described are reported, following a prevalence criterion. The representation finds a "natural" correspondence with a bit matrix (which means a great ease in the implementation); but good precision may be only achieved at the cost of reducing the cell size, thus increasing (quadratically) the number of elements to be stored. In our opinion, the map can be viewed as a set partitioned in equivalence classes with respect to a given criterion or "colour". The problem then is how to represent those equivalence classes- for that, it is only necessary to describe the boundaries of the zone and give it a unique identification to what other information (e.g. population, name, gross income, etc...) may be attached. Methods of this type have been proposed, for example in (CAR74), in (SME76), and in (GOS78). Boundaries of a given zone may be viewed as a set of curves passing through some points- in this case, methods from numerical analysis may help us in storing the least set of points necessary (and sxfficient) to reproduce the given curve within an acceptable tolerance- storing, for example, only the interval boundaries and the parameters of the

best-fitting polynomial of the curve. This type of
approach, where zones of homogeneity with respect to an
assigned criterion are described by means of their
boundaries, allows us to discard large chunks of points
describing the inner part of the zone and to save only the
meaningful parameters of the boundaries. To fix the ideas,
let us suppose to have to represent the political map of
Italy. Based on a criterion of political homogeneity (for
example- membership to a region) we could partition Italy in
a set of non-overlapping regions, each of which described by
its boundaries, described, in turn, by a set of best-fitting
polynomials. A structure that could fit this approach has
to give, for each polynomial: the definition interval
extremes, an identifier to retrieve the parameters of the
curve, the identifiers of the zones to the left and to the
right of the boundary - supposing to follow it clockwise,
so to have the zone to be described always on the right. In
general, there will be a number of ways in wich a given
zone boundary may be divided, with the constraint that each
boundary segment has the form: y=f(x). However, an
equivalence criterion may be established, based on the fact
that two different ways of dividing a boundary imply that
overlapping intervals are joined by the same best-fitting
polynomial- in this sense we can find (in this equivalence
class) the subdivision which entails the least number of
segments and then speak of "the" subdivision of a zone
boundary. In this process, curves belonging to more than one
region are described only once. To re-build the boundaries,
one simply starts from the lower-bound of any given
interval, builds the curve up to the respective upper bound,
retrieves the following interval (the one which has the
lower bound coincident with the upper bound of the
preceeding one), builds the curve and continues the process
until a closed curve is obtained. Note that the method
works also for such items as "line" and "point", as the line
may be considered as a (degenerated) surface with zero
width and a point as a (degenerated) line with zero length.
A problem may then arise as to how the position of points
are given- i.e. the reference system. Quite obviously, the
only reference system which has a physical meaning is the
one based on latitude (PHI), longitude (LAMBDA) and height
(RHO), as every other is context dependent- anyway,
interfaces taking account of the spherical trigonometry are
to be provided so data can be entered or accessed based on
other reference systems. Apart from these interfaces, the
internal form of representation should be the one
aforementioned; so a map obeying a given criterion (e.g.
"political") is represented by the following relation MAP:

MAP (STARTX, STARTY, ENDX, ENDY, F#, LID, LEN)

where STARTX is the latitude of the lower bound of the
interval, STARTY is its longitude; ENDX and ENDY are the
same for the upper bound, F# is the identifier, in another

table, of the relevant parameters of the best-fitting polynomial, LID is the identifier of the line described by that tuple and LEN is the length of that boundary segment. Note that the relation MAP may store maps with different scale factors, as they differ only by the mean length of the boundary segments. In the cases where the zones of the map do not completely cover the territory, (for example, cities or grown zones maps) a standard identification for "background" is used for those zones not present in the map. The table MAP is in turn complemented by the table ZONE (LID, ZID, SIDE) which carries, in each tuple, the line identifier (LID), the zone identifier (ZID) and the side where this zone is found when the line LID is followed from the starting point (STARTX, STARTY) to the end. To draw the map from these data, one can proceed as follows:
1. Locate all tuples in ZONE which have the zone wanted (call it A) as ZID and take their LID's.
2. Search these LID's in MAP and take the respective start-end intervals.
3. For each interval, use the appropiate polynomial to compute a certain number of intermediate points according to the raster unit of the display and the scale factor.
4. Project these points, according to the projection chosen, and display them.

Note that no ordering of tuples in the relation is necessary, as the contiguity of the boundary segments is assured by the coinciden ce of their starting and ending points.
The number of parameters needed to describe the best-fitting polynomial depends on the polynomial itself: if it can be expressed in the form $y=f(x)$, this number is n+1, where n is the degree of the polynomial itself. In our case, we consider that a degree of 3 could represent boundaries with a reasonable approximation, without increasing too much the number of parameters to be stored. The relation needed to accomodate this structure is of the following type:

POLY (P#, A, B, C, D)

where P# is the identifier of the polynomial and A,B,C,D correspond respectively to the parameters of the polynomial written in the form:

$y=ax^3+bx^2+cx+d$

Each time a new fitting polynomial is found, a tuple is added to the relation POLY. To find the polynomial, the methods of polynomial regression can be used, by imposing the further condition of the passage through the definition interval boudaries, not to have discontinuities in these points.
In the map representation, the problem arises how to take

into account the third dimension, in a context where few
height are relevant and/or known. Strictly speaking, the
problem can be viewed as the representation of surfaces in
the three-dimensional space, so having the points expressed
by two coordinates and lines expressed as the intersection
of two surfaces. This, apart from the sudden increase of the
complexity of algorithms needed to face the problem,
requires a knowledge of input locational data we are far
from. On the other hand, the availability of height data as
level curves suggests by itself to consider height as a
particular "colour" of the zone enclosed by the level
curve.
Supposing to give the default value zero, we shall obtain a
"heights" map, where each zone has "height" as an attribute:

HEIGHTS (ZID, HEIGHT)

exactly in the same way the attributes "NAME" and
"POPULATION" are attributes for the zone of a "political"
map.
The height of a given point (P) in the zone between two
successive level curves is determined by linear
interpolation. The tables MAP, POLY and HEIGHTS serve merely
to describe locational data: then, depending upon the theme
we want to express in the maps a certain number of tables
will describe non - locational data. For example, a
description of a political-economical zone could involve the
relation POLZONE which we have already described, while an
agricultural description could consist of AGRIZONE, also
already described. Both are linked, via ZONE , to the
appropriate LID's of MAP. It is often the case that
territorial entities are organized into broader classes of
entities, in a hyerachical way. A typical example is the
administrative organization, where the elementary entity
(which could be "city", but also "district" or "province" as
well) is included in a higher- level entity ("province") and
this, in turn, included in another one ("region"), and so
on. Another example could refer to the agricultural map, as
the corn, oats and barley fields can be collec tively
referred to as "cereal fields" and these, in turn, included
into "graminaceous", and so on.
To accomodate these concepts, it is necessary to introduce
the concept of "level" in the description of map, as an
integer, associated to a given entity, which represents
the number of hierarchy levels that entity is
involved in. It is also necessary to represent the
hierarchical dependencies by means of a table which gives,
for each entity (e.g. "city") the entity at the upper level
("province"). Suppose this table be ADMIN(ENTITY, LEVEL,
PARENT) where ENTITY is the ZID of the entity we want to
describe, LEVEL is its hierarchical level (0 for the basic
entities), PARENT is the upper-level entity identifier.
It is often convenient, or necessary, to have a
"frame" into which a given zone may be displayed or, in

other words, the frame can be considered a compact way to
refer to the set of information relevant to a given zone. It
is quite obvious to think of a frame as a rectangular
window, such that two parallel sides are at a given (small)
distance from the points at lowest and highest latitude
(call them X1 and X2 respectively) of the given zone and the
other two sides are at the same distance from the points at
lowest and highest longitude (Y1 and Y2 respectively) of the
given zone. The frame can be biunivocally associated to
each "elementary" (i.e. 0-level) zone, simply by taking the
values of X1,X2,Y1,Y2, as the coordinates of the frame are
(X1, Y1), (X1,Y2), (X2, Y1), (X2,Y2).
For example, a frame for Italy could very well be the one
limited by the parallels passing through Innsbruck at North,
through Malta at South, and by the meridians passing through
Geneva at West and through Tirana at East. For zones
whose level is greater than zero, the "union" of the
dependent zones (i.e. the figure enclosed by the set of
boundaries not in common between two dependent zones) is
taken, and the four frame parameters are determined. Then,
according to the homogeneity criterion (e.g.
"administrative") the map was based upon, those values are
added to the appropriate relation, by suitably expanding its
schema. In our case, the relation is ADMIN which now
becomes:

ADMIN(ENT, LEV, PARENT, X1, X2, Y1, Y2)

where the last four attributes correspond to the four frame
parameters. In this way we can dynamically compute, for
each level, the largest frame as the one which has as sides
the maximum difference between X1 and X2 (for the same
entity) and the maximum difference between Y1 and Y2 (also
for the same entity). Frames may help to solve the point -
in - zone problem: given the coordinates of a point,
determine the zone it is in.
The query itself determines the level the user is interested
in (e.g. "province", "region", etc....), so, to solve the
problem, if we take the maximum frame at that level and
center it on the point coordinates (X, Y), we can exclude
large chunks of the map, while being sure that some
boundaries of the relevant zone have been taken. To
determine which zone it is, take the boundary segments which
have at least one extreme in the frame and choose among them
those having the extremes ordinates one greater and the
other less than Y. Determine the nearest of those segments
and, based on the fact that the point is on the left or on
the right of this segment, use the relation ZONE to find
where it is.
Till now we have referred our considerations mainly to one
(thematic) map (e.g. "political" or "agricultural", etc..).
In general, however, queries may refer to more than one map
(e.g. "corn fields in sedimentary soil in Apulia"). So,
after having considered operations on maps, we have to

consider operations between maps. The first one to consider
is the union between two maps, possibly selected with some
conditions. Union of two adjacent, non-overlapping figures
involves determining the boundary segment in common, while,
for overlapping figures, the intersections of boundaries
must be found. This problem can be dealt with by finding
the intersections of those segment boundaries wich have only
one extreme into the other figure (or on its boundary). Once
these intersections have been determined (so splitting in
two two boundary segments), the boundary segments which
have the extremes into the other figure ("internal"
segments) are ignored, while the remaining ones form the
union figure. Intersection is dealt with in a strictly
anologous way, except the fact that now the internal
segments are the only to be kept. In this way, we can
account for queries involving maps overlay (e.g.
"sedimentary soils in Tuscany"). As a particular case, union
of two adjacent zones of the same map (e.g. France and
Switzerland) can be obtained. If all the boundaries are to
be kept, then a simple overlay operation is required, which
can be seen as one of the two preceeding operation, without
discarding any segment boundary. Another operation which
often occurs in the map processing is the map coloring,
made by associating a different colour to the points
internal to each zone. Determining which points are internal
to which zone can be made by determining the intersections
of horizontal segments with the boundaries of each zone.

7. IMPACTS ON THE LANGUAGE OF THE MAP OPERATIONS

The operations outlined until now have to have a
corresponding set of keywords and/or semantic extensions at
the level of the language It is our opinion that, for the
user's ease of use, the number of key-words of a given
language, has, in general, to be kept to a minimum (while
preserving a given expressive power): this entails that the
semantics (rather than syntax) of the keyworks has to be
expanded and made context - sensitive so to account for the
operations on the maps. Also, "aggregate" concepts are of
importance as the user has to be able to speak of
"boundaries", "regions", "states" as if they were
"primitive" items. For that, the attributes and view
definition capability of AQL may help us very efficiently.
Of course, for non - geographic data, AQL may be used all
the same way we have already seen. First of all, the use of
the aggregate concept of "zone" needs some structures and
operations to be supported at the language level. As we have
already seen, operations on zones may involve the creation
of new boundary segments and the deletion of other ones:
namely, union discards "internal" segments (and parts
thereof), and intersection discards "external" segments (and

parts thereof). This depends on how we approached the representation problem: in fact, representing each point of the zone (and its features) as a tuple in some relation would have not required any semantic (or syntactic) extension to be added at the price of less accuracy and a much larger mass of data to be stored, most of them repetitive. To account for the segments resulting from "zones" operations, two special temporary tables are used: TMAP and TZONE, strictly analogous to their "permanent" counterparts (MAP and ZONE respectively). Whenever a new segment (or zone) is created, a tuple is added to those relations, and its tid (suitably flagged) is added to the set of tid's already obtained. The final set of tid's is then used by the function WHEN as usual, with the provision that the flagged tid's are to be retrieved from the temporary relations. The relations TMAP and TZONE are deleted at the end of the query. However, if the user makes a copy of the result of the query, their information is transfered to the "permanent" relations. On the side of operations, the set membership operation has to give same results as if the function ISONEOF was applied into a point - at - a - time representation: i.e. give the necessary information describing the possible overlap of two given zones. Of course, this information will be (partly) stored in TZONE (as far as the zone of overlap is concerned) and in TMAP (as far as new boundary segments, arising from crossings of "old" ones, are concerned). This function is called ISPARTOF and has the following syntax:

[zoneid1] ISPARTOF [zoneid2]

where zoneid1 and zoneid2 are expressions, queries or attribute names denoting a set of zone identifiers. ISPARTOF computes, for each zoneid on the left, the possible intersections with zones identified on the right, determines which boundary segments break up (and where) due to intersection, stores the segment pieces so formed into TMAP, stores the intersection zone information into TZONE and finally returns, as a result, the tid's (in MAP) of the boundary segments delimiting the intersection zone, together with the tid's (in TMAP) of the newly formed segment pieces which close the intersection zone border. To compute the intersection zones and the boundary segments of a given zone which are contained in another one, the function CONTAINS is used, which will be seen later on. Of course, the function ISONEOF still maintains its features and meaning for "discrete" (or "non-geographic") data. Another function is useful, which performs the complementary operation of ISPARTOF, i.e. which excludes the boundary segments of the common zone. This function is named ISNOTPARTOF and has the following syntax:

[zoneid1] ISNOTPARTOF [zoneid2]

The result is constituted by the tuple identifiers (in MAP
and TMAP, respectively) of the boundary segments of the two
zoneid 's which do not belong to the intersection zone.
Two zones may be said to have the same "shape" if they have
the same sequence of polynomial segments of the same length.
In this case, two segments are in "sequence" if the starting
point of the second coincides with the ending point of the
first. To put in sequence the boundary segments of a zone,
we may use the function BORDEROF with the following syntax:

BORDEROF zid

where zid stands for any expression denoting a zone
identifier. The function BORDEROF retrieves into ZONE the
LID's corresponding to zid , retrieves into MAP the
starting and ending points corresponding to those LID's and
then returns them arranged in sequence with the LID having
the least STARTX as first. These LID's may be used to draw
a map, by suitably telling the system how to draw (e.g. by
solid red lines, by broken green lines, etc...)
Note that these lines are built by repeating a number of
times a certain unit which we may call a "line pattern". The
definitions of the line patterns are stored in the following
relation:

PATTERN (PID, ORD#, TYP, LEN, COLOUR)

where each tuple represents one of the parts the pattern may
be constituted by. In it, PID is the pattern identifier,
ORD# the ordinal number of the pattern part, TYP tells if
it is a line, space, or dot, LEN is the length (expressed in
raster units) of the pattern part, COLOUR is the colour of
that part. To display a given segment, we use the function
DRAW with the syntax:

[draw-parameters] DRAW [sequence-of-LID's]

where draw-parameters is any expression denoting a table
containing a pattern identifier, a scale factor and a zero
for the reference system, expressed in terms of raster units
from the lower left corner of the display. These parameters
may be given by a standard default, assigning a standard
pattern as a system parameter, while the reference system is
put to the lower left corner of the display, and the scale
factor is such that the zone frame coincides with the
display. These values may be changed by setting a system
parameter. The term sequence-of-LID's is a set of line
identifiers resulting, for example, from the BORDEROF
function. The lines corresponding to these ZID's may be both
recorded in the relation MAP or in the relation TMAP, if
they have been created as a result of previous operations in
the same query. To display a zone of given ZID, the system
has to establish the reference system local to the display
unit, by taking into account the draw-parameters±. The X's

and Y's of the sequence of LID's to be drawn are transformed
into the coordinates for the new system and then, by using
the interpolating polynomials, a sequence of points is
determined. Starting from an arbitrary point, the line
pattern is applied counting the raster units, deleting the
points corresponding to blank pattern, and saving the other
ones. In this way we may draw, for example, the map of
Florence (supposing that the relation POLZONE carries
information referring to cities):


```
G1.    AQL 'LANDUSE'
'' DRAW BORDEROF (ZID OF POLZONE)
            WHEN
            NAME EQ FLORENCE
```


where the empty vector means that the default drawing
parameters are to be used. If we wanted to put the
reference system in another point and to scale down the
image, we simply had written:


```
G2.    AQL 'LANDUSE'
(RR REF SF SCALE SORED) DRAW BORDEROF
            (ZID OF POLZONE)
            WHEN
            NAME EQ FLORENCE
```


The function SCALE, like the function REF, merely fills the
drawing parameters table, while SORED is name of a drawing
pattern (solid red). An implicit assumption has been made
until now regarding the projection, which has been assumed
to be orthographic, with the projection plane tangent in the
point corresponding to the frame center. The type of
projection is a parameter for the function BORDEROF which
uses it to modify the values obtained from the calculation
of the boundary segments and may be set as a system
parameter. We may, for example, use the definition
mechanism of AQL, to define SHAPE as BORDEROF ZID and
restate (G1) as follows:


```
G3.    AQL 'LANDUSE'
'' DRAW (SHAPE OF POLZONE)
        WHEN
        NAME EQ FLORENCE
```


In this way, we may compare (for EQ or NOTEQ) the SHAPE's of
two zones. In these cases where more than one zone is
retrieved, then we may not refer to the frame of a single
zone, but we have to frame the entire figure, based on the

"outermost" frames. In this way, the overall reproduction
scale is stated, and so are the relative positions of the
zones displayed. A problem which is often encountered is to
determine in which zone a point of given coordinates is
found, or, more generally, which zone contains another given
zone. To solve the problem, the user writes:

G4.   AQL 'LANDUSE'
(NAME OF POLZONE)
WHEN
(ZID OF MAP) CONTAINS ZONEID

i.e. "name of the zone whose map contains another zone".
ZONEID stands for any expression or query resulting in a
zone identifier or in a couple of coordinates. In the case
of a point, the problem is solved by determining the LID of
the first boundary segment at the left (or, alternatively,
the right) of the point: i.e. the one which has the largest
(respectively, least) abscissa at the same ordinate as the
point. To limit the number of candidates boundary segment,
the largest frame associated with that type of zones is
used: only those segments are kept, which have both extremes
in the frame and at opposite sides with respect to the
horizontal line passing through the point. For the zone
problem, if all boundary segments extremes are internal, and
none is on the border, then the zone is contained;
otherwise, if, for each couple of points on border, the
corresponding boundary segment is common to the two zones,
the zone is still contained, otherwise it is not. Besides
inclusion, it can be sometimes convenient to represent union
of a number of zones, like in the following example:

"Draw the map of territorial zone whose soil is made up of
clay or sand"

G5.   AQL 'LANDUSE'
'' DRAW BORDEROF
   (ZID OF GEOZONE)
   WHEN
   TERTYPE ISONEOF CLAY UNITE SAND

In this way, boundary segments between adjoining sandy and
clayey zones are reported. If we wanted only borders of
clayey or sandy zones, without distinction between them, we
had to exclude the common borders. This is made by imposing
that no intersection (or common) part has to be considered:

G6.   AQL 'LANDUSE'
'' DRAW BORDEROF

```
(ZID OF GEOZONE)
WHEN
((ZID OF GEOZONE) WHEN TERTYPE EQ SAND)
ISNOTPARTOF
(ZID OF GEOZONE) WHEN TERTYPE EQ CLAY
```

Instead of writing a series of WHEN clauses denoting a set of ZID's, separeted by the function ISPARTOF (respectively ISNOTPARTOF), the user may want to group these sets of ZID's in an array such that each plane corresponds to a set of ZID's and then apply a function which takes the common parts. This function is called COMMON and has the following syntax:

```
                    COMMON   zoneidlist
```

and the semantics of zoneid1 ISPARTOF zoneid ...ISPARTOF zoneidn Quite analogously, we can define its complementary function NOTCOMMON, with the syntax:

```
                    NOTCOMMON   zoneidlist
```

and the semantics of zoneid1 ISNOTPARTOF zoneid2 ...ISNOTPARTOF zoneidn so the preceeding query may be restarted as follows:

```
G7.    AQL 'LANDUSE'
'' DRAW BORDEROF
(ZID OF GEOZONE) WHEN NOTCOMMON (ZID OF GEOZONE)
                                     WHEN
                                     TERTYPE  EQ  CLAY  UNITE
                                     SAND
```

Same considerations should apply if we use the function OR between the two conditions requesting the soil to be clayey or sandy, respectively. However, with the function OR, the conditions may span two (or more) relations, like in the following example: "Draw a map comprising both rocky soil and corn fields"

```
'' DRAW BORDEROF
   (ZID OF ZONE)
   WHEN
   NOTCOMMON (ZID OF ZONE)
          WHEN
          (ZID ISONEOF (ZID OF GEOZONE)
                   WHEN
                   TERTYPE EQ ROCK)
          OR ZID ISONEOF (ZID OF AGRIZONE)
                   WHEN
```

PRODUCE EQ CORN

or, making use of inference, we may write:

G9.   AQL 'LANDUSE'
'' DRAW BORDEROF
*   (ZID OF ZONE)*
*   WHEN*
*   NOTCOMMON(ZID OF ZONE)*
*   WHEN*
*   (TERTYPE EQ ROCK) OR PRODUCE EQ CORN*

Note that, when conditions span more than one relation, it is necessary that all of them refer to the relation ZONE. An important use of the concept of zone union is found in the implementation of territorial hierarchies. Suppose we want to use the concepts of "province", "region" and "state". To do that, we start by defining PROVINCE as synonym of PARENT, REGION as PARENT FOR PROVINCE, and STATE as PARENT FOR REGION, in the relation ADMIN. The function FOR merely determines, at each application, the first ascendents of its right argument, as we can see from the following example: "Draw the map of Tuscany"

G10.   AQL 'LANDUSE'
'' DRAW BORDEROF
*   (ZID OF POLZONE)*
*   WHEN*
*   NOTCOMMON (ZID OF POLZONE)*
*   WHEN*
*   REGION EQ TUSCANY*

which, by the application of the definition of REGION and by the inference, becomes:

G11.   AQL 'LANDUSE'
'' DRAW BORDEROF
*   (ZID OF POLZONE)*
*   WHEN*
*   NOTCOMMON (ZID OF POLZONE)*
*   WHEN*
*   ZID ISONEOF (ENT OF ADMIN)*
*   WHEN*
*   PARENT ISONEOF (ENT OF ADMIN)*
*   WHEN*
*   PARENT EQ TUSCANY*

In this query,both definition and inference mechanisms have been triggered to produce this "complete" form of the query. The innermost query determines the entities whose "parent" is Tuscany, i.e. the provinces of Tuscany. Then, entities whose "parents" are Tuscany provinces (i.e. Tuscan cities) are determined and their "external" borders are drawn, in a standard fashion. Quite analogously, we can define the relation CULTIVATION, like ADMIN, so to be able to query using concepts like "cereals", "graminaceous", etc.... The definition mechanism works well also for non - geographic data, like in the following example:

"Total population in Tuscany"


```
G12.    AQL 'LANDUSE'
SUMUP (POP OF POLZONE)
        WHEN
        REGION EQ TUSCANY
```


which, by the same mechanisms as (G11.), is transformed into a query asking for the population of all the cities in Tuscany, which are then summed up. The definition capability may be used to find the names of the regions which are adjoining another region. To determine them, we first find the "elementary" zones (cities) which have something in common with the given region (only borders may be in common, as we are dealing with only one map, so no intersections are possible) and then we find their province and region. This can be seen from the following example:

"Build a function which gives the names of the regions
 adjoining a given one"


```
        ∇'Z←ADJOINING R' AQLDEF 'LANDUSE'
DISTINCT (NAME OF POLZONE)
        WHEN
        ZID ISONEOF (PARENT OF ADMIN)
                WHEN
                ENT ISONEOF (PARENT OF ADMIN)
                        WHEN
                        ENT    ISONEOF  (ZID    OF
POLZONE)
                                WHEN
                                ZID ISPARTOF
        (ZID OF POLZONE)
        WHEN
        NOTCOMMON (ZID OF POLZONE)
                WHEN
                REGION EQ R
```

Note that the query requests the name(s) of the parent of
the parent of cities which have something in common with the
external borders of the given region. In this way, we may,
for example, find very easily the regions adjoining Tuscany:

        ADJOINING'TUSCANY'
LIGURIA
EMILIA
MARCHE
UMBRIA
LAZIO

The companion operation of union is intersection, which is
relevant whenever zones with two or more properties,
belonging to different themes (and hence maps) are to be
found. For this, the function ISPARTOF is useful, as can be
seen from the following example: "Draw the map of corn
fields on clayey soil in Tuscany"


```
G15.   AQL 'LANDUSE'
''  DRAW BORDEROF
    (ZID OF ZONE)
    WHEN
    NOTCOMMON (ZID OF ZONE)
            WHEN
            ((ZID OF ZONE)
            WHEN
            ZID ISONEOF (ZID OF POLZONE)
                    WHEN
                    REGION EQ TUSCANY)
            ISPARTOF (ZID OF ZONE)
                WHEN
                ((ZID OF ZONE)
                WHEN
                ZID ISONEOF (ZID OF GEOZONE)
                        WHEN
                        TERTYPE EQ CLAY)
                ISPARTOF (ZID OF ZONE)
                    WHEN
                    ZID ISONEOF (ZID OF AGRIZONE)
                            WHEN
                            PRODUCE EQ CORN
```


which can be read as follows: Draw the map of those parts of
Tuscany which are parts of clayey soil, cultivated with
corn. Note that several zone identifiers resulting from
intersection operations refer to the relations TMAP and
TZONE, so they are specially flagged to be suitably
processed by the display functions. The zone identifiers,
determined by the selections on various relations, have to
be referred to the relation ZONE through the function

ISONEOF, so the result of the function ISPARTOF is
constituted by a set of tid's on ZONE and/or TZONE. Using
the inference mechanism, (G15) may be written as follows:


```
G16.   AQL 'LANDUSE'
'' DRAW BORDEROF
   (ZID OF ZONE)
   WHEN
NOTCOMMON (ZID OF ZONE)
            WHEN
            ((ZID OF ZONE)
             WHEN
             REGION EQ TUSCANY)
            ISPARTOF (ZID OF ZONE)
                     WHEN
                     ((ZID OF ZONE)
                      WHEN
                      TERTYPE EQ CLAY)
                     ISPARTOF (ZID OF ZONE)
                              WHEN
                              PRODUCE EQ CORN
```

The function ISPARTOF may be used also for performing the
complement operation, like in the following example:

"Draw the map of the province of Florence, except Florence
itself"


```
G17.   AQL 'LANDUSE'
'' DRAW BORDEROF
   (ZID OF POLZONE)
   WHEN
NOTCOMMON NOT ((ZID OF POLZONE)
               WHEN
               PROVINCE EQ FLORENCE)
              ISPARTOF (ZID OF POLZONE)
                       WHEN
                       NAME EQ FLORENCE
```

Another function which is, in a sense, complementary to
CONTAINS is the function ISIN which is used to know which
zone is contained by another one, like in the following
example:

"Which river flows through Florence?"


```
G18.   AQL 'LANDUSE'
(NAME OF RIVERS)
WHEN
```

```
ZID ISIN (ZID OF POLZONE)
         WHEN
         NAME EQ FLORENCE
```

The function ISIN determines, first of all, which rivers'
frames intersect, contain, or are contained by the
Florence's frame. Then, the boundary segment of the river(s)
in the frame(s) selected are checked for intersection with
the boundary segments of Florence and the segments which
intersect determine the ZID('s) of the river(s) in Florence.

8. SUMMARY AND CONCLUSIONS.

The representation of geographic data faces us with various
problems; among them, the problem of equivalence classes of
data has impacts at the conceptual model level. In fact,
geographic data are such that many of the individual points
described differ only by their positions, so they can be
grouped in some kind of equivalence classes which are far
less numerous than the original points. However, this
entails that the individuality of each point is lost and the
traditional relational operations (e.g. join) have to be
revisited to account for this new situation. This means, in
turn, extensions in syntax and semantics of the language, by
the introduction of new keywords which both perform
traditional operations in the new context, and perform new
operations, related with map processing. On the other hand,
this consideration needs not to be limited to geographical
concepts but holds in all cases where information may be
described by giving its properties, rather than by
enumeration. It is our opinion that this problem deserves
further investigation, as its solution could make it
possible to approach the problem of continous quantities.
Other problems are related with geometrical properties of
the objects to be represented in the database. To account
for these problems, a set of standard relations is used, to
describe the geometrical properties of the equivalence
classes of points (called zones), together with a number of
more traditional (descriptive) relations, which account for
non-geometrical properties of objects. This structure
accounts also for other problems (e.g. distance between two
points along a given road), also related to map processing.
Moreover, the definition and view definition capabilities
seem to be central to support the use of aggregate concepts,
which have widespread use in geographic data processing. The
proposed structure offer a powerful means to query
geographical databases together with the full capabilities
of default options, inference, definitions and computational
power, inherited from AQL.

REFERENCES

ALD74: Aldred, B. K., "The case for a Locational Data Type" Technical Report, IBM UK Scientific Center, UKSC0054, April 1974

ANT78: Antonacci, F., Dell' Orco, P., Spadavecchia, V. N., Turtur, A., "AQL: A Problem-solving Query Language for Relational Data Bases" IBM Journal of Research and Development, vol. 22, n. 5, Sept. 1978 pp. 541-559

BON76: Bonfatti, F., Tiberio, P., "A data structure for land description and investigation", Proceedings of the fifth biennial international Codata Conference, B. Dreyfus ed., Pergamon Press, 1976

CAR74: Carlson, E. D., Bennett, J. L., Giddings, G. M., Mantey, P. R. "The design and evaluation of the interactive geo-data analysis and display system", Proceedings of IFIP Congress 1974, Rosenfeld, J. L. ed., North Holland, 1974

CAS75: Casazza, I., Faedo, C., Marini, G., "Una base di dati relazionali per la gestione dei dati ambientali", Atti del Convegno AICA, 1975

CHA74: Chamberlin, D. D., Boyce, R. F., "SEQUEL, a Structured English Query Language", Proceedings 1974 ACM SIGFIDET Workshop, Ann Arbor, MI, April 1974, pp. 249-264

COD70: Codd, E. F., "A Relational Model of Data for Large Shared Data Banks", CACM 13, 377 (1970)

COD72: Codd, E. F., "Relational Completeness of Data Bases Sublanguages" Data Base Systems, Vol. 6, Courant Computer Science Symposia Series, Prentice-Hall, Inc., Englewood Cliffs, NJ, 1972

GOS78: Gosen, F., Gradenigo, G., "Proposta per un sistema informativo territoriale. Sistema di gestione di Data Bases geografici" Atti del Seminario: "Sistemi informativi per la gestione fisica ed economica dell' ambiente", Padova, March 20, 1978

IBM1: "APL Language", Report No. GC26-3847, IBM Corporation, White Plains, NY

IBM2: "APL Shared Variables (APLSV) User's Guide, Report No. SH20-1460-1, IBM Corporation, White Plains, NY

IBM3: "APL Shared Variables (APLSV) Programming RPQ WE 1191 TSIO Program Reference Manual, Report No. SH20-1463, IBM Corporation, White Plains, NY

OHK77: Ohkohchi, M., Udo, M., "CARPS: Computer Assisted Regional Planning System", IFAC Symposium on Environmental Systems Planning, Design and Control, M. Akashi ed., Pergamon Press, 1977

SME76: Smedley, B. S., "An Urban Management System and Geographic Data Processing in Urban Planning", IBM UK Scientific Center Report UKSC0079, April 1976

ZLO75: Zloof, M. M., "Query by Example", Proceedings National Computer Conference (AFIP Press), 44, 431 (1975)

596

Figure 1

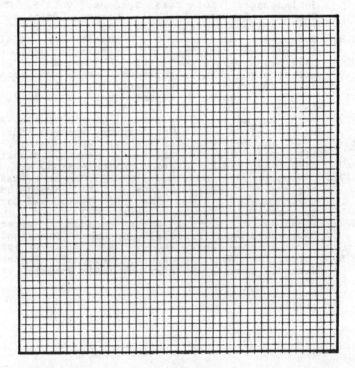

Figure 2a

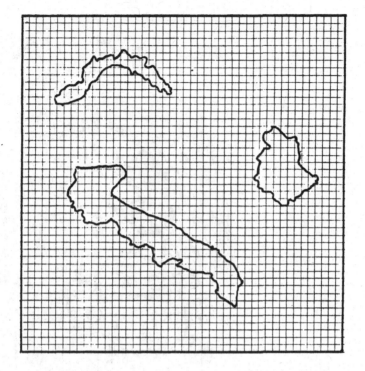

Figure 2b

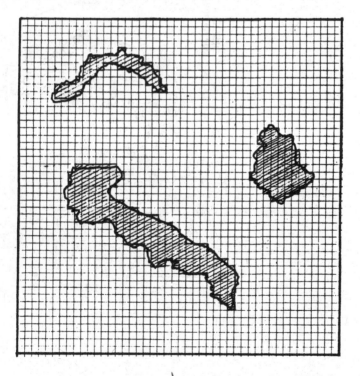

Figure 2c

Figure 3a

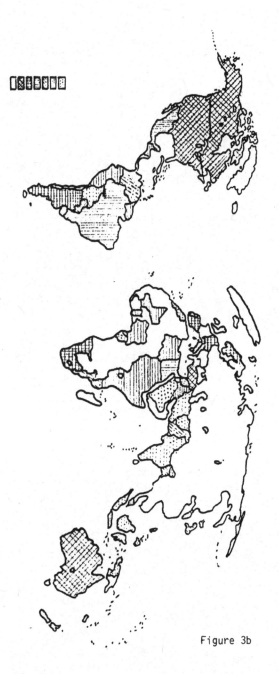

Figure 3b